To my parents:

"Stones would seldom stand by the highway
if sons did not set them there."

America in Time

by Malcolm C. Jensen

America's history year by year through text and pictures

Houghton Mifflin Company • Boston

Atlanta • Dallas • Geneva, Illinois • Hopewell, New Jersey • Palo Alto

Houghton Mifflin Company
Dictionary Division

Editorial Director
Fernando de Mello Vianna

Supervising Editor
Anne D. Steinhardt

Assistant Editor
Carole La Mond

Art Director
Geoffrey Hodgkinson

Contributing Editors
Glenn Davis
Susan Wilfong Gurewitsch
Max Rudmann

All correspondence and inquiries should be directed to

Dictionary Division, Houghton Mifflin Company
Two Park Street, Boston, MA 02107

Library of Congress Cataloging in Publication Data
Jensen, Malcolm C.
  America in time.
  Includes index.
  1. United States — History — Chronology. I. Title.
E174.5.J46   973'.02'02   77-10595
ISBN 0-395-25408-6

Contents

Foreword

America in Time has two main parts. The first, "Chronology," attempts to survey certain main historical developments, year by year, from the first voyage of Christopher Columbus through 1976. The second, "Thematic Chronologies," presents facts relating to more specialized areas of American achievement, like sports, literature, economic growth, and so on, also in chronological order.

Unlike most reference books for the general reader, *America in Time* incorporates in the "Chronology" section a framework once almost universally found in basic textbooks used in the public schools and in introductory college courses in American history. It is hoped that this framework of periods — "European Discovery and Exploration," "The Federal Period," "Westward Expansion," and so on — will have a pleasing familiarity to some readers and will enhance the value of *America in Time* for those who have sons and daughters currently engaged in learning something about their country's history.

Of late, historical facts and dates have in the opinion of some undergone a certain regrettable de-emphasis. This has happened for a variety of reasons, not the least of which is that most general surveys of American history are mainly political in nature. That is, they tend to focus on those events which have engaged the attention and energies of public American figures, especially those having important roles in the national government. As a result the period framework used in general surveys has a tendency to underemphasize social and economic developments, to be uncomfortable with collective achievements, particularly those of ordinary citizens, and to overlook the perspectives and experiences of people having minority status. Nevertheless, this framework has not been successfully supplanted by any other, and its mere absence from general surveys does not guarantee that those aspects of the American historical experience having impact on the lives of ordinary citizens will automatically move into sharper focus. Frequently it simply means that important facts and dates slip into limbo, and average students and readers are left to wrestle with questions of cause and effect that the discipline of history is not itself theoretically prepared to answer.

The time is near, perhaps, when history, as one of the ways in which people organize information about themselves, will incorporate insights and theories from the behavioral sciences that will facilitate historical generalizations of great power — power not only to explain but also to predict. But that time has not quite come, and even when it does, facts and dates will still form the key ingredients of historical understanding.

In *America in Time* brief essays preface each chronology or listing of events. These essays have from time to time sought to call attention to nonpolitical developments and on some occasions have introduced metaphors, sympathies, opinions, or other amusements not usually to be found in general reference works. These essays may be read in conjunction with the facts and dates they introduce, or they may simply be considered condiments, to be used or not, that have been placed near the meat and potatoes.

Several people have made important contributions to this work. I should like here to mention specifically Fernando de Mello Vianna for his role in shaping this book and want especially to make known my gratitude to Anne D. Steinhardt for her unshakable and friendly professionalism.

Malcolm C. Jensen

I

Chronology

The United States in Time: The Major Periods

1492		
	European Discovery and Exploration	Explorers from Spain, France, Portugal, and England begin to learn something about the shape, size, and nature of America north of present-day Mexico. Mexico and the Caribbean are colonized by Spain during this period.
1607		
	The Colonial Period	England, France, Spain, and the Netherlands create permanent settlements in North America. The thirteen original English colonies are formed and rather quickly become economically and socially independent. Toward the end of this period France is driven out of eastern North America, and England seeks to assert political and economic control over its colonies.
1776		
	The Revolutionary Period	The thirteen English colonies rebel and form the United States of America, which defeats British forces on United States soil.
1789		
	The Federal Period	The United States Constitution goes into effect; George Washington is elected the nation's first President, and the American political system is formed.
1801		
	Westward Expansion	The United States acquires by purchase or war most of its present territory, expanding to the Pacific coast; political and socioeconomic conflict develops between the northern and southern sections.
1861		

1861	The Civil War	The southern states are prevented by war from forming a separate nation; slavery is abolished; political and economic control of the nation passes to the industrial North.
1865		
	Reconstruction and Industrialization	The southern states are placed under martial law and then readmitted to the Union; the Great Plains and Far West are settled, and the last free Indians are broken; the United States becomes the world's leading industrial nation; the population becomes increasingly urbanized.
1899		
	World Power and the Progressive Era	The United States acquires foreign colonies and asserts itself militarily and diplomatically throughout the world; considerable efforts are made to reform industrial, political, and environmental abuses.
1919		
	Postwar Reaction and the Twenties	The United States emerges from World War I and rejects the Versailles Treaty and the League of Nations; Prohibition is enacted; there is a great renaissance in the sciences, technology, popular entertainments, and all creative arts.
1930		
	The Depression and the New Deal	The federal government vastly expands in order to prevent a total economic collapse.
1940		
	World War II	The United States develops enormous military-industrial capability in the process of defeating fascist (Axis) powers in Europe and Asia; the country emerges as a dominant economic and military nation.
1946		
	Cold Wars and Others	The world becomes divided into two camps, Communist and non-Communist, each perceiving the other to be intent on world hegemony; a series of economic, political, and localized military offensives are undertaken by each side, each possessing the military capability of destroying human life on a planet-wide scale; environmental deterioration becomes increasingly evident; the U.S. becomes involved in a costly, unpopular war in Southeast Asia and experiences a series of internal political disturbances, including assassinations, domestic riots, and the resignations in disgrace of a President and a Vice President.
1976		

European Discovery and Exploration
1492–1607

This period begins in 1492 with Christopher Columbus' first landfall in the Bahamas. It closes a hundred and fifteen years later with the founding of the first permanent English settlement, in Jamestown, Virginia.

Before 1492 European knowledge of lands west across the Atlantic took the form of legends and rumors. By 1607 Europeans were smoking American tobacco, wearing American furs, and eating American codfish. At the end of this period European scholars could draw a map of the world showing the outlines and position of North and South America more accurately than the average American today can draw them from memory. And on this map Europeans could place names like Florida, California, St. Augustine, Puerto Rico, Cuba, the Mississippi, the Rio Grande, Mexico, the Pacific Ocean, Veracruz, Newfoundland, Labrador, the St. Lawrence River, Cape Cod, Virginia, and the name of America itself.

During this period Spain conquered and colonized vast American territories, including Mexico and the large islands of the Caribbean. It established a major urban center in Mexico City and planted several forts and missions along the southeastern coast of the United States. The Spanish discoveries prompted England, France, and Portugal to send out explorers whose voyages added to the sum of European knowledge, provided the basis for North American claims, and led to several abortive colonizing attempts.

On most of its American territories Spain permanently impressed its language, institutions, customs, and faith. It also extracted from them, following the conquest of Mexico in 1521, enormous quantities of gold, silver, and gemstones. In this, Spain was perhaps too successful. The shiploads of American gold undermined Spanish commerce and industry, paid for several European wars that Spain lost, and stimulated the imagination and the economies of England, France, and Holland. By 1607 these countries were eager to grab whatever parts of North America Spain could not police—in effect, everything north of Florida.

We honor Columbus' cranky, wrong-headed voyage of 1492 as one that made a huge difference in the history of the American continents. But many Americans find it difficult to call this difference by its right name: conquest. Instead we tend to speak of a *New World* that was, in fact, as ancient as any other. We speak of "finding" a landmass that was explored, populated, and ordered by human beings eleven thousand years ago at the very least. We refer to thousands of years of intricate American cultural development as pre-Columbian and mean by that term something less neutral than "what happened before Columbus arrived in 1492." Most significantly, we persist in thinking of fifteenth-century America as mostly empty wilderness. However, the consensus is that about twenty-five million people lived in pre-Columbian America, with nine hundred thousand to a million and a half of them living in the United States and Canada. And among some anthropologists even these estimates have been steadily rising, until today some speculate that pre-Columbian America contained nearly ninety million people, of whom five to nine and a half million lived in the United States and Canada.

Greenland, no more than five days' easy sailing from mainland North America, supported a Christian European community for about five hundred years, beginning in 985 or 986. At its most flourishing, in about 1200, Greenland had a population of three thousand souls; that is, it then contained more Europeans than the Greater Antilles did in the 1570's.

In 1000 the Greenlander Leif Ericson explored and named parts of eastern Canada, including what are now Baffin Island, Labrador, and Newfoundland. About ten years later Thorfinn Karlsefni planted a Norse settlement in Newfoundland, probably at L'Anse aux Meadows. Karlsefni and about a hundred and eighty settlers remained there for three years. Greenlanders made a number of subsequent visits to the North American mainland, taking timber and furs, some of which went back to Iceland and Norway as export items. But of the Norse adventure in North America little remains, apart from documentary and archaeological evidence. Only the name of Greenland (translated from the Norse *Grønland*), chosen by its colonizer Eric the Red, reminds us that the Norse possessed something in North America for long enough.

Why didn't the Norse succeed in North America? The briefest, clearest answers take the form of military metaphors. Greenland was an advanced base. Its existence depended on logistic support from Iceland, Norway, and ultimately the Northern European community. But this community had neither the means nor the will to support and reinforce the Greenland base. And so Greenland died.

In relation to Greenland the settlement of Newfoundland was a beachhead. The settlers were sharply outnumbered by an aggressive native population and had no significant technological superiority to offset this disadvantage. The Greenland sagas make it clear that the Norse settlers on Newfoundland decided they could not turn their visit into a successful invasion, even though they delighted in the good grass, the timber, the furs, the bog iron, and the grapelike berries of their Vinland. Indeed, they were unable to make the name of Vinland stick to any particular place.

When we look at the European community that supported the first successful invasion of America in the fifteenth and sixteenth centuries, we see something quite different. Now the will to succeed in America is fueled by those passions—greed, dreams of secular and spiritual empire, the competition for national prestige and power—that are most productive of grand enterprises and most destructive of anything getting in their way. This will to triumph is now backed up by an array of superior technology—true ships, navigational aids, written communication, explosives, portable cannon, wagons, pack animals, steel armor, war-horses. And so this time the Europeans keep coming, first as navigators, soldiers, and priests, then as administrators, clerks, farmers, miners, masons, printers. The Spanish-advanced bases and beachheads in America are supplied, resupplied, consolidated, extended—a magnificent and relentless operation resembling in several respects the big campaigns of World War II. And as the Spanish kept coming in the sixteenth century, so did the English in the seventeenth.

By the mid 1400's royal governments in Portugal, Spain, France, and England had achieved varying but substantial degrees of centralized control; at the same time, the populations, economies, and patriotisms of these nations were growing. Luxury items like spices, perfumes, silks, and chinaware had for several centuries been trickling into Europe from the Orient over long, expensive land-water routes, winding up in the Moslem-controlled Mediterranean and moving thence to distribution points in Italian city-states like Venice and Genoa. Determined to break the Moslem and Italian monopolies on this delicious trade, the new European nations geared up to reach the Indies—all of Asia—entirely by sea. Portugal, largely under the leadership of Prince Henry the Navigator, beat them to the punch. By the late 1490's the Portuguese had thriving trading posts along the coast of Africa and had reached India by sailing east around the Cape of Good Hope.

In 1492 the Spanish monarchs, Ferdinand and Isabella, succeeded in driving the Moors out of Spain and finally presided over an entire country. In the flush of national enthusiasm occasioned by this success, they also expelled the Jews and decided furthermore to back Christopher Columbus' notion of sailing west to the Indies, even though his geographic ideas were, expert opinion agreed, extremely fishy.

The Spanish settlements planted in the Caribbean by Columbus were moderately successful almost from the start and remained so, proving valuable trading partners with the English colonies more than a century later. But not until the 1520's and Magellan's globe-circling voyage did it become clear that the Americas were not next door to China and Japan. It was also at this time that Spain hit real pay dirt in Mexico, looting the Aztec empire. After the 1520's many European explorers still hoped to find a strait that would take them through the American landmass to Asia. But now they were also willing to settle for another golden Mexico.

As a result of Portuguese and English explorations at the turn of the sixteenth century, English, French, and Portuguese fishermen began to take large quantities of cod from the Grand Banks. They dried and salted their catches ashore and learned that they could trade for furs with the local inhabitants. Conveniently for the New England settlers who came in the 1600's, these fishermen also spread measles, cholera, and smallpox throughout the northeastern United States. When the Pilgrims and Puritans arrived in the 1620's and 1630's, the coastal American populations were already decimated.

Toward the end of this period France and England began to emerge as the two most powerful nations in Europe. The brilliant Elizabeth I of England made all the right moves and ultimately checkmated Spain. England's defeat of the Spanish Armada in 1588 cleared much of the Atlantic for English shipping, a peace treaty was signed with Spain in 1604, and it was then just a matter of time before the English were to try their hand at North American conquest. That time came in 1606, when corporations were formed to finance a beachhead in Jamestown, Virginia.

In one sense, however, the initial Jamestown venture ended rather than began an era. It had about it much of the naive, even crackbrained enthusiasm characteristic of earlier Spanish and French attempts, and little of the enlightened practicality typical of most later English efforts. In 1607, after a voyage lasting more than eighteen weeks, the Jamestown settlers landed in a swamp; discovering that they couldn't saunter about picking up gold nuggets, they set about starving to death.

European Discovery and Exploration (1492–1607)

Columbus shows the Spanish court riches from the New World.
LIBRARY OF CONGRESS

1492

Christopher Columbus, an Italian sailing under the Spanish flag in vessels *Santa Maria, Niña,* and *Pinta,* lands on San Salvador in the Bahamas (October 12). Columbus, believing he is near Indies, names native Arawaks "Indians." Columbus makes three more Caribbean voyages (1493, 1498, 1502), establishing an exploitative settlement on Hispaniola in 1493. Insisting he has found an Other World somewhere near Japan, Columbus dies in Spain (1506), his discoveries considered interesting but not very promising.

1497

John Cabot, an Italian sailing under the English flag in vessel *Matthew,* makes a North American landfall, probably at Newfoundland; Cabot's obscure voyage forms the basis for England's claim to North America. In 1498 Cabot makes a second voyage but never returns.

1500

The Portuguese send Gaspar Corte-Real on a voyage to North America to check out Cabot's discovery. Corte-Real reaches Greenland and possibly Newfoundland.

1501

A small English expedition reaches Labrador and Newfoundland; Labrador gets its name from a crew member, a Portuguese ex-farmer (*lavrador*) who makes sighting; Newfoundland is referred to as such in report to English king.

In the Caribbean, Spanish occupation proceeds as Puerto Rico is conquered by Juan Ponce de León.

1502–04

French and Portuguese fishermen begin visiting the Grand Banks.

1507

Martin Waldseemüller, German map maker, suggests name "America" for western landmass, on basis of letters printed in Europe (1504–05) that purportedly describe the new continent and suggest Amerigo Vespucci had discovered it.

1512

Spanish Caribbean holdings prosper and expand; Hispaniola exports about $1 million worth of gold; Cuba is settled; Caribbean Indians, being rapidly exterminated, are replaced by African slaves to work mines, sugar plantations, and cattle ranches.

1513

Vasco Núñez de Balboa leads expedition across Panama; he sights Pacific Ocean and claims it all for Spain, believing it to be the Indian Ocean.

Juan Ponce de León, sailing from Puerto Rico, discovers and names Florida, believing it to be part of magical island named Bimini. Later explorations by Alonzo de Piñeda (1519) and Lucas Vásquez de Allyón (1520) show Florida to be part of larger mainland.

1519

Hernando Cortés, sailing from Cuba, lands in Yucatán; he proceeds northward, founding Veracruz, and then treks westward to Aztec capital, now Mexico City; completes final conquest of Aztec Mexico, partly with aid of black slaves, in 1521; Cortés' triumph vastly stimulates Spanish interest in New World, and exploration, occupation, and colonization become deadly serious.

1522

Remnants of Ferdinand Magellan's fleet reach Spain after three-year round-the-world voyage, giving Europeans first clear idea of what and where America is in relation to the Orient.

1524

The Italian Giovanni da Verrazano, sailing for France, explores New York Harbor and the American coast

Amerigo Vespucci
UFFIZI GALLERY

Sebastian Cabot
LIBRARY OF CONGRESS

Giovanni da Verrazano
LIBRARY OF CONGRESS

Jacques Cartier
LIBRARY OF CONGRESS

Hernando de Soto
LIBRARY OF CONGRESS

northward to Newfoundland; this voyage further contributes to notion that a strait, variously called Strait of Anian or Northwest Passage, exists through North American landmass, which is presumed to have a narrow, Panama-like isthmus.

1528

Pánfilo de Narváez lands near Tampa Bay, Florida; lured ever northward by Indian tales of yellow metal in the next village (Indians got very good at pandering to the European appetite for the wild-goose chase), he reaches Pensacola Bay with only half his force alive; thence he sails on makeshift boats to the Mississippi delta and later to Galveston Bay, where a few survivors, not including the luckless Narváez, are nursed by Indians.

1533

Fortún Jiménez, sailing north from Mexico, discovers and names (lower) California, believing it to be an island.

1534

Jacques Cartier, seeking the Strait of Anian and gold, explores and names the Gulf of St. Lawrence for France; he makes a second voyage in 1535, wintering among friendly Huron Indians near future site of Quebec; Indians feed Cartier a story about a rich white Kingdom of Saguenay somewhere to the west.

1535

Álvar Núñez Cabeza de Vaca, with three or four other survivors of the Narváez expedition, including a Moroccan slave named Esteban, begins to walk from Texas to Mexico City; he arrives in Mexico City in 1536, bringing with him Indian tales of seven fabulously rich cities of gold.

1539

Hernando de Soto, having assembled a force of 600

enthusiasts to investigate de Vaca's reports, arrives in Florida from Cuba; his group wanders through the U.S. southeast for four years, getting as far north as Tennessee and discovering in the process the Mississippi River; the survivors (about 300) finally reach Mexico by boat in 1543.

1540

Francisco Vásquez de Coronado leads huge expedition, including 800–1,000 Indians and blacks, north from Compostela, Mexico, into U.S. southwest, in search of the rumored Seven Cities; he finds instead Zuñi pueblos in Four Corners area; one of his officers discovers Grand Canyon; Coronado leads small group through Texas Panhandle into Kansas, drawn on by Indian lies of another golden empire, Quivira; although some of Coronado's men wish to carve out estates in the rich Kansas grasslands, he insists they return and leads expedition back to Mexico in 1542.

1541

Cartier makes a third voyage to eastern Canada; he again winters near Quebec, this time collecting fool's gold and crystals he believes to be diamonds; returns to France in 1542, to be a laughingstock. A follow-up colonizing expedition, arriving in 1542 under Sieur de Roberval, is abandoned in the following year.

1542

Juan Rodriguez Cabrillo and Bartolomé Ferrelo sail north from Mexico along California coast, Ferrelo getting as far north as Oregon and claiming entire coast for Spain.

1562

French Huguenots, under Jean Ribaut, found colony named Port Royal on Parris Island, in South Carolina; colonists, starving, take off for France the following year.

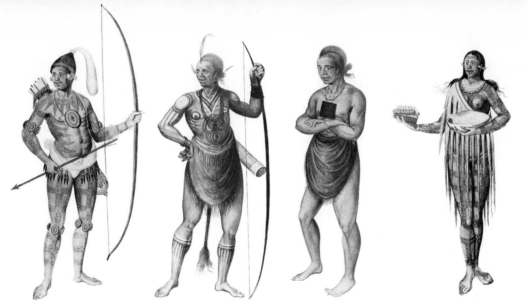

Florida Indians painted about 1585 by John White, a member of the Roanoke expedition, who depicted life in America

1564

Second French Huguenot colony is founded at Fort Caroline, in northern Florida; is heavily resupplied in 1565.

1565

Spanish, alarmed at French moves in Florida and seeking to protect route of treasure galleons, establish St. Augustine, first permanent European settlement in U.S., as military base for action against French; French colonists are hunted down and slaughtered.

1567

British fleet under Sir John Hawkins is virtually destroyed by Spanish in Gulf of Mexico; Hawkins had led two previous very profitable voyages to Spanish West Indies (1562–1565), selling there black slaves captured in Africa and defying Spanish colonial law against trade with foreigners.

1572

Sir Francis Drake, who had sailed to Caribbean under Hawkins, steals 30 tons of Spanish silver in Panama; Drake's piratical venture marks beginning of an increasingly transparent effort by Elizabeth I of England to challenge Spain, primarily on the seas.

1576

Sir Martin Frobisher makes first of three voyages to Baffin Island area, in search of Northwest Passage.

1577

Sir Francis Drake begins three-year round-the-world

voyage, in course of which his *Golden Hind* sacks Spanish towns on Pacific coast of South America, robs a Peruvian treasure galleon, sails up the California coast past San Francisco, and returns by way of the Spice Islands and the Cape of Good Hope in 1580.

1578

Elizabeth I grants Sir Humphrey Gilbert a patent to colonize North America; patent provides that all colonists are to enjoy the same rights and privileges as English citizens at home.

1583

Gilbert leads expedition to Newfoundland; he claims it and its multinational fishing community for England; Gilbert's ship is lost with all hands on return voyage.

1584

Sir Walter Raleigh obtains his half-brother Gilbert's patent, names non-Spanish North America Virginia in honor of "virginal" Elizabeth I, and sends out small fleet that reconnoiters Albemarle Sound area of South Carolina; as a result of good reports Raleigh sends out colony under Ralph Lane to Roanoke Island in 1585.

1585

Sir Francis Drake sacks Spanish settlements, including St. Augustine, on Florida coast; stops at Roanoke colony in 1586 and brings back to England Raleigh's colonists, who are depressed and hungry; although unsuccessful, the first Roanoke attempt results in glowing description of Virginia by Thomas Hariot (1588) and magnificent drawings of Indians by John White.

1587

Raleigh sends out second Roanoke colony (117 men, women, and children); first English child, Virginia Dare, is born in North America; because of war with Spain, colony cannot be resupplied until 1591, by which time colonists have disappeared, leaving a few ambiguous traces. Raleigh spends £40,000 of his own money on Roanoke, a lesson not lost on future English colonizers.

1598

Spain, partly as a result of Drake's Pacific rampage, begins a push to colonize northward into the American southwest and California; Juan de Oñate leads a few miners and settlers into Texas and New Mexico, where some of their sheep, cattle, and horses wander off, quickly multiply, and ultimately form basis for longhorn cattle industry and supply Plains Indians as far north as Canada with mustangs.

1602

Expedition led by Sebastián Vizcaíno sails up California coast, naming San Diego Bay, discovering and naming Santa Catalina Islands, and reporting favorably on Monterey as a site for future Spanish colony.

On the other side of North America, Bartholomew Gosnold lands in New England, explores coast from Maine to Massachusetts, names Cape Cod and Martha's Vineyard, and builds small fort on Cuttyhunk in the Elizabeth Islands. Six years later Gosnold is one of the original Jamestown settlers, dying there in a climate he correctly denounced as malarial.

1603

Henry IV, king of France, casting an eye on the increasingly lucrative trade in Canadian beaver pelts, promises fur monopoly to four old army friends, including Samuel de Champlain, if they will set up a French colony; Champlain makes his first voyage to St. Lawrence region and learns from Indians about the Great Lakes.

1605

After a false start a solid French colony is established in Port Royal, Nova Scotia; although Champlain and his friends thrive there, they are recalled in 1607 as a result of political intrigues at the French court.

1606

King James I of England, having made peace with Spain in 1604, grants a royal charter to the Virginia Company, a corporation of small private investors governed by a royal supervisory board, to form two colonies in North America. One group of investors, located mainly in Plymouth, is granted the right to settle northern Virginia (New Jersey to Maine); a second group, soon called the London Company, is entitled to settle Virginia between New Jersey and Georgia.

1607

In ships *Susan Constant, Godspeed,* and *Discovery,* financed by the London Company, 105 colonists sail 30 miles up the James River and select the marshy Jamestown site, largely because the ships can be moved right up to shore and tied to trees (May 14–24); by the end of the year only 36 colonists remain alive, the rest having been killed by disease, starvation, Indians, or each other.

The Plymouth group of investors also sends out colonists, who settle on the Kennebec River in Maine (May); the colonists demand to be taken home the following year, after having experienced a Maine winter; the Plymouth Company remains inactive thereafter until 1620.

(1) THE BRAFFERTON   **(2) THE COLLEGE**   **(3) PRESIDENT'S HOUSE**

(4) THE CAPITOL   **(5) THE COLLEGE (REAR)**   **(6) THE PALACE**

From an Engraving made in the Year 1740, or thereabout, the Original of which was presented by the Bodleian Library, Oxford, to Mr. John D. Rockefeller, Jr., in 1937.

Buildings in Williamsburg, Virginia, in 1740
COLONIAL WILLIAMSBURG

The Colonial Period
1607–1776

This period in the United States, beginning with the Jamestown colony and ending with the Declaration of Independence, lasted a hundred and sixty-nine years. Until the end of World War II this period comprised more than half of our country's total historical experience.

From 1607 until about 1640 five European nations tinkered with colonial empires in North America. The French founded Quebec in 1608, repopulated Nova Scotia (Acadia), and settled several islands in the Caribbean. The Dutch founded trading posts in Albany and New York City in the mid 1620's and soon thereafter began to settle the Hudson River Valley; they too planted themselves in the West Indies. Spanish settlers founded Santa Fe, New Mexico, in 1609, and Spanish

Franciscans established a string of missions from western Florida to coastal South Carolina. Beginning in 1638 the Swedes planted several small colonies in what is now Delaware. The English founded colonies in Jamestown (1607), Bermuda (1612), Plymouth (1620), St. Kitts (1625), Barbados (1629), Massachusetts Bay (1630), and Maryland (1634). Of these the British colonies in the West Indies were the stars, having more people and producing much more wealth than any of the mainland settlements. The mainland colonial population in 1640 was about twenty-eight thousand.

From 1640 to 1660, a period roughly corresponding to the civil war and rule of the Cromwells in England, European immigration slowed to a trickle for the most part, but the existing French, Dutch, and English colonies prospered on their own. The French founded Montreal in 1642, and French Jesuits and fur-traders opened up the Great Lakes. The Dutch colonies also did well, becoming strong enough and rich enough from the Hudson River fur trade to gobble up the Swedes and to

The cruelty of early explorers to the Indians was notorious. Left, Spaniards torture Florida Indians. Right, the Indians retaliate by pouring molten gold down a Spaniard's throat.
BOTH: LIBRARY OF CONGRESS

crush an attempt by New Englanders to set up a trading post on the Delaware River. In the Northeast English settlers scattered in increasing numbers throughout New England, filling in parts of Rhode Island, Connecticut, and New Hampshire. This movement, begun in the late 1630's, was fueled in part by a desire to get out from under the rather nasty Puritan government in Massachusetts and in part by the astonishingly high rate at which colonial New Englanders made babies. To the south the Virginia and Maryland colonies also grew, aided in part by an influx of Anglican farmers fleeing Cromwell's England.

From 1660, when the Stuarts were restored to the throne of England, to 1690, when they were gone for good, the English were aggressively active in North America. In 1663 Charles II of England chartered a colony called Carolina, which extended from the present northern border of Florida to the southern border of Virginia. In 1664 the English seized from the Dutch a huge chunk of mid-Atlantic territory, comprising what are now the states of New York, New Jersey, Pennsylvania, and Delaware. In 1670 King Charles granted all the lands drained by Hudson Bay to a private fur company, which immediately began to plague the French, as it was supposed to. From 1662 to 1679 royal charters were granted to Connecticut, Rhode Island, and New Hampshire. In 1681 Pennsylvania was chartered as a separate colony, which soon included Delaware and the southern half of New Jersey. By 1690 almost all the Atlantic seaboard except Florida was in English hands.

During the years 1660–90 France was also busy in North America. It encouraged farming settlements in the Quebec region and vastly extended its reach in the North American interior. With the Mississippi voyages of Père Marquette, Louis Joliet, and especially Robert Cavalier, Sieur de La Salle, who claimed the entire Mississippi Valley (Louisiana) for France, the French laid the foundation for a vast fur-trading empire that by 1750 extended south from the Great Lakes to the Mississippi delta and west to the Rocky Mountains.

Until 1690 Spanish moves north of Mexico were confined mainly to unstinting Jesuit and Franciscan missionary activity in Arizona, New Mexico, and Texas. This activity received a big setback with the great Pueblo Revolt of 1680, which drove the Spanish out of New Mexico and afforded a moment of triumph remembered and cherished by Hopi and other southwestern Indians to this day.

In 1690 the colonial population had grown to about 214,000. By 1770, however, there were 2,205,000 American colonials. This tenfold growth from 1690 to 1770 was in part caused by a colonial birth rate that continued to be very high. But it was also spurred for the first time by significant immigration into the English colonies by people who weren't English-born and who either hated England or didn't know much about it. The Presbyterian Scots-Irish, who settled the backcountry frontier areas from Pennsylvania to the Carolinas, began arriving after 1690 in increasingly large numbers. To them England and the English were at best a wincing pain, and still are. Beginning in the 1680's there was a trickle of German immigration, mainly to William Penn's new Pennsylvania. After 1710, and after an unpleasant experience in New York, where the English bottled up three thousand German immigrants to make tar and masts for the navy, this trickle became a mass migration, largely into western New York, western Pennsylvania, and thence into the Shenandoah Valley and south. Beginning in the mid 1680's large numbers of French Protestants, many of them skilled men or members of the educated middle class, fled Catholic persecution in France and came to America, settling in New England (the Bostonians Paul Revere and Peter Faneuil were the sons of Huguenot refugees), the middle colonies, or South Carolina, where they established rice plantations and contributed significantly to the growth and character of Charleston. After 1690 black slaves bought in West Africa by English traders and carried to America in ships of English or New England make also began to arrive in larger and larger numbers. By 1776 slaves of African origin constituted 20 per cent of the mainland population; of these half-million slaves forty-seven thousand were in the New England and middle colonies, and the rest in the South.

After 1690, the midpoint of the colonial period, France, Spain, and England intensified their efforts to consolidate and expand their North American holdings. For the next hundred and twenty-five years these na-

Jacques Marquette and Louis Joliet explore the Mississippi.
LIBRARY OF CONGRESS

tions were at war with each other all over the world, and colonial North America was an important third-world theater for these wars. As in most such theaters, the European power blocs fought each other here mainly at long distance and mainly by spilling other people's blood.

As though imitating the beaver, the furry dam-building rodent upon which their North American empire was based, the French got very busy building forts and outposts at both ends of the Mississippi. In 1699 they established forts at Biloxi and Mobile; in 1718 they planted a settlement at New Orleans, which soon became the capital of French Louisiana. In the north Detroit was founded in 1701. In the next forty years a series of fortified trading posts was extended south from Lake Michigan and Lake Erie, staking out as French a wedge-shaped territory including the present states of Wisconsin, Michigan, Indiana, and Illinois, with the point of the wedge located near St. Louis, Missouri, and aiming straight down the Mississippi to Louisiana. Some hundred years later the Union forces struggled for almost five years to duplicate this configuration, and when they did the Civil War was won.

Spain, usually allying itself with France against England but hating both, became alarmed at the French moves in Louisiana, which bid fair to cut off Spain's Florida possessions and appeared to threaten its centuries-old supremacy in Mexican waters. Rather falteringly, Spain began to act, beefing up its garrisons in Pensacola and elsewhere in Florida. It also seriously began to fortify and colonize southeastern Texas, building between 1716 and 1718 the town of San Antonio and its Franciscan mission, later known as the Alamo. For the next forty years Spanish priests competed with French traders, usually unsuccessfully, for the loyalties of nomadic Indians from Texas to Kansas. In 1763 Spain got title to virtually all of the United States west of the Mississippi and by 1769 had begun to lay out a string of California missions and garrisons from San Diego to San Francisco Bay.

For England and the American colonies the late 1680's and early 1690's were a time of trouble. In England the Glorious Revolution of 1688–89 deposed the increasingly despotic James II, placed William and Mary on the throne, enshrined certain political and civil liberties in the Bill of Rights, ensured the near-supremacy of Parliament, and promptly brought on a war with France. In the English colonies, beginning in the mid 1680's, there was a mirror-image set of complex, unseemly, and often lethal squabbles in New England, South Carolina, Maryland, and New York. Right on schedule, starting in 1689, there was also a war with France. This war, called King William's War, devastated New England frontier settlements but otherwise proved only that France and England could mobilize their Indian allies to attack each other's colonists.

After 1690, however, the new English government gradually took a firmer hold on its American colonies. It made Maryland a royal province in 1692 and about ten years later partly sorted out the messy questions of what and where the Delaware and New Jersey colonies actually were. It separated North and South Carolina in 1712 and in 1729–30 finally untangled the affairs of these increasingly prosperous colonies by making them separate royal provinces. The Carolinas, now with large Scots-Irish, German, and French Huguenot populations, had for sixty years been laboring under a complex constitution drawn up by the English philosopher John Locke. Locke's constitution, like Plato's republic, is a reminder to all civilized people that philosophers, when given the chance, almost always make up governments that nobody can stand.

In 1732 England granted James Oglethorpe a charter to form the colony of Georgia as a buffer against Spanish Florida and French Louisiana. Georgia, originally settled by English refugees from the poorhouse and German, Swiss, French, and Jewish refugees from religious persecution, did not thrive under Oglethorpe's idealistic rules—no slavery, no large plantations, no buying or selling of land, no liquor—but it did relatively soon involve itself in a war in Spanish Florida.

By 1750 land speculators, frontier squatters, and fur traders from Virginia and Pennsylvania were pushing into the Upper Ohio Valley, where the French determined they must not pass. There, in 1754, the last and biggest of the French and Indian wars got started. When it was over in 1763, Great Britain controlled all of North America from Hudson Bay to the Florida Keys, from the Atlantic to the Mississippi.

Or thought it did. After 1763, as Britain tried to make its American colonies absorb the costs of driving out the French and sought otherwise to regulate the behavior of its American subjects, it met with resistance. Only twelve years later, on a hill near Boston, this resistance took the form of musket and rifle fire, costing 1,054 British soldiers killed or wounded. Another war for political, social, and economic control of North American territory had begun. It was not the first such war, it was not the biggest, and it was by no means the last.

In 1763 colonial America, flushed with victory over the French, the Spanish, and their Indian allies, was a strange, complicated place. Its population, then about a million and a half, was basically English-speaking, rural, and middle or lower class. There was no hereditary aristocracy, but there was a hereditary slave class, numbering at least 350,000 and growing fast. This population was scattered throughout a territory already huge in relation to England, the mother country, which is somewhat smaller in area than North Carolina.

In 1763 there were only fifteen large towns in all the American colonies, with Philadelphia (twenty thousand) and Boston (eighteen thousand) being far and away the largest. None of these towns, even the largest and richest, represented *the* colonial capital—the principal seat of government, culture, fashion, ideas, or trade for the American colonies as a whole. In this the American colonies differed sharply from the Mexican colonies, of which Mexico City was the brain and heart, or from the French empire in North America, which fell when Quebec did.

Each of the colonies had its own governmental assembly or legislature. These assemblies varied in structure, history, and quirkiness from colony to colony, but all had several things in common.

First, they had real power. They had earned the right by necessity and usage to raise and spend money, to appoint or to pay the salaries of local governmental officials, to form and control local armies, and to regulate the behavior of their constituents in most of the ordinary activities of life. Colonial legislatures could and did pass laws about what their constituents wore, how they were schooled, what they printed and read, how they practiced their religious beliefs and which ones they could practice, how they married and divorced, how they treated their servants and slaves, how they dealt with neighboring Indians, how they acquired and disposed of land, and so on.

Second, these colonial assemblies were elective, in the sense that some members of the colonial community were elected to be lawmakers by some other members of the same community. Qualifications for participating in this elective process, however, varied widely from colony to colony and from time to time. In some colonies, as in Massachusetts, there was a gradual widening of the male franchise as religious qualifications were relaxed. In others there was a gradual restriction of the franchise, as in Virginia, where property qualifications were imposed in the late 1600's. In others, as in New York, there had always been stiff property, religious, and other qualifications. In Virginia, whose representative assembly was called the House of Burgesses and was the oldest such assembly in America, representatives were elected publicly, with each voter announcing his preference in the presence of the candidates and a host of boisterous, wagering onlookers.

Third, the colonial assemblies were dominated by the leading members of the colonial community—those whose education, manners, and wealth qualified them for the upper middle class, above which, with the excep-

tion of royal governors or visiting lords proprietor, there was no other. In Virginia a small group of tidewater planters—about a hundred families—thoroughly controlled that colony's assembly and other institutions of local government. In Massachusetts it was a few shipowners, ministers, and merchants. In Pennsylvania it was mainly a small group of rich English Quakers. It was such small ruling groups, based largely on the Atlantic seaboard, who made the American Revolution. And they made it against another small group—the English king, his cronies, and Parliament—that reached clumsily across three thousand miles of ocean and, through royally appointed governors, judges, and customs officials, sought to deprive the local colonial rulers of some of their power, status, and wealth.

Colonial self-government was neither democratic nor representative in the sense these political terms have today. Colonial artisans, craftsmen, or small farmers did not expect one of their number to represent them in their colonial assembly, any more than today the branch managers of individual stores in a huge national chain expect to have a representative on their corporation's board of directors. The eighteenth-century American colonies were rather like today's great social or economic institutions—private universities, giant white-collar corporations, and so on. Employees of such institutions do not *expect* them to be democratic or representative. What they do expect is a certain amount of fairness, a certain minimal responsiveness. That is what average American colonials expected of their governments. When they didn't get it, they made a rebellion and briefly ran amuck. This happened fairly often, particularly after 1690, when the differences between settled areas and the frontier backcountry became increasingly pronounced. After 1690 settlement began to outdistance local colonial institutions, leaving the frontier settler with taxes, fees, or price squeezes but without courts, schools, judges, roads, or defenses.

There were several broad American communities of interest, but then as now they had little to do with formal lines of political authority. The small frontier farmers in the South Carolina or Virginia Piedmont had much more in common with the small frontier farmers in western Pennsylvania or Massachusetts than they did with the people who ran things in Charleston or Williamsburg. Despite their obvious differences, the Puritan shipowner in Newport, the landed baron of Dutch ancestry in New York, and the Huguenot owner of a rice plantation in South Carolina had more in common with each other than they did with the ordinary ruck in their respective colonies. And yet, on the other hand, there was also a curiously intense localism or territoriality among the colonists, regardless of class.

During the Revolutionary War, for example, this warm loyalty to place prevented Massachusetts men from serving under New Hampshire officers and caused all sorts of comical bickering among the colonies, to the despair of Washington and other military commanders.

Apart from the east-west, establishment-frontier divergence that ran throughout the colonies from north to south, there were also pronounced latitudinal differences. These socioeconomic differences between settled northern and southern regions traveled full-blown into the nineteenth century, caused a civil war, and have lingered fitfully to this day. These differences were mainly about how people made a living.

Neither the Jamestown nor the Plymouth colonies showed any signs of vigorous life until their settlers were allowed to own land and to work for their own profit rather than for the common or company good. Once this happened, both New England and Virginia became, literally, lands of opportunity for the English middle and working classes.

In England, and in Europe generally, land was scarce and expensive. Even its wildlife was jealously guarded, so that hunting and freshwater fishing was a prerogative of the estate owner and poaching a serious criminal offense for everybody else. On the other hand, labor in England was abundant and cheap; there was considerable unemployment in the towns and in the country. In North America the situation was reversed: land was abundant and labor scarce. Hence North America acted as a magnet, attracting those who had skills, wanted to work, and hoped to get some land and other property they could own.

The original Massachusetts colonies of Plymouth,

Left, curing and inspecting tobacco; right, taking it to market.
BOTH: LIBRARY OF CONGRESS

Salem, and Boston were founded by a group of stiff-necked, middle-class English Puritans whose forms of worship and passion for learning, sobriety, and exclusivity had a strong Hebraic quality. At first the Massachusetts Puritans were concerned more with self-sufficiency than with profit making, and so they concentrated mainly on building small, neat townships whose inhabitants raised enough corn, cattle, and vegetables to feed themselves, with perhaps a little surplus. By the 1640's Massachusetts had achieved a certain shaky subsistence and had sent to London the first of a long line of messengers telling the English Parliament that Massachusetts wanted to be left alone. But Puritan saints also had to repay their English stockholders, and they had to buy from England guns, gunpowder, books, paper, type, printer's ink, woolens, beer, wine, and other manufactures necessary for their exemplary "city upon a hill." At first the Puritans paid for such purchases with furs, skins, fish, and timber.

Soon, however, New England geography and New England orneriness combined to upset Britain's grand mercantile scheme for its colonies, which was to buy raw materials from them and sell back manufactured items. It was essential to this scheme that the colonies be allowed to trade only with the mother country, which could then set low prices for raw materials it wanted to buy and high prices for finished goods it wanted to sell. It was also essential that the colonies be prevented from setting up industries of their own. If that happened, the colonies would become producers as well as consumers, and their finished goods might compete in home and foreign markets with the mother country's. England was not alone in planning such an arrangement for its American colonies; France, Spain, and Portugal wanted the same thing. But unlike England these countries vigorously enforced their economic imperialisms; as a result former French, Spanish, and Portuguese colonies in the Western Hemisphere were until recently still economic colonies of the industrialized world, exporting raw materials and cheap labor, importing manufactured goods and technological expertise.

The English passed a lot of laws designed to prevent the New England colonies from growing up economically, but for a number of reasons they didn't get serious about enforcing them until 1763. For one thing, England was preoccupied during most of the sixteenth and seventeenth centuries with internal conflicts and wars for European supremacy. For another, the mercantile scheme was working nicely in the West Indian and in the southern colonies. Thirdly, the prosperity of the New England colonies, though heterodox, did enable these colonies to purchase English manufactures. Basically England wished its North American colonies well, and it seemed hardly worth the trouble to impoverish a bunch of crabby Puritans who were, in any case, altogether too quick with quotations from the literature of English civil liberty.

The raw materials Massachusetts had to sell were beaver furs, timber, huge amounts of fish, and some meat, grains, and vegetables. New England beaver soon ran out, and further expansion of this trade west and north was blocked by the Dutch and French. Unmilled timber was not a particularly profitable export in relation to its bulk. England had its own fishing industry and farms; in 1660 it moved to protect them by forbidding importation of New England fish and produce. According to mercantile theory Massachusetts should then have given up the ghost. But the Puritans were not going to let British imperial theory stand in the way of God's work and the accumulation of capital, so they sold what they had wherever they could. They sold their fish to Catholic Spain and to planters, including non-English ones, in the West Indies. To the West Indian planters, who had large slave populations to feed, they also sold their grains, vegetables, cattle, and worn-out horses.

From the very first the Massachusetts colonists started making things. They made books—religious tracts, a Bible for the Indians, a spelling book that sold three million copies before it quit. They made schools—elementary schools, grammar schools, colleges. They minted coins, which was strictly forbidden. They made pots, pans, and other utensils. They milled lumber and made hoops and staves for barrels. They made shirts and hats. They started making these things because, obviously, they needed them. But soon some of these items, like barrels, pots, and shirts, began to find their way into the world marketplace, winding up in Africa or the West Indies.

More threatening to British mercantile interests, New Englanders also made capital goods—productive facilities whose function is to make more and more of something, including profits. They made shipyards, iron foundries, and rum distilleries. In 1660 the English encouraged the colonial shipbuilding industry, for some of the same reasons for which manufacturers today set up plants in less developed countries. With its large, accessible supply of good timber, New England could build sound ships for about half the English cost. By 1713 a New Englander had invented the schooner—small, fast, lovely, and good for smuggling, among other things; by 1776 one third of all British tonnage was American-made, and British shipbuilders didn't like that any more than General Motors likes Toyotas.

England did not encourage the building of iron foundries, but New England made them anyway. Produced at first for local needs—nails and other tools—colonial iron soon made its way into the grown-up world where the real money was. West African chieftains used iron bars as currency and traded slaves for them; iron chains and shackles were also useful adjuncts to the African trade. By 1776 iron foundries in the thirteen colonies were producing more iron than Great Britain did.

Rum distilleries were at first a useful way of handling the surplus sugar of the British West Indian colonies. Rum became the most popular drink in the colonies; it was also purchased in quantities by the British navy, which issued it to its wretched naval proletariat as grog. Rum also became a hot trading item. African slave traders would exchange slaves for it. It was also a crucial ingredient in the Indian fur trade and in Indian land swindles. By the 1730's New England distilleries were putting out more than a million gallons of the stuff and were consuming more sugar and molasses than British West Indian planters could supply. In flagrant violation of British policy, New England merchants bought from French and Spanish planters and, to compound the outrage, smuggled most of this cargo in without paying customs duty on it. British measures after 1763 to crack down on the molasses-rum trade were so infuriating to New Englanders that John Adams said it caused the Revolution.

After 1690, when the British monopoly on the slave trade ended, New Englanders began working a series of triangular trade routes, going from ports like Boston or Newport to southern Europe or West Africa and thence to the West Indies and home. They sent out, in addition to fish and foodstuffs, water, large quantities of rum, iron in the form of bars or shackles, pots and pans, even shirts. From Spain or Africa they carried wine, gold dust, spices, and slaves to the West Indies and from there brought back to their home ports sugar, molasses, salt, silver, gold, spices, a few slaves, and anything else that might be worth something to somebody. Also after 1690 a deep-sea whaling industry got started, mainly out of Nantucket, which supplied oil for colonial lamps and a waxy substance for candles.

Most of the capital New Englanders acquired in the triangular trade was spent on British manufactures, but not all of it. Some of this capital went into more rum distilleries, more iron foundries, more shipbuilding. Equally contrary to long-term British interests, some of this capital also financed a growing host of small colonial makers—hatters, tailors, shoemakers, cabinetmakers, coopers, wheelwrights, silversmiths, tanners, weavers, gunsmiths, glass blowers, blacksmiths, printers. And some of this capital—born out of cod or rum, nurtured on small manufacture, domestic retail, or western land speculation, and always obeying the stern Puritan injunctions against idleness and frivolity—grew up to finance in the 1820's the first New England textile mills and mass-production factories and to participate thereafter in the swift growth of the industrial Northeast.

In 1763 two surveyors named Mason and Dixon began laying out a line establishing the southern border of Pennsylvania. A hundred years later this line divided two societies at deadly war with each other, but even during the late colonial period it marked off two rather distinct regions. North and south of this line most of the people were small farmers. They wanted mainly to be let alone—by the Indians whose lands they had conquered or were in the process of conquering, by those forces of nature in which it is easy to find a malevolent intelligence, and by colonial legislatures that took more than they gave and didn't know scratch about the important things.

But also north of this Mason and Dixon border were people—about 10 per cent of the population—who were not farmers, big or small. They lived in towns, and they were inventive, aggressive people who by 1763 had engendered a complex, modern, and prosperous society. In many respects, in language, belief, and basic law, this was an English society, though with differences that might be expected to develop in any offspring growing up in a strange, wild place three thousand miles from home. Here, in New England and the middle colonies, were most of the colonial colleges, most of the high schools, and most of the elementary schools for ordinary folk. Here were most of the lighted streets, the hospitals, the roads. Here were most of the colonial doctors, lawyers, scientists, jurists, surgeons, professors, printers, inventors, merchants, apothecaries, and ministers, though all practicing their arts in ways that had undergone a sea change and ignoring many of the professional traditions and categories typical in England. Here were most of the skilled workers and craftsmen, making silver teapots and ships, glassware, stoves and covered wagons, rifles, clocks, pewterware, Queen Anne and Chippendale furniture. Here was a middle-class prosperity pervasive enough by the 1770's to have undermined the intellectual and egalitarian status of middle-class women, who for much of the colonial period had worked as printers, innkeepers, accountants, lawyers, blacksmiths, midwives, barbers, butchers, or gunsmiths, but were now increasingly pushed into more ornamental roles. And here too was most of the fluid colonial capital, a lot of it in the hands of former shipmasters accustomed to making lonely decisions involving life, death, and fortunes, accustomed above all to commanding men and receiving from them deference and obedience. These were the captains whom William Pitt, very popular in the colonies as a Parliamentary friend of the Americans, described as "children" who must "obey" their mother, especially in matters "relating to trade and navigation."

Between 1763 and 1776 Great Britain tried both to control colonial commerce and to skim some of the cream off the top. But psychologically it was simply too late for that. Prosperous New Englanders were backed up now by the prime movers of New England-style commerce and industry in the middle colonies, where, in addition, rich farmlands had been turned into magnificent breadbaskets by skilled German farmers. The seaboard Northerners were now willing to risk reaching for their petitions, their urban mobs, and finally their own muskets in order to protect what was theirs.

The northern merchants had allies in the South too, people with names like Lee, Burdwell, Jefferson, Washington, and Carter. These people dressed in English clothes, sat down to English tables set with English silver, got letters from their sons in English universities, rode in English saddles, browsed through libraries of English books bound in English calf, danced English dances, and got pressure put on them by English merchants. After 1763, as it became clear that England was moving in and that control of North America was once again the central issue, these people also began to think cold thoughts about power and the land. They knew, and pointed out to the New England hotheads, that the colonies had no alliance with a naval power and no navy of their own; they were, in that regard, easy targets. But when the chips started to fall, only one thing really mattered. Their high place in this good land, their honor, their good life—all these were power, which had, in the final analysis, come out of the barrel of a gun. It would be kept or lost in the same way, either today, or tomorrow, or whenever, but it was not to be given away.

And so it is not very surprising that on July 4, 1776, a small group of cultivated, prosperous American colonials, gathered from a hodgepodge of places and peoples a half-million square miles in extent, met in a handsome brick building in Philadelphia and there approved—but did not sign—a document entitled *The unanimous Declaration of the thirteen United States of America in Congress Assembled*. It had been written by Thomas Jefferson of Virginia and edited by an Adams of Massachusetts, a Sherman of Connecticut, a Livingston of New York, and a rich printer, scientist, diplomat, author, inventor, and land speculator named Benjamin Franklin, of Pennsylvania. Their declaration was given a final smoothing and toning down by the fifty-five-member Continental Congress and then sent out into the world—the most nobly worded and spiritually resonant expression of the territorial imperative ever written.

The Colonial Period (1607–1776)

1607

Jamestown is a disaster area; Indians attack, killing or wounding seventeen; ruling council squabbles, executes one leader, tries another for slander; wheat planted, grows seven feet tall with no grains; 60 people die of malaria or dysentery; John Smith saved, so he claims, by intervention of Pocahontas, daughter of Indian chief; 40 remaining colonists saved at year's end by arrival of ship bringing supplies and 120 more settlers (May–December).

1608

Samuel de Champlain founds fur-trading post at Quebec (July); almost single-handedly keeps it going; following year explores upper New York (Lake Champlain), alienates powerful Iroquois confederation, which allies itself with Dutch and then English and 150 years later helps drive French from North America.

First women (two) and first foreigners (Poles, Dutch) arrive in Jamestown, in second of two shiploads of reinforcements (October).

1609

Henry Hudson, English navigator sailing for Dutch company, explores and names Hudson River; ship *Half Moon* reaches site of Albany in September.

Spanish settlers abandon earlier New Mexico site, form Santa Fe, oldest U.S. capital, under Spanish governor Peralta.

"Starving time" begins in Jamestown: Captain John Smith becomes leader; learns from Indians to plant corn but leaves after serious injury; winter famine sets in; settlers dig up Indian corpses to eat; one man kills wife, preserves meat in salt, is shot for it; in England king reorganizes Jamestown charter, providing for military governor instead of ruling council.

1610

Jamestown is saved by arrival of fleet under Lord De La Warr, with 300 new colonists (June); survivors and remnant of nine-ship fleet sunk in storm were actually sailing away when met by De La Warr and ordered back; strict military discipline enforced for next six years, workers being marched from barracks to fields by drumbeat.

1612

John Rolfe of Jamestown develops cross of Spanish and local tobacco; well liked in England, this tobacco quickly becomes the cash crop, the economic mainstay, and the money (medium of exchange) of the Virginia colonies and later of Maryland and North Carolina.

Virginia Company colonizes Bermuda Islands.

1613

Although barely hanging on, Jamestown sends Captain Samuel Argall sailing 800 miles north to wipe out French fur and missionary outposts on Mount Desert Island in Maine and in Port Royal in Nova Scotia.

1614

Pocahontas and John Rolfe marry, securing temporary peace with Powhatan Indians; Pocahontas (now Lady Rebecca) later dies in England (1616–17).

Pocahontas, renamed Rebecca, as she looked when visiting London in 1616
LIBRARY OF CONGRESS

1616

Beginnings of private property in Virginia: settlers granted 100 acres apiece to work; settlements spread up James River to higher, healthier ground in Henrico, which becomes leading town, with real houses; total population about 350.

John Smith publishes *A Description of New England*, based on 1614 explorations, thus naming and creating interest in this region.

1619

Military rule abolished in Virginia; first legislative assembly convened as House of Burgesses (*burgess*, meaning "citizen," is term describing English class of substantial officeholding merchants, next in rank below gentlemen); headright system begun, in which grant of 50–100 acres is made to each new arrival and dependents; first blacks (nineteen) arrive in Dutch ship manned by Englishmen, are purchased as indentured servants; first shipload of English women arrives, purchased as wives for 150 pounds of tobacco each; total Virginia population about 1,000.

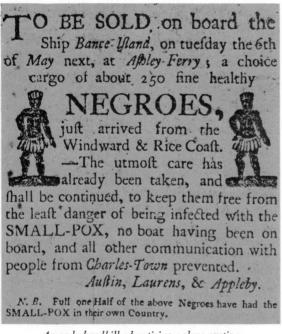

An early handbill advertising a slave auction
LIBRARY OF CONGRESS

1620

Mayflower, with 102 Puritans, including Separatist Pilgrims from Holland, arrives in Provincetown, Cape Cod, November 21 (modern calendar); since charter from Virginia Company applies only as far north as New York area, where Pilgrims intended to settle, Pilgrim (Saints) and Puritan (Strangers) factions draw up *Mayflower Compact*, providing for majority-rule self-government, which is signed by 41 adult males; exploring party locates Plymouth Harbor, and *Mayflower* arrives there December 26; winter and illness kill more than half by spring of 1621.

1621

Pilgrims, now under governorship of William Bradford, learn corn planting and Indian diplomacy from two English-speaking Indians, Squanto and Samoset; conclude peace treaty with Massasoit of Wampanoag Indians; Plymouth receives charter from Council for New England (old Plymouth Company); Pilgrims have harvest thanksgiving feast in October, but serious food shortage in winter of 1621–22 would have wiped out colony without supplies from Indians.

1622

Powhatan Indians, under new leadership, launch massive surprise attack on Virginia settlements, killing 357, about a quarter of the population; war against Indians continues for two years, settlers learning to attack Indian villages in fall, destroying harvests.

1623

Pilgrims institute private enterprise, with each family growing its own food on its own plot; colony prospers and spreads out as settlers seek more land for growing corn and raising cattle; Pilgrims trade corn for local wampum, then trade wampum with Maine Indians for furs.

1624

Virginia, its charter revoked, is made royal province, largely because of scandalous colonial death rates; between 1618 and 1624 at least 3,000 colonists died, mostly from overwork or starvation, because, in defiance of company policy, labor and land are diverted to tobacco growing; king reluctantly allows House of Burgesses to continue in existence.

Dutch West India Company establishes fur-trading settlement at Fort Orange (Albany), New York, and similar settlement on Governors Island, off Manhattan.

1625

New Amsterdam built by Dutch West India Company on southern tip of Manhattan Island; island bought in 1626 from Manhattan Indians; colony grows slowly (from 270 in 1628 to 1,000 in 1656) but is autocratically and wretchedly governed by Dutch.

Barbados, St. Kitts, Nevis, and Antigua in West Indies colonized by English and prosper from start; population 3,000 by 1629.

The earliest existing view of New Amsterdam, dated 1651
LIBRARY OF CONGRESS

1628

Plymouth Pilgrims send Miles Standish to break up Thomas Morton's settlement (Merriemount) near present site of Quincy; Puritans object to Anglican settler's maypole frolics, relations with Indian women, and gunrunning; Morton is deported to England.

Salem, Massachusetts, founded by John Endicott and first Puritan settlers sent out by Massachusetts Bay Company (September).

1629

Dutch institute patroon system—enormous baronial holdings along Hudson River Valley, worked by tenant farmers; after 1664 English continue practice of granting huge manorial estates in New York, far larger than any in southern colonies until early nineteenth century.

John Winthrop
LIBRARY OF CONGRESS

1630

Large group—about 900—of Puritans, under John Winthrop, found Boston; Winthrop and other Puritan leaders possess unique charter (confirmed by king in 1629) that enables them to transfer government of Massachusetts Bay Company (a private trading company with stockholders) to Massachusetts. Charter calls for management of company by quarterly meeting (called a General Court) of stockholders who are to elect governor and council of assistants (a board of directors), but charter doesn't say stockholders have to meet in England. Puritan leaders, the main stockholders, decide to meet in Massachusetts, thus taking corporate management with them and using it as government of colony. Since Puritan religious leaders control company, they also control colony, running it through a corporate board of directors who are priests, lawmakers, judges, and chief executives all in one, responsible only—and vaguely—to the king. Strict religious qualifications are at first placed on membership in General Court; unprecedented power and independence of Massachusetts ruling group lead to long series of struggles with English Parliament. Colony is rapidly populated by "Great Mi-

gration" (1630–40) of Puritans fleeing religious persecution in England, estimates varying from 10,000 to 24,500 immigrants.

1634

Colony of Maryland founded under ownership of Calvert family (family of the barons of Baltimore); colony prospers immediately, having learned from Jamestown mistakes; designed partly as haven for English Catholics, is first colony to practice religious toleration, although this is later (1654) temporarily abridged by Anglican majority.

1636

Connecticut settled by mass migrations from Massachusetts; settlers found new towns of Hartford, Windsor, Wethersfield, and Springfield (later part of Massachusetts).

A Prospect of the Colledges in Cambridge in New England.

The earliest known view of Harvard, published in 1726
LIBRARY OF CONGRESS

First college in American colonies founded in Cambridge, Massachusetts; opens under new name of Harvard two years later.

Roger Williams, banished from Massachusetts in 1635, founds Providence, Rhode Island; two years later second Rhode Island town, Portsmouth, founded by another refugee from Massachusetts, Anne Hutchinson; under Williams colony becomes model of civilized tolerance—of Indian culture, Baptists (sect organized by Williams), Quakers, Episcopalians, and Jews; 1663 royal charter for Rhode Island explicitly sanctions "lively experiment" of separation of Church and State.

1637

Pequot War: aggressive Pequot tribe, in southeastern Connecticut, destroyed by colonists from Connecticut and Massachusetts with enthusiastic aid of Mohegan and Narraganset (Rhode Island) Indians.

1638

Swedish colony established at Fort Christina on Delaware River (present site of Wilmington, Delaware); colony begins aggressive expansion in 1640's and 1650's but is taken over by Dutch in 1655; Swedish and Finnish settlers there are principal source of two structures that later become frontier standards: log cabin and corncrib.

1639

Fundamental Orders of Connecticut drawn up; provide for democratic, representative form of "orderly and decent" government for Connecticut settlements, with freemen electing assembly, governor, and judges and empowered in some circumstances to override decisions of governor and judges.

First printing press in American colonies established by Mrs. Jose Glover (and her employee Stephen Daye) in what is now Harvard Yard; prints Freeman's Oath, almanac, and, in 1640, the book known as the *Bay Psalm Book (The Whole Book of Psalmes)*.

1641

"Body of Liberties," first compilation of Massachusetts laws, marks beginning of deepening concern by Puritan leaders and colonists alike that idiosyncratic judge-made law, based largely on Bible, should not conflict too violently with traditional English civil and political liberties; in next twenty years Bay Colony undergoes slow liberalization, including a broadening of General Court to include deputies from each town (1644) and a widening of church membership (Halfway Covenant, 1662) that admit many more Puritans to church membership and hence to voting or officeholding privileges.

1642

French found Montreal; thereafter French expansion of fur trade into Great Lakes area largely is checked until 1653 by Iroquois confederation; Iroquois, armed with guns by Dutch traders, rampage against traditional enemies, especially Hurons, north to Montreal and as far west as Lake Michigan; Iroquois goal is to gain exclusive trading rights with French so that they can bid up prices against Dutch in Albany and New York.

1643

Several Massachusetts and Connecticut settlements make first effort to form confederation (United Colonies of New England) to deal with mutual defense, boundary disputes, runaway servants, and other intercolonial problems.

First tide-powered gristmill; first "factory" for fulling (shrinking) wool.

1644–46

First ship built in Massachusetts and first ironworks.

1647

Massachusetts General Court passes law requiring each town with 50 families to hire a teacher and each town with 100 families to set up a grammar (high) school; called "Old Deluder Satan Act" because it aims to frustrate Devil's work (ignorance of Scriptures), law is widely copied in New England colonies except Rhode Island.

1648

Margaret Brent of Maryland, wealthy landowner, executor of Governor L. Calvert's will, and lawyer (barrister) for Calvert family in Maryland, demands right to vote in Maryland assembly; is refused.

1650

First book of original poems written in American colonies, *The Tenth Muse Lately Sprung up in America: or, Several Poems, compiled with great variety of Wit and Learning, full of delight*, by Anne Bradstreet of Massachusetts, published in London.

1651

Massachusetts General Court passes law reflecting both increasing colonial prosperity and concern for status distinctions: people of "meane condition" are not to wear gold or silver lace or buttons, high leather boots, or silk scarves or hoods; only those of "more liberall education" or persons worth more than £200 in taxable property are entitled to wear such clothing.

1652

Massachusetts issues Pine Tree Shilling, minted until 1684; most common colonial coin is Spanish dollar, from Mexico via West Indies.

1654

First Jews (Sephardic) arrive in New Amsterdam from Brazil; by 1776 American Jewish population is about 2,500, mainly in New York City, Newport, Rhode Island, Philadelphia, Charleston, and Savannah.

Brief civil struggle between Protestant majority and

Catholic elite in Maryland; protection of law briefly withdrawn from Catholics, but Calvert family regains control in 1657.

1656

First Quakers, Mary Fisher and Ann Austin, arrive in Boston and are imprisoned and banished; until 1661 Quakers generally suffer persecution, including mutilation and hanging, especially in Massachusetts.

1659

French traders Grosseilliers and Radisson traverse Lake Superior, reaching Wisconsin; French governor in Quebec confiscates their furs, so they go to England and persuade King Charles II to open up Hudson Bay Trading Company to get at Wisconsin furs; Grosseilliers guides first Hudson Bay Company trip in 1688.

1660

Parliament passes Navigation Acts, which give English and American ships monopoly on trade among colonies and England; greatly encourages colonial shipbuilding.

1662

Connecticut granted royal charter; terms are so liberal that later monarchs attempt to rescind it.

1663

Carolina granted to eight owners; proprietors originally offered free land, representative assemblies, and freedom of conscience to encourage settlement; some settlers from Virginia have been in Albemarle Sound (North Carolina) area since 1653, but little growth until after 1690. Southern portion prospers after founding of Charleston in 1670, despite Locke's Fundamental Constitutions (1669), which calls for elaborate landowning aristocracy, among other things.

Canada becomes royal French province; thereafter Iroquois confederacy checked (1666), and rapid exploration and expansion through American interior follow.

1664

Maryland and Virginia begin passing codes designed to answer questions relating to small but growing slave populations: Does Christian baptism confer freedom? Are American-born children of African slave women free? Are slaves killed or injured by their masters victims of criminal assault? Answer to all these questions is No.

English fleet captures New Amsterdam (August); all Dutch settlements are included in huge grant from Charles II to his brother, Duke of York (later James II). Grant went from Connecticut to Delaware River, including Long Island and parts of Cape Cod and northern Maine. New Amsterdam, with population of about 1,000, speaking eighteen different languages, has been chafing under Dutch governor, Peter Stuyvesant, and refuses to help him defend city against English; city is surrendered with no shots fired and renamed New York.

1665

New Jersey, given by Duke of York to friends George Carteret and John Berkeley, gets capital at Elizabethtown and representative assembly; southwestern portion passes through several hands, eventually going to William Penn (1682).

1670

Distillation of rum from West Indian molasses begins in Massachusetts.

Virginia assembly passes law prohibiting prosperous free blacks from owning white indentured servants.

Metacomet, or King Philip, leads the Indians into battle against the colonists.
LIBRARY OF CONGRESS

1673

Jesuit Father Jacques Marquette and trader Louis Joliet travel from Green Bay to Mississippi River and then down it as far south as Arkansas River, hoping that Mississippi will lead to Pacific; they learn instead that it provides all-water route to Gulf of Mexico, possibilities of which lead to later La Salle expeditions.

1675

King Philip's War begins in New England; started by young leader Metacomet (called King Philip by English) of Wampanoags in Plymouth area, whom colonists attempted to disarm; Wampanoags attack Swansea, Massachusetts; war spreads quickly after invasion of Narraganset territory in Rhode Island by Massachusetts (which hoped thus to cause trouble for Rhode Island colony); soon rest of Connecticut and Massachusetts tribes (Mohegans, Podunks, Nipmucks) are on warpath. War destroys or damages 64 towns, kills one sixth of male adult population in New England, and costs £150,000. War is finally won in 1676 after Indian food supplies in upper Connecticut Valley are destroyed; Indian power in New England is broken; Philip's head is displayed on pole in Plymouth for next 25 years.

1676

Bacon's Rebellion begins in Virginia (March): Nathaniel Bacon leads a group of frontier farmers against royal governor William Berkeley, briefly seizes power, burns Jamestown; Bacon is tool in three-cornered power struggle involving Berkeley, the planter aristocracy he has frozen out of power, and frontier farmers, who want to exterminate all Indians they can get their hands on, including friendly ones under Berkeley's protection. Bacon dies of dysentery (October); 37 followers hanged; new assembly passes reforms wanted by planter elite; in 1677 Berkeley, harshly criticized by Charles II, is summoned back to England.

1678

Lyric poems by Anne Bradstreet, *Several Poems Compiled with Great Variety of Wit and Learning By a Gentlewoman in New England*, published posthumously in Boston; intimate love poems addressed to husband, they apparently typify many Puritan marriages, in which love and sexuality were not compartmentalized. Puritan marriages often include extended courtship or precontract stage in which premarital sexual relations are permitted, since sexual incompatibility is grounds for divorce and childlessness is a disaster for frontier family.

1681

Robert Cavalier, Sieur de La Salle, leaves Fort Miami (which he founded) on Lake Michigan and begins voyage with 23 others down Mississippi River, arriving at Gulf of Mexico April 9, 1682; La Salle claims Louisiana (entire Mississippi Valley) for France. In 1684 La Salle leads fleet from France in attempt to found colony in present-day Louisiana but fails to find mouth of Mississippi and lands in Texas instead, where he is murdered by his own men.

1682

William Penn, Quaker convert, arrives in Pennsylvania (granted to him in 1681 by Duke of York, in repayment of £16,000 debt owed Penn's father, Admiral William Penn, conqueror of Spanish Jamaica), purchases land from Delaware Indians, and lays out Philadelphia; Penn's brochure for Pennsylvania advertises religious freedom and good land on liberal terms. Settled by English and Welsh Quakers, German Protestants, and Scots-Irish, colony prospers from start; by 1685 population is about 9,000.

1684

Massachusetts charter is revoked, partly because of Puritan religious intolerance, partly because of violation of trade restrictions.

1685

Political and religious conflicts in southern Carolina (where assembly is dissolved) and in Maryland (where Protestant farmers rise up against Catholic planter elite).

1686

Dominion of New England formed by James II; combines Massachusetts, Plymouth, New Hampshire, and

Sir Edmund Andros
LIBRARY OF CONGRESS

Maine into one administrative unit under royally appointed Governor Edmund Andros and council, but with no assembly; Rhode Island, Connecticut, New York, and New Jersey added to Dominion (1687–88). Andros is very unpopular because he tries to enforce English mercantile policies, levies (small) taxes, cuts out money for schools, and defines most Dominion land as king's property and demands rents for it.

1689

Massachusetts expels Andros, following arrival (April) of news of English "Glorious Revolution" and deposition of James II; New England colonies revert to former governments, and Maryland kicks out Catholic governor. Rebellion in New York against Andros' deputy leads to civil war between popular government in New York City, led by Jacob Leisler, and great estate-owning and fur-trading interests in Albany; in 1691 Leisler undergoes rigged trial for treason, is hanged, disemboweled, decapitated, and quartered, then posthumously acquitted.

King William's War begins, American phase of European War of the Grand Alliance (also called War of the League of Augsburg); French governor, Frontenac, sends Indians against New York and New England frontier settlements in retaliation for earlier English-inspired Iroquois raids against French settlements near Great Lakes; under leadership of Leisler, New England colonies and New York attempt two-pronged invasion of Canada, which fails (1690); war ends in 1697 with some French gains, especially in Maine, but with Indians and French and English colonists only clear-cut losers (of life, peace, property).

1690

New England Primer published, first elementary textbook; teaches ABC's through rhymes ("In Adam's Fall/We sinned all") and includes child's prayer ("Now I lay me down to sleep . . .").

1692

Witchcraft hysteria in Massachusetts (May–October): in a community troubled by inflation-caused poverty and by war (King William's), young girls start chain reaction of accusations and terror resulting in hanging of nineteen men and women for witchcraft; Puritan leaders later publicly confess moral and judicial error in matter.

1693

College of William and Mary, second in American colonies, founded; opens in 1695 in Williamsburg, Virginia, which becomes Virginia's capital in 1699.

1699

French begin to garrison and settle Illinois Territory; under Pierre Lemoyne d'Iberville, French also fortify lower Louisiana Territory with posts on Biloxi Bay (now Mississippi) and Fort Mobile (now Alabama).

1701

Detroit founded as fort by Antoine de la Mothe Cadillac, as part of ongoing French effort to secure Great Lakes region.

Yale College founded (as Collegiate School) in Connecticut; later (1716) moves to New Haven and is renamed Yale. Yale, like Harvard, had very shaky legal foundations; only royally chartered corporations (like Oxford and Cambridge in England) had a right to give exams and confer degrees, but New England colleges did it anyway. Yale set pattern for later colonial colleges in that it arose from and was controlled by leading members of community (trustees) rather than by a self-governing faculty, and it later abandoned original sectarian narrowness as result of competition for students.

An early view of Yale College
LIBRARY OF CONGRESS

1702

Queen Anne's War begins, American phase of the War of the Spanish Succession; in American colonies is fought mainly on New England and Carolina frontiers; New Englanders capture Port Royal, Nova Scotia, in 1710, but English invasion of Quebec fails in 1711; Carolina colonists, with Indian allies, fight Spanish and French, with their Indian allies, in Florida. War is officially ended in 1713 by Treaty of Utrecht. England emerges as dominant world sea power, but big questions are left unsettled in North America. Although England gets Hudson Bay, Newfoundland, and Nova Scotia, the whole St. Lawrence-Great Lakes-Illinois territory and whole southeast Florida-Louisiana territory are left available for anyone to take.

1718

French found New Orleans; French settlements in Louisiana prosper and grow until 1729, winning allegiance of many southeastern Indian groups, including the Yamassee, who attack Carolina settlements; after 1729 French in the South come under severe attack by Natchez and Chickasaw Indians, who prefer British trading goods. Natchez War (1729–39) ties up French, making possible, among other things, settlement of Georgia by English.

Spanish found San Antonio, Texas, in a move to counter French.

1729

North and South Carolina become separate royal colonies; by this time most English colonies are of this type, with royally appointed governors and other officials, plus elective colonial assemblies; only Maryland and Pennsylvania are still privately owned, though largely run by their representative assemblies; only Connecticut and Rhode Island are operating under corporate charters, which enable assemblies to elect governors and ruling council.

1730

Estimated colonial population: 654,950, including about 90,000 slaves. Settled seaboard in New England, middle colonies, and tidewater South is flourishing; newspapers being printed in Boston, Philadelphia (including Ben Franklin's *Pennsylvania Gazette*), and New York; considerable work being done in applied and natural sciences and in early colonial history; first exhibition of American painting held in Boston; designs drawn for Independence Hall in Philadelphia; Newport, Rhode Island, begins attracting colonials as resort. In the next few years dramatic productions, musical concerts, and operas are being performed, then as now following the pattern of first comes money, then comes culture. For frontiersmen German gunsmiths in Pennsylvania begin development of long rifle, deadly accurate, that later becomes known as Kentucky rifle.

1733

Savannah, Georgia, founded by James Oglethorpe, who was granted charter to establish colony of Georgia in 1732; colony is designed in part to be buffer against Spanish and French in disputed Southeast, in part as philanthropic utopia; colony does not thrive until 1749, when slavery and large landholdings are permitted.

Parliament passes Molasses Act, designed to protect British West Indian colonies by placing high duties on rum, molasses, and sugar imported from non-British West Indies; act results mainly in increased colonial smuggling.

1734

"Great Awakening," a religious revival, is begun in New England by Jonathan Edwards and carried on throughout colonies by spellbinding revivalist George Whitefield until 1745; movement causes a variety of religious schisms, tends to reinforce cultural distinctions between frontier and more conservative settled areas, and is in part responsible for founding of University of Pennsylvania (1740), Princeton (1746), Columbia (1754), Brown (1764), Rutgers (1766), and Dartmouth (1769).

1735

Trial of Peter Zenger, publisher of a New York newspaper: Zenger's acquittal establishes truth as sufficient defense against libel; however, most colonial printers remain closely tied economically and socially to legislative assemblies and rarely exercise what today we would recognize as an independent freedom-of-press function.

1739

Fur traders from western Pennsylvania begin penetrating upper Ohio River Valley and begin competing with French for Indian fur business.

1740

War between Spain and England (War of Jenkins' Ear, begun in 1739) leads to invasion of Spanish Florida by Oglethorpe and Creek Indian allies; Spanish invade Georgia in 1742 but are repulsed.

1741

Danish navigator Vitus Bering, sailing under Russian flag, discovers Alaska and Aleutian Islands; Russian fur traders soon follow; presence of Russian traders in Pacific Northwest alarms Spanish in Mexico and is partly responsible for decision to colonize California.

1744

King George's War begins, American phase of War of the Austrian Succession and in part an extension of War of Jenkins' Ear; French attempt to retake Nova Scotia but fail; New Englanders capture Fort Louisburg, French stronghold on Cape Breton Island (1745); colonial plans to capture Montreal and Quebec fail (1747), but English fleet protects colonial seaboard; there are savage raids against colonial settlers in western New York; war settles nothing, and peace treaty of 1748 actually returns Fort Louisburg to France.

1750

Parliament passes Iron Act to protect English merchants against colonial iron industry; law is widely ignored.

Conestoga wagon developed by German craftsmen in Pennsylvania; carries four- to six-ton load and later becomes standard frontier vehicle; a hundred years later carries settlers across Great Plains to Pacific Northwest.

1753

Benjamin Franklin publishes how-to-make-one description of lightning rod in his *Poor Richard's Almanac*, thus in typical colonial fashion turning his interest in electricity and results of kite-and-key experiment into piece of practical technology.

French governor Duquesne orders construction of string of forts from Lake Erie to forks of Ohio River; this action causes alarm in Pennsylvania and Virginia; Virginia governor sends George Washington (21 years old) to investigate; Washington reports that French intend to keep Ohio territory.

1754

Albany Congress, using plan proposed by Benjamin Franklin, attempts to confederate seven New England colonies and Pennsylvania, New York, and Maryland and provide "one general government" for purpose of wooing Iroquois confederacy, dealing with Indians in general, and providing for common defense against French (June). Albany plan is turned down by English government because it feels proposed union would have too much power; all colonial assemblies turn it down for same reason. But plan, copied in part from Iroquois organization, provides precedent and guidelines for later united colonial action against British.

Beginning of French and Indian War, in Ohio: small force, led by George Washington, is sent to build fort at forks of Ohio River, where French are already completing Fort Duquesne; Washington's force is defeated (July 3) and then released. War between French and English colonists and Indian allies in North America goes on for two years until, in 1756, France and England formally declare war, then fight each other and each other's European allies in many parts of world. Hence war is also called Seven Years War (1756–63) or Nine Years War, to include first two years of French and Indian War. War goes badly for English in North America until 1758.

Braddock is fatally wounded at the Battle of the Wilderness.
LIBRARY OF CONGRESS

1755

English force, under General Braddock, is badly mauled in Battle of Wilderness in Ohio (July 9); George Washington is one of survivors. Braddock's defeat leaves whole Virginia-Pennsylvania frontier open to merciless French-Indian attacks.

French colonists (Acadians) in Nova Scotia are deported; some of the deportees ultimately reach Louisiana, forming "Cajun" communities.

1756

Failure (for philosophical-pacifist reasons) of ruling Quaker elite in Pennsylvania to provide for defense of western frontier causes Quakers to resign from any further active governance of colony.

1758

England, now under leadership of William Pitt, pours money, ships, and men into French and Indian War; tide

The British block the harbor at the siege of Fort Louisburg.
LIBRARY OF CONGRESS

turns with fall of Louisburg (July) and French forts on Ohio River and Lake Ontario (August–November); thus approach to Quebec is open from east (Atlantic) and from west (via St. Lawrence River from Lake Ontario). Middle approach, north through New York via Lake Champlain, is blocked by French victory at Fort Ticonderoga.

1759

English fleet, with 18,000 British troops under General James Wolfe, sails up St. Lawrence and besieges Quebec (June–September). Wolfe sneaks army of 4,500 up cliffs and onto Plains of Abraham outside Quebec; French commander, Montcalm, marches his army out of fortress, engages in pitched battle (September 13), loses life, army, Quebec, and New France.

1760

French and Indian War ends in North America with surrender of Montreal in September. Britain, France, and allies continue war elsewhere for two years; Britain wins everywhere.

1763

Treaty of Paris formally ends French and Indian War; France cedes Canada and Louisiana east of Mississippi to England; French ally Spain cedes east and west Florida to England in exchange for Cuba; France repays Spain for loss of Florida by ceding Louisiana west of Mississippi and town of New Orleans (February 10).

General Wolfe dies on the battlefield as his army defeats the French troops, commanded by General Montcalm, who is also killed.
LIBRARY OF CONGRESS

The Declaration of Independence was approved by the Continental Congress in Philadelphia on July 4, 1776. The next day copies were circulated among the colonies. In this engraving a man on horseback reads the Declaration to a cheering, flag-waving crowd while a man at left posts a sign reading "America Independant, 1776."

The Colonial Period:
The Critical Years

1763–1776

Glanced at quickly, these thirteen years have a click-click inevitability about them. An island cannot control a continent, as Tom Paine said in 1776, and the years 1763–76 are, in one sense, an eyeblink of history during which the continent shrugged its shoulders and the island was gone.

Looked at more closely, however, these thirteen years are a bit puzzling. From 1763 to 1776 the American colonists were drawn, for reasons most of them didn't care about, into a war most of them didn't want. They made this war against Christendom's most powerful empire, of which they had been proud to be a part, and in order to do so they formed out of thin air a government that almost nobody respected or liked.

During these critical years most American colonials were not directly affected by anything the British government did or didn't do. In the settled countryside, where most of the people were, farmers were little concerned with the issues that bothered the city folk, who were always getting notions about one thing or another. On the western frontier, now near or crossing the Appalachians, speculator-backed exploration was taking place, and the frontier settlers or squatters there had their own problems—mainly with Indians, confused land titles, and the ineffectiveness or corruption of local government. During these years there was at least one fairly large Indian war, and there were two serious frontier rebellions against the colonial governments of North and South Carolina.

Resistance to the British imperial policies came from the seaboard towns and cities. It was there that the first articulate grumbling took place, and it was there that this grumbling turned into violent attacks upon various symbols of British authority.

Beginning in 1763 and 1764 the British government initiated a series of measures designed to recoup part of the costs of the French and Indian War and to generate revenue for the administration of an empire that included most of North America and the West Indies, parts of West Africa, and the Indian subcontinent. Most of these measures were not especially burdensome, even to the export-import merchants they directly affected. The colonies had in fact been taxed more heavily in the past, and the English were paying tax rates five times higher than American colonials were. Only the Stamp Act involved fairly large numbers of people—those whose business in some way involved paper—and created the potential for widespread frustration, comparable perhaps to a law today that threatened to make citizens renew their driver's licenses in person every week at their local departments of motor vehicles. But the Stamp Act was quickly repealed, as were most other measures designed to tax the colonies.

What really bothered the colonial elite was a political question, namely, who had the right to *initiate* taxing measures? The right to tax was equivalent to the right to rule, and who ruled was the main issue. Initially some colonial leaders objected that Parliament was taxing them without representation, for there were of course no members from the colonies seated in Parliament. But nobody really wanted to send colonial representatives to Parliament, where they would be both outvoted and out of touch. What the colonists wanted was the old system, in which Parliament would ask the various colonial assemblies to raise money for a given purpose and the colonists, through their assemblies, would *consent* to doing so. Parliament didn't like this idea at all, mainly because colonial assemblies had proven notoriously stingy, ungracious, or unpredictable as fund raisers in the past. The arguments developed by leading colonial thinkers and polemicists for taxation by consent were good ones, drawn largely from English theory and precedents. These arguments blossomed into a firm, powerful rhetoric that defined colonial demands as liberty, freedom, and basic human rights and defined British failure to meet these demands as tyranny and oppression. It is not possible to develop a noble and genuinely effective rhetoric without at some level actually believing what you are saying, and so it is unwise to underestimate the sentiments for liberty and equality that achieved their finest flowering in the Declaration of Independence. Not a few colonists were so troubled by the illogic of demanding freedom for themselves and yet owning other human beings that they freed their slaves, both in the North and in the South. And, of course, many colonists put their lives on the line in the belief that they were fighting for liberty against tyranny.

But, as a wit once savagely remarked, an idea is not necessarily true just because a man dies for it. The American colonies were not unfree, not oppressed, not tyrannically ruled. But they were ruled, and there was the rub. The people who had most of the social and economic power in the colonies, and had been accustomed to exercising most of the politicial power through the colonial assemblies, decided, in many cases reluctantly, to go for the brass ring—political power not subject to override by any outside force, be it king or Parliament. And they got it.

But the American Revolution was not a coup. The farmers who fired the shots heard 'round the world at Concord Bridge were not soldiers helping one bunch of colonels grab power from another. When we ask what goaded the American elite into making its Revolution and what caused about 40 per cent of the American colonial population to join them in a war against the most powerful of the Western empires, it is helpful to look at several aspects of colonial American society that are sometimes underemphasized.

Today it is hard for us to think of American colonial society as one that had been at war, more or less continuously, for a hundred and fifty years. But the English colonial societies had been at war with Indian societies for that long, and Indian and settler had taught each other a total, ruthless guerrilla-type warfare more characteristic of ninth-century Viking raids than anything in recent European experience. The American people of the eighteenth century were unique, among those of European stock, in being an *armed* people and one accustomed to defending its territory by war. The peasantry of England, Spain, France, or Germany was not armed and was used to standing aside while professional armies maneuvered through the countryside. European warfare did not usually involve the deliberate destruction of towns, farms, and harvests and did not include women and children as potential foes to be killed lest they kill you. But American warfare did, and the ferocity of American colonial women and children in combat was something that seems more at home in the Icelandic sagas or in the Greek myths.

The educated middle class in Boston, New York, Williamsburg, or Charleston was far closer to physical violence than its counterpart is today. When, as in the 1930's, executives of the Ford Motor Company had fist fights in the board room, or when there is a scuffle on a commuter train or in the House of Representatives, we consider it shocking or amusing. But in colonial days many a shipowner or planter had forced his will upon other human beings with pistol, whip, or fists. Members of colonial legislatures not infrequently went after each other with walking sticks, and the first recorded duel was probably fought in Pilgrim Plymouth in 1621. The Sons of Liberty were, like most vigilante groups, composed mainly of middle-class persons, though they often disguised themselves as laborers or blacks and often enlisted local riffraff in some of their demonstrations.

Eighteenth-century American colonial society was not only accustomed to applying physical violence, but it was also accustomed to directing this violence away from the community toward something outside itself. The colonial frontier—whether it was Pelham Bay Park in New York City, where Anne Hutchinson and thirteen of her children were butchered in 1643 by Narragansets, or western Pennsylvania and Virginia a hundred years later—was not settled by *loners*. The solitary fur trapper or explorer was a unique, often legendary figure, but the farmers who came after came in groups. These large family units sparsely settled a definite territory and cooperated in building cabins and barns, helped each other when disaster struck, and coalesced when the community as a whole was threatened. This kind of settlement, especially the norm in New England, led to the formation of intense "us" bonds and a correspondingly intense aggressiveness toward "them." For most of the colonial period "them" meant Indians or their European allies but also included people who were in some way different enough in culture or religion to be unacceptable. After 1763 the British increasingly became the "them" against whom local communities applied typical colonial techniques: lecture 'em, tell 'em to get lost, and if that doesn't work, get the neighbors and the guns and kick 'em out. The farmers who shot at the British troops were shooting at "them"—invaders of their territory.

From 1763 on, one can follow a whole trail of local sporadic, violent attacks upon "them"—some person, or some piece of property, that had become a symbol of something unwanted coming in from the outside, invading community turf. Tax stamps or the people who sold them; British troops strolling the streets or scabbing as dock workers; customs cutters chasing about after honest smugglers; customs officials, once bribable but now incorruptibly snooping around and breaking into warehouses and inns looking for illegal goods; citizens, high or low, who failed to align themselves with prevailing community sentiment, be it Patriot or Loyalist; some particular chests of tea—all these were physically attacked. It was such a series of violent attacks that led King George III—and British public opinion—to remove the glove from the imperial fist and finally to strike back in anger. But as other kings had already learned—kings named Opechancanough, Metacomet, Pontiac, or Cornstalk—George III soon found that American colonials had become the toughest kids on the block.

The Colonial Period: The Critical Years (1763–1776)

1763

Pontiac's War: Ottawa chief, Pontiac, attacks British at Fort Detroit (May 7); Shawnee, Delaware, and Chippewa Indians, alarmed at encroachment by settlers and surveyors and angered by cutback in British bribes, rise up and seize most of Great Lakes area, killing 600 settlers (May–July); after several Indian defeats a truce is arranged, and by September British regain the West; settlers begin drifting back (1765–66).

Proclamation of 1763: occasioned partly by Pontiac's rebellion and partly because British want settlers to spread into Canada and Florida, proclamation forbids settlement west of Appalachians (where some farmers already are), forbids private purchase of land from Indians, and allows unregulated trade with Indians, which usually means cheating and then trouble (October 7); settlement line is extended westward following year; proclamation is widely ignored, especially by royal governors, who are heavy speculators in land.

Vermont named after Green Mountains (October); Green Mountain Boys, militia, formed to protect settlers from Indians but mainly to fight New York and New Hampshire, both of which claim area; Vermont declares independence during Revolutionary War (1777).

1764

Sugar Act, part of general Revenue Act designed to raise money from colonies, disrupts smuggling of West Indian sugar and molasses; adds new duties on luxury imports like silk, linen, and Madeira wine; adds technical rules allowing seizure of American ships for improper loading procedures (April 5); leads to colonial boycotts of luxury items and to no-taxation-without-representation arguments, summarized in James Otis' *The Rights of the British Colonies Asserted and Proved* (July).

1765

Stamp Act: first "internal" tax, passed by Parliament on March 22, requires tax to be paid (in hard cash) on all legal and commercial paper, from newspapers to diplomas to playing cards; special paper has to be bought from distributor or special stamp bought to place on regular paper; act goes into effect in November and is met with violent resistance throughout colonies, often led by Sons of Liberty, middle-class groups who smash, burn, tear down stamp offices, and terrorize distributors and other officials; act is repealed in March, 1766.

Quartering Act (March 24) calls for colonial assemblies to vote appropriations for shelter, bedding, cooking pots, and rum for British soldiers (about 10,000) now permanently stationed in colonies.

Stamp Act Congress meets in New York City (October); representatives from nine colonies petition for withdrawal of Stamp Act and assert colonies cannot be taxed without their consent; do not demand representation in Parliament, which is too far away, but demand taxing be done by colonial legislatures; Parliament later denies taxation-without-consent argument in Declaratory Act of March, 1776.

Fort George, New York City, about 1760

1766

New York assembly fails, in opinion of British commander, to vote sufficient funds for support of troops garrisoned in New York City (August 11). From British standpoint this is one of a long series of actions by colonial assemblies demonstrating unreliability and unwillingness to "consent" to raising fair share of imperial costs.

1767

Townshend Acts, four Parliamentary measures, passed in June and July under influence of British minister Charles Townshend. First measure dissolves New York assembly for failure to support Quartering Act; second places revenue-raising duties on imports of lead, paper, glass, tea, and paint; third sets up board of customs in Boston, with wide powers to appoint officials, hire vessels, search for contraband, and in general enforce trade laws; fourth cheapens cost of British tea in colonies by removing duties in England. Second or revenue act is designed to pay costs of Crown judges, governors, and other officials, thus freeing them from control of colonial assemblies, which hitherto had paid their salaries.

1768

John Hancock's ship *Liberty* seized by customs officials for technical violation; Boston mob rescues ship and attacks customs officials, who then ask for and get about 1,000 British troops (June–October).

Massachusetts assembly dissolved (July 1) after it refuses to rescind Circular Letter sent to other colonies, urging resistance to Townshend Acts.

Nonimportation agreements (August) lead to boycott of British goods throughout colonies, although effectiveness varies from colony to colony; mobs in some localities often violently enforce boycott, while other localities smuggle in British goods; imports actually increase in southern colonies; boycott continues in crazy-quilt pattern until 1770, when most Townshend Acts are repealed.

1769

Daniel Boone, intrigued by tales of bluegrass Kentucky country, sets out in May with small group to explore. Group finds Cumberland Gap; Boone remains virtually alone in Kentucky until 1771, exploring, trapping, and being robbed by Indians.

California explored and settled by group led by Gaspar de Portolá and Father Junípero Serra. Serra founds mission of San Diego de Alcalá (July 1); Portolá explores on foot northward along coast, discovers San Francisco Bay (November 1), which had eluded ship-borne explorers for more than a century.

1770

Riot in New York City: British troops cut down liberty pole; mob attacks troops, one civilian killed (January).

Boston Massacre (March 5) is culmination of series of incidents—often instigated by Boston radicals like Sam Adams—between British troops and local working people. British troops often moonlighted, especially in shipyards, where strikes were frequent. Large crowd taunts, stones, and clubs small group of British soldiers; in confusion, soldiers finally fire, killing five of mob. British soldiers later defended by patriots and acquitted by colonial jury. However, Adams, Revere, and other radicals milk incident for huge propaganda gains.

Townshend Acts repealed (April 12) except for tax on tea; colonies enjoy greatly increased prosperity for next three years; agitators have hard time stirring up anti-British feeling.

California presidio and mission built at Monterey by Portolá and Serra (June 3); becomes temporary capital of upper (Alta) California; in next six years Serra founds missions at San Antonio (1771), San Gabriel (1771), San Luis Obispo (1772), San Francisco de Assisi (1776), and San Juan Capistrano (1776); settlement hindered until clear-cut overland route from northern Mexico is pioneered by Juan Bautista de Anza in 1774.

1771

Battle at Alamance Creek in North Carolina (May 16) climaxes ten years of frontier discontent with high fees and taxes, corrupt colonial officials, lack of representation in colonial legislature; vigilante-militia group, called Regulators, routed by governor's forces; six leaders hanged. Similar Regulator movement in South Carolina had been successful in 1769, when Regulators got local courts they wanted after series of battles.

1772

Gaspee, customs boat under British commander, runs aground in Rhode Island while chasing smuggler; group of Rhode Islanders attacks, beats up crew, shoots commander, and burns boat (June 9–10); British attempt to find those responsible, intending to try them in England, away from sympathetic colonial juries (September, 1772–June, 1773); British unable to obtain evidence

The British fire on an angry mob during the Boston Massacre.

sufficient to try anyone, but threat to remove trial by local jury greatly spurs development of Committees of Correspondence, informational and propaganda groups formed on town, county, and colony levels.

1773

Tea Act (April 27): Parliament allows British East India Company to export tea wholesale to colonies, thus making their tea the cheapest Americans could buy, even with Townshend tax, which Americans had been busily paying since 1767. However, cheap but taxed tea, which also threatens to undercut smugglers, is seized upon by radicals as symbol of Parliamentary "tyranny," or taxation without consent.

Tea is dumped into the harbor during the Boston Tea Party.
LIBRARY OF CONGRESS

Boston Tea Party (December 16): Sons of Liberty, disguised as Indians and blacks, dump 342 chests of East India tea from ship *Dartmouth* into Boston Harbor; first of several colonial "tea parties" in which colonials either refuse to let tea ships enter harbors or destroy them when they arrive. Boston incident is important because it goads King George III and British public opinion into crackdown designed to settle issue of where political power really is—in colonies or in England.

1774

Coercive ("Intolerable") Acts, four laws passed (March–June) to punish Massachusetts for Boston Tea Party, close Boston Harbor to all shipping until it pays for ruined tea; deprive Massachusetts of right to elect certain officials; require that officials accused of capital offenses be tried in England rather than in Massachusetts; and permit troops to be quartered in inns and other private property (Boston authorities had circumvented earlier quartering acts, so that troops had to live in tents on Boston Common).

Lord Dunmore's War: Shawnee Indians, under great provocation, finally rise up against settlers in Kentucky (April); isolated from other Indian allies by colonial diplomacy, Shawnees are defeated by Virginia militia under governor of Virginia, Earl of Dunmore (October).

Quebec Act (June 22) is deemed part of "Intolerable" Acts because it extends Canadian border to Ohio River and Mississippi, thus denying colonial claims to Ohio and Illinois territory; act also grants full civil liberties to French settlers in Canada, which colonies regard as plot to establish "popery" in North America, much as later Americans feared Catholic President would establish "tunnel to the Vatican."

First Continental Congress meets (September 5–October 26) in Philadelphia in response to Coercive Acts; 55 delegates, from all colonies except Georgia, have no real authority to do anything, but issue *Declaration of Rights* and agree to stop all British imports and exports and to meet the following May if British fail to remove Coercive Acts.

New Hampshire militia raids British arsenal at Fort William and Mary, carries off munitions (December 14).

1775

Kentucky purchased for £10,000 worth of trading goods by Judge Richard Henderson of North Carolina (March), as result of Shawnee defeat in Lord Dunmore's War; Henderson sends Daniel Boone and party to cut 300-mile Wilderness Road from eastern Tennessee through Cumberland Gap to Kentucky River, where Boone founds settlement of Boonesborough. This brings colonial settlement very close to area defined as Canada by Quebec Act and allows easy access to Ohio, Illinois, and Indiana territory.

Patrick Henry gives "Liberty or Death" speech in Virginia, urging preparations for defense against predicted "clash of arms" (March 23).

The Battle of Lexington, the first battle in the Revolutionary War

Battles of Lexington and Concord (April 18–19): British send 700 troops from Boston to find and destroy militia arms stored in Concord, Massachusetts; Paul Revere, William Dawes, and Dr. Samuel Prescott manage to alert countryside to British advance, enabling John Hancock and Samuel Adams to escape from Lexington; British fire upon militia at Lexington, killing eight, then proceed to Concord, where militia and British exchange fire at North Bridge; British retreat from Concord all the way back to Boston is harried by guerrilla tactics from militia; 73 British, 49 colonials killed. Massachusetts militia then begins to deploy around Boston.

Fort Ticonderoga on Lake Champlain seized by Ethan Allen, Benedict Arnold, and Green Mountain Boys (May 10); although Continental Congress considers abandoning fort, cannon are moved in winter of 1775–76 to Boston, where they force evacuation of the British.

Second Continental Congress meets in Philadelphia (May 10); although still without any actual authority to do anything except talk and send messages to king and Parliament, Congress acts anyway: it extends its blessing to Massachusetts militia, calling it "Army of United Colonies"; urges formation of Committees of Safety, essentially guerrilla headquarters, at local and colony-wide levels; appoints George Washington commander in chief of Continental forces (June 15); votes $2 million for support of army, authorizes invasion of Canada, and sends king the "Olive Branch Petition," which de-

nies that colonies want to be rebellious or independent, but merely wish a redress of grievances (July 8). Petition does not reach England until mid-August and is rejected by king.

Bunker Hill (June 17): bloody battle, actually fought on nearby Breed's Hill, sees frontal attack by British regulars against colonial militia behind fortifications; colonials hold fire until enemy is very close and inflict heavy casualties. Colonials run out of ammunition and are forced to withdraw, but not before leaving 1,054 British troops killed or wounded, with American losses less than half that. Considered great victory by colonials, leads to mistaken idea that militia can defeat trained British regulars in open-field combat.

George III declares colonies to be in state of rebellion and demands punishment of traitors (August 23); Parliament follows up with act prohibiting all trade with colonies and authorizing seizure of all colonial vessels (December 22), despite protest from strong pro-American faction in England.

Falmouth, Maine, prosperous seaport near present Portland, set afire by shelling from British warship and completely destroyed in retaliation for aid to rebels in Boston (October 18).

Montreal captured by colonial forces under General Montgomery (November 12–13); Montgomery joins forces with Benedict Arnold's army in attack on Quebec; colonial assault is smashed back (December 31).

Left, British troops cross the harbor on their way to the Battle of Bunker Hill. Right, a soldier in the Continental army.

Governor Dunmore of Virginia driven out of Virginia by patriot forces; Norfolk burned, with blame falling on Dunmore and Loyalists (December 11).

1776

Common Sense published by Tom Paine (January 10); pamphlet, which sells 100,000–120,000 copies in first three months, greatly influences colonial opinion toward independence, which until late 1775 had been goal of only few radicals in New England. Paine's arguments against monarchy and tyranny are buttressed by arrival of news of Parliament's decision in December to isolate colonies.

Battle at Moore's Creek Bridge (February 27): North Carolina governor raises 1,600 backcountry Loyalists, who are defeated by 1,100 Patriots in quick, decisive battle, spoiling plans for British naval invasion of Wilmington-Cape Fear area.

Boston evacuated by British (March 17) when cannon brought from Fort Ticonderoga by Henry Knox, a Boston bookseller, are placed by George Washington on heights commanding city and harbor.

Continental navy, begun in December, 1775, with four ships, raids British colony Nassau in Bahamas, captures large quantity of munitions (March).

French king, Louis XVI, authorizes secret donation of munitions to rebellious colonies (May 2); France and Spain donate or lend-lease about 5,000,000 livres' (about $950,000) worth of munitions between 1776 and 1778; these munitions, smuggled in with help of French secret agent Beaumarchais (author of *The Barber of Seville*), largely supply Continental armies in first years of war.

American forces driven out of Canada (May 5–June 15); spring thaw enables British to send fleet up St. Lawrence, break siege of Quebec (May 5), smash American army at Three Rivers (June 7), and force evacuation of Montreal (June 15); thereafter Canada is secure base for British operations against American colonies.

Settlers led north from Mexico by Juan de Anza build presidio and mission at San Francisco, California (June).

Virginia delegate Richard Henry Lee offers resolution in Continental Congress that colonies "are, and of right ought to be, Independent States" (June 7); Congress appoints committee to draft Declaration of Independence (June 11); Congress debates and, after several maneuvers, approves Lee's resolution (July 2); Declaration of Independence approved July 4; copies distributed July 5; Declaration is signed later, in August.

British naval attack on Charleston repulsed by newly built Fort Moultrie, in Charleston Harbor (June 28).

A French summary of the Revolution, with views of major battles
LIBRARY OF CONGRESS

The Revolutionary Period

1776–1789

This period has two main parts. The first, the military struggle against the mother country, ended formally in 1783 and was successful, as most such colonial wars are. The second, equally revolutionary part ends in 1789, when political power gained on the battlefield was incorporated into the formal national structure described by the Constitution of the United States. It is during this second, postmilitary stage of consolidation that many revolutions, colonial or otherwise, fail.

The American Revolution was unlike most large civil conflicts in at least one important respect. The people who started the Revolution not only remained in control of the military phase but also kept power during the postrevolutionary stage and used this power to shape the new nation into something permanent and decent. Many revolutions follow a different pattern: they are started by a privileged but disaffected group of intellectuals and businessmen, enter a violent stage in which control is usurped by obscure fanatical elements, and then pass into a postrevolutionary phase characterized by a thoroughgoing narrow-minded beastliness on the part of whatever group has emerged on top.

This didn't happen in the American Revolution. Most of the revolutionary leaders were too experienced, too tough, too wise, too conservative, and too closely identified with regional interests to allow anything like a military junta to emerge and turn on them. Instead, they did what they and their forebears had always done: they took what existed and made something out of it that worked. What existed, of course, was the same sprawling hodgepodge of diverse, warlike peoples and places that had just fought a war to be let alone. Out of that hodgepodge the colonial elite made a confederated government they hoped would work. It didn't, so they abandoned it and made another one.

The military effort was, as might be expected, given the nature of American colonial society, a farce. It had, like most wars, moments of glory and piercing nobility, and moments of horror and unspeakable cowardice, but as an overall effort—civilian and military—it was a mess. Most of the time the colonists fought the British and the Hessian mercenaries in much the same way as the Indians fought the colonists. The colonists fought with small, locally raised armies, reluctant to stray very far from their turf no matter how strategically sound such a move would be. They were, in the main, unable to put aside traditional intergroup rivalries, so that every ac-tion was debated more in terms of its positive or negative effects on some neighboring rival than on the damage it might do the common enemy. Within these ad hoc colonial armies individual groups of warriors drifted away when they felt they had to tend to hunting, harvests, and families or when the war was no fun anymore. There was scant military discipline among these colonial armies, in the conventional sense of remote group control by a strict chain of command, with officers of one rank passing along commands to officers of lower rank. Instead, leadership on the battlefield and off tended to be a matter of individual character, proven success as a warrior, and proven largess as a supplier of the necessities and luxuries of war.

Unlike the Indians, however, a few American leaders with vision and the ability to command intertribal respect and obedience were able to raise quasi-permanent armies, train them in the forms of combat—a disciplined charge with fixed bayonets, for example—necessary to defeat British professionals on the open field, and move these armies across local territorial lines, say from New York to Virginia. Colonial leaders were, however, just barely able to supply these armies, partly because they bickered among themselves about who should pick up what part of the tab and partly because local farmers, bakers, and tailors were extremely reluctant to part with their goods for anything less patriotic than hard cash.

The British weren't much better. Their hearts weren't really in this war; many leading English thinkers and political leaders found a war against their relatives distasteful at best. Some of the ablest British commanders, especially those with actual combat experience in America, flatly and magnificently refused to serve in the American theater. The generals Britain did put in command in America were, for the most part, not incompetent but were unequipped by experience and inclination to fight a successful war in America, much as most United States generals were similarly disadvantaged in Southeast Asia about two hundred years later. Furthermore, whatever instinct for the jugular the British generals had was often restrained by orders from England, which usually urged them to go slow and try to make peace at every opportunity.

The British had a strategy—the strategy, in reverse, that had won the French and Indian War. It called for securing the forts in the Great Lakes area and pushing east while a second major force drove down from

Montreal via Lake Champlain and the Hudson toward New York; at the same time, Britain's almost complete naval control of the Atlantic would enable it to seize the major American cities, especially New York. In theory this strategy would hem the northern colonies in from west and east, capture New York and Philadelphia, and thus split the colonies lengthwise, leaving the South to dangle and be mopped up at will.

This strategy, neat in theory, didn't work, in part because it was applied in the wrong war against the wrong enemy and in part because it was applied on far too small a scale. Had the British been willing and able to mount an invasion on the scale of the Normandy operation, it would have succeeded. On the modest scale they actually used, it didn't, because, unlike the French colonial empire, the American colonies had no center. The British did in fact capture almost every major American city at some point during the war—Boston, New York, Philadelphia, Savannah, Charleston. But it didn't do them very much good, because to control New York or Philadelphia was not to control the American colonies. British control of the Atlantic did of course hinder, but not completely cut off, the importation of military and other supplies from France and Spain. The British could land armies wherever they wanted, all along the American coast, but in order for this to do them any good the British armies had then to seek out, engage, and destroy the American armies. The British soon found this out and tried, after their fashion, to do it, which accounts for all the seemingly pointless marching back and forth from New York to Philadelphia, or from Charleston to Virginia, that characterizes much of the war.

The occupation of New York by British troops early in the war
LIBRARY OF CONGRESS

But the British also found out that they couldn't march their armies too far from the seaports, because they then ran into something unique to the experience of eighteenth-century professional armies. They ran into an armed peasantry, who could and did shoot at them, who could and did prevent their being equipped by supply train from the secure seaports. Logistic difficulties and an armed peasantry contributed heavily to the crucial defeat at Saratoga in 1777, and after that British commanders were very reluctant to penetrate the American interior. Besides, it was *so* unprofessional to be picked off at a hundred yards by some peasant under a bush just because one was an officer and a gentleman and had the insignia to prove it.

The way to kill the American colonies was to make total war against the land and the people. You had to burn the fields and harvests, destroy the homes and livestock, smash the little forges, level the forts and blockhouses, and kill anyone who could conceivably take up arms against you—children, women, the old, everybody. This is the lesson colonist and Indian had taught each other, and this is the way Tory and Patriot fought each other in New York, in the Carolinas, and elsewhere on the frontier. The Revolutionary War was, in two senses, a civil war, and the most savage and bestial conflicts of the war took place when colonial Loyalist and Patriot forces went after each other. The British had for the most part neither the will nor the understanding to wage this kind of war.

The Loyalist segment of the colonial population was large—estimates run as high as one third—but many Loyalists took no active part in the war, and neither did many of the Patriots. It has been suggested that no more than 50 per cent of the population had any real interest in the struggle. In 1777 many state legislatures, upon the advice of the Continental Congress, voted to confiscate Loyalist and Crown property. A lot of it, especially conspicuously large holdings, was confiscated and sold. But many of the measures taken against Loyalists—deprivation of civil liberties, tar and feathers, whatever—rested, like so much else involving the war effort, within the discretion of community and county committees. As a result treatment of Loyalists varied widely from locale to locale and often turned on local community likes and dislikes having little to do with the main issues.

The war dragged on, and people in the United States and England grew more and more sick of it. By 1781 it was getting to be a question of which side would get fed up first and give up. Then the French committed a large fleet to the American cause. In short order this fleet, cooperating beautifully with Washington's army in New York, bottled up a large British force at Yorktown, Virginia. The British commander, Charles Cornwallis, later a distinguished and enlightened governor general of India, more or less promptly and professionally surrendered. Although they were by no means defeated militarily, for the British the Yorktown surrender was simply the last straw, a kind of Tet offensive, and they rather generously threw in the towel.

The Yorktown operation was a classic, thoroughly professional military maneuver, and the colonial militia played little part in it. The military effectiveness of this part-time soldiery has, in the past, been overrated. They weren't all deadly marksmen by any means, they often cut and ran when the going got tough, and they otherwise messed things up. But, in this age of specialists, we must also guard against underestimating them or their cause.

At the Battle of Bennington, during the crucial Saratoga campaign of 1777, militia stopped an attempt by the British commander, Burgoyne, to provision his army. The failure of the British Saratoga campaign gave France the excuse it was looking for to enter the war openly as an ally of the United States and led ultimately to the Yorktown victory. The militia at Bennington and at later Saratoga battles didn't really care about all that. Their attitude was summed up in the immortal words of a Massachusetts farmer named Reuben Stebbins. Hearing the battle sounds of Bennington coming across his land, he got his gun, got on his horse, and, as he rode off toward the battle, called out: "We'll see who's goin't' own this farm!"

It is easy to chuckle at this homely battle cry, with its complete irrelevance to large strategy or large anything else. But suppose we set ourselves a task like the one in the old story about the Arab potentate who demanded that his economic advisers summarize, on pain of death, all the economic knowledge in the world into one short sentence. The terrified advisers, so the story goes, saved their skins by doing it: *There is no such thing as a free lunch.* If we ask ourselves to perform a similar analysis of the Declaration of Independence, the words of Farmer Stebbins take on, it may be argued, a certain peculiar significance.

The Continental Congress had during the war years evolved into a government, but it had virtually no legal standing. In 1777 it came up with a formal plan of government called the Articles of Confederation and sent it to the states for ratification. None of the states liked it, of course, and they bickered about it until 1781, when it was finally approved. The Articles set up what were in effect thirteen sovereign states, loosely joined together at the top by a Congress that, on paper, constituted a national government. But in fact it was no more a sovereign government than the United Nations is. It could not, either on paper or in practice, control the behavior of the states in three important respects: it could not raise money from them, it could not raise troops from them, and it could not regulate their commerce. In practice it could do few of the things it

theoretically was empowered to do—manage foreign affairs, manage Indian policy, manage war, and so on—because in such important matters any combination of four states could veto any congressional action. The congressional government set up by the Articles was more or less the kind of arrangement the colonies had wanted with Great Britain. But it soon became as obvious to American leaders as it had been to British ones that such an arrangement was extremely irritating.

Samuel Adams
LIBRARY OF CONGRESS

The nation was deeply in debt—the war had cost $104,042,000—and it had to get commerce and trade going. That meant it had to make deals of one sort or another with other countries, and it couldn't have New York or Massachusetts or Virginia making their own weird, self-serving arrangements. The national government needed money to run itself, to provide for embassies or consulates abroad, to pay for a navy, and so on. Under the Articles there was simply no way of getting it. A national government that did in fact have certain sovereign, centralized powers was needed, and so that was what the Constitutional Convention came up with in 1787, regardless of what it had been told to do.

The Constitution of the United States as drawn up in 1787 was a problem-solving device. As such, in marked contrast to the Declaration of Independence, it has the flat, matter-of-fact tone of a do-it-yourself manual: first you do this, then that, then that. It solved the problem of a centralized government with some real clout by making one. It solved the problem of putting too much power in one place by putting some of it here, some there, and some over there. It gave the large states the influence they expected by making a lower House with proportional representation and gave the smaller ones an upper Senate in which they had two votes like everybody else. With a certain grim methodicalness, it solved some problems, like whether slaves should or should not be counted as part of a state's population, by splitting the difference and counting a slave as three fifths of a person. It solved other problems, like defining the powers of the President, by being rather vague about the whole thing. After all, everybody knew George Washington was going to be the first President, and he was furthermore sitting right there in the convention listening to every word.

The men who made the Constitution knew it wasn't going to be very popular. Within the American governing class, which had made the revolution, there were basically two factions. One, represented by Sam Adams and Patrick Henry, was deeply opposed to *any* centralized power, and in this it reflected the attitude of most average Americans. The other faction, to which most of the founders belonged, was deeply opposed to any centralized power not under *their* control. The Constitution centralized power, no doubt about it, but didn't give anybody all of it and was therefore likely to be rejected on one count or another. One of the problems the framers had to deal with was whether they should waste their time on something likely to be so controver-

sial, and the other was getting the remaining members of the convention actually to sign it, even though most of them had doubts or peeves about it.

There was one other problem to be solved. Most other governments in the world were kingdoms of one sort of another. In these governments power—social, political, and economic—was located at the apex of a pyramid, in a royal family and in the particular member of that family who actually functioned as king, monarch, emperor, or whatever. Time, tradition, church, and age-old consensus had put this power there and given it a legitimacy few even dreamed of challenging. The Constitution created a government with considerable power. Where did the ultimate authority for that power lie? Was there nothing *above* it? What was there on earth or in heaven that could confer legitimacy on this power? The men who made the Constitution could have written reams of rhetoric and theory on these questions. But they had a job to do and, in their typical, matter-of-fact way, simply tucked the whole issue away in three simple words: "We, the people . . ."

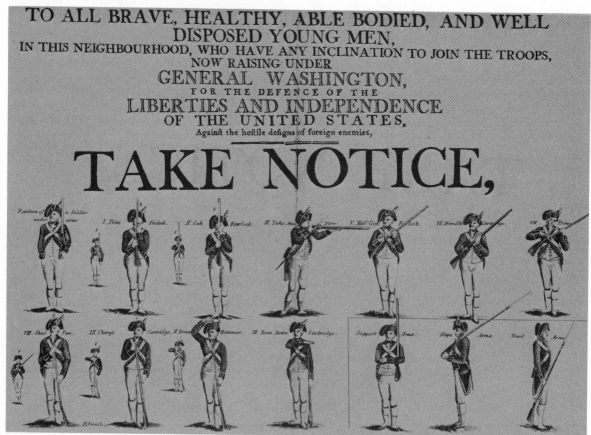

Recruiting poster offering a bounty of twelve dollars for enlisting in the Continental army
LIBRARY OF CONGRESS

The Revolutionary Period (1776–1789)

1776

Battle of Long Island (August 27) is first of string of American defeats in which British push Washington's army out of New York and (November–December) chase it through New Jersey and across the Delaware River into Pennsylvania.

Nathan Hale, 21-year-old captain in Continental army, posing as Dutch schoolmaster (he was a Yale graduate), scouts British position in New York and is caught and hanged (September 22); is reputed to say on gallows: "I only regret that I have but one life to give for my country."

British attack citizens suspected of setting fire to New York.

First of Tom Paine's *Crisis* pamphlets appears; written while Paine was aide to General Nathanael Greene, contains line "These are the times that try men's souls" and argues that freedom can only be won at high cost, because "Tyranny, like hell, is not easily conquered" (December 19).

Washington crosses Delaware (December 25) and captures Hessian force at Trenton, New Jersey (December 26); this victory, combined with Washington's smashing defeat of British at Princeton on January 3, 1777, vastly buoys American morale; American and British armies then mainly settle down for the winter, the British in New York City and the Americans in Morristown, New Jersey.

1777

Vermont drafts constitution abolishing slavery and establishing something close to universal male suffrage (July); goes into effect in 1778, but Vermont does not become state until 1791.

British grand strategy, calling for advance from west along Mohawk River, south from Montreal down Hudson, and up Hudson from New York City, receives check at Fort Stanwix (August 6) and is ruined by a series of battles culminating in General Burgoyne's surrender of more than 5,000 troops at Saratoga (October 17). Saratoga victory marks turning point of war, since it persuades France to back U.S. formally.

British capture Philadelphia (September 11); Washington tries but fails to prevent this, succeeding, however,

British General Burgoyne surrenders at Saratoga, New York.

in main job of keeping army intact and uncornered.

Articles of Confederation adopted by Congress (November 15) and sent to states for ratification, which is not accomplished until March 1, 1781. Delay is caused largely by question of what to do with western lands claimed by some states, some of whose original charters granted them land clear across continent "from sea to sea." States having no western claims refuse to ratify until landed states agree to cede western claims to national government, which could then make new states out of them.

Conway Cabal, movement in part designed to remove Washington as commander in chief and replace him with Horatio Gates, victor at Saratoga, causes public opinion to rally behind Washington (November).

Washington winters army of 11,000 at Valley Forge, Pennsylvania (December 19–June 19, 1778); December blizzards, January mud, and administrative foul-ups prevent wagon trains from reaching camp; typhus and smallpox epidemics break out; clothing and blankets are lacking; Washington forages countryside; Baron von Steuben begins drilling soldiers, especially in use of bayonet, against which they had no defense; army reduced to 4,000 when Washington leaves Valley Forge in 1778.

1778

France signs treaties with U.S. commissioners Benjamin Franklin, Silas Deane, and Arthur Lee, recognizing U.S. independence and guaranteeing it through military alliance (February 6).

Benjamin Franklin
LIBRARY OF CONGRESS

British government authorizes peace mission to U.S., empowered to grant all colonial demands except independence (February 17).

News of French treaties arrives (May 2) before British peace commission, whose terms Congress rejects (July 17).

Iroquois Indians, firm English allies, ravage frontier settlements in Mohawk Valley, New York (May–June); Loyalist and Iroquois troops under Tory Colonel John Butler slaughter defenders of fort in Wyoming Valley, Pennsylvania (July 3–4); devastation of western frontier leads to expedition by George Rogers Clark, who briefly gains control of Illinois Territory (August).

1779

Washington sends armies into Mohawk Valley to subdue Iroquois and Tories, whose depredations are seriously cutting into grain supplies needed by army; Iroquois temporarily dispersed (August).

John Paul Jones, with fleet of five ships, attacks shipping and ports around British Isles (August–September); Jones, in old tub named *Bonhomme Richard*, fights ship-to-ship with H.M.S. *Serapis* and when called upon to surrender answers: "I have not yet begun to fight." *Serapis* finally surrenders (September 23).

1780

British capture Charleston, South Carolina (May 12), and set up Loyalist government there; from Charleston base British and Tory armies roam almost at will through Carolinas, despite check at Battle of Kings Mountain (October 7).

Benedict Arnold goes over to British (September 25) after his plans to turn over West Point are discovered; later leads several attacks against Patriots, including an invasion of Virginia in 1781.

Benedict Arnold
LIBRARY OF CONGRESS

1781

Articles of Confederation go into effect on March 1; do not really change much in existing congressional government; two months later George Washington notes that situation is grim—no transportation, no troops, no supplies, no weapons. Individual states are not complying with congressional requests, and Washington is in many cases taking what he needs from countryside: "We are daily and hourly oppressing the people—souring their tempers—and alienating the affections."

Skillful campaign in Carolinas, led by General Nathanael Greene, causes British army under Cornwallis to move north into Virginia, where Cornwallis sets up major base camp at Yorktown (August 7).

Ignoring main British army in New York, Washington moves his army and a French one under General Rochambeau from White Plains, New York, across Hudson and then down through Philadelphia toward Chesapeake Bay, aiming at Cornwallis in Yorktown (August 19–September 5); French fleet under Admiral de Grasse defeats British fleet near mouth of Chesapeake Bay (September 5); French and American armies are then ferried down Chesapeake Bay to sur-

Right: a French summary of the battles that led to the defeat of the British and the signing of the Treaty of Paris in 1783
LIBRARY OF CONGRESS

round Yorktown (September 28); about 16,000 French and American troops begin siege, supported by French naval gunfire; Cornwallis, with about 7,250 men and nowhere to go, eventually surrenders (October 19); surrender at Yorktown virtually ends British will to continue war.

British General Cornwallis surrenders at Yorktown, Virginia.

Los Angeles, California, founded by 44 settlers, of whom more than half are descendants of African slaves.

1782

Neglect of Ohio forts by impoverished states, absence of American trading goods, and cold-blooded murder of peaceful Delaware Indian community cause northwest frontier to explode (April–May); British, harnessing Indian outrage, consolidate hold on much of Northwest, basically controlling by war's end everything north and west of the Ohio River (June–November).

Peace negotiations begin in Paris between British and American representatives in April; preliminary treaty signed November 3, in effect ending war on American soil. American negotiators John Jay, John Adams, and Benjamin Franklin, with exceedingly generous and farsighted help of British negotiator Lord Shelburne, got for United States whole trans-Appalachian west to Mississippi, which otherwise France would have given away to Spain.

1783

Treaty of Paris signed between U.S. and Great Britain (September 3); formally ending Revolutionary War,

treaty stipulates American independence, evacuation of British troops, American payment of prewar debts, right of New Englanders to fish in traditional Grand Banks area. U.S. borders defined roughly as present one in north, Mississippi in west, and current northern border of Florida in south. In separate simultaneous treaty Great Britain gives Spain the Floridas, which include New Orleans.

Massachusetts court outlaws slavery, based on "all men are born free and equal" clause in state constitution.

Noah Webster publishes what becomes known as *Webster's Spelling Book* or *Blue-Backed Speller*; it becomes raging best seller.

George Washington bids farewell to his officers at Fraunces Tavern in New York City (December 4), resigns his commission as commander in chief to Congress in Annapolis, Maryland (December 23), and goes home to Mount Vernon.

1784

American ship *Empress of China* sails from Sandy Hook, New York (February 22), to Canton, China, arriving August 30; her cargo out is four tons of ginseng root, and she brings back tea and silk; profitable voyage opens up China trade; by 1786 U.S. has consulate in China.

Congress selects New York City as temporary capital of U.S. (December 23).

1785

University of Georgia founded as nondenominational state institution; oldest such in U.S. (January 27).

Ordinance of 1785 provides means by which western lands are to be surveyed, subdivided, and sold (May 20). Ordinance provides for township units six miles square, divided into 36 square-mile (640-acre) sections. Townships can be bought whole or by 640-acre sections, at auction, for minimum price of one dollar an acre. Congress sets aside one section in each township for support of public schools. Method provides for orderly disposition of western lands, although it favors speculators, since many settlers neither need nor can afford a 640-acre section and instead purchase subdivisions from speculators. Congress, which needs a lot of money fast, later agrees to sell much larger blocks of land to private companies, most notably the Ohio Company. Problem of what to do about Indians on township land is only partly settled by diplomacy—several shaky treaties, soon repudiated by Indian nations whose lands had been ceded without their consent.

Regular stagecoach routes established between New York City, Boston, Albany, and Philadelphia. Boston to New York City trip takes six days.

Automatic flour mill, invented by Oliver Evans, becomes operational in Maryland; like many early American inventions, it solves a problem relating both to agriculture and to a shortage of labor.

1786

Virginia adopts Thomas Jefferson's Statute of Religious Freedom, which later becomes model for First Amendment to U.S. Constitution; statute says that *"Whereas Almighty God has created the mind free,"* legislators and rulers should leave it that way and compel no man to *"suffer on account of his religious opinions or belief"* (January 16).

Shays' Rebellion, revolt of poor Massachusetts farmers (August): involves those whose property is being seized for nonpayment of relatively heavy taxes in time of economic depression and who often lack enough property to qualify to vote; under leadership of Daniel Shays farmers escalate conflict and attempt to seize munitions from national arsenal (January 25, 1787); neither national nor state governments are able to supply money for troops; private individuals put up $20,000 for state troops, who repulse arsenal attack and later break up rebel forces in February, 1787. Reforms are subsequently instituted at state level, and rebels mostly pardoned. However, inability of Confederation government or state government to deal effectively either with rebellion or with economic conditions that caused it increases pressure for a change in Articles of Confederation.

Troops fire on farmers participating in Shays' Rebellion.

1787

Constitutional Convention meets in Philadelphia (May 25); Virginia Plan offered (May 29), which calls for new form of government with national executive, national judiciary, and a bicameral legislature made up in proportion to each state's wealth and population; New Jersey Plan offered (June 15), calling essentially for a revision of Articles, in which states vote as blocks with same number of votes; Connecticut Compromise offered (July 16), calling for a House of Representatives with proportional representation and a Senate in which each state is to be represented equally with two votes; first draft is debated (August 6–September 10); final draft is prepared by a committee under leadership of Gouverneur Morris and is approved (September 17); most delegates, including George Washington and Benjamin Franklin, think they'll be lucky to get it ratified at all and expect it to stand up no more than twenty years.

Congress passes Northwest Ordinance of 1787 (July 13); measure has three parts, the first providing that the Northwest eventually become no fewer than three states (frontier settlers didn't want large states) and no more than five (eastern states were afraid of losing congressional voting power to group of new states); second part provides three-stage method by which new territory can become a state (first—territory is ruled by Congress-appointed governor, secretary, and three judges; second—after population reaches 5,000, it is to elect assembly with some power and a nonvoting delegate to Congress; third—after population reaches 60,000, territory is to frame state constitution and apply for equal membership in Union); final part of Ordinance is bill of rights, guaranteeing religious freedom, trial by jury, habeas corpus, and other protections of law. Slavery and primogeniture are forbidden. It is basically under this ordinance that the country expands to Pacific. It greatly encourages westward settlement because, like the original English colonists, pioneers don't want to go from a place that has more rights and freedoms to one that has fewer. The problem of Indian occupancy of territorial lands is ultimately settled in a way that is also in accord with colonial tradition: military conquest.

Confederation Congress, after debating for a week whether to censure Constitutional Convention for exceeding its authority and actually breaking the law (Articles needed unanimous thirteen-state approval for revision, whereas Constitution, which is a revision with a vengeance, needs only nine states to get approval), finally votes to accept Constitution (September 28) and send it to states for ratification by special conventions; framers call for special ratifying conventions because they figure there is no way Constitution can get approved by regular state legislatures. By end of year three states—Delaware, Pennsylvania, and New Jersey—have ratified.

As part of ratification struggle, first of *Federalist* (pro-Constitutional) essays appears in New York newspapers (October 27); written mainly by Alexander Hamilton, John Jay, and James Madison under pen name "Publius," essays, ultimately numbering 85, are first collected in book form on May 28, 1788; in general, essays represent political argument of the highest order and are aimed at those who are capable of appreciating such argument.

1788

New Hampshire becomes ninth state to ratify Constitution (June 21); although Constitution is technically now in effect, ratification by Virginia and Massachusetts is practical necessity and occurs on June 25 and 26, respectively. As part of the New York ratification battle, New York City threatens to secede from New York State and ratify on its own; Rhode Island and North Carolina do not ratify until new federal government is in operation.

Old Confederation Congress accepts Constitution as ratified (July 2) and designates March 4, 1789, as date when new government is to go into effect.

Maryland cedes a ten-mile-square site on Potomac River to form District of Columbia (December 23).

1789

Although supposed to meet on March 4, most newly elected members of Congress are still making their way to New York City at this time; quorum achieved by House (30 out of 59) and Senate (9 out of 22) during first week of April, during which ballots of presidential electors are counted and results announced, and Congress is formally organized for business.

Congressional committees debate (April) form of address appropriate to President, including "Majesty," "Excellency," and "Elective Highness"; Senate committee proposes "His Highness the President of the United States and the Protector of the Rights of the Same," but House of Representatives balks.

George Washington inaugurated as first President of the United States (April 30) on balcony of Federal Hall in New York City. Oath of office is administered by Robert Livingston of New York, there being as yet no Chief Justice. Although Washington is escorted with great ceremony on the last stages of his journey from Virginia to New York City, he has to borrow £100 from a friend to meet his travel expenses, since he is deeply in debt and is considered a poor credit risk by Virginia moneylenders.

George Washington takes the oath of office as first President of the United States in New York on April 30, 1789.

The Federal Period

1789-1801

The Federal period began when George Washington took the oath of office as the first President of the United States in New York City and ended with the inauguration of the third President of the United States, Thomas Jefferson, in the new national capital of Washington, D.C.

During the years 1789-1801 a paper called the Constitution was turned into a functioning government, several of the institutions and traditions characteristic of our political life were laid down, and the American republic did something rather unexpected: it survived.

The United States was the first republic of any size to try and make a go of it since Rome experimented—and failed—with a similar form of government. Contemporary European views of the American experiment were of two kinds. A small minority of radical types watched hopefully, urgently desiring this experiment to work, much as a similar minority in the twentieth century watched the communist developments in Russia after 1917 or in China after 1949. The majority, however, looked on with the same feelings of complacency or distaste that many Americans today display toward some newly emerged People's Republic of this or that, confidently expecting it to turn into something ridiculous or worse.

The American republican experiment succeeded in a welter of paradox that would have quite overthrown a leadership less practiced in making do or more committed to theory than to what was. Some forty years later Ralph Waldo Emerson rather smugly expressed this aspect of the American experience when he wrote: "A foolish consistency is the hobgoblin of little minds adored by little statesmen and philosophers and divines." There was nothing little-minded about George Washington, his first cabinet appointees, the first United States Congresses, or even John Adams, when the crunch came. These men successfully contained within themselves, as individuals sometimes but as a collective leadership certainly, a mind-boggling set of contradictions. And they bequeathed these contradictions, more or less intact, to subsequent political generations.

In 1789 the nation was broke. What was worse, it was regarded as a poor credit risk by those in a position to lend it money. At the urging of Alexander Hamilton, Washington's visionary Secretary of the Treasury, the new government quickly established itself as financially sound by firmly assuming a really respectable amount of debt—more than $73,000,000 worth—and by paying this debt off at face value plus interest. This move enriched a small group of financiers and speculators who had bought much of this debt at about twenty-five cents on the dollar. As Hamilton hoped it would, this move also made those rich in capital, at home and abroad, the principal supporters of a radical new government presiding over the destiny of a sprawling nation of dirt farmers.

From Alexander Hamilton came a vision of the United States as a booming industrial nation firmly controlled by a strong centralized government allied beneficently with business interests à la modern Japan, and above all run by the few—"the rich and well-born." (Alexander Hamilton was born on an uncertain date in a scraggly British colony in the Leeward Islands and was, as John Adams more or less correctly remarked, "the bastard brat of a Scotch peddler.")

From Thomas Jefferson, a member of the Virginia squirearchy, tutored as a child in the classics, French, dancing, chess, and the violin, came a vision of the United States as a nation of industrious and incorruptible farmers, in whose capable and well-meaning hands the reins of government ought ultimately to rest. For Jefferson the new central government must not, above all else, do two things: it must not become too energetic, because then it would get too big and strong and complex for ordinary people to understand and control. And it must not encourage commerce and industry and finance, because to depend for one's living on the "casualities and caprice of customers" was to become subservient and venal, qualities fortunately lacking in "those who labor in the earth." The last thing Jefferson wanted was a booming industrial nation, because "the mobs of the great cities add just so much to the support of pure government, as sores do to the strength of the human body."

When Jefferson began to develop a political party (the ancestor of today's Democratic Party) in reaction to Hamilton's policies, the first thing he did was visit New York City, where he garnered support from disaffected politicians with a direct pipeline to the urban mob and forged a political link between the urban North and rural South that has persisted to this day. On the other hand, in many parts of pastoral New England, with its tidy farming villages, Jefferson was in 1800 denounced from the pulpit as the candidate who would, if elected, confiscate all the Bibles in New England.

Hamilton, John Adams, and most of the other Federalists had no use for the mass of the people and said so. In 1791 Hamilton gave Jefferson's laborers in the earth the back of his hand by persuading Congress to pass an internal tax on whiskey, which was the form in which backcountry farmers brought their surplus corn to market and was furthermore a medium of exchange on the frontier. From this, Hamilton got a farmers' rebellion. But this rebellion was suppressed not by the state in which it occurred but rather by the federal government, thus proving to Hamilton's satisfaction that the government was no paper tiger. George Washington pardoned the leaders of the rebellion, who were found guilty of treason and sentenced to death, thus mixing federal mercy with federal muscle.

By 1792 Jefferson and Hamilton had become overt political enemies and covert personal ones. Around them and their respective interests and positions two political parties gradually formed. The Hamiltonians called themselves Federalists, although they were not in favor of a *federal* union with substantial power distributed among the states. They were actually in favor of the *republic*, meaning the central, national government. The anti-Hamiltonians were of course unwilling merely to be labeled anti-Federalists and so took the name Republicans.

Alexander Hamilton
LIBRARY OF CONGRESS

Nevertheless Hamilton and Jefferson between them created a fund of political argument, like a binary-star system, about which the American polity has ever

after orbited, drawing heat and light first mainly from one star, then mainly from the other. And it is entirely typical of the men, and their period, that in the savage election of 1800 Hamilton should throw his support to Jefferson, whom he described as "a contemptible hypocrite" but whom he also considered better qualified to lead the nation than Aaron Burr.

The political parties that formed around Hamiltonian and Jeffersonian positions were at first informal groups whose shared interests were explored and crystallized through correspondence and small gatherings. But beginning in 1795 they were hardened into something like today's political parties by foreign-policy issues. The central question was, Should we make peace and money with our former enemy Great Britain, or should we make war with our former friend and ally France? Typically enough, the federal government acted in such a way as to do some of both, but not too much of either.

Until 1795 it was the British who were most provocative. The British had not left their forts in the Northwest, a territory they had ceded to the United States by treaty in 1783. They still controlled fur trading in the area, largely as a result of their superior trade goods. This fur trade got the Indians guns, powder, shot, and tacit British encouragement to use these nice new toys on occasional raids against American frontier settlements.

After 1793 France declared war on Great Britain, and Britain went after American shipping in the West Indies. For a time American vessels were boarded and confiscated, theoretically because they were carrying French goods or foodstuffs destined for France but more often than not because underpaid British naval officers and seamen got a cut from any prize they took. So Washington had enormous pressures on him from two groups—frontier farmers and some New England shippers and fishermen—to strike out at Great Britain.

There was a hitch, though. Wicked old England accounted for three quarters of all United States foreign trade, and 95 per cent of our imports were British. The whole Hamilton financial structure was based on revenues generated by import duties placed on incoming British goods. Had war broken this trade, it would also have broken the United States Treasury and left the nation's credit in tatters. Besides, Hamilton rather liked the British Empire, and wanted an American one along somewhat the same lines. For Hamilton and many other Federalists war with England spelled ruin, and they did everything possible to avoid it. In 1794 they sent John Jay over to England to negotiate Anglo-American grievances and, to make sure that Jay came back with a peace treaty, leaked information to the British that guaranteed Jay wouldn't be holding any high cards at all. As a result

Jay came back with a treaty that brought peace and British removal from the Ohio territory forts but said very little about other American grievances. Looked at with a jaundiced eye, Jay's treaty was a sellout of American honor and interests, and the Republicans made sure that people looked at it in just that way. At enormous political damage to themselves the Federalists ratified and signed Jay's treaty.

Knuckling under to England seemed bad form because England's enemy and our friend France was looking especially good to many Americans during Washington's administration. In 1789 the French had made a revolution that sounded just like ours, and they did us the honor of using some of our rhetoric and some of our heroes—Tom Paine, the Marquis de Lafayette—in the process. Enthusiasm for a sister republic seemed to demand a corresponding lack of enthusiasm for monarchial Britain, whose "tyranny" we had so recently thrown off with the indispensable aid of France, who had made a military alliance with us at a time when we had no friends in the world. And it didn't help Hamilton or Washington one bit that their Secretary of State loved France and things French, and had been known to say that "a little rebellion now and then is a good thing."

While all this was going on Washington had another foreign-policy problem. In the South and West a hundred and twenty thousand Americans in Kentucky, Tennessee, and Georgia encircled the Spanish empire, based in New Orleans but including what is now Florida, Alabama, and Mississippi. There some twenty-five thousand French, Spanish, British, and Greek settlers lived under a quasi-military Spanish colonial government and had as allies some fourteen thousand Chocktaw, Creek, Cherokee, and Chickasaw Indians, for whom the southeastern woodlands were home. The Americans wanted free use of the Mississippi, along which the Spanish had forts, and most of all they wanted the land, no matter who owned it. That it happened to belong to Spain, who also happened at the time to be an ally of England, just rendered the idea of grabbing it even more irresistible. Washington had to spend a lot of his political credit restraining Kentuckians and Georgians, led in many cases by his old and capable Revolutionary comrades-in-arms, from jumping off into Spanish Louisiana and setting off God only knew what.

In 1796 Washington, after administering a good Federalist scolding in his Farewell Address, stepped down with great relief. In that election year Hamilton's political maneuvering backfired and managed to get Federalist President John Adams a Republican Vice President, Thomas Jefferson. At about this time France started turning nasty. The French had chopped off Louis XVI's head, and Robespierre was getting busy on a Reign of Terror. In 1793 the Federalists had given Citizen Genêt, France's minister to the United States, the cold shoulder because he was stirring up trouble against England. In 1796 the French government had tried to meddle in American politics and get the pro-French Jefferson elected President. That didn't work, but they didn't learn anything from it and still thought they could embarrass Federalist John Adams and his Federalist Congress by being nasty and by interfering with American shipping in the same way Britain had done.

In 1797 the French set a bunch of privateers loose on American ships in the West Indies. They didn't really want war with the United States, but French armies were mopping up Europe under a bright young general named Napoleon Bonaparte, there was still considerable popular and Republican support for the French, and it seemed to the French foreign minister, Talleyrand, that tweaking the Federalists would be fun.

But it wasn't. In 1797 Adams sent over three American diplomats to patch things up, and Talleyrand—partly on the advice of some U.S. Republicans, including Jefferson—stalled them. But he did it in such a way as to ruffle American feathers and went so far as send three flunkies (known as *X, Y,* and *Z* in the American reports) to suggest that a few bribes might be in order. In early 1798 all this came out, American public opinion swung violently against France, and the United States prepared for war. It built a navy, including a crack new frigate called the *Constitution*, and called up George Washington from retirement to head its army.

The Federalists, especially the higher, sterner sort led by Hamilton, saw in the popular anti-French feeling a splendid chance to discredit the pro-French Republicans and pay them back for the licking Federalists had taken over Jay's Treaty. Hence the Federalist pamphleteers and presses got busy building anti-French feeling into anti-French hysteria, promising the American public among other things an invasion by black French-speaking soldiers from Haiti in which these "dusky Othellos" would of course have their way with every American Desdemona from Georgia to Boston. As a result, from 1798 to 1800 the Americans fought an undeclared naval war with France, with the undeclared naval help of their former enemy Great Britain.

This war was always threatening to break into a real, down-and-dirty one, given the success of Federalist propaganda. However, it was Federalist John Adams, who disliked the French and loathed what the French Revolution had become, who in 1799 personally took advantage of French peace feelers and rammed peace negotiations down his own party's throat by threatening to resign the Presidency to Jefferson if the Federalists in Congress didn't send somebody over to France and make peace lickety-split.

The Federalist-inspired war hysteria had another paradoxical effect on Federalist party fortunes. In 1791 the Hamiltonians had allowed the first ten amendments to be added to the Constitution as the Bill of Rights. Most Federalists regarded the Bill of Rights as unnecessary because most state constitutions had bills of rights, and it was assumed that the states would be most zealous about protecting the civil liberties of their citizens. But a federal bill of rights had been a part of deals made during the ratification struggles, and the Federalists honored their bargain because they figured the Bill of Rights couldn't do any harm. And so were added to the Constitution ten one-sentence paragraphs that have come to be regarded by many Americans as the true and living soul of the national charter.

During 1798, when war fears were at their highest, the Federalist Congress passed the Alien and Sedition Acts, aimed largely at French subversives but also containing provisions abridging the freedom of press and speech that could be and were used to clamp down on anti-Federalist spokesmen. These acts did, as correctly claimed by Republicans, violate freedoms guaranteed in the Bill of Rights, and so the Federalists were guilty of that most un-Federal and un-American thing: they were unconstitutional.

The Alien and Sedition Acts had another consequence, one that was later to haunt everybody. Thomas Jefferson got together with James Madison late in 1798 and wrote what became known as the Virginia and Kentucky Resolutions. Although designed mainly as a defense of the Republican Party and a kind of Republican platform for the 1800 election, these resolutions also contained the argument that the states as well as the people "consented" to the federal arrangement and that if the national government did something to contravene the Constitution, maybe it was the states' right and duty to step in. Later spokesmen elaborated on these ideas and put them finally to the test of civil war.

But it was not only in politics that this crucial period seems so fatefully paradoxical. Socially and economically, strange things were happening. For example, many Americans, north and south, were finding slavery increasingly hard to swallow. Many slaves had fought well in the Revolutionary War, and those who had followed their Patriot masters into battle had won their freedom thereby. Slavery was widely expected to wither away as the un-American and uneconomical thing it was. Several northern states—those with relatively small black populations—had already passed laws abolishing slavery, and several southern states, including Virginia, had come within a few votes of doing so. But in 1793 a Connecticut Yankee named Eli Whitney, visiting the widow of the Revolutionary War general Nathanael Greene on her plantation in Georgia, tinkered with an idea for a machine that would easily remove seeds from cotton fibers. Whitney applied for a patent for his cotton gin the same year. Within the next few decades this machine had put King Cotton on the throne and had set in stone the southern plantation system and the institution of black slavery.

Also during this Federal period an Englishman named Samuel Slater smuggled over in his head the plans for a new kind of water-powered spinning machine and set up a factory in Pawtucket, Rhode Island, thus beginning the New England textile industry and giving New England an economic stake in cotton, however it was planted or harvested. In 1798 Eli Whitney, having legal troubles with his cotton-gin patent, began tinkering with a system for making interchangeable parts and gained as a result of the French war fever a contract to mass-produce ten thousand muskets by machine, using relatively unskilled labor. Thus Whitney laid the foundation of the American manufacturing system, located in the Northeast and profoundly affecting the social and economic development of that region too. Some sixty years later a civil war was fought to find out who was really king, the people who owned Whitney-ginned cotton or the people who owned Whitney-style factories.

During the Federal period something rather strange was also happening to American women. In the 1790's huge numbers of settlers began spilling into Kentucky, Tennessee, and Ohio (and promptly voting Republican when they got the chance). While large numbers of frontier women were killing cows by bashing them over the head with an ax, or pulling wagons out of the mud, or steering flatboats down the Ohio River, middle-class urban women found themselves being defined as ethereal, fragile creatures, far too delicate for anything like real thought, real work, or real sex. As the tightly knit, mutually dependent families and communities typical of pioneer existence moved west young middle-class ladies found themselves having to get husbands not on the basis of mutual need—economic and sexual—but rather on the basis of so-called desirable qualities or fashion. And the fashion, imported with some distortions from Europe, was the dependent, graceful, delicate idealized woman—a fashion against which, in 1792, in England, Mary Wollstonecraft began her epic battle with her *Vindication of the Rights of Women.*

By 1795 French and English observers had begun to notice and comment on a curious American twist in relations between the sexes. Unmarried American girls—at least some of them—enjoyed a solid "manly" education and freedom from chaperonage unprecedented among their peers in Europe. They got these things from their fathers as a sort of vestigial relic from the less repressed colonial days, when educated Puritans like Cotton Mather wrote lengthy historical and educational treatises for their daughters. A hundred years later the colonial squire, Thomas Jefferson, was planning his daughter's education carefully, mixing in "the graver sciences" with "the best poets and prosewriters" because she might marry a "blockhead" and hence might

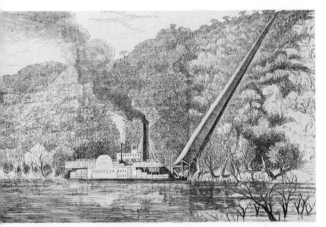

Cotton being loaded from a chute (above) onto a boat (below)
LIBRARY OF CONGRESS

really have to run the household and in any case would be responsible for educating her own children.

The cleverness, freshness, and freedom of American girls derived from their status as a daughter in their father's house. But American *wives*, in the houses of their husbands, suffered what European observers considered a strange and sometimes shocking loss of status and freedom. Although nothing was too good for middle-class American wives, and their every whim was indulged, and their lives were adorned with every new thing that their husbands' level of prosperity allowed, they were excluded from male companionship, serious

conversation, and seemingly all serious matters of life in a way that middle-class European wives were not. They were even disqualified as sexual objects, since sacred motherhood and wifeliness did not seem to mix well with anything but a dutiful, perfunctory sort of sexual function. In 1795 French observers noted that the real sex was now going on in the burgeoning brothels of Philadelphia or in illicit short- or long-term liaisons arranged by high-class madams.

By the 1830's European visitors were explicitly making comparisons between American wives and American slaves, the one indulged constantly, the other indulged pettily and capriciously but both sharing the essential characteristic of being chattel. And by this time some American women were also venturing this parallel, and indeed the entire abolitionist and women's suffrage movements were soon to be profoundly mixed up in each other.

Even in matters less weighty, paradox abounded in the Federal period. George Washington liked going about in a coach-and-six, that age's equivalent of the limousine, and was an immensely imposing and aloof man. Washington thus took it on the chin for his "monarchial" tastes—a bit like the last king, was George. At the same time, his regular appearance at the theatre in New York City earned him the censure of respectable folk. At that time the theatre was something like boxing matches in the nineteenth century: widely attended and reported but a distinctly lower-class sort of entertainment. But Washington's attendance did much to legitimize the theatre, and many states rescinded their laws against public dramatic productions. In this matter, as in the wider affairs of state, Washington displayed the even-handed, even-headed balancing of interests that in a modern President like Franklin Roosevelt we have no trouble calling political genius.

When we look at the Federal period from the olympian perspective of pure rationalism, we can see a lot of Mad Hatters, Cheshire Cats, and Mock Turtles. But we can also see the thin line of something solid and steady and victorious. The country transferred power to three executives and to two rather distinct political machines. And it did so constitutionally. Unlike rationalist France, no guillotines glinted in public squares, no wagonloads of victims rolled through the towns, and no Robespierre or Napoleon arose from corpse-strewn streets or battlefields. The nation emerged from this period with the curious honor that attaches to the skillful boxer—always moving, always thinking, never doing anything terribly gallant or terribly stupid—who outpoints in fifteen rounds a heavier, deadlier champion. It also emerged with a purse rich enough to buy itself, just a few years later, almost half a continent.

The Federal Period (1789–1801)

1789

Society of Tammany formally organized in New York City (May 12); originally a club of Patriots, it becomes by 1800 a focus for anti-Federalist political activity, although later registering as a charitable organization; in 1860's becomes center of New York big-city machine.

Congress passes first tariff law (July 4); law gives break to imports carried in U.S. ships, thus encouraging shipbuilding industry; also places England and France on equal footing as trading partners, which annoys France.

French Revolution begins with storming of the Bastille (July 14); French assembly later issues Declaration of Rights modeled largely on American Declaration of Independence (August 27).

Department of State organized by Congress as Department of Foreign Affairs (July 27); Washington appoints Thomas Jefferson as Secretary of State, but Jefferson, who is abroad, does not take office until March 22, 1790. State Department originally handles not only foreign affairs but also interior domestic affairs not covered by other executive departments; in 1790 department consists of Jefferson, four clerks, a messenger, and two diplomats.

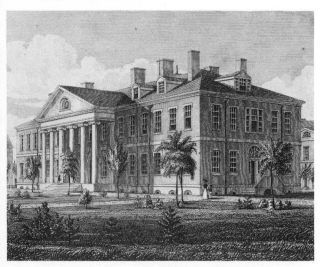

The Department of State, Washington, D.C.
LIBRARY OF CONGRESS

War Department organized (August 7); Washington appoints Henry Knox as first Secretary of War; idea is for a small (560-man) regular army, to be augmented by a well-regulated militia, the latter being largely a contradiction in terms.

Treasury Department organized (September 2); Alexander Hamilton appointed first Secretary of Treasury; department is responsible for taking in revenues but also for running lighthouses and conducting land surveys; by 1801 becomes largest and most important branch in the executive part of government, with 1,693 employees.

Congress passes Federal Judiciary Act (September 24) creating Supreme Court (six members), three circuit courts (Supreme Court justices were to ride around to them), and thirteen district courts; President is to appoint Supreme Court and district court judges; John Jay is appointed first Chief Justice, with Edmund Randolph as first Attorney General, whose main job was to render legal advice to President (September 26).

Congress submits to states (September 25) twelve proposed amendments to Constitution, of which ten are ultimately ratified two years later as Bill of Rights.

North Carolina ratifies Constitution (November 21), becoming twelfth state to do so.

Georgia sells huge section of land (25.4 million acres) along Mississippi River to land speculators, including Patrick Henry and George Rogers Clark (December 21); move threatens war with Spain and Creek Indians; treaty signed in New York City the following year eliminates war threat; Spain considers its plan for colonizing Louisiana failure.

1790

Alexander Hamilton presents to House of Representatives his *Report on Public Credit* (January 14), which recommends, among other things, the assumption of Revolutionary War debts run up by Continental Congress ($11,710,379 foreign, $40,414,086 domestic) and by individual states ($25,000,000, of which $21,500,000 is to be assumed); southern states particularly balk at paying for northern states' debts but finally trade off for permanent U.S. capital to be located on Potomac River and temporary capital to be moved from New York City to Philadelphia. Hamilton's assumption proposal passes Congress (July 26).

Death of Benjamin Franklin (April 17): 20,000 people attend his funeral in Philadelphia.

Rhode Island becomes thirteenth state to ratify Constitution (May 29).

First U.S. copyright law signed by President Washington (May 31); legislation comes about partly as result of agitation by Noah Webster, who was worried about protecting his *Spelling Book*.

Congress creates position of Postmaster General; postal service begins operation in 1791, but formal organization of Post Office Department does not occur until 1795.

Robert Morris buys (November 18) from overextended speculators and from state of Massachusetts whole of western New York, from Lake Seneca to Lake Erie; sells it to European (English and Dutch) capitalists (1791–92). Holland Land Company, eventual owner of 4 million acres of western New York and Pennsylvania, begins development, setting up improvements—stores, taverns, roads, mills, etc.

Philadelphia becomes temporary capital of the United States (December 6).

Samuel Slater (carrying plans for machinery in head) sets up first water-powered cotton factory, in Pawtucket, Rhode Island (December 21).

Patrick Henry drafts "remonstrance" against federal assumption of debt; claims that creating and perpetuating "large monied interest" in an agricultural country would lead to "prostration of agriculture at the feet of commerce" (December 23); Hamilton's response: "This is the first symptom of a spirit [that] must either be killed, or will kill the Constitution of the United States."

Results of first national census: population 3,929,625, including 697,624 slaves and 59,557 free blacks. Half the total population is in the South; New England and middle colonies have about one quarter each. Philadelphia is largest city (42,444), with New York, Boston, Charleston, and Baltimore next largest in that order. Percentage of population living in towns larger than 2,500 people: 5.4 per cent.

Gazette of the United States (founded in 1789) moves from New York to Philadelphia; under editorship of John Fenno becomes weekly newspaper most associated with Federalist cause.

First federal patent granted to Samuel Hopkins for element of glassmaking process.

1791

President Washington signs law chartering Bank of the United States (February 25); central bank, part of Hamilton's fiscal program, opens its doors in Philadelphia (December 12); issue of bank provokes constitutional argument, since Constitution did not specifically empower Congress to set up a central bank that would in effect control amount of money in circulation. Strict constructionists, led by James Madison and Thomas Jefferson, argue that any power not specifically granted to the government is therefore unconstitutional. Hamilton argues successfully that there are "implied powers," i.e., if the *goals* of a given policy are constitutional, and if the *means* selected to further those goals are not specifically prohibited, then the means are by implication constitutional.

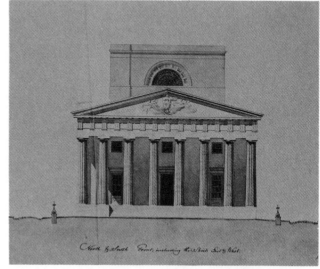

Benjamin Latrobe's design for the Bank of the United States
LIBRARY OF CONGRESS

Whiskey tax bill passed by Congress (March 3); first internal tax since the Stamp Act, it mostly affects western farmers; since failure to pay tax is federal crime, violators have to travel immense distances to federal district courts, compounding their outrage.

Vermont admitted as the fourteenth state (March 4).

Thomas Jefferson and James Madison visit New York City on a "botanizing" expedition (May–June), cultivating there disaffected anti-Federalist elements; marks beginning of anti-Federalist Republican political party; Madison persuades poet Philip Freneau to set up (October 31) *National Gazette*, which emerges as Republican organ.

As result of Indian raids in Northwest Territory, Washington sends territorial governor, Arthur St. Clair, to build forts and suppress Indians; St. Clair's army of 3,000 is surprised and routed, suffering 630 dead and 283 wounded (November 4). Indian success leads to constant raiding of whole territory north of Ohio River; since Indians are armed and supplied mainly by British, who still occupy forts in Ohio Territory, frontier rage against British grows.

Alexander Hamilton presents his *Report on Manufactures* to Congress (December 5); brilliantly argued, it calls for use of high tariffs not only to generate revenue but also to protect and nourish domestic industries, thus providing many more and different jobs, hence larger internal markets; Hamilton's proposals are not adopted, being about 100 years ahead of their time. But arguments for and against high tariffs created by this proposal linger on and are revived again and again, most notably during various crises leading up to Civil War.

First ten amendments to the Constitution (Bill of Rights) ratified by eleven states and go into effect as part of the law of the land (December 15).

1792

Mint Act (April 2) authorizes construction of federal mint, which opens in Philadelphia in 1793. Designed to implement a bimetallic decimal coinage system proposed by Alexander Hamilton, mint's output is low, largely because coinage system is failure, for a variety of complicated reasons. Result is that mint mainly puts out gold coins, and old Spanish dollars remain legal tender and most common coin in circulation.

A copper penny, the first coin issued by the new mint in 1793
CHASE MANHATTAN BANK, NEW YORK

Columbia River in state of Washington discovered and named by Captain Robert Gray (spring) on his second voyage to Oregon Territory; Gray traded in sea-otter pelts with Indians, then traded pelts in China for enormous profits. As result of Gray's voyages Oregon coast is swarming with New England traders; Indians there decide all white men are called "Bostons."

New York Stock Exchange organized at a coffee house in New York City (May 17); brokers deal mainly in bank stocks and federal securities and do business under a tree on Wall Street.

Kentucky becomes fifteenth state (June 1).

Presidential electors vote as follows: 132 for George Washington, 77 for John Adams (December 5); although Federalists also win congressional elections, some anti-Federalist opposition strength begins to show itself, particularly in 50 vice-presidential votes for

George Clinton, leader of anti-Hamilton faction in New York.

1793

Citizen Edmond Genêt arrives in Charleston, South Carolina, as French minister to U.S. (April 8); on way to Philadelphia, Genêt gets friendly popular welcome from crowds sympathetic to French Revolution; crowds have not yet heard of the execution of Louis XVI, considered by many America's friend because of help during American Revolution.

Washington issues proclamation to people, declaring that all citizens must remain "friendly and impartial" in war between France and Great Britain (April 22); although Thomas Jefferson signs proclamation and contributes to its wording, Hamilton's pro-British policies and advice to Washington grate sharply against his own pro-French feelings; Jefferson believes French Revolution "the most sacred cause that ever man was engaged in."

Citizen Genêt coolly received by President Washington in Philadelphia (May 18); Genêt, misled by considerable pro-French popular sentiment, continues to organize anti-British activities, including outfitting privateers to raid British shipping and raising southern and western armies to invade Florida and Louisiana, which belong to Britain's ally Spain. He appoints George Rogers Clark a major general in private frontier army; Kentuckians, longing to get at New Orleans, are delayed by Washington just long enough to prevent war with Spain. Cabinet, outraged by Genêt's meddling, votes to demand his recall (August 2). In meantime Jacobins, led by Robespierre, have taken power in France and begin instituting Reign of Terror. U.S. allows Genêt to remain here, since he would now probably be executed in France, but Genêt's anti-British movement collapses (November).

Eli Whitney applies for patent on cotton gin (June 20); patent is granted (March 4, 1794); later improvement added in 1796 by another inventor causes confusion of patent and much litigation, and Whitney does not receive as much money from invention as he had hoped; machine, which removes seeds from cotton fibers, enables cotton to be processed quickly but at same time increases need for labor to clear land and plant and harvest cotton, thus encouraging plantation system and institution of slave labor.

Jefferson resigns as Secretary of State (July 31), effective at end of the year; Jefferson is irked by Hamilton's views, his interference in foreign affairs, and his success in advising Washington.

1794

Congress passes Neutrality Act (June 5), in effect legislating Washington's executive proclamation of year before; anti-British feeling is now running high because of British activities in Ohio Territory and because of British seizure of American ships and cargoes in West Indies, under wartime theory that goods destined for enemy (France) are contraband, even though carried in neutral (U.S.) ships. Issue sharply divides Republicans, who wish to retaliate commercially against England even if this brings war, and Federalists, who are determined to protect and foster trade with England at all costs.

Whiskey Rebellion in western Pennsylvania, long brewing as focus of several frontier grievances, finally erupts into violence when mob (led by local Republican organization) attacks and burns home of local tax collector (July 17); resistance to whiskey tax continues, mostly nonviolently, and Washington mobilizes militia army and commands it to suppress rebels in western counties, which it does (September–November).

Battle of Fallen Timbers (August 20): Indian confederation, formed (1785–87) in hope of securing separate Indian state in Northwest and encouraged by British to believe that an Anglo-American war is inevitable, is defeated by General "Mad Anthony" Wayne, in command of Regular Army in Ohio Territory; Wayne advances slowly, sending word through forest that he will attack Indian position—a natural breastwork of fallen trees near British-held Fort Miami—on August 17; Indians, who fast on day before battle, are outfoxed by Wayne, who keeps them waiting and hungry for three days; when one quarter of Indian force leaves to eat, he attacks and scatters defenders; nearby British do not help, thus convincing Indians that all hope of British help is lost and breaking their spirit.

General Wayne surprises the Indians at Fallen Timbers.
LIBRARY OF CONGRESS

Jay's Treaty is signed in London (November 19); John Jay, Chief Justice of Supreme Court, is sent to England, ostensibly to negotiate wide range of grievances against British, but Federalists desire only that he prevent a war and undercut his bargaining power by secretly informing British of this; Jay obtains promise that British will evacuate Northwest forts by 1796, peace, and the ruination of his career, because Republicans attack treaty viciously as a sellout of American interests, especially since treaty says little about U.S. maritime rights. Treaty is bitterly debated in Senate, where it is finally ratified (June, 1795); Washington, upon signing it (June 25), becomes target of considerable popular outrage and Republican venom in press.

1795

Yazoo land fraud (January): Georgia legislature sells western lands (most of Alabama and Mississippi) to form speculating companies; land is claimed and occupied by Spanish and southeast woodlands Indians, and Georgia has nothing like a clear title to it. Public reaction to fraud is intense, and legislature is swept away in 1796 election.

Alexander Hamilton resigns from Cabinet in shuffle but remains predominant in Federalist affairs (January 31).

Post Office Department formally established (May 8); concerned mainly with building post roads. Even post office becomes focus for Hamiltonian-Jeffersonian conflict. Hamilton wants post office to earn money; Jefferson wants postal revenues to go toward expanding delivery to less settled regions.

Indian defeat at Fallen Timbers greatly spurs settlement of trans-Appalachian plateau; many settlers drift down Ohio in flatboats; others, aided by wilderness roads (rough clearings in forest), pour into Kentucky and Tennessee from South and New England.

Treaty of Greenville (August 3): General Anthony Wayne signs treaty with defeated northwestern Indians; Indians cede all Ohio lands west of line running roughly north from Cincinnati to tip of Lake Erie; area ceded is roughly area to which settlers have penetrated.

Thomas Pinckney negotiates Treaty of San Lorenzo with Spain (October 27); Spain gives up disputed area north of 31°, grants free navigation rights on Mississippi, allows American merchants to warehouse goods in New Orleans, and agrees to dismantle forts along Mississippi; treaty is immensely popular but is soon rendered moot when France, under Napoleon, bullies Spain into ceding all its Louisiana territory back to France (1800).

1796

Cleveland, Ohio, laid out (in spring) by Moses Cleaveland, agent for Connecticut Land Company, which bought huge tract in northeastern Ohio; many other towns spring up in Ohio, often starting as "paper towns" laid out and sold by speculators.

Tennessee joins Union as sixteenth state (June 1).

Presidential campaign shapes up along party lines, with John Adams and Thomas Pinckney as agreed-upon Federalist candidates and Thomas Jefferson and Aaron Burr as Republicans. Campaign is conducted by spokesmen for the candidates, by correspondence, and in the press. Alexander Hamilton secretly plans to dump John Adams by arranging electoral vote so that Pinckney, whom Federalist electors assume is merely Vice President, will actually receive more votes than Adams and hence become President. As electoral politicking goes on and is evidently going to be close, Jefferson secretly urges some of his supporters to vote for Adams, for reasons that are, in the end, anybody's guess.

Washington's Farewell Address is published (September 19) in Philadelphia newspaper; written mainly by Hamilton and Madison, it urges people to obey Constitution, to be wary of political ties with foreign nations but be willing to extend commercial relations to them, to beware of having a "passionate attachment" to any other foreign nation, and finally to shun political parties, all of which are bad but the "popular form" being of "greatest rankness."

French government attempts (October) to swing election to Republicans by authorizing Pierre Adet, French minister to U.S., to make various threatening announcements; attempt backfires and apparently costs Republicans some votes.

Electors cast votes as follows (December 7): John Adams (Federalist) 71, Thomas Jefferson (Republican) 68; Thomas Pinckney (Federalist) 59, Aaron Burr (Republican) 30, and scattered votes for others. Thus President and Vice President are of different "factions."

1797

Thomas Jefferson, after trying to get himself sworn into office in Virginia, yields to pressure and makes long trip to Philadelphia (February 20).

John Adams inaugurated as second President of United States, in Philadelphia (March 4); Washington attends ceremony as private citizen; of Washington, leading Republican newspaper *Aurora* says his retirement should cause a "Jubilee" because the "man who is the source of all the misfortunes of our country, is this day reduced to a level with his fellow citizens."

XYZ Affair: France, retaliating against what it considers Federalist pro-British policies, begins raiding American shipping carrying British goods or engaged in trade with Britain (January–October); President Adams sends Charles C. Pinckney, John Marshall, and Elbridge Gerry to France to patch things up; American diplomats are received unofficially (October 8), then toyed with and visited by flunkies (named *X, Y,* and *Z* in reports) who suggest U.S. pay bribes in order to secure audience with the French foreign minister, Talleyrand; by year's end American diplomats are still in France, getting nowhere, because Talleyrand believes he can embarrass Federalist government and gain Republican support without running serious risk of war.

1798

Two of American diplomats return to U.S., and reports of XYZ Affair are published (April); American public opinion swings violently against French and is fed to

Charles Cotesworth Pinckney

John Marshall

Elbridge Gerry

hysteria point by Federalist warnings about French armies (which are conquering most of Europe), French-inspired slave uprisings, an invasion by blacks from Haiti, and even French tutors, who are whispering "the poison of atheism and disaffection" into the tender minds of American children; attempt to discredit pro-French Republicans helps push nation to brink of war with France and also splits Federalists, one section of which, led by Adams, does not want war with France, and the other section of which—mainly Federalists in Congress—does (May–June).

Eli Whitney presents plan (May 1) for producing interchangeable musket parts, using power machinery and jigs; gets contract to produce huge number of muskets in 28 months; sets up factory near New Haven, Connecticut, and although misses his contract deadline by about nine years, eventually perfects system, revolutionizing American and later world manufacturing.

Navy Department created (May 3), and construction of naval vessels hastened; frigates *United States, Constitution*, and *Constellation* are put to sea.

The U.S. frigate Constitution, *known as "Old Ironsides"*
LIBRARY OF CONGRESS

Alien and Sedition Acts (June–July): Congress enacts four laws, partly in reaction to war hysteria; first (June 18) requires that a foreigner reside in U.S. fourteen years instead of five to become a citizen; second (June 25) allows President to deport any foreigners he considers dangerous; third (July 6) allows President to deport or imprison any foreigners with whose country of origin U.S. is at war; fourth (July 14) makes it crime to "conspire" to oppose government or publish false or malicious "writing" against President or Congress with the intent to "bring [them] into contempt or disrepute" and provides for fines and imprisonment; this last, or Sedi-

tion Act, is selectively enforced against a few Republican congressmen, editors, and loudmouths, who quickly become martyrs in public view (October).

A 1798 cartoon: one man's response to a charge of sedition
LIBRARY OF CONGRESS

George Washington is called from retirement to head U.S. Army in threatened war with France (July 2).

Virginia and Kentucky Resolutions: legislatures of Kentucky (November 16) and Virginia (December 24) pass resolutions written by Jefferson and Madison, respectively, protesting Alien and Sedition Acts and exploring possibility that states must consider whether national government can be ultimate judge of what the limits of its powers are and whether states have duty or right to check unconstitutional actions.

Undeclared naval war with France begins (November), with British navy protecting Atlantic and new U.S. Navy taking care of Caribbean; war goes on for two years, with U.S. Navy acquitting itself extremely well.

Ohio settlers force Governor St. Clair to take census and as result compel him to hold elections for legislature. Anti-Federalists are elected (December) and send 26-year-old William Henry Harrison to Congress as delegate (1799–80).

1799

Adams averts full-blown war with France by accepting French peace feelers and nominating a minister to France (February 18); war-hungry Federalist faction in Senate tries to block appointment, but Adams threatens to resign government to Jefferson; Senate compromises on three-man peace mission to France, which eventually accomplishes its purpose (1800).

Fries Rebellion in Pennsylvania (February): group of farmers violently protest new tax on land and houses; Adams calls out federal troops, which squash uprising;

Adams further widens rift in Federalist ranks by pardoning leaders, whom Federalist judges have twice sentenced to death for treason.

Death of George Washington (December 14): Washington's last will and testament expresses wish that "a university in a central part of the U.S." will be set up so that young people will not acquire "local attachments and state prejudices."

1800

Indiana Territory created (May 7), largely as a result of Republican efforts to prevent Ohio Territory from being split into three small states that Federalists could dominate or at least prevent from joining Union as Republican.

Congress passes Land Act of 1800 (May 10); act allows direct purchases of frontier land by individuals at local land offices; settlers can buy 320 (half-lot) acres at one quarter down and the rest over four-year period. This means a 320-acre farm can be bought for $160 at land offices near actual settlement. Eliminates large-scale land speculators from Ohio and greatly increases western settlement; also originates phrase "doing a land-office business" (because people flocked to take advantage of law).

Campaign of 1800: begins early in year, with Republicans under Jefferson and Burr determined to swing key states of New York, New Jersey, and Pennsylvania; Federalists are split; campaign, carried out mainly by surrogates and newspapers, is extremely savage and scurrilous, with Federalists predicting that with Jefferson "rape, adultery, and incest will be openly taught and practiced"; much nastiness about Adams comes from Federalist faction headed by Hamilton, who, in leaked letter, calls Adams full of "distempered jealousy," "vanity without bounds," and general unfitness; Republicans win majority in House of Representatives.

Convention of 1800 ends undeclared Franco-American naval war (September 30).

Louisiana Territory secretly changes hands from Spain to France under Napoleon Bonaparte by Treaty of San Ildefonso (October 1), with France to take actual possession in 1802.

Congress meets for first time in Washington, D.C. (November 17).

Presidential electors cast ballots as follows: Jefferson and Burr, 73 each; John Adams, 65; Charles Cotesworth Pinckney, 64; although results show sharp tightening of party discipline, it is too tight for Republicans. The 73

votes each for Jefferson and Burr, with neither man specifically designated as President or Vice President, means a tied election, which must therefore go to House of Representatives, where each of sixteen states has one vote and where Federalists control six to eight states.

Results of second U.S. census: population 5,308,483, of which 896,849 are slaves.

1801

John Marshall appointed Chief Justice of the United States (January 20) by lame-duck President Adams.

Balloting begins in lame-duck House of Representatives for presidential choice (February 11); goes on through 35 ballots, until one Federalist decides to switch to Jefferson and so informs his party; Federalists then arrange voting so that Jefferson is elected on 36th ballot, without any Federalist votes going to him (February 17); final count is Jefferson 10 states, Burr 4, with two states casting blank ballots.

Lame-duck Congress passes Judiciary Act (February 27), which creates a variety of new judgeships and other clerical positions; Adams fills them on last day in office, seeking to maintain Federalists in power through "midnight appointments" (March 3) even though Republicans have won control of both House and Senate and will later wipe most of these appointments out.

Thomas Jefferson inaugurated as third President of United States (March 4); Jefferson is first President to be inaugurated in new capital of Washington, D.C., and walks through muddy Washington streets to his inauguration in unfinished Capitol building; in inaugural address Jefferson promises wise, tolerant, frugal Republican government, calls upon all to "unite in common efforts for the common good," and skillfully blends Republican and Federalist themes and principles.

The Capitol in 1800
LIBRARY OF CONGRESS

Emigrants accepted hardship and danger on the wagon trails in the hope that the West would offer prosperity.

Westward Expansion
1801–1860

This period begins in 1801, with the inauguration of Thomas Jefferson, and ends in 1860, with the election of Abraham Lincoln as the sixteenth President.

The big story of the period is, in one sense, extremely rapid territorial expansion. In roughly two generations the nation leapt across the continent, adding 2,133,576 square miles of territory and acquiring its present continental borders. Much of this territory was taken by war, or by threat of war, from its native inhabitants and from France and Spain. Almost all of it was paid for, in money and in blood. With the exception of Jefferson's purchase of the trans-Mississippi Louisiana Territory, American people got to this land before the American government did, in most cases quickly outnumbering the Europeans or Indians who had been there before.

But territorial expansion was only a part of a more significant kind of growth. During these years the United States not only grew bigger, but it also grew much more complex. In the two generations that comprise this period, an interconnected series of developments took place that are difficult to condense into a single narrative.

Politically, the nation was governed at the executive level for most of this period by the direct or indirect heirs of Thomas Jefferson and Andrew Jackson. They were usually democrats, both small-d and large-D. They were usually from the South or from what was then the West—Tennessee or Indiana. Until 1824 the Demo-

59

cratic "Virginia" dynasty of Jefferson, Madison, and Monroe busily implemented a largely Hamiltonian program, for the most part encouraging or at least rarely hindering various forms of expansionist economic, commercial, and technological development and at the same time mostly retaining the favor of the Westerners by encouraging or by failing to obstruct a gradual broadening of the white male franchise and a gradual liberalizing of western land policies, making this land easier and cheaper to get. The one main break in this pattern was the War of 1812.

Andrew Jackson and his successors did not depart radically from the main outlines of the program of the Virginia group but for the most part merely intensified some of the elements of this program. The pro-western, pro-Average Man politics were carried forward strongly, with the white male franchise becoming virtually universal and few if any roadblocks being placed in the way of expansion into western lands. The traditional Democratic aversion to strong, centralized financial institutions blossomed into an almost personal war by Jackson on the Bank of the United States, which Jackson won, thus contributing heavily to an economic crash in 1837.

Increasingly, however, the Democratic Party was unable to contain fully or respond adequately to the contradictory demands of its main power bases among the middle and lower classes in the rural South, urban North, and pioneer West. Splinter third parties—always a sign in American politics that its coalitional, consensual, cross-regional system is approaching a condition of overload—began to appear, some arising from within Democratic ranks, like the Locofoco urban working-class party, others mainly just anti-Jackson, like the Anti-Masonic Party.

In 1834 a broad-based opposition party—the Whigs—coalesced around various anti-Jacksonian interests. Since these anti-Jackson elements were, in effect, mirror images of the pro-Jackson ones, the new party was also composed of contradictory regional and class interests—northern manufacturing and financial types, portions of the southern estate-owning and mercantile classes, and western farmers wanting less tariff and more cheap land than the Democrats were able to deliver. The Whigs promptly appropriated Democratic election tactics and hooplahed and just-plain-folksed the Democrats to death in the campaign of 1840. But the Whig Party, like the Democrats, simply could not contain the antagonistic factions within itself. More splinter parties arose, and ultimately both the Whig and Democratic parties split along regional lines, North and West versus South, and a new splinter party, the Republican Party, itself a coalition of northern splinters, captured the

executive in the election of 1860, without winning a single southern state.

In 1846, under a strong Democratic executive, James K. Polk, the United States picked a fight with Mexico, which, under a new militaristic regime, was more than willing to go to the mat. To the surprise of most European military experts, the United States won this war and took as the victor's spoils California and what is now the American Southwest. National opinion was divided by the war, with some wanting to take all of Mexico and others bitterly opposed. This opposition, centered to some extent in the Northeast but also cutting across regional lines and embracing the same educated, liberal middle-class constituency that articulated opposition to the Vietnam war in this century, further agitated the Whig and Democratic parties and virtually tore them apart in the 1850's when the time came to organize the newly acquired territory into political units.

Economically the main story is one of growing regional specialization, with each region producing surpluses of a particular kind for both internal and foreign consumption. The Northeast increasingly produced surpluses of manufactured goods—cotton cloth, shoes, glassware, pig iron, revolvers, and everything in between. The Northwest, by now including all of the Great Lakes region, produced enormous surpluses of wheat, flour, corn, and pork. The Deep South or Gulf States produced huge surpluses of cotton. The older or tidewater South grew and processed tobacco and produced surplus labor in the form of human slaves for interstate sale. The Far West was beginning to produce, among other things, large quantities of gold and silver, a shortage of which had always plagued the nation.

Theoretically each of the regions ought to have been mutually dependent, but it didn't work out that way. What did happen was a shifting pattern of economic alignments that wound up in 1860 with the Northeast, Northwest, and Far West needing each other and the South needing Great Britain. Technological developments—capital-intensive labor-saving devices—were largely responsible for this pattern.

What existed in the 1850's therefore was something that both the Federalists and the Jeffersonian Republicans of the early 1800's could mainly approve of: a largely agricultural nation with a booming manufacturing sector, each region producing its own specialty and the whole increasingly tied together by a communications network—canals, railroads, newspapers, steamboats, telegraphy—capable of moving goods and information at relatively high speeds and low cost. But this is precisely the whole that blew apart into a civil war, a war that remains, in relation to population, the deadliest and most expensive Americans have ever fought.

Westward Expansion (1801–1860)

1801

Naval war with Tripoli begins (May 14); Barbary state of Tripoli declares war on U.S. because it feels U.S. tribute payments to protect American shipping are not high enough; war finally ends in 1805 after naval blockade and overland attack; annual bribes to Tripoli abolished.

Tripoli forces an American ship to make a tribute payment.
LIBRARY OF CONGRESS

Johnny Appleseed (John Chapman) begins planting apple seeds brought from Pennsylvania throughout Ohio, Indiana, and Illinois.

1802

Congress establishes U.S. Military Academy at West Point, New York (March 16).

Congress repeals Hamilton's excise tax on whiskey, thus increasing Jefferson's popularity among Westerners.

1803

Marbury v. *Madison* (February 24): William Marbury, one of President Adams' "midnight" appointees, sues for right to his job, which Jefferson administration refuses to give him. Supreme Court, under John Marshall, Federalist, distant relative but no friend of Jefferson, says Marbury has right to job (thus condemning Jefferson administration) but also says Court has no power to compel administration to give Marbury his job back because a congressional law (Judiciary Act of 1789) giving the Supreme Court that power is unconstitutional and hence void. Thus Court avoids a direct confrontation with the executive and at the same time asserts a principle only later understood in its entirety, namely, that the Supreme Court has the power and duty to invalidate acts of Congress deemed unconstitutional.

Ohio joins Union as seventeenth state, first state formed out of Northwest Territory, where slavery is forbidden

(March 1); Chillicothe is first capital.

Louisiana Purchase (April 30): western fears of a French strangle hold on New Orleans prompt Jefferson to send ministers to France to buy New Orleans, allowing French agents to see letters promising to "marry ourselves to British fleet and nation" if sale is not accomplished; Napoleon, having failed to suppress black kingdom in Haiti and realizing he could not hold Louisiana against British attack, agrees to sell all of Louisiana Territory; final treaty does not specify boundaries, French just saying they would sell the territory they got from Spain; no one is exactly sure if it includes Floridas or Texas; total cost $15 million, which includes $3.75 million in claims against France for damage to U.S. shipping, which U.S. agrees to assume; Jefferson is fairly sure it includes lands drained by Mississippi and Missouri (present-day Missouri, Nebraska, Iowa, Arkansas, North and South Dakota, Kansas, Minnesota, Montana, Wyoming, and Louisiana, about 828,000 square miles); territory formally passes to U.S. on December 20, 1803, in New Orleans.

Mandan Indians on the Missouri River in about 1800
LIBRARY OF CONGRESS

Lewis and Clark expedition: after careful preparation (Jefferson sent Meriwether Lewis to Philadelphia to be briefed by scientists), expedition begins (July 5); Lewis and Clark winter in St. Louis, training force of 51; on May 14, 1804, expedition starts up Missouri into what is now North Dakota and picks up Shoshone woman, Sacajawea, with two-month-old child; woman promises to guide them through Rockies (winter, 1804); another member of party, York, a slave belonging to William Clark, serves as translator and also as curiosity, because

Indians are fascinated by black skin; party crosses continental divide in what is now Montana (summer, 1805) and ultimately reaches Pacific, via Clearwater and Columbia rivers (November 7, 1805); party expects arrival of Yankee fur-trading vessel, but none arrives, so they return overland, arriving back in St. Louis September 23, 1806; trip costs $49,000 and provides much scientific data.

1804

Jefferson tries to get at largely Federalist judiciary through impeachment, including impeachment of Supreme Court Justice Samuel Chase; attempt fails when Senate acquits Chase (March 1, 1805) of flimsy charges, and Jefferson gives up.

New England Federalists (sometimes called Essex Junto) plan to form separate Northern Confederacy, with New York, and to secede from Union; plan temporarily collapses when Aaron Burr fails to win New York governorship (April 25); Federalists are alarmed at Republican inroads among their own people and fear that the newly acquired Louisiana Territory will go Republican and that the West with the South will dominate national government.

Duel between Alexander Hamilton and Aaron Burr (July 11) in Weehawken, New Jersey: Burr, blocked by Hamilton in his attempt to gain governorship of New York, issues challenge; Hamilton accepts and is fatally wounded; Burr is indicted by New York and New Jersey but continues as Vice President.

Twelfth Amendment ratified (September 25); provides separate balloting for President and Vice President.

Presidential electors vote (December 5) for Thomas Jefferson as President and George Clinton as Vice President, defeating Federalists Charles Cotesworth Pinckney and Rufus King by vote of 162 to 14.

1805

Thomas Jefferson inaugurated for second term, with George Clinton of New York as Vice President (March 4); Jefferson's second inaugural address alienates some Republican support by urging Congress to spend money on roads and other internal improvements; Jefferson also soon has to deal with England, which begins impressing American seamen of British birth to serve in war against Napoleonic France, and deals with it badly by further reducing U.S. Navy.

1806

Lieutenant Zebulon Montgomery Pike begins second exploratory expedition (July); travels from St. Louis

across Kansas into Colorado, where he names Pikes Peak; crosses Sangre de Cristo Mountains (1807) and builds fort on upper Rio Grande, in Colorado; Spanish army captures party, marches it to Santa Fe, and finally releases it east of Red River in Texas, which Spanish consider border of their Texas territory.

1807

Aaron Burr tried for treason (August 3–September 1) before Chief Justice Marshall as circuit judge; case involves scheme of Burr to get himself declared president of independent Louisiana and then invade and conquer Mexico; several prominent Westerners are involved, including Andrew Jackson, but plans are betrayed before Burr has a chance to gather army; Chief Justice Marshall insists on strict constitutional definition of treason, and hence Burr is acquitted.

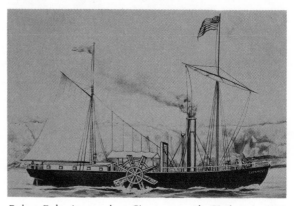

Robert Fulton's steamboat Clermont *on the Hudson in 1809*
LIBRARY OF CONGRESS

Robert Fulton successfully tests steamboat *Clermont* on Hudson River between New York City and Albany (August 17–19); although steamboats had been tested as early as 1787, *Clermont* trip excites popular imagination and stimulates subsequent rapid development.

Jefferson recommends embargo of all foreign trade (December 18); Congress passes Embargo Act (December 22); idea that cutting off trade with Britain would bring her to her knees was pet Jeffersonian notion, but wrong; embargo mainly hurt New England and seaports; French, on pretext they were enforcing American law, confiscated American vessels; throughout 1808 embargo was violated by smugglers and others, aroused tremendous opposition from Federalists, and had a divisive effect on Republicans, especially in North.

1808

Prohibition of African slave trade (January 1) does not

affect interstate slave trade, and smuggling continues.

Elections of 1808: Jefferson, having declined to run for a third term, indicates James Madison as choice to succeed him; antiembargo Republicans get George Clinton on ticket as Vice President and also run him as presidential candidate; electoral vote as follows: James Madison (Republican) 122; Charles Cotesworth Pinckney 47. Clinton becomes Vice President with 113 votes over Federalist Rufus King. Federalists score gains in Congress as a result of antiembargo sentiment.

American Fur Company founded by John Jacob Astor; Astor plans to build forts from Great Lakes to Pacific; sets up fort (Astoria) at mouth of Columbia River, in Oregon (1811).

1809

Nonintercourse Act signed by Jefferson (March 1); repeals embargo on all foreign trade and substitutes nonintercourse with warring Great Britain and France.

Inauguration of James Madison as fourth U.S. President (March 4); George Clinton is Vice President.

Madison renews trade with Great Britain (April 19) after being led to believe that British will stop abuses such as impressing American sailors; British refuse to go along, so Nonintercourse Act is reinstated (August 9).

1810

Macon's Bill Number 2 (May 1): authorizes President to renew trade with both England and France but to cut off trade with whichever nation does not recognize American neutral shipping rights. Napoleon hoodwinks Madison into believing that France will stop interfering with American shipping (November 2).

West Florida rebels against Spanish rule (September 26); inhabitants, now 90 per cent American, seize Spanish fort at Baton Rouge after President Madison opines that Florida is part of Louisiana Purchase; Madison annexes West Florida, from Baton Rouge, Louisiana, to Pensacola, Florida (October 27); Spain, however, retains strong fort right in middle, in Mobile, Alabama.

Census of 1810: population 7,239,881, including 1,191,364 slaves and 186,746 free blacks.

1811

Congress refuses to renew charter of Bank of the United States (January 24–February 20).

Congress declares nonintercourse with Great Britain (March 2), even though French continue to pillage American shipping.

Several "war hawks" are elected to Congress from South and West, including Henry Clay of Kentucky and John C. Calhoun of South Carolina; war hawks, mostly young, mostly expansionist, are outspoken in favor of war with England but numerically have little influence.

Tecumseh, Shawnee chieftain, in response to ten years of land grabbing by William Henry Harrison, governor of Indiana Territory, forms confederacy of northwestern tribes, from whom 110 million acres had been wrung by bribes, bullying, and treaties with venal tribal factions; with Tecumseh away in South gathering support, Harrison leads army of 1,000, which successfully withstands Indian attack at Tippecanoe, on Wabash River, in Indiana (November 7); Indian attacks increase in number and ferocity, especially in spring of 1812; Westerners believe British are behind Indian attacks and call for war against Canada.

Russians establish fort and agricultural colony (Fort Ross) in California, north of San Francisco, which is used as base for extensive trade in sea-otter skins; Russians later give up territorial claims to West Coast (1824) and sell Fort Ross to John Sutter (1841).

Construction of Cumberland or National Road begun; paved road, first national highway, financed by sales of federal land, is to run from Cumberland, Maryland, to Wheeling, on the Ohio River (which it reaches in 1818).

1812

Britain, now severely strained by Napoleonic war and wishing to reinstitute trade with U.S., protests in vain that France has not stopped violating U.S. shipping; finally revokes measures against U.S. ships (June 16); despite great opposition to war, especially in New England, U.S. Congress declares war on Great Britain two days later (June 18), before news of revocation arrives.

Connecticut and Massachusetts refuse to support war, hint at secession (July–August).

Invasions of Canada fail; western army, under William Hull, defeated by British under Isaac Brock, who captures both Detroit and Hull's army (August 16); militia force of 6,000 captured at Niagara River when regular army refuses to support them (October 18); third militia army of 5,000 marches up Lake Champlain but refuses to cross into Canada and retreats (November 19).

Series of naval victories (U.S.S. *Constitution* over H.M.S. *Guerrière*, August 19; U.S.S. *United States* over H.M.S. *Macedonian*, October 25; U.S.S. *Constitution* over H.M.S. *Java*, December 29) elate Americans but are really of no military significance; later British blockade keeps most of U.S. Navy bottled up for duration of war.

The Constitution *capturing the* Guerrière *on August 19, 1812*

Commodore Perry defeats the British at the Battle of Lake Erie.

Elections of 1812 (December 2): President Madison wins re-election, 128 votes to 89, over De Witt Clinton, who is supported by both Federalists and antiwar Republicans; Elbridge Gerry elected Vice President over Charles Jared Ingersoll, 131 to 86.

1813

British gradually extend naval blockade of U.S. coast; by November blockade extends from New Orleans to New York; New England is excluded in hopes that it will break away from Union; when it does not, blockade is thrown over New England too (May, 1814); effect is devastating on economy and on government revenues (e.g., value of Virginia exports falls from almost $5 million in 1812 to roughly $18,000 in 1814).

Battle of Lake Erie (September 10): Captain Oliver Hazard Perry slugs it out with British fleet on Lake Erie, and British lose; Perry sends message: "We have met the enemy, and they are ours." Victory enables U.S. land forces to invade Canada and causes British retreat; by end of 1813, however, British are still in control of most of Canada and have burned Buffalo, New York.

Battle of the Thames (October 5): American army under William Henry Harrison pursues fleeing British force in Canada and destroys it; Tecumseh is killed, and his confederacy collapses.

1814

Battle of Horseshoe Bend, Alabama (March 27): Andrew Jackson, with army of 3,000, defeats 1,000 barricaded warlike Creeks; Jackson forces the few survivors to cede half of Creek lands in Southeast, including most of Alabama and half of Georgia (August 9).

Congress, on recommendation of Madison, repeals all embargoes and other trade restrictions (April 14); New

England continues to trade with "enemy," Great Britain, via British-held Maine and Canadian ports.

British sail into Chesapeake Bay and land an expeditionary force that proceeds to Washington, D.C., and burns public buildings (August 25); raid on Washington has little military significance, and British move on to Baltimore, where they bombard Fort McHenry at entrance to Baltimore Harbor and Francis Scott Key writes words to "Star-Spangled Banner" (September 13); British fail to take Fort McHenry and land invasion fails, so they end Chesapeake campaign (September 14).

Battle of Lake Champlain (September 11): American gunboats, under Captain Thomas Macdonough, defeat English fleet, thus preventing invasion of New York by 11,000 British troops; probably the most decisive battle of war, ultimately leading to peace treaty with Great Britain; Macdonough wins big, using device that allows him to turn ships around while they are at anchor, thus presenting second broadside to British ships.

Creek Indians massacre whites at Fort Mims, Alabama, in 1813.

Washington burning during the British raid on the capital

Bombs burst over Fort McHenry as the British attack Baltimore.

Andrew Jackson invades Florida, captures Pensacola (November 7); raid further convinces Americans that Spain's grasp on Floridas is shaky at best.

Treaty of Ghent signed (December 24); peace negotiations, begun in Ghent, Belgium, in summer of 1814, drag on until news of U.S. naval victory on Lake Champlain arrives; Duke of Wellington, in overall command of British armies in Canada, recommends signing of peace treaty, since invasion is not possible until naval control of Lakes Erie and Champlain is regained; treaty says little except that hostilities should cease and prewar boundaries should be recognized.

Federalists hold secret Hartford Convention (December 15–January 5, 1815); although war had to some extent enriched New England and stimulated its manufacturing interests, Federalists were bitter about being dragged into it in the first place; convention issues set of resolutions urging constitutional amendments whose main purpose would be to prevent another such war and

Jackson's men defeat the British at the Battle of New Orleans.

suggests that New England use federal revenues to provide for its own defense. Resolutions are issued at about same time that news of peace treaty and Battle of New Orleans arrive; they are ridiculed as unpatriotic and severely damage Federalist prestige.

Boston manufacturing company, headed by Francis Cabot Lowell, establishes water-powered textile factory at Waltham, Massachusetts; combines all processes (spinning, weaving, dyeing) leading to finished cotton cloth under one roof, using single waterpower source and nonessential labor (young women); factory is typical of early New England textile system in that it is located in countryside rather than in city and attempts to provide pleasant living and working conditions.

1815

Battle of New Orleans (January 1–8): large British army is virtually wiped out as it attacks fortified American militia under General Andrew Jackson. Although battle has no military significance, it causes great popular exaltation, makes Americans believe they have won the war, and ultimately gains Jackson the Presidency.

Second war against Barbary states (March–June): Congress sends fleet against Algiers, whose dey has captured American ships and sailors and has declared war against U.S. for underpayment of bribes; fleet under Stephen Decatur mops up dey's navy (June 19), and Decatur forces treaty with Algiers (June 30) and later similar ones with Tunis and Tripoli; treaties end all tribute payments, release all U.S. prisoners, and in general put an end to Barbary piracy; later (1816) Decatur makes toast relating to Barbary expedition: "Our country! In her intercourse with foreign governments may she always be in the right; but our country, right or wrong!"

1816

Second Bank of the United States chartered by Congress (April 10); bank is capitalized at $35 million, of which $28 million is owned by private shareholders, the rest by federal government; bank is badly managed until 1819 and overextends credit; afterward, especially under Nicholas Biddle, bank is soundly run, thus incurring wrath of Westerners and especially state and private banks, which it requires to issue sound bank notes, redeemable in gold.

Congress passes first protective tariff (April 27), designed not only to raise revenue but also to protect budding U.S. industries, especially iron and textiles; John Calhoun of South Carolina argues for protectionist tariff because he hopes South will develop textile mills, and Daniel Webster argues against because New England shippers oppose measure.

James Monroe chosen by Republicans as successor to Madison in party caucus; swamps Federalist Rufus King in Electoral College, 183 to 34 (December 4); election represents virtual death of Federalist Party, although many Hamiltonian measures are now being incorporated by Republican Party.

Steamboat *Washington,* with boilers on deck and shallow draft, begins era of riverboats suitable for use on Mississippi and Ohio rivers; by 1825 there were about 100 such vessels, usually carrying goods south to New Orleans; riverboat traffic is expected to link Ohio and other northwestern states economically with South and does so for a while, until Erie Canal and later railroad systems change this.

1817

President Madison, on last day in office, vetoes bonus bill (March 3); bill, project of John Calhoun, called for using $1.5 million, some of it profits from U.S. shares in Bank of United States, to build internal improvements such as roads and canals; Madison vetoes it because he feels it is unconstitutional.

James Monroe of Virginia inaugurated as fifth President (March 4); Daniel D. Tompkins of New York becomes Vice President. Absence of any significant opposition party and heightened sentiment of nationalism cause Monroe's administration to be called Era of Good Feelings.

British Canada and U.S. sign Rush-Bagot Agreement (April 28–29), designed to eliminate armaments race on Great Lakes, where naval shipbuilding is threatening to get out of hand; each nation agrees to have only eight warships on Lakes.

Construction begun on Erie Canal (July 4); canal, which ultimately is 363 miles long and 4 feet deep, with 83 locks, is built largely by farmers under leadership of engineers who learn on the job and solve problems as they crop up; canal is designed to connect New York City via Hudson with Buffalo on Lake Erie and costs more than $7 million, which is paid back very quickly after canal opens, eight years later.

Excavation of a part of the Erie Canal at Lockport, New York
LIBRARY OF CONGRESS

1818

General Andrew Jackson invades Florida (April 7–May 24) to punish Seminole Indians for raids against frontier settlers; raids usually were in retaliation for U.S. Army invasions in search of runaway slaves, but several British traders also stirred up trouble; Jackson captures Spanish forts of St. Marks and Pensacola and hangs two British traders; ease with which Jackson tears through Florida convinces Spain it might as well sell colony as lose it.

1819

Spain cedes Florida to U.S. in Adams-Onis Treaty (February 22); Spain in effect gives up all claims to Florida for $5 million, in form of claims against Spain by U.S. citizens to be paid by U.S.; treaty also defines Spanish holdings in Southwest as including all of Texas (west of Sabine River) and what are now states of New Mexico, Arizona, Utah, Nevada, and California.

Economic Panic of 1819 causes depression lasting three years; one result is that Bank of United States forecloses on many mortgages in West and South, leaving many farmers in these areas howling about "monster" bank and, as John Calhoun noted, "looking for a leader," whom they find in Andrew Jackson.

McCulloch v. *Maryland* (March 6): Supreme Court, under John Marshall, unanimously decides that Maryland cannot tax branch of Bank of United States, because this would in effect give states power to destroy federal institutions; Marshall also asserts bank's constitutionality, using Hamilton's argument of implied powers—if the ends are constitutional and the means to achieve these ends do not violate the letter or spirit of the Constitution, the means are constitutional.

1820

U.S. census: population 9,638,453. New York is largest city, with 124,000; Philadelphia is next largest (113,000), followed by Baltimore (63,000), Boston (43,000), and New Orleans (27,000).

Missouri Compromise (March 3): measure designed to maintain balance of slave and free states (and hence balance of power in Senate) by admitting Maine, formerly part of Massachusetts, as a free state and allowing Missouri to draw up a state constitution as it wishes (slavery had existed there since earliest French days), with the stipulation that in the rest of the Louisiana Territory slavery will be prohibited above line 36°30′ latitude. In 1821 Missouri draws up a constitution with a provision that allows it to exclude free Negroes and mulattos, which Congress balks at and causes to have removed; Missouri then enters Union as slave state on August 10, 1821; the 36°30′ line satisfies almost everyone and comes to be considered inviolate and almost part of Constitution.

American missionaries—from New England—established in Hawaii; Hawaii becomes part of three-cornered Yankee trade: Pacific Northwest (furs), Hawaii (sandalwood), and China (silks, tea, porcelain, etc.); also used as provisioning station by American whalers; in 1826 Hawaii and U.S. sign treaty of friendship, which remains in effect although U.S. Senate fails to ratify; by 1840's American interests firmly established there.

President Monroe is re-elected (December 6) without any formal opposition, getting all but one of the 232 electoral votes cast. Daniel Tompkins is re-elected Vice President.

1821

President James Monroe inaugurated for second term (March 5); Daniel Tompkins is Vice President.

Yankee shippers establish regular tallow and hide trade in California; Mexico, having gained independence from Spain in September, 1821, welcomes trade with Americans, as Spain had not; California missions are broken up, and huge private cattle ranches are established; most early Anglo-American settlers in California are seamen who jump English and American ships.

1822

With permission of Mexican governor of Texas, Stephen F. Austin leads settlers to Texas, founding colony at Austin; by 1825 there are about 2,000 American settlers in Texas, including about 400 slaves.

Denmark Vesey's plan for slave uprising aborted in Charleston, South Carolina; Vesey and 36 others executed (May 30).

1823

Monroe Doctrine promulgated (December 2); included in speech to Congress by President Monroe, it represents Secretary of State John Quincy Adams' position that (1) American continents are not to be considered available for any further colonization by European powers and (2) any attempt by European nations to interfere with new South American republics will be regarded as hostile to U.S. interests, peace, and safety. Doctrine has little immediate effect, and even though U.S., during period 1822–26, formally recognizes Colombia, Mexico, Chile, Argentina, and Peru, it gives them little economic and political support; doctrine did not become basis for actual U.S. interference in Latin-American affairs until early 1900's.

1824

Election of 1824: old Jeffersonian Republican Party drifts apart, ultimately providing four presidential candidates: John Quincy Adams of Massachusetts, William Crawford of Georgia, Henry Clay of Kentucky, and Andrew Jackson of Tennessee; John C. Calhoun of South Carolina runs as Vice President on both Adams and Jackson tickets. Campaign is quiet, with no sharp delineation of issues, except that Clay and Jackson are both Westerners, representing in a vague way something new and popular. Electoral vote (December 1) is as follows: Jackson 99; Adams 84; Crawford 41; Clay 37. Since no candidate has a majority, election goes to House of Representatives.

1825

House of Representatives elects John Quincy Adams President (February 9) after Clay throws support to Adams; Jackson supporters claim "corrupt bargain" and begin to plot election campaign of 1828.

John Quincy Adams inaugurated as sixth President (March 4); John C. Calhoun is Vice President.

Erie Canal opens (October 26); canal is soon great success, making New York City leading port, enriching Buffalo, and enhancing land values all along its path; canal becomes main route for massive migrations from

New England to northwestern states; sets off huge boom in canal and railroad building as other eastern cities attempt to get linkup with lucrative western trade, in some cases coming up with schemes for canals going up 2,000-foot elevations; many states and cities float bond issues (bought mainly by Europeans), which ultimately become worthless in Panic of 1837; immediate and long-term effect of canal is to link Northeast and West together economically.

1828

Congress passes "Tariff of Abominations" (May 13), comprehensive bill setting high rates on all imports; legislation is proposed by Jacksonians, who hope New England, which favors a strong tariff, will vote against it under pressure from manufacturers; northern manufacturers object to excessively high rates on raw materials and on molasses, sharing the position advocated by the South, which has to import everything and thus opposes a strong protective tariff. It is calculated that amendments making the bill more palatable to northern interests will be voted down and thus Jacksonians can claim credit in North for having supported a protective-tariff measure and in South for having defeated it; this would ensure that in the forthcoming election Jackson would get antiprotectionist votes from middle states, West, and South. Instead measure passes because New Englanders decide to accept it as the best they can get and in the end give the bill enough votes to ensure its passage. Adams signs. The Jacksonians' proposed strategy has come to naught, and the end result threatens to alienate certain southern states, especially South Carolina, whose state legislature draws up a statement (December 19) protesting the action of Congress in passing the law (under the Constitution, Congress has no power to pass tariff laws that favor one section or group over another; if Congress goes beyond its specific powers to pass a law, it is the right of any state to nullify that law). In the end Jackson does not get hurt in the South, where he is (incorrectly) touted as a states'-rights advocate; because of the support he receives from the West and from discontented elements in the Northeast, his political position is undamaged.

Construction begun on Baltimore and Ohio Railroad (July 4); first passengers carried in 1830, in single horse-drawn cars.

Campaign of 1828 pits Andrew Jackson and John C. Calhoun against John Quincy Adams and Henry Clay, representing popular Democratic faction and Hamiltonian National Republican faction, respectively, of old Jeffersonian Republican Party; although some real issues lurk somewhere under all campaign slander, campaign is conducted largely on basis of Jackson as man of the people and Adams as corrupt, sissified, and unlikable; popular vote (December 3): Jackson 647,000, Adams 508,000; this is first election in which large numbers of voters participate and in which majority of electors are chosen by this popular vote; Electoral College results: Jackson 178, Adams 83.

1829

Andrew Jackson inaugurated as seventh President (March 4); John C. Calhoun becomes Vice President; mob scene at White House reception, where "uncouth" Jacksonian frontiersmen pour into White House and make an exuberant mess.

Spoils system: practice of replacing federal officials on basis of party affiliation supposedly introduced by President Jackson, who believed ordinary citizen could perform most governmental jobs; actually appointments based on party loyalty have been common since Jefferson's administration, and Jackson replaces only about 20 per cent during his administrations.

1830

U.S. census: population 12,866,020; center of population is in what is now West Virginia.

Webster-Hayne debates in U.S. Senate (January 19–27): begun over issue of sale of public lands, which the East wants to restrict because it fears population drain and also because it wants government to make lots of money from land sales, debates ultimately deal with states' rights vs. national union, with Daniel Webster of Massachusetts arguing for "liberty and Union, one and inseparable" and Robert Y. Hayne of South Carolina arguing that the federal government is encroaching upon sovereign powers and rights of states.

Mexico forbids further settlement in Texas and further importation of slaves and resolves to occupy territory militarily (April 6); law emanates from Centralist (authoritarian) political faction in Mexico, with whom the Federalists (Democrats) are in constant conflict; there are now about 8,000 Americans in Texas, and Mexican action causes them to press for independence as a separate Mexican state rather than remaining part of the larger province of Texas-Coahuila.

Church of Jesus Christ of Latter-day Saints, based on Joseph Smith's *Book of Mormon*, organized by Smith (April 6) in Fayette, New York; large Mormon settlement established in Jackson County, Missouri, in 1833; Mormons eventually driven from Missouri to Nauvoo, Illinois (1838); new settlement prospers and then undergoes further persecution, partly because of cultural differences, especially plural marriage; Joseph Smith and brother are murdered by mob (June 27, 1844); Mormons begin migration farther west in 1846.

Indian Removal Bill signed (May 28); Congress authorizes removal of all eastern Indians to lands west of Mississippi, by force if necessary; largely aimed at southeastern Indians, whose property states were ruthlessly expropriating; President Jackson signs bill because other alternatives—extermination and assimilation—seem unworkable.

First steam locomotive, *Tom Thumb*, built by Peter Cooper in Baltimore, for use on Baltimore and Ohio Railroad; can pull only one car and loses race with horse-drawn train after a mechanical failure.

The locomotive Tom Thumb *racing a horse-drawn carriage*

1831

William Lloyd Garrison founds antislavery weekly newspaper, *The Liberator*, in Boston; first issue appears January 1; small-circulation paper never makes money but is one of first demands for immediate rather than gradual emancipation; considered extremist even by other abolitionists, Garrison is later (1835) almost killed by Boston mob.

The Liberator's masthead clearly shows its antislavery slant.
BOTH: LIBRARY OF CONGRESS

Peggy Eaton affair (April): Margaret Eaton, wife of Jackson's Secretary of War, becomes target of social ostracism, led by Calhoun and his wife, on account of her lowly origins and supposedly scandalous immorality; part of larger political breach between Jackson and Calhoun, affair leads ultimately to resignation of Secretary of State, Martin Van Buren, an Eaton and Jackson supporter; this move precipitates the resignation of rest of

Jackson's Cabinet, who are Calhoun men (April 11); Jackson gets new Cabinet (May–August) and decides to run for second term, with Martin Van Buren as heir-apparent.

Nat Turner's Rebellion in Virginia (August 22): Turner, slave preacher, leads 60 or 70 slaves on rampage, killing 55 whites, many of them women and children, in Southampton County; militia puts down rebellion, killing at least 100 blacks, some of whom had no connection with Turner; rebellion terrifies tidewater Virginia, where blacks outnumber whites by 65,000, and puzzles it as well, since Turner was well treated by and spoke well of master and family; many southerners feel that Turner, who could read, was influenced by abolitionist propaganda, and rebellion ultimately leads to increasing censorship within South of antislavery views.

Anti-Masonic Party formed (September 26); first third party with a platform, party is formed partly out of indignation against secret societies, especially Freemasonry (to which Washington, Franklin, and other Founding Fathers had belonged), but mainly as a focus for anti-Jackson forces when it is discovered that Jackson is a Mason.

Debate on slavery begins in Virginia legislature (December); last free, open, full debate on pros and cons of slavery as social and economic institution and on question of whether or not to abolish; motion to abolish ultimately defeated 73 to 58, although there is actually a proabolition majority (January 25, 1832); debate is significant in that there is substantial agreement that blacks, like Indians, are unassimilable and that therefore emancipation must be linked with removal of blacks through colonization, starting with those already free; ultimate effect of debate is to strengthen proslavery forces, since it is shown that removal of Virginia blacks is logistically and economically impossible, and hence southern apologists go on propaganda offensive: slavery is best because other alternatives (deportation or freedom and assimilation) are impossible.

1832

Worcester v. *Georgia* (March 3): Supreme Court, under John Marshall, decides in suit filed on behalf of Cherokees in Georgia that Indians are under protection of federal government and state of Georgia has no right to seize their land and otherwise molest them; Jackson ignores decision, reputedly saying: "Marshall has made his decision, now let him enforce it." Cherokees are prosperous tribe of 15,000 who attempt to save themselves by adopting many aspects of white civilization, possessing cattle, 1,300 slaves, textile mills, gristmills, sawmills, a newspaper printed in Cherokee in a writing system invented by half-breed named Sequoya, and a legislative assembly that drafted (in 1827) a constitution for Cherokee republic. Pressure from Georgia and Congress is relentless, however, and Cherokees finally cede all lands to U.S. for $5.6 million and begin to move into Oklahoma (1835).

Black Hawk War begins in Illinois (May 14); climax of ten-year process of removal of Indians from fertile Great Lakes territory (Illinois, Wisconsin, Michigan), war is begun after Black Hawk, Sauk chieftain, attempts to reoccupy Indian lands on eastern side of Mississippi in what is now Illinois (April 6); although attempt is peaceful (Black Hawk's party includes women and children, and purpose is to plant corn), move terrifies frontier; small group of Black Hawk's followers are fired upon under flag of truce and war begins (May 14). Black Hawk and his group are pursued through northwestern Illinois into Wisconsin, where, nearly dead from hunger, they are slaughtered at Bad Axe River (August 3); all other northwestern Indians now realize resistance means extermination and in next five years cede all remaining lands (for $70 million) in Northwest, ultimately winding up in reservations, first in Kansas (1846) and finally in Oklahoma (1869).

Black Hawk

The massacre of Black Hawk's followers on the Bad Axe River

Campaign of 1832: Democratic Party nominates Jackson and Van Buren; anti-Jacksonians, under National Republican banner, nominate Henry Clay; Anti-Masonic Party nominates William Wirt; issues mainly involve Bank of United States, which Jackson opposes (vetoing a bill sponsored by Clay for renewing its charter on July 10), protective tariffs, which Jackson tepidly supports, and nationalism or supremacy of federal Union, which Jackson strongly supports; popular vote (December 5) gives Jackson 707,000, Clay 329,000, and Wirt 255,000; Electoral College vote: Jackson 219, Clay 49, Wirt 7.

South Carolina legislature passes law nullifying federal tariffs (November 24); law forbids U.S. customs officials to collect duties and threatens secession if U.S. tries force; Jackson reinforces forts in Charleston Harbor and issues proclamation to people of South Carolina warning that secession is treason and that no state has right to withdraw from Union (December 10).

1833

Jackson signs two bills temporarily settling nullification issue (March 2); one bill promises to reduce tariff gradually, and the other (Force Act) authorizes President to use Army and Navy to collect customs duties; controversy fizzles away, since nullifiers get reduction of tariffs and Unionists get assertion of federal sovereignty, and neither gets armed conflict, which all want to avoid.

Andrew Jackson inaugurated for second term (March 4); Martin Van Buren becomes Vice President.

Oberlin College founded in Oberlin, Ohio (May); first to admit male and female students; in 1835 first to admit black students.

Jackson wins battle with Bank of U.S. (September 26) by getting federal funds out of bank and deposited

A cartoon of the collapse of the Bank of the United States

ALL: LIBRARY OF CONGRESS

instead in local state banks, called pet banks because they were often selected on a political basis; destruction of Bank of U.S. is partly responsible for Panic of 1837 and development of New York City instead of Philadelphia as financial capital of U.S.

American Anti-Slavery Society formed; national organization, it is a merger of Garrison's New England group and a similar, somewhat more moderate group under Arthur and Lewis Tappan, New York merchants and philanthropists.

1834

Federal troops first used in labor dispute (January 29); Irish canal workers strike for closed shop, violence results, and Jackson orders War Department to intervene; nevertheless, Jackson and Democratic Party continue to enjoy support of many crafts organizations.

Whig Party formed out of anti-Jackson elements (April–June); includes conservative business interests in North and South (Daniel Webster is their chief spokesman), antitariff Westerners (Henry Clay), and Southerners, including some states' righters.

National Trades Union formed (August); first national federation of local and city labor organizations, usually formed by skilled workers along guild lines; earliest crafts unions date from 1790's, but many are organized in 1820's and 1830's, seeking local political influence and forming workingmen's parties; Panic of 1837 and subsequent depression cause disappearance of National Trades Union and many local organizations.

1835

First assassination attempt against a U.S. President (January 30): would-be assassin fires twice while Jackson is attending funeral of congressman, but guns misfire; assassin later judged insane.

Locofoco Party, radical prolabor offshoot of Democratic Party, formed (October 29); so called because when conservative Tammany Hall Democrats sought to dissolve caucus by turning off gaslights, Locofocos lit candles with new friction matches called locofocos and continued meeting.

Florida War, or Second Seminole War, begins in Florida when Seminoles are asked to give up reservation; war goes badly for U.S. until Seminole leader Osceola is seized under flag of truce and imprisoned (1837); Osceola dies in prison (1838), but war, costing $40–$60 million, drags on until 1842, when most of the Seminoles are deported to Oklahoma, although a few remain deep in Everglades.

1836

Siege of Alamo (February 23–March 6): Texas, along with many other states of Mexico, rises up in protest against assumption of dictatorial powers by General Santa Anna; Santa Anna, fearing that Texas will become rallying center of general revolt, advances with army of about 3,000 toward San Antonio, where the small force (187) under Colonel William Travis elects to defend

Davy Crockett
LIBRARY OF CONGRESS

Alamo mission; walls finally breached on thirteenth day, and all defenders killed, including Davy Crockett and Jim Bowie; about 30 noncombatants spared; 1,500 in Mexican army killed. Santa Anna's march into Texas and Alamo defense decide Texans to declare complete independence from Mexico (March 2).

Samuel Colt awarded patent for six-shot revolver (February 25); manufacture begins in Paterson, New Jersey.

President Jackson sends W. A. Slacum to Oregon to make a report of the land, sparsely occupied by several Methodist missionaries and a few settlers; Slacum's report, made to Congress in December, 1837, stimulates interest in new territory; hard times following Panic of 1837 spur movement of settlers from Mississippi Valley and beginnings of "Oregon fever."

Battle of San Jacinto in Texas (April 21): General Sam Houston leads attack of 800 Texans against 1,450 Mexican soldiers under Santa Anna; Houston attacks during siesta, and his men charge among Mexicans crying "Remember the Alamo! Remember Goliad!" (About 400 Americans had surrendered at Goliad in March, and many had been put to death.) Texans win battle in seventeen minutes, killing 630, and capturing Santa Anna; Santa Anna promises to grant independence and send rest of his army back to Mexico; although Santa

Anna later repudiates promise, he is never able to reassert authority over Texans, and independence is in fact won. Republic of Texas, under President Sam Houston and several other presidents, remains independent country until 1845, plagued throughout its existence by financial problems.

Gag rule passed by House (May 26); prevents discussion of flood of antislavery petitions, many generated by American Anti-Slavery Society; ex-President John Quincy Adams, now serving in House as representative from Massachusetts, fights gag rule vigorously, although he is not an abolitionist; rule is ultimately repealed in 1844, when northern Democrats cease to support it.

Campaign of 1836: Democrats have nominated Martin Van Buren and Richard M. Johnson (who claims to have personally killed Tecumseh at Battle of Thames); Whigs have Hugh L. White, Daniel Webster, and General William Henry Harrison in race; Van Buren promises to continue policies of Jackson and wins, with popular vote of 765,483 against combined Whig and Anti-Masonic popular vote of 739,795 (December 7); electoral vote: Van Buren 170, Harrison 73, White 26, and Webster 14. No vice-presidential candidate receives majority, so election goes to Senate (February 8, 1837), where Democrat Richard M. Johnson is chosen.

Transcendental Club is formed as discussion group of many leading New England writers and thinkers, including Ralph Waldo Emerson, whose essays in the volume *Nature* form a sort of blueprint for movement, Margaret Fuller, who later (1840) founds famous magazine *The Dial*, and Nathaniel Hawthorne.

1837

Angelina and Sarah Grimké begin speaking tour; Grimké sisters, born of aristocratic South Carolina family, have learned to hate slavery and have become associated with abolitionist cause.

Martin Van Buren inaugurated as eighth President (March 4); Richard M. Johnson is Vice President.

John Deere begins production of steel plows, which can cut though thick sod of plains and turn over sticky, heavy midwestern soils.

State Board of Education established in Massachusetts (April 20); Horace Mann becomes first secretary, institutes many changes, including teacher training, increase in salaries, and so on; beginnings of public-school system, partly in response to demand by labor groups, who resented "poor schools," public institutions run for those students who could demonstrate poverty.

Panic of 1837 (May) begins economic depression, which

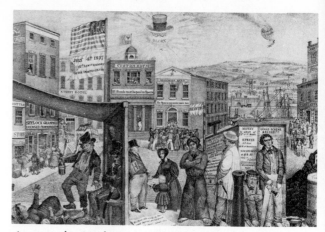

A cartoon showing the causes and effects of the Panic of 1837
LIBRARY OF CONGRESS

lasts until 1843; caused by large state debts incurred during orgy of canal and railroad building and by massive land speculation, which Jackson had tried to check in 1836 by requiring land purchases to be made in cash, thus drawing deposits out of local and state banks just when European creditors started calling in loans; depression hits hardest in South and West, where there are also crop failures. Panic and depression spur westward movement of settlers and help elect Whigs in election of 1840.

Elijah P. Lovejoy, editor of antislavery newspaper Alton *Observer*, is shot and killed (November 7) in Alton, Illinois, while attempting to protect his printing press, which mob was trying to destroy.

Caroline affair (December 29): American steamer *Caroline* attacked and sunk on American side of Niagara River by Canadian forces, and one American killed; raid is in retaliation for U.S. help to Canadian rebels against royal governor in Ottawa; raid causes much outrage and threatens to bring on war with Britain, but President Van Buren issues neutrality proclamation (January 5, 1838) and seeks to avoid conflict through diplomacy.

Mount Holyoke, first college for women, founded by Mary Lyon in Massachusetts.

1838

Federal troops force remaining Cherokee Indians from Georgia; during winter march to reservation in what is now Oklahoma, one out of four Indians dies en route; Indians call march Trail of Tears.

1839

Aroostook War (January–March): Canadian lumberjacks enter disputed Aroostook River between Maine and New Brunswick; Canadian and Maine militias called out, and Congress authorizes war preparations; U.S. General Winfield Scott arranges truce (March), and boundary issue is referred to commission for settlement.

Liberty Party formed (November 13) in New York as moderate abolitionist party, nominating for President James G. Birney, an ex-slaveholder from Kentucky.

1840

U.S. census: population 17,069,453; includes 599,125 immigrants, mainly from Ireland, Great Britain, Scandinavia, and Germany, first substantial immigration since Revolutionary War; census shows first decline in birthrate since 1790; black population about 16 per cent of total; urban population now almost 11 per cent.

Permanent Indian Frontier or reservation in Kansas and Oklahoma acts as barrier to westward expansion from South; pioneers from lower Mississippi Valley move instead to Texas, Oregon, and California.

First scheduled transatlantic steamship service established between Boston and Liverpool (July); crossing takes fifteen days.

Campaign of 1840: Whigs run General William Henry Harrison of Indiana and John Tyler of Virginia, Democrats run Martin Van Buren, and Liberty Party, James G. Birney. Whigs crank up "Log Cabin and Hard Cider, Tippecanoe and Tyler Too" campaign, presenting wealthy 67-year-old Harrison as man of the people, portraying Van Buren (a lower-class New York politician) as effete, dandified aristocrat, and using modern rallies and campaign symbols (log cabins, cider barrels) to get out vote; Harrison, expected by Whigs to be tool of Henry Clay and Daniel Webster, has correspondence screened so he won't inadvertently take a position on some issue; popular vote (December 2) is 1,275,016 for Harrison, 1,129,102 for Van Buren, and 7,059 for Birney; electoral vote is 234 for Harrison and 60 for Van Buren, who lost big states of New York, Pennsylvania, and Ohio by very slender margins.

1841

William Henry Harrison inaugurated as ninth President (March 4); John Tyler is Vice President; Harrison delivers lengthy (almost two hours) inaugural address in bitter cold, without hat or overcoat, and catches cold, which turns into pneumonia.

Amistad case (March 9): Supreme Court orders release of 53 Spanish slaves who under leadership of slave Cinque had seized ship *Amistad* (1839) and had sailed it to Long Island, from which they were taken to Connecticut; although Spanish government demands return of slaves to be tried for piracy, Supreme Court, swayed by arguments of John Quincy Adams, allows slaves to return to Africa as free men. In similar case, *Creole* affair, the British free the slaves who take over Virginia slave ship *Creole*, headed for New Orleans, and direct it to Nassau. Secretary of State Daniel Webster demands return of slaves as U.S. property; British, who have outlawed slavery in West Indies and compensated slave owners for property, ignore Webster's demands.

President Harrison dies, first to die in office (April 4); John Tyler becomes tenth President, first Vice President to become President under such circumstances. Tyler was chosen by Whigs to garner states'-rights anti-Jackson vote but has little sympathy with Whig programs.

New York *Tribune* founded (April 10) by Horace Greeley; becomes one of most influential newspapers in North and West.

Brook Farm established in West Roxbury, Massachusetts (April); most famous of utopian, communal, anti-materialist communities established in 1840's and 1850's; often visited by famous intellectuals of New England but closes after fire in 1846.

John Bidwell leads wagon train of settlers from Kansas to California (May–November 4); settlers are first to arrive by overland route.

Preemption Law passed (September 4); law, long demanded by Westerners, allows squatters on unsold federal lands to have first crack at buying land (for $1.25 an acre) when government puts it up for sale; in past squatters often lost land they had improved to speculators, who were able to outbid them; measure is outcome of complicated political maneuvering but also represents another link between West and industrializing Northeast, which previously opposed liberal western land policy, fearing loss of laborers, but now looks upon West as market for manufactured goods and worries less about shortage of labor now that Irish and other immigrants begin pouring in.

President Tyler vetoes second Whig attempt to establish national bank (September 9); almost whole Whig Cabinet resigns (September 11), except Daniel Webster.

1842

Dorr's Rebellion in Rhode Island: Thomas W. Dorr sets up rival state government in Rhode Island, whose antique charter severely limits franchise; militia puts down Dorr and followers (May), but more liberal constitution is installed (November), though it denies franchise to foreign-born.

Webster-Ashburton Treaty (August 9) settles northeastern U.S.-Canadian border.

Mexico declares that U.S. annexation of Texas will bring war with U.S. (August 23); issue of Texas creates political dilemma for many; some fear annexation will vastly increase political power of South; others fear that failure to annex will involve Texas in diplomatic and economic ties with Great Britain, which promises to recognize republic if it abolishes slavery; others fear a nonslave independent Texas will provide haven for runaways and compete with South as cotton producer; others wish to avoid war with Mexico; others wish to annex as part of general expansionist belief that it is "Manifest Destiny" of U.S. to spread over whole of North America; most Texans favor annexation because republic is broke and fears invasion by Mexico.

Commonwealth v. *Hunt*: Massachusetts Supreme Court legalizes labor unions by ruling that union efforts to recruit or control members do not constitute criminal conspiracy; decision is widely copied in other states.

Personal-liberty laws: passed by several northern states prohibiting state officials from aiding federal officials attempting to return fugitive slaves, these laws, like similar ones passed in 1820's, are aimed partly at professional slave catchers, who often seize free blacks, and come in direct response to Supreme Court decision in *Prigg* v. *Pennsylvania*, which held that all state laws in conflict with federal fugitive slave law were unconstitutional. Personal-liberty laws are in effect deliberate nullifications of federal law but are not explicitly proclaimed as such.

1843

Dorothea Dix begins movement for reform of treatment of insane in jails, asylums, and poorhouses with report of conditions to Massachusetts legislature (January); usually treatment consists of beatings, to remove "devils."

First large (1,000 settlers) overland wagon train to Oregon leaves Independence, Missouri (May 22); arrives Willamette Valley, Oregon, in November; 2,000-mile Oregon Trail becomes deeply rutted as thousands of settlers, bitten by "Oregon fever," pass over it; by 1845 population has grown to about 6,000.

1844

Samuel F. B. Morse sends message ("What Hath God Wrought") by telegraph from Baltimore, Maryland, to

Wagons bound for Oregon cross the Missouri River.
LIBRARY OF CONGRESS

Washington, D.C. (May 24); telegraph invented in 1835 by Morse, but practical demonstration leads to quick adoption in many parts of country.

Samuel F. B. Morse
LIBRARY OF CONGRESS

Charles Goodyear patents (in France) process of vulcanizing rubber, discovered in 1839.

Campaign of 1844: Democrats run dark-horse candidate James K. Polk of Tennessee and George M. Dallas of Pennsylvania; Whigs run Henry Clay and T. Frelinghuysen of Pennsylvania; Liberty Party runs James Birney; Democrats have firm platform favoring annexation of Texas, Oregon territory border that includes half of what is now British Columbia ("54'40° or fight!"), and lowered tariffs. Whig platform calls for protective tariffs and national bank but waffles on Texas. Clay comes out with statement vaguely supportive of Texas, which alienates some New York Whigs, and Birney's abolitionist party takes away other New York votes, so Clay loses New York and election. Popular vote (December 4): Polk 1,337,243; Clay 1,299,062; Birney 62,300; electoral vote: Polk 170, Clay 105.

1845

Republic of Texas annexed by joint resolution of Congress, signed by lame-duck President Tyler on March 1; if Texas were considered foreign country, a treaty would be required, and Senate could not muster two-thirds majority; resolution stipulates that Texas can become state if it submits constitution by January 1, 1846, thus becoming state without passing through territory stage.

James K. Polk inaugurated as eleventh President (March 4); George M. Dallas is Vice President.

Antirent rebellion in upper New York State climaxes with murder of sheriff (August); agitation against ancient land laws, which require farmers to pay feudal rents to great landowners and turn over one quarter of proceeds from sale of lease, has been going on since 1839, with secret societies tar-and-feathering law-enforcement agents; farmers' rebellion in 1845 causes legislature to reform land laws, which date back to Dutch colonial days.

U.S. Naval Academy opens at Annapolis, Maryland (October 10).

President Polk sends John Slidell to Mexico (November 7) for purpose of buying California and New Mexico and negotiating Texas boundary, authorizing payment of $30–40 million; Mexican government, under new head of state, refuses to receive Slidell because to do so would bring on another coup by strong nationalist faction (December 16).

Texas admitted as twenty-eighth state and as fifteenth slave state (December 29).

Frederick Douglass publishes *Narrative of the Life of Frederick Douglass, an American Slave*; Douglass, who was very effective speaker for American Anti-Slavery Society, publishes book partly because many do not believe so polished an orator could ever have been a slave; he then has to leave for England to escape capture under fugitive slave law.

1846

President Polk orders troops into disputed Texas-Mexico boundary area (January 13); Mexican troops attack American patrol (April 25) and then cross Rio Grande in force and are repulsed (May 8).

Mormons, under Brigham Young, begin migration from Illinois (February 4); first Mormons arrive in Utah, in the Great Salt Lake area, on July 24, 1847.

Congress declares war on Mexico (May 13), thus formally beginning Mexican War; President Polk had told Cabinet on May 9 of his decision to recommend war on basis of Mexico's refusal to deal with Slidell and to pay claims of American citizens for property damage during Mexico's frequent civil struggles, but later on same day news arrives of Mexican attack on U.S. troops in disputed border area, so Polk's message to Congress (May 11) now calls for war on basis of Mexico's invasion of U.S. territory and shedding of American blood. Although there is no doubt that Mexican government wanted war and thought it could win, there is also no question that Polk, too, wanted war and felt the U.S. could win.

Bear Flag Revolt in California (June 14): settlers in northern California, in Sacramento Valley, fearing—quite falsely—repression by California authorities, seize pueblo of Sonoma ("To whom shall we surrender?" they are asked); settlers proclaim Republic of California (June 15) and display makeshift flag with grizzly bear painted on it; whole affair is unnecessary, since prominent Mexican landowners and Americans in southern California, who have intermarried with land-grant families, are already planning peaceful amalgamation with U.S.

Senate ratifies Oregon treaty with Great Britain, fixing Oregon-Canadian border at 49th parallel (June 15).

Wilmot Proviso (August 8) tacked on revenue bill; Wilmot amendment stipulates that slavery shall not be permitted in any territory acquired from Mexico as result of war; although proviso is defeated on this and other occasions, principle is much debated and causes heightened antagonism to the war itself and among sections. Proviso is proposed by David Wilmot, Democrat of Pennyslvania, partly to embarrass Polk, with whom some northern Democrats are unhappy for lowering tariffs and for settling for 49th parallel in Oregon, and partly to get Wilmot re-elected, since his constituents are not only displeased with his party-line vote for lower tariff but also nourish strong antislavery feelings. Proviso debate begins splitting Whig and Democratic parties along sectional lines, the northern elements of both parties generally favoring it, the southern elements generally opposing it.

California annexed by naval commander, and John C. Frémont appointed governor (August 17); southern Californians rebel against harsh military rule, and conquest of California begins all over again, ending finally on January 13, 1847.

1847

Mexico City surrenders to General Winfield Scott (September 14), thus ending Mexican War.

Cyrus McCormick begins manufacture of horse-drawn mechanical reaper in Chicago.

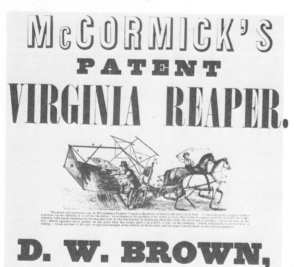

An 1850 handbill advertising Cyrus McCormick's reaper
INTERNATIONAL HARVESTER

First use of Richard Hoe's rotary press, invented in 1846; press can print 8,000 newspapers an hour.

1848

Gold discovered in millrace for sawmill on John Sutter's property in Sacramento, California (January 24).

Treaty of Guadalupe-Hidalgo signed, formally ending war with Mexico (February 2); Mexico accepts Rio Grande border with Texas, cedes California, Nevada, Utah, and most of Colorado, New Mexico, and Arizona to U.S. for $18,250,000 (ultimate actual U.S. costs, including military operations and payments to Mexico under treaty, are $162,140,053); little-known clause to treaty provides for protection of property of Mexicans who remain in new U.S. territory.

First Women's Rights Convention, organized by Lu-

cretia Mott and Elizabeth Cady Stanton, meets at Seneca Falls, New York (July 18–19); produces declaration of rights, modeled on Declaration of Independence, calling for equal educational and professional opportunities, reform of laws that make it impossible for married women to own property in their own right, and the right to vote.

Free-Soil Party organized in Buffalo, New York (August 9); formed of antislavery Democrats ("Barnburners"), dissident Whigs ("Conscience" Whigs), and Liberty Party; platform calls for no further extension of slavery or increase in number of slave states and for free homesteads for western settlers; nominates Martin Van Buren and Charles Francis Adams.

Campaign of 1848: Whigs run General Zachary Taylor, military hero of Mexican War, and Millard Fillmore of New York; Democrats run Lewis Cass of Michigan; Free-Soil Party runs Martin Van Buren. Whig platform consists mainly of Taylor's military record (Taylor had never voted in a presidential election); Democrats fudge Wilmot Proviso issue. Free-Soilers deprive Democrats of New York electoral vote and hence election. Popular vote: Taylor 1,360,099; Cass 1,220,544; Van Buren 291,263. Electoral vote: Taylor 163, Cass 127; Democrats and Whigs each carry roughly equal number of states in North and South, indicating that strictly regional political alignments have not yet set in.

President Polk announces (December) discovery of gold in California, setting off gold rush; thousands flock to goldfields—by ship around Cape Horn or mainly by overland wagon train—where many die of cholera, thirst, hunger, and so on; nevertheless, by end of 1849 population of California reaches 100,000.

1849

Zachary Taylor inaugurated as twelfth President (March 5); Millard Fillmore is Vice President.

Astor Place Riot, in New York City (May 10): mob supporting American actor Edwin Forrest attacks Astor Place Opera House, where rival British actor, William Macready, is playing *Macbeth*; militia is called out and fires on crowd, killing 22 and wounding more.

California, now with large, unruly population, cannot wait for Congress to set up territorial government, passes constitution forbidding slavery, and asks for admission as a state (September–October 13); President Taylor recommends admission (December 4), but Congress delays because balance of slave-free states is now 15-15, and House cannot even agree on an acceptable Speaker, taking 63 ballots to elect one.

The discovery of the Comstock Lode made nearby Virginia City, Nevada, the area's center of luxury and entertainment.

Westward Expansion:
The Critical Years
1850–1860

This decade began with a reasonable political compromise proposed by Henry Clay and defended in a great self-sacrificial speech by his old enemy Daniel Webster. The Compromise of 1850, designed to bleed off some of the political pressures for disunion, served instead to introduce additional irritants and stress into the American system. Southerners lost the symbolic importance of slave trading in the nation's capital, and Northerners gained the Fugitive Slave Act, which sent agents of the national government into their territory as active representatives of an alien institution. Many of the larger and smaller events of this decade followed the same pattern. Whatever caused these events, whatever motivated their human actors, whatever particular economic, political, or social problem these events came in response to, the net result was the same: more rather than fewer dissatisfied individuals and groups, more rather than fewer citizens who saw no practical or satisfying alternative to a southern withdrawal or a national slugfest. When on December 20, 1860, the Charleston *Mercury* announced the secession of South Carolina with the headline "The Union Is Dissolved!" it was not exaggerating unduly.

There have been numerous efforts to explain why the Civil War happened when and how it did. In general, these explanations have fallen into two main categories.

The first category emphasizes the motives and decisions of a relatively small number of individuals—mainly abolitionists, slave owners, and political leaders—who acted in such a way as either to "cause" the Civil War or fail to prevent it. Nineteenth-century historians tended to blame slaveholders or abolitionists for "conspiring" to achieve their various ends, blowing up the slavery issue all out of proportion and poisoning the deep well of American consensus and compromise. Some twentieth-century historians, especially those reacting to the seemingly pointless horrors of World War I, found much merit in this explanation, especially when it was buttressed by what seemed to them the lack of stature, astuteness, and decisiveness on the part of those responsible for guiding the American political system in the 1850's. Explanations of this sort today are not considered particularly compelling, largely because many historians doubt that any small group of individuals can cause a large, complex society with traditions like ours to achieve the sort of critical mass needed for civil war.

The second category of explanation for the Civil War emphasizes the many systemic differences between the North and the South, holds the two socioeconomic systems to have been fundamentally incompatible, and finds that the Civil War was, like most wars, simply an extension of the struggle between these two systems for the right to rule from the political arena to a military one. Developed largely by historians formed in the progressive era and modified in various ways subsequently, the systemic explanation has been in place since the 1950's and has not undergone sweeping or substantial revision since then. Slavery, as one of the many factors to be taken into account by such an explanation, has been described variously as a relatively minor political issue—an almost accidental focus for deeper, broader forces in conflict—and as a burning central issue of the highest moral significance that could no more be skirted or compromised than Nazi designs upon the Jews during the 1930's.

The issue of black slavery was certainly a complex one. By the mid-nineteenth century human slavery of any sort was correctly and widely considered to be a grave moral evil. But what to do specifically about the institution of slavery as it had developed in the United States and what to do about the black human beings who were, in the South and in the Border States, the legal property of a small percentage of the white population were questions to which few Americans had answers they felt very confident about.

The abolitionist movement itself was splintered, with some, like William Lloyd Garrison, urging secession from a Union that embraced slavery and publicly burning a copy of the Constitution to dramatize his views.

Others were far more moderate and hoped merely to arrest the spread of the institution into new territory or hoped that somehow slavery could be peacefully eliminated as the British government had done, in effect by buying the slaves and then releasing them.

Many if not most of the less radical abolitionists viewed emancipation as merely the first step in a process by which all black persons could somehow be removed from the body politic by some scheme of colonization or segregation. This assumption on the part of many abolitionists that black people were unassimilable led one free black to tell members of the Massachusetts Anti-Slavery Society that *they* were a greater enemy to blacks than slaveholders, because at least slaveholders wanted to keep blacks where they were, whereas the abolitionists wanted to ship them off somewhere. Most Americans of that time had no doubts whatever about the intellectual and moral—but not physical—inferiority of black human beings. This set of cultural beliefs had been formed in large measure by the same institution of slavery that many whites agreed was intolerable in the moral abstract, and it enormously complicated things. In the North it victimized black people who had been free, prosperous, and productive since colonial or Revolutionary times.

Most Americans who were not indifferent to the question of what to do about black slavery were confused by it. Many thoughtful Northerners and Southerners perceived slavery as a complicated, ambiguous problem with many moral, legal, economic, and practical aspects. At any rate, it is a fact that slavery in the United States was not abolished until the Civil War was well under way, and then for reasons and in a manner directly related to the Union war effort.

To say that the United States as a whole became from 1803 to 1860 a more complex, fragmented, interdependent, and integrated society and that this process accelerated sharply during the 1850's is to provide a generalization that has little explanatory or predictive value. Such a generalization will have predictive value only when we have theories that explain how people react to an enormous increase in social complexity and also satisfactorily relate these reactions to the behavior of a large national system. Such theories will probably reduce historical facts to the status of information, classify this information as "positive" or "negative," quantify it in terms of the rate and volume at which it pours in on any given observer, key in the known ways in which individuals respond to high information rates, provide a multiplier factor, and thus be able to predict accurately when a national system is likely to achieve a condition of critical overload and hence metaphorically "blow a fuse."

Westward Expansion: The Critical Years (1850–1860)

1850

U.S. census: population 23,191,876, including about 3.2 million slaves and about 400,000 free blacks. Immigration during the decade 1840–50 totaled approximately 1.7 million, largely from northern Europe: Irish, 780,000; German, 435,000; English, Welsh, Scots, 267,000; Scandinavian, 14,000.

Henry Clay introduces resolutions that later become the Compromise of 1850 (January 29); resolutions are debated until September; Clay hoped for single omnibus bill designed to satisfy various sections by admitting California as free state, allowing rest of territory acquired from Mexico to decide for itself whether slavery would be permitted, settling a Texas boundary dispute

Henry Clay addresses Congress on the Missouri Compromise.
LIBRARY OF CONGRESS

with New Mexico, paying Texas to abandon its claims on certain Mexican territory, abolishing the auctioning of slaves in Washington, D.C., but not the institution of slavery there, and stiffening the existing fugitive slave law. Among other things at stake is balance of slave-free states, now standing at 15–15, and hence balance of power in Senate, which, owing to longer terms of senators, unlimited debate, smaller membership, and advise-and-consent feature with respect to foreign treaties and executive appointments, has become in many respects the more powerful body of Congress, although most founders had assumed House of Repre-

sentatives would be. Clay's bill is supported by leading Union men, mostly Democrats, including Stephen A. Douglas, Lewis Cass, and Free-Soiler Daniel Webster; eventually passes as series of separate measures.

Daniel Webster gives famous "Preservation of the Union" speech in support of Clay's proposed compromise (March 7); sharply alienates many of his Free-Soil constituents.

President Zachary Taylor, whose last months in office are marred by smelly political scandal involving his Secretaries of War and Treasury, dies (July 9); Millard Fillmore becomes President (July 10). Unlike Taylor, Fillmore is not opposed to Clay's compromise measures, and his assumption of Presidency is partly responsible for their passage.

California admitted as sixteenth free state (September 9); in separate "compromise" acts passed on same day, New Mexico and Utah become territories, with slavery optional, depending on popular choice to be expressed in state constitution; New Mexico-Texas border dispute settled, New Mexico getting Santa Fe region in return for U.S. government paying pre-1845 Texas debts.

New Fugitive Slave Act passed (September 18); empowers special commissioners to issue certificates of arrest for blacks claimed as fugitives (commissioners get $10 for every certificate issued, and only $5 if they deny certificate); testimony of alleged fugitive cannot be admitted as evidence, and no jury trials are permitted; federal marshals made liable for full value (as much as $2,000) for any slave who escapes their custody; all persons aiding fugitives or hindering arrest become liable to heavy criminal and civil penalties.

Slave trading abolished in Washington, D.C. (September 20); slave auctions, exhibiting most degrading features of institution, are eliminated from U.S. capital as sop to abolitionists and Northerners and tradeoff for new Fugitive Slave Act; slavery per se is still permitted in District of Columbia.

Underground railroad, informal network of escape routes throughout Northeast and upper Mississippi Valley, in operation since 1830, now passes most fugitives on to Canada, as result of fugitive slave law; slave song "Follow the Drinkin' Gourd" contains explicit instructions for one escape route, following "drinkin' gourd" (Big Dipper) across Ohio River to Detroit, Michigan, and thence to Windsor, Canada, across Detroit River; safe houses along route also hang actual drinking gourd outside. During 1850's escaped slave Harriet Tubman makes nineteen trips south, "conducting" 300 slaves to freedom; total number of escapees during 1830–60 from 60,000 to 75,000.

Federal government grants public lands to Illinois, Alabama, and Mississippi, which in turn grant them to railroads as means of financing trans-Mississippi lines; during 1850's about 27,000 miles of track are laid down under municipal, state, and federal subsidies.

1851

López expedition (August 3–September 1): privately financed invasion of Cuba, led by refugee General Narciso López, attempts to liberate Cuba from Spain but results in "Bay of Pigs" type of fiasco, with 50 Americans executed and about 80 imprisoned; South is interested in acquiring Cuba for its purposes, North is dead set against it, and federal government remains neutral, ultimately paying Spain $25,000 for mob damage to Spanish consulate in New Orleans.

New York Times (originally called *New York Daily Times*) founded as Whig newspaper.

1852

Harriet Beecher Stowe's *Uncle Tom's Cabin* published in book form (March 20); serialized since June 5, 1851, book becomes raging best seller, with 300,000 copies sold in 1852 and more than a million by 1854; although author expects book to be well received in South because of "balanced" treatment (wicked overseer Simon Legree is Yankee Vermonter and slave Uncle Tom is devoted to white master), it greatly sharpens North-South antagonisms.

An engraving from Uncle Tom's Cabin: *slaves being freed*
LIBRARY OF CONGRESS

Campaign of 1852: after all strong candidates eliminated, Democrats nominate Franklin Pierce of New Hampshire and William R. King of Alabama; Whigs nominate General Winfield Scott of Mexican War fame;

Free-Soilers nominate John P. Hale. Whigs and Democrats both support Compromise of 1850. Democrats sweep electoral vote 254 to 42 for Whigs, carrying all but two New England and two border states. Popular vote (November 2): Pierce 1,601,274, Scott 1,386,580, Hale 155,825. Election returns considered popular vindication of Compromise of 1850; Whig Party is virtually destroyed by wholesale defection of southern Whigs to Democrats; inability of Democrats to nominate any leading figures like Douglas or Cass also indicates strain under surface.

1853

Franklin Pierce inaugurated as fourteenth President (March 4); William R. King is Vice President.

Commodore Matthew C. Perry arrives in Tokyo Bay, Japan (July 8); purpose is to secure trading rights and to negotiate treaty dealing with American and Japanese seamen shipwrecked on each other's shores; Perry's orders include possibility of tough talk, but Japanese are impressed by his squadron, which includes two steam frigates; Perry withdraws (July 14) to give Japanese time to think about it.

Gadsden Purchase (December 30): U.S. buys southern portions of Arizona and New Mexico (needed for proposed transcontinental railroad linking New Orleans and San Diego) from Mexico for $10 million; treaty, which also deals with other American-Mexican disputes arising from Guadalupe-Hidalgo, barely passes Senate because of northern opposition, but 29,640 square miles acquired round out U.S. continental borders.

1854

Kansas-Nebraska bill proposed by Stephen Douglas (January 23); Douglas, anxious to secure a transcontinental railroad passing through central U.S. and ending up in Chicago, proposes legislation to organize territory in what is now Kansas and Nebraska; in order to secure

Stephen Douglas
LIBRARY OF CONGRESS

southern support Douglas is required to press not only for "popular sovereignty" (people of territory choose for or against slavery, as in New Mexico and Utah territories in 1850) but also for a specific repeal of the Missouri Compromise of 1820, since territory is above 36° 30′. Douglas assumes that Kansas, next to Missouri, will probably go slave, and Nebraska, next to Iowa, will go free, thus pleasing everybody and quite possibly earning him Presidency in 1856. Democratic administration under Pierce and Democratic majorities in Senate and House pass bill (May 22). South hails bill as great victory; North attacks it savagely as sellout to slavery interests; many are disturbed by repeal of quasi-sacred 36° 30′ line; struggle begins to settle Kansas and Nebraska Territory as free or slave.

Black Warrior affair (February 28): Spain seizes American ship *Black Warrior,* supposedly for technical violations but really in fear of more López-type adventures; some demand war with Spain, others fear whole episode is pretext for Southerners to gain more territory suitable for slave-labor agriculture. Affair ultimately results in Ostend Manifesto.

Republican Party formed (February 28–July 6) in spontaneous opposition to Kansas-Nebraska Act; draws strength from Free-Soilers and adopts Free-Soil opposition to extension of slavery; about two thirds of its membership drawn from northern Whigs, with some abolitionists. Name "Republican" first proposed (February 28) in gathering at Ripon, Wisconsin, and ratified (July 6) by state convention at Jackson, Michigan, is deliberate reference to old Jeffersonian Party and to Jefferson's role in fostering Ordinance of 1787, which prohibited slavery in old Northwest Territory. By end of 1854 party has respectable organization in most midwestern and northern states.

Perry returns to Japan with large squadron (March 8); Americans and Japanese exchange gifts at Yokohama, and Treaty of Kanagawa is signed (March 31), leading to opening of commercial and diplomatic relations.

New England Emigrant Aid Society founded by Free-Soil and abolitionist elements (April 26); designed to help antislavery New Englanders settle Kansas, it manages to send out between 1,200 and 2,000 settlers, who found Lawrence, Kansas, and other communities; most emigrating New Englanders (90,000), however, want no part of potentially violent territory and settle in older, organized portions of Midwest. In next few years overwhelming majority of Kansas settlers come from adjacent states (about 31,000 from Ohio, Indiana, and Illinois, about 20,000 from Missouri, Kentucky, and Tennessee), and there is little abolitionist sentiment,

even among those who oppose slavery in the abstract; there is almost no settlement by actual slaveholders, who have no intention of risking property in turbulent area.

Anthony Burns affair in Boston (May 26–June 2): mob attempts to rescue fugitive slave Burns from courthouse, killing federal marshal in process; despite impassioned pleas by leading abolitionist lawyers, Burns is returned (June 2) to owner in Alexandria, Virginia, but it takes battalion of artillery, four platoons of U.S. Marines, and 22 militia companies to do it, at cost of $40,000 to federal government. Burns is last slave to be returned from Massachusetts and is later (1855) repurchased by several Boston citizens for $1,300.

American (Know-Nothing) Party riot in St. Louis, Missouri (August): secret party, evolved from Order of Star-Spangled Banner of 1849 and named because members, when questioned about order, say "I know nothing about it," enjoys vastly increased membership and considerable success in local elections; Know-Nothings are pledged to vote only for native-born Protestants, reflecting alarm at large—mainly Catholic—Irish and German immigration, and thereby draw many disturbed members of electorate to it with focus on "enemy" within and avoidance of the sectional issue, slavery; Know-Nothing violence at polls in Baltimore includes "plug-uglies" with carpenters' awls to "plug" voters who don't give proper password; culminates in huge St. Louis riot between Know-Nothings and Irish Catholics, finally suppressed by 700 armed townspeople. Know-Nothing Party splits over slavery issues in 1856, with proslavery elements gaining control and thus losing northern support.

Ostend Manifesto (October 18): document drawn up by American ministers to Spain, Britain, and France (Pierre

A cartoon: domestic disapproval of the Ostend Manifesto

Soulé, James Buchanan, and John Mason, respectively) at Ostend, Belgium, recommending U.S. purchase of Cuba from Spain or, failing that, annexation by force. U.S. forced to repudiate document after storm of foreign and domestic protest; Republicans use document as proof Democratic administration is seeking new slave territory.

Clipper ship *Champion of the Seas,* built by Donald McKay, sets single day's sailing record never surpassed, 465 nautical miles in a 24-hour run (December 11–12); although first clipper, *Anne McKim,* was built in 1833, era of clipper ships reaches finest flowering in 1850's, when, under impetus of California gold rush, the loveliest and fastest are built, cutting about two months off standard sailing time of 159 days from New York or Boston around Cape Horn to San Francisco.

First substantial Chinese immigration to U.S.: 13,000 Chinese arrive in San Francisco (then with population of 37,000).

1855

Five thousand armed Missourians, called Border Ruffians by Free Staters, swarm into Kansas for territorial election (March 30) and fraudulently elect proslavery legislature, which soon passes harsh anti–free-speech measures; Free-State settlers later (October) form second legislature. Free-State settlers are located mainly in Lawrence, Topeka, and other towns on Kansas River; proslave settlers are located mainly in Leavenworth and Atchison, in Missouri River Valley.

William Walker, mercenary adventurer, takes over government of Nicaragua under orders from Cornelius Vanderbilt, who runs a freight company there and wishes for stable, compliant government (October); Walker had previously seized Baja California (1853) and attempted to set up slave "republic" there.

1856

William Walker, dictator of Nicaragua, sends representative to U.S., where he is received (May 14); Walker opens Nicaragua to slavery, talks about conquering Central American empire, and is denounced as tool of slaveholders. Walker ousted (1857) during power struggle with Vanderbilt.

"Bleeding Kansas" (May 21–September 11): civil conflict begins May 21 with sack of Lawrence, free-state town, by 800 Border Ruffians, in retaliation for shooting of proslavery sheriff visiting Lawrence; abolitionist John Brown retaliates with cold-blooded murder of five Southerners at Pottawatomie Creek (May 24–25); Reverend Henry Ward Beecher urges new eastern settlers

Confrontation during a peace convention in Fort Scott, Kansas

to carry breechloading Sharps rifle as a moral equivalent to Bible, and rifles—having great range and accuracy—become known as Beecher's Bibles; violence in Kansas ultimately results in 200 deaths and about $2 million worth of property damage; much of violence probably has to do with local issues, especially battles over land titles between squatters and newcomers on unsurveyed territory, but northern and southern press and public opinion focus on pro- and antislavery issue, making Kansas appear battleground in which all Southerners are proslavery murderers, all Northerners antislavery innocent victims, and vice versa. Armed civil conflict largely suppressed after September 11, when federal troops are called in.

Sumner episode (May 22): Representative Preston S. Brooks of South Carolina enters Senate and beats Senator Charles Sumner of Massachusetts senseless at his desk with cane; act comes in response to vicious speech by Sumner on "rape of Kansas" in which Sumner also ridicules moderate Senator Andrew P. Butler of South Carolina, an uncle of Brooks; Sumner, gravely injured, becomes hero and martyr to Northerners; Brooks becomes hero in South, being rewarded with gift of several new canes and re-election.

Western Union Telegraph Company formed (April 1); merger of several local telegraph companies, in which Ezra Cornell is a prime mover, grows enormously in next few years; by 1860 lines connect country from Atlantic to Mississippi, with large number of lines in Great Lakes-Ohio region; company reaps enormous profits, some of which go into founding of Cornell University in 1865.

Campaign of 1856: American (Know-Nothing) Party runs Millard Fillmore and Andrew J. Donelson of Tennessee; Whig Party runs same candidates; Republicans run John C. Frémont of California and William L. Dayton of New Jersey on platform that criticizes Ostend

Manifesto, criticizes Douglas' popular sovereignty, criticizes slavery and Mormon polygamy as "twin relics of barbarism," and supports admission of Kansas as free state and building of transcontinental railroad; Democrats run James Buchanan of Pennsylvania and John C. Breckinridge of Kentucky on platform supporting states' rights, condemning sectionalism, and urging popular sovereignty. Popular vote (November 4): Buchanan 1,838,169, Frémont 1,341,264, Fillmore 874,534; electoral vote: Buchanan 174 (fourteen slave states and five free), Frémont 114 (eleven free states), Fillmore 8 (Maryland).

1857

James Buchanan inaugurated as fifteenth President (March 4); Andrew J. Donelson is Vice President.

Dred Scott v. *Sandford* decision (March 6): Supreme Court declares in majority opinion written by Chief Justice Taney that (1) Dred Scott, a Missouri slave who has resided in free territory for several years, is neither free on that account nor a citizen on any account, because black persons are incapable of citizenship anywhere; (2) neither Congress nor state or territorial legislatures anywhere can legally exclude slavery, because such exclusion violates Fifth Amendment protections against deprivation of property, thus in effect declaring not only the Missouri Compromise but also a host of

Dred Scott
LIBRARY OF CONGRESS

northern state laws unconstitutional and undercutting Douglas' popular-sovereignty solution. Case, which begins because Mrs. John Emerson wishes to be rid of Scott but cannot legally free him under manumission laws of Missouri, results in unnecessarily broad opinion by Taney and southern majority on Court and creates well-deserved furor; has effect of swelling Republican ranks, enraging North, frightening Westerners, delighting Southerners, and further weakening Democrats, since Douglas supporters in North don't know whether popular-sovereignty idea is legal.

Panic of 1857 (August): bust follows overspeculation in railroad stocks and western lands, compounded by poorly regulated banks in West; depression that follows hits mainly industrial East, where unemployment and bread lines develop, and western wheat-growing areas, where there are bank failures and foreclosures; has effect of driving manufacturing interests into Republican ranks, where they are promised higher tariffs and other subsidies, and accelerating Republican enlistments by Westerners, who are promised free land for homesteads. It does not help that the Democratic South, which opposes both free western land and protective tariffs, is undergoing economic boom, largely as a result of high (British) prices for cotton.

Lecompton Constitution for state framed by proslavery forces in Kansas (October 19–November 8); as a result of boycott by free-state elements and tricky provisions based partly on Dred Scott decision (no matter whether voters choose "Slavery" or "No Slavery," they still get slavery), Lecompton Constitution in no way represents majority of Kansas settlers.

E. V. Haugwout Department Store opens in New York City, among first of new large stores featuring variety of goods, with fixed prices, and specifically designed to entice public into store; Haugwout's five-story department store is soon followed by R. H. Macy's (1858) and others.

1858

President Buchanan recommends that Congress admit Kansas under Lecompton Constitution (February 2); Senate approves, but House does not; Douglas, true to his principles, rejects Lecompton Constitution because it does not represent true people's choice and leads opposition to it through friends in House, thus alienating southern portion of Democratic Party. Kansas later (May 4) given choice of accepting Lecompton Constitution and joining Union (with a fat federal land grant thrown in) or rejecting constitution and remaining a territory; Kansans ultimately reject constitution (August 2).

Minnesota joins Union as thirty-second state and seventeenth free state (May 11).

"House Divided" speech by Abraham Lincoln (June 16): speech, made on occasion of his nomination as Republican candidate for senator from Illinois, avows that nation cannot exist half-slave or half-free but must become all of one or the other; Lincoln's opponent in senatorial race, Douglas, so effectively attacks this speech that Lincoln is forced to challenge Douglas to series of debates.

Lincoln-Douglas debates in Illinois (August 21–October 15): seven debates, one in each congressional district, are followed closely by nation; Douglas attacks Republicans for sectional bias and forces Lincoln to make slavery a moral, social, and political issue. In second debate, in town of Freeport, Lincoln presses Douglas into so-called Freeport doctrine, in which Douglas affirms that slavery cannot exist unless state laws are written to permit it to exist, thus in effect repudiating Dred Scott decision and upholding notion of popular sovereignty and states' rights at same time; Freeport answer wins Douglas senatorial election but utterly alienates southern wing of Democratic Party and loses Douglas all chance of winning Presidency in 1860 with southern support.

Left, a gold miner; right, a typical California mining claim

Lincoln speaks against slavery during a debate with Douglas.

1859

Oregon becomes thirty-third state and eighteenth free state (February 14).

Ableman v. *Booth* (March 7): U.S. Supreme Court finds fugitive slave law constitutional; Wisconsin legislature, citing states'-rights theory, declares Supreme Court decision null and void.

Huge gold rush to Colorado and Nevada (spring) is a result of small strikes in Pikes Peak and Denver area in 1858; thousands more are later attracted in July, when fabulously rich Comstock Lode is struck in Nevada.

Southern Commercial Convention urges repeal of laws prohibiting slave trade (May 12) and forms African Labor Supply Association toward this end; demand for reopening foreign purchase of African slaves (from

Cuba, Brazil, and Africa) is partly in response to U.S. crackdown on slave smuggling since 1858, partly in response to increasing costliness of slaves, which are now out of reach of middle and lower classes, and partly logical, since it is all right to buy slaves in Virginia or Missouri but not in Africa. Issue is further complicated by unwillingness of Deep South to alienate Border States, which are main suppliers of slaves, and Confederate constitution later forbids foreign slave trade in bid for Border State support.

Edwin L. Drake drills first oil well (69 feet deep) in Titusville, Pennsylvania (August 27).

An 1891 oil well and (inserts) the first oil well, drilled in Titusville, Pennsylvania, in 1859, and Edwin L. Drake
ALL: LIBRARY OF CONGRESS

John Brown's raid (October 16–18): John Brown of Kansas leads eighteen men, including five free blacks, in raid on federal arsenal at Harpers Ferry, in what is now West Virginia; plan is to arm slaves in immediate vicinity and set up base for eventual armed liberation of all southern slaves; Brown is financed by a few abolitionists in New England and Canada but is very vague about details of plan, although he apparently dis-

John Brown's Fort, a building in Harpers Ferry, West Virginia

closes plan to Frederick Douglass, who rejects it on grounds it cannot succeed; Brown's group captures arsenal, taking hostages and killing some townspeople (including a free black), and holds off local militia; no slaves join uprising, and Brown and his group are ultimately captured by U.S. Marines under Colonel Robert E. Lee. Brown, rejecting plea of insanity, is hanged on December 2. Although Brown's actions are generally condemned in northern press and by leading northern politicians, raid touches deepest southern fears and at same time excites northern admiration for the man's quixotic bravery.

Henry David Thoreau publishes essay *A Plea for Captain Brown,* in defense of Brown's Harpers Ferry raid.

1860

U.S. census: total population 31,433,321, including 3,953,760 slaves and 448,070 free blacks, and for first time in U.S. census certain "civilized" Indians, meaning those on reservations. Urban population now almost 20 per cent, and center of population has shifted west, into Ohio. In years 1851–60 immigration represents roughly 35 per cent of net population increase, with a total of 2,598,214 immigrants arriving: 952,000 German; 914,000 Irish; 424,000 British; 117,000 Dutch, Swiss, French, and Belgian; 41,000 Chinese; and 25,000 Scandinavian being largest groups. With the principal exception of some German immigration to Texas, few of these immigrants settle in states that join Confederacy, and German votes in seven northwestern states are a significant factor in carrying that swing region for Lincoln.

Twenty thousand shoe-factory workers, including women, strike for higher wages in Massachusetts (February 22).

Pony Express begins mail service between St. Joseph,

Missouri, and Sacramento, California (April 3).

Campaign of 1860: Republicans run Abraham Lincoln (chosen on third ballot) and Hannibal Hamlin of Maine on platform opposing spread of slavery but not suggesting abolition, supporting protective tariff, internal improvements, and free western land; newly formed Constitutional Union Party, made up mainly of former Whig and Know-Nothing elements, runs John Bell of Tennessee and Edward Everett of Massachusetts on centralist, pro-Union, antisectionalist platform; northern Democrats run Stephen Douglas and Herschel V. Johnson of Georgia on platform pledged both to popular sovereignty and to support of past and future Supreme Court decisions on property; southern Democrats in eight cotton states bolt Democratic convention when rabid proslavery plank is defeated and run John C. Breckinridge of Kentucky and Joseph Lane of Oregon, representing extreme expansionist position on slavery. Estimated popular vote (November 6): Lincoln 1,865,908, Douglas 1,380,202, Breckinridge 848,019, Bell 590,901; electoral vote: Lincoln 180 (eighteen free states), Breckinridge 72 (eleven slave states, including Delaware and Maryland), Bell 39 (Virginia, Kentucky, Tennessee), Douglas 12 (Missouri and three New Jersey votes). Had not the seven midwestern states (Ohio, Indiana, Michigan, Wisconsin, Minnesota, Illinois, and Iowa) gone for Lincoln over Douglas by slender margin, election would have gone to House.

South Carolina legislature calls (November 10) for special secessionist convention, which meets December 20 and declares union between it and the United States of America "hereby dissolved"; this is done with understanding that other southern states will soon follow, partly in belief that secession will result in better compromise terms from U.S., and by December 30 South Carolina has occupied all federal arsenals and forts except Fort Sumter.

A Charleston newspaper announces South Carolina's secession.
BOTH: LIBRARY OF CONGRESS

Life continues amid the rubble of Richmond, Virginia; most of the city was burned when the Confederates evacuated in 1865.

The Civil War

1861–1865

The American Civil War began at 4:30 in the morning of April 12, 1861, when Confederate cannon opened fire on Fort Sumter, in Charleston, South Carolina. This was not the first time the Confederacy had fired on the United States flag, but it was the first time the federal government had done anything about it. The new President, Abraham Lincoln, treated the attack on Fort Sumter as though it were an act of war against the United States government. Lincoln's response precipitated a conflict that lasted four years and virtually ended on April 12, 1865, when the Army of Northern Virginia, under Robert E. Lee, formally laid down its arms in surrender. Within the next month or so all Confederate forces had surrendered. The Confederate government, which now consisted chiefly of Jefferson Davis, was dissolved upon Davis' capture.

The secession by the southern states, and the war against them that followed, presented the United States with an interesting philosophical problem. The Constitution is utterly silent on the issue of a state's right to withdraw from the federal Union. But the preservation of this constitutional Union—and the denial of the right of any state or combination of states to wreck it by secession—was the main point of the war, from the Federal point of view. The only legal or constitutional basis for prosecuting a necessarily aggressive war against the Confederacy was to argue that the states comprising it had never left the Union and to insist instead that certain individuals within the Confederate states were engaging in civil insurrection—a sort of oversized Shays' or Whiskey Rebellion. The Constitution gives Congress the power to call out the militia in such a case and gives the President the power to command this militia when it serves as part of the armed services of the United States.

The United States was in fact at war with a separate sovereign nation, the Confederate States of America, which had its own government, constitution, flag, territorial boundaries, army, diplomatic representatives, and so on. For the most part, however, the fiction of civil insurrection by individuals suited United States purposes well and was maintained vigorously throughout the war. It did raise some practical problems, though. An essential part of United States strategy was a naval blockade, and it was a bit tricky getting international acceptance of a blockade restricting commerce with a nonexistent entity. If the Confederacy was not a separate country, then its people were United States citizens engaged in treason, a grave crime seemingly demanding harsh punishment. In fact, however, captured Confederate soldiers were not treated as traitors but were exchanged or otherwise treated according to the conventions of international war, and neither Lincoln nor Congress ever contemplated widespread postwar executions or other extreme reprisals.

Toward the end of the war, when Federal victory was clearly in sight, questions arose about exactly how and under what conditions the Federal government could readmit Confederate states that in theory had never left it. Lincoln rather testily dismissed such questions as "pernicious abstractions," which indeed they were when weighed against the hideous human costs of the war. But these questions were also part of a very real political and philosophical struggle between Congress and the executive branch, a struggle that had large postwar consequences both for the South and for the nation as a whole.

Viewed as two nations or two societies at war with each other, the United States and the Confederate States of America were unequally matched, with the Confederacy being the underdog.

The Confederate States of America occupied about one quarter of what was then the continental United States. One state, Texas, which never became a major theater of war, constituted more than one third of Confederate territory. The population of the eleven Confederate states in 1861 was about eleven million, of whom about three and a half million were slaves. The slave population freed a relatively high proportion of white males for military service. No effort was made to include black males in the combat forces until the war was already lost. Had the Confederacy armed its slaves, and had Confederate blacks fought as gallantly as their Union counterparts, the outcome of the war might have been different. Arming the slaves and taking advantage of the natural human urge to prove one's courage and gain acceptance in one's community would have been an imaginative stroke. But throughout the war the civilian Confederate leadership demonstrated again and again its inability to think big or think flexibly.

Although the Confederacy had a railroad network, it did not have the industrial base to expand this network or even to keep it in repair. By 1863 breakdowns in the southern railroads were resulting in failures of food and supplies to reach some southern cities and the Confederate armies. The Confederacy was also gravely weakened by the lack of a navy and by a failure to appreciate the need for a quick naval build-up until it was too late.

The Confederate economy was mainly agricultural and mainly cash crop—cotton, tobacco, sugar cane, and so on. Although southern agriculture soon diversified in order to provide food for its people, doing so dried up the principal source of southern wealth, since cash-crop production dropped and since what cotton and tobacco were being grown had to be run out through the Union naval blockade. In 1860 five of the ten richest states in the Union, on a per capita basis, were South Carolina, Georgia, Mississippi, Louisiana, and Texas. As a consequence of the war, even twenty years later no southern state was to be found among the thirty richest states in the Union.

In contrast to the United States, to which two states, several new territories, and about eight hundred thousand immigrants over and above natural population increase were added during the war years, the Confederate States of America grew neither in size nor in population. Indeed, the territory under its effective control dwindled steadily, until by 1864 or 1865 Union armies rampaged almost at will through the breadbasket states of Georgia and the Carolinas.

On the other hand, the United States in mid-1861 consisted of twenty-three states, with a population of about twenty-two million. It then included four slave states—Delaware, Maryland, Kentucky, and Mis-

never penetrated north of the Mason-Dixon line or north of the Missouri and Ohio rivers. This was partly by design, since Confederate strategy called for a basically defensive war. By 1862, however, the Confederacy lacked the manpower, supplies, and logistic network to carry the war into the northern heartlands. The two large-scale Confederate attempts to invade the North—at Antietam Creek in Maryland (1862) and at Gettysburg, Pennsylvania (1863)—both ended in military and diplomatic defeats.

In 1861 and 1862 most of the battles fought lay within a rainbow-shaped arc about a hundred miles wide, stretching from lower Louisiana, curving up the Mississippi River through Tennessee, Kentucky, West Virginia, and Virginia, and ending up in Maryland, with a front about a hundred and fifty miles wide somewhat west of Washington, D.C. In 1863, 1864, and 1865 the central part of this rainbow pushed steadily eastward, through Tennessee and into Georgia, eventually reaching the sea at Savannah and Charleston and then looping north into the Carolinas. At the same time the naval blockade, stretching from Delaware around Florida to the Mexico-Texas border, gradually tightened, preventing less and less from getting into and out of the Confederacy.

The overall Union strategy, grasped at the outset by Lincoln and General Winfield Scott, never changed. It consisted of (1) retaining the political loyalty of the

A dollar issued in 1862; such notes were called greenbacks.

A one-hundred-dollar bill issued by the Confederacy in 1861

BOTH: CHASE MANHATTAN BANK, NEW YORK

souri—with a combined slave population of about a half million. The United States had a diversified, balanced economy, with mechanized agriculture producing large grain and corn surpluses, a vigorous and expanding industrial base, and a virtual monopoly on technological expertise. By 1863 it had a reasonably effective banking system, with about two thirds of the nation's capital to work with. The United States not only had a navy that gave it access to international markets, but it also had an extensive rail network tying its agricultural, industrial, and financial centers together. These centers of manufacturing, food growing, and moneymaking were all positively stimulated by the war and were almost entirely out of reach of Confederate military power.

In the four years of war Confederate forces almost

border slave states or, failing that, controlling them under martial law; (2) gaining military control of the Mississippi River system, thereby cutting off Arkansas, Louisiana, and Texas from the rest of the Confederacy; (3) using the Tennessee and Cumberland rivers as attack routes leading through Tennessee and thence into the guts of the Confederacy, Georgia and the Carolinas; (4) attacking southward from Washington, D.C., into Virginia and seizing the Confederate capital, Richmond; and (5) encircling the entire Confederacy with a naval blockade, preventing goods from moving up or down the Mississippi and moving into or out of the Confederacy by way of the Atlantic or the Gulf of Mexico.

Confederate strategy, on the other hand, consisted

mainly in preventing any of this from happening. Although the North was open to attack in the latter part of 1861, Jefferson Davis insisted on an almost purely defensive posture, expecting (1) that England and France, dependent on southern staples, would eventually recognize and aid the Confederacy out of economic necessity, mixed with a certain sympathy for the southern aristocracy, and (2) that southern military prowess would check invasion attempts by the North for long enough and at a high enough cost to the enemy that northern lack of success and war-weariness would ultimately cause the Federal government to give up.

Davis' strategy almost worked. Twice, once in the summer of 1862 and again in the summer of 1864, the North came close to throwing in the towel. In both cases the immediate cause of northern despair and disgust was the inability of Union generals to win battles in the eastern theater, and specifically to take Richmond, Virginia. In Virginia, Union armies under a variety of generals faced the magnificent Robert E. Lee and the great Thomas "Stonewall" Jackson, who with depressing regularity outmaneuvered and outfought superior Union forces on Virginia soil. One measure of Lee's greatness as a military commander, and an equivalent yardstick for gauging northern impatience, is this: as the crow flies, Richmond is somewhat less than a hundred miles south of Washington, D.C., and it took the larger, better-supplied Army of the Potomac four years to push Lee out of the way and get at Richmond. An average advance of less than twenty-five miles a year is not one to inspire popular confidence or enthusiasm.

It was Robert E. Lee, not Jefferson Davis, who came to represent, for people in the North as well as in the South, all that was generous, brilliant, noble, and worthy of sympathy in relation to the Confederate cause. The man was greater than his cause, and to the extent that any one human being could, he ennobled it. But his cause had the weevil of human slavery in it. Lee personally deplored the idea of secession. When offered overall command of the Union army in 1861, he declined it, saying that he never again wanted to draw his sword, save in defense of his native state. His military defense of Virginia was indeed masterful. But when Lee ventured north, into Maryland in 1862 and into Pennsylvania in 1863, his heart, his genius, and even his common sense seemed to leave him, and he was beaten each time on the field of battle by less audacious men. Each time, too, the Confederate cause was beaten on a broader field, by perhaps the greatest war leader this country has ever produced, Abraham Lincoln.

After Antietam, Lincoln checked the Confederate cause with his preliminary Emancipation Proclamation, causing England and France to back off from recognition of the Confederacy and at the same time appeasing abolitionist elements within his own party. About four months after Gettysburg he gave a short war speech that cannot be underestimated as a summation of national ideals.

As President, Lincoln had to run a big, complex country; as commander in chief he had to win a long, increasingly nasty war. To do both he had to be a political genius and a first-rate strategist who was also capable of identifying and supporting first-rate commanders on the battlefield. It was ultimately Lincoln who held all the reins of war in his hands, and it was he who was responsible for getting the right commanders in the right jobs, for coordinating their efforts within an overall strategy,

Detective Allan Pinkerton with President Abraham Lincoln and Brigadier General John A. McClernand, Antietam, 1862
LIBRARY OF CONGRESS

and for channeling the resources of a complex nation into the single task of winning the war.

Lincoln's ability to contain within himself—and on occasion to give immortal expression to—an enormous intellectual and emotional range is perhaps best exemplified in his Second Inaugural Address. Here, among other things, are to be found the sentiments of tenderness, mercy, and charity without which any nation engaged in war becomes a beast. Here too is the righteous, thundering call to battle without which no war is ever won: the war may go on, Lincoln said, if God wills it so, "until all the wealth piled up by the bondsman's two hundred and fifty years of unrequited toil shall be sunk, and until every drop of blood drawn with the lash shall be paid by another drawn with the sword . . ."

Lincoln meant what he said, sounding a harsh, clear call that old John Brown might have envied. In 1864 and 1865 the Civil War became increasingly modern; that is, it was increasingly waged against the total war-supporting physical and emotional resources of the southern people. That was the whole point of Sherman's marches through Georgia and the Carolinas and Sheridan's devastation of the Shenandoah Valley. After 1864 the war also became more wasteful of the individual soldier's life, particularly in the eastern and Virginia theaters. There massed infantry was increasingly hurled across open space swept by rifle and artillery fire from entrenched enemy positions. In the last year of the war trench warfare of the sort characteristic of World War I became the norm in the eastern theater, and so did the characteristic horrors of such warfare. At the heart of this eastern campaign, under Grant's overall command, was a calculated gamble involving a race against time. Grant could afford to lose more men and materiel than Lee and was prepared to spend them until Lee's forces were so worn down by attrition that they no longer existed as an army. The question was simply this: which would give out first, Lee's military resources or the North's tolerance for mounting casualties? In the summer and early fall of 1864 the northern will to spend blood almost cracked, and Lincoln was certain that anti-Republican and antiwar elements would unseat his administration in the 1864 elections. Nevertheless, he did submit himself to the electoral process and gained a narrow victory, made possible in part by nick-of-time Union military successes in the Shenandoah Valley and in Georgia.

The total cost in money of the American Civil War has been estimated to be about $10 billion, including veterans' benefits. In lives lost the Confederate casualties are estimated to have been between eighty and ninety thousand battle deaths, with perhaps as many as a hundred and eighty thousand dead of disease—typhoid, dysentery, and tuberculosis—and at least a hundred thousand wounded. Union casualties are estimated at 140,414 battle deaths, with 224,097 dead of disease and 275,175 wounded. About one out of every three soldiers who served in the Civil War—and most of them were under twenty-one years of age—died or was wounded in it. To the Union casualty list must be added the name of Abraham Lincoln, whose life the war took by extending itself through the inflamed mind but steady hand of John Wilkes Booth.

The murder of Abraham Lincoln is hateful to contemplate. But the fact that it happened in a theater during the performance of an English comedy and was committed by an actor who supported himself in Shakespearean roles reminds us, however grotesquely,

that the life of the nation was not wholly absorbed by the Civil War. In the North especially, people pursued their social, cultural, intellectual, and business interests more or less without dropping a stitch. In 1862 Stewart's Department Store—a glassy cast-iron palace for the consuming public—opened in New York City. At least seven colleges were founded during the war in the East, including one for deaf-mutes. At Vassar, Maria Mitchell became the first woman professor of astronomy. New operas by Verdi—*Un Ballo in Maschera* and *La Forza del Destino*—received their first American performances during this period, and Richard Wagner's *Flying Dutchman* was introduced to New York audiences in symphonic form. Henry James tried to enlist, was turned down for physical reasons, and went off to the Harvard Law School, where he began writing short stories. *Scientific American* continued to advise its readers of the latest developments, including, for example, the first photograph taken of the moon. George Pullman patented his Pullman sleeping car, and a Massachusetts man hit upon the idea of selling paper dress-patterns and made a mint out of them.

Popular amusements—high and low—bubbled along, with fashionable crowds taking in thoroughbred races at the newly opened Saratoga racetrack. Baseball introduced several innovations (umpires called both balls and strikes, players tried base stealing, and a team hired the first professional player), and the game of rackets enjoyed a minor boom in New York City. On May 5, 1863, while Stonewall Jackson was dying painfully from wounds suffered at Chancellorsville, Virginia, a sixty-three-round bare-knuckles American boxing championship match was held in nearby Maryland.

During the Civil War years at least three hundred thousand people migrated to the Far West. Many, like Mark Twain, who was born in Missouri, left to avoid the war and to get rich on the mining frontiers of Nevada, Colorado, Montana, or Idaho (Twain was a flop as a prospector but struck gold in 1865 with his tall tale "The Celebrated Jumping Frog of Calaveras County"). The development of frontier mining communities usually followed a pattern: a strike of loose or placer gold that could be separated from the surrounding gravel or dirt by panning or sluicing it; a rush to the new area by many thousands of new prospectors, most of them doomed to disappointment; an influx of farmers and shopkeepers attracted by the extravagant prices miners would pay; an influx of mining capital and expertise, to get at the large deposits or lodes of gold and silver of which the loose stuff was just a symptom and which required hard-rock tunneling and expensive ore-crushing and smelting equipment; the establishment of formally organized and governed communities, which eventually combined to request territorial status and then statehood.

During the Civil War the transportation system linking the Rocky Mountain territories with California and the East was a series of government-subsidized stagecoach lines, including the Butterfield Overland Mail Company and the five thousand miles of stagecoach routes owned by the legendary Ben Holladay, servicing mainly the Northern Rockies area. Much of this system soon became obsolete, however, since by 1863 the Central Pacific Railroad of California was already laying track and in the next few years had begun, with Chinese coolie labor, to hack its way through the Sierra Nevadas. In the East the Union Pacific had laid track as far west as Omaha, Nebraska, by 1865.

As the Far West underwent a mining boom there were accompanying Indian troubles. A Cheyenne-Arapaho war erupted in Colorado in 1864, briefly isolating Denver, resulting in the massacre at Sand Creek of 450 peaceful Cheyennes, including women and children, and culminating in 1865 in the surrender of most Cheyenne and Arapaho lands in Colorado. At about the same time Texans forced Kiowas and Comanches to give up much of central Texas and parts of New Mexico. Also during 1864 and 1865 ex-mountainman Kit Carson, now a colonel in the Union army, was doing to Navaho peach orchards, melon fields, vineyards, and sheep herds in Arizona what Sherman was doing to Georgia, for the same reasons and with about the same results. By 1865 the Navahos had surrendered and were sent off on their long walk to a parched reservation in Texas. In late 1862 there was a Santee Sioux uprising in Minnesota as a result of corrupt dealings by Indian agents, and late in 1862 Lincoln took time from his schedule to review the convictions of 306 Santee prisoners and order the hanging of thirty-nine.

When the Civil War ended in mid-1865, the United States of America was not yet one hundred years old, but it was intact. It was also greatly strengthened. Civil wars are bitter things, not only because they are wars, but also because they have a way of being especially savagely fought. And yet most relatively young and heterogeneous nations have them.

Today many Americans tend to look upon the Civil War as a glamorous, romantic, or deeply moving episode in our history. This positive attitude toward the Civil War is in part made possible by blaming all the bad things associated with it—including the economic ruination of the South—on the Reconstruction period that immediately followed. But several groups did in fact benefit directly or indirectly from the war. With some exceptions, business, technology, and agriculture were all stimulated by high prices and high levels of government spending. Workers as a group tended rather idealistically to view the Civil War as something that would ultimately affect their status positively, if only by eliminating forever the threat of competition from slave labor. Blacks, women, and immigrants all experienced, in various degrees, increases in political and social status as a result of the war. Quite apart from the elimination of slavery, which, as one ex-slave put it, could make you proud but didn't make you rich, the combat record of black soldiers resulted in subtle, slight upward changes of status, even in the South. The war record of Irish immigrants had a similar effect. Women gained from their participation in the victorious abolitionist movement and from their labors on behalf of the war, both as fund raisers and as nurses. Southern women largely managed the southern economy during the war and were instrumental in picking up the pieces afterward.

More than a century of American experience separates us from the Civil War as a military event. But time has largely erased the horrors of this war and has left intact, in its healing way, a considerable residue of romance, gallantry, and beau geste in which all Americans may share.

The Civil War (1861–1865)

1861

Delaware, one of four slave states to remain within Union, unanimously rejects secession (January 3).

Federal forts and arsenals in Georgia, Alabama, and Florida seized (January 3–7); these and subsequent seizures of Federal property are largely bloodless.

Six southern states—Mississippi, Florida, Alabama, Georgia, Louisiana, and Texas—formally secede from the United States (January 9–February 1). Governor Sam Houston of Texas refuses to go along with secession and is eventually forced to resign (March 18). Four other southern states—Virginia, Tennessee, Arkansas, and North Carolina—do not secede but make it clear that any attempt to coerce seceded states will cause them to drop out too. In addition there are three slave states (Missouri, Kentucky, and Maryland) whose ultimate status is in doubt, with Maryland being especially critical, since it contains Federal capital.

Federal ship *Star of the West,* sent by lame-duck President Buchanan to reinforce Fort Sumter, is prevented by bombardment from entering Charleston Harbor (January 9); Buchanan has previously expressed opinion (December 3, 1860) that Federal government has no legal right to prevent secession by force; his position has generally stiffened but not to the point that he is prepared to use *Star of West* incident as cause of war.

Vassar Female College founded in Poughkeepsie, New York (January 18).

Kansas admitted as thirty-fourth state, under a free-state constitution (January 29).

Peace convention, last-ditch effort to prevent war by delegates of 21 border, southern, and northern states, meets in Washington, D.C. (February 4–23); convention adopts proposals suggested in late December, 1860, by Senator John J. Crittenden of Kentucky, including pledges in form of constitutional amendments never to interfere with slavery where it existed, to reimburse slave owners for escaped slaves, and to extend 36°30′ line across country to Pacific; as President-elect, Lincoln refuses to go along with extension of 36°30′ line but indicates willingness to accept measures protecting slavery where it exists in return for nonsecession.

Confederate States of America formed in Montgomery, Alabama (February 4–9); Jefferson Davis of Mississippi chosen provisional president, with Alexander H. Stephens of Georgia as vice president.

Jefferson Davis
LIBRARY OF CONGRESS

Lincoln's first inauguration on March 4, 1861, at the Capitol
LIBRARY OF CONGRESS

Congress organizes Colorado Territory (February 28); subsequently forms Nevada Territory and Dakota Territory (March 2).

Morrill Tariff (March 2): Congress passes tariff law having strong protectionist features and high rates designed to produce revenue for a government treasury depleted by Panic and Depression of 1857.

Abraham Lincoln inaugurated as sixteenth President (March 4); Hannibal Hamlin is Vice President. In his inaugural address Lincoln promises that his administration poses no threat to southern "property," "peace," or "personal security" but denies that right of secession from Union exists.

Missouri splits on secession (March 22), and a state of civil war, carried on primarily by guerrilla raiders, continues for several years; Union forces retain overall command, however, and Missouri ultimately contributes three times as many soldiers to Union army as to Confederate. Proslavery government in exile adds a star to Confederate flag, but state is never member of Confederacy.

Lincoln informs South Carolina that he will send nonmilitary supplies to Union garrison at Fort Sumter in Charleston Harbor (April 6); action creates dilemma for Confederate leadership, which they resolve in part by demanding immediate surrender (April 11). Union commander, Major Robert Anderson, offers to surrender in two days, when his food supply will be exhausted. Confederate shore batteries commence firing on April 12, in part because local authorities fear Federal reinforcement and in part because Confederate staff officers on scene fear chance for war will somehow be compromised away. Firing upon Fort Sumter, considered beginning of Civil War, goes on for 34 hours. Major Anderson, his supplies exhausted, is forced to surrender (April 13), but no casualties are sustained.

President Lincoln declares that an "insurrection" exists and calls for 75,000 90-day volunteers to put it down (April 15); northern response is enthusiastic.

Virginia secedes (April 17), bringing to Confederacy many of its ablest military commanders, including Robert E. Lee and Thomas J. "Stonewall" Jackson, and its capital, which is moved to Richmond on May 1.

Lincoln orders naval blockade of all Confederate ports (April 19); blockade is soon recognized and in the main respected by European powers, who accord Union and Confederacy equal status as belligerents, without, however, formally recognizing Confederacy as separate and independent nation.

Arkansas, Tennessee, and North Carolina secede from U.S. and join Confederacy (May 6–20).

Maryland legislature attempts to remain neutral (May 10) but is blocked partly by Unionist governor and antisecessionist popular opinion and mainly by suspension of habeas corpus, which allows local military commanders to jail secessionists. Practice leads to *Ex parte Merryman* (May 27), in which Chief Justice Taney ar-

The interior of Fort Sumter in Charleston, South Carolina, after the Confederate bombardment that began the Civil War

gues that only Congress, not President, has power to suspend habeas corpus. Lincoln ignores Taney and is later backed up by emergency legislation passed by Congress.

Kentucky votes to remain neutral (May 20); this neutrality, understandable in state that was birthplace of both Abraham Lincoln and Jefferson Davis, as well as Henry Clay, is first violated by Confederate forces (September 3) and leads to Federal occupation by request of legislature. A pro-Confederate government in exile is formed late in 1861, adding the thirteenth star to Confederate battle flag.

Great Britain closes its ports to naval prizes seized either by U.S. or by Confederate ships (June 1); act hinders Confederate privateering effort.

Dorothea Dix appointed superintendent of women nurses (June 10).

Western part of Virginia forms separate pro-Union government (June 11); process of secession from Virginia, begun May 13, eventually leads to formation of state of West Virginia.

First Battle of Bull Run, near Manassas, Virginia, ends in Union rout (July 21); popular demand for quick "on to Richmond!" action causes Lincoln to send General Irvin McDowell and 25,000–35,000 volunteers marching into Virginia, accompanied by reporters and sightseers; although battle is topsy-turvy for a while, Confederate battlefield leadership, especially by Generals Johnston and Jackson (who earns nickname by holding his line like a stone wall), ultimately tells, as does lack of training and discipline on part of green Union troops,

whose retreat becomes headlong, panicky rush back to Washington, D.C. Battle dispels Union hopes for speedy victory and is only major land engagement of 1861; rest of year is given over to recruiting, equipping, and training Army of Potomac, ably done by George B. "Little Mac" McClellan. However, problems highlighted at Bull Run—popular demand for Union action and victory, combined with superior Confederate battlefield leadership—continue to plague operations in theater east of Appalachians for several years to come.

Congress passes joint resolution declaring that purpose of war is to preserve Union, not to abolish slavery (July 22).

First income-tax bill (3 percent of income over $800) signed into law by Lincoln (August 5), effective January 1, 1862.

Transcontinental telegraph becomes operational (October 24); Lincoln receives message from Sacramento, California, over about 3,500 miles of telegraph wire.

Trent affair (November 8): Union seizure of Confederate diplomats from British mail packet *Trent* out of Havana threatens to provoke confrontation with England, where there is strong prosouthern sympathy, especially among ruling classes; affair is smoothed over with U.S. apologies and release of Confederate diplomats (December 26), since last thing Union wants is Confederate alliance with British naval power. By end of 1861 U.S. naval blockade of Confederacy is beginning to hurt, allowing only 800 ships to clear southern ports as opposed to 6,000 in 1860.

Congress appoints Joint Committee on the Conduct of

A bridge over the Virginia stream known as Bull Run, where two fierce battles were fought

"Stonewall" Jackson

the War (December 20); formed partly because of congressional exasperation with slow pace of war and a minor Union defeat and partly in resentment against executive war powers assumed by Lincoln, committee is dominated by radical (abolitionist) Republicans, who urge Lincoln to abolish slavery and zealously, if not vindictively, prosecute war; almost by definition, the radical Republicans are out of step with majority opinion and political and tactical necessities and have a very unfortunate tendency to back those generals least able to win battles, but they are not the benighted, self-serving, and vicious group they are sometimes considered to be.

1862

Edwin M. Stanton takes office as Lincoln's Secretary of War (January 15), replacing Simon Cameron, who is forced to resign because of inefficiency and corruption.

As a result of inaction by Union forces Lincoln issues General War Order No. 1 (January 27), which designates Washington's Birthday (February 22) as day on which all U.S. army and navy forces will fight, whatever the circumstances; this desperate order is widely ignored by Union commanders.

Julia Ward Howe publishes "Battle Hymn of the Republic" (February); sung to tune of "John Brown's Body."

General Ulysses S. Grant captures Fort Donelson, on Cumberland River in Tennessee (February 16); important victory ensures fall of Nashville and secures Union opening of attack route into Confederacy from West, eventually used by Sherman to march through Georgia in 1864.

Five-hour battle at Hampton Roads, Virginia, between ironclads U.S.S. *Monitor* and C.S.S. *Virginia* (formerly Union ship *Merrimack*) is inconclusive (March 9); although *Virginia* retreats, in need of repairs, it still blocks James River, preventing invasion of Richmond by this route; Confederates later scuttle *Virginia* when Norfolk, Virginia, main Confederate naval base, is captured by Union forces (May 11).

Virginia Peninsular Campaign (April 5–July 1): complicated series of maneuvers and battles, with George McClellan in command of Army of Potomac against Robert E. Lee's Army of Northern Virginia; main result is that despite superior numbers Union forces fail to capture Richmond, although it is several times within their grasp (four miles away at one point), and fail to destroy Lee's army. Although McClellan maneuvers brilliantly and on occasion inflicts heavy losses on Lee,

he fails in main objectives, in part because Lee and Stonewall Jackson perform miracles and in part because McClellan lacks the relentless bulldog instinct for the jugular characteristic of Grant and Sherman in the western theater. Failure to take Richmond deeply depresses northern public opinion and swings British and French close to recognition of Confederacy.

Battle of Shiloh, in Tennessee (April 6–7): at enormous cost U. S. Grant pulls out victory from almost certain defeat. Despite political pressures to remove Grant (there are rumors of drunkenness and objections to high casualty rate) Lincoln makes key decision: "I can't spare this man; he fights."

Confederate congress passes conscription law (April 16); class-related exemptions sharply antagonize southern poor.

Commodore David G. Farragut of Alabama rams Union gunboat fleet through Confederate blockade of lower Mississippi, capturing New Orleans (April 24–25); although this and subsequent Union victories in West are gradually tightening noose around Confederacy, these strategically vital events are more than offset in public mind by series of Union disappointments or disasters in Virginia theater.

Confederate gunboat *Planter* seized by Robert Smalls, slave seaman (May); Smalls, with black crew, sails boat out of Charleston, South Carolina, and delivers it to Union forces; blacks serve with comparatively little discrimination in U.S. Navy, especially early in war, and ultimately comprise about 25 per cent of Union sailors in blockade, participating in all major naval engagements, including *Monitor* battle and destruction of C.S.S.

The battle between the ironclads Monitor *and* Merrimack

Alabama; Smalls ends war as captain and later serves in House of Representatives from South Carolina during Reconstruction period.

Homestead Act signed (May 20); grants 160-acre quarter section of Great Plains free to any settler who improves land for five years; a fulfillment of Republican campaign promise, Homestead Act of 1862 is intended to benefit urban workers and small farmers, but 160-acre plot is wrong size for semiarid plains; about one out of every nine acres of western land goes to small farmers under Homestead, rest—a half billion acres—being engrossed by railroads, states, and speculators.

C.S.S. *Alabama,* steam warship built in Great Britain for Confederacy, slips out to sea despite Union protests (July); C.S.S. *Alabama* and other British-built and largely British-manned raiders take heavy toll (about $19 million worth) of U.S. shipping and cause large numbers of U.S. merchant ships to be transferred to other flags, thus contributing heavily to decline of U.S. Merchant Marine after Civil War.

Congress passes Pacific Railroad Act (July 1); authorizes construction of transcontinental railroad (Chicago to San Francisco), with Union Pacific building west and Central Pacific building east to meet it; railroads granted land sections and other subsidies for each mile of track laid, with result that railroads become single largest landholders in West.

Morrill Land Grant Act becomes law (July 2); loyal Union states granted 30,000 acres of western lands for each senator and representative; interest on invested proceeds from sale of land to be used to set up agricultural and engineering land-grant colleges; act benefits more populous eastern states; ultimately 69 colleges established under this act.

Lincoln signs Confiscation Act (July 17); sweeping law has many provisions relating to rebel property, but one main purpose is to substitute fines, confiscation of property (including slaves), and imprisonment as punishment for treason instead of the death penalty, in effect eliminating possibility of wholesale executions of Confederate leaders; Lincoln largely ignores major provisions of act, but one result of act is to allow organization of escaped slaves and free blacks into U.S. combat units. By war's end approximately 186,000 blacks—about half from Confederacy—have served in combat units, often with great distinction.

Second Battle of Bull Run, at Manassas Junction, Virginia (August 25–31): Generals Lee and Jackson badly defeat Union armies in Virginia under command of General John Pope. Union defeat increases likelihood that Europeans will recognize Confederacy and encourages Confederacy to invade Maryland.

Battle of Antietam, near Sharpsburg, Maryland (September 17): McClellan, restored to command of Army

Antietam, one of the bloodiest battles of the Civil War, left thousands of soldiers dead. Left, bodies of Confederate soldiers lie beside their artillery at the Dunker Church. Below left, in the only photograph that exists of a Civil War battle, the armies meet on the field at Antietam. Below right, Robert E. Lee, who led the Confederate army in the Antietam campaign.

ALL: LIBRARY OF CONGRESS

of Potomac, stops Lee's invasion of Maryland in extremely bloody battle (23,386 killed or wounded in one day); McClellan fails to pursue advantage and allows Lee to retreat back into Virginia. Failure of Lee's invasion forestalls European recognition of Confederacy and provides Lincoln with long-awaited "victory" in eastern theater.

Lincoln proclaims preliminary Emancipation Proclamation (September 22); proclamation declares intention to free slaves in states still in rebellion as of January 1, 1863; although qualified in relation to Border States and containing references to colonization, preliminary proclamation has desired effect of further influencing foreign public opinion against diplomatic recognition of Confederate States of America.

Gatling gun (rapid-fire machine gun) patented (November 4); largely as result of War Department opposition gun sees limited use during war, as do other technologically superior firearms, including the Winchester repeating rifle, patented in 1860, and several effective breechloading rifles.

Battle of Fredericksburg, Virginia (December 13): Army of Potomac, now under command of General Ambrose Burnside (McClellan having been removed, for the last time, for his failure to move quickly and relentlessly against Lee at Antietam and afterward), is shattered in senseless assault against Lee's numerically

inferior Army of Northern Virginia. Year thus ends with deep northern gloom owing to failure of Virginia campaigns against Richmond, yet with long-term factors favoring Union cause.

Lincoln foils demand by radical Republicans that he reorganize (i.e., appoint more radicals to) his Cabinet (December 17).

Union exports 40 million bushels of wheat and flour to Great Britain, which as a result of poor European harvests needs food more than it does southern cotton.

1863

Lincoln issues Emancipation Proclamation (January 1), which proclaims that all slaves in rebel-held states "are, and henceforward shall be, free." Proclamation specifically exempts Border States and Union-held portions of Confederacy and urges southern free blacks to "abstain from all violence, unless in necessary self-defense" and promises that blacks "will be received into the armed services of the United States."

P. T. Barnum creates sensation in New York City (February 10) by staging marriage of midget Tom Thumb to Mercy Warren, who is also about 2'5" tall.

Territory of Arizona formed (February 24); Congress acts in response to expulsion of Confederate army at Battle of Glorietta Pass (1862) and to influx of miners

Ambrose Burnside

Right, Tom Thumb with circus giant; insert, P. T. Barnum

into Tucson area as result of gold strikes on Colorado River.

Congress sets up national banking system as part of war-financing effort (February 25); requires national banks to hold U.S. securities and issue bank notes (greenbacks) against these holdings; state bank notes are driven out of circulation. U.S. greenbacks reach a low of 39 cents on the dollar in July, 1864, corresponding to an ebb tide in Union fortunes, but Federal inflation is nothing like that in Confederacy, which prints a billion dollars' worth of paper money that becomes progressively more worthless.

Lincoln signs Conscription Act (March 3); act makes all white males 20 to 45 eligible for draft but includes provision enabling draftees to avoid service by paying $300 or providing a substitute; act functions mainly to spur enlistments, since volunteers are paid a bonus and draftees are not; vast majority of Union soldiers have enlisted.

Idaho Territory formed (March 3) as result of heavy influx of gold miners in 1862. Territory originally includes Wyoming, Idaho, and Montana. Large gold rush to Montana (May 26) leads to boom-town development of Virginia City, Montana, and ultimately to separate territorial status for Montana (1864).

Battle of Chancellorsville, Virginia (May 2–5): Confederate Generals Lee and Jackson with force of 60,000 defeat 130,000-man Army of Potomac, now under General Joseph Hooker; last major Confederate victory of war, Chancellorsville is extremely costly in that Lee loses more than 10 per cent of his army killed or wounded, including General Stonewall Jackson, who is accidentally shot by his own men and dies (May 10) of his wounds.

A Union army camp at Cumberland Landing, Virginia

Fifty-fourth Infantry Regiment, one of first black combat units, leaves Boston for South (May 28); later suffers extremely high casualties at Fort Wagner, Morris Island, South Carolina; black troops earn praise from many quarters for discipline and courage and have a positive effect on social status of blacks, especially in North; originally black private's pay set at half white rate, but parity is later achieved, and black officers get battlefield commissions; 22 blacks receive Congressional Medal of Honor.

54th Infantry Regiment storms Fort Wagner on July 18, 1863.

French troops invade Mexico, capturing Mexico City (June 7); invasion originally a joint English, Spanish, and French effort to force Mexico to pay its foreign debts; France goes ahead alone with plans of conquest and installs puppet government, which invites Archduke Maximilian of Austria to become emperor. U.S. protests but can do little else until end of Civil War except continue to recognize republican government of Benito Juárez as legitimate Mexican government.

West Virginia admitted as thirty-fifth state (June 20) and fifth slave state in Union.

Battle of Gettysburg, Pennsylvania (July 1–3): in effort to secure European recognition and encourage rising sentiment for peace among northern Democrats, President Davis orders Lee to invade North with army of 75,000 (against 90,000 Union troops); for first—and last—time large Confederate army gets a few miles north of Mason-Dixon line but is stopped at Gettysburg by Army of Potomac, now under command of General George L. Meade; on third day of battle Lee orders suicidal frontal assault by 15,000 Confederate soldiers (under Generals Pickett, Pettigrew, and Trimble) on

Dead soldiers lie on the field after the Battle of Gettysburg.

center of fortified Union line, which holds and virtually destroys entire Confederate charge. Total Union and Confederate casualties: about 51,000 killed or wounded. Lee attempts to retreat July 4 but is blocked by flooded Potomac; Meade fails to pursue, and Lee eventually escapes (July 13). Meade's victory is, however, a near-fatal blow to Confederate hopes and, combined with fall of Vicksburg, dooms Confederacy in eyes of potential European allies.

Fall of Vicksburg, Mississippi (July 4): after brilliant two-month campaign and siege by General U. S. Grant, Confederate army under General John C. Pemberton surrenders city and 30,000 troops; fall of Vicksburg, followed by surrender of Port Hudson, Louisiana, gives Union complete control of Mississippi River. Vicksburg victory, resulting in virtually complete naval encirclement of Confederate heartland, and defeat of Lee at Gettysburg cause England and France to seize or sell off ironclads under construction for Confederacy (September), signaling the end of all European aid to Confederate States of America.

Antidraft riots in New York City (July 13–16): first drawing of names under Conscription Act provokes riot by poor workers, largely by Irish immigrants, which spreads throughout city, with mobs lynching first blacks, then Chinese and Germans, and destroying about $1.5–2 million worth of property; order finally restored by troops detached from Meade's army at Gettysburg, the absence of which contributed to Meade's failure to pursue Lee.

Lincoln delivers Gettysburg Address (November 19); brief remarks are read to crowd following two-hour oration by Edward Everett, commemorating national cemetery at Gettysburg battlefield.

Battle of Chattanooga, Tennessee (November 23–25): Chattanooga, occupied by Federal forces since September 9 and under siege by Confederate army under Braxton Bragg since September 20, is relieved and firmly secured by Union armies under overall command of U. S. Grant. Rout of Confederate forces around Chattanooga opens southern Confederacy to attack and provides jumping-off place for Sherman's march through Georgia.

Ulysses S. Grant

Lincoln issues Proclamation of Amnesty and Reconstruction (December 8); proposes to pardon most rebels (except high officials) and to reabsorb into Union any state in which 10 per cent of 1860 voters pledge oath of allegiance to Federal government and to acts of Congress and President regarding slavery; Lincoln's plan widely denounced by radical Republicans as too lenient and marks beginning of struggle between executive and Congress over terms and overall direction of Reconstruction.

Vicksburg and the Mississippi lie quiet after the Union siege.

1864

Arkansas voters approve state constitution abolishing slavery (March 18).

Virginia campaigns (May 5–June 18): U. S. Grant, now general in chief of all Union armies, begins slow and costly but relentless drive on Richmond and war of attrition on Lee's 60,000-man Army of Northern Virginia; a series of battles (Wilderness, May 5–6; Spotsylvania, May 8–12; Cold Harbor, June 1–3; and Petersburg, June 15–18), including first trench warfare in the World War I mode, cost Grant more than 68,000 killed or wounded; Lee's casualties are about 25,000–30,000 killed or wounded, but that is roughly 50 per cent of his army, whereas Grant's army is constantly being reinforced; the upshot of this long, bloody campaign is that Lee is pinned down about twenty miles from Richmond for next nine months while Sherman is tearing up Georgia and Carolinas and Grant's siege forces are gradually built up; enormous losses of Virginia campaign strengthen northern peace Democrats, however.

General William T. Sherman begins march through Georgia, with army of 100,000 (May 7); Confederate General Joseph E. Johnston, with 60,000 men, fights a skillful delaying action, but Sherman presses on, eventually reaching Atlanta on September 1 and occupying evacuated city following day; fall of Atlanta buoys northern spirit and contributes to Lincoln's re-election.

Sherman's men cripple Atlanta by tearing up railroad tracks.
LIBRARY OF CONGRESS

Abraham Lincoln and Andrew Johnson nominated at convention in Baltimore (June 7); nominating convention avoids using term "Republican" and calls itself National Union Convention, in effort to draw in pro-Union Democrats willing to proceed with war; Andrew Johnson, military governor of Tennessee and lifelong Democrat, is nominated for Vice President.

C.S.S. *Alabama* sunk in naval battle off Cherbourg, France (June 19), by U.S.S. *Kearsarge.*

Early's Raid (July 2–13): Confederate General Jubal Early drives north from Shenandoah Valley into Maryland and gets within five miles of Washington, D.C., before troops sent by Grant from Petersburg force Early back into Virginia; near success of Early's raid causes panic and deepening war-weariness in North, making further Union efforts to prosecute war questionable.

Lincoln vetoes Wade-Davis bill (July 8); congressional plan calls for military governors of seceded states, stiffer oaths of allegiance, and special conventions repudiating secession and slavery; since bill is passed by Congress on last day of session, Lincoln is able to kill it by simply not signing it; radical Republicans denounce Lincoln for (pocket) veto, assert that Reconstruction is purely a congressional function, and hint that new nominating convention might reconsider Lincoln as Republican Party's nominee.

Admiral Farragut attacks Mobile Bay, Alabama (August 5); Farragut ignores mines in channel ("Damn the torpedoes [mines], full speed ahead!"); destruction of Confederate gunboat fleet there and closing of ports give Union complete control of Gulf of Mexico.

David Glasgow Farragut
LIBRARY OF CONGRESS

Democratic Party, meeting in Chicago, Illinois, nominates General George B. McClellan as President and George H. Pendleton, a Copperhead (a Northerner who sympathizes with the South), as Vice President (August 29); platform calls for immediate cessation of hostilities and is actually repudiated by McClellan; fall of Atlanta on September 2 to Union forces helps considerably to undercut Democratic peace demands.

Louisiana voters ratify constitution abolishing slavery (September 5); Congress refuses to seat representatives from either Louisiana or Arkansas, although these states have complied with Lincoln's 1863 version of Reconstruction.

Shenandoah campaign (September 19–October 19): Union army, now under command of General Philip H. Sheridan, begins devastation of Shenandoah farms, principal suppliers of grain to besieged Confederate capital; Sheridan makes famous ride to rally troops at Battle of Cedar Creek (October 19), firmly and finally securing Shenandoah Valley for Union and adding another item of good news for Republican electoral campaign.

Nevada admitted as thirty-sixth state (October 31); Nevada does not have sufficient population to qualify for statehood, but Congress and Lincoln argue that a state producing so much wealth from gold and silver mines soon will have large enough population; Congress anxious to add state because it needs votes for Thirteenth Amendment, abolishing slavery, which is now working its way through Congress and will soon be submitted to states for ratification.

Campaign of 1864: Union military victories, temporary closing of radical and moderate Republican ranks, and truculent, intransigent statements by Jefferson Davis in September and October swing election to Lincoln (November 8); electoral vote: Lincoln 212, McClellan (carrying New Jersey, Kentucky, and Delaware) 21. Popular vote: Lincoln 2.2 million, McClellan 1.8 million, with Lincoln carrying key states of New York, Pennsylvania, and Ohio by margin of 86,000 votes. Election is very near thing; although Confederate states do not participate, the fact that there is a national election at all during a state of civil war is in itself a major triumph for democratic government.

Sherman begins march to sea (November 16); leaves Atlanta and marches toward Savannah, cutting 60-mile-wide swath in which anything conceivably of use to Confederate war effort is systematically destroyed; reaches Savannah on December 10 and occupies it on December 22.

Battle of Nashville (December 15–16): Union army under General George Thomas utterly smashes Confederate force under General Hood; Hood's 40,000-man army was intended to cut Sherman's supply line, which stretched back into Tennessee.

Sherman marches north through Carolinas (January 16–March 21); jumping off from Savannah, he begins 435-mile scorched-earth march north, wreaking even greater destruction than in Georgia; Columbia, capital of South Carolina, is burned (February 17), and Charleston is taken (February 18); Sherman enters Goldsboro, North Carolina, on March 21.

William T. Sherman
LIBRARY OF CONGRESS

Congress passes Thirteenth Amendment, barring slavery in the U.S. (January 31); amendment goes to states for ratification.

Peace talks at Hampton Roads, Virginia (February 3): Confederate commissioners continue to insist on independence, and Lincoln dismisses them.

Congress establishes Freedmen's Bureau (March 3); originally called Bureau of Refugees, Freedmen, and Abandoned Lands and designed to deal with all those rendered destitute or homeless by war, its powers are later greatly expanded (1866) and bureau focuses particularly on problems of emancipated slaves.

Abraham Lincoln inaugurated (March 4); delivers great Second Inaugural Address, in which he promises to finish war and bind up nation's wounds "with malice toward none; with charity for all"; Andrew Johnson becomes Vice President.

Lee forced to retreat from siege lines at Petersburg and abandon Richmond (April 2); Richmond, goal of Union armies since 1861, occupied (April 4); Grant pursues, and Lee's Army of Northern Virginia, now down to about 30,000 starving men, is quickly surrounded; Grant requests surrender (April 7).

John Wilkes Booth shoots Abraham Lincoln in the head (April 14); Booth, an actor, gains easy access to Lincoln during performance of play at Ford's Theatre in Washington, D.C., and fires at pointblank range; murder part of broader, deranged conspiracy to kill Vice President Johnson and Secretary of State Seward and seems to have been motivated by desire to avenge South's defeat; Lincoln dies following day, without regaining consciousness. Booth is trapped and killed in barn near Bowling Green, Virginia (April 26).

Photograph of Lee and his sons in Richmond after the war

Lee and Grant meet at private home in Appomattox Courthouse, Virginia (April 9); Grant offers generous surrender terms, which Lee accepts; Army of Northern Virginia formally lays down arms (April 12) and Confederate soldiers are saluted by Union forces.

Lincoln's assassination, April 14, 1865

Soldiers in Appomattox at the time of Lee's surrender

Left, a playbill from the night of Lincoln's assassination; above, John Wilkes Booth

Andrew Johnson becomes seventeenth President (April 15).

General Johnston surrenders last substantial Confederate army, in North Carolina (April 26); by May 4 all Confederate forces east of Mississippi surrender.

Jefferson Davis and his wife captured in Georgia (May 10); President Johnson declares Civil War at an end, although scattered Confederate forces west of Mississippi do not surrender until May 26.

ROBERT C. DE LARGE, M.C. of S. Carolina.   JEFFERSON H. LONG, M.C. of Georgia.

U.S. Senator H.R. REVELS, of Mississippi   BENJ. S. TURNER, M.C. of Alabama.   JOSIAH T. WALLS, M.C. of Florida   JOSEPH H. RAINY, M.C. of S. Carolina.   R. BROWN ELLIOT, M.C. of S. Carolina.

THE FIRST COLORED SENATOR AND REPRESENTATIVES,
In the 41ˢᵗ and 42ⁿᵈ Congress of the United States.

LIBRARY OF CONGRESS

Reconstruction and Industrialization

1865–1898

This period began in mid-1865, after the federal government had won a bloody four-year civil war against eleven southern states. It ended in 1898, after a short and successful war against Spain had left the United States an imperial power.

Politically the big stories of this period are the Reconstruction effort, the Compromise of 1877, the trend away from strong presidential rule, the general dominance of the Republican Party, the graft, corruption, and scandals often associated with long tenure in office, the rise of reformist pressures leading to the agrarian-populist movement in the 1890's, and the gradually increasing United States involvement in hemispheric and world affairs, which culminated in the Spanish-American War of 1898. However, most of these stories lack the sharp outlines, decisive confrontations, and other exciting features characteristic of political drama. Political developments were in the main shaped in local, state, and federal legislatures and have as a result a certain impersonality about them. The political leaders of this period are among the most obscure in American history. Eight men served as President of the United States during the years 1865–98, but many Americans today would be hard pressed to name more than half of

103

them or to associate any positive achievement with their administrations.

The tangle of events referred to as Reconstruction has particularly suffered from the lack of star political performers and show-stopping scenes. The Reconstruction era offered in several respects a brief glimpse a hundred years into the future, and its accomplishments on the political level were large and enduring. The Thirteenth Amendment to the national charter cleansed from it the institution of slavery. The Fifteenth Amendment provided black males with access to political power. The Fourteenth Amendment provided the federal government with a mechanism by which it could intervene on behalf of an individual American citizen anywhere in the country to ensure that his or her federally guaranteed rights were not violated either by other individuals or by local and state governments. The Fourteenth Amendment was a great new valve through which federal power could flow into large areas of American life; although this valve was not really opened wide until the twentieth century, it was now in the system, and it was put there during the Reconstruction era.

It is strange therefore that until recently Reconstruction has been a negative term in American history, standing for a sad, villainous time in which a handful of radical senators and representatives somehow got hold of an entire nation, twisted its magnanimous instincts, and pushed it along a course of greed, hypocrisy, and general fanaticism that impoverished the South for a hundred years and permanently poisoned relations between black and white Americans.

Because traditional historical surveys tend to pass rapidly from one high point of political or military activity to the next, one often gets the impression that nothing much happens during periods in which people's energies are directed toward solving problems in the less public areas of social and economic life. But the years 1865–98 were years of collective social and economic activity having great significance for the lives of most Americans; during these years modern America was born—or at least American society became more complex and interconnected.

Socially and economically these years were revolutionary. Immense fortunes—in oil, steel, railroads, lumber, insurance, real estate, mining, meat-packing— were amassed and created long-lasting corporate institutions. A large, shifting class of urban and rural poor sought by trial and grievous error to recognize itself and to form political and economic alliances having the power to compel modest improvements in status, working conditions, wages, and quality of life. The city as we know it—with skyscrapers, apartment buildings, mass-transit systems, chain stores, and tenements—took

shape. The speed of light was measured to within 99.999 per cent of true.

Social historians can point to these years as years in which American society was given a new texture by an almost Homeric catalogue of new things: the telephone, the electric light, the Kodak camera, the phonograph, the fountain pen, the safety razor, the automobile, the electric trolley, the cash register, the motion picture, the mail-order catalogue, the Mayo Clinic, the library catalogue, the adding machine, the battleship, processed foods, mass-produced ready-to-wear clothing, the chemical industry, organized professional or recreational sports (like baseball, tennis, basketball, football, and roller-skating), the Linotype machine, dime novels, the Metropolitan Opera, the company town, the silo, the diesel engine, *Tom Sawyer*, *Huckleberry Finn*, *The Red Badge of Courage*, *The Portrait of a Lady*, the modern insurance business, a widespread, excited tinkering with the ideas of Karl Marx and Charles Darwin, the electric chair, national parks, the harvester-thresher combine, toothpaste in tubes, the tuberculosis sanatorium, the Brooklyn Bridge, the key-punched card, the typewriter, the A&P, the appendectomy, alternating current, the Christmas card, and the legal trademark.

In this period rapid technological development affected the lives of many millions of American citizens. And the major motifs of this period—the conquest and settlement of the Far West, the rapid growth of old and new industries and the resultant creation of monopolies and concentrations of capital, the rise of labor organizations, the growth of American cities and the increasing urbanization of the population, the heavy foreign immigration, the entry of women during the 1880's and 1890's into wider participation in political, economic, and social affairs, the increased political and social repression of blacks in the South after 1890, the colonial adventures in 1898—all gain in clarity when we look at them as having been at least in part shaped or even directed by rapid technological change.

For example, the interlocking effects of a greatly expanded railroad network on the American environment defy any brief description, but in the 1870's and 1880's the railroads in effect created the long-drive cowboy by opening up eastern markets for beef and providing magnetlike terminals to which huge herds could be moved from the Southwest and the far northern plains. (Another piece of technology, barbed wire, was instrumental in killing off the open-range cattle industry and with it the need for large numbers of people to supervise, round up, and drive to market the hitherto free-roaming herds.)

From 1870 to the turn of the twentieth century the United States population grew from about forty million to seventy-six million; of this increase nearly twelve million were immigrants, mainly English, Irish, Scandinavian, and German but also including a million Italians, a million Russians, Yugoslavs, Poles, and other east-central Europeans, and about two hundred thousand Chinese. But the steamship, with the cheap and quick passage it provided, has frequently been overlooked in discussions of the heavy immigration that characterizes this period.

The new steel industry and the new steam navy in effect cross-fertilized each other, and the existence of a spanking new steam-and-steel navy was largely responsible for the pattern of United States territorial possessions established by the end of 1898—Puerto Rico in the Caribbean and Hawaii, Guam, and the Philippines in the Pacific.

Increasingly large numbers of American middle-class women were partially released from the home by one wave of technology, the kind that began to eliminate time-consuming tasks like baking bread and making clothes, and were carried into the lower levels of the business world by another wave—one of typewriters, adding machines, telephone switchboards, and cash registers. For working-class women there were, of course, the power looms, lasting machines, canning factories, sweatshop sewing machines, and other products of the industrial age.

It is in this technological period that we may place the beginnings of the long-term trend in American society away from a scarcity of labor and toward the creation of an increasingly large proletariat. Until after the Civil War labor scarcity had been a 250-year-old feature of the American socioeconomic environment, and much American ingenuity had been expended on developing labor-saving devices in agriculture and manufacturing. By 1898 a condition of overall labor surplus had become—and has since remained—the norm, broken only by temporary scarcities associated with war. There was as a result a large and growing pool of unskilled or semiskilled workers among whom there was competition for a shrinking number of jobs. It is no accident that among the various reforms associated with the local populist movements of the 1880's and 1890's there is a clear, unmistakably urgent call for restrictions on foreign immigration. It is similarly not coincidental that the populist movement, when it undertook to gain power in the South during the 1890's, turned against the largest and most visible group of unskilled workers and embarked on a thirty-year period of the grossest sort of political, economic, and social discrimination against blacks.

The new working class of this period was not a proletariat in the classic sense of capitalless, exploited laborers. In fact many workers had low-paying but relatively pleasant white-collar positions. But these people constituted a large and growing group whose jobs—in factories, in offices, and in service industries—had few intrinsic satisfactions, little genuine social utility, and great vulnerability to economic downturns.

The period 1865–98 was in effect the troubled adolescent stage of today's industrial society. It was also the time of cowboys, the long drive, the stampede, the cow town, gunslinging sheriffs and desperadoes, Custer's last stand, range wars, boot hills, the sodbuster, the Colt Peacemaker, cattle rustlers, and gunfights at the OK Corral. This aspect of the American experience has proven to be an inexhaustible mother lode of myth and has been exploited by at least four generations of mass media—pulp fiction and penny-dreadful newspapers, traveling circuses, movies, and television. The mythical Wild West, now indelibly impressed by such media on the American imagination, was first created during the 1880's and 1890's for an audience not unlike the one that feeds on it today. For the great majority of Americans of this period gunfights, Indian raids, and cowherding were as exotic as they were to mid-Victorians everywhere else in the Western world.

The fact is that more people (four hundred) were killed in the 1888 blizzard that struck New York City than died by violence in all the so-called rip-roaring cattle towns like Dodge City or Abilene or Tombstone during their thirty-year heydays. Cowboys and gunslingers really didn't have lightning-fast draws, because their big, floppy holsters, designed to protect and secure their revolvers, would not permit fast draws. A third of all long-drive cowboys (about thirty-five thousand) were Mexican-Americans and blacks; a good many of them were members of a union, the Knights of Labor. The cavalry units that achieved perhaps the most effective record against the Plains Indians and the Apaches were the "Buffalo Soldiers," black professionals serving in the 9th and 10th Cavalry. The Haymarket Massacre in Chicago and the Homestead strike in Pennsylvania were far more typical expressions of American violence than the celebrated range wars, in which a few hired guns battled each other over water rights, cut fences, rustling, or sheepherders. And so forth.

The idea of the frontier, as distinguished from Far West cowboy-and-Indian entertainments, did not become an important one until after 1890, when the director of the census announced that the frontier was gone—all areas of the country were settled, however sparsely. This announcement came as a considerable shock to many Americans. There was, of course, plenty of land left, and large quantities of it were homesteaded after 1890. But the *idea* of the frontier was gone, and this idea now came to figure heavily in the thinking of many political and economic leaders, especially those who had never been in a frontier area. Many Americans came to believe, on scant evidence, that the frontier had functioned as a safety valve for society, bleeding off from the more settled areas many lawless or radical social elements and providing an ultimate haven for the urban poor in times of economic depression. Actually the urban worker rarely had either the money to get to the frontier or the skills or capital to make a go of the agricultural life when he got there. And the lawless elements, then as now, tended to congregate where pickings were good: in the cities, where people had more money and more vices. But the belief that the United States was spatially unlimited and that it contained a large area where discontented and undesirable citizens might be absorbed was a comforting one. This belief now had to be abandoned, and as a result people started to take it seriously and to worry about it.

Consequently it is not entirely coincidental that the 1890 announcement tolling an end to the existence of an internal frontier was followed in 1891 by the beginnings of the forest-preserve system and that people began to pay increased attention to the idea of conservation, an idea first broached by George Perkins Marsh in 1864. By 1897, when farm prices began to rise steeply and farm acreage increased in value, many Americans suggested—incorrectly—that these developments were related to the disappearance of the frontier. Were food

and land becoming scarce? Could the United States conceivably run out of these commodities entirely? It is also not unlikely that the enthusiastic public response to a war with Spain for its Caribbean and Pacific possessions had something to do with an increased sense of confinement related to the 1890 announcement.

The 1865–98 period ended with many of the features of modern American life in place. The nation had achieved world-rank industrial and naval power and was soon to experience the contradictory responsibilities such power posed for a country having anti-imperial, individualistic, democratic, and materialistic traditions. It had, through the creation of an essentially technological society, achieved enormous increases in agricultural and industrial output. Although conferring large benefits on the country as a whole, this output had left certain imbalances in the distribution of power and wealth that were soon to be widely perceived as inherently unstable, if not unjust. The nation's internal frontier had disappeared, and with it had gone a certain complacent assumption that all problems could somehow be solved by limitless internal expansion or that all social tensions would dissipate of their own accord in the fresh, pure wind of an infinite inner space. For about a generation American talents and energies had been chiefly absorbed in transforming the nation's social and economic life. Now it was time to look more closely at what had in fact been wrought and to attempt to align the nation's political life to this new reality.

The celebration begins as the last spike on the railroad linking the East and the West is driven at Promontory Point, Utah.

UNION PACIFIC RAILROAD

106

Reconstruction and Industrialization (1865–1898)

1865

President Johnson issues proclamation of amnesty and Reconstruction (May 29); Johnson's plan follows Lincoln program of 1863 but is harsher on property-owning classes, refusing general amnesty and pardon to those owning taxable property valued at more than $20,000 but allowing members of this group to seek individual pardons; during summer, while Congress is in recess, Johnson recognizes governments of Arkansas, Tennessee, Louisiana, and Virginia and sets up provisional governments in remaining seven Confederate states, in which conventions of "loyal" citizens (white males having sworn allegiance to Union) change state constitutions, repudiate Confederate war debts, ratify Thirteenth Amendment, and hold elections; Johnson hopes to destroy southern planter aristocracy through federal disenfranchisement and confiscation and assumes that southern small farmers will repudiate aristocratic leadership; Johnson's policy is failure on its own terms, since southern states re-elect high Confederate leaders and are in effect carbon copies of prewar states; result is totally unacceptable to radical and moderate Republicans.

Four convicted conspirators in Lincoln assassination plot are hanged (July 7); three others are sentenced to life imprisonment, and a fourth conspirator gets six years.

First Sioux War begins in Powder River area of Wyoming and Montana (August 14 or 15); Sioux under Red Cloud resist army attempt to build road and forts from Fort Laramie through sacred Big Horn country to mining communities in Montana (Virginia City, Bozeman, Helena); Army is forced to retreat back to Fort Laramie by end of 1865.

Captain Henry Wirz, former commandant of Andersonville, Confederate prisoner-of-war camp in Georgia, is hanged as result of camp's high death rate (November 10); more than one third (at least 12,912) of Andersonville prisoners died, mainly as a result of exposure, malnutrition, and disease; Wirz is only Confederate military or civilian official to be executed by federal authority.

Series of statutes known as black codes passed by Mississippi legislature (November); these laws grant blacks some legal rights—to marry, to own certain kinds of property, and to bring certain grievances to courts—but are on the whole designed to "reconstruct" former slaves into a landless, rural labor force having a permanent relationship of inferiority to white society as a whole. One of the Mississippi statutes prohibits blacks from owning or leasing farmland, and various others deny blacks anything like equality before the law. Other southern state governments approved by Johnson soon enact their own version of Mississippi codes; although these codes vary in harshness, all have effect of creating an inferior caste bound to the landowning classes in ways sometimes amounting to involuntary servitude. A South Carolina code prohibits blacks from doing anything but farm work without a license; a Louisiana code requires blacks to enter into binding labor contracts in first ten days of each year; vagrancy codes in several states in effect allow unemployed blacks to be auctioned off to highest bidder. President Johnson refers noncritically to these codes (December 18), although they clearly benefit the planter classes he has made a career of denouncing.

Congress forms Joint Committee of Reconstruction (December 4), also called Committee of Fifteen (six senators and nine representatives); its immediate purpose is to investigate conditions in South and make recommendations to Congress about seating of representatives from Johnson-recognized governments; controlled by moderate, not radical, Republicans, committee ultimately assumes leadership role in congressional Reconstruction. The committee does not somehow gain dictatorial control over the U.S. Congress; instead it garners support of large, moderate congressional majorities by offering the only acceptable practical and humanitarian alternative to the policies of President Johnson and the ex-Confederate southern leadership, policies that on every level—political, economic, and social—are often deliberately offensive to Congress and represent in the eyes of many Unionists a continuation of Civil War issues by nonmilitary means.

Thirteenth Amendment to Constitution, which abolishes slavery and involuntary servitude, goes into effect (December 18).

Union Stockyards open in Chicago (December 25); this stockyard, largest of its kind, is capitalized at $1 million and is largely owned by various railroads having a terminal in Chicago; makes Chicago supreme in the meatpacking industry and gives rise to the Armour (1867) and Swift (1875) empires.

1866

Fisk School opens in Nashville, Tennessee (January 9); college for blacks, named for General Clinton B. Fisk, of Freedmen's Bureau; school later (1867) chartered as

Fisk University, with liberal-arts curriculum; to raise money for school Fisk Jubilee Singers are formed and introduce black spiritual and gospel music to North and ultimately to Europe.

Congress passes bill extending life of Freedmen's Bureau (February 19); bill gives bureau power to try in military court those accused of depriving freedmen of their civil rights; President Johnson vetoes bill on grounds that military trial violates Fifth Amendment and that Congress has no right to pass laws for whole country without southern states being represented; Congress repasses bill over Johnson's veto (July 16).

The confrontation that resulted in the New Orleans race riot
LIBRARY OF CONGRESS

Johnson vetoes Civil Rights Act (March 27); act makes blacks U.S. citizens (overturning *Dred Scott* decision), guarantees them equal protection of the law, and gives federal courts jurisdiction over violations; Johnson's veto, on states' rights grounds, is overridden (April 9); act is intended to nullify those portions of black codes that deny blacks legal rights enjoyed by other citizens, but they do not tamper with social segregation as established in the codes.

Western Union becomes first U.S. communications monopoly (June 12); absorbs U.S. Telegraph Company (servicing East) and provides national service at uniform rates.

President Johnson proclaims end of "insurrection" in all ex-Confederate states except Texas (April 2); a later proclamation (August 20) includes Texas and declares complete restoration of Union; ten years later Supreme Court decides that these two dates mark legal end of Civil War; for Congress these proclamations amount to a presidential declaration of war against legislative branch.

Three-day race riot begins in Memphis, Tennessee (April 30); more than 40 blacks are killed, and freedmen's schools are burned.

Congress passes Fourteenth Amendment (June 16); designed to eliminate doubts about constitutionality of Civil Rights Act, it makes all native-born or naturalized persons except Indians citizens of U.S., guarantees federal protection of rights of individual citizens against state interference, provides that citizens denied the vote in any state shall not be counted in determining the number of representatives that state shall have, disqualifies for federal or state office most of the ex-Confederate leadership, validates federal debt incurred in fighting Civil War, and repudiates all debt incurred by Confederacy. With exception of Tennessee, southern states refuse to ratify, and ratification is made condition for readmission to Union. Amendment reflects, among other things, congressional anger that ex-rebels are assuming high positions (vice president of Confederacy, Alexander Stephens, is elected U.S. senator from Georgia) and that Democratic representation in House will increase by twelve to fifteen seats as result of counting nonvoting blacks as whole free persons instead of three fifths (as in old slave rule).

Joint Committee of Reconstruction recommends exclusion of southern representatives (June 20); committee asserts that Congress, not the President (especially a nonelected one, and a Democrat to boot), must control Reconstruction process.

Tennessee readmitted to Union (July 24), five days after ratifying Fourteenth Amendment.

Race riot in New Orleans, Louisiana (July 30): 35 blacks and whites are killed, and more than 100 are wounded; this and other riots help convince voters in North that South is still rebellious and that blacks need federal protection.

National Union Convention held at Philadelphia (August 14); President Johnson attempts to form new party of moderates, but effort convinces many voters in Union states that Johnson's policies are supported mainly by Copperheads (Northerners who sympathize with South) and ex-rebels. Country goes overwhelmingly Republican in fall congressional elections, giving Republicans two-thirds control of both House and Senate and repudiating Johnson as a leader to whom it is willing to entrust national economic and political policy.

National Labor Union formed in Baltimore (August 20); federation of crafts unions, it seeks to achieve eight-hour working day, to influence national politics, and to establish producers' cooperatives; many constituent unions drop out after 1870, in part as a result of failure of cooperatives.

Sioux, under Red Cloud, end year of successful guerrilla

tactics against U.S. with ambush of 81 soldiers and their leader, Captain W. J. Fetterman, near Fort Philip Kearny in what is now Wyoming; Fetterman and entire command are killed; about 200 Sioux and allies are killed or wounded.

First oil pipeline (five miles long) becomes operational in Pennsylvania.

1867

Congress gives black males right to vote in Washington, D.C. (January 8); measure is passed over Johnson's veto. Until after congressional elections of 1866 Republicans are unwilling to press issue of black suffrage, because most northern and midwestern states have not extended the franchise to their black citizens; but participation of southern blacks is vital to Republican plan of Reconstruction, so black manhood suffrage is gradually extended, first being required in territories (January 31) and finally being made prerequisite for readmission of southern states.

A black man votes for the first time in a state election.
Harper's Weekly, NOVEMBER 16, 1867

Congress calls itself into special session (January 22); usurping this presidential prerogative, Congress elected in 1866, fearing Johnson's interference with its programs, votes to convene in March rather than December.

Congress passes first Reconstruction Act, over presidential veto (March 2); act divides South (excluding Tennessee) into five military districts under martial law; in order to be readmitted southern states must (1) elect constitutional conventions by universal manhood suffrage, (2) draw up state constitutions guaranteeing black male suffrage, (3) ratify Fourteenth Amendment, and (4) submit themselves and their elected representatives to congressional review. This and subsequent Reconstruction acts actually represent defeat for radical Republican minority, since its hopes for land reform—giving freedmen an economic base through confiscation and redistribution of large estates—are not realized.

Congress passes Tenure of Office Act (March 2); act is designed to protect Republicans against patronage sweep by Johnson and specifically to prevent Johnson from removing Secretary of War Stanton, only Johnson cabinet member sympathetic to radicals; Congress also passes Command of the Army Act, requiring Johnson to issue all military orders through Stanton and General of the Army U. S. Grant, thus cramping Johnson's power as commander in chief; Congress fears military coup by Johnson and also fears Johnson will bungle Reconstruction through contrary orders to commanders of southern military districts.

Howard Normal Institute (later Howard University) founded in Washington, D.C., by the Freedmen's Bureau (March 2); named after General Oliver O. Howard, head of bureau, which, with failure of land reform, is only government agency directly concerned with economic welfare of destitute, often starving ex-slaves. Bureau eventually disburses about $15 million worth of aid, mostly in rations, clothing, hospitals, and school buildings. Private northern philanthropy donates books and teachers (for example, George Peabody of Massachusetts creates $3.5 million fund for educational purposes).

Congress requires military commanders in southern districts to set up voting-registration procedures (March 23) after southern states fail to hold constitutional conventions.

Senate ratifies treaty (April 9) with Russia to purchase Alaska for $7.2 million; called "Seward's Folly" after Secretary of State Seward, who negotiated treaty, Alaska is considered liability, especially by Russians, who lobby and possibly bribe Congress to ratify purchase and later (July 14, 1868) to appropriate money for sale.

Ku Klux Klan formally organized in Nashville, Tennessee (May); fancy names are given to local, county, and state cells comprising "Invisible Empire" under Grand Wizard General Nathan B. Forrest; is just one of several secret white supremacist groups organized to intimidate and terrorize freedmen, scalawags (southern Republicans), and carpetbaggers (Northerners who go South for any purpose).

Armed Ku Klux Klan members in robes and white hoods
LIBRARY OF CONGRESS

President Johnson suspends (but does not dismiss) Secretary of War Edwin Stanton (August 12); hopes to test constitutionality of Tenure of Office Act and also to close leak in his Cabinet.

Midway Islands occupied by U.S. (August 28) as possible naval coaling station.

First shipment by rail of Texas cattle from Abilene, Kansas, east to Chicago stockyards (September 5): beginning of long-drive era, in which herds of Texas longhorns are driven north along Chisholm Trail and other western trails to railroad terminals at cattle towns like Abilene, Ellsworth, Newton, and Dodge City. In next five years more than 1.5 million longhorns are shipped (live) east from Abilene alone.

Peace commission, created by Congress in March, signs Treaty of Medicine Lodge with Kiowa and Comanche Indians (October 21); represents beginning of small-reservation policy, in which all Plains Indians are to be resettled on small reservations concentrated in Oklahoma and in Black Hills area of Dakota Territory; Indians are expected to settle down and become agriculturalists.

Grangers organized in Washington, D.C. (December 4); begun as secret society, Order of the Patrons of Hus-

An 1873 lithograph shows an idealized view of farm life.
LIBRARY OF CONGRESS

bandry, Grange eventually develops into open pressure group representing interests of western farmers and small-town merchants and calling for ceilings on railroad shipping rates and for agricultural and technical schools.

1868

President Johnson dismisses Secretary of War Edwin Stanton (February 21); Stanton refuses to give up office; Johnson attacks U. S. Grant for role in Stanton affair, causing Grant to move toward radicals for protection.

House of Representatives votes to impeach President Johnson (February 24); after vote, eleven articles of impeachment prepared, charging President with violations of Tenure of Office Act, contempt of Congress, and behavior tending to degrade office of President; House had voted down similar impeachment resolution recommended by Judiciary Committee in December, 1867.

Senate impeachment trial of President Johnson (March 30–May 26): Chief Justice Salmon P. Chase presides over trial, in which prosecutors argue that (1) Johnson has committed high crimes and misdemeanors and (2) Congress has right to remove President through impeachment process as a political measure, whether or not President is actually guilty of indictable offense. Senate votes (May 16) 35 to 19 for conviction, one vote short of two-thirds majority needed; same vote, 35 to 19, occurs on May 26, and proceedings are abandoned. Seven Republicans, including chairman and one other member of Joint Committee of Reconstruction, vote with twelve Democrats against impeachment.

The Johnson impeachment was open to the general public.
LIBRARY OF CONGRESS

Horatio Alger publishes *Ragged Dick* in book form, first of about 35 similar rags-to-riches novels ultimately totaling about 30 million copies sold (May).

Seven southern states readmitted to Union (June 22–25); Arkansas, Alabama, Florida, Georgia, Louisiana, North Carolina, and South Carolina have drawn up good state constitutions and satisfied other requirements of Reconstruction acts.

Congress votes eight-hour day for workers on federal projects (June 25).

Fourteenth Amendment goes into effect (July 28).

Campaign of 1868: Republicans run General Ulysses S. Grant and Schuyler Colfax of Indiana on platform endorsing radical Reconstruction, payment of national war debt in gold, and hedging on tariff and suffrage for blacks; Democrats run Horatio Seymour (New York) and Francis P. Blair, Jr. (Missouri) on platform attacking radical Reconstruction and urging payment of war debt

in greenbacks; Republicans make "bloody shirt" a campaign issue (Republican suggestions that Democrats were responsible for starting Civil War, had killed Union soldiers in it, and were still killing Northerners in the South, became known as the "bloody shirt" issue); popular vote (November 3): Grant 3,013,650, Seymour 2,708,744 (southern black vote in excess of 500,000 for Republicans clinches victory). Three southern states do not participate. Electoral vote: Grant 214, Seymour 80.

Military reoccupation of Georgia (September): Georgia, having expelled blacks from state legislature after readmission to Union, is placed once more under martial law.

End of First Sioux War: U.S. government removes troops from Powder River forts, and Red Cloud signs treaty (November 6) at Fort Laramie, although terms of treaty are either misrepresented or misunderstood by Sioux, who believe Powder River and Big Horn country are theirs; treaty actually stipulates Indian use of this land until U.S. wants it.

President Johnson grants unconditional amnesty to those accused of treason against U.S. (December 25); causes trial of Jefferson Davis to be dropped.

George Westinghouse invents air brakes for trains.

1869

Congress passes Fifteenth Amendment to Constitution (February 27); proposed amendment specifically gives black males the right to vote in North and South, partly in response to black role in presidential election of 1868; ratification is made condition for readmission to Union of four southern states (Virginia, Mississippi, Texas, and Georgia) still remaining out.

U. S. Grant is inaugurated as eighteenth President (March 4); Schuyler Colfax is Vice President.

Public Credit Act (March 18): Congress provides that national debt be paid in gold; long debate follows about whether to redeem $356 million in greenbacks, with farmers and other debtors who favor inflationary currency strongly opposed.

First transcontinental railroad completed (May 10); ceremony is held at Promontory Point, near Ogden, Utah, where Union Pacific meets Central Pacific.

National Woman Suffrage Association founded in New York (May); headed by Susan B. Anthony and Elizabeth Cady Stanton, NWSA represents more radical element of women's-rights movement, in which suffrage is but a small part of general reformist demands with respect to divorce, sexual rights (especially a married woman's

Women casting their votes at the polls in Cheyenne, Wyoming

right to regulate her sexual behavior in relation to her husband), the nature of home and family, and other social issues; more conservative New England-based American Woman Suffrage Association is formed soon afterward by Julia Ward Howe, Lucy Stone, and Antoinette Blackwell. In general the women's-rights movement is in disarray for next twenty years; Elizabeth Cady Stanton, who originally raised issue of woman suffrage, splits with the New Englanders over the issue of black male suffrage (she believes white women should get vote as soon as or before black ex-slaves) and later calls the ballot a "crumb" beside the main issue—the relations between the sexes, especially as institutionalized in American-style marriage.

National Prohibition Party formed in Chicago (September 1).

"Black Friday" (September 24): price of gold plunges after attempt of Jay Gould and Jim Fisk to corner gold supply fails; Gould and Fisk spread rumor, through President Grant's brother-in-law, that Grant is in on deal and will not release Treasury gold; rumor is false, and Grant orders government gold to be sold when cornering plot comes to his attention; even though Grant was personally innocent of corruption, such is moral tenor of the times that many speculators are willing to believe that President of U.S. is part of corrupt deal and are ruined on Black Friday, although Gould and Fisk get out in time.

Noble Order of Knights of Labor founded (December 9); at first a secret organization because legal status of labor unions is up in air, it later (1881) goes public and becomes one of largest labor organizations, with a peak membership of more than 700,000 in 1886; membership open to all workers except lawyers, bankers, stockbrokers, professional gamblers, and saloonkeepers.

Territorial legislature of Wyoming Territory, organized in 1868, grants women right to vote (December 10).

1870

U.S. census: total population 39,905,000, including 4,901,000 blacks and 2,314,824 immigrants arrived since 1861; most immigrants are from northern Europe, including about 787,000 from Germany (largest national group), but 64,300 Chinese also arrive to work on western railroads. Population center now 40 miles northeast of Cincinnati, Ohio; there has been a net shift of the population from east to west of about 2,299,000 people and from south to north of about 752,000 people; percentage of urban population is now slightly over 25 per cent.

John D. Rockefeller organizes Standard Oil Company of Ohio (January 10); by 1879 Standard Oil controls 90–95 per cent of refined oil.

Four remaining ex-Confederate states readmitted to Union (January–July); as part of readmission package representatives swear oath never to deny blacks vote, right to hold office, or educational opportunity.

First black U.S. senator, Hiram R. Revels of Mississippi, is seated (February 25); first black representative, Joseph H. Rainey of South Carolina, is seated in December.

Fifteenth Amendment is declared ratified and goes into effect (March 30).

New York parade honors ratification of the 15th Amendment.

Congress passes first Force Act (May 30); in response to growing terrorism by Klan (formally disbanded in 1869) and other white supremacist groups, Force Act prohibits use of force to prevent citizens from voting, authorizes President to enforce Fifteenth Amendment by military, and provides federal supervision of elections.

Annexation of Dominican Republic refused by Senate (June 30); President Grant wants Dominican Republic as naval base, but Senate, after long debate on pros and cons of international expansion, rejects treaty.

Tariff bill reduces duties on imported raw materials (July 14); protection of manufactured goods is largely retained.

1871

Victoria Claflin Woodhull appears before House Judiciary Committee to appeal for women's suffrage (January 11–12); she and her sister, Tennie Claflin, have been outspoken in discussing women's rights in sexual terms, insisting on a woman's right to fulfill and regulate her sexual needs, especially outside the institution of marriage (a topic often widely denounced as "free love"); controversies swirling about such a "scandalous" woman further split suffrage movement.

Second Force Act (February 28): Congress extends federal supervision to local southern elections, again in response to intimidation and terrorism directed toward black voters and sympathetic northern and southern whites; Congress later (April 20) passes Ku Klux Klan Act, which imposes heavy fines and imprisonment on those who conspire secretly to deny black civil rights. Act succeeds in breaking up Klan by 1872, but by this time open, organized violence directed by local Democratic clubs and working through local militias has taken its place and proves impossible to control, largely because respected traditional local leadership approves it.

President Grant appoints head of Civil Service Commission (March 4), recently authorized by Congress to reform civil service, which is riddled with corruption; Congress refuses to fund commission, however, and ignores commission's recommendations.

P. T. Barnum opens circus in Brooklyn (April 10).

Camp Grant Massacre in Arizona (April 30): war against Apaches in Southwest culminates in massacre by citizens' group from Tucson of more than 100 women and children under U.S. military protection; although eastern public opinion is outraged, war against small bands of Apaches goes on until 1886, when Apache leader Geronimo surrenders. War against Apaches is costliest, in terms of money and lives lost, of all the Indian wars.

Chicago fire (October 8–9): three and a half square miles of city, including business center, burn to ground; city is built almost entirely of wood (even sidewalks are pine); fire starts near hovel occupied by poor Irish family named O'Leary, but how it starts is never firmly established; more than 17,000 buildings are destroyed, about one third of population of 300,000 is left homeless, at least 300 die, and about $200 million in property damage results.

Fire razes Chicago as citizens flee with their belongings.

William Marcy "Boss" Tweed indicted (October 26); indictment is result of anticorruption campaign by *New York Times*, principally against "ring" led by Tweed, Democrat and leader of Tammany Hall, but also involving many influential state and city leaders; Tweed Ring is partially broken by Tweed's indictment and subsequent arrest (December 16); Tweed is convicted in second trial (November 19, 1873), but many henchmen go free; Tweed Ring is estimated to have looted $45–50 million from city treasury between 1869 and 1871; other estimates place total skim as high as $200 million, utterly dwarfing graft and corruption so widely decried among southern radical Reconstruction governments.

The Tweed Ring accuse each other of stealing public funds.

Stanley finds Livingstone (November); Henry Morton Stanley, reporter for New York *Herald*, finds explorer David Livingstone ("Dr. Livingstone, I presume?") in Central Africa, where Livingstone, lost for last five years, has been searching for source of Nile.

By year's end conservative governments now have control of Tennessee, Virginia, North Carolina, and Georgia, largely as a result of Klan violence.

1872

Yellowstone National Park (3,471 square miles) established (March 1); for first time Congress sets aside an area as "a pleasuring ground for the benefit and enjoyment of the people."

Amnesty Act (May 22): removes restriction against officeholding for all but top ex-Confederate leaders, 500–600 in number.

Commercial killing of Great Plains buffalo begins; professional hide hunters take at least 3 million buffalo per year, leaving carcasses rotting on the plains, until by 1883 less than 200 exist in all the West. At least 13 million killed in years 1867–83, completely destroying economic base of Plains Indians.

Crédit Mobilier scandal builds (September 4); New York newspaper accuses Vice President Colfax and many other prominent politicians of taking bribes in stock from Crédit Mobilier construction company, which was secretly set up by promoters of Union Pacific Railroad to rake off additional profits; congressional committee set up in late December to investigate matter.

Alabama claims settled (September 14); international tribunal, set up previous year by treaty with Britain, awards U.S. $15.5 million for damages inflicted on U.S. shipping during Civil War by British-built *Alabama* and other Confederate raiders.

Campaign of 1872: liberal Republicans, disgusted with radical Reconstruction and corruption under Grant, run editor Horace Greeley and B. G. Brown (Missouri); Greeley-Brown ticket is also supported by many Democrats and by Liberal Colored Republicans; a Democratic faction, the "straight" Democrats, runs Charles O'Conor (New York) and John Quincy Adams II; Republicans run U. S. Grant and Henry Wilson (Massachusetts); the Prohibition Party runs James Black (Pennsylvania); the National Labor Reform Party nominates Judge David Davis (Illinois), who later withdraws; the Equal Rights Party nominates Victoria Claflin Woodhull as President and designates black author, reformer, and ex-slave Frederick Douglass as Vice President, but Douglass de-

clines. Popular vote (November 5): Grant 3,598,235, Greeley 2,834,761, O'Conor 18,602, Black 5,607; electoral vote: Grant 286, Greeley 66 (Greeley dies before Electoral College meets, and vote is distributed to other candidates).

Celluloid (invented 1870) is produced commercially, marking beginning of synthetics industry.

1873

Fourth Coinage Act (February 12): Congress eliminates silver as a monetary standard, placing country on gold standard; advocates of large money supply point to large quantities of silver being mined in West, denounce act as "crime of '73," and agitate for silver coinage for next twenty years.

House of Representatives censures two members for role in Crédit Mobilier scandal (February 18).

"Salary Grab Act" (March 3): Congress doubles salary of President (to $50,000) and votes increases for judges,

Stock exchange closing its doors during the Panic of 1873

congressmen (50 per cent increase, to $7,500), and other officials; public reaction causes law to be repealed following year, allowing only raises for President and judges to remain.

Coal Lands Act and Timber Culture Act (March 3): Coal Lands Act enables individuals or associations to buy U.S. coal-bearing land for $10–20 an acre; Timber Culture Act enables homesteaders to acquire additional 160-acre section if they plant trees on 40 acres of it.

Panic of 1873 (September 18): failure of banking house Jay Cooke and Company, combined with rampant speculation in railroad construction and agricultural overexpansion, brings on depression, which lasts five years; failure of many state banks ultimately strengthens national banking system.

Virginius affair (October 31): Spanish capture ship *Virginius*, illegally flying U.S. flag and running arms to revolutionaries in Cuba; authorities execute crewmen, some of whom are Americans; American public opinion considers executions act of war, but eventually Spain indemnifies families of executed Americans ($80,000).

First school of nursing opens at Bellevue Hospital in New York City.

Cable cars first used in San Francisco (August 1).

1874

Massive grasshopper plague destroys wheat crop in much of Great Plains (spring); although grasshopper infestations in spring and summer were like autumnal grass fires, a recurrent threat to farmers, the 1874 plague was one of the worst in history.

Federal troops intervene in clash between Republican and Democratic elements in Arkansas (May); Democratic control is eventually established and formally recognized by President Grant (May 15).

Steel-arch bridge across Mississippi River at St. Louis completed (July 4); largest such bridge in world, it has been under construction for seven years under James B. Eads.

The 1,628-foot bridge spanning the Mississippi at St. Louis
LIBRARY OF CONGRESS

First Chautauqua Assembly on shore of Lake Chautauqua, New York (August 4-18): movement begun by John H. Vincent, Methodist minister, is designed to provide summer-camp instruction in how to set up Sunday schools; movement soon extends into popular education and entertainment, including home-study courses; hundreds of local assemblies spring up, equivalent in many respects to earlier lyceum movement but with more entertainment in form of concerts and recitals.

Republicans in Louisiana split into pro- and anti-Grant factions (September 14); federal troops install pro-Grant faction.

Democrats gain control of House of Representatives (November 3); voter dissatisfaction, caused by Depression, Reconstruction, and scandals, costs Republicans 89 seats in House during congressional elections; "bloody shirt" issue no longer works.

Joseph F. Glidden receives patent for barbed wire (November 24); invention, which goes into commercial production following year, eventually revolutionizes cattle industry, eliminating open range and cattle drives.

Greenback Party formed in Indianapolis, Indiana (November 25); platform calls for greenback inflation and reflects agrarian discontent in South and West.

National Women's Christian Temperance Union formed in Cleveland, Ohio.

First electric streetcar, in New York City; made possible by Stephen Dudley Field's invention of third rail, which ultimately transforms urban transportation systems.

1875

Specie Resumption Act (January 14): act authorizes resumption of specie payments (representing wish of "sound money" financial interests in North) and cuts back on number of greenbacks in circulation (from $382 million to $300 million).

Civil Rights Act (March 1): act guarantees equal rights to blacks in public places (inns, theaters, public transportation, etc.) and prohibits exclusion of blacks from jury duty; last gasp of radical reformist and egalitarian impulse (bill had originally been sponsored by late Senator Sumner of Massachusetts), act is never enforced and is ruled unconstitutional in 1883, when Supreme Court rules that discriminatory acts by individuals are not a legitimate federal concern.

U.S.-Hawaii Treaty is ratified by the Senate (March 18); reciprocity treaty establishes favorable trade relations with the U.S. and stipulates that Hawaii will cede no territory to any other foreign power.

"Whiskey Ring" scandal (May 1): widespread conspiracy of distillers to evade payment of taxes exposed; Grant appointees are involved, including Grant's private secretary.

Black Hills gold rush (fall): 15,000 miners push into Black Hills after government gives up attempt to stop them from entering Sioux treaty lands; influx of miners, corruption of Indian agents (who deliver rotten meat, flour, and blankets to Indians), and approach of Northern Pacific Railroad all combine to bring on Second Sioux War.

"Molly Maguires" crushed (fall); secret violent organization (formed 1862) of Irish coal miners in Pennsylvania is broken after group is infiltrated by Pinkerton detectives and leaders are hanged or imprisoned.

Alexander Graham Bell demonstrates telephone (March 10); forms Bell Telephone Company in following year.

Centennial Exposition, celebrating first 100 years since Declaration of Independence, opens in Philadelphia (May 10); theme is technological progress, with many inventions displayed (self-binding reaper, telephone, typewriter, refrigerated railroad cars, Corliss steam engine, etc.); 50 foreign countries send exhibits, and 10 million people attend exposition.

Custer's Last Stand (June 25), episode in second Sioux War: George Armstrong Custer vaingloriously attacks major Sioux encampment with 265 soldiers and is completely annihilated at Battle of Little Bighorn; Indian victory has little military effect, and most Sioux are forced to surrender on October 31; small band under Sitting Bull escapes to Canada and remains there until 1881.

"Molly Maguires" hold a meeting in the Pennsylvania hills.

Custer's men charge the Sioux at the Battle of Little Bighorn.

"Mississippi plan" goes into effect (September); during state elections overt organized violence is employed by local Democratic clubs, which openly vow to use as much force as is necessary to win (by driving blacks and others expected to vote Republican from polls); governor of Mississippi, appealing to Grant administration for help in preventing killing of blacks, is told by Grant's Attorney General that people are "tired of these annual autumnal outbreaks in the South." Variants of Mississippi plan are used successfully in South Carolina, Florida, and Louisiana the following year.

1876

Secretary of War William W. Belknap is impeached by House (March 2); Belknap, who resigns immediately, is accused of corruption in sale of and kickbacks from Indian trading-post concessions; reservation trading posts are rich sources of profit (at the expense of Indian wards) and thus are highly sought-after political plums.

George Armstrong Custer
ALL: LIBRARY OF CONGRESS

Campaign of 1876: Democrats run Samuel J. Tilden, governor of New York and breaker of Tweed Ring, and Thomas A. Hendricks (Indiana) on platform stressing economy in government, high tariffs, and repeal of Specie Resumption Act of 1875; Republicans run Rutherford B. Hayes (Ohio) and William Wheeler (New York) on sound-money and "bloody shirt" platform; Greenback Party runs Peter Cooper (New York); Prohibition Party runs Green Clay Smith (Kentucky). Tilden, who campaigns unenthusiastically, receives 4,288,546 popular votes and 184 undisputed electoral votes; Hayes gets 4,034,311 popular votes and 165 electoral votes; Republicans refuse to accept 20 disputed electoral votes from Florida, Louisiana, South Carolina, and Oregon. If these electoral votes are counted as Republican, Hayes will win, 185 to 184.

Melvil Dewey invents Dewey decimal system for cataloguing library books and becomes first secretary of American Library Association, established October 6 in Philadelphia.

Florida, Louisiana, South Carolina, and Oregon send in two sets of election results, Democratic and Republican, both more or less fraudulent; Florida and Louisiana reportedly offer to sell their electoral votes for $200,000 and up; Congress must decide who will count votes and how to legitimate count.

1877

Congress establishes fifteen-member electoral commission to examine and evaluate disputed electoral returns (January 29); consists ultimately of five senators, five representatives, and five Supreme Court justices, with an 8–7 Republican majority.

Compromise of 1877 (February 9–28): electoral commission votes, along straight party lines, to accept Hayes's votes and give Republicans the election; although there is talk in the Senate of renewed civil war and an endless filibuster, southern Democrats make it clear behind the scenes that they are willing to accept a Republican President in return for Republican pledges (1) to withdraw all federal troops from South, thus guaranteeing home rule, (2) to appropriate federal funds for internal improvements, especially southern railroads, and (3) to appoint at least one Southerner to a cabinet post. Commission declares Hayes elected, 185–184, on March 2.

Desert Land Act (March 3): provides that individuals can acquire claim to 640-acre section in Great Plains or Southwest and gain title to it if they irrigate a portion of it during three-year period; act is actually cattlemen's bill, designed to allow them extensive acreage for graz-ing through dummy claims by cowboy employees and witnesses who testify they saw water, often sloshed onto ground from buckets.

Rutherford B. Hayes is officially inaugurated as nineteenth President (March 5); William A. Wheeler becomes Vice President.

Withdrawal of last Federal troops from South (April 24) marks end of Reconstruction effort and beginning of long period of conservative Democratic state and local rule; about 4 million ex-slaves are left to their fate, which is not a kind one.

Supreme Court rules in *Munn* v. *Illinois* that states have right to regulate "businesses affected . . . with a public interest"; case involves one of "Granger laws" passed in Midwest to counteract monopolistic railroad practices by fixing maximum rates for intrastate shipping, storage, etc.

Chief Joseph and Nez Perces begin four-month running battle to escape to Canada (June); force of 250 warriors and 450 women, children, and old people travel almost 2,000 miles and surrender close to Canadian border (October 5).

Chief Joseph
LIBRARY OF CONGRESS

Baltimore and Ohio Railroad strike (July 17): workers in West Virginia protest wage cuts and increased workload; strike spreads to eight states and finally must be put down by federal troops after state militias fail in Martinsburg, West Virginia, and in Pittsburgh, where a total of 26 die and $5–10 million property damage is done; violence causes several states to pass antilabor (anticonspiracy) laws; total union membership drops from 300,000 to 50,000 as result.

First intercity telephone lines are established between Salem and Boston, and Chicago and Milwaukee.

1878

Constitutional amendment granting women right to

vote introduced for first time in Congress (January 10); amendment is introduced every year thereafter until finally passed by Congress in 1919.

U.S. establishes naval base on Samoa, in Pago Pago Harbor (January 17).

Thomas Edison receives patents for phonograph (February 19).

Greenback Labor Party formed in Toledo, Ohio (February 22); delegates from 28 states adopt platform calling for proinflationary policies, shorter hours, and restrictions on Chinese immigration; party gains fourteen seats in Congress in fall elections, with James B. Weaver (Iowa) becoming leading spokesman.

Bland-Allison Act passed (February 28); requires government to buy $2–4 million worth of silver each month to be minted into coins; passed over Hayes's veto, act comes in response to western mining interests and proinflation worker and farmer (debtor) groups; conservatively implemented, act does not produce significant inflation.

Timber and Stone Act (June 3): law permits 160-acre purchase of lands "valuable chiefly for timber" at $2.50 an acre—about what one log costs; by using alien seamen and others to make dummy purchases, timber magnates acquire about 3.6 million acres of choice forest lands by 1900.

District of Columbia government set up by Congress (June 11); residents are not permitted to vote.

President Hayes, who has appointed able Cabinet, makes first effort to curb Republican corruption by dismissing members of New York State machine run by Senator Roscoe Conkling (July 11); move splits Republican Party, with radical (now called "stalwart") faction being especially alienated; Republican corruption and disunity contribute to Democratic success in congressional elections (November 5), in which Republicans lose control of both houses for first time in twenty years.

Albert A. Michelson publishes paper on measuring speed of light; ultimately is able to determine its speed with 99.999 per cent accuracy.

1879

Resumption of specie payments (January 1): greenbacks are now redeemable in gold, but since government has adequate gold reserves, there is no large-scale move to redeem them.

Hayes vetoes bill with Democratic rider attached prohibiting use of federal troops in congressional elections (April 29); this and five other attempts to pass such a bill

or rider are defeated with Republican help.

California adds measure to state constitution prohibiting employment of Chinese workers (May 7); six days earlier President Hayes had vetoed bill restricting Chinese immigration.

Edison gives large public demonstration of incandescent electric bulb in laboratory at Menlo Park, New Jersey (December 31); patent for device is issued early in following year.

"Exodus of 1879": mass migration of 20,000–40,000 blacks from South, under a variety of leaders, including Benjamin "Pap" Singleton, to Kansas, movement is in response to increasingly deplorable economic, social, and political conditions in southern states; approximately one third of migrating blacks remain in Kansas; rest are forced to return by increasing scarcity of land and rising white hostility.

First Church of Christ, Scientist, founded by Mary Baker Eddy in Boston; *Science and Health with Key to the Scriptures,* Eddy book upon which Christian Science movement is based, was published four years earlier.

Frank W. Woolworth opens successful five-and-ten-cent store in Lancaster, Pennsylvania; idea is that low fixed price will actually sell goods and that salesclerks have only to record sale; Woolworth owns seven such stores by 1886, and chain grows by leaps and bounds thereafter.

Progress and Poverty published by Henry George; book, which sells 3 million copies, is among first to deal with central paradox of the age, namely, the observation that as the nation grew richer the number of desperately poor and disadvantaged grew apace; George's solution, a single 100 per cent tax on profits gained on the sale of land, is too radical for his age—or ours.

Milling process for hard-kerneled wheat is perfected, allowing speedy, economical milling of wheat varieties most suitable for commercial agriculture on Great Plains.

Standard Oil Trust formed; trust system, perfected by 1882 and thereafter widely copied, is one of solutions to industrial overproduction and profit-cutting competition; stock voting rights in related corporations within a given industry are transferred to small number of trustees, who are thus able to integrate corporate decisions on an industry-wide basis; by 1882 nine Standard Oil trustees control actions of 40 companies in oil-refining industry (representing 90 per cent of this business), thus virtually eliminating competition and posing regulatory problems for state and national governments.

1880

First U.S. Salvation Army missions founded in Philadelphia (March 24).

Campaign of 1880: Republicans run James A. Garfield (Ohio) and Chester A. Arthur (member of "stalwart" faction) on campaign of civil-service reform, benefits for veterans, restrictions on Chinese, and protective tariff; Democrats run William S. Hancock (Pennsylvania) and William H. English (Indiana) on virtually identical platform, excepting tariff, which Democrats want lowered; Greenback Labor Party runs James B. Weaver (Ohio), and Prohibition Party runs Neal Dow (Maine); popular vote (November 2): Garfield 4,446,158, Hancock 4,444,260; electoral vote: Garfield 214, Hancock 155; Republicans regain control of House.

Treaty signed with China allowing U.S. to restrict but not suspend Chinese immigration (November 17).

U.S. census: total population 50,156,000, including 2,812,000 immigrants, mostly from northern Europe but also including 123,201 Chinese; 28 per cent of population is urbanized, and center of population is now near Cincinnati, Ohio.

Western cattle boom begins; removal of Indians and buffalo, accessibility of eastern markets via railroads, and skyrocketing beef prices lead to remarkable growth of cattle business throughout Great Plains, especially in northern plains; enormous amounts of European capital pour in between 1880 and 1885; boom eventually leads to overstocking; by 1885 many areas of Great Plains have herds exceeding grazing capacity, and many ranchers start fencing in (public) lands to protect their pasturage.

1881

Springer v. *United States* (January 24): U.S. Supreme Court upholds constitutionality of income tax.

Inauguration of James A. Garfield as twentieth President (March 4); Chester A. Arthur becomes Vice President.

President Garfield is shot at train station in Washington, D.C. (July 2); Charles J. Guiteau, "stalwart" Republican who failed to get political appointment, shoots Garfield so "stalwart" Arthur will become President; action causes further decline in "stalwart" prestige and more public revulsion against spoils system; Garfield survives until September 19, ultimately dying of blood poisoning; Guiteau is tried and convicted; is executed in 1882.

Chester Alan Arthur sworn in as twenty-first President (September 20); although a former spoilsman and "stal-

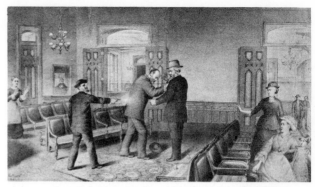
An engraving of the assassination of President James Garfield

wart," Arthur publicly recommends (December) reform of federal civil service, arousing opposition within his party.

Clara Barton organizes the American Red Cross, based on her experience with International Red Cross; organization soon becomes involved in civilian disaster relief.

Booker T. Washington establishes Normal and Industrial Institute for Negroes in Tuskegee, Alabama (July 4); school later becomes Tuskegee Institute and furthers Washington's policy of black self-help through industrial-vocational education—a policy that both northern and southern philanthropists find congenial.

Wharton School of Finance and Commerce, first of its kind, established at University of Pennsylvania.

A Century of Dishonor published by Helen Hunt Jackson; popular book arouses public sympathy for plight of reservation Indians.

1882

Chinese Exclusion Act (May 6): act, passed over President Arthur's veto, prohibits all immigration of Chinese

Strong anti-Chinese feeling in Denver results in a brutal riot.

laborers for ten years and denies right of citizenship to foreign-born Chinese.

U.S. signs treaty with Korea (May 22); treaty establishes commercial relations with "Hermit Kingdom" and recognizes that country's independence.

Commission appointed by President Arthur recommends sharp reduction in tariff (December 4); federal Treasury has huge surplus, which Congress has begun to tap for pork-barrel projects.

1883

Pendleton Act (January 16): establishes Civil Service Commission, provides for competitive examinations, removes many civil-service jobs from party patronage, and forbids practice of making federal jobholders give campaign contributions to party organizations.

Congress authorizes first build-up of U.S. Navy since Civil War (March 3); orders construction of three steel warships; U.S. ranks twelfth as naval power, and U.S. shipbuilding industry has lost technological initiative to Europe, especially in relation to marine engines, naval armaments, armor plate, and steel construction in general.

Brooklyn Bridge officially opens (May 25); longest steel suspension bridge in world at the time (1,595 feet), bridge connects lower Manhattan and Brooklyn.

Supreme Court declares Civil Rights Act of 1875 unconstitutional (October 15); Court declares that Congress has no jurisdiction over discriminatory practices by individuals.

Standard time zones adopted by U.S. and Canadian railroads (November 18); division into four zones (Eastern, Central, Mountain, and Pacific) ends scheduling confusion resulting from 75 different railroad time systems, from which local communities often set their clocks.

Joseph Pulitzer buys New York *World*; Pulitzer introduces large "scare" headlines, crime stories, and Sunday editions with comics. One comic strip, "Yellow Kid," leads to term "yellow journalism," which describes various forms of sensationalism engaged in by Pulitzer and William Randolph Hearst in their battle in the late 1890's to increase circulation and hence advertising revenues.

Ladies' Home Journal established by Cyrus H. K. Curtis.

1884

Organic Act (May 17): act organizes Alaska Territory, now to be run by appointed governor under laws of Oregon.

Rivalry runs high between publishers Pulitzer and Hearst.

Campaign of 1884: Republicans run James G. Blaine (Maine) and John A. Logan (Illinois); Democrats run Grover Cleveland (New York) and Thomas A. Hendricks (Indiana); National Greenback-Labor Party runs Benjamin F. Butler (Massachusetts); Prohibition Party runs John P. St. John (Kansas). Some reformist Republicans bolt party and support Cleveland, who has reputation for honesty; these Republicans become known as Mugwumps. Campaign consists mostly in personal attacks upon major candidates: Blaine is accused of having used position as Speaker of House for personal profit; Cleveland is accused of having fathered illegitimate child, which he promptly admits; Blaine ultimately loses key state of New York because he fails to repudiate statement that Democrats are party of "rum, Romanism, and rebellion," thus alienating Irish voters. Popular vote (November 4): Cleveland 4,874,621, Blaine 4,848,936, Butler 175,096, St. John 147,482; electoral vote: Cleveland 219, Blaine 182.

1885

Washington Monument is dedicated (February 21); work on monument was completed late in 1884, although it was begun in 1848.

Contract Labor Act (February 26): law prohibits immigration of unskilled laborers (domestic servants excepted) who agree to work on indentured basis in return for cost of passage.

Inauguration of Grover Cleveland as twenty-second President (March 4); Thomas A. Hendricks becomes Vice President but dies in November.

Land Commissioner William Sparks revokes western land titles suspected of being fraudulent (April 3); opens 2,750,000 acres of speculator-controlled land to settlers.

Bunker Hill and Sullivan lead deposits, largest in world, are discovered in Kellogg, Idaho.

1886

Presidential Succession Act (January 19): law provides that in event of disability or death of both President and Vice President they will be succeeded by cabinet officers, beginning with Secretary of State.

Haymarket Square Massacre in Chicago (May 4): mass demonstration, held to protest police shooting of pickets at McCormick reaper factory on previous day, turns into riot when bomb explodes, killing seven policemen and injuring others; police open fire on demonstrators, some of whom shoot back; although identity of bomb thrower is never established, eight anarchists are arrested and seven are sentenced to death; labor movement suffers because it becomes associated in public mind with anarchists, violence, and radical agitators.

A bomb explosion in Haymarket Square leads to gunfire.
LIBRARY OF CONGRESS

Santa Clara County v. *Southern Pacific Railroad Co.* (May 10): Supreme Court interprets Fourteenth Amendment as applying to corporations as legal "persons," hence shielding corporations from many forms of state regulation; in another railroad case, *Wabash, St. Louis and Pacific Railroad Company* v. *Illinois* (July 10), court invalidates Illinois law against discriminatory rates on grounds that such law infringes on right of Congress to regulate interstate commerce. Net result of both rulings is to place railroads and other corporations seemingly beyond reach of state or federal law and to increase agrarian discontent in West, where farmers pay high rates for short hauls to middlemen, who then pay low rates for long-distance shipping to the East.

Intermittent Apache wars in Southwest come to an end with surrender of Geronimo and his band of no more than 24 warriors, against whom U.S. had used 5,000

troops, roughly one fifth of U.S. Army (September 4).

Statue of Liberty dedicated on Bedloe's (now Liberty) Island in New York Harbor (October 28); gift of people of France, statue was shipped to U.S. in pieces in 1885 and assembled here.

American Federation of Labor founded in Columbus, Ohio (December 8); under leadership of Samuel Gompers, AFL stresses organization of skilled workers (who cannot easily be replaced in the event of a strike) and narrow economic goals (higher wages, job security, etc.); begins to raid Knights of Labor for membership and abandons unskilled or semiskilled workers as liability to trade-union movement.

Disastrous winter of 1886–87 delivers death blow to open-range cattle industry; herds weakened by summer drought that parched already overgrazed plains are now devastated by immense blizzards; many large stockraising companies are bankrupted. Henceforth ranchers fence in their land, reduce herds to manageable size, and grow hay in order to provide cattle with winter food.

1887

U.S. ratifies modified treaty with Hawaii, which now grants U.S. right to build naval base at Pearl Harbor (January 20).

Electoral Count Act (February 3): law makes each state responsible for providing proper vote count and deprives Congress of any control over electoral vote unless there is fraud or a state cannot reach a decision.

Interstate Commerce Act (February 4): law establishes federal regulatory agency, Interstate Commerce Commission, having certain limited powers to investigate railroads passing through more than one state; law also prohibits monopolistic practices like rebates, pooling, and discriminatory short-haul rates; commission's decisions are frequently reversed during 1890's by Supreme Court, and it does not have real power until early decades of twentieth century.

Dawes Severalty Act (February 8): law permits President to grant 160-acre homestead out of reservation land to each Indian head of family, and smaller sections to others; Indians who receive homesteads are to become American citizens. Well-intentioned act is designed to break up tribal organization and institute private ownership of land; the hope is that Indians will learn agricultural techniques and cultural values of whites and thus be assimilated into American life. Actual result is cultural disorganization of many Indian groups and a further alienation of Indian lands, since unallotted parts of reservation are sold and money is held in trust for such purposes as Indian education.

Between 1887 and 1937 approximately 90 million acres of former reservation land pass into white hands.

At President Cleveland's insistence Congress repeals Tenure of Office Act (March 5), thus formally restoring some of the power of the executive branch.

Ten-year cycle of drought begins in Great Plains (summer); farmers, who are heavily mortgaged, cannot repay loans, especially with dollars whose purchasing power steadily increases owing to relatively small amount of money in circulation; many foreclosures result and lead to stronger demands for an inflationary increase in money supply via unlimited coinage of silver.

Construction begun on "skyscraper," thirteen-story Tacoma Building in Chicago; building, which is completed in following year, is first to use wrought-iron skeleton throughout. (Chicago's Home Insurance Building, completed in 1885, is frequently honored as first to use skeletal framework but was of mixed cast-iron and wrought-iron construction.)

Battle-flag controversy (June 7): President Cleveland authorizes return of captured Confederate battle flags; routine order arouses storm of protest from Union veterans and some Republican politicians and is rescinded on June 15.

1888

Bayard-Chamberlain Treaty (February 15): treaty signed to end Canadian-American conflict over fishing rights off Newfoundland; although Senate rejects it (August 21), details worked out in treaty permit defusing of conflict, which had threatened to become serious.

Congress establishes separate U.S. Department of Labor (June 13); department does not achieve cabinet rank until 1913.

Campaign of 1888: Democrats run Grover Cleveland and Allen G. Thurman (Ohio); Republicans run Benjamin Harrison (Indiana) and Levi P. Morton (New York) on platform calling for high protective tariff (which Cleveland has specifically criticized), urging large bonus-type pensions for Civil War veterans (which Cleveland has vetoed), and criticizing Cleveland on battle-flag issue. Several small labor parties run candidates, as Prohibition Party and Equal Rights Party, which runs Belva Ann Lockwood. Cleveland does not campaign vigorously, and Republicans pull off coup (October 24) with "Murchison letter," a letter to British ambassador written by a California Republican pretending to be naturalized Englishman puzzled about whom to vote for. British ambassador unwisely suggests that Cleveland is best choice, and Republicans raise cry of

"foreign interference." Many Irish-Americans are alienated by Murchison letter, which probably costs Cleveland New York and election. Popular vote (November 6): Cleveland 5,443,892, Harrison 5,534,488; electoral vote: Harrison 233, Cleveland 168.

Looking Backward, 2000–1887 published by Edward Bellamy; best-selling novel postulates future U.S. in which socialist government controls production and distribution of goods and in which competition has been eliminated because all citizens have economic security; Bellamy clubs spring up all over, but movement is not translated directly into political action, although idea of nationalizing some industries is adopted later by populists.

1889

Department of Agriculture achieves cabinet rank (February 9).

"Omnibus Bill" authorizes North Dakota, South Dakota, Montana, and Washington to apply for statehood (February 22); these territories have been clamoring for admission for several years, but since they were Republican politically, Democratic Congresses have blocked them; slight Republican majorities in both houses now permit entry, and these states join Union in November.

Benjamin Harrison inaugurated as twenty-third President (March 4); Levi P. Morton becomes Vice President.

American, British, and German warships in Apia Harbor, Samoa, are blown away by hurricane, which averts naval battle (March 16); diplomatic problem centering on German control of Samoa (with tacit British support), brewing since 1885, is finally settled by Treaty of Berlin (June 14), which provides for Samoan independence under three-power protectorate.

Oklahoma land rush (April 22): 2-million-acre tract in middle of Indian territory, unassigned to any tribe, is

Settlers in Guthrie, Oklahoma, during the land rush in 1889

thrown open to 100,000 would-be settlers, or "boomers"; at noon signal is given, and mad rush to stake out claims begins; by nightfall Oklahoma City and Guthrie have populations (in tents) of 10,000 and 15,000, respectively; in next four years 10 million additional Oklahoma acres, pried loose via the Dawes Severalty Act, are opened to similar "boomer" rushes.

Johnstown flood in Pennsylvania (May 31): shoddily built dam breaks, sending huge reservoir roaring down Conemaugh Valley. City of Johnstown, leading steel-making center, is drowned under 30 feet of water, at least 2,142 persons die (estimates range as high as 5,000), and about $10 million in property damage occurs.

"The Gospel of Wealth," article by Andrew Carnegie, published (June); Carnegie argues that great wealth, such as his own, is in effect held in trust and ought to be used to benefit the community as a whole by providing opportunities for the "fittest" members of society to rise through their own efforts (e.g., endowing libraries where the poor can educate themselves) and by providing (ultimately through foundations) venture capital for research and other projects that neither government nor profit-making concerns can afford to risk money on.

Jane Addams and Ellen Starr open Hull House, on Halsted Street in Chicago (September); is among the first of the privately supported settlement houses, in which poor immigrants are helped in various ways to adjust to American life and to improve slum conditions.

First International Conference of American States opens in Washington, D.C. (October 2); attended by seventeen Latin-American nations, conference eventually establishes permanent agency (later becoming Pan American Union) for exchanging information and lays groundwork for later tariff agreements between U.S. and South American countries.

Elizabeth Cochrane Seaman ("Nellie Bly"), reporter for New York *World,* begins attempt to beat record of Phileas Fogg, fictional character in Jules Verne's *Around the World in Eighty Days* (November 14); she does it, getting around the world by ship and train in 72 days, 6 hours, and 11 minutes.

Leaders of two great agrarian protest groups, Farmers' and Laborers' Union of America (southwestern) and Farmers' Alliance (northwestern), meet in St. Louis, Missouri (December); merger of two groups, having a hoped-for combined membership of perhaps 5 million, does not occur, but general agreement on goals is reached, namely, graduated income tax, government ownership of railroads, the breaking of large landholdings, and inflationary currency (greenbacks and silver); members disperse to work (successfully) for election of local candidates in congressional elections of 1890; many of farmers' goals are later incorporated in Populist Party platform of 1892.

1890

Dependent Pension Act (June 27): law makes eligible for pension all Union veterans mentally or physically unable to work (whether disability is war-related or not) and having 90 days' service; also gives benefits to dependent children and parents and widows of such veterans; by 1895 pension rolls number 970,000, up from 538,000 in 1890; from 1889 to 1903 the annual pension appropriation increases by about $50 million, to $135 million.

Federal election or force bill passes House (July 2); bill proposes federal supervision of southern elections to protect black voters, but bill's failure to pass Senate is interpreted in some southern states as a go-ahead to disenfranchise blacks openly and systematically.

Sherman Anti-Trust Act (July 2): ostensibly passed to regulate trusts, measure is actually worded so as to render labor unions and farmers' alliances illegal as forms of "conspiracy in restraint of trade or commerce." For first twenty years of its life measure is quite ineffective against economic monopolies—partly because it is not enforced and partly because Supreme Court decisions gravely weaken it—except when it is applied to labor unions.

Wyoming admitted as forty-fourth state (July 10); state's constitution is first to grant woman suffrage.

Sherman Silver Act (July 14): requires Treasury to buy 4.5 million ounces of silver per month at market price, issuing for it legal-tender notes redeemable in gold or silver; a compromise measure, it pleases neither the gold-standard faction nor the free-silverites, but it does have the effect of increasing money supply and weakening U.S. gold reserves.

McKinley Tariff (October 1): puts very high protective duties (about 50 per cent) on most manufactured goods; popular outrage at resultant higher prices is considered to be reflected in a Democratic and farmer-alliance sweep of local and congressional elections one month later.

Mississippi enacts "understanding" clause, making right to vote dependent upon potential voter's ability to understand and explain selected parts of state constitution (November 1); as applied locally, it disenfranchises many blacks or poor whites, depending on which group it suits local election officials to block out. Many other states enact similar clauses.

Massacre at Wounded Knee Creek, near the Pine Ridge Reservation in South Dakota (December 29): more than 200 Sioux men, women, and children are slaughtered by U.S. Army in one of last episodes in Ghost Dance War, which begins when Sioux and other Plains Indians try to make whites disappear by performing a special dance; inexperienced Indian agents panic at dancing, cause arrest and needless death of Sitting Bull (December 15), and send Sioux into one last frightened and desperate uprising.

U.S. census: total population 62,948,000. Approximately 40 per cent of increase over 1880 census comes from immigration, a total of 5,246,613 immigrants arriving in years 1881–90. For first time a significant number (almost a million) of these immigrants are from central and southern Europe rather than from northern Europe. Thirty-five per cent of population is now urbanized, and center of population has shifted to near Columbus, Indiana. U.S. census director declares that there no longer is a frontier, since all areas are settled, however sparsely.

How the Other Half Lives published by Jacob A. Riis; presents shocking report on conditions of urban poor.

U.S. Post Office Department censors *The Kreutzer Sonata* by Leo Tolstoy.

Alfred T. Mahan publishes *The Influence of Sea Power Upon History, 1660–1783*; book has considerable impact upon decision makers and reinforces trend toward accelerated U.S. naval build-up.

1891

Circuit Court of Appeals established (March 3); intermediate system of appellate courts is designed to ease case load of U.S. Supreme Court.

Forest Reserve Act (March 3): act repeals Timber Culture and Timber Cutting acts and authorizes President to close forested areas and establish national preserves; President Harrison sets aside 13 million acres of forest land, which later become national parks.

International Copyright Act (March 4): act protects British, French, Belgian, and Swiss authors against U.S. pirating of their works and protects sales and royalties of U.S. authors in those countries.

Thomas Edison applies for patent on "kinetoscopic" or moving-picture camera (July 31).

Congress authorizes construction of first nonmilitary federal prisons.

University of Chicago founded; funded primarily by John D. Rockefeller, school models itself after Johns Hopkins University (1876) in that it pays high salaries to top scholars in wide range of disciplines and stresses graduate studies and complete academic freedom.

1892

President Harrison demands, in so many words, a declaration of war against Chile (January 25); action comes in response to an 1891 attack on American sailors on shore leave in Valparaiso that leaves two dead and seventeen wounded; Chile offers apologies and an indemnity of $75,000, both of which are accepted.

Bering Sea controversy (February 29): U.S. refers conflict with Great Britain about who controls right to take seals in Bering Sea to international commission, which eventually denies U.S. right to control entire Bering Sea.

U.S. ends diplomatic crisis with Italy by offering $25,000 indemnity (April 12) for eleven Italian immigrants, of whom three were Italian nationals, lynched by a mob in New Orleans in previous year; Italian government accepts, and diplomatic relations are resumed.

Geary Chinese Exclusion Act (May 5): extends exclusion of Chinese workers for another ten years and provides for registration and deportation under certain circumstances.

Populist Party meets at nominating convention in Omaha, Nebraska (July 2–5); formally organized as the People's Party in February, Populists put forth platform (the "Omaha program") calling for graduated income tax, free and unlimited coinage of silver, government ownership of railroads and telegraph lines, expropriation of excessive railroad land grants, postal savings banks, shorter working hours, direct election of senators, widespread use of the referendum and initiative, limitation of the Presidency to one term, and restrictions on immigration. Populists nominate James B. Weaver (Indiana) and James G. Field (Virginia).

Homestead Strike (July 6): strike against Andrew Carnegie's steelworks in Homestead, Pennsylvania, erupts into violence when Pinkerton strikebreakers arrive; ten are killed and hundreds are wounded in ensuing battles; order is restored by state troops three days later, and strike is broken under their protection in next four months; steelworkers' union virtually destroyed as a result.

Coeur d'Alene, Idaho, strike (July 14): lead and silver miners battle strikers, and federal and state troops break strike under martial law.

Scenes from the steelworkers' strike, Homestead, Pennsylvania

Campaign of 1892: Democrats run Grover Cleveland and Adlai Stevenson (Illinois) on platform firmly supporting gold standard and hedging a bit on tariff, though clearly favoring a lower, nonprotective one; Republicans run Benjamin Harrison and Whitelaw Reid (New York) on platform supporting high protective tariff; Populists run Weaver and Field on Omaha program; Prohibition Party runs John Bidwell (California); Socialist Labor Party runs Simon Wing (Massachusetts). Popular vote (November 8): Cleveland 5,551,883, Harrison 5,179,244, Weaver 1,024,280, Bidwell 270,770, Wing 21,163; electoral vote: Cleveland 277, Harrison 145, Weaver 22. (Populists carry Kansas, Colorado, Idaho, and Nevada and win many state and local offices.) Democrats gain majorities in both houses of Congress.

1893

Revolution in Hawaii (January 16–17): Hawaiian-born American missionary and sugar interests overthrow native Hawaiian ruler with help of U.S. Marines, landed without U.S. approval by American envoy to Hawaii; provisional government declared by Sanford B. Dole, who then submits treaty of annexation to U.S. Senate (February 15); Senate does not ratify it.

Diplomatic Appropriations Act (March 1): creates diplomatic rank of ambassador.

Grover Cleveland is inaugurated as twenty-fourth President (March 4); Adlai Stevenson becomes Vice President.

President Cleveland withdraws proposed treaty of Hawaiian annexation (March 9); he sends special commissioner to Hawaii to investigate; four months later commissioner reports that coup was instigated by American sugar interests and has no popular support;

Cleveland orders American-led provisional government to restore native rule, but it refuses, and Cleveland is unwilling to use force against it. Cleveland denounces provisional government (December 18) and states that he will not permit annexation, but provisional government remains a *fait accompli.*

Panic of 1893 (April 21): U.S. gold reserves fall below $100 million, a number widely believed to represent the sound currency line, as a result of high tariffs, high pension payments, and foreign selling of U.S. securities. Commodity prices dive, and the stock market crashes (June 27); by end of year almost 500 banks have closed, 15,000 businesses have failed, and one third of nation's railroads are in bankruptcy. Depression lasts four years.

Illinois Governor John Peter Altgeld pardons three Haymarket conspirators, citing rigged jury, fake evidence, and judicial bias (June 26); for this act and for his protest against federal strikebreaking during Pullman strike of following year Altgeld is branded a radical and hounded from public life.

Duryea brothers successfully test improved version of their 1892 horseless buggy in Massachusetts; Henry Ford successfully tests gasoline buggy in Detroit.

Congress repeals Sherman Silver Purchase Act (October 30); during two-month special-session congressional debate President Cleveland strongly urges repeal and is successful, but his antisilver position splits Democratic Party.

Colorado becomes second state to adopt woman suffrage (November 7).

"Coxey's Army" marching from Ohio to Washington, D.C.

1894

"Coxey's Army" marches on Washington, D.C. (March 25–May 1); populist Jacob Coxey leads 400–500 unemployed to Capitol, demanding public-works program; "army" fizzles when Coxey and other leaders are arrested for trespassing on government property.

Pullman strike begins as strike of Pullman car workers against wage cuts and financial exploitation by company town of Pullman, a suburb of Chicago (May 11); Eugene Debs's recently formed American Railway Union joins in sympathy, refusing to handle Pullman sleeping cars (June 26); an injunction is issued against Debs on basis that his union is interfering with U.S. mails; President Cleveland orders in federal troops over protest of Illinois Governor Altgeld, and violence results (July 3); Debs is arrested (and later jailed), injunction is enthroned as strikebreaking tool, and Pullman workers are rehired if they sign no-union pledge and blacklisted if they don't.

Provisional government of Hawaii proclaims itself Republic of Hawaii, with Sanford Dole as president (July 4); President Cleveland recognizes new government on August 7.

First graduated income tax (August 28): attached as rider to Wilson-Gorman Tariff, which lowers tariffs somewhat and which Cleveland allows to become law without his signature; Supreme Court declares income tax unconstitutional in following year, ultimately necessitating Sixteenth Amendment to Constitution.

Republicans gain majorities in both houses in congressional elections (November 4); Populists elect six senators and seven representatives.

1895

Federal government buys $62 million worth of gold from private banking syndicate headed by J. P. Morgan and August Belmont (February 8); repeal of Sherman Silver Act has not replenished government gold reserves, and the fact that Morgan and Belmont make $1.5 million profit on deal outrages Populists and free-silverites and results in widening split within Democratic Party.

Cubans begin fight for independence against Spain (February 24); President Cleveland urges Americans, who are mainly sympathetic, not to help rebels, who are destroying American sugar plantations and mills in an effort to get U.S. to intervene (June 12).

U.S. Secretary of State Richard Olney sends Great Britain belligerent note saying that U.S. intends to involve itself in a boundary dispute Britain is having with Venezuela (July 20); when Great Britain rejects application of Monroe Doctrine, Cleveland practically threatens to go to war (December 17); British soon thereafter agree

to arbitration by special U.S. boundary commission, which in following year substantially upholds Great Britain's claims against Venezuela.

Sears, Roebuck Company opens mail-order business; gives isolated farm families and communities access to wide range of consumer goods.

1896

Utah admitted as forty-fifth state (January 4); Congress has been unwilling to admit it until Mormon church outlaws polygamy and until church elders somehow dispose of wives they had acquired before Congress made this practice illegal.

U.S. Congress resolves to accord Cuban rebels belligerent rights and offers to mediate a settlement with Spain (April 6); Spain rejects offer (May 22); yellow journalism of Hearst's and Pulitzer's New York papers fans sympathy for rebels with accounts of Spanish General Valeriano "Butcher" Weyler's notorious concentration camps.

Plessy v. *Ferguson* (May): Supreme Court rules that "separate but equal" segregation of blacks in public accommodations is constitutional, thus legalizing Jim Crow practices, which have increasingly been in force since 1890 and are directly related to Populist gains in South.

Campaign of 1896: Republicans run William McKinley (Ohio) and Garret A. Hobart on platform supporting gold standard, high protective tariff, and U.S. annexation of Hawaii; Democrats run William Jennings Bryan (Nebraska) and Arthur Sewell (Maine) on free-silver platform with Populist overtones; Bryan has electrified nominating convention with "cross of gold" speech and stolen free-silver issue Populists had unwisely made their main one; Populists back Bryan but run Tom Watson as Vice President; "gold Democrats" and "silver Republicans" bolt their respective parties. Bryan travels 18,000 miles during campaign; McKinley, under direction of campaign manager Marcus Hanna, runs "front-porch" campaign, a very cleverly managed affair in which representative groups from all over country are brought to McKinley's home and their views and McKinley's replies (especially those emphasizing Bryan's "radicalism") are given wide press coverage. Popular vote (November 3): McKinley 7,108,480, Bryan 6,511,495; electoral vote: McKinley 271, Bryan 176. Republicans maintain control of Congress.

1897

Cleveland vetoes immigration bill (March 2); veto is based on literacy-test requirement, which Cleveland correctly calls "a radical departure from our national policy."

William McKinley is inaugurated as twenty-fifth President (March 4); Garret A. Hobart becomes Vice President.

Yukon gold rush begins (June); news of strike, made in 1896 on Klondike River in Yukon Territory, reaches West Coast and causes thousands to trek to this region through Alaska; in July shipments of gold worth $1.5 million reach West Coast.

Gold miners en route to the Yukon pose in their Alaska camp.

Dingley Tariff (July 7): special session of Congress passes highest protective tariff ever.

First subway is completed, in Boston; streetcars run on one-and-a-half-mile roadway cut below street level and then covered over.

Economy revives, in part because gold-standard issue has been settled by 1896 election and in part because nation's gold supply expands as a result of new gold discoveries and new methods of refining gold-bearing ore.

1898

Private letter written by Dupuy de Lôme, Spanish minister to U.S., describing McKinley as "weak" and a "cheap politician," is printed by Hearst's New York *Journal* (February 9), further inflaming pro-Cuban, anti-Spanish public opinion.

U.S.S. *Maine* blows up in Havana Harbor (February 15); 260 American crewmen die in explosion, which is assumed to have been caused by Spain; a later inquiry establishes (May 28) that a mine attached to hull set off *Maine*'s powder magazine, but who planted mine is never established, although Cuban revolutionaries stood to gain most by such an action.

The sinking of the Maine *arouses U.S. demand for revenge.*

BOTH: LIBRARY OF CONGRESS

Pacific fleet ordered to prepare for war in Philippines (February 25); Assistant Secretary of State Theodore Roosevelt orders Hong Kong-based U.S. fleet to make ready to attack Spanish fleet in Philippines if war breaks out.

U.S. government tells Spain that it does not wish to annex Cuba but demands an armistice between rebels and Spanish forces and an end to Weyler's concentration camps (March 27); Spain agrees to U.S. demands on April 9.

McKinley yields to intense public pressures for war and, ignoring Spanish concessions, asks Congress for resolution authorizing use of force to free Cuba (April 11); Congress obliges on April 19, although the Senate vote is fairly close, 42 to 35.

U.S. sets up naval blockade of Cuba, captures one Spanish ship, and authorizes volunteer army of 200,000 (April 22); two days later Spain declares war on U.S., with U.S. (April 25) issuing formal declaration of war against Spain made retroactive to April 21.

Battle of Manila (May 1): U.S. fleet (four modern steel cruisers and two gunboats) under command of Commodore George Dewey makes mincemeat of decrepit Spanish fleet and obsolete shore batteries; no American ships are damaged, and only seven to nine American seamen are wounded; Spanish lose 381.

Grandfather clause adopted by Louisiana (May 12); new state constitution disenfranchises black voters through literacy tests and poll taxes but protects illiterate white voters through provision that those whose grandfathers voted before 1867 may be exempted from literacy test; number of black voters in Louisiana goes from 130,000 in 1896 to 5,000 in 1900, and similar legislation is adopted by many southern states.

Spanish fleet is blockaded in Santiago Harbor (May 29); Spanish fleet attempts to break out but is demolished (July 3); Spanish losses in this engagement are 323 killed, 151 wounded, and 1,750 captured; U.S. losses are 1 killed, 1 wounded.

Island of Guam captured by U.S. warship (June 20); when U.S. cruiser shells island, Spanish commander sends message that he cannot return salute, because he has no ammunition.

U.S. expeditionary force (17,000) arrives in Cuba (June 22); on July 1 this force, including volunteer Rough Riders under Theodore Roosevelt, takes San Juan Hill and village of El Caney, sustaining relatively heavy casualties; force now commands heights overlooking Santiago and Spanish fleet.

Congress passes joint resolution annexing Hawaii, and McKinley signs it (July 7); joint resolution is used because Senate cannot muster two-thirds majority required for treaty of annexation.

City of Santiago, Cuba, surrenders to U.S. forces (July 17).

Puerto Rico captured by U.S. forces (July 25–28).

U.S. expeditionary force returns from Cuba (August 1–4); many of troops are dying of food poisoning and yellow fever.

U.S. peace terms accepted by Spain (August 12); terms include cession of Puerto Rico and Guam, end of Spanish rule in Cuba, and U.S. control of Philippines until matter can be settled.

Battle of Manila (August 13–14): U.S. and Filipino rebels under Emilio Aguinaldo take Manila, unaware that fighting has stopped; U.S. ultimately decides to keep Philippines.

Treaty of Paris signed, formally ending Spanish-American War (December 10); Spain cedes Philippines to U.S. for $20 million, gives up Cuba and assumes $400 million Cuban debt, and cedes Guam and Puerto Rico to U.S.; direct military costs of Spanish-American War are about $400 million and 5,462 dead, of whom only 379 die in battle.

Teddy Roosevelt and his Rough Riders capture San Juan Hill.

Troops hear that the U.S. has won the Spanish-American War.

THE BIG STICK.

PRESIDENTS CHAIR

25 per cent PROFIT

PLEASE HELP THE POOR FOREIGN BOND HOLDER. T.R.

SOUTH AMERICA REPUBLIC

A cartoon criticizes Teddy Roosevelt for threatening intervention if the Caribbean countries default on their European debts.

World Power and the Progressive Era

1899–1918

This period began in January of 1899, when President William McKinley announced that the United States intended to keep the Philippines and develop, civilize, and educate the Filipinos, training them in the "science of self-government." It ended in December of 1918, when President Woodrow Wilson departed a surprised and somewhat disgruntled United States for the Paris Peace Conference, where he hoped to secure a liberal peace treaty and thereby give Europe a lesson in the science of self-government.

The years 1899–1918 were dominated by foreign-policy issues and war, boisterous political struggles at the national level, and vigorous, often opinionated public men in high office. The period has an aggressive,

action-filled quality to it that has guaranteed it a prominent place in the textbooks. But though a lot of dust and feathers flew during this period, they have long since settled. It is now possible to see that much of the political activity was in fact reactivity and that much of it was essentially conservative in nature.

William McKinley was a kind and generous soul, but he fought a nasty guerrilla war in the Philippine Islands to secure them for the United States, keeping out all other interests.

Teddy Roosevelt found himself with a powerful navy and used it exuberantly to pressure several South American nations, thus earning from Hispanic America a suspicion and resentment of United States intentions that have long lingered. It is true that Roosevelt also grinningly rattled the Big Stick at just about everybody, including Canada and Great Britain during a 1903 dispute about an Alaskan boundary, and that he also referred several foreign disputes to international tribunals. But in relation to Latin America, Roosevelt and his successors, including Wilson, clearly proceeded on the assumption that the Southern Hemisphere was to remain within the sphere of United States political and economic influence, securely away from European meddling.

World War I was a somewhat different story. This war was a ghastly thing, and Wilson was perfectly right to want to stay out of it. But German U-boats were after all killing American citizens and weren't going to stop doing it; France and England, with whom the United States shared many traditions and interests, were going to fall if America didn't pitch in. And so, after three years of hesitation, the United States plunged into the war militarily—and all of a sudden it was over before the war effort had really hit high gear.

But the World War I that Woodrow Wilson wanted to fight wasn't the same muck-and-blood affair of trenches and treacherous U-boats that everybody else was fighting. *His* war was not only going to end all wars, but it was also going to make the world safe for democracy. It was a war to which Wilson asked Americans to commit "everything that we are and everything that we have" in order to conserve "the principles that gave [America] her birth and happiness and the peace which she has treasured." This war for the triumph of Jeffersonian ideals was going to be fought according to a perfectly progressive platform (the Fourteen Points), one that included a kind of superprogressive legislature for the entire world, namely, the League of Nations.

During Wilson's administration wartime propaganda pictured our enemies as the living embodiment of undiluted evil, setting off thousands of unofficial "patriotic" ripple effects that resulted in the burning of German-language books and the banning of German-language studies in public schools, gave impetus to the national Prohibition movement, which was seen as harming brewers and distillers—many of whom were Germanic in origin—and touched off a whole series of local, minor social persecutions of German-American citizens. At home Wilson's appeals for freedom, justice, liberalism, and democracy were so high and glorious and palpably fine that anything less than wholehearted agreement with them was looked on with suspicion.

In many respects Woodrow Wilson's idealism, his tendency to wrap everything in noble progressive or Jeffersonian rhetoric, and his administrations generally had fewer beneficial effects. Although it is possible to find in Wilson's fight for the League of Nations and for his vision of a new world order certain elements of high personal tragedy, it is also possible to find in his tenure much that was tragic for the country. Wilson's dream of a parliament of nations was a noble and correct one. But political arrangements, either on the national or the global scale, usually ratify existing economic and social reality; they can rarely transform it. The United States and the rest of the world were not socially and economically ready for a world legislature, and they still aren't.

World War I, especially after 1917, rang down the curtain on what is usually called the Progressive Era. But there is no longer full agreement on what the progressive movement was or what it accomplished or even hoped to accomplish. It used to be thought, for example, that the progressives were basically forerunners of New Deal liberals under a variety of party labels—Republican, Democratic, Bull Moose, Progressive, and even Socialist—who just got sidetracked by the war and the roaring twenties. But such an interpretation is no longer widely accepted, and a number of progressives were in fact appalled by the New Deal.

Both progressivism and later the New Deal were essentially political movements attempting to deal governmentally with new socioeconomic conditions, but these conditions were strikingly different. In the 1930's the nation was in a state of economic collapse and deep social shock. This was not the case in the years 1899–1914 or thereabouts. In this period the nation was, economically speaking, fat and sassy. Collectively, Americans were feeling rather secure. They perceived that the nation had changed and that this change posed certain problems, but large numbers of Americans were prosperous enough, aware enough, and free enough from fear to engage in a clear-eyed, fascinated probing of these new conditions that subsequent generations of Americans have some reason to envy.

There were two main problems. First, it had become obvious to many Americans that the nature of their social relationships had changed markedly. For increasingly large numbers of Americans, especially city dwellers, the old social controls typical of small communities—in which one knew one's neighbors, depended on them for a wide variety of services, and had to face them day in and day out for most of one's life—had vanished. It had become more and more likely that one was dependent for livelihood, housing, food, clothing, and various services like fire and police protection on giant institutions or on paid specialists who were personal strangers.

Individual middle-class urbanites could do very little about the factory conditions that produced the ham their families were going to eat. As individuals they could do little about the way in which the city environment as a whole was shaped and directed—they couldn't ostracize a corrupt machine boss or shame a whole slum into cleaning the streets. Only an organization of many individuals able to articulate certain shared demands and bring them to bear on a pressure point would enable the good citizen to have an impact on the things that mattered. In other words, political power was needed to effect change.

The progressives agitated at every level—municipal, state, and finally federal—for various devices like the initiative, the referendum, and the direct election of senators that would enable citizens acting as voters to gain access to political power. What they intended to do, and in many cases did do when they got power, was to make laws, commissions, and regulatory agencies that would institutionalize small-town social controls. Some of these controls were "natural" or fair, in effect placing the same kind of sanitary regulations on giant meat-packers that folks would naturally impose on the town butcher; others were not so liberal and emerged in the form of national Prohibition or state and local Jim Crow statutes.

Secondly, the new industrial nation was faced with a problem of distribution. America's industrial machine was now producing goods, services, and wealth in increasingly huge quantities; it also seemed to be producing a great sea of squalor and misery. Most of this squalor and misery was distributed among a large class of working poor, both native-born and immigrant. Was this inevitable or desirable? If not, what could or should be done about it? These were the questions that the progressives set about answering, and the various answers they came up with were partly a function of who the progressives were.

The progressive movement was pre-eminently a middle-class one; its theoreticians and leaders, many of them Protestant clergymen, were middle class and, more specifically, upper middle class. Before World War I the American upper middle class, mainly college-educated professionals and independent merchants, could command a lifestyle that today we would call rich—frequent and luxurious trips to Europe, large, comfortable town and country houses with many servants, and so forth. This group was largely committed to a set of social beliefs revolving around the notion that hard work ought to bring substantial rewards and that a "good" person was one of good morals and good education and hence was a believer in democracy, humanitarianism, equality of opportunity, social justice, and having a rather large say in running the country.

The progressives sympathized to a certain extent with

workers and were certainly appalled by the environments in which this class often lived and worked. But the progressives were of more than two minds about the whys of it all. Many suspected that these environments were, in the final analysis, the result of innate weakness of character, intelligence, or religion. Many progressives were unwilling to believe wholeheartedly that the slum-dwelling peasant Jew from Russia or peasant Catholic from Sicily wasn't really personally responsible for the ill health, squalor, vice, and other well-publicized inequities of the time. Others suspected that the various socialist or Marxian theories being popularized by labor leaders and local politicians were close to the truth and incorporated into their speeches rhetoric that today strikes us as verging on communistic. (We must keep in mind that Marxian or socialist ideas were very much in the air during this period, both in the United States and in Europe, and that before the Leninist revolution in Russia in 1917 these ideas were not tainted with the same suspicion and fear they later acquired in American life.)

Other progressives, especially women, were less concerned about why the poor were poor and simply plunged into material reforms at the local level, often with a clearly expressed understanding that they were doing so in order to prevent serious revolutionary or class upheavals. Most of the charities, reforms, and social-service functions later taken over by New Deal agencies were until the 1930's performed largely by middle-class women's groups who did everything from reforming the juvenile- or family-court system to making sure that garbage was picked up in poor neighborhoods.

In relation to the working class the progressives tentatively favored certain kinds of legislation also favored by labor organizations, especially laws seeking to control or eliminate child labor and to set certain limits on how many hours women could work, particularly in hazardous industries. But the progressives were in general hostile to organized labor, seeing in it just another form of the economic concentration or monopolizing tendency that seemed, like the trusts, to be somehow stifling America.

In relation to the very rich, the "plutocrats" whose wealth derived from the great industrial combines, the progressives were similarly ambivalent. They didn't like the trusts and monopolies, feeling that they had clearly gotten too big, too bossy, and too elusive. Some progressives were pained by the conspicuously lavish manner in which the very rich displayed their wealth, especially when there was so much abysmal poverty and privation also to be seen. But many believed that the very rich deserved to be, and not a few progressives hoped that they too might some day find themselves in that exalted class. Most progressives had absolutely no intention of tampering with the institution of private property, although a good many of them, including Teddy Roosevelt, toyed with the idea of nationalizing certain monopolies, especially the railroads.

As a result of all this progressive ambivalence, what emerged were a few relatively mild controls on the trusts, mostly in the form of laws whose stated purpose—if not effect—was to restore economic competition to American life. The progressives were instrumental in establishing the notion that the great industrial fortunes were at least in part social artifacts— accumulations made possible by the efforts of millions of Americans in the capacity of shareholders, workers, or consumers. Progressives thundered their approval when plutocrats like Andrew Carnegie or John D. Rockefeller cagily wondered out loud if their wealth was not something to be held in trust, and applauded long

and hard when such men did in fact philanthropically turn back part of their wealth into the public weal in the form of foundations, libraries, universities, museums set up to house their great private art or manuscript collections, and so on.

World War I actually accelerated the processes of economic concentration and organization against which many progressives had set their faces, and so to that extent their efforts were as naught. The progressive vision was essentially a Jeffersonian one, finding its nostalgic ideal not in the small farmer but in the small town and seeking by means of elections, legislative enactments, and regulatory agencies to conserve in American life something of the small town's predictability, equanimity, and pleasantness. In a sense, the main progressive achievement was one chiefly of style. After the progressives had done their work and had their say, the extreme disparity between the very poor and the very rich would never again be permitted to exist.

By 1900, when this Labor Day crowd filled Main Street in Buffalo, New York, the city was a prosperous business and trade center.

World Power and the Progressive Era (1899–1918)

1899

Philippine movement for independence from U.S. begins (January 5); revolutionary assembly and Emilio Aguinaldo, leader of Filipino rebellion against Spanish, declare independence from U.S. rule (January 23); Filipinos attack U.S. forces in Manila (February 4); U.S. war against Filipinos goes on until 1902, with atrocities characteristic of guerrilla warfare committed on both sides; about 70,000 U.S. troops used in war.

American infantry in the Philippines fire on Filipino rebels.
U.S. ARMY

Treaty of Paris ratified by Senate (February 6); ratification passes by two votes when William Jennings Bryan urges Democratic and Populist supporters to vote for treaty as means of technically ending war with Spain; many labor and Populist elements oppose Philippine annexation for selfish or ethnic reasons, while more principled opposition cites imperialism as alien to U.S. traditions; proimperialists argue for annexation on grounds of national prestige, economic advantage, and likelihood of foreign intervention should U.S. withdraw.

Anti-Imperialist League formed (February 17); includes wide spectrum of prominent Americans (Andrew Carnegie, Samuel Gompers, Mark Twain, Jane Addams, and Populist spokesmen) who oppose U.S. overseas expansion but also argue that "constitution follows flag," i.e., that if U.S. does own colonies, colonials should be U.S. citizens with all rights.

U.S. representatives attend world conference at The Hague, Netherlands (May 18–July 29); purpose is to discuss disarmament and abolition of certain weapons of war (bombs from balloons, poison gas), but conference fails to get anywhere on these topics; Permanent Court of International Arbitration is established, but submission of disputes to court is not compulsory.

Open Door Policy initiated (September 6); U.S. Secretary of State John Hay urges that European powers, having carved out spheres of influence in China, not discriminate against one another commercially; Hay's suggestion is not rejected in so many words, so he later (1900) announces that the Open Door Policy is in effect.

Samoan Treaty (December 2): Germany, Britain, and U.S. sign treaty, in effect splitting Samoa between U.S. and Germany; U.S. portion is administered by Navy, which has a similar role in Guam.

1900

Gold Standard Act (March 14): declares gold dollar the standard unit of value, makes all currency redeemable in gold, establishes $150 million gold reserve, and creates small rural banks as sop to agrarian interests.

Taft Commission appointed by McKinley (April 7); five-man commission, under Judge William Howard Taft, eventually establishes civilian government in Philippines, with Taft serving as governor (July 4, 1901); extends Bill of Rights protections, organizes city government, and promotes Filipino participation.

Foraker Act (April 12): establishes civilian government in Puerto Rico, with President appointing governor and eleven commissioners (five of whom are Puerto Rican); act creates popularly elected lower house, extends tariffs to Puerto Rican products, and defines Puerto Rico as unorganized territory without giving populace U.S. citizenship.

Campaign of 1900: Republicans run William McKinley and Theodore Roosevelt (against their wishes) on platform of gold standard, expansionist foreign policy, need for Panama Canal, and "the full dinner pail"; McKinley campaigns from his front porch, as he did in 1896, and Roosevelt travels, wearing Rough Rider hat; Democrats run William Jennings Bryan and Adlai Stevenson on anti-imperialist, free-silver platform, which alienates conservative Democrats; Socialist, Populist, and Prohibition parties also run candidates. Popular vote: McKinley 7,218,039, Bryan 6,358,345; votes for other candidates total 394,086; electoral vote: McKinley 292, Bryan 155. Republicans retain control of Congress.

U.S. troops sent to China to put down Boxer Rebellion (August 14); siege of Peking, in which American missionaries and other foreigners are under attack, is broken by international force, including U.S. Marines.

U.S. troops leave Peking at the end of the Boxer Rebellion.
LIBRARY OF CONGRESS

International Ladies' Garment Workers' Union founded in New York City; union is one of several crafts unions chartered by American Federation of Labor, with largely immigrant Jewish membership.

Census of 1900: total population 76,094,000, including about 3,688,000 immigrants who have arrived since 1891. About 40 per cent of population is urbanized. Three largest cities are New York City (3,437,202), Chicago (1,698,575), and Philadelphia (1,293,697). Center of population is now near Columbus, Indiana. In most northeastern states, and especially in cities, women outnumber men and have longer life expectancies.

1901

First large oil strike, at the Spindletop Well, near Beaumont, Texas (January 10).

United States Steel Corporation formed (February 23) by financial syndicate headed by J. P. Morgan and Elbert H. Gary; formed out of ten companies, including Andrew Carnegie's steel company, it represents world's largest industrial corporation and is capitalized at more than $1 billion.

Platt Amendment (March 2): attached to army appropriations bill, rider specifies conditions under which U.S. will withdraw troops from Cuba: Cuba is to make no treaties with other foreign nations, keep its public debt down, allow U.S. to intervene in Cuban affairs to preserve order and maintain Cuban independence, and allow U.S. to establish naval base on Cuban soil. Amendment is later incorporated in Cuban constitution (June 12), and U.S. withdraws troops in following year.

Inauguration of President William McKinley (March 4); Theodore Roosevelt is Vice President.

"Insular Cases" (May 27): Supreme Court upholds Foraker Act and in effect declares that territories acquired in Spanish-American War are neither foreign countries nor part of U.S. and that people living in these territories are not U.S. citizens.

McKinley shot in Buffalo, New York, by anarchist Leon F. Czolgosz (September 6); McKinley dies of gangrene on September 14, and Theodore Roosevelt becomes twenty-sixth President.

China signs treaty with U.S. and other nations, indemnifying losses incurred during Boxer Rebellion (September 7); U.S. share is $24.5 million, of which $18 million is used to educate Chinese students in U.S.

President Roosevelt invites Booker T. Washington to lunch at White House (October 16); action evokes strong southern protests.

Booker T. Washington
LIBRARY OF CONGRESS

Hay-Pauncefote Treaty signed with Great Britain (November 18); grants U.S. sole right to build, own, and run a canal across Isthmus of Panama; U.S. agrees to admit all shipping on nondiscriminatory basis.

Rockefeller Institute for Medical Research founded; among its first efforts is a campaign (1902) to eliminate hookworm, which is widespread among poor southern whites.

Roosevelt's first address to Congress (December 3) calls for a certain amount of supervision and regulation of large corporations.

Up From Slavery, best-selling autobiography of ex-slave, published by Booker T. Washington, now head of Tuskegee Institute in Alabama and leading black spokesman during late nineteenth century; represents a high point of "accommodation," or policy stressing economic self-help, largely through industrial and farm-oriented vocational education; policy also acquiesces in social segregation and political discrimination; although Washington succeeds in gaining extensive donations from northern philanthropists and enjoys support from many black businessmen, his policies are increasingly challenged by events (lynchings and Jim Crow laws get worse, and skills needed to run small farms do not provide much economic security in increasingly urbanized industrialized nation) and by other black spokesmen, notably William E. B. Du Bois, who insist more and more sharply upon political equality and elimination of social discrimination.

1902

Roosevelt causes prosecution of Northern Securities Company, a huge and unpopular railroad holding company, under Sherman Antitrust Act (February 18); U.S. Supreme Court later (1904) accepts government arguments and breaks up Northern Securities.

Oregon adopts initiative and referendum (June 2); enables people to initiate legislation by petition and to overturn actions of state legislature; procedure is copied by several states in next few years.

Reclamation Act (June 17): also called Irrigation Bill or Newlands Act, it authorizes government funding of irrigation projects in arid states and allows President to set aside public lands for parks.

Panama Canal authorized (June 28); Spooner Act allocates $40 million for construction of canal on Isthmus of Panama.

One of the huge locks in the Panama Canal under construction

Philippines Government Act (July 1): defines Philippines as unorganized territory, ratifies work of Taft Commission, and provides for increased self-government through popularly elected 80-member assembly; first elections held in 1907.

Roosevelt intervenes in Pennsylvania anthracite coal strike in manner perceived to be even-handed if not sympathetic to organized labor (October); after six-month strike by United Mine Workers for higher wages, eight-hour day, and union recognition has gained public sympathy, and railroads, which own mines, have lost it through arrogant refusals to cooperate in settlement, Roosevelt threatens to use troops to operate mines; commission to settle dispute is then established (October 16), and miners soon go back to work; commission later (1903) recommends 10 per cent wage increase but does not require recognition of union.

1903

U.S. Army General Staff Corps established (February 14); sets up general staff of military professionals for planning and coordinating tasks formerly performed by civil servants in War Department.

Department of Commerce and Labor established by President Roosevelt (February 14); includes a Bureau of Corporations empowered to investigate interstate corporations.

Elkins Act (February 19): strengthens Interstate Commerce Commission by specifying fines or imprisonment for railroad officials and others who give or receive rebates on published railroad shipping rates; courts generally interpret act in favor of railroads, however.

First direct primary adopted in Wisconsin (May 23); is one of several reforms developed under Wisconsin governor, Robert M. La Follette, later lumped together as so-called Wisconsin Idea and adopted by many other states; other Wisconsin reforms include limitations on campaign and lobbying expenditures and development of special regulatory and advisory commissions to aid lawmakers in areas requiring specialized technical knowledge.

First transcontinental auto trip (August 1): Packard car arrives in New York City after 52-day journey from San Francisco.

U.S. recognizes three-day-old Republic of Panama (November 6); after Colombia refuses to ratify treaty giving U.S. a canal zone, region of Colombia that is now Panama declares itself independent, with Roosevelt's tacit approval; U.S. warships promptly appear on scene to discourage any attempt on the part of Colombia to regain Panama; on November 18 U.S. and Panama sign treaty granting U.S. perpetual control of ten-mile-wide Canal Zone for $10 million, plus $250,000 annual lease; U.S. also guarantees independence of Panama.

First airplane flights at Kitty Hawk, North Carolina (December 17): Orville and Wilbur Wright make four flights (the longest, by Wilbur Wright, lasts 59 seconds and goes 852 feet) in first successful heavier-than-air flying machine.

Wilbur Wright examines the Wright brothers' 1903 airplane.
SMITHSONIAN INSTITUTION

"Muckrakers" Ida M. Tarbell and Lincoln Steffens begin publication of exposés in *McClure's* magazine; Tarbell's target is Standard Oil Company, while Steffens goes after corrupt big-city machines and their tie-ins with leading citizens.

The Great Train Robbery produced; first motion picture employing movement of camera (e.g., to provide close-ups) and fully developed plot.

1904

U.S. Supreme Court rules that although Puerto Ricans are not U.S. citizens, they are not aliens either and so cannot be denied entry to U.S. mainland (January 4).

Panama Canal Commission appointed (February 29); under its guidance rights of a French canal company, which had begun excavations in 1881, are acquired and construction is resumed, albeit with several false starts.

Campaign of 1904: Republicans run Theodore Roosevelt and Charles W. Fairbanks (Indiana) on conservatively drawn platform largely ignored by most voters, who perceive Roosevelt as vigorous progressive; Democrats run conservative Alton B. Parker (New York) and Henry G. Davis (West Virginia) on platform calling for more trustbusting and support of gold standard; big business contributes heavily to Roosevelt campaign, preferring impulsive candidate of conserva-

tive party to conservative candidate of impulsive party; five other parties run candidates, with negligible results. Popular vote (November 8): Roosevelt 7,626,593, Parker 5,082,898; electoral vote: Roosevelt 336, Parker 140 (representing "solid" South). Republicans retain control of Congress.

Roosevelt Corollary (December 6): in address to Congress, Roosevelt lays down variant of Monroe Doctrine holding that although European powers may not intervene in Latin-American affairs, the U.S. may, in order to exercise a "police power" and rectify "chronic wrongdoing" on part of South American governments. Policy statement comes in response to threat by European countries to force Dominican Republic to repay $22 million loan.

1905

Inauguration of Theodore Roosevelt (March 4); Charles W. Fairbanks is Vice President.

U.S. takes over Dominican Republic customhouses, collecting receipts and paying European creditors 55 per cent, turning over the rest for Dominican use (February 4); arrangement is later formally ratified by Senate in 1907, when U.S. withdraws.

Lochner v. *New York* (April 17): U.S. Supreme Court rules that a state may not regulate maximum hours; famous dissent by Justice Oliver Wendell Holmes calls attention to fact that Supreme Court is expressing social Darwinist economic assumptions that belong to another, earlier age.

First nickelodeon established, in Pittsburgh, Pennsylvania (June); three years later there are 8,000–10,000 of these establishments, which show silent flicks with piano accompaniment for a nickel.

Industrial Workers of the World ("Wobblies") formed in Chicago (June 27–July 8); started by Eugene Debs and William "Big Bill" Haywood, this fabled union enjoys some organizational success, principally among western miners and eastern textile workers, but also becomes a rich source of union legend, representing as it does a dream of "one great industrial union" subsuming the entire working class and doing romantic battle with the capitalists on a worldwide basis.

Treaty of Portsmouth signed in Portsmouth, New Hampshire (September 5); President Roosevelt, at Japan's request, mediates end of Russo-Japanese War and receives Nobel Peace Prize (1906) for his efforts.

Mount Wilson Observatory built near Pasadena, California.

Tammany official George Washington Plunkitt distinguishes between "honest graft" and "dishonest graft"; honest graft, according to Plunkitt, is taking advantage of inside information to buy up real estate that the city intends to acquire for some project; dishonest graft is shaking down brothels, saloons, and other shady establishments, and is something only the small fry engage in.

Niagara movement begun in meeting on Canadian side of Niagara Falls by W. E. B. Du Bois and 28 educated blacks; directly opposed to accommodationist policies advocated by Booker T. Washington, Niagara group calls for restoration of black voting rights and an end to all social, political, and economic discrimination based on color. Niagara movement derives much of its support from Du Bois' "talented tenth," or educated black elite—largely Northerners of free lineage—and fails to connect with majority of blacks, who are rural, poor, and are first- or second-generation ex-slaves. However, movement provides nucleus of black leaders who four years later participate in founding of NAACP.

1906

Act of Algeciras signed in Algeciras, Spain (April 7); U.S. is involved, as mediator, in entirely European issue involving status of Morocco but ends up siding against Germany.

San Francisco earthquake (April 18): devastating quake and resultant fires kill 700 and destroy most of central city, causing about $400 million in property losses.

Radio transmitter making voice transmission possible patented by Reginald A. Fessenden.

Fires burn in the rubble after the San Francisco earthquake.
LIBRARY OF CONGRESS

Hepburn Act passed (June 29); also known as Railway Rate Regulation Act, it empowers the Interstate Commerce Commission to set fair maximum shipping rates and to extend its jurisdiction to pipelines, sleeping-car trains, and bridges and to require uniform accounting procedures; commission's decisions are made binding,

so railroads are required to go to court in order to change them.

Pure Food and Drug Act passed (June 30); requires correct labeling of foods and drugs intended for interstate sale. This law, along with Meat Inspection Act passed the same day, comes partly in response to public disgust aroused by Upton Sinclair's muckraking fictional exposé (*The Jungle*) of the meat-packing industry in Chicago.

Cuban president asks U.S. help in putting down revolt; Roosevelt sends troops and appoints W. H. Taft provisional governor (September 29); Taft is later replaced by another U.S.-appointed governor, who rules until 1909.

Brownsville affair (November 5): Roosevelt dismisses with dishonor every soldier in A, B, and C companies (167 men) of the black 25th Regiment after it is charged that some black soldiers had fired into houses of white citizens in Brownsville, Texas; this incident, combined with serious race riots and a steady undercurrent of lynchings and floggings in some southern states, causes blacks to despair of equitable treatment by the federal government and by Teddy Roosevelt in particular; Army ultimately clears Brownsville soldiers of guilt in 1972.

Roosevelt visits Panama Canal Zone (November 9); it is the first time a U.S. President leaves the country while in office.

Heresy trial of Reverend Algernon S. Crapsey ends (December 4); ecclesiastical trial, which has been widely reported since its beginning in April, results in defrocking of former High-Church clergyman who has denied divinity of Christ.

First radio broadcast of voice and music by Reginald A. Fessenden (December 24); broadcast from Massachusetts is picked up by ships in West Indies.

1907

"Gentleman's agreement" with Japan (February 24): following 1906 earthquake San Francisco public-school system has ordered segregation of all Oriental pupils, which arouses Japanese public opinion to point of creating international crisis; Roosevelt works out agreement whereby schools will be desegregated if Japan clamps down on immigration of laborers to U.S., especially through U.S. territorial possessions; agreement is formalized on March 13, when school board rescinds segregation order, and on March 14, when Roosevelt issues executive order prohibiting further immigration of unskilled Japanese workers to continental U.S.

Panic of 1907: despite general prosperity, prices of stocks and corporate securities begin to tumble in March, which causes severe run on banks and stock-market panic in October; U.S. and J. P. Morgan each loan New York banks $25 million to prevent widespread collapse; panic ultimately leads to creation of Federal Reserve System.

U.S. Marines intervene in Honduras (March 21); Honduran revolution threatens banana plantations, largely owned by United Fruit Company, and Marines are dispatched to protect this property.

Panama Canal Commission reorganized (April 1); construction has lagged since 1905 owing to ravages of yellow fever and malaria and disagreement about whether canal should use locks or be cut at sea level; Roosevelt backs lock construction and appoints Lieutenant Colonel George Goethals to supervise work; Dr. William Gorgas, applying discoveries of Walter Reed, virtually eliminates mosquito-borne tropical diseases from site, and work proceeds.

Second Hague Peace Conference (June 15–October 18): U.S. proposal for world court is defeated, but conference passes resolution against use of force to collect debts owed to European nations by South American ones, thus reinforcing Roosevelt Corollary to Monroe Doctrine.

Oklahoma admitted as forty-sixth state (November 16).

Albert A. Michelson, of University of Chicago, becomes first American to win Nobel Prize in Physics (December 10).

"Great White Fleet" begins round-the-world cruise (December 16); fleet, which includes sixteen new battleships, is particularly designed to impress Japan; cruise takes two years.

Ziegfeld's *Follies* opens in New York City.

New York chorus girls pose with their leading man in 1909.

Western cattle and mining interests force repeal of Forest Reserve Act of 1891, under which Roosevelt has reserved 150 million acres of forest land; repeal is in form of rider attached to vital appropriations bill, but Roosevelt transfers an additional 17 million acres to federal reserves by executive order before he signs bill.

1908

"Danbury Hatters' case," or *Loewe* v. *Lawlor* (February 3): Supreme Court rules that industry-wide boycott by labor union constitutes restraint of trade under Sherman Antitrust Act.

Congress passes child-labor law in Washington, D.C. (May 28); this is only part of Roosevelt's plan to make Washington, D.C., a model progressive community (including factory inspection and slum clearance).

Child laborers in a coal mine, left, and a glassworks, right

Aldrich-Vreeland Currency Act (May 30): emergency measure in response to banking crisis of 1907, it authorizes banks to circulate additional paper currency; establishes National Monetary Commission to study banking system; commission's findings are later incorporated in Federal Reserve System.

National Conservation Commission created (June 8), with Gifford Pinchot, chief of U.S. Forest Service, as head; commission begins first systematic study of nation's natural resources, a study deriving in part from the realization that no one environmental problem can be dealt with entirely separately and that nobody knows what U.S. resources really are.

Campaign of 1908: Republicans run Roosevelt's hand-picked successor, William Howard Taft (Ohio), and James S. Sherman (New York) on platform promising some sort of tariff reduction, further antitrust efforts, and continuation of Roosevelt's conservation and other policies; Democrats run William Jennings Bryan and John W. Kern (Indiana) on antimonopoly, pro–tariff-reduction platform; six other parties nominate candidates. Popular vote (November 3): Taft 7,676,258, Bryan 6,406,801; electoral vote: Taft 321, Bryan, 162. Republicans retain control of House and Senate.

Henry Ford introduces Model T (October 1); new no-frills car is designed for masses and revolutionizes auto industry and eventually many aspects of American society, including rural life; originally $850, price steadily goes down, and Ford furthermore encourages installment purchases; 19,000 Model T's are produced by 1909, 15 million by 1928.

Henry Ford
FORD MOTOR COMPANY

Jack Johnson becomes first official black American heavyweight boxing champion of the world (December 26); match takes place in Sydney, Australia.

Muller v. *Oregon*: Supreme Court declares that Oregon law setting maximum working hours for women is constitutional; case is further notable for "Brandeis brief," in which Louis D. Brandeis, attorney for Oregon, presents masses of statistical, sociological, economic, and historical data rather than standard legal arguments.

Women millworkers often spent long hours on their feet.
NATIONAL ARCHIVES

1909

Robert E. Peary, his black assistant Matthew Henson, and four Eskimos plant U.S. flag on North Pole (April 6); Peary's claim to be first to reach Pole is later disputed but sustained; in 1945 Congress honors Henson for his role.

National Association for the Advancement of Colored People (NAACP) founded in New York City (May); begun as a result of an appeal by Oswald Garrison Villard, grandson of William Lloyd Garrison, and signed by 60 prominent persons, including seven blacks, NAACP concentrates on court action designed to re-establish principle of legal equality; W. E. B. Du Bois is the sole black national officer and edits NAACP journal *The Crisis*; Booker T. Washington attempts to sabotage organization but fails, in part because of NAACP's prominent white leadership.

Congress passes Sixteenth Amendment, providing for an income tax (July 12); amendment is not ratified until 1913.

Payne-Aldrich Tariff Act signed by Taft (August 5); although act reduces tariff on some items, it raises rates on many others, disappointing public and infuriating many progressive Republicans who, like Taft himself, favor lower rates; calling it "the best tariff bill that the Republican Party ever passed," Taft begins split of Republican Party.

U.S. troops sent to Nicaragua (November 18); effect of military intervention is the dismantling of liberal regime hostile to foreign penetration (and a possible U.S. canal route).

Bakelite, an important industrial plastic, is patented by Leo H. Baekeland.

Herbert R. Croly publishes *The Promise of American Life*; not widely read, book is nevertheless influential in that its idea of New Nationalism, or control by the state of all large and powerful institutions according to criterion of public interest, is adopted by Theodore Roosevelt in 1912 campaign.

1910

Taft fires Gifford Pinchot from U.S. Forest Service (January 7); action comes after Pinchot and others had accused Secretary of the Interior Richard Ballinger of giving away federal lands to coal and hydroelectric interests; Pinchot-Ballinger controversy further alienates progressives.

Boy Scouts of America organized in Washington, D.C. (February 8).

Barney Oldfield sets new automobile speed record of about 133 mph at Daytona Beach, Florida (March 16).

Camp Fire Girls founded in Maine (March 17).

Progressive revolt in House of Representatives deprives conservative Speaker Joseph Cannon of crucial control over House Rules Committee (March 19).

Mann-Elkins Railroad Act (June 18): law further strengthens Interstate Commerce Commission and extends jurisdiction to communications industry (telegraph, telephone, and cable).

Congress sets up postal savings-bank system, which pays 2 per cent interest (June 25); long a populist demand, it allows people to deposit funds at post offices, which then usually transfer them to savings banks.

Publicity Act (June 25): requires that U.S. representatives enumerate campaign contributions received.

Mann Act, or White-Slave Traffic Act (June 25): prohibits transportation of women across state lines for purposes of prostitution; act represents legislative compromise in part reflecting enormous pressure by women's groups to do something about prostitution; although women's groups are sometimes sympathetic to plight of prostitutes, they do not want to appear to sanction prostitution by treating it as some reformers have suggested, i.e., by licensing, mandating health inspections, etc.

"New Nationalism" speech by Theodore Roosevelt in Kansas (August 31) is critical of conservative Supreme Court decisions and, in publicizing some of Herbert Croly's ideas, is widely assumed to be criticizing Taft administration for lack of initiative and vigor.

Democrats gain control of U.S. House of Representatives in fall elections (November 8); Victor Berger of Milwaukee, Wisconsin, is first Socialist to be elected to U.S. Congress; Senate is actually controlled by coalition of Democrats and progressive Republicans; 26 Democratic governors elected, including Virginia-born Woodrow Wilson of New Jersey.

First airplane is launched from deck of U.S. warship (November 14); ship is anchored at Hampton Roads, Virginia.

Census of 1910: total population 92,407,000, of which 8,795,386 are immigrants who have arrived since 1901, about 70 per cent coming from southern Europe, including more than 2,000,000 Italians, and from eastern Europe. About 46 per cent of population is urbanized. Illiteracy rate in persons over ten years of age has decreased to 7.7 per cent (down from 10.7 per cent in

1900); less than half the adult population has finished elementary school, and about 4 per cent is college-educated. About 75 per cent of U.S. black population is rural and lives in South.

1911

Senator Robert M. La Follette of Wisconsin organizes National Progressive Republican League (January 21); platform calls for direct election of U.S. senators and for other progressive reforms.

Robert M. La Follette
NATIONAL ARCHIVES

Electric self-starter for automobiles demonstrated (February 3); device eliminates need for laborious start with hand-turned crank.

U.S. troops are sent to Mexican border, where revolutionary forces under liberal Francisco Madero are battling against those of President Díaz (March 7); fighting is so close to border that U.S. crowds come to watch it; Taft demands that Mexicans fight elsewhere; U.S. troops are finally withdrawn in June, after Madero has won.

Triangle fire in New York City (March 25): 147 employees, mostly women and girls, lose their lives when fire sweeps top three floors of Triangle Waist Company; although owners are acquitted of any culpability, disaster leads to many reforms in municipal fire codes.

A parade held in memory of the victims of the Triangle fire
LIBRARY OF CONGRESS

U.S. Supreme Court orders breaking up of Standard Oil Company (May 15); Court holds that Standard Oil, monopoly that controls 33 companies, has engaged in unreasonable restraint of trade.

U.S. Supreme Court holds that tobacco trust represented by American Tobacco Company has unreasonably restrained trade and must be dissolved (May 29); this second application of the "rule of reason" thus places large combinations on notice that "reasonable" holding companies—those that do not ruthlessly eliminate competitors—will not be dealt with harshly.

Treaty is signed by U.S., Great Britain, Russia, and Japan barring pelagic sealing for fifteen years north of 30° parallel (July 7); move comes in response to threat of complete extermination of fur-bearing seals.

President Taft vetoes admission of Arizona to statehood (August 22) on grounds that Arizona constitution, which provides for (populist) recall of judges, violates independence of judiciary.

Canada rejects Taft proposal for reciprocal lowering of tariffs (September 21); well-meaning initiative by Taft to overcome Canadian resentment at Payne-Aldrich Treaty goes astray when U.S. proponents of Taft measure indulge in loose talk about annexing Canada, which maddens Canadian nationalists.

U.S. abrogates 1832 treaty with Russia following Russia's refusal to honor passports of Jewish Americans and certain American clergymen (December 18).

Frederick Taylor publishes *The Principles of Scientific Management*; Taylor, an inventor, engineer, and efficiency expert, has since 1900 been serving as consultant to increasing number of industries, showing them how to improve productivity through time-and-motion studies ("Taylorism"), including minute dissection of proper method of using a shovel to perform various tasks. Although Taylor's methods are basically humanitarian in impulse, seeking to eliminate impossible demands on workers, the total effect of his system is to lock workers more firmly into various man-machine processes, further subordinating workers' specifically human skills and qualities to the demands of technological systems.

Commercial production of synthetic fiber rayon begun.

1912

New Mexico admitted as forty-seventh state (January 6).

Textile workers at American Woolen Company, in Lawrence, Massachusetts, walk out after company cuts wages and institutes piecework system (January 12); millworkers and families—mostly Poles, Italians, and Russians—make up about half the population of Lawrence; Wobblies move in and conduct careful and atypical Wobbly campaign, in that violence against strikers is not paid back in kind; Wobblies finally win when they devise plan to send children of strikers to other communities in order to lessen drain on strike fund; police mercilessly bludgeon mothers and children who are on their way out of town; public opinion is outraged, and American Woolen Company yields to virtually all union demands.

Force is used to hold back American Woolen Company strikers.
LIBRARY OF CONGRESS

Arizona is admitted to U.S. as forty-eighth state (February 14); soon after admission it reinserts recall of judges into state constitution, a measure that Theodore Roosevelt has pointedly approved of.

Theodore Roosevelt publicly announces his candidacy for Republican presidential nomination (February 25); in preconvention primaries and caucuses he accumulates more than 200 delegates.

Senator Henry Cabot Lodge of Massachusetts torpedoes agreement with Great Britain and France calling for referral of international disputes to The Hague (March 7); agreement, designed essentially to restrain Japanese aggression in Korea and Manchuria, is wrecked by Lodge amendments involving Monroe Doctrine, Oriental exclusion, and senatorial veto.

British ocean liner *Titanic* smashes into iceberg and sinks (April 14–15); more than 1,500 die, including many prominent Americans; 20-year-old David Sarnoff (later head of Radio Corporation of America) catches radio message on set he is operating as publicity gimmick in Wanamaker's department store in New York City; President Taft orders all other stations off the air, and for 72 hours Sarnoff relays details of disaster to nation.

Awaiting the arrival of the survivors from the Titanic
LIBRARY OF CONGRESS

Republican National Convention meets (June 18); Roosevelt supporters are excluded by Taft-dominated national committee; Taft is nominated, with James S. Sherman, who dies shortly before election, as Vice President (June 22); progressive Republicans, supporting either Roosevelt or La Follette, denounce Taft nomination and bolt party. Republican platform calls for conservation, regulation of trusts, reform of currency and banking system, lower protective tariff, and anticorruption laws.

Democratic National Convention meets in Baltimore (June 25–July 2); Woodrow Wilson is nominated on 46th ballot, after William Jennings Bryan throws his support to Wilson. Thomas R. Marshall of Indiana is nominated for Vice President. Democratic platform is virtually identical to Taft Republican one.

Lodge Corollary (August 2): Senate passes resolution affirming U.S. right to veto sale of land by Latin-American countries to foreign powers if site is deemed "strategic"; resolution comes in direct response to proposed purchase by Japanese company of site on Baja California.

Progressive (Bull Moose) Party nominates Theodore Roosevelt and Hiram W. Johnson (California) in Chicago (August 5–7). Bull Moose platform calls for tariff revision; direct election of U.S. senators; nationwide primaries for selecting presidential candidates; the vote for women; elimination of child labor; the initiative, referendum, judicial and legislative recall; minimum wages for women; and stricter regulation of trusts. Platform is in effect a monument to La Follette progressivism, and party derives nickname from Roosevelt's statement that he feels "as fit as a bull moose."

Marines landed in Nicaragua again (August 14); U.S. bankers have loaned government $1.5 million, in return for control of Nicaraguan national bank and railroad and

American supervision of customs collection; popular discontent with these terms requires presence of U.S. troops, which do not finally withdraw until 1933.

Congress passes Panama Canal Act, which gives coastal U.S. shipping toll-free passage (August 24); a violation of treaty with Great Britain, act is repealed in 1914.

Campaign of 1912: although platforms of all three major parties are remarkably similar and progressive, Wilson introduces subtle but vague "New Freedom" slogan, which, by emphasizing federal regulation of competition, places him to right of Roosevelt, who urges more direct control of monopolistic corporations (New Nationalism), and somewhat to the left of Taft, who although having initiated some 90 antitrust actions is perceived as being the most conservative candidate. Campaign is further complicated by an attempted assassination of Roosevelt and by strong campaign by Eugene Debs, running as candidate of one of two socialist parties in race. Popular vote (November 5): Wilson 6,293,152, Roosevelt 4,119,207, Taft 3,486,333, Debs 900,369; electoral vote: Wilson 435, Roosevelt 88, Taft 8. Democrats gain control of both houses of Congress.

Alexis Carrel receives Nobel Prize in physiology and medicine (December 10); Elihu Root, president of Carnegie Endowment for International Peace (established 1910), receives Nobel Peace Prize.

1913

Parcel-post delivery by U.S. Post Office goes into effect (January 1).

President Taft vetoes immigration bill that imposes literacy tests for prospective immigrants (February 14); calls it contrary to U.S. traditions.

Armory Show in New York City opens (February 17); introduces Americans to contemporary European painting (cubist, abstract, impressionist).

Sixteenth Amendment, giving Congress power to levy income taxes, goes into effect (February 25).

Webb-Kenyon Act passed over Taft's veto (March 1); law prohibits interstate shipment of liquor to dry states, of which there are now nine.

Woodrow Wilson inaugurated as twenty-eighth President (March 4); Thomas R. Marshall becomes Vice President.

Congress separates Departments of Commerce and Labor into two separate cabinet-rank departments (March 4).

Dayton flood (March 21–26): Miami River in Ohio and

Indiana floods, killing 700, leaving 200,000 homeless, and causing at least $175 million in property damage; city of Dayton, Ohio, is devastated.

President Wilson personally delivers tariff message to Congress (April 8); is first time since 1800 that a U.S. President has appeared before Congress.

Secretary of State William Jennings Bryan negotiates "cooling off" treaties with 21 foreign countries (April 24); treaties provide that signatories will refer international disputes to international commission and wait one year before going to war.

John D. Rockefeller gives $100 million to establish Rockefeller Foundation (May 14).

Seventeenth Amendment, providing for direct public election of U.S. senators, goes into effect (May 31).

Underwood-Simmons Tariff Act (October 3): lowers duties to about 30 per cent average; act also levies 1 per cent tax on personal incomes over $3,000; average worker's annual income is well below $1,300.

President Wilson demands resignation of Mexican dictator Victoriano Huerta (November 7); Huerta, who has come to power through the assassination of reformist president Francisco Madero, has been recognized as legitimate ruler of Mexico by most European governments, although Madero's followers still control parts of Mexico; Huerta has gained support of American business interests, who have more than $1 billion invested in Mexico, but Wilson says he "will not recognize a government of butchers."

Wilson signs Federal Reserve Act (December 23); act sets up current national banking system, with twelve Federal Reserve Banks under supervision of Federal Reserve Board; system allows available supply of currency to be expanded or contracted as economic conditions warrant and bases currency on total commercial assets of member banks rather than strictly on amount of gold reserves; measure is passed over vigorous objections from banking community.

Henry Ford announces that he will pay workers unprecedented wage of $5 a day for a 40-hour week; move shrewdly compensates for drudgery of newly developed assembly line, gives Ford workers an income enabling them to purchase a Model T (they are fired if they are found owning anything but a Ford), and makes more tolerable Ford's paternalistic but totalitarian supervision (which leads to development of "Ford whisper," a way of talking without moving the lips).

Woolworth Building in New York City completed; 60-story, 792-foot-high building is tallest in world.

Workers on an early assembly line at the Ford Motor Company
FORD MOTOR COMPANY

1914

Mexican crisis (April 9–July 15): U.S. sailors are arrested by mistake in Tampico, Mexico, and released with apology; American naval commander demands ridiculous 21-gun salute as apology; Huerta refuses, and Wilson orders U.S. fleet to Tampico (April 14); U.S. Navy shells and occupies Veracruz (April 21) in order to stop delivery of German armaments to Huerta regime, against which U.S. has proclaimed an arms embargo; Tampico and Veracruz incidents unite all Mexicans, even those battling Huerta, against U.S. and bring countries to brink of war; ABC powers (Argentina, Brazil, and Chile) offer to mediate crisis, and offer is accepted (April 25); ABC commission rejects U.S. claims for indemnity but suggests that Huerta resign (June 30); liberals under Venustiano Carranza force Huerta's resignation, and crisis dissipates temporarily. In October, 1915, U.S. recognizes Carranza as head of Mexican government.

Acting upon a congressional resolution designating second Sunday in May as Mother's Day, President Wilson issues proclamation calling for observance by displaying American flag (May 9).

President Wilson issues proclamation of neutrality as World War I begins (August 4); controversy over neutral shipping rights begins almost immediately, and Wilson publicly asks Americans to be "impartial in thought as well as in action" (August 19).

Panama Canal opens to traffic (August 15).

Federal Trade Commission created (September 26); five-man commission is empowered to regulate business practices of those corporations engaged in interstate commerce not covered by Interstate Commerce Commission.

Clayton Antitrust Act (October 15): greatly strengthening Sherman Antitrust Act, it also exempts farm and labor organizations from "restraint of trade" clause and reduces use of injunction as strikebreaking tool.

British declare North Sea a military area and seize foodstuffs delivered to neutral northern European nations (November 3); U.S. does not protest and permits U.S. bank to loan France $10 million (November 4).

Theodore W. Richards becomes first American to receive Nobel Prize in chemistry, for work on atomic weights (December 10).

Robert H. Goddard patents liquid-fuel rocket.

Charlie Chaplin and Marie Dressler star in Mack Sennett's full-length comedy *Tillie's Punctured Romance*.

1915

First transcontinental phone call made from New York City to San Francisco (January 25); callers are Alexander Graham Bell and Thomas A. Watson, and message is same one delivered in 1876: "Mr. Watson, come here, I want you."

Congress creates U.S. Coast Guard (January 28).

D. W. Griffith's *Birth of a Nation* opens in Los Angeles (February 8); it is a cinematic masterwork, but its sympathetic treatment of Ku Klux Klan during Reconstruction period and racist portrayal of blacks evoke strong and legitimate protest.

U.S. announces that German interference with U.S. shipping is unacceptable and that Germany will be held strictly accountable for loss of American life (February 10); announcement comes in response to declaration by Germany six days earlier that neutral shipping entering war zone around British Isles does so at own risk.

Nevada establishes "quickie" divorce law (February 23).

British passenger liner *Lusitania* sunk by German U-boat (May 7); 1,198 die, including 128 Americans; American public opinion is outraged.

Third "Lusitania note" from Wilson to Germany (July 21): strongest of three protests (Secretary of State Bryan has resigned over second note, which he fears will bring war), it is virtually an ultimatum, stating in effect that further loss of American life on high seas will be considered result of deliberate hostility.

U.S. Marines land in Haiti to protect U.S. business interests during a revolution there (July 28); Haiti becomes in effect a U.S. protectorate.

"Plattsburg idea": military training camp for civilians who pay own expenses while being trained by regular army officers is experimented with in Plattsburg, New York, by group of New York professional and businessmen who favor preparedness (August 10); notion is widely condemned by various pacifist organizations and receives no support from Wilson until November; by summer of 1916, 16,000 are enrolled in Plattsburg-type camps.

U.S. Secret Service leaks details of German sabotage and spy ring to New York *World* (August 15); several German consulate officials and German-Americans are implicated.

German ambassador announces that passenger liners will no longer be sunk without warning (September 1); new German policy, following inadvertent sinking of British liner *Arabic*, which cost two American lives, is adhered to for rest of year.

American bankers, organized by J. P. Morgan and Company, float $500 million loan to France and Great Britain (October 15).

Henry Ford charters "peace ship" *Oskar* II and sails for Norway, hoping to negotiate end of war (December 4).

Wilson addresses Congress on necessity for comprehensive plan for national-defense preparedness (December 7).

New York Society for the Suppression of Vice hauls Margaret Sanger into court for writing *Family Limitation*, pioneer work on birth control; court finds book contrary to laws of state and God and jails Sanger.

Margaret Sanger, left, well-known birth-control advocate

NAACP wins first significant court battle when U.S. Supreme Court declares "grandfather clause" unconstitutional; immediate effect seems to be a revival of Ku Klux Klan in several southern states, beginning with Georgia.

1916

Wilson appoints Louis D. Brandeis to Supreme Court (January 28); Brandeis is sworn in on June 3, becoming first Jew to sit on Court.

House-Grey Memorandum (February 22): Wilson's personal advisor, Colonel Edward House, draws up agreement with British Foreign Secretary Edward Grey stipulating that U.S. will call for negotiated peace if Britain and France request such a move; if Germany rejects U.S. offer to negotiate, U.S. will "probably" fight Germany.

Despite Germany's warning that all Allied shipping will be sunk without warning as of March 1, Wilson demands that Congress not adopt resolutions restricting right of Americans to travel on Allied (French and British) ships subject to German attack (February 24).

Francisco "Pancho" Villa, angered by U.S. support and recognition of Mexico's Carranza government, crosses U.S. border and shoots up town of Columbus, New Mexico (March 9); with President Carranza's initial consent, Wilson orders General John J. "Black Jack" Pershing to cross into Mexico in pursuit of Villa; Villa cleverly draws Pershing deeper and deeper into Mexican territory, eventually causing alarm and anger among Mexican populace and a demand for Pershing's withdrawal, which does not come about until 1917.

General Pershing pursuing Francisco "Pancho" Villa in Mexico
LIBRARY OF CONGRESS

Wilson issues sharp ultimatum to Germany (April 18); threatens to break off relations as result of *Sussex* episode (March 24), in which French steamer in English Channel is sunk, with injury to American passengers; Germany agrees not to torpedo unarmed merchant ships any more (May 4).

National Defense Act (June 3): act provides for three-part organization of U.S. armed forces, expanding Regular Army to 175,000, establishing a National Guard (450,000) to replace state militias, and creating organized reserve force, including a Reserve Officers' Training Corps.

Wilson signs bill providing $5 million in matching federal funds for state highway construction (July 11); there are now about 3.5 million cars and trucks operating in U.S.

Federal Farm Loan Act (July 17): establishes regional banks in which farmers can get cheap, long-term credit and finances large-scale investment in farm machinery and opening of marginal crop lands to meet war-related demands for greater agricultural production.

Munitions dump in New Jersey blown up by German saboteurs (July 30).

U.S., fearing Germany has designs on territory as naval base, buys Virgin Islands from Denmark for $25 million (August 4).

Council of National Defense established (August 29); provides for overall civilian and military planning related to all phases of possible war effort.

Wilson signs law mandating eight-hour day for most railroad workers (September 3); measure averts threatened nationwide strike and gains Wilson additional labor support.

Shipping Act (September 7): creates Emergency Fleet Corporation, with $50 million to build, buy, or lease merchant vessels.

Campaign of 1916: Republicans nominate Supreme Court Justice Charles E. Hughes and Charles W. Fairbanks; Theodore Roosevelt refuses nomination of Progressive Party, which thereupon virtually collapses as a significant political organization at the national level; Democrats renominate Wilson and Marshall, who run on platform defending domestic record and foreign policy of "He Kept Us Out of War." Wilson receives heavy support from women in western states with suffrage, whereas Hughes receives heavy support from Irish-Americans and German-Americans (who feel Wilson's policies are too pro-British) and from those at other end of spectrum, who wish U.S. to get into war with Germany faster. Popular vote (November 7): Wilson 9,126,300, Hughes 8,546,789; electoral vote (which hangs in balance for three days until California passes into Democratic column by 3,773 votes): Wilson 277, Hughes 254.

U.S. troops occupy Dominican Republic after revolution breaks out (November 29).

Germany announces willingness to enter into peace negotiations (December 12); Wilson asks all warring parties to state their war aims (December 18); Germany refuses to do so.

1917

Foundry in New Jersey is exploded by German saboteurs (January 11), causing $33 million worth of damage.

Wilson urges "peace without victory," meaning an end to the war without a vindictive settlement, in speech to Congress (January 22); he also mentions need for international organization to guarantee "a lasting peace among equals."

Wilson vetoes immigration bill requiring literacy test (January 29); bill is later passed over veto, as is second immigration act, which excludes virtually all Asian immigration (February 5).

Germany informs U.S. (January 31) that virtually unrestricted submarine warfare will be resumed as of February 1.

U.S.S. *Housatonic* is sunk by German submarine after warning is given (February 3).

U.S. breaks off diplomatic relations with Germany (February 3).

"Zimmermann note" published (March 1); telegram, decoded by British and turned over to Americans on February 24, contains proposal by German foreign secretary, Arthur Zimmermann, that should U.S. go to war against Germany, a Mexican-German-Japanese alliance be formed, with Mexico promised return of New Mexico, Texas, and Arizona.

Organic Act for Puerto Rico (March 2): act organizes Puerto Rico as American territory and confers U.S. citizenship on Puerto Ricans.

Woodrow Wilson inaugurated (March 5) for second term; Thomas R. Marshall is Vice President.

Senate, called into special session by Wilson, adopts cloture rule (Rule 22), enabling a majority of senators present to cut off debate (March 8); action is taken as a result of filibuster against arming merchant ships.

Wilson directs that all U.S. merchant ships headed for war zones be armed (March 12–13); takes action under executive statute after Senate group, led by Robert La Follette, filibusters to death Wilson's request for congressional authorization to arm ships.

Wilson asks Congress for declaration of war against Germany as result of sinking of four U.S. merchant vessels (April 2); says that "world must be made safe for democracy" and that U.S. will "fight without rancor and selfish object"; Congress passes resolution on April 6, Wilson signs it, and U.S. is formally in World War I.

Wilson creates Committee of Public Information (April 14); under leadership of journalist George Creel, committee begins massive patriotic propaganda campaign in which war is wrapped in idealistic and progressive rhetoric and Germans are pictured as cave men seeking world domination; as a result of the superpatriotic enthusiasms generated by the Creel committee sauerkraut becomes "liberty cabbage," but, more importantly, dissent becomes treason.

Liberty Loan Act (April 24): authorizes sale of bonds to pay for war; public ultimately subscribes to more than $20 billion worth from 1917 to 1919.

Selective Service Act (May 18): under law almost 3 million men are drafted, and eight times that many are registered.

President Wilson prepares to select the first draft numbers.

General John "Black Jack" Pershing arrives in Paris, in advance of American Expeditionary Force (June 14); Pershing's nickname derives in part from esteem in which he holds U.S. black combat units, which he commanded in Spanish-American War and in Mexico.

Espionage Act (June 15): provides for maximum 20-year prison sentence and maximum fine of $10,000 for hindering the war effort; also provides for post-office censorship of materials deemed seditious.

War Industries Board created (July 28); is designed to set manufacturing priorities for war-related industries.

Lever Food and Fuel Control Act (August 10): gives President wide powers to fix prices and otherwise promote production and conservation of foodstuffs and fuels; act also forbids manufacture or importation of hard liquor.

War Revenue Act (October 3): increases personal and corporate income taxes, imposes excess-profits tax, and steeply raises excise taxes on luxuries, liquor, and entertainment.

Four women picketing White House for right to vote are arrested and given jail sentences of from six days to six months (October 16).

First U.S. troops, which Pershing insists remain under U.S. control, are moved to battlefront near Verdun, France (October 21).

Lansing-Ishii agreement with Japan (November 2): ambiguous agreement seemingly recognizes Japan's aggressive gains in Manchuria and yet seemingly commits Japan to respect China's territorial integrity and U.S. Open Door Policy.

Congress sends Prohibition amendment to states for ratification (December 18); culmination of long temperance campaign that has resulted in passage of dry laws in 29 states, measure gains strength from fact that many brewers and distillers are of German ancestry and that grains and other foodstuffs are needed for U.S. armed forces and Allies.

U.S. Railroad Administration created (December 26); government takes over operation and coordination of U.S. railroad industry.

1918

Wilson, in speech to Congress, outlines fourteen points he considers will form basis for lasting peace (January 8): some of points include (1) "open covenants of peace openly arrived at," (3) removal of trade barriers, (4) disarmament, and (14) a general association of nations. The French premier, Georges Clemenceau, is reported to have remarked, upon hearing of Wilson's Fourteen Points, that the Good Lord himself only had ten.

Bolshevik government of the Soviet Union, under Nikolai Lenin, signs separate peace with Germany (March 3); Bolsheviks, who took over middle-class revolutionary regime in November of 1917, have denounced war as "imperialistic" and publicized a number of secret Allied treaties that make it look that way, thus making Wilson's idealistic Fourteen Points seem all the more attractive to many of world's peoples; immediate effect of Communist peace treaty is to free large numbers of German troops from Russian front, thus giving Germany a numerical advantage in France and making American military aid vitally important.

Wilson reorganizes War Industries Board and appoints financier Bernard Baruch as head, with sweeping powers (March 4).

In order to conserve electricity Congress enacts law, to take effect March 31, establishing Daylight Saving Time.

National War Labor Board established (April 8); function is to arbitrate labor disputes, prohibiting strikes but also recognizing right of labor to organize and bargain collectively.

First scheduled air-mail delivery, between Washington, D.C., and New York City (May 15).

Sedition Act (May 16): makes it crime to "utter, print, write or publish any disloyal, profane, scurrilous, or abusive language" in relation to war bonds, the government, the flag, the draft, or anything, such as Red Cross, remotely connected with war; aimed largely at Socialists and pacifists (Socialists Eugene Debs and Representative Victor Berger were snared by it), it also catches up many others, including a Hollywood movie producer who is sentenced to ten years in jail because his movie about Revolutionary War shows British lobsterbacks in bad light.

American Railway Express Company formed with government support (May 28); a merger of more than six shipping companies, it is the kind of combination progressives had tended to denounce not very long ago.

About 27,500 American troops are involved in Allied counteroffensives at Château-Thierry and Belleau Wood (June 3–July 1), in which German advance on Paris is checked.

Second Battle of Marne (July 18–August 6): about 270,000 U.S. troops take part in counteroffensive that pushes German line back about 30 miles, from Marne River to Aisne River, thus eliminating threat to Paris (which could be shelled by supercannon Big Bertha) and turning tide of war. From now on, Allies are on offensive. Poet Joyce Kilmer, author of one of America's beloved poems, "Trees," is killed during this battle (July 30); no unshattered tree could be found, so he was buried near a stump.

About 550,000 American troops, under direct command of General Pershing, capture 16,000 German prisoners in successful assault on Saint-Mihiel salient (September 12–16).

U.S. troops pour into Saint-Mihiel in September, 1918.
U.S. SIGNAL CORPS

Eugene V. Debs is sentenced to ten years in prison for sedition as a result of making a speech in which he said Socialists did not support the war and in which he denounced arrests taking place under 1917 Espionage Act (September 14).

Huge Meuse-Argonne offensive, involving 896,000 Americans, begins (September 26); horrible battle in Argonne Forest costs 120,000 Americans killed or wounded, but advance threatens vital German railroad supply network, and before official end of Meuse-Argonne campaign (November 11) Germans know they are beaten and have called for peace negotiations.

American soldiers in the ravaged Argonne Forest in France
U.S. SIGNAL CORPS

Influenza pandemic sweeps through U.S. (October); coming from Europe and appearing in eastern cities in September, it spreads throughout U.S., ultimately taking about 500,000 lives and leaving many with permanently impaired health before it peters out in 1919; worldwide, the pandemic kills 20 million people.

Democrats lose control of House and Senate in congressional elections (November 5); Wilson had specifically appealed to electorate for Democratic majorities "for the sake of the nation" in "the most critical period our country has ever faced."

Armistice signed with Germany (November 11); huge celebrations throughout U.S.

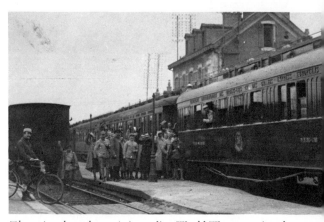

The train where the armistice ending World War I was signed
U.S. SIGNAL CORPS

Wilson announces that he will attend Peace Conference in Paris (November 18); the fact that he is not taking with him any U.S. senators, especially prominent Republican senators, does not go unnoticed. Wilson sails on December 4.

Germans meeting Russians for peace talks at the end of the war
NATIONAL ARCHIVES

The automobile, which was a feature of life in America during the 1920's, and the fashionable raccoon coat symbolized the time.

Postwar Prosperity and the Twenties
1919-1929

In 1919 the curtain abruptly fell on Act One of what had been billed as "America's Century," which up to now had featured progressivist ferment and World War I. The audience decided it didn't like the play so far and said No. In 1919 it said No to the Versailles Treaty and the League of Nations, No to a good stiff drink, No to organized labor, No to foreigners and other radicals, and, in the *Schenck* v. *United States* decision, No to free speech as a form of political dissent. In 1929 it was still saying No, in the form of its third discriminatory immigration law in ten years, when the stagehands, just doing their job, raised the curtain on the next scene—a devastating stock-market crash and the Great Depression.

With the notable exception of the Nineteenth Amendment, which enfranchised half the adult population of the United States, American political institutions and political leaders contributed little that was both positive and enduring in the years 1919-29. Furies in

part whipped up to fight the beastly Hun "over there" spent themselves largely right here, in savage race and labor riots, Ku Klux Klan activities, Red scares, the Sacco-Vanzetti case, the Scopes trial, and the Eighteenth Amendment, which outlawed the manufacture and sale of alcoholic beverages and thus launched Prohibition. It is tempting now to look upon Prohibition as a quaint aberration, a bit of twenties foolishness belonging on the trivia shelf along with hip flasks, raccoon coats, and the Charleston. But it wasn't. Prohibition crashed into American life with sufficient force to spill out great evil in the form of a rich criminal community that is still with us today.

During the 1920's the creative energies and constructive passions of the American people were, for the most part, engaged outside the political arena. In the United States, and in Western civilization as a whole, an astonishing renaissance was well under way—in the sci-

149

ences, in technology, in popular entertainments, and in all the creative arts, including the art of making money. In practically every area of constructive human effort we may find great individual and collective achievements. At least four American poets of world stature—T. S. Eliot, Ezra Pound, Wallace Stevens, and Robert Frost—did major work during the years 1919–29, as did a host of other fine American poets. Ernest Hemingway, Thornton Wilder, F. Scott Fitzgerald, Thomas Wolfe, Sinclair Lewis, William Faulkner, Willa Cather, and Edith Wharton wrote some of their first or finest novels in these years. Eugene O'Neill, considered by some America's finest playwright, produced his first full-length drama in 1920. It is entirely typical of these years, in which Americans were creating works of art that constitute an enduring glory of our culture, that the United States Post Office was spending its time seizing, burning, and barring from our shores one of the greatest novels of the twentieth-century renaissance: James Joyce's *Ulysses*.

The 1920's was a time of great popular music making—of blues, jazz, Broadway musicals—and of names like "Ma" Rainey, Bessie Smith, Louis Armstrong, Bix Beiderbecke, Jelly Roll Morton, George Gershwin, Jerome Kern, W. C. Handy, Cole Porter, Sigmund Romberg, and Duke Ellington. In motion pictures, a popular entertainment medium that, like the Elizabethan drama, also produced fine works of art, Erich von Stroheim made *Greed* in 1923. Cecil B. De Mille gained his cast-of-thousands reputation during this period, which was also the heyday of such stars of the silents as Douglas Fairbanks, Mary Pickford, Rudolph Valentino, Greta Garbo, Lillian Gish, and the great comedians like Charlie Chaplin, Buster Keaton, and Laurel and Hardy. Walt Disney produced his first "Mickey Mouse" cartoon in 1928. The first Oscars were awarded in this year by the newly formed Academy of Motion Picture Arts and Sciences. Important magazines like *The New Yorker, Time, The Saturday Review of Literature*, and H. L. Mencken's *American Mercury* were founded during this period; the Modern Library series, the Book-of-the-Month Club, and *Reader's Digest* were also created in the 1920's. In sports it was Babe Ruth having his 1927 season, with sixty home runs, Walter Johnson and Ty Cobb retiring in the late twenties, leaving monumental records of achievement, and Gertrude Ederle swimming the English Channel; it was the era of Knute Rockne in football, Bill Tilden in tennis, and Bobby Jones in golf (although Jones's great grand-slam year came in 1930). And, of course, there was Charles Lindbergh, packing a few sandwiches for his solo flight across the Atlantic Ocean.

There was an equivalent burst of productivity in the sciences and related technology. In psychology behavioral theory got a huge boost from John B. Watson in 1919. Franz Boas and his students at Columbia University (Alfred L. Kroeber, Robert H. Lowie, Edward Sapir, Ruth F. Benedict, and Margaret Mead) did much to put anthropology on the map of the social sciences in the 1920's; in 1928 Boas made one of the first major scientific attacks on the notion of inherent racial inferiority or superiority. The foundations of linguistics as a separate discipline were laid in the twenties, largely by Sapir and Leonard Bloomfield. Almost all the basic research in radar was done in the 1920's, as was the work making television a practical communications medium. In 1926 Hermann J. Muller altered the genetic code of fruit flies by x ray and for the first time created a mutant. American scientists discovered or isolated vitamins D and E in the twenties, Robert Goddard launched the first rocket, one of the first great American physicists, Albert A. Michelson, measured the diameter of a star (260 million miles), and Vesto Slipher discovered that the universe was moving apart at greater and greater speeds. Important basic research in atomic physics was done by Americans in the 1920's. The New School for Social Research was founded in 1919, the National Bureau of Economic Research in the following year, and the Brookings Institution in 1928.

To emphasize the "disillusionment" of a "lost generation" of American intellectuals or to take too seriously contemporary shock at the "loosened morals" of the flapper age (when women smoked and drank publicly and spoke of Sigmund Freud and other earthshaking horrors through reddened lips) is to displace the Roaring Twenties in America from their central position in a splendid creative renaissance (circa 1905–45) in which all of Western civilization was participating.

The much-vaunted prosperity from 1923 on was real enough; the estimated gross national product went from $784 billion in 1919 to $103.1 billion in 1929. The automobile industry led the pack, but there was also spectacular growth in related industries (from petroleum to roadside franchises), in electrical equipment, and in the chemical industry. By 1929 the United States was producing more electricity than the rest of the world combined, and it has been estimated that as much as 40 per cent of the world's wealth was held by Americans.

Large numbers of Americans shared in this aggregate wealth, of course. Average Americans could have things that were quite beyond their European peers—everything from cars (especially the cheap Model T Ford) to electric vacuum cleaners, refrigerators, plumbing, telephones, and so on. However, they could afford these things not because their paychecks were particularly large but because mass-production techniques had lowered the prices of these things to the level where they were within reach (between 1919 and 1929 the average industrial wage rose 19 per cent, to about fifty-seven cents an hour, but the industrial productivity of wage earners increased 72 per cent), especially when they were purchased by installment credit. If a clerk earning eight hundred dollars a year in 1925 could, with a lot of scrimping, manage to buy a used Model T, it is easy to see how many Americans could come to believe not only in the miracle of unending American prosperity but also that they were destined for greater things—that they were meant to become rich. This optimistic, speculative enthusiasm was shared especially by those who were in fact relatively rich—the 2.3 per cent that earned more than ten thousand dollars a year or the 8 per cent that earned more than five thousand dollars and controlled well over a third of all income earned in the United States. This group was attracted to the Florida land-boom frenzy in the mid-twenties and transferred its speculative mood to the Wall Street casinos in the late twenties. When the market crashed, these people lost their money or got scared enough to cut down on their spending. Since they were doing a disproportionate amount of the spending and investment that fueled economic growth, the economy stopped growing.

When growth stopped, the legendary American technological productivity (which had seen industrial output between 1919 and 1929 far outstrip the relatively small increase in the labor force) worked against itself. There were now far more goods available than consumers were willing or able to buy. The fact that in precrash 1929 as many as 60 per cent of all American families were at the bare-necessity level or that 40 per cent were at or below the poverty level didn't help a bit to provide needed consumer dollars.

The economy was also vulnerable because during the 1920's it had become increasingly consolidated, with more capital, more trade, more productivity, and more jobs under the control of fewer and fewer corporations, many of them intricately linked by various stockholding and investment devices. There were now fewer and fewer independent, decentralized sources of jobs, investment capital, or consumer dollars. When, for example, the three automobile companies producing almost 90 per cent of all cars in the United States were forced to cut back on wages and jobs or a giant insurance empire went bankrupt, the reverberations throughout the economic system were bound to be enormous. When, in 1929 and thereafter, the economic dominoes began to fall, the American political system, which had not undergone a comparable process of concentration and centralization, was unprepared philosophically or institutionally to intervene. Few cities or states had the resources to deal with the growing number of wage earners who now had no wages and no other means of securing the basic necessities of life. The federal government did have the financial resources to break into the self-fueling cycle of declining sales, subsequent layoffs or wage cuts, and then further declining sales, but was unaccustomed to act in this way. It had neither the will nor the bureaucratic means to get federal dollars into the hands of individual American citizens who needed them for food, rent, mortgage and other installment payments, clothing, and all the other purchases on which the economic system depended for sustenance. The result was a sickening, snowballing series of economic failures that left many Americans, including most leaders of the economic and financial communities, in a state of bewilderment. Enter the Great Depression.

Charlie Chaplin, left, and Jackie Coogan in The Kid, *1920*

Postwar Prosperity and the Twenties (1919–1929)

1919

Paris Peace Conference (January 18–May 7): treaty ending World War I is worked out and includes, at Wilson's insistence, a charter for the League of Nations; treaty, although not as harsh as it could have been, bears relatively little resemblance to Wilson's Fourteen Points and hence causes disgust among U.S. liberals; Germany, which has been partially occupied and subjected to naval blockade during negotiations, has not taken part in treaty discussions.

David Lloyd George, Vittorio Orlando, Georges Clemenceau, and Woodrow Wilson meet at the Paris Peace Conference.
LIBRARY OF CONGRESS

The Eighteenth, or Prohibition, Amendment is declared ratified (January 29).

American Legion formed in Paris by members of American Expeditionary Force (March 15–17).

Germany signs Treaty of Versailles (June 28); new liberal democratic Weimar government is substantially discredited among many Germans for having accepted treaty terms, though it had no choice.

Volstead Act (October 28): passed over Wilson's veto, act implements Prohibition Amendment and outlaws beer and wine, which many thought Eighteenth Amendment probably permitted; enormously complex law has many loopholes (allowing home brewing, medical prescription of alcohol, private liquor stocks, etc.); principal accomplishment is to make organized crime an immensely profitable industry.

Wilson submits Treaty of Versailles to U.S. Senate for ratification (July 10); Republican opposition falls into two categories, moderate (under Henry Cabot Lodge) and total, or "irreconcilable" (led by progressives Hiram Johnson and Robert La Follette); more than two thirds of Senate favor U.S. participation in one form or another in League of Nations.

Communist Labor Party formed in Chicago (August 31); splits off from Socialists and adopts pro-Bolshevik program.

Wilson begins nationwide speaking tour in favor of League of Nations (September 3); his appeal to people is undercut by parallel tour of progressive "irreconcilables," financed largely by trust money (Mellon and Frick fortunes); Wilson, exhausted, collapses on tour and later suffers stroke in Washington (October 2), which incapacitates him for at least two months.

Calvin Coolidge, Massachusetts governor, uses National Guard to break strike by Boston police (September 9–14); Coolidge's stand against (AFL) unionization of police, who are fired because of union membership, earns him 1920 Republican vice-presidential nomination.

Steelworkers strike U.S. Steel and other companies (September 22); demand union recognition and end to twelve-hour day and seven-day, $28 week; strike eventually involves 365,000 workers and is led by William Z. Foster, who has Communist affiliations; strike is violently broken in January, 1920.

U.S. Attorney General A. Mitchell Palmer commences "Red scare" raids and arrests (November); U.S. public, convinced through efforts of local politicians and industrialists that race riots (25), strikes (involving more than 4 million workers), and several bombings are part of

A. Mitchell Palmer
LIBRARY OF CONGRESS

overall Bolshevik plot, responds enthusiastically to sweeping and lawless arrests by Palmer (who has presidential ambitions) and his special assistant, J. Edgar Hoover; most of those arrested are later released for lack of evidence, but some aliens are deported (December 22).

Senate blocks ratification of Versailles Treaty and League of Nations (November 19); failure to ratify is result of Wilson's insistence that Democrats vote against treaty, which now includes some essentially harmless amendments attached by Senator Lodge, whom Wilson hates.

U.S. Supreme Court upholds wartime Espionage Act of 1917, saying that it does not unconstitutionally abridge free speech.

1920

Coordinated "Palmer" raids in 33 cities result in arrest of at least 2,700 alleged Communists (January 2); most of those arrested are merely working-class immigrants; raids continue until May, when public support of Palmer fizzles out and Department of Labor ceases to cooperate with Palmer's Department of Justice; Palmer's cry-wolf pronouncements and actions have lasting effects at state and local levels, resulting in wave of political conformity aimed at "purifying" school books and suppressing free exchange of political ideas at university level.

Esch-Cummins (Transportation) Act (February 28): returns railroads to private control, expands powers of Interstate Commerce Commission, and sets up Railway Labor Board.

Versailles Treaty defeated again in Senate (March 19); vote is closer because some—but not enough—Democrats defy Wilson's instructions to vote against it; Congress attempts to declare end of war by joint resolution (March 20), but effort is vetoed by Wilson; war is not officially ended until 1921.

Nicola Sacco and Bartolomeo Vanzetti, Italian immigrants and anarchists, are arrested in connection with payroll robbery and charged with murder in Massachusetts (May 5); Sacco-Vanzetti case, which goes on for seven years, is deeply disturbing to many, who feel that system of American justice, rather than actual defendants, becomes the accused.

Federal Power Commission created (June 10); commission is to regulate waterways on public lands and to license dam sites for hydroelectric power.

The Nineteenth Amendment, granting women the right to vote in national elections, is declared ratified (August 26).

Nicola Sacco, left, and Bartolomeo Vanzetti, right, in 1921
LIBRARY OF CONGRESS

Eight members of Chicago White Sox baseball team indicted on charges of throwing 1919 World Series (September 28).

Campaign of 1920: Republicans run Senator Warren G. Harding (Ohio) and Calvin Coolidge (Massachusetts) in "front-porch" campaign that waffles on League of Nations and calls for "normalcy" and a general cooling down; Democrats run James M. Cox (Ohio) and Franklin Delano Roosevelt (New York) in vigorous campaign backing Wilson's League and seeking to make election what Wilson has called a "solemn referendum" on that issue; five other parties nominate candidates, including Socialists, who run Eugene V. Debs from jail cell. Popular vote (November 2): Harding 16,133,314, Cox 9,140,884, Debs 913,664; electoral vote: Harding 404, Cox 127.

First national radio broadcast (November 2): station KDKA broadcasts U.S. election results.

Census of 1920: total population 106,461,000, including 5,735,811 immigrants arrived since 1911, mostly Italians, Russians, and other Slavs. For first time in U.S. history more than half (51.2 per cent) of population is urbanized. Actual working farmers make up about 30 per cent of population.

1921

Warren G. Harding inaugurated as twenty-ninth President (March 4); Calvin Coolidge becomes Vice President.

Tariff law raises duties on agricultural products (March 27).

U.S. pays Colombia $25 million for loss of Panama (April 20).

Quota law (May 19): immigration law places overall limit of 357,803 on number of persons allowed to immigrate to U.S. and limits immigration from any country to 3 per cent of its 1910 contribution.

Budget and Accounting Act (June 10): provides for a national budget, to be prepared by Bureau of Budget, an agency of the executive branch; act also establishes General Accounting Office.

Joint resolution of Congress declares end of war with Germany and its allies (July 2); separate treaties later worked out with Germany, Austria, and Hungary.

Sacco and Vanzetti convicted of murder (July 14); trial is widely protested as judicial disgrace.

General William "Billy" Mitchell, using a condemned German battleship and other vessels as targets, demonstrates that aircraft armed with bombs can sink armored warships (July 21).

Veterans' Bureau established (August 9).

Postwar depression peaks (August–September); prices are high, wages are low, and unemployment is about 5 million; although economy begins to recover after 1922 and achieves boom, especially in consumer goods and construction, farm earnings remain generally low.

First Armistice Day celebrated (November 11); ceremony held at Tomb of Unknown Soldier at Arlington National Cemetery.

Washington Conference for Limitation of Armaments opens (November 12); U.S. proposes reduction of naval armaments and eight other treaties, dealing for most part with Far East.

1922

Naval Limitation Treaty signed (February 6); U.S., Great Britain, and Japan agree on ten-year moratorium on battleship construction and agree to 5:5:3 ratio in warship tonnage. Although agreement causes resentment in Japan, it actually favors that country, which has only one ocean, the Pacific, to worry about.

World War Foreign Debt Commission established (February 9); as result of loans during and immediately after World War I, other countries owe $10,350,479,074, much of it uncollectable because of European financial conditions; over next four years commission gradually reduces or cancels much of Allied debt.

Lincoln Memorial dedicated in Washington, D.C. (May 30).

Fordney-McCumber Tariff Act (September 21): marks return of protectionist tariff on manufactured goods and

sets even higher duties on agricultural products; high tariffs are not particularly helpful to countries attempting repayment of war debts and are resented abroad.

1923

Several newspapers begin exposé of widespread Ku Klux Klan activities (January 7); Klan, now with an estimated membership of 5 million in South, Midwest, and North, has begun to overreach itself in terrorist campaigns against blacks, Catholics, Jews, immigrants, and practically everyone who might have an interesting idea; public reaction begins to set in, especially after Oklahoma governor has to place state under martial law as result of Klan terrorism (September 15).

A lynched man's body draws ghoulish approval from a crowd.
LIBRARY OF CONGRESS

Intermediate Credit Act (March 4): establishes regional credit banks to aid farmers' cooperatives and ease effects of agricultural depression.

President Harding falls ill in Seattle, Washington, and is taken to San Francisco, where he dies (August 2); cause of death is embolism, although later ugly rumors are circulated that Mrs. Harding poisoned him; there is a massive and genuine outpouring of grief at his death, and 3 million people gather along route of funeral train.

Calvin Coolidge takes oath of office as thirtieth U.S. President (August 3); he is sworn in by his father, a Vermont notary public.

U.S. Senate subcommittee, under Senator Thomas J. Walsh, opens hearings into leasing of U.S. naval oil reserves at Teapot Dome, Wyoming, to private oil companies (October 25); rumors of major scandals have been circulating for several months.

Calvin Coolidge delivers message to Congress, first to

be broadcast on radio (December 6); message calls for noninvolvement in League of Nations, enforcement of Prohibition, economy in government, and collection of Allied war debts.

1924

Congress passes joint resolution condemning Teapot Dome and other oil leases and authorizes President Coolidge to seek prosecutions (February 8); Teapot Dome and other scandals eventually implicate Harding's Secretary of Interior, Attorney General, Secretary of Navy, and chief of Veterans' Bureau and a group of Harding's political cronies known as Ohio Gang in bribery, fraud, and conspiracy; by 1929 five of the "gang" are jailed, four commit suicide, and one is hospitalized for insanity; although Harding, like Grant before him, is personally without taint of corruption, his reputation ultimately suffers and is further beclouded by rumors suggesting adultery in White House and black blood in Harding family; immediate public reaction to blossoming scandal in 1924 is, however, disbelief, anger at investigators, and widespread feeling that it is all a Democratic witch hunt.

A cartoon implies the Teapot Dome scandal may reach Harding.
LIBRARY OF CONGRESS

Dawes Plan (April 9): U.S. proposal successfully lessens European tensions resulting from complete collapse of German economy, subsequent failure of Germany to pay war reparations, and occupation of Ruhr Valley by France and Germany; plan involves stabilization of German currency, Allied supervision of Germany's central bank, and a U.S. loan of $110 million.

Congress passes Soldiers' Bonus Bill over President

Coolidge's veto (May 19); designed to compensate veterans for difference between soldiers' pay and wages earned by civilians during World War I, it establishes a 20-year annuity against which veterans can borrow up to 25 per cent; veterans later demand full cash payment.

New Immigration Quota Law (May 26): law halves total immigration, to about 150,000 a year, and restricts immigration from any country to 2 per cent of its 1890 contribution, thus substantially excluding immigration from southern, central, and eastern Europe; Japanese immigration is flatly prohibited.

Snyder Act (June 2): makes all American Indians born in the U.S. American citizens.

Campaign of 1924: Republicans run Calvin Coolidge and General Charles G. Dawes (Illinois) on platform calling for lower taxes, reduced federal spending, high tariffs, armaments control, and U.S. involvement with World Court; Democrats, gravely split on Prohibition question, take 103 ballots to nominate Senator John W. Davis (West Virginia) and Charles W. Bryan (Nebraska), with platform favoring lower tariffs, disarmament, and the League of Nations and denouncing KKK and Harding corruption; six other parties nominate candidates, including a revived Progressive Party, which runs Robert M. La Follette and Burton K. Wheeler on platform calling for government ownership of railroads and hydroelectric plants, end of injunction in labor disputes, a national child-labor law, and controls on commodity speculation. Popular vote (November 4): Coolidge 15,717,553, Davis 8,386,169, La Follette 4,814,050; electoral vote: Coolidge 382, Davis 136, La Follette 13 (Wisconsin).

J. Edgar Hoover appointed head of Bureau of Investigation (later FBI).

J. Edgar Hoover
FEDERAL BUREAU OF INVESTIGATION

1925

Calvin Coolidge inaugurated (March 4); Charles G. Dawes becomes Vice President.

Scopes "monkey trial" in Dayton, Tennessee (July 10–21): schoolteacher John T. Scopes is tried for teaching concepts of evolution in test-case defiance of recent Tennessee law making such teaching illegal; case attracts nationwide attention as result of Clarence Darrow's participation in Scopes defense and William Jennings Bryan's in the prosecution; trial becomes essentially a public argument between small-town fundamentalist values and those of urban, liberal, and scientific America; Darrow puts Bryan on stand as authority on Bible and twists him inside out; Scopes is found guilty and fined $100; conviction is later reversed, but anti-evolution law stands until 1967.

The Scopes trial: W. J. Bryan researches the prosecution's case.

Court martial of "Billy" Mitchell (October 28–December 17): charged with insubordination because he has publicly blamed War and Navy departments for underfunding and neglecting air forces and thereby causing pilot deaths, Mitchell is found guilty and suspended from Army for five years; he resigns from service the following year.

1926

Florida land boom falls off (January); one of most frenzied real-estate speculations in American history begins to fizzle; a destructive hurricane in September delivers coup de grâce.

U.S. Senate votes approval of U.S. participation in World Court at The Hague, Netherlands (January 27); however, Senate conditions are such as to deny court any significant role in U.S. disputes, and court rejects conditions.

Revenue Act (February 26) fulfills Coolidge pledge to lower income and inheritance taxes.

Richard E. Byrd and Floyd Bennett make first airplane flight over North Pole (May 8–9).

Gertrude Ederle of New York becomes first woman to swim English Channel, setting a record time of 14 hours, 31 minutes (August 6).

1927

First commercial transatlantic telephone service begins, between New York and London (January 7).

Radio Act (February 23): provides for public ownership of airwaves and establishes Radio Commission for licensing purposes.

Nixon v. *Herndon* (March 7): U.S. Supreme Court declares unconstitutional Texas law forbidding blacks to vote in primaries.

Heavy floods in lower Mississippi Valley leave more than 600,000 people homeless and take several hundred lives (April–May).

First experimental television transmission demonstrated, from New York to Washington, D.C. (April 7).

Charles A. Lindbergh makes first solo transatlantic flight, from New York to Paris (May 20–21); flight, in *Spirit of St. Louis*, takes 33 hours and 39 minutes and wins Lindbergh $25,000 prize and world acclaim.

Charles Lindbergh after the first solo transatlantic flight
BOTH: LIBRARY OF CONGRESS

Naval conference between U.S., Great Britain, and Japan, designed to limit navies, is complete failure (June 20–August 4).

Sacco and Vanzetti are executed in Massachusetts (August 27).

The Jazz Singer, starring Al Jolson, opens (October 6); first motion-picture film with sound track.

Income of Al Capone's Chicago mob this year is estimated to be $105 million, of which $60 million is derived from bootlegging and the rest from gambling, prostitution, and the protection racket.

1928

Alien Property Act (March 10): provides $300 million to compensate Germans for property seized in U.S. during World War I.

Flood Control Act (May 15): provides $325 million for work on Mississippi levees over ten-year period.

First color motion pictures demonstrated by George Eastman in Rochester, New York (July 30).

Briand-Kellogg Pact (August 27): agreement, developed by French foreign minister, Aristide Briand, and U.S. Secretary of State, Frank B. Kellogg, is signed by fifteen nations in Paris; treaty bans war as instrument of national policy; 62 countries ultimately sign.

Campaign of 1928: Republicans run Herbert Hoover (California) and Charles Curtis (Kansas) on platform calling for some kind of farm relief (Coolidge had consistently vetoed proposed price-support measures) and favoring Prohibition and protective tariffs; Hoover adds "rugged individualism," which he asserts is responsible for U.S. prosperity; Democrats run Alfred E. Smith (New York), first Roman Catholic presidential candidate, and Joseph T. Robinson (Arkansas); Democratic platform favors collective bargaining for labor, independence for Philippines, and farm relief; although platform supports enforcement of Prohibition, Smith is well-known "wet" and calls for repeal of Eighteenth Amendment; four other parties nominate candidates, including Norman Thomas of Socialists. Popular vote: Hoover 21,411,991, Smith 15,000,185, Thomas 266,453; electoral vote: Hoover 444, Smith 87. Republicans maintain control of Congress.

U.S. State Department repudiates Roosevelt Corollary to Monroe Doctrine (December 17).

1929

U.S. Senate ratifies Briand-Kellogg Pact (January 15).

Young Plan (February 11): revision of Dawes Plan, U.S. proposal reduces amount of war reparations Germany must pay and lengthens payment time.

"St. Valentine's Day Massacre" (February 14): members of one Chicago gang, disguised as policemen, machine-gun seven members of rival "Bugsy" Moran mob; massacre is actually drop in Chicago's bloody bucket.

Herbert Hoover inaugurated as thirty-first President (March 4); Charles Curtis is Vice President.

Agricultural Marketing Act (June 15): designed to support farm cooperatives through purchase of surpluses, it fails to support farm prices, in part because farmers do not reduce acreage under cultivation.

First "blind," or by-instrument-only, airplane flight made by James Doolittle (September 24).

Stock-market crash (October 24–29): heavy selling wave occurs on "Black Thursday," October 24, but is shored up by a syndicate of the largest New York banks, who place buy orders above current ticker price; on Black Thursday record 13 million shares are traded, and although prices rally, many investors have been wiped out on downslide; on Tuesday, October 29, bottom falls out of market, more than 16 million shares are traded, and about $8 billion worth of losses are sustained. Market rallies for a few days but on November 11–13 takes another deep plunge, wiping out about $30 billion in value. Losses incurred curtail spending on which economy depends for growth and exacerbate other serious weaknesses in economy.

An artist shows the despair of a 1929 stock-market speculator.

During the Great Depression it was not at all unusual to see destitute and jobless people sitting dispiritedly on park benches.

The Depression and the New Deal
1930–1939

Herbert Hoover, who presided over America's slide into the Great Depression, did not cause it. Hoover was more sophisticated economically than most Presidents before or after his time, and he took a variety of steps to slow what was obviously becoming an economic depression of disastrous proportions. Despite these steps—an urgent appeal to employers not to cut wages or lay off more wage earners, the infusion of federal money into large and faltering financial institutions, often repeated attempts to restore confidence by promising that conditions would soon improve—the Depression kept cutting deeper and deeper, with increasing numbers of layoffs, bank failures, and repossessions. Rightly or wrongly, people blamed Herbert Hoover and wanted someone else. That someone else was Franklin Delano Roosevelt, a cheery man with a good, solid American name, who promised to fix things up. In 1932 Americans voted for him in droves.

Franklin D. Roosevelt and his New Deal didn't exactly cure the Depression as an economic phenomenon. Renewed prosperity, in the form of high levels of industrial output and low levels of unemployment, did not come about until World War II had started. What

F.D.R.'s New Deal did do, and do quickly—by the fall of 1933—was make it clear that the federal government was not going to let the Depression cut any deeper. The government wasn't going to let *anyone* starve. There were going to be no more bank failures, no more repossessions of home and farm mortages, and no more layoffs if that could humanly be prevented.

Many New Deal programs have endured substantially unchanged. The Tennessee Valley Authority (TVA), price supports for farmers, social security, unemployment insurance, laws favorable to labor, and bank-deposit insurance are just some examples. Other New Deal programs were emergency relief measures that poured money into then virtually bankrupt state and municipal coffers, thence to be distributed as relief to those who needed it most. Still other measures in effect made the federal government an employer. The Civilian Conservation Corps (CCC) hired young people eighteen to twenty-five years of age whose families were on relief and sent them around the country planting trees, restoring historic battlefields, clearing beaches, and so forth. Secretary of the Interior Harold Ickes' PWA built major public-works projects like dams, hospitals, schools, and sewage systems, providing jobs for skilled workers and for engineers, architects, contractors, and so on. Harry Lloyd Hopkins spent more than eleven billion dollars during the New Deal era, some of it on direct relief but much through various agencies like CWA and WPA. Hopkins used these agencies to create jobs, millions of them. He even employed actors, writers, painters, and other artists. (When there were objections to the fact that the federal government was employing artists, Hopkins had a typical answer: "Hell, they've got to eat just like other people.")

The predictable but vastly accelerated changes that constituted the New Deal were hated by some, but not most, Americans. The Stalinists, for example, hated the New Deal because they wanted the whole American system to fall apart, believing they would be the ones to pick up the pieces when it did. Old-style progressives like Al Smith came to hate the New Deal because it brought the federal government into American life as a major, pervasive institutional presence. The progressives had hoped that the federal government could monitor the American system, checking the various abuses deriving from concentrated economic power without itself growing very large. Instead the progressives got their whole package, bingo, and just as fast got a mouthful of alphabet-soup agencies to administer this package; not a few of them gagged on it.

Many business executives, especially owner-officers of industrial or agricultural enterprises they had created themselves, were infuriated at what they rightly regarded as a new set of rules. Now, for example, you couldn't just fire a union organizer and blacklist him throughout the industry so he couldn't get a job anywhere. You had to let him do his work, and if he was successful, you had to share—give up—some of your power to hire, fire, and otherwise control the environment of the workplace. And then there was social security and unemployment insurance, which not only meant a lot of extra paperwork and people snooping around in your books but also meant you had to pay some more of your money to Uncle Sam.

By and large, however, most Americans liked this new thing. They were glad that their government had steppd in to protect them, their homes, their farms, their savings, their investments, and their self-respect from the blight called the Great Depression. The government was helping almost everybody, including the poor; for almost the first time the poor got the sort of attention from federal agencies that previously had come almost exclusively from private civic charities and big-city machines. Labor, especially unskilled and semiskilled labor, got a change of rules, so that the game was no longer stacked so heavily against it.

By 1936 the New Deal had done two main things. First, it had restored the confidence of the middle class. Second, it had pumped a lot of dollars into the economy, many of these dollars gotten by increasing the national debt. Although economic conditions improved, however, attacks on the New Deal from fiscal conservatives grew in intensity and volume. In the 1936 elections Roosevelt turned these attacks to his own advantage and more or less asked the voters to choose between him and what he called the forces of "organized money." The result was an overwhelming triumph at the polls, with F.D.R. carrying every state but Maine and Vermont.

During the thirties the federal government and the American people learned a big lesson. They learned that the government could—and would henceforth be expected to—intervene in the economic life of the nation when the security of too many Americans was threatened. In the course of this learning process the federal government became not only a big government but also an exciting one. It attracted bright, eager, productive, creative people who wanted to work in a stimulating environment at tasks perceived to be socially useful, socially good, and socially helpful. This was true not only of the brain trusters—the lawyers, economists, political scientists, and conservationists—who found homes in the higher levels of government, but also of the artists, musicians, actors, and writers who through various WPA projects found and did decent work throughout the land. The various federal arts projects did not undercut or stifle the private creative impulses of the country but augmented them, bringing art, music, drama, and scholarship to new places.

The American nation had in this period experienced a series of shocks to its well-being and its understanding. But out of these experiences came innovative solutions to problems. Through measures instituted by the federal government people got jobs, public buildings were constructed, murals were painted, plays were put on the boards, and books were written. Sometimes the actions of the federal government were confusing, sometimes costly, and sometimes infuriating. They were not, however, destructive; citizens got a little more security, a little more peace of mind, a little more red tape—a little more of everything except, perhaps, fear.

By 1937, according to President Roosevelt, two thirds of the nation was no longer ill-housed, ill-clad, or ill-nourished. Roosevelt's attention began to be increasingly absorbed by political developments abroad and by a concern that the United States, now as isolationist as it could get, would be caught in a war it was fatally unprepared for.

The Depression and the New Deal (1930–1939)

1930

London Naval Conference (January 21–April 22): U.S., Great Britain, and Japan agree to continued limitations on naval armaments.

Supreme Court holds that purchase of liquor does not violate Eighteenth Amendment or Volstead Act (May 26).

Stock market begins relentless downward slide (June); market had recovered after 1929 crash but now begins two-year decline that tears the bottom out of various industrial averages like the Dow Jones and the *New York Times* index.

The New York Stock Exchange during a session in the 1930's
LIBRARY OF CONGRESS

Smoot-Hawley Tariff Act (June 17): raises tariffs, especially on agricultural products, to record highs; Hoover signs act despite objections by many economists, who correctly predict it will deepen economic crisis.

Veterans' Administration created (July 3); centralizes all federal agencies dealing with ex-servicemen.

Republicans, who have controlled both houses of Congress since 1918, lose majority in House of Representatives (November 4).

Hoover asks Congress for $100 million public-works appropriation (December 2); during first year of Depression, Hoover has for the most part been successful in persuading business to refrain from large-scale pay cuts or panicky layoffs, and labor into refraining from wage-hike demands; call for public works is first attempt to stimulate economy through federal action; unemployment is about 4.5 million, but middle class is not yet heavily affected by deepening depression.

Bank of United States in New York City closes (December 11); bank, with 60 branches and more than 400,000 depositors, is largest yet to fail; more than 1,300 have closed by year's end.

Census of 1930: population 122,775,000. More than 56 per cent of population is urbanized. About 4.1 million immigrants have arrived since 1921; as a result of new quota laws most have come from northern Europe and from Canada, Mexico, and South America.

1931

Wickersham Commission, appointed in 1929 by President Hoover to look into the connection between crime and Prohibition, makes its report (January 19); report

Herbert Clark Hoover
LIBRARY OF CONGRESS

spells out corrupting influence of bootlegging traffic on municipal governments and state law enforcement and concludes that Prohibition laws are unenforceable because of graft and public hostility to them; commission does not, however, recommend repeal of Eighteenth Amendment.

Congress appropriates funds to run government-owned Muscle Shoals power and fertilizer plants on Tennessee River, nucleus of what later becomes Tennessee Valley Authority (TVA) project (February 23); Hoover vetoes on grounds that federal government must not go into business in competition with its citizens.

Veterans' Compensation Act passed over Hoover's veto (February 27); act allows veterans to borrow up to half of their bonus at low interest; Hoover vetoes act on grounds that it will unbalance budget.

"Star-Spangled Banner" becomes official U.S. national anthem (March 3).

Empire State Building, at 102 stories tallest in world, opens in New York City (May 1).

Hoover proposes one-year moratorium on payments of war debts (June 20); moratorium agreement is finally signed in August, after series of bank failures and panics, in part stemming from U.S. 1929 stock-market crash, strike at European economies.

Banking panic accelerates (September–October); more than 800 banks close; some banks have in effect been looted by their officers, who used depositors' money to play stock market; some banks have made huge loans to foreign governments of questionable credit-worthiness, and these loans are now in default; and some have many domestic loans outstanding that are collateralized by now worthless stocks; other basically sound banks are forced to close because they cannot convert assets fast enough to meet withdrawal demands by panicked depositors. By year's end almost 2,300 banks have closed, spreading fear among the middle class. Large-scale wage cuts, increasing numbers of business failures, unemployment now reaching 9 million, sharply reduced local and state tax revenues, and hoarding of gold all contribute to sickening downward spiral in which more and more people find themselves without the means to purchase the bare necessities of life.

Al Capone sent to prison for eleven years for federal income-tax evasion (October 17).

Nevada legalizes gambling; casinos are developed in Reno and Las Vegas that offer low-stakes gambling and an atmosphere designed to attract respectable tourists.

1932

U.S. protests Japanese occupation of Manchuria (January 7); League of Nations eventually seconds the U.S. protest (March 11) but ultimately proves unwilling and unable to do anything about Japanese aggression in China.

Reconstruction Finance Corporation (RFC) established (January 22); recommended by Hoover in late 1931, RFC, designed to provide loans to large business and financial institutions, lends about $1.5 billion in 1932, but this does little to increase purchasing power of ordinary consumers; Hoover insists that relief for individuals should come from neighbors, private charities, and local and state governments.

At disarmament conference in Geneva, Switzerland, sponsored by the League of Nations, U.S. proposes sweeping arms cutbacks, including elimination of all offensive weapons (February 2); conference adjourns with no agreements reached.

Glass-Steagall Act (February 27): authorizes U.S. to sell off $750 million of gold reserves to counteract hoarding; also authorizes Federal Reserve System to extend easier credit.

Lindbergh kidnapping (March 1): infant son of Charles

and Anne Lindbergh abducted; child's body later found near Lindbergh home, even though $50,000 ransom was paid (May 12).

Congress sends Twentieth ("Lame Duck") Amendment to states for ratification (March 3); amendment provides that newly elected President will take office on January 20 instead of March 4 and that new Congress will convene on January 3.

Norris-La Guardia Act (March 23): limits use of injunctions in labor strikes and prohibits employers from making nonmembership in a union a condition of employment.

Amelia Earhart becomes first woman to fly solo across Atlantic (May 20–21).

Amelia Earhart
LIBRARY OF CONGRESS

Hoover announces 20 per cent salary cuts for himself and cabinet members (July 15); unemployment is now at about 12 million; farm prices are so low that crops and livestock are destroyed because costs of harvesting or shipping exceed selling price; farmers begin to resist foreclosures violently; unemployment in large cities is running as high as 40 per cent; families evicted from their homes are living in shantytowns ("Hoovervilles"), bread lines and soup kitchens are everywhere, and food riots are becoming common.

Hungry people waiting for a meal stand in a bread line.
LIBRARY OF CONGRESS

Emergency Relief Act (July 21): provides $300 million for states whose relief funds are exhausted.

Federal Home Loan Bank Act (July 22): sets up regional banks to lend $125 million to institutions giving home mortgages.

"Bonus army" routed in Washington, D.C. (July 28); about 2,000 veterans and their families are set upon by federal troops under General Douglas MacArthur; remnants of a much larger group of veterans who had come to Washington (from May 29 through June) to demonstrate for immediate cash payment of full bonus annuity, they are dispersed by tear gas, their squatters' shacks are burned, and in general they are needlessly maltreated. MacArthur reacted excessively, and Hoover failed to reprimand him. MacArthur's performance later caused F.D.R. to call him (privately) "the most dangerous man in America" and contributed to public view of Hoover as indifferent or callous toward ordinary citizens.

Campaign of 1932: Republicans renominate Herbert Hoover and Charles Curtis on platform calling for balanced budget, reduced government spending, protective tariff, the gold standard, restriction of immigration, and revision of the Prohibition law; Democrats run Franklin Delano Roosevelt and John Nance Garner (Texas) on formal platform that differs from Republican mainly on issue of Prohibition, advocating repeal; six other parties nominate candidates. In contrast to Hoover, whose campaign is lackluster and inactive, Roosevelt stumps vigorously, traveling about 25,000 miles and promising a "New Deal" and help for "the forgotten man on the bottom of the economic pyramid." Although confined by a conservative platform, Roosevelt clearly stands for some form of active intervention on behalf of the citizenry ("But above all, try something"), whereas Hoover doesn't. Popular vote (November 8): Roosevelt 22,825,016, Hoover 15,758,397; various Socialist and Communist candidates total more than 1 million, of which Socialist Norman Thomas gets 883,990 and Communist William Z. Foster gets 102,221. Electoral vote: Roosevelt 472, Hoover 59.

1933

Twentieth Amendment goes into effect (February 6).

Attempt to assassinate Roosevelt in Miami, Florida, fails (February 15).

Franklin Delano Roosevelt inaugurated as thirty-second President (March 4); John Garner is Vice President. In his inaugural address Roosevelt promises quick action along a wide front, vowing if necessary to fight the economic emergency as though it were a "foreign foe."

Franklin Delano Roosevelt
LIBRARY OF CONGRESS

Roosevelt declares bank holiday (March 5); all banks in the nation are to be closed from March 6 to March 9 (most of them are anyway) and are to be reopened and furnished with currency when they are judged to be sound by the Treasury Department; by March 13 about 5,000 banks have reopened, and public confidence in banking system has been restored (depositors are no longer afraid to leave their money in banks).

First "fireside chat" (March 12): F.D.R. explains in radio broadcast what he is doing with banking system; the explanation is a friendly, masterful one that, as Will Rogers put it, allows everybody to understand banking, even the bankers.

The radio brings Franklin Roosevelt's voice to a farm family.
LIBRARY OF CONGRESS

Economy Act (March 20): reduces salary of government workers, cuts veterans' pensions, and reorganizes some government agencies. Act is F.D.R.'s nod to conservative economic theory about balancing budget and is prelude to whole series of deficit-spending measures designed to pump money into economy and increase purchasing power.

Beer-Wine Act (March 22): legalizes beer and wine with 3.2 per cent alcoholic content and slaps revenue-producing tax on it.

Civilian Conservation Corps (CCC) established (March 31); hires jobless males 18–25 years old and puts them to work on various conservation projects; by end of July 300,000 young men are employed and sending part of their earnings back to their families.

Federal Emergency Relief Administration (FERA) established (May 12); under Harry L. Hopkins, FERA provides $500 million for grants to state and local relief agencies; Hopkins, a former social worker, is a wizard at moving funds out quickly to those who can benefit by them.

Agricultural Adjustment Administration (AAA) established (May 12); designed to raise farm prices by reducing huge surpluses and paying farmers to remove acreage from cultivation, it also provides emergency loans to refinance farm mortgages.

Tennessee Valley Authority (TVA) created (May 18); a monument to vision and persistence of Senator George W. Norris (Nebraska), TVA is authorized to build dams and power plants and in general to develop Tennessee Valley in seven-state area.

Federal Securities Act (May 27): requires that issues of new stocks and bonds provide public with information about these securities.

Joint resolution of Congress takes U.S. off gold standard (June 5).

Home Owners Loan Corporation (June 13): refinances home mortgages of those who are not farm owners; also advances low-cost loans to pay taxes and make repairs.

Federal Deposit Insurance Corporation (FDIC) established (June 16); insures bank deposits of up to $5,000, a feature widely denounced by bankers; FDIC is established under Banking (Glass-Steagall) Act (June 16), which also introduces a variety of banking reforms.

Farm Credit Act (June 16): extends loans to farmers for production and marketing.

National Industrial Recovery Act (NIRA) passed (June 16); has two main parts; Title I provides system of industry-developed codes, having force of law, that are designed to regulate production, fix prices, establish working conditions, etc., on industry-wide basis under supervision of National Recovery Administration (NRA); Title II sets up Public Works Administration (PWA) with $3.3 billion to spend. Title I and NRA are a failure in economic sense, but many codes have enduring social consequences, eliminating child labor and greatly encouraging unionization and collective bargaining. NIRA marks end of spurt of legislation drawn up by Congress during special session called the Hundred Days.

Civil Works Administration (CWA): Harry Hopkins, arguing that people want jobs, not handouts, persuades Roosevelt to create CWA (November 8); within a month and a half Hopkins uses CWA to put 4 million people to work doing everything from fixing roads to painting wall murals in post offices.

F.D.R. establishes diplomatic relations with Soviet Union (November 16).

Prohibition repealed by ratification of Twenty-first Amendment (December 5).

1934

Gold Reserve Act (January 30): enables President to deflate dollar, which he promptly does.

Roosevelt creates Export-Import Bank to provide loans to U.S. exporters (February 2).

Hopkins' CWA is cancelled (March); F.D.R. is frightened by cost (almost $1 billion) of CWA, which has also been attacked for wastefulness by those not unemployed; Hopkins uses some of his FERA funds to continue some CWA projects, however.

Tydings-McDuffie Act (March 24): provides for eventual independence of Philippines.

Congress passes bill increasing government salaries and veterans' pensions over Roosevelt's veto (March 28).

Nye Committee begins hearings (April 23); committee, under Gerald P. Nye (North Dakota), investigates role of munitions makers, industrialists, and bankers during World War I; committee is active until 1936 and gives public the (false) impression that those who made money in war actually caused the war or dragged U.S. into it. Committee's work both reflected and contributed to strong isolationist feelings among many citizens.

Drought worsens in Great Plains (April); topsoil from farms in western Kansas, western Oklahoma, and Texas

Clouds of dust darken the sky over Elkhart, Kansas, in 1937.

Panhandle begins to blow away in larger and larger quantities, creating Black Blizzards of silt that sometimes carry to Atlantic coast and leave Great Plains a dust bowl.

Congress enacts series of crime laws strengthening federal police powers (May 18); also makes kidnapping a capital offense, largely as a result of Lindbergh case.

Du Pont laboratories announce development of synthetic fiber later called nylon (May 23); nylon is first commercially used, for toothbrush bristles, in 1938.

Securities and Exchange Commission (SEC) created to supervise and regulate stock market (June 6).

Reciprocal Trade Agreements Act (June 12): gives President power to work out higher or lower tariff agreements with other nations.

Federal Communications Commission (FCC) set up to regulate telegraph, radio, and cable communications systems (June 19).

Federal Housing Administration (FHA) established (June 28); insures mortgages granted by private lending institutions.

Democrats score gains in both House and Senate during midterm elections (November 6); although many (at least 16 million) are still on relief and unemployment stands at more than 11 million, there has been a perceptible upswing in various economic indicators; vast numbers of Americans have concluded that F.D.R. and Democrats are on right track, and the utter dread and hopelessness characteristic of 1930–32 are gone.

Several well-known robbers, having stature of folk heroes, bite the dust; these include John Dillinger, "Pretty Boy" Floyd, "Baby Face" Nelson, and Bonnie Parker and Clyde Barrow (Bonnie and Clyde).

1935

Senate once again rejects U.S. membership in Hague World Court (January 29).

Emergency Relief Appropriations Act (April 8): act gives President wide latitude to establish agencies providing jobs rather than direct relief; under its provisions—and encouraged by the 1934 election results—F.D.R. establishes Works Progress Administration (WPA) under Harry Hopkins. Hopkins, who was a bureaucratic genius, is said to have chosen WPA name deliberately so that it would be confused with PWA, run by Secretary of Interior Harold Ickes, with whom Hopkins constantly fought jurisdictional and funding battles. Using WPA, Hopkins ultimately provides employment for more than 8.5 million people, mostly unskilled

workers, and spends about 85 per cent of $11 billion budget on wages, an extremely important and far-sighted tactic; under various WPA-coordinated agencies Hopkins also provides employment for young people, artists, actors, and writers, many of whom do useful and enduring work.

Soil Conservation Service (April 27): fights soil erosion on Great Plains and elsewhere.

Resettlement Administration (May 1): helps to resettle farming families on better land and places marginal farmland under soil-erosion or reforestation programs; also builds some low-cost suburban housing.

F.D.R. creates Rural Electrification Administration (May 11); REA almost literally brings light (and sound, in the form of radio) to rural America, which has long been neglected by private power utilities.

U.S. Supreme Court unanimously invalidates Title I of NIRA (May 27).

National Labor Relations (Wagner) Act (July 5): law, sponsored by Senator Robert F. Wagner (New York), creates National Labor Relations Board (NLRB), whose function is to guarantee right of labor to organize and bargain collectively.

Social Security Act (August 14): establishes federal old-age insurance paid for through federal tax on wage earners and employers; establishes federal-state unemployment-insurance program, as well as partial funding for state relief and welfare programs.

Revenue (Wealth Tax) Act of 1935 (August 30): steeply increases personal income tax in upper brackets, raises estate and gift taxes, and increases corporate taxes. Both this "soak the rich" act and the Social Security Act were in part responses to various popular schemes put forward by Dr. Francis E. Townsend, who advocated huge (by 1930's standards) pension payments of $200 a month for senior citizens, by Father Charles E. Coughlin, the "radio priest," whose National Union for Social Justice demanded drastic currency inflation, and by Senator Huey Long of Louisiana, whose "Share-Our-Wealth" clubs proposed confiscation of all fortunes in excess of $5 million and of all income in excess of $1 million, this wealth to be used to provide every family with a minimum annual income, a "homestead" (house, car, and other necessaries), and various educational and retirement benefits.

Congress passes Neutrality Act of 1935 (August 31); first of a series of laws betraying increasing congressional nervousness at rising dictatorships in Germany, Italy, and Japan, it contains various provisions designed in effect to keep the U.S. out of the first World War rather than the second one now looming on the horizon.

Senator Huey Long is fatally shot by Dr. Carl A. Weiss, Louisiana eye, ear, nose, and throat specialist whose father-in-law was a judge and a critic of Long's and whom Long intended to gerrymander out of his judicial district (September 8); Weiss is killed instantly by Long's bodyguards, and Long dies later of wounds.

Senator Huey Long on a speaking tour in Magnolia, Arkansas
UNITED PRESS INTERNATIONAL

Committee for Industrial Organization formed within American Federation of Labor to organize unskilled and clerical workers along industry lines (November 9); later expelled from AFL (1937), committee renames itself Congress of Industrial Organizations, thus retaining now-familiar CIO initials.

1936

U.S. Supreme Court invalidates Agricultural Adjustment Act (January 6).

Over F.D.R.'s veto Congress passes law paying full veterans' bonus in cash (January 24); more than $1.5 billion paid out by June 15.

Neutrality Act of 1936 (February 29): extends previous act and forbids loans to any nations at war.

Soil Conservation and Domestic Allotment Act (February 29): continues AAA output-control plan by paying farmers to plant productive acreage with soil-conserving crops like alfalfa; also seeks to share payments to farmer-owners with tenant farmers, who, under old AAA, were often pushed off land that owners had been paid to remove from cultivation.

Robinson-Patman Act (June 19): prohibits national chain stores from selling at or below cost to drive out smaller competitors in local areas.

Walsh-Healey Public Contracts Act (June 30): establishes minimum wage, 8-hour day, and 40-hour work week for employees of companies having government contracts.

Campaign of 1936: Republicans run Alfred M. Landon (Kansas) and Frank Knox (Illinois) on platform condemning New Deal; Democrats renominate Roosevelt and John Garner, who run on record, although F.D.R. lashes out at "economic royalists" and takes a strong antibusiness tone; five other parties run candidates. Popular vote (November 3): Roosevelt 27,747,636, Landon 16,679,543; electoral vote: Roosevelt 523, Landon 8 (Maine and Vermont). Democrats get huge majorities in House and Senate. Election also marks almost total switch among black voters from Republican to Democratic Party.

1937

Congress passes joint resolution forbidding exports to either side in Spanish civil war (January 6); resolution, F.D.R.'s idea, prevents aid to democratic Loyalist government, while fascist governments in Germany and Italy supply arms and men to right-wing Franco forces. Soviet Union, although theoretically allied with Loyalists, acts in such a way as to undermine forces of leftist but democratic Spanish government.

Franklin Delano Roosevelt inaugurated for second term (January 20); John Garner continues as Vice President. In his second inaugural F.D.R. calls for increased social justice for Americans, saying one third of nation is "ill-housed, ill-clad, ill-nourished," which is probably an understatement. F.D.R. makes no mention of foreign affairs in address.

Supreme Court fight: overconfident as result of huge 1936 victory and angered at threat posed by Supreme Court to New Deal legislation, F.D.R. proposes (February 5) scheme for adding new members to Supreme Court and speaks disparagingly of "lowered mental or physical vigor" of aged justices (the great Brandeis, at 81, is oldest member); court-packing scheme outrages conservative and liberal Democrats, but F.D.R. persists in effort, wrecking Democratic coalition and giving conservative Democrats, already disenchanted with New Deal legislation, a rallying point. Savagely denounced by Senate Judiciary Committee, bill is finally killed (July 22). Supreme Court, under Chief Justice Hughes (a masterful politician himself), had already begun to move toward political center, and bill was neither necessary nor instrumental to that shift. Instead F.D.R.'s stubborn demand for substantial judicial control makes it far more difficult to gain congressional approval of further New Deal legislation, because conservative Democrats and Republicans now know they can block liberal domestic legislation, and liberal Democrats and progressive Republicans can block any attempt to end isolationist foreign policy. F.D.R. must increasingly court conservatives as foreign-policy issues become important.

Indignation over Roosevelt's court-packing scheme ran high.
LIBRARY OF CONGRESS

United Automobile Workers, a CIO affiliate, win 44-day strike for recognition at General Motors Plant in Flint, Michigan (February 11); workers use sit-down method, in which striking workers occupy inside of plant rather than picket outside it; tactic works because employers are reluctant to provoke violent confrontations that might cause damage to plant premises.

F.D.R., in effort to balance budget and accommodate conservative critics, cuts back severely on relief appropriations (April); by August economy is in tailspin again, with stock prices and industrial production falling sharply and unemployment approaching 10 million.

Congress passes further Neutrality Act, which requires that nonmilitary supplies bought by belligerent nations be transported on their ships and forbids Americans to travel on ships of any nation at war (May 1).

German dirigible *Hindenburg* explodes and burns at Lakehurst, New Jersey (May 6).

"Memorial Day Massacre" (May 30): although large steel companies, led by U.S. Steel, have signed contracts with CIO union, "Little Steel," a group of smaller steel manufacturers led by Republic Steel Company, refuses to; Memorial Day picketers, including women and chil-

dren, are fired on by Chicago police and savagely beaten outside gates of Republic plant. Although 10 die and 84 are seriously injured, public blames strikers for violence, and F.D.R. expresses general public dissatisfaction with both labor and management on this issue by saying of them: "A plague on both your houses."

Bankhead-Jones Farm Tenant Act (July 22): provides low-interest loans to sharecroppers and other tenant farmers to encourage farm ownership.

Roosevelt makes "quarantine-the-aggressor" speech (October 5); overwhelmingly negative response to F.D.R.'s suggestion that international community may have to act to quarantine "epidemic of world lawlessness" convinces him that major effort will have to be made to prepare U.S. for defense against possible fascist aggression.

Roosevelt calls Congress into special session to enact needed domestic legislation (November 15–December 21); Congress doesn't give him anything he asks for.

Japan attacks U.S. warship *Panay* in Chinese waters, killing 2 Americans and wounding 30 (December 12); Japan apologizes and guarantees incident will not be repeated.

All 36 passengers on the Hindenburg *died in this explosion.*
UNITED PRESS INTERNATIONAL

1938

Agricultural Adjustment Act (AAA) of 1938 (February 16): establishes "ever-normal granary," with government in effect buying surplus crops and storing them; also provides for insurance against wheat-crop failures.

F.D.R. asks for expanded deficit spending to continue combating the Depression (April 14).

Vinson Naval Act (May 17): responding to F.D.R.'s January call for a "two-ocean" Navy, act provides $1 billion for naval construction.

House Committee on Un-American Activities established (May 26); Martin Dies is chairman.

Revenue Act of 1938 (May 27): lowers taxes on large corporations and capital gains; becomes law without F.D.R.'s signature.

Federal Food, Drug, and Cosmetic Act (June 24): prohibits false advertising and misbranding.

Fair Labor Standards (Wages and Hours) Act (June 25): sets minimum wage of 25 cents an hour for workers in interstate commerce; causes about 750,000 workers to get immediate raise.

Munich Agreement (September 29): Britain and France give Sudetenland, western part of Czechoslovakia, to Hitler in order to keep peace in Europe; Gallup Poll shows that most Americans approve of action, as do many Europeans.

"Invasion from Mars": radio broadcast based on H. G. Wells's *War of the Worlds* in news-bulletin format by Orson Welles causes thousands in New Jersey, who believe they are hearing actual account of Martian invasion, to flee their homes in panic (October 30).

Republicans score important gains in midterm elections (November 8); Roosevelt has campaigned in Democratic primaries against certain conservative Democratic candidates, who all win re-election, since F.D.R.'s interference is resented by local voters.

Japanese, who are now in control of large areas of China and at war with the rest, reject U.S. protests and declare America's traditional Open Door doctrine "inapplicable" (November 18).

1939

F.D.R. warns Congress and nation about fascist threat (January 4); asks for $1.3 billion for defense (out of $9 billion budget) and soon requests additional $525 million appropriation.

Supreme Court outlaws sit-down strikes (February 27).

Administrative Reorganization Act (April 3): consolidates a number of small agencies.

Roosevelt asks Hitler and Mussolini to guarantee an end to aggression against other European nations (April 15); Hitler has demanded part of Poland, and England and France have agreed to back Poland.

Pan American World Airways establishes first regularly scheduled transatlantic commercial flight, a seaplane between New York and Lisbon, Portugal (June 28).

Emergency Relief Appropriation Act (June 30): Congress votes restrictions on WPA wages and hiring practices and eliminates Federal Theater Project; this action, along with reduced appropriations, causes WPA workers to strike, and many are dismissed.

U.S.-Panama treaty ratified by Senate (July 25); U.S. agrees not to intervene in Panamanian affairs, raises amount of annual payment to Panama, and pledges mutual defense of Canal Zone.

Hatch Act (August 2): prohibits government employees from taking part in political campaigns.

Britain and France declare war on Germany (September 3) two days after Hitler launches blitzkrieg attack on Poland, and World War II is on; F.D.R. says that although U.S. will remain neutral, he cannot ask Americans to "remain neutral in thought" or to close their minds or consciences to what is happening; U.S. issues formal declaration of neutrality on September 5.

F.D.R. receives letter signed by Albert Einstein warning that an atomic bomb may be possible and that Germany seems to be moving to control uranium supplies (October 11); actually Einstein is not involved in nuclear fission, and prime mover in affair is Leo Szilard; Einstein later calls signing of famous letter the "one great mistake in my life." Letter ultimately results in top-secret Manhattan Project, which produces world's first nuclear weapon.

Neutrality Act of 1939 (November 4): special session of Congress, called by Roosevelt, repeals arms embargoes mandated by previous neutrality acts and authorizes cash-and-carry sale of munitions to belligerents; cash-and-carry provision favors Great Britain and France, who control the seas and have money.

Economy, stimulated by defense expenditures and war orders from abroad, has rebounded and in last quarter enjoys sharp increases in manufacturing output; unemployment declines about 9 per cent from 1958 level, to about 9.5 million.

"A date that will live in infamy": Roosevelt's characterization of December 7, 1941, when the Japanese attacked Pearl Harbor

World War II

1940–1945

For most Americans of the time World War II was a simple, bald affair of first beating Germany and then beating Japan. This was good, in the sense that there were relatively few of the grandiose expectations characteristic of World War I, almost no domestic hysteria, and little hoopla about what a glorious adventure this thing was going to be. With the exception of the Japanese-American internments on the West Coast, a disgrace in which ignorance and greed played no small role, there were few domestic witch hunts, official or otherwise, and pacifists and other conscientious objectors were dealt with calmly and on the whole justly. During the war the tenor of Supreme Court decisions, usually a fairly reliable index of the public mood, was generally liberal. Although the Court upheld the government's right to incarcerate West Coast Japanese-

Americans, it also placed some limits on that right; it invalidated state laws that required schoolchildren to salute the American flag, interfered with the internal migration of Dust Bowl refugees, and infringed on black voting rights.

The United States and its allies won the war, achieving the formal surrender of Germany on May 7, 1945, and of Japan on August 14, 1945. But despite the relative modesty of American war goals and the complete American success in achieving them, World War II had effects both at home and abroad that were complex and in some cases surprising.

At home the federal government virtually ran the economy from 1943 on and invested hugely in it. From 1940 to 1946 the federal government spent $370 billion, dwarfing the outlays made during the New Deal period, which in the years 1933–38 totaled somewhat more than $46 billion. As a result of this enormous investment industrial output almost doubled, with spectacularly high increases in certain industries: synthetics, plastics, and alloys and light metals like aluminum. By 1945 the government controlled nine tenths of all synthetic-rubber, airplane, shipbuilding, and magnesium plants, 70 per cent of aluminum-manufacturing plants, and half of the machine-tool factories. The spectacular wartime economic growth not only cured the Depression but also brought large numbers of women, blacks, and other minorities into the labor force. The labor shortage and the need for labor-management harmony vastly increased union membership and caused such holdouts against unionization as the Ford Motor Company and Little Steel to cave in. Black membership in labor unions, particularly in CIO affiliates, increased considerably.

About 40 per cent of the war costs were paid for on an ongoing basis through various corporate, individual, and excise taxes; there were steep individual and excess-profit taxes at the high income levels, and income taxes were extended for the first time to the majority of wage earners through the payroll-deduction system. There seems to have been a fairly substantial redistribution in national income, with the richest 5 per cent of the population receiving 17.4 per cent of the national income in 1945 as opposed to 24.4 per cent of it in 1936. (It should be pointed out, however, that for a nation so manifestly fascinated by statistics, figures on overall distribution of national wealth are remarkably difficult to come by and to interpret.) The national debt increased from about $43 billion in 1940 to $258 billion in 1945.

The war accelerated the east-to-west, south-to-north, and country-to-city movements of the population, with California enjoying a 50 per cent gain in population, largely as a result of the many munitions and aircraft factories located there.

As in any war, technology got an enormous boost, with research and development piling up important gains in electronics, rocketry, jet engines, wonder drugs (sulfa drugs, penicillin, and other antibiotics), and, of course, atomic power. The enormous backlog of scientific and technological expertise created during World War II nourished the American system until the 1960's, when a similar though smaller-scale government crash program in space exploration again caused the rapid growth of research and development in many areas from which commercial spin-offs are now beginning to trickle into American life.

World War II was the biggest, bloodiest, costliest war in human history. It was war on a planetary scale, with global strategies and enormous groups of military personnel being shifted and supplied with unparalleled speed by sea, air, and mechanized ground transport. Supporting the large strategies, which involved the invasion of whole continents or, in the Pacific theater, a battlefield containing some twenty-five million square miles of ocean, there were thousands of traditional land battles, differing from those of previous wars mainly in the increased firepower available to the individual soldier, improved communications available to combat commanders, and vastly improved medical and evacuation procedures available to the wounded. But in other respects the nature of warfare as a purposeful human activity underwent significant changes.

Combatants became increasingly specialized; that is, they were intensively trained to use specialized tools of war in specialized environments, from underwater demolition or jungle fighting to all the other kinds of air, land, and naval operations, with the almost infinite variety of weapons and tasks associated with them. But as the weapons and techniques of combat became more specialized, and as the individual warrior gained more and more power in terms of the destructive energies he could command, the target of his military skills and power became increasingly less well defined. The enemy ceased in many respects to be another human being close enough to have recognizable human features and became instead a piece of machinery that contained human operators or a city that from thousands of feet in the air contained human beings too small to be distinguished as such. In World War II the distinction between combatant and noncombatant, between soldier and civilian, dwindled to the vanishing point, with the result that total civilian casualties may have exceeded military ones. They certainly did in the European theater, where aerial bombing was intensively used and where perhaps as many as twenty million civilians died as a direct result of the war, including 4.5–6 million Jews who died in Nazi extermination camps. In the process of liberating Nazi-held Europe at least two hundred thousand non-German civilians were killed by the Allies alone. In such cases the word "enemy" has lost all its traditional meaning. In a perverse way the conventions of warfare as applied to combatants during World War II were observed more or less honorably and scrupulously; for the most part armies that were trapped, out of supplies, or otherwise placed in a militarily untenable position were given the opportunity to surrender; if surrender occurred, the killing came to an end. But the civilian inhabitants of a city in a nation at war could not surrender to bombers flying over their heads, even if they wanted to; this is true whether the city was London, Coventry, Rotterdam, Brussels, Dresden, Hamburg,

Amiens, or Tokyo. Defenseless, civilians could only hide during a raid and, if they survived it, resume their appointed tasks until the next one.

The civilian population of the United States for the most part did not share the hardships, deprivation, and violence that was the experience of many ordinary European and Asian citizens during World War II. A few munitions plants blew up, there was some rationing, and some restrictions were placed on travel by automobile, but that was about it. After 1942, when the Atlantic coastal waters had been more or less cleared of U-boats and the Battle of Midway had taken a big chunk out of Japan's carrier force, the United States was in no serious danger of invasion, even on the commando-raid level. But this is not to say that the United States was a stranger to war grief; 405,399 Americans lost their lives in World War II, dying on obscure islands or in little towns whose names even today cause a chill.

When World War II came to an end in 1945, there was a brief, pleasant moment in which Americans could look around them and say: Well done. The fascist powers had been defeated, and the United States had been largely responsible for that defeat, achieving it without destroying its own economic, political, or social institutions—indeed, in many respects having strengthened them. There was a new and untried President at the helm, to be sure. But there was also a new international organization being formed that, it could reasonably be hoped, would both help keep the peace and help in the task of rebuilding a shattered world. The United States now occupied a very satisfying, unquestionably dominant position among the nations of the earth. Many Americans looked forward to a new era in which American wealth, power, and democratic experience would help transform the global community into a better, friendlier, and somehow more American place.

President Truman addresses the San Francisco Conference in June, 1945; the United Nations Charter was drafted at this time.

World War II (1940–1945)

1940

"Phony war" in Europe, as isolationists have called period of military inaction since September, 1939, ends with Nazi invasion of Denmark and Norway (April 9); by June 22 Belgium, the Netherlands, and France have fallen, and only England, now under Winston Churchill, remains free, although under threat of invasion.

Electron microscope demonstrated by Radio Corporation of America (April 20).

U.S. begins to supply Great Britain with arms, munitions, and airplanes (June 3).

Congress permits sale of weapons to South American nations (June 16); U.S. informs Germany that it will not permit takeover of French or Dutch possessions in Latin America.

Smith (Alien Registration) Act (June 29): requires registration and fingerprinting of foreigners in U.S.; also makes it a crime to advocate or belong to any organization supporting the violent overthrow of U.S. government.

Amendment to Hatch Act limits campaign expenditures to $3 million per party in presidential elections and limits individual contributions to $5,000 (July 20).

F.D.R. signs bill authorizing $4 billion worth of naval construction (July 20).

U.S. trades Britain 50 World War I-vintage destroyers in return for 99-year leases on British air and naval bases on Newfoundland and in West Indies (September 3); British need destroyers desperately because German U-boats are cutting up Atlantic shipping; trade circumvents existing laws prohibiting outright sale or loan of destroyers and also appeases U.S. "fortress-America" elements, who like idea of additional defensive bases.

Selective Training and Service Act (September 16): first U.S. peacetime draft calls for registration of males between 21 and 35 years old; by October more than 16 million have been registered, and F.D.R. picks first draft numbers.

F.D.R. places embargo on exports of scrap iron and steel to Japan, which has moved into French Indochina (September 26); the next day Japan signs military pact with Germany and Italy, thus forming Axis alliance.

Campaign of 1940: Republicans run Wendell L. Willkie (New York) and Senator Charles McNary (Oregon) on platform criticizing methods but not substance of New Deal and denouncing F.D.R. for seeking a third term and thus violating American political tradition; Democrats run F.D.R. and Henry A. Wallace (Iowa); Willkie, a foe of TVA, is appealing and energetic campaigner (one critic calls him "a simple, barefoot Wall Street lawyer"), and F.D.R. is forced to hit campaign trail too; both candidates basically support national defense, all aid to Britain "short of war," etc., but Willkie accuses F.D.R. of trying to drag U.S. into war, which F.D.R. denies; Socialist and Communist parties run candidates, mainly on pacifist platforms, but make little impact. Popular vote (November 5): Roosevelt 27,263,448, Willkie 22,336,260; Socialists and Communists get less than 200,000 total. Electoral vote: Roosevelt 449, Willkie 82.

Franklin Delano Roosevelt
FRANKLIN D. ROOSEVELT LIBRARY

Census of 1940: total population 132,122,000, including 528,431 immigrants. This is smallest immigration since 1830; largest single group (114,000) is from Germany, including many refugees from Hitler. Net population increase is smallest ever (slightly more than 7 per cent) and represents in part decline in immigration but also sharp decline in birthrate during Depression decade. Five largest cities are New York (7.5 million), Chicago (3.4 million), Philadelphia (1.9 million), Detroit (1.6 million), and Los Angeles (1.5 million); there has been virtually no increase in the ratio of urban to rural population, largely because many returned to family farms during the Depression.

1941

F.D.R. recommends lend-lease program to Congress (January 6) and links war effort to Four Freedoms (freedom of expression and worship, freedom from want and fear); lend-lease program is ingenious idea designed to get around remembered difficulties with World War I war debts and to emphasize defensive nature of increased war production (U.S. will become arsenal of democracy and will distribute part of that arsenal abroad, where it will do the most good, giving it to anti-Axis powers); F.D.R. asks for about $10.5 billion for defense.

U.S. and British military staffs meet secretly in Washington (January 27–March 29); agree to concentrate on Germany rather than Japan if U.S. becomes directly involved against Axis powers.

After two months' debate Congress approves Lend-Lease Act (March 11); initial appropriation is $7 billion; ultimately U.S. gives more than $50 billion in aid under program.

Office of Price Administration (OPA) established to control inflation by fixing prices and wages (April 11); first step taken is to freeze steel prices (April 16).

U.S. extends naval security patrols to longitude 26°W, a line running down east coast of Greenland, in effort to cut down shipping losses (April 11); U.S. warships shadow U-boats and radio their positions to Allies but do not themselves attack.

F.D.R. declares state of national emergency (May 27).

F.D.R. freezes German and Italian assets in U.S. and suspends diplomatic relations with Germany and Italy (June 14–16).

Following German invasion of Soviet Union, F.D.R. promises lend-lease aid to Russia (June 24).

F.D.R. issues Executive Order 8802, which bans anti-black hiring practices in defense industries (June 25); does so only because union leader A. Philip Randolph threatens 100,000-member march on Washington; 8802 sets up Fair Employment Practices Committee to enforce ban but gives committee few powers.

F.D.R. freezes Japanese credit in U.S., places total embargo on oil shipments to Japan, and calls up Philippine national guard, placing it under command of General Douglas MacArthur (July 26); move comes two days after Japan's military occupation of French Indochina; Japan, now completely under control of militarist clique, needs oil to continue its expansion, which includes plans for invasion of East Indies, Malaya, and Philippines.

Atlantic Charter (August 14): document, drawn up by F.D.R. and Winston Churchill on warships off Newfoundland coast, renounces territorial war aims and looks forward to permanent structure of peace.

U.S. destroyer *Greer* torpedoed by German U-boat near Iceland (September 4); *Greer* had been directing a bombing attack on the U-boat, which turned on it, although Roosevelt claims *Greer* was only carrying mail; on September 11 F.D.R. orders U.S. Navy in North Atlantic to shoot German warships on sight; undeclared naval war with Germany now begins; by the time war is formally declared, two U.S. warships have been torpedoed (one, the U.S.S. *Reuben James*, was sent to the bottom), and seven U.S. merchant vessels have been sunk.

Japanese attack U.S. fleet at Pearl Harbor, Hawaii (December 7); Sunday morning attack by 190 Japanese carrier-based planes sinks or damages 19 ships, including 8 battleships, destroys about 150 planes, kills 2,335 military personnel, and wounds 1,178; although Japanese diplomatic code has been broken and intelligence reports have spotted movement of Japanese naval units, information has not been properly interpreted or acted upon.

Ships explode in flames as the Japanese bomb Pearl Harbor.

F.D.R. asks for and gets a declaration of war against Japan (December 8); sole dissenting vote is cast by Representative Jeannette Rankin of Montana.

Germany and Italy declare war on U.S. (December 11).

1942

Declaration of the United Nations (January 1): 26 anti-Axis countries agree, in Washington, D.C., to support Atlantic Charter, defeat the fascists, and make no separate peace treaties with Axis powers.

Japanese take Manila, Philippines (January 2); General MacArthur retreats to Bataan Peninsula.

National War Labor Board established (January 12); has authority to settle labor disputes.

War Production Board created (January 16); has authority to set priorities in production and supply.

Women and men work together in a plant producing tanks.
CHRYSLER CORPORATION

F.D.R. issues Executive Order 9066, under which 112,000 Japanese-Americans on West Coast are interned in concentration camps (February 19).

Japanese-American internees at the Manzanar, California, camp
LIBRARY OF CONGRESS

Bataan falls (April 9); 85-mile "death march" of U.S. prisoners results in thousands of fatalities; fortress of Corregidor finally surrenders to Japanese (May 6).

Carrier-based bombing raid on Tokyo (April 18): raid, under General James Doolittle, does little damage but boosts U.S. morale.

Battle of the Coral Sea (May 7–8): first naval battle in which enemy ships do not sight each other but duel long-distance with carrier-based aircraft, it ends with withdrawal of Japanese fleet, thus forestalling Japanese invasion of Australia.

Battle of Midway (June 3–6): superior Japanese fleet is stopped by U.S. Navy; four Japanese aircraft carriers are sunk, ending Japanese naval domination of Pacific and marking beginning of Allied offensive in Pacific theater.

Republicans score gains in congressional elections (November 3); although Congress remains nominally under control of Democrats, it is actually run by loose coalition of conservatives of both parties.

"Operation Torch" is launched (November 8); amphibious Anglo-American force lands in North Africa; purpose is ultimately to provide staging ground for assault on Sicily and Southern Europe and to accommodate Stalin's demand for a second front to take some of the pressure off the Soviet Union, which has been bearing brunt of land war in Europe for more than a year.

Draft age is lowered to eighteen (November 13).

WPA is terminated (December 4); unemployment has vanished, and civilian labor force has expanded significantly, with women taking many jobs in defense industries.

1943

Casablanca Conference in Morocco (January 14–24): F.D.R., Churchill, and military staffs decide to attack Sicily and promulgate "unconditional surrender" strategy (F.D.R.'s idea); "unconditional surrender" probably prolongs German resistance long after war is actually lost militarily.

Guadalcanal, one of the Solomon Islands, is finally taken by U.S. forces (February 9); fierce naval and land warfare has been going on there for about six months; Guadalcanal is one of first bases in southern prong of "island-hopping" campaign (via New Guinea and Philippines) aimed at Okinawa and ultimately Japan.

F.D.R. orders freeze on all wages and prices (April 8).

F.D.R. issues executive order requiring nondiscrimination clauses in all government-industry war contracts (May 27).

Smith-Connally Anti-Strike Act passed over F.D.R.'s veto (June 25); prohibits strikes in war industries and gives government right to operate struck industries; act is partly in response to strike by 80,000 coal miners in April and May.

Allies invade Sicily (July 10); by end of July, Sicily-based bombers are hitting Rome and have caused resignation of *il Duce* (Mussolini).

"Big Inch," world's longest oil pipeline, from Texas to Pennsylvania, opens (July 19); pipeline is part of overall successful effort to get oil and other materials from U.S. Southwest and South America to northern industries without losing a lot of it to German U-boats.

Large-scale Allied invasion of Italy (September 9): although Italy in fact surrendered the day before, Allies meet fierce and brilliant opposition from German troops. The "underbelly" is far from "soft"; Allies do not reach Rome until June, 1944, even though new Italian government has entered war on Allied side by October, 1943.

United Nations Relief and Rehabilitation Administration formed by 44 nations in Washington, D.C. (November 9); member nations eventually agree to provide $4 billion for war victims.

Tarawa, a three-mile-long atoll in Gilbert Islands, is finally taken (November 23); island is defended to the death by 4,000 Japanese against 200-ship U.S. task force with 108,000 men.

Teheran Conference in Iran (November 28–December 1): first face-to-face meeting of "Big Three" (F.D.R., Churchill, and Stalin), who plan second-front invasion of Western Europe, putting General Dwight D. Eisenhower in overall command; Stalin promises to declare war on Japan once Germany is defeated; participants agree on necessity for international postwar peace-keeping organization.

Stalin, Roosevelt, and Churchill at the Teheran Conference

Race riots erupt in several U.S. cities (Los Angeles, Chicago, Detroit, New York, and others); most are caused by white resentment at large numbers of blacks moving to cities for defense jobs and at housing shortage, which leads to black presence in previously all-white neighborhoods; some are caused by attacks on black servicemen, who resent poor quality of segregated barracks, messes, and other military facilities. Worst riot happens in Detroit, where 34 are killed and F.D.R. has to send in troops. In Los Angeles blacks and Mexican-Americans wearing zoot suits are attacked.

Rationed items now include tires, sugar, coffee, gasoline, meats, certain fats and oils, butter, cheese, and various processed foods. Cars are no longer being manufactured. Although conservation of war materials causes some changes (e.g., cuffs and vests disappear from men's styles), there is no serious deprivation among U.S. civilian populace.

1944

Marshall Islands recaptured from Japanese (February 22).

American troops in the war-devastated Marshall Islands

German capital, Berlin, is bombed for first time by U.S. planes (March 4); many German cities have been under heavy bombing attack for many months.

D-Day, or Normandy invasion (June 6): 4,600 ships and 176,000 men cross English Channel and attack 40-mile strip of Normandy coast; within seven days Allies land 326,000 men, 50,000 vehicles, and more than 100,000 tons of supplies.

A French peasant says a prayer for a dead American soldier.
ALL: U.S. ARMY

Germans send first V-1 (subsonic) rocket against London (June 13).

Battle of Philippine Sea (June 19–20): Japan loses many of its carrier planes, opening the way for capture of Mariana Islands.

Bretton Woods Conference in New Hampshire (July 1–22): sets up $8.8 billion International Monetary Fund to stabilize European currencies.

German officers attempt to assassinate Hitler (July 20); many German military men consider war lost and wish to surrender; Hitler has General Erwin Rommel (the "Desert Fox") killed (forcing him to take poison) for trying to get peace negotiations started.

Soviet Union recognizes Communist puppet regime as government of Poland (July 27).

Key islands (Guam and Saipan) in Marianas are now in U.S. hands (August 1); Japan can be reached by bombers based on these islands, and first large-scale raid by Marianas-based B-29's takes place on November 24.

Siege of Warsaw (August 2–October 2): Polish underground, encouraged by approach of Soviet army, rises up against German occupation force; Soviets deliberately withhold support so that a source of potential resistance to Soviet domination will be destroyed, as it is by October 2.

Germans launch first V-2 (supersonic) rocket against London (August 8).

War Production Board authorizes partial reconversion of industry to consumer-goods output (August 14).

Dumbarton Oaks Conference, near Washington, D.C. (August 21–October 7): U.S., China, Britain, and U.S.S.R. discuss proposals that form basis for charter of United Nations.

Paris liberated by French troops (August 25).

First U.S. forces enter Germany (September 12); Aachen, first large German city to be captured by Allies, falls to U.S. Army on October 21.

Moscow Conference (October 9–18): Churchill and Stalin get together to divide up Eastern Europe; F.D.R. says U.S. will not be bound by Moscow agreements.

Battle of Leyte Gulf in the Philippines (October 23–25): greatest naval battle in history, having three separate parts, results in virtual destruction of entire Japanese fleet and allows MacArthur, who had arrived in Leyte October 20, to stay there.

Campaign of 1944: Democrats nominate F.D.R. and Harry Truman (Missouri); Republicans choose Thomas E. Dewey (New York) and John W. Bricker (Ohio); three other parties also run candidates. Although both parties support postwar international peace organization, Republicans attack F.D.R.'s longevity in office, suggest that new, younger men should guide the postwar destinies of nation, and raise questions about F.D.R.'s health. Popular vote (November 7): Roosevelt 25,611,936, Dewey 22,013,372; electoral vote: Roosevelt 432, Dewey 99.

Battle of the Bulge (December 16–26): massive German counterattack on Allied line in the Ardennes almost succeeds but fails to break fierce U.S. resistance at Bastogne; original Allied line restored in January, 1945.

Office of Price Administration estimates that U.S. black market in scarce consumer goods does more than $1 billion business a year.

1945

Yalta Conference (February 4–11): F.D.R., Stalin, and Churchill make wide range of agreements (many not made public until later), including four-part occupation of Germany, treatment of war criminals, and concessions to Soviet Union in Eastern Europe and Far East, many of which are later denounced in West but are

U.S. troops march through Paris after its liberation in 1944.

The "Big Three" at Yalta: Churchill, Roosevelt, and Stalin

made in part because Soviet help is thought to be essential to the defeat of Japan. Yalta meeting also sets up meeting in San Francisco in which UN charter is to be drafted.

Iwo Jima captured (February 19–March 14); extremely costly battle places U.S. forces 750 miles from Japan.

Okinawa invaded (April 1); at cost of 12,520 killed and 36,311 wounded, U.S. forces finally secure island, 350 miles from Japan, on June 21.

F.D.R. dies of stroke at Warm Springs, Georgia (April 12); Harry S. Truman becomes thirty-third President.

Harry S. Truman is sworn in as President on April 12, 1945.
NATIONAL ARCHIVES

United Nations Conference, in San Francisco, California (April 25–June 26): 50 nations draft UN charter.

Germany signs unconditional surrender at Reims, France (May 7); Hitler had committed suicide on April 30, and Berlin was captured May 2.

German General Jodl signing the act of military surrender
U.S. ARMY

First atomic bomb exploded, at Alamogordo, New Mexico (July 16).

Potsdam Conference, near Berlin, Germany (July 17–August 2): a new "Big Three" (Truman, Stalin, and Clement Attlee, the last replacing Churchill, who had been defeated in British general election) call for unconditional surrender of Japan and work out details for occupation of Germany and settlement of European territorial questions.

U.S. Senate ratifies United Nations Charter (July 28).

Atomic bomb dropped on Hiroshima, Japan (August 6); four square miles of city are leveled, with 60,175 killed outright.

Atomic bomb is dropped on Nagasaki, a naval base in Japan (August 9); approximately 36,000 are killed. Five days later Japan declares its intention to surrender unconditionally.

Hiroshima: the total devastation caused by the atomic bomb
NATIONAL ARCHIVES

Japanese formally surrender on battleship *Missouri* in Tokyo Bay (September 2).

The formal surrender of Japan being signed on the Missouri
U.S. ARMY

London Conference (September 11–October 2): Soviet Union and other western nations fail to reach agreement about peace treaties.

War-crimes trials begin in Nuremberg, Germany (November 20).

The Brandenburg Gate in the British sector is visible behind the concrete wall and barbed wire separating East and West Berlin.

Cold Wars and Others
1946–1976

In the thirty years since World War II the United States has undergone many changes as a society. The world order and our place in that world order have become very different from what they were in 1946.

In 1946 America was a winner; it had emerged from a colossal war, fought mainly to preserve the status quo in Europe and Asia, an economic and military giant. Abroad, many looked hopefully to the United States not only as a source of material aid that would help heal a war-torn world but also as a nation whose traditions of political and social idealism would cause it to look kindly upon the efforts of impoverished and unfree peoples to achieve just, independent, and prosperous societies. At home Americans looked forward to the easing of various wartime restrictions, to being able to spend their paychecks on cars, housing, refrigerators, and other consumer goods, and in general to enjoying themselves.

By the end of 1976, the year in which the United States celebrated its two hundredth anniversary as an independent democratic state, the country had passed

through a series of shocking internal and international crises. It was still a world military and economic giant, but it wasn't the only one, and it was now almost as vulnerable to complete military destruction as the least of nations. It had engaged in a long, expensive, brutal war against a little country with whom many members of the international community sympathized and had been forced by public opinion at home to withdraw from this war. It had experienced a series of racial and political conflicts that had set Americans to rioting in major cities across the land, had seen the alienation of a significant portion of the educated middle class, and had witnessed some Americans doubting the wisdom and truthfulness of their national government and others seeing in that government something baneful and threatening. It had seen one President assassinated and several other key national leaders, including a potential President, murdered; it had seen a President and a Vice President resign in disgrace as alternatives to impeachment or imprisonment. It had experienced a strange economic malaise—a supposedly impossible condition of depres-

177

sion and inflation—in the course of which the nation's largest city went to the edge of bankruptcy. It had been alerted to widespread environmental degradation and also found itself being criticized by some of its own citizens as the principal and most wasteful consumer of raw materials and energy in a world whose resources were now seen to be not only finite but increasingly scarce. In the world forum it had once dominated it had found itself outvoted and tongue-lashed by a host of poor, small, or underdeveloped African, Asian, and South American nations with whose aspirations it had somehow failed to align itself. Instead it had found itself with a small group of friends consisting of a handful of democratic, industrialized countries, including Germany and Japan, and certain conservative and repressive regimes little loved by their own people and largely dependent on American military and economic aid for survival.

During the years 1946–76 the United States was governed by three Democratic Presidents—Truman, Kennedy, and Johnson—and three Republican Presidents—Eisenhower, Nixon, and Ford. Each of these Presidents had his own style, and each confronted foreign and domestic problems in a different manner. During their administrations American society went through various changes in texture or feel—the "give 'em hell" decisiveness of the early Truman years, the paranoia of the McCarthy era, the placid materialism of the Eisenhower fifties, the stylish excitement of the Kennedy years, the deep social divisiveness of the late sixties under Johnson and Nixon, and in the early seventies the bewildering combination of détente abroad and Watergate at home.

American foreign policy since 1946 has been dominated by a set of assumptions, perceptions, and actions that may perhaps best be summed up in the term "anti-Communist." Historians argue about the correctness of some of these American perceptions and decisions, especially during the immediate postwar period. But the fact remains that whether or not Truman and his advisers were right about Soviet intentions and capabilities in the late 1940's and early 1950's, what American decision makers feared then was what in fact existed by the mid-fifties: a world dominated by at least two giant nations, each capable of wreaking destruction on the other and on any other part of the world. Although the Soviet Union and the United States have increasingly acted to minimize the likelihood of an all-out nuclear war, both nations continue to have good reason to distrust each other's intentions, and almost any decision by a Soviet or American leader about almost any domestic or foreign issue must ultimately be weighed in relation to its effect on a delicate set of balances—psychological, economic, political, and military—that have so far not tipped into Armageddon.

Another and related constant of the 1946–76 period has been the United States' lack of success in connecting in any positive way with the various popular and nationalist movements that began to spring up in many parts of the world after World War II had gravely weakened the European colonial powers. Almost every time the United States has intervened either diplomatically or militarily, beginning with Greece in 1947 and ending with Angola in 1975, it has wound up backing losers or propping up unpopular rather than popular authoritarian regimes. The behavior and reputation of the American government have thus stood in increasingly sharp contrast to the behavior and reputation of American individuals, who as missionaries, scholars, entrepreneurs, or Peace Corps volunteers have generally earned high marks for generosity, inventiveness, kindness, hard work, know-how, and imagination.

A third constant of the 1946–76 years has been economic. The huge federal expenditures of World War II seem to have become permanent features of the economic environment. Military budgets remained fairly high from 1946 to 1950 and thereafter rose steadily. The combined federal budgets for 1974–76 amounted to more than $958.6 billion, well over twice the total costs of government during World War II; of that sum about $255.5 billion went for military expenditures. Economists can and do argue about whether our economy has become a permanent wartime economy, but at least some of the effects seem to be similar to those created by an economy *temporarily* geared to high military expenditures: namely, inflation and debt. The dollar that bought $2.38 worth of goods in 1940 bought about 59 cents' worth in 1976. In the thirty years since the end of World War II there have been few years in which expenditures did not exceed revenues, with the result that the national debt rose from about $43 billion in 1940 to $258 billion at the end of World War II, in 1945, but to more than $620 billion in 1976. It will be up to future economic historians to decide whether this thirty-year trend was something the American system could and did absorb without massive dislocation or whether it meant, as some fiscal conservatives and some Marxists have naggingly said, that the country was slowly going bankrupt.

A fourth major pattern of the 1946–76 years has been the explosive growth in the communications media, particularly in data processing, xerography, and television. The first true computer (ENIAC) was operational by 1946, and by 1951 the Bureau of the Census had installed UNIVAC, a machine with a memory and a program capable of searching this memory and handling a fairly wide range of problems. Invented in 1940, the xerographic copying process was commercialized in 1947 by the Haloid Corporation, which as the Xerox Corporation put its first automatic office copying machine on the market in 1959–60. In less than ten years Xeroxing and other dry-copying processes had revolutionized office procedures and the publishing industry, created a whole nest of tricky problems relating to copyright, and, not incidentally, made it much harder for government and industry to hang on to their secrets. High-fidelity sound reproduction (developed during World War II so that the different sounds of German and British submarines could be taught to trainees) combined in 1948 with the long-playing phonograph record, with the result that major symphonic and operatic works could now be recorded on a relatively few records. The transistor, invented in 1948, made possible great gains in the compactness, storage capacity, and portability of both computers and radios. Television, a medium delivering a set of visual and aural stimuli that were not only complex but immediate, became the most popular form of mass communication and entertainment. Live television coverage of domestic and foreign events also greatly amplified both the individual and the social responses to these events. And the communications revolution has only begun; it may yet fulfill its promise to organize resources and disseminate knowledge on a global scale.

The years 1946–76 have certainly taught us much about the ability of ordinary citizens and political leaders alike to cope with bewildering changes in the national and world community. It may well be that future historians will point to these years as a time in which the American nation was tested as few others have been. It was tested by a brief moment in the late 1940's when American power could have reached into a helpless world and taken what it wanted but instead gave, not took. It was tested in the 1950's by deep and legitimate fears about a new, threatening world, fears that could have turned the United States into an autocratic power abroad or a police state at home but instead saw it fight a police action in Korea and turn its face soon enough from Senator Joseph McCarthy's homegrown demagoguery. It was tested in the 1960's and early 1970's by a series of schismatic internal and foreign disasters that would have had most nations reaching for their generals but saw America instead reach for the nicest man it could find, one whose ideas of rough stuff derived from the football field, not the parade ground. In 1976, when most other countries would have bet on an incumbent, the people of the United States took a chance on a Deep South agriculturist-engineer who called for economic justice, asked for ordinary decency in the nation's politi-

cal life, promised changes in the national policies toward energy and the environment and hence in the way ordinary Americans live, and even went so far as to suggest that love, faith, and intellect were not things he was ashamed of having.

During the years 1946–76 Americans encountered many unfamiliar and discouraging constraints, but we also burst out of the greatest physical constraint of all. During this period we sent a probe into the deep universe, a gesture not only proud but also sublimely hopeful. Somebody might be out there, and if so, we'd like to say our How-Do-You-Do's. During this period we also took the first crucial steps out of the planetary cradle, an achievement that future historians may measure against all other achievements in the entire history of the human species so far.

Apollo 16, *a manned flight headed for the moon, blasts off.*
NASA

Cold Wars and Others (1946–1976)

1946

Employment Act of 1946 (February 20): creates Council of Economic Advisers for President and in effect makes federal government responsible for promoting full employment, controlling inflation, and otherwise concerning itself with health of the economy.

Winston Churchill, in Fulton, Missouri, speech, refers to an "iron curtain" behind which Soviet Union is organizing governments of Central and Eastern Europe (March 5).

U.S. proposes to ban atomic weapons (June 14); plan, offered to United Nations, calls for international inspection system run by UN and subsequent destruction of U.S. bomb stockpile; Soviet Union rejects proposal because it will not accept inspection.

Philippines granted full independence by U.S. (July 4); leases military bases to U.S.

Atomic Energy Commission established (August 1); civilian agency is to control all military and nonmilitary nuclear development.

Fulbright scholarship program established (August 1); proposed by Senator J. William Fulbright (Arkansas), plan establishes system of grants enabling American students to study abroad and foreign students to study in U.S.; program initially financed by sale of U.S. wartime surpluses to Allies.

President Truman fires Henry A. Wallace, now Secretary of Commerce, for continued advocacy of "friendly, peaceful competition" with Soviet Union and satellites (September 20).

Republicans gain control of House and Senate in midterm elections (November 5).

Truman creates Committee on Civil Rights by executive order (December 5); in following year committee issues report, "To Secure These Rights," that recommends federal antilynching law, elimination of poll tax, end to segregation in armed forces, integration of interstate travel, and establishment of permanent Fair Employment Practices Commission.

John D. Rockefeller donates $8.5 million site for United Nations headquarters in New York City (December 14).

Price controls are removed, and consumers bid up prices for relatively scarce consumer goods; most unions in basic industries strike for higher wages. There are almost 5,000 strikes, involving more than 4.5 million workers.

1947

Truman Doctrine (March 12): in message to Congress, Truman announces policy of containment of Soviet expansion through support of anti-Communist governments around the world and specifically asks for $400 million in aid to Turkey and Greece. Right-wing Greek government has been under attack by Greek Communists supported by Soviet satellites.

Truman establishes program to investigate loyalty of all present and future government employees (March 21).

United Nations grants U.S. trusteeship over Micronesia within a three-million-square-mile area of Pacific Ocean (April 2).

Jack Roosevelt "Jackie" Robinson is signed by the Brooklyn Dodgers, thus becoming the first black player in twentieth-century major-league baseball (April 11).

"Jackie" Robinson
BASEBALL HALL OF FAME

Marshall Plan proposed (June 5); Secretary of State George C. Marshall proposes that European nations draw up economic recovery plan that U.S. will then fund; Soviet Union turns down offer, but sixteen European nations participate, ultimately receiving about $12 billion in aid.

Taft-Hartley (Labor Management Relations) Act passed over Truman's veto (June 23); bans closed shop (establishment in which only union members can be hired), permits employers to sue for broken contracts, allows federal government to seek 80-day cooling-off injunction against damaging strikes, ends check-off system (in which employer collects union dues), forbids political contributions, and requires union leaders to swear they are not Communists.

National Security Act (July 26): establishes Air Force as separate branch coequal with Army and Navy and places all three branches in national military establishment under a Secretary of Defense; creates National Security Council and Central Intelligence Agency (CIA).

First piloted airplane breaks sound barrier in California (October 14).

1948

U.S. recognizes new state of Israel minutes after Israel, created by UN General Assembly, declares its independence (May 14).

United Automobile Workers and General Motors sign first wage contract pegged to cost of living (May 25).

Western Allies agree to form state of West Germany (June 7).

Displaced Persons Act (June 25): grants visas to 205,000 Europeans who cannot or will not return to their homes (now in Soviet-controlled Europe).

Berlin airlift: U.S. begins (June 26) to fly in supplies to Allied-controlled portion of Berlin, which lies within Soviet-controlled East Germany and to which Soviets have cut off highway and railroad access; blockade is broken almost a year later, after 272,264 flights that carry in more than 2.3 million tons of food, fuel, and other supplies.

President Truman bans segregation in U.S. armed forces by Executive Order 9981 (July 30); Congress had failed to do so in new draft law, passed on June 24, which authorized peacetime armed forces of 2 million.

Campaign of 1948: Republicans nominate Thomas E. Dewey (New York) and Governor Earl Warren (California); Democrats nominate Harry S. Truman and Senator Alben W. Barkley (Kentucky); southern Democrats, offended by civil-rights plank in Democratic platform, bolt to form States' Rights, or Dixiecrat, Party, running Strom Thurmond (South Carolina); liberal Democrats bolt to form Progressive Party, which opposes cold-war foreign policy and runs Henry A. Wallace. Three other parties nominate candidates, including Norman Thomas of Socialists. Truman, though widely considered hopelessly out of the running, conducts hard-hitting whistle-stop campaign, lambasting "do-nothing" (Republican) Congress, attacking Taft-Hartley law, and generally "giving 'em hell." Popular vote (November 2): Truman 24,105,587, Dewey 21,970,017, Thurmond 1,169,134, Wallace 1,157,057; electoral vote: Truman 303, Dewey 189, Thurmond 39. Democrats regain control of House and Senate.

Alfred C. Kinsey and others publish *Sexual Behavior in the Human Male,* which documents wide variety of sexual practices.

1949

Harry S. Truman inaugurated for first term (January 20); Alben W. Barkley is Vice President. In his inaugural address Truman calls for foreign aid in form of technical assistance to underdeveloped countries, which becomes known as "Point Four" program.

Harry S. Truman
TRUMAN LIBRARY

North Atlantic Treaty Organization (NATO) pact is signed (April 4); U.S., Great Britain, France, Canada, Denmark, Norway, Iceland, Belgium, the Netherlands, Luxembourg, Italy, and Portugal sign mutual-defense treaty that commits signatories to defend each other against military attack; for first time U.S. enters into permanent "entangling" alliance, thus for the first time abjuring advice in Washington's Farewell Address.

President Truman announces that the Soviet Union has the atomic bomb (September 23).

People's Republic of China proclaimed by Mao Tse-tung (October 1); on December 7 corrupt, incompetent Nationalist government is finally driven out of China to Formosa (Taiwan), which Chiang Kai-shek takes over by slaughtering Formosans, who are Japanese in language and culture. There is a great outcry in U.S. about Truman administration's having "lost" China by failing to support Chiang sufficiently, and to many Americans it seems that the whole world is going Communist.

Eleven leaders of U.S. Communist Party are tried and found guilty under Smith Act of 1940 (October 14); convictions are later (1951) upheld by Supreme Court.

1950

Alger Hiss, former State Department official, is found

guilty of perjury and sentenced to five years in prison (January 21); Hiss case began in 1948, when he was accused by self-confessed Communist Whittaker Chambers of passing classified documents in the 1930's. Representative Richard Milhous Nixon (California) of House Un-American Activities Committee has made a name for himself in Hiss case by charging a Democratic cover-up.

In Wheeling, West Virginia, speech Senator Joseph McCarthy of Wisconsin charges that he has the names of 205 (later the number was changed to 57) Communists who are working in U.S. State Department (February 9).

North Korean forces invade South Korea (June 25); UN Security Council (which Soviet Union is boycotting) asks for cease-fire and withdrawal of North Korea; Security Council calls for armed resistance to North Koreans (June 27), and Truman, who has already made decision to commit U.S. Air Force and Navy, orders air and naval gunfire support of South Korean troops; U.S. ground forces committed to battle (June 30).

President Truman sends 35 military advisers to Vietnam, where Communist forces under Ho Chi Minh have been battling French soldiers and a French colonial puppet regime since 1945 (June 27); later in year (December 23) U.S. signs treaty with France, Vietnam, Laos, and Cambodia providing for American aid to Indochina for purposes of defending "the principles of freedom." Until 1954 U.S. pays an estimated two thirds to three quarters of costs of French war against Ho.

Truman asks for U.S. mobilization and $10 billion rearmament appropriation (July 19); General Douglas MacArthur has been appointed head of UN forces in Korea, 90 per cent of whom are American.

General MacArthur receives the Distinguished Service Medal.
LIBRARY OF CONGRESS

Defense Production Act signed (September 8); gives Truman wartime control of prices and wages.

McCarran (Internal Security) Act passed over Truman's veto (September 23); requires registration of U.S. Communists and "Communist-front" organizations; Truman protests that act will "put the government of the United States in the thought-control business."

Puerto Rican nationalists fail in attempt to assassinate President Truman (November 1).

Republicans, charging Democratic softness on Communism, win large gains in congressional midterm elections but do not win control of either house (November 7); in Maryland senatorial election McCarthy aides campaigned against Senator Millard Tydings, who had investigated McCarthy's charges and found them to be fraudulent. McCarthy's intervention in Maryland election is held to be responsible for Tydings' defeat, and thereafter elected officials become increasingly reluctant to challenge McCarthy's methods or charges.

Chinese Communists, who have warned that they will not "stand idly by," throw in 250,000 troops when MacArthur presses into Yalu Valley, near Chinese-Korean border (November 26); by January, 1951, UN troops have been forced back below 38th parallel and have lost Seoul, capital of South Korea.

NATO members agree on plan for rearming Europe, including West Germany (December 18); General Dwight Eisenhower is appointed overall commander of NATO forces (December 19).

Census of 1950: total population 150,697,000. The rate of population increase is about double that of the 1930–40 decade and has been affected by a rising birthrate, a declining death rate, and a substantial increase in immigration (1,034,503, many of them displaced Europeans). About 65 per cent of the population is now urbanized. Black Americans have, for first time since 1790, ceased to decline as a percentage of the total population and have risen slightly, to about 10 per cent, largely as a result of declining death rates. Many northern cities have doubled their black populations.

1951

Twenty-second Amendment is ratified (February 26); limits U.S. Presidents to two full terms; if President has succeeded to office and serves for more than two years, that tenure will be considered a full term.

Julius and Ethel Rosenberg are sentenced to death for conspiring to steal atomic secrets (April 5); they are executed two years later.

President Truman fires General MacArthur for insubordination (April 11); MacArthur wants to run risk of provoking wider war by attacking China. He returns to a hero's welcome, and Truman's popularity plunges.

Truce talks on Korea begin (July 10); talks later break down but are resumed in Panmunjom on October 25; negotiations go on for next two years, but so does fighting, although neither side achieves significant territorial gains; U.S. continues to bomb North Korea and subject it to naval bombardment.

First simultaneous nationwide television broadcast (September 4): carries Truman's address to international conference in San Francisco, gathered to sign peace treaty with Japan; treaty is signed September 8.

1952

Truman orders government seizure of steel mills in order to prevent strike (April 8); Supreme Court later rules his action unconstitutional (June 2).

Federal Communications Commission authorizes use of 70 frequencies and grants licenses to more than 2,000 new stations (April 13).

Keel of first atomic submarine, U.S.S. *Nautilus,* is dedicated at Groton, Connecticut (June 14); *Nautilus* is commissioned about two years later.

McCarran-Walter (Immigration and Nationality) Act passed over Truman's veto (June 27); retains 1924 quotas but lifts ban on Asian immigration; imposes stiff new measures for screening subversives and empowers Attorney General to deport naturalized U.S. citizens who have "Communist-front" affiliations.

Truman signs GI Bill of Rights for veterans of Korean War (July 16).

Puerto Rico becomes self-governing commonwealth (July 25).

U.S. explodes hydrogen bomb on Eniwetok Atoll in Marshall Islands (November 1).

Campaign of 1952: Republicans nominate Dwight D. Eisenhower and Senator Richard M. Nixon on July 11; Democrats nominate Governor Adlai E. Stevenson (Illinois) and Senator John J. Sparkman (Alabama) on July 26. An estimated 65 million Americans watch nominating conventions on television. Republicans attack Truman, bureaucratic corruption, and foreign policy, call for lower taxes and reduction of national debt, and support Taft-Hartley law; Democrats call for civil rights and repeal of Taft-Hartley. Nixon is almost dropped from Republican ticket when secret California slush fund is disclosed, but he defends himself in maudlin

televised "Checkers" speech (September 23) in which he tearfully refers to dog Checkers, a gift he says he won't return because his family loves it. Eisenhower promises to go to Korea and end a war many Americans are now sick of. Six other parties run candidates. Popular vote (November 4): Eisenhower 33,936,137, Stevenson 27,314,649; electoral vote: Eisenhower 442, Stevenson 89. Republicans gain control of both houses of Congress by slim margins.

President-elect Dwight Eisenhower leaves for three-day inspection trip to Korea (November 29).

1953

Dwight D. Eisenhower inaugurated as thirty-fourth President (January 20); Richard M. Nixon becomes Vice President.

Secretary of State John Foster Dulles says in radio-TV broadcast aimed at Iron Curtain countries that "captive peoples" there can "count on us" (January 27); congressional resolution embodying this principle is shelved upon Stalin's death (March 5); "captive peoples" in several East German cities subsequently revolt and are suppressed. U.S. cannot and does not intervene.

Department of Health, Education, and Welfare becomes operational, with Mrs. Oveta Culp Hobby as Secretary (April 11); consolidates previously separate agencies, including Social Security Administration.

Tidelands Oil Bill (May 22): gives states offshore oil lands, generally within three-mile limit but extending to ten and a half miles off Texas and Florida. Oil reserves are estimated to be worth $40 billion and had been set aside by President Truman (whose actions were upheld in several Supreme Court decisions) as belonging to nation.

Korean armistice signed (July 27); demilitarized zone is created around 38th parallel, and complicated provisions are worked out for repatriation of prisoners. Twenty-three Americans refuse to return; it is later learned that many American prisoners of war collaborated with North Korean captors, and term "brainwashing" enters the language. U.S. casualties: 54,246 dead, 103,284 wounded out of approximately 5,720,000 who served in some capacity. Actual costs of war are difficult to separate from huge military budgets of 1945–55 period, but estimated current costs through 1974 are $67.5 billion.

Refugee Relief Act (August 7): allows refugees from Communist nations to enter U.S. even if normal quotas from such countries are exceeded; some 214,000 are admitted in next three years.

Soviet Union announces it has tested a hydrogen bomb (August 20).

Earl Warren, governor of California, is appointed Chief Justice of the U.S. Supreme Court (October 5).

Senator McCarthy charges Communist influence in U.S. Army (December); McCarthy has been riding high throughout year, getting away with unfounded accusations and various smear tactics, but overreaches himself when he suggests Communist conspiracy is behind routine promotion of New York dentist drafted in 1952; dentist, summoned before McCarthy's Senate Permanent Investigating Subcommittee in January, 1954, pleads Fifth Amendment, thereby becoming a "Fifth Amendment Communist" and "proving" McCarthy's case that whole army chain of command is infiltrated with Communists. McCarthy's hearings are paralleled by hearings in other Senate and House committees, including the House Un-American Activities Committee, which investigates Communists in entertainment industry and spawns blacklisting of actors, directors, and writers in movie industry.

Senator Joseph McCarthy
NATIONAL ARCHIVES

1954

Secretary of State John Foster Dulles announces strategy of "massive retaliation" (January 12); instead of containment by fighting "brush-fire" wars, as in Korea, U.S. will now respond to Communist aggression with heavy nuclear attack delivered by long-range bombers; reliance on nuclear deterrent is known in the parlance of the times as getting "more bang for the buck."

Mass immunization program is begun to test Salk vaccine against polio (February 23); test results, announced following year, show vaccine to be safe and effective.

Puerto Rican nationalists shoot up U.S. House of Representatives, wounding five congressmen (March 1).

U.S. explodes H-bomb on Bikini Atoll in Marshall Islands (March 1); it is later revealed that Japanese fishing boat 80 miles away has received fallout that seriously injures 22 fishermen and kills one. Other Japanese fishermen, operating 1,000 miles from Bikini, take fish that prove on examination to be contaminated with radioactivity.

Establishment of U.S. Air Force Academy is authorized (April 1); permanent facilities open four years later near Colorado Springs, Colorado.

Eisenhower makes reference, in a press conference, to a concept that thereafter becomes known as the domino theory (April 7); defending U.S. policies in Indochina, he says that if one Southeast Asian nation (Vietnam) falls to Communists, the others will go too: "You have a row of dominoes set up. You knock over the first one, and what will happen to the last one is the certainty that it will go over very quickly."

Army-McCarthy hearings (April 22–June 17): Army, stung by McCarthy allegations in dentist case, brings charges that Roy Cohn, counsel to McCarthy's subcommittee, had improperly sought favors for Private G. David Schine, a former member of McCarthy's committee who had toured the United States Information Services libraries abroad, removing from them as subversive books like John Steinbeck's *Grapes of Wrath*. Hearings, conducted by Senator Karl Mundt, are televised, and for first time millions of Americans get to see McCarthy in action and don't like what they see. Key day is June 9, when McCarthy falsely accuses counsel for Army, Joseph Welch, of having a Communist in his old-line Boston law firm. Welch tears into McCarthy: "Have you no sense of decency, sir, at long last?" At that moment millions of Americans *see* that McCarthy does not, and it is all over. Later the Mundt committee in effect absolves both McCarthy and the Army of charges, but McCarthy is finished. The "big lie" no longer attracts any attention, and McCarthy becomes an alcoholic.

Communist forces (Vietminh) take Dien Bien Phu, vital French-defended fort in North Vietnam (May 7); U.S. has twice wished to intervene directly in aid of French, but neither Britain nor France will support further military action in Vietnam.

St. Lawrence Seaway authorized (May 13); Canada and U.S. agree to construct deep channel between Montreal and Lake Ontario; seaway ultimately includes system of inland waterways connecting Atlantic to all Great Lakes.

Brown v. *Board of Education of Topeka* (May 17): U.S. Supreme Court rules unanimously that racial segregation in schools is a violation of the equal-protection clause of the Fourteenth Amendment; decision specifically overturns "separate but equal" *Plessy* v. *Ferguson* ruling and declares that "separate educational facilities are inherently unequal."

Atomic Energy Commission removes security clearance of J. Robert Oppenheimer, who developed first atomic bomb at Los Alamos, New Mexico (June 1); AEC finds that Oppenheimer, although "loyal," has Communist "associations" and is not sufficiently enthusiastic about H-bomb.

CIA helps overthrow elected regime in Guatemala, which is regarded as pro-Communist (June 29).

Geneva Agreements (July 20): U.S., France, Britain, U.S.S.R., China, Cambodia, Laos, and Communist and non-Communist governments in Vietnam reach accords whereby Vietnam will be partitioned along a 17th-parallel demilitarized zone, foreign military bases will be prohibited anywhere in Vietnam, and general elections will be held in 1956. U.S. does not sign Geneva accords but promises to do nothing to "disturb" them. However, a CIA team is already conducting covert operations against Vietminh, and on August 20 President Eisenhower agrees to undertake defense of South Vietnam, now headed by Ngo Dinh Diem.

Communist Control Act (August 24): deprives U.S. Communists of various civil rights.

Atomic Energy Act (August 30): permits U.S. to share information on military and peaceful uses of atomic energy with friendly nations and authorizes development of atomic power plants by private U.S. companies.

Southeast Asia Treaty Organization (SEATO) pact signed (September 8); SEATO includes only three Asian nations (Philippines, Thailand, Pakistan), specifically excludes Taiwan, and commits U.S. to defense of signatory nations only in case of Communist aggression. SEATO later extends protection to Vietnam, Cambodia, and Laos, although this is a violation of Geneva Agreements.

Canada and U.S. agree to set up DEW (Distant Early Warning) line, a string of radar stations extending from Alaska to Greenland across northern Canada (September 27); DEW line is operational in 1957.

Furor over violence and vulgarity in comic books leads comic-book publishers to adopt self-censorship (October 27); comic books have greater circulation than *Reader's Digest, Life, Look, Ladies' Home Journal, McCall's,* and *Better Homes and Gardens* combined.

Democrats regain control of Congress in midterm elections (November 2), despite charges by Vice President Nixon that Democrats have poor record on Communism.

Senate "condemns" McCarthy for "conduct that tends to bring the Senate into dishonor and disrepute" (December 2); measure falls short of formal censure and does not strip McCarthy of any senatorial privileges.

1955

Congress passes Formosa Resolution (January 28); requested by President Eisenhower, resolution authorizes U.S. protection of small Nationalist-controlled islands near Formosa, which have been under intermittent Red Chinese bombardment since September, 1954; U.S. is committed by treaty to defend Chiang's regime on Formosa, but status of offshore islands has been unclear; in March, Red Chinese cease bombardments of islands.

First U.S. military advisers sent to Vietnam to train South Vietnamese army (February 23); in following year (May, 1956) U.S. sends additional 350 advisers, in violation of Geneva accords.

U.S. Supreme Court orders that its 1954 *Brown* v. *Topeka* decision be implemented "with all deliberate speed" (May 31).

Eisenhower cancels Dixon-Yates contract (July 11); contract to private utility in Memphis, Tennessee, was criticized in 1954 as an attempt to "dismember" TVA and is further tainted by conflict-of-interest scandal.

Geneva summit meeting (July 18–23): Eisenhower, Soviet leader Nikolai Bulganin, British prime minister Anthony Eden, and French premier Edgar Faure meet to discuss various international issues. Eisenhower proposes "Open Skies" plan for mutual aerial inspection to guarantee against surprise attacks. No significant agreements are reached, but summit tone is cordial, and international tensions are relaxed.

Poliomyelitis Vaccination Assistance Act (August 12): the Salk vaccine having proved effective, act provides $30 million to states for vaccination program.

Eisenhower suffers heart attack (September 24); returns to active presidential duties on November 22.

As result of Eisenhower's heart attack, stock market plunges (September 26); single day's losses ($14 billion) are greatest in history of stock exchange, but market recovers quickly. In general, this is a year of unprecedented prosperity, with high consumer spending and record outputs in many industries, including steel and automobiles.

Tired after a long day's work, Mrs. Rosa Parks, a black seamstress in Montgomery, Alabama, refuses to give up her seat to a white passenger and move to the back of the bus; she is arrested (December 1); a young black minister, Dr. Martin Luther King, Jr., and other members of black community organize boycott of Montgomery bus lines (December 5); nonviolent boycott lasts for almost a year and is ultimately successful.

American Federation of Labor and Congress of Industrial Organizations merge to form single 16-million-member AFL-CIO, with George Meany as president (December 5).

1956

Manifesto, "Declaration of Constitutional Principles," is issued by 101 southern members of Congress (March 12); calls upon states to resist Supreme Court desegregation rulings "by all lawful means." Several have already closed schools or voted to fund private schools for whites.

U.S. Supreme Court rules that public servants may not be fired simply because they invoke Fifth Amendment (April 9).

Agricultural (Soil Bank) Act (May 28): pays farmers to remove croplands from production; measure, similar to old Agricultural Adjustment Act of New Deal era, is designed to reduce enormous food surpluses.

Federal-Aid Highway Act (June 29): authorizes thirteen-year program for 41,000-mile state and interstate highway systems at cost of more than $30 billion; federal government will pay 90 per cent of costs of interstate highways and split costs of state road-building programs.

U.S. retracts offer to lend Egypt money to build Aswan Dam on Nile (July 19); Egyptian leader Gamal Abdel Nasser nationalizes Suez Canal (July 26), intending to use Suez revenues to build dam.

U.S. and Soviet Union force Britain, France, and Israel to withdraw from Suez Canal, which they have captured from Egypt (November 6).

Campaign of 1956: Republicans run Dwight D. Eisenhower and Richard Nixon; Democrats run Adlai E. Stevenson and Estes Kefauver (Tennessee); four other parties nominate candidates. Republican and Democratic platforms are similar, being in favor of civil rights, hydroelectric power, and supports for farmers. Questions are raised about Eisenhower's health, and Democratic candidate proposes ban on H-bomb testing. Popular vote (November 6): Eisenhower 35,585,245, Stevenson 26,030,172; electoral vote: Eisenhower 457,

Stevenson 73. Eisenhower's sweeping victory is personal one, since Democrats increase majorities in both House and Senate.

Supreme Court voids Alabama law segregating public transportation (December 13).

1957

U.S. voids Michigan obscenity law that prohibits publication or sale to adults of anything that has potential for "corrupting" children (February 25).

Eisenhower Doctrine (March 7): Congress passes resolution empowering President to give economic and military assistance to any Middle Eastern nation requesting help against Communist aggression; "doctrine" is necessary because of power vacuum caused by humiliation of British and French during last year's Suez crisis.

Watkins v. *United States* (June 17): U.S. Supreme Court restricts right of congressional investigating committees to query a witness for the sole purpose of exposing the person's views or associations to public censure; Court holds that questions must be related to a topic about which Congress intends to legislate.

International Geophysical Year begins (July 1); 60,000 scientists from 70 nations begin 18-month study of earth, atmosphere, oceans, the sun, and outer space.

U.S. proposes ten-month ban on nuclear testing (July 2); public concern about nuclear fallout has risen.

Arkansas governor, Orval E. Faubus, blocks integration of Central High School in Little Rock with National Guard troops he has called up (September 4); after

A black student entering Little Rock's Central High School

violence results, President Eisenhower sends in federal troops (paratroopers) and removes Guard from Faubus' control (September 24), and 1,000 paratroopers escort nine black children past howling mob into Central High on September 25.

Black students being escorted from class at Central High
WIDE WORLD

Civil Rights Act of 1957 (September 9): establishes Civil Rights Division in Department of Justice and prohibits interference with a person's right to vote.

Soviet Union places *Sputnik 1,* 184-pound artificial satellite, world's first, into elliptical orbit around earth (October 4); U.S. and world are astonished at evidence of Soviet technological sophistication. On November 3 Soviets place in orbit 1,120-pound *Sputnik 2,* containing live dog ("Laika"), thus indicating that they have very powerful rockets.

U.S. Office of Education publishes survey of Soviet education, showing great emphasis on scientific and technical study (November 10); report causes much hand wringing in U.S. educational circles.

Eisenhower suffers mild stroke (November 25).

AFL-CIO expels Teamsters' Union for corruption (December 6); Teamster leader Dave Beck has been investigated by Senate and later convicted of embezzlement, and Teamster official Jimmy Hoffa is also under cloud.

First atomic power plant begins to produce electricity in Shippingport, Pennsylvania (December 18).

1958

U.S. launches *Explorer 1,* its first successful artificial satellite (January 31); 18-pound satellite confirms presence of Van Allen radiation belts.

Fallout controversy (April): AEC and Dr. Edward Teller defend continued nuclear testing and state that present radioactive levels are not dangerous; critics claim that present radiation levels will cause cancer and birth defects.

Vice President Richard Nixon begins good-will tour of Latin America (April 27); tour ends May 15, after hostile crowds, especially in Peru and Venezuela, throw eggs and rocks at him.

At request of Lebanese government, U.S. sends Marines to protect Lebanon from leftist "indirect aggression" from Egypt and Iraq (July 15); troops are withdrawn in October.

National Aeronautics and Space Administration (NASA) created (July 29); civilian agency is to handle all space exploration of a nonmilitary nature.

Nuclear submarine U.S.S. *Nautilus* ends trip from Hawaii to Iceland, in the course of which it travels under North Pole and Arctic ice (August 5).

National Defense Education Act (September 2): provides more than $600 million for low-cost loans to college and graduate students interested in teaching, sciences, and mathematics, for building up science and modern-language facilities, and for multimedia education.

Eisenhower's chief presidential assistant, Sherman Adams, resigns (September 22); resignation comes after scandal involving regulatory agencies and gifts to Adams by Boston industrialist who has cases pending before agencies.

U.S. shoots *Pioneer 1* rocket toward moon (October 11); rocket gets 70,700 miles from earth.

Democrats score large gains in congressional midterm elections (November 4); reflects public dissatisfaction with nuclear testing, racial tensions, and deepening recession (unemployment rate reaches almost 8 per cent).

U.S. successfully tests intercontinental ballistic missile (ICBM) with 6,325-mile range (November 28).

1959

Alaska becomes forty-ninth state (January 3).

NASA selects seven astronauts for training program; NASA has estimated that it will be able to get men to the moon in ten years (April 9).

Fidel Castro, head of revolutionary Cuban government, receives warm welcome in U.S. (April 15–28).

U.S. Postmaster General bans D. H. Lawrence's *Lady*

Fidel Castro, Manuel Bisbe, and Dag Hammarskjöld at the UN
UNITED NATIONS

Chatterley's Lover from mails as obscene (June 11); U.S. court later (1960) reverses ban.

St. Lawrence Seaway formally opened by President Eisenhower and Queen Elizabeth II (June 26).

Vice President Nixon visits Soviet Union (July 23–August 2); Nixon addresses Soviet people on TV and engages Soviet Premier Nikita Khrushchev in impromptu debate at U.S. exhibition in Moscow; debate is called "kitchen debate" because it takes place in kitchen of model ranch house that, Nixon points out, a U.S. steelworker could afford; Soviet Union has great shortage of consumer goods and is very touchy about it.

Hawaii becomes fiftieth state (August 21).

Landrum-Griffin Act (September 14): a response to investigations of racketeering and corruption in labor unions, act requires secret-ballot elections, disclosure of union finances, and variety of other controls and penalties.

Nikita Khrushchev visits United States (September 15–27); meets with President Eisenhower at Camp

Nikita Khrushchev waves after addressing the United Nations.
UNITED NATIONS

David, Maryland; general air of détente and cordiality, along with announcement that Eisenhower will visit Soviet Union next year, is dubbed "spirit of Camp David."

1960

Sit-in movement begins (February 2); four black college students in Greensboro, North Carolina, sit in whites-only Woolworth lunch counter and, although not served, remain there in peaceful protest. Sit-in tactic quickly spreads throughout South.

Black students stage a sit-in at a segregated lunch counter.
WIDE WORLD

U-2 incident (May 1–17): Soviets announce that they have downed U.S. plane more than 1,000 miles inside their territory; U.S. claims it is a weather plane, whereupon Soviets produce pilot, Francis Gary Powers, a self-confessed CIA operative; on May 11 Eisenhower says he personally authorized U-2 overflight, which forces Khrushchev (who is having trouble with Red China and with his own military hawks) to bluster and demand an apology; Eisenhower refuses. Khrushchev then calls off Paris summit meeting, which began on May 16, and cancels scheduled visit of Eisenhower to Soviet Union. (Khrushchev had been eager enough for Eisenhower's visit to order the construction of a golf course; Ike's love of golf was legendary, and Soviet Union didn't have a course.)

Civil Rights Act of 1960 (May 6): permits federal judges to order supervision of voter registration and elections and stiffens penalties for interference with voting rights.

U.S. stops buying Cuban sugar and embargoes most exports to Cuba (October 20); Cuban-American relations have soured since June, when U.S.-owned refineries in Cuba refused to process Soviet oil; Cuba then proceeded to nationalize all big industries, issued nationalistic anti-American statements, and received diplomatic support from Soviet Union.

Campaign of 1960: Democrats nominate Senator John F. Kennedy (Massachusetts) and Senator Lyndon B. Johnson (Texas); Republicans nominate Richard M. Nixon and Henry Cabot Lodge (Massachusetts). Democratic platform has strong civil-rights plank, favors federal medical care for aged and loosened credit to combat recession; Republican platform calls for strong civil-rights enforcement, a fiscally sound health program, strong defense, and continued support of Eisenhower foreign policy. Kennedy calls for strong chief executive who will get country "moving again" and charges (nonexistent) "missile gap" with Soviet Union; Kennedy's Catholicism is also an issue, but he pledges strict separation of Church and State. There are four nationally televised debates (September 26–October 21) in which Nixon's nervous mannerisms place him at a disadvantage. Popular vote: Kennedy 34,221,344, Nixon 34,106,671. Election remains in doubt until December 19, when electoral vote is announced: Kennedy 300, Nixon 219—not including Hawaii's 3 votes, which by January 6, 1961, have gone to Kennedy.

U.S. abstains from General Assembly resolution calling for "speedy and unconditional" end to colonialism (December 14).

Census of 1960: total population 179,323,175, of whom about 2.5 million are immigrants. Almost 70 per cent of population is now urbanized; however, almost 28 per cent of large American cities have lost population, the slack being taken up by huge (85 per cent) growth of suburbs surrounding central cities. Nevada, Arizona, California, and Florida gain heavily in population and acquire additional representatives in House; Pennsylvania, New York, and Massachusetts each lose two or more representatives.

1961

President Eisenhower breaks off diplomatic relations with Cuba (January 3).

In farewell address President Eisenhower warns nation of "military-industrial complex" (January 17); says that combination of immense military establishment and large civilian arms industry has "grave implications" for "very structure of our society." (Defense budget for 1960 is $40 billion, more than three times what it was in 1950.)

John F. Kennedy is inaugurated as thirty-fifth President (January 20); Lyndon B. Johnson becomes Vice President.

President Kennedy creates Peace Corps by executive order (March 1); calls for civilian volunteers to aid underdeveloped countries in health, education, and tech-

A Peace Corps member, right, works as a mechanic in Tunisia.
PEACE CORPS

nical areas; Congress makes program permanent and appropriates $30 million in September, by which time 13,000 Americans have volunteered.

President Kennedy proposes Alliance for Progress (March 13); objectives of alliance are to promote economic and social development of Latin America, with U.S. pledging $20 billion to program; organization is chartered on August 17.

Twenty-third Amendment ratified (March 29); gives residents of Washington, D.C., right to vote in presidential elections.

Bay of Pigs invasion: 1,500 U.S.-trained and U.S.-equipped Cuban exiles land in Cuba (April 17) and, contrary to CIA expectations, do not set off popular uprising but instead are quickly crushed (April 20); Kennedy accepts (April 24) full responsibility for fiasco, which boosts Castro's prestige among Third World nations and causes embarrassment and dismay among U.S. allies.

Freedom riders, biracial group sponsored by CORE (Congress of Racial Equality), leave Washington, D.C.,

Alabama police surround a fire-bombed freedom-riders' bus.
WIDE WORLD

on interstate buses to force integration of interstate facilities in South (May 4); riders are attacked and beaten in several cities; U.S. Attorney General Robert Kennedy sends U.S. marshals to protect riders.

President Kennedy calls for additional $3.5 billion defense appropriation and reserve call-up in response to Berlin crisis (July 25); action comes about as result of June meeting in Vienna with Soviet Premier Khrushchev that convinces Kennedy Soviets intend to force Western powers out of West Berlin; Soviets respond by building Berlin Wall (August 13), which seals off access to West Berlin and ends flight of East German population to West via Berlin.

Soviet Union resumes atmospheric testing of nuclear weapons (September 1); U.S. resumes underground tests (September 5), and test-ban discussions in Geneva are shelved.

Although Kennedy turns down recommendation by General Maxwell Taylor and Walt W. Rostow that U.S. commit 6,000–8,000 troops to South Vietnam in support of Diem regime, which is under attack by Vietcong (South Vietnamese Communists), he does increase number of military advisers, sends in Special Forces (counterinsurgency group) and helicopter units, and uses navy and air force units for reconnaissance; by end of 1961 3,200 Americans are serving in some military capacity in South Vietnam.

1962

John H. Glenn, Jr., becomes first American astronaut to achieve outer-space orbit around earth (February 20);

John H. Glenn, Jr., with the space capsule Friendship 7
NASA

Soviet Union has achieved similar feat in 1961, but U.S. is now closing "space-race" gap.

Baker v. *Carr* (March 26): U.S. Supreme Court holds that federal courts have jurisdiction over suits involving apportionment of state legislatures; case is first in series of decisions resulting in "one-man, one vote" doctrine.

President Kennedy forces rollback of steel prices (April 13); U.S. Steel and others have announced price hike despite earlier agreement with Kennedy administration not to.

U.S. Supreme Court bans reading of specially composed prayer in New York State schools (June 25); in later decisions Court holds that all prayer and readings from Bible represent violations of separation of Church and State.

Telstar 1, communications satellite handling TV and telephone signals, is placed in orbit (July 10).

James H. Meredith enters University of Mississippi as first black student (October 1); Mississippi governor, Ross Barnett, has been held in contempt of court for denying Meredith admission; riots and two deaths have resulted; Meredith is escorted to class by federal marshals.

Cuban missile crisis: President Kennedy announces that Soviets are building nuclear missile bases in Cuba and proclaims naval blockade of Cuba and U.S. intention to halt and search Soviet vessels approaching island (October 22); Soviet ships turn away from blockade zone, thus averting crisis (October 24); Kennedy accepts one (of two) Soviet proposals suggesting removal of missiles in return for U.S. promise not to invade Cuba (October 27), and Khrushchev publicly accepts these conditions on following day. Showdown, during which world hovers at brink of nuclear war, is widely hailed by Americans as Kennedy administration's "finest hour"; NATO allies, however, are appalled, having no wish to go up in a nuclear flash over Cuban missiles, which do not, as American officials admit, alter actual military-strategic balance, since it is immaterial where missiles are launched from.

Rachel Carson publishes *Silent Spring,* warning of ecological dangers of DDT and other pesticides; although widely denounced at first by scientific community, book makes deep impression on American public and marks beginning of environmental-awareness movement and subtle shift in status of technologists, who heretofore have been considered beneficent wizards of American life.

1963

Civil-rights demonstrations in Birmingham, Alabama (April 3–May 12): peaceful demonstrations led by Martin Luther King, Jr., are broken up by police using fire hoses, dogs, and electric cattle prods; King and other black leaders are jailed; ultimately President Kennedy orders in federal troops.

Limited Nuclear Test Ban Treaty signed in Moscow (August 5); treaty between U.S.S.R., U.S., and Great Britain bans atmospheric and outer-space but not underground testing. China and France refuse to sign treaty.

March on Washington (August 28): some 200,000 persons gather in Washington to underscore demand for civil rights; Martin Luther King, Jr., gives "I Have a Dream" speech.

Civil-rights demonstrators gathered in Washington, D.C.
U.S. INFORMATION AGENCY

Hot line, direct teletype linkup between Moscow and Washington, becomes operational (August 30).

John F. Kennedy is assassinated in Dallas, Texas

Lyndon B. Johnson taking the oath of office as President
LYNDON B. JOHNSON LIBRARY

(November 22); Lyndon B. Johnson is sworn in as thirty-sixth President.

Lee Harvey Oswald, accused murderer of President Kennedy, is shot and killed by Jack Ruby, nightclub owner, while Oswald is being transferred from one jail to another (November 24).

John F. Kennedy is buried in Arlington National Cemetery; funeral ceremonies are attended by many heads of state and watched on television by many millions of Americans, most of them feeling, as one journalist put it, that what was worst in the nation had somehow triumphed over what was best in it.

John F. Kennedy is buried in Arlington National Cemetery.
JOHN F. KENNEDY LIBRARY

President Johnson appoints commission, headed by Chief Justice Earl Warren, to investigate Kennedy assassination (November 29).

President Johnson addresses a joint session of Congress.
LYNDON B. JOHNSON LIBRARY

1964

President Johnson, in speech to joint session of Congress, calls for "War on Poverty," a many-faceted attack on causes and conditions of poverty (January 8); Johnson has previously urged Congress to enact many J.F.K. proposals, which have largely been stalled in either House or Senate.

Twenty-fourth Amendment, barring use of poll taxes to prevent citizens from voting, is ratified (January 23).

Civil Rights Act of 1964 (July 2): bars discrimination in public places, authorizes Department of Justice to file suits in case of school segregation, outlaws job discrimination on basis of race, sex, religion, or ethnic origin, and increases protection of voting rights.

U.S. spacecraft *Ranger* 7 provides first close-up photographs of the moon (July 31).

Tonkin Gulf Resolution (August 7): congressional resolution authorizes President Johnson to "take all necessary measures" to "prevent further aggression" by North Vietnamese; Tonkin Resolution is sought by Johnson administration as quasi-declaration of war and is used to legitimate bombing of North Vietnam; later investigations reveal that resolution was obtained by distorting, if not falsifying, circumstances under which U.S. destroyers were attacked in Gulf of Tonkin off North Vietnam.

Economic Opportunity Act (August 11): appropriates almost $948 million for ten programs including job training, work-study programs, community-action programs, incentives to business for hiring hard-core unemployed, and VISTA (a domestic Peace Corps).

Warren Commission report (September 27): report concludes that Lee Harvey Oswald acted alone in firing upon presidential motorcade in Dallas and was solely responsible for murder of President Kennedy. Although few professional historians have examined Warren Commission findings and amateur rebuttals, doubts persist about commission's methods and conclusions.

Campaign of 1964: Republicans nominate Senator Barry Goldwater (Arizona) and Representative William E. Miller (New York); Democrats nominate Lyndon B. Johnson and Senator Hubert H. Humphrey (Minnesota); four other parties nominate candidates. Although Republican platform calls for endorsement of Civil Rights Act of 1964, Republican campaign is clearly conservative, if not right-wing, refusing to eschew support from extremist right-wing groups like John Birch Society and virtually conceding entire political center to Johnson and Democrats, who pre-empt it by, among other things, denying (falsely) any plans to escalate

Vietnam conflict. Popular vote (November 3): Johnson 43,126,584, Goldwater 27,177,838; electoral vote: Johnson 486, Goldwater 52. Democrats gain seats in House and Senate.

White-instigated violence relating to civil-rights activism in South continues, and black riots occur in many northern cities.

1965

President Johnson calls for "Great Society," or manifold qualitative improvements in American life (January 4).

Lyndon B. Johnson inaugurated for first full term (January 20); Hubert H. Humphrey becomes Vice President.

First U.S. ground combat troops (Marines) arrive in South Vietnam (March 8).

Selma march (March 21–25): marchers, black and white, are led by Martin Luther King, Jr., from Selma to Montgomery, Alabama, to protest discrimination in voting; ultimately numbering 25,000, marchers are protected by federalized National Guard troops. Two white persons associated with march are murdered.

Elementary and Secondary School Act (April 11): grants $1.3 billion for aid to public and private school pupils.

President Johnson sends Marines to Dominican Republic (April 28); U.S. troops, eventually numbering 22,000, are used to suppress leftist revolt that administration claims has been taken over by Communists.

Medicare (July 30): provides medical and hospital care for elderly through Social Security; also provides for Medicaid, federally supported medical care for poor under age 65.

Voting Rights Act of 1965 (August 6): suspends literacy tests; authorizes federal supervision of election districts where less than half of eligible voters are registered.

Omnibus Housing Act (August 10): provides rent supplements and other housing programs for poor.

Watts riot (August 11–16): riot in black ghetto in Los Angeles costs 35 killed, 1,032 wounded, and about $250 million in property damage. Although touched off by racial incident (involving arrest by white policeman of young black drunk driver near Watts section) and accompanied by attacks upon white motorists, firemen, policemen, and national guardsmen, riot is in effect an attack upon ghetto environment itself.

Department of Housing and Urban Development created (September 9); Robert C. Weaver, black economist, becomes first Secretary.

National Foundation of the Arts and Humanities established (September 29); provides financial aid to artists.

Water Quality Act of 1965 (October 2): requires states to set antipollution standards for interstate waters within their jurisdiction.

Immigration law revised to eliminate 1921 quota system (October 3); sets overall immigration limits (120,000 from Western Hemisphere, 170,000 from rest of world) but allows up to 20,000 immigrants from most nations on first-come, first-served basis.

Clean Air Act of 1965 (October 20): allows federal government to set emission standards for new cars and to set up research into control of emission from power plants.

Higher Education Act (October 20): provides federal scholarships to undergraduate students.

Massive power failure in Northeast (November 9–10): malfunction in part of power grid, which extends into Canada, triggers overloads and automatic cutoffs that ultimately black out area with 30 million people.

By end of year there are 184,300 U.S. troops in Vietnam, almost an eightfold increase over 1964 commitment; there has been heavy bombing of targets in North Vietnam; U.S. casualties are 1,350 dead, 5,300 wounded; general public is uneasy but supportive of administration policy; dissent is confined largely to universities.

1966

U.S. bomber carrying four unarmed H-bombs crashes near Palomares, Spain (January 17); several bombs rupture, poisoning farmlands.

France, in part reflecting increased European distaste for heavy U.S. involvement in Vietnam, announces it will withdraw its troops from NATO and requests that NATO headquarters be removed from French soil (March 31).

James Meredith begins walk from Tennessee to Jackson, Mississippi, to demonstrate to Mississippi blacks that "there is nothing to fear" (June 6); he is shot, though not seriously wounded; various civil-rights organizations take up march where Meredith left off, but serious split develops between militant and nonviolent factions, with Stokely Carmichael, head of Student Nonviolent Coordinating Committee (SNCC), calling for "black power," which sounds sinister or at least separatist to many black and white moderates but is really just old-fashioned interest-group politics with a militant tinge.

Miranda decision (June 13): Supreme Court rules that a suspect must be informed of his legal rights by police before interrogation may begin; decision is widely criticized by law-enforcement spokesmen.

Traffic Safety Act and Highway Safety Act (September 9): Traffic Safety Act sets federal safety standards for automobile manufacturers and comes in response to Ralph Nader's 1965 book, *Unsafe at Any Speed* (book has received much attention after General Motors confesses to having tried to discredit author and after book almost single-handedly kills sales of rear-engined Chevrolet Corvair); Highway Safety Act provides funds for state traffic-safety programs.

Department of Transportation created (October 15); combines 34 agencies concerned with airlines, railroads, and highways.

Republicans register strong gains in congressional midterm elections (November 8); although Democrats retain majority, strong Republican showing reflects increased public dissatisfaction with Vietnam war, rising inflation, a "credibility gap" perceived between statements and actions of administration, class and racial tensions, and an overall upsurge of bad news. Edward Brooke of Massachusetts becomes first black elected to U.S. Senate in twentieth century.

There are now 385,300 U.S. troops in South Vietnam, and B-52 bombing raids have been extended to North Vietnamese cities of Hanoi and Haiphong; although U.S. military continues to issue optimistic statements, little progress appears to have been made, and dissent becomes increasingly vocal and increasingly associated with educated middle class, not just students.

1967

Three American astronauts die when fire sweeps their Apollo capsule during simulated launch (January 27).

Twenty-fifth Amendment is ratified (February 10); enables Vice President to take over duties of disabled President and allows President to appoint a Vice President, subject to congressional approval, if that office becomes vacant.

Antiwar parades held in New York and San Francisco (April 15); crowd estimates for New York demonstration are 150,000–350,000; Dr. Martin Luther King, Jr., is a leader of New York march and makes explicit the connection between costs of Vietnam war and sharp curtailment of Great Society programs.

Arab-Israeli ("Six-Day") War (June 5–10): Israelis capture Jerusalem, Sinai Peninsula, west bank of Jordan River, and Golan Heights in Syria; U.S. and Soviet Union make first use of hot line, promising each other no direct involvement in conflict; as a result of war

Israelis fighting to capture the Golan Heights in June, 1967
ISRAEL GOVERNMENT PRESS OFFICE

U.S.S.R. resupplies Arab states with more sophisticated military hardware, and U.S. does same for Israel.

Detroit riot (July 23–30): worst of 164 urban ghetto riots that have taken place since April, Detroit riot takes 43 lives, injures 2,000, and leaves 5,000 burned out of their homes; requires 4,700 U.S. paratroopers to control.

Thurgood Marshall becomes first black justice on U.S. Supreme Court (October 2).

March on Pentagon (October 21–22): 50,000 antiwar protesters gather in Washington, D.C., and approach Pentagon, which is guarded by troops; march is peaceful for the most part, although there are some minor incidents.

Blacks score important gains in state and local elections (November 7); first black mayors are elected in Gary, Indiana, and Cleveland, Ohio; blacks win seats in Virginia, Mississippi, and Louisiana state legislatures.

There are now 485,600 U.S. troops in Vietnam; battle deaths are 9,350. U.S. planes have begun to bomb

Vietnam: paratroopers of the 173rd Airborne Brigade on duty
U.S. ARMY

North Vietnam near Chinese border, increasing fears of a widening war.

1968

Pueblo incident (January 23): *Pueblo,* navy electronic spy ship, is seized by North Korea in international waters off its coast; U.S. crew is detained and brutalized for about a year.

Tet offensive begins (January 30); Vietcong and North Vietnamese launch broad attack against major South Vietnamese cities and U.S. military outposts; attack confirms for many Americans that they simply cannot believe official U.S. military statements about progress of war, especially when U.S. commander in Vietnam, General William Westmoreland, calls Tet offensive a Communist defeat and then asks for 206,000 more U.S. troops (February 27).

President Johnson announces that he will not seek or accept nomination for second term (March 31); surprise announcement follows strong showing by antiwar candidate Eugene McCarthy in New Hampshire presidential primary (March 12) and reflects the fact that the President is now unable to make public appearances without encountering large, bitter demonstrations.

Martin Luther King, Jr., is assassinated in Memphis, Tennessee (April 4); riots break out in more than 100 U.S. cities, including Washington, D.C.

Martin Luther King, Jr.
NAACP

Open Housing Law (April 11): prohibits discrimination in sale and rental of most housing and has rider tacked on that makes it a criminal offense to cross state lines with intent to start or to participate in a riot.

Preliminary peace talks between U.S. and North Vietnam begin in Paris (May 10).

Truth-in-Lending Act (May 29): requires that consumers be told true annual interest rate on installment purchases.

Robert F. Kennedy, a candidate for Democratic presidential nomination, is mortally wounded in Los Angeles following a victory in California primary (June 5); assailant, an Arab named Sirhan B. Sirhan, is seized on the spot; Kennedy dies on June 6.

James Earl Ray is arrested in London, England, and charged with murder of Martin Luther King, Jr. (June 8); Ray ultimately pleads guilty to murder, and questions are raised—but not answered—about how he could elude capture and travel to England unaided.

Democratic National Convention (August 26–29): bitterly divided party selects Hubert Humphrey as presidential nominee and Senator Edmund Muskie (Maine) as vice-presidential candidate; convention, held in Chicago and controlled by Johnson and party regulars, defeats platform plank calling for a bombing halt in Vietnam and therefore fails to dissociate Humphrey sufficiently from Johnson war policies; outside the convention Chicago police riot and indiscriminately attack antiwar demonstrators, bystanders, and TV reporters. The Chicago violence, although approved of by many Americans, probably costs Humphrey the election, because it fatally alienates liberal Democratic and independent elements who cannot in good conscience vote either for Humphrey or for the Republican nominee, Richard Nixon, and who sit the election out or scatter their votes among a handful of protest candidates.

Congress passes a group of conservation laws preserving certain wilderness areas, including scenic rivers, and establishing Redwood National Park (October 2).

L.B.J. withdraws nomination of Abe Fortas as Chief Justice of Supreme Court after Senate mounts filibuster (October 4).

Campaign of 1968: Republicans run Richard M. Nixon and Spiro T. Agnew (Maryland); George Wallace (Alabama) makes a third-party run as head of American Independent Party; six other parties, mainly leftist, also nominate candidates, including black comedian and civil-rights activist Dick Gregory and black militant Eldridge Cleaver; in addition, Eugene McCarthy is on ballot in some states. Nixon hints that he will change U.S. policies in Vietnam, and Wallace appeals to blue-collar workers who feel threatened by economic competition from blacks; in closing weeks of campaign Democratic candidate Humphrey moves away from Johnson slightly, and Johnson halts bombing in North Vietnam, thus attracting some—but not enough—of the antiwar

vote. Popular vote (November 5): Nixon 31,785,148, Humphrey 31,274,503, Wallace 9,901,151; electoral vote: Nixon 301, Humphrey 191, Wallace 46. Democrats maintain control of Congress.

Apollo 8 spacecraft, carrying three astronauts, leaves the earth, orbits the moon (making live telecasts from lunar orbit), and returns safely to the earth (December 21–27); journey represents the first time that human beings have broken free of the gravitational hug of the planetary home and have looked upon the earth from a great distance and seen it whole and fragile-looking.

1969

Richard M. Nixon is inaugurated as thirty-seventh President (January 20); Spiro T. Agnew becomes Vice President.

Oil well in California (Santa Barbara channel) develops massive leak (January 28); attitude of environmentalists toward economic versus ecological trade-offs begins to harden.

Nuclear Nonproliferation Treaty ratified by U.S. Senate (March 13); 60 nations, not including France and Red China, agree to ban spread of nuclear weapons to nations that do not now possess them; treaty is signed by President Nixon and Soviet President Nikolai V. Podgorny in November.

My Lai Massacre (March 16): U.S. troops, under Lieutenant William L. Calley, shoot down 450 unarmed South Vietnamese villagers; story does not break into print until November 16.

U.S. astronauts Neil Armstrong and Edwin Aldrin land on moon (July 20); astronauts walk on moon, collect

An American astronaut makes the first historic moon walk.
NASA

195

samples, leave scientific instruments there, rejoin *Apollo 11* command module in lunar orbit (July 21), and return home safely (July 24).

Nixon announces Vietnamization plan (November 3); U.S. troops are to be withdrawn concurrent with increased effort to train and equip South Vietnamese army (ARVN); by this date Nixon has announced planned withdrawal of 60,000 American troops.

Vice President Spiro Agnew begins attack on news media for biased and unrepresentative coverage (November 13); persistent theme of Nixon administration, attack comes about partly in recognition of role mass media, especially TV, have played in reporting various foreign and domestic disturbances and partly in response to fact that the mass media no longer broadly reflect or support official government policy.

Antiwar demonstrations (November 15): huge crowds, including 250,000 people in Washington, D.C., gather in many U.S. cities to protest continuation of Vietnam war.

U.S. troops in Vietnam number 475,200 at year's end, down from 1968 level of 536,100. More than 40,000 Americans have died in Vietnam since 1961, and war is now costing about $30 billion a year.

1970

National Environmental Policy Act (January 1): requires federal agencies to issue environmental-impact statements about proposed projects and requires President to issue annual report on quality of the nation's environment.

Second Nixon appointee to U.S. Supreme Court, G. Harrold Carswell, is rejected by U.S. Senate (April 8); first nominee, Clement Haynsworth, was rejected November 21, 1969; third appointee, Harry A. Blackmun, is unanimously confirmed May 12, 1970.

Earth Day (April 22): people across nation celebrate in favor of conservation and cleaner environment.

Cambodian incursion (April 30): although on April 20 Nixon has announced planned withdrawal of 150,000 U.S. troops from Vietnam, U.S. and South Vietnam mount large invasion of Cambodia; invasion is supposed to capture Communist sanctuaries and major headquarters but merely results in more extensive Communist control of Cambodia, outrages public opinion, and sets off hundreds of antiwar demonstrations and some counterdemonstrations; student demonstrators are killed at Kent State University in Ohio (May 4) and at Jackson State College in Mississippi (May 14).

A wounded Kent State University demonstrator gets help.
LIBRARY OF CONGRESS

Postal Reorganization Act (August 12): post office is eliminated as cabinet-level department and set up as independent agency.

Environmental Protection Agency (EPA) established (October 2); consolidates control of various antipollution programs.

Despite Nixon administration appeals to "silent majority" for support of Vietnam policy and "law and order," Democrats retain control of Congress in midterm elections (November 3); Republicans lose nine House seats but gain two in Senate.

Occupational Safety and Health Act (December 29): authorizes federal government to set and enforce health and safety standards for industrial and other workers.

Census of 1970: total population 203,211,926, including about 3.3 million immigrants, of whom approximately half have come from Mexico and South America. About 75 per cent of population is now urbanized. Suburban portions of metropolitan areas continue to grow; older, denser cities (e.g., Chicago, Detroit, Philadelphia, and Manhattan and Brooklyn boroughs of New York City) continue to lose population. California has become most populous state (19,953,134) and gains five congressional representatives; Florida gains three representatives. Increase over 1960 census is 13.3 per cent, although birthrate has declined further since 1950–60 period.

1971

Public funding for supersonic transport (SST) plane voted down by Congress (March 24); concern over environmental effects, economic viability of project, and actual necessity for superfast plane result in first major no-confidence vote against technological "progress."

AMTRAK begins service (May 1); semigovernmental

corporation, created in 1970 to relieve railroads of unprofitable passenger lines, is designed to encourage travel by railroad.

"Pentagon Papers" begin appearing in *New York Times* (June 13); part of classified 47-volume history of U.S. involvement in Vietnam, commissioned by Secretary of Defense Robert McNamara in 1967, "Pentagon Papers" further undermine public confidence in government statements about war because they reveal deliberate deception of American people, especially during Johnson years; U.S. Supreme Court denies government-sought injunction to halt further publication (June 30).

Twenty-sixth Amendment, lowering voting age to eighteen, is ratified (June 30).

President Nixon announces that he will visit Red China in 1972, thus signaling a major shift in U.S. policy (July 15); announcement follows visit to Red China of U.S. Ping-Pong team (April 14) and lifting of U.S. trade embargo against China; on August 2 U.S. announces it will support admission of Red China to United Nations.

President Nixon imposes 90-day freeze on prices, wages, and rents (August 15); move is intended to combat rising cost of living, rising unemployment, and falling economic productivity, a combination previously considered impossible and later called stagflation; Nixon also calls for tax cuts and increased public spending and ends all conversion of dollars into gold, thereby in effect deflating the dollar.

1972

President Nixon and foreign-policy adviser Henry Kissinger make visit to People's Republic of China (February 21–28); event, given wide TV coverage, is designed to lead to normalization of relations with Red China; U.S. agrees that Taiwan is part of China; in 1973 China and U.S. exchange diplomatic liaison offices.

Congress sends Equal Rights Amendment (ERA), banning discrimination on basis of sex, to states for ratification (March 22).

Nixon announces intensification of war against North Vietnam (May 8); in face of major North Vietnamese offensive into South, U.S. continues to withdraw its ground troops but mines Haiphong Harbor, tightens naval blockade of North, and steps up bombing of North.

Governor George Wallace of Alabama, campaigning in Maryland primary, is shot and crippled by Arthur Bremer (May 15); Bremer is convicted and given 63-year sentence.

President Nixon makes visit to Moscow, first American President to do so (May 22–30); U.S. and U.S.S.R. agree to cooperate in scientific, technological, health, commercial, and environmental areas, propose a joint venture in space, sign a treaty limiting number of antiballistic missile (ABM) defense systems, and sign an executive agreement (to expire in 1977) limiting offensive armaments to those already deployed or being built. Last agreement is result of 1969 Strategic Arms Limitation Talks (SALT) in Helsinki, Finland.

Environmental Protection Agency announces (June 14) that use of the pesticide DDT will be banned by end of year.

Watergate break-in (June 17): five men carrying cameras and electronic bugging equipment are arrested in Democratic National Committee offices in Washington, D.C., apartment-hotel complex named Watergate. Although there is some evidence linking burglars with Committee to Re-elect the President (CREEP), Nixon's campaign organization, both CREEP and White House deny any connection with break-in. In late September and October, Washington *Post* reporters Bob Woodward and Carl Bernstein begin to report on campaign irregularities by CREEP, but the issue does not become a major one in 1972 presidential election.

U.S. Supreme Court rules that death penalty as currently applied among states is unconstitutional (June 29).

Last U.S. combat troops leave South Vietnam (August 13); some support personnel remain, and many Americans (50,000) are still stationed in Thailand.

Federal Water Pollution Act passed over Nixon's veto (October 18); aims to eliminate all pollution of U.S. waters by 1985, authorizes expenditure of $24.7 billion, and permits suits by citizens against either polluters or U.S. government.

Revenue Sharing Act (October 20): authorizes sharing $30.2 billion of federal tax revenues with state and local governments over a five-year period.

Campaign of 1972: Democrats nominate Senator George McGovern (South Dakota) and Senator Thomas Eagleton (Missouri) in convention in which minorities, young, and women are represented in proportion to the general population and from which many party stalwarts or regulars are excluded (July 10–13); Democratic platform calls for immediate end to war in Indochina, amnesty for draft evaders and war resisters, and a guaranteed income for poor. Senator Eagleton withdraws from ticket after history of mental illness is revealed and is replaced by R. Sargent Shriver (Maryland). Republicans renominate Richard M. Nixon and Spiro T. Agnew (August 21–23) on platform supporting Nixon foreign policy, revenue sharing, and welfare reform and opposing amnesty and busing of schoolchildren to achieve racial balance in schools. Seven other parties nominate candidates. Republicans successfully portray McGovern as radical leftist and bumbler, while Nixon ostensibly remains above political fray, with administration officials making most of the campaign speeches. Popular vote (November 7): Nixon 47,170,179, McGovern 29,171,791; electoral vote: Nixon 520 (49 states), McGovern 17 (Massachusetts and Washington, D.C.).

U.S. resumes bombing of North Vietnam (December 18–30); round-the-clock bombing of Hanoi area by B-52's follows breakdown of peace negotiations in Paris and is heaviest of war.

1973

Paris peace talks conclude (January 27); U.S., North Vietnam, South Vietnam, and the Vietcong sign agreements calling for immediate cease-fire, withdrawal of all U.S. military personnel, end of all military activities in Laos and Cambodia, and release of U.S. prisoners of war held by North Vietnam and the Vietcong. By March 29 most American POW's are released, and remaining U.S. troops (23,500) are removed. U.S. casualties in Vietnam war are 46,079 battle deaths and more than 303,000 wounded as of 1973.

U.S. and Cuba sign antihijacking agreement (February 15); each country agrees to try or extradite those who have hijacked airplanes and forced them to land either in U.S. or in Cuba.

Judge John Sirica, presiding judge of trial of seven Watergate defendants, releases letter by James McCord, one of the burglars, charging perjured testimony and involvement of higher-ups (March 23).

President Nixon accepts resignations of top aides H. R. Haldeman and John Ehrlichman and of Attorney General Richard Kleindienst and fires presidential counsel John Dean (April 30).

Senate Watergate hearings (May 17–August 7): televised hearings, presided over by Senator Sam J. Ervin, Jr. (North Carolina), elicit testimony by John Dean (June 25–29) that President Nixon was full party to attempted cover-up of Watergate break-in; presidential assistant Alexander Butterfield reveals (July 16) that President Nixon has tape system that records all conversations in White House and Executive Office Building.

Soviet leader Leonid I. Brezhnev visits U.S. (June 17–25); summit meetings with Nixon lead to few major agreements but symbolize détente, or relaxation of U.S.-Soviet tensions.

Nixon vetoes congressional bill cutting off funds for continued bombing of Cambodia (June 27); Nixon later agrees to halt all U.S. military efforts in Cambodia by August 15 and signs a law to that effect July 1.

Selective Service Act expires (June 30); U.S. armed forces revert to volunteer basis for first time in 25 years.

Congress confirms nomination of Henry A. Kissinger as Secretary of State (September 21).

Resignation of Vice President Spiro T. Agnew (October 10): resignation is part of deal in which Agnew pleads no contest to income-tax evasion; alternative would have been prosecution as felon for accepting bribes.

Arab oil embargo (October 17): Arab oil producers announce embargo on oil sales to nations that are supporting Israel in "Yom Kippur" war, which began October 6 with Arab attack on Israeli-occupied Sinai; U.S. armed forces are placed on worldwide alert on October 25, when U.S.S.R. threatens to move troops into Middle East, but crisis subsides with appointment of UN peace-keeping force. Oil embargo against U.S. lifted in March, 1974, but substantial price hikes by Arab oil producers follow.

"Saturday Night Massacre" (October 20): new Attorney General, Elliot L. Richardson, and Deputy Attorney General William D. Ruckelshaus resign after refusing to comply with Nixon's order to fire Special Prosecutor Archibald Cox, who has rejected Nixon's proposal to turn over summaries of White House tapes; Cox is then fired by third-ranking official in Justice Department. Public outrage results in passing of impeachment reso-

White House demonstrators demand Nixon's impeachment.

lutions by House; resolutions are turned over to House Judiciary Committee, which begins preliminary investigations ten days later.

Leon Jaworski is appointed special prosecutor and is promised complete freedom to conduct investigation of Watergate affair (November 1).

War Powers Act passed over presidential veto (November 7); act requires that President get congressional approval for any commitment of U.S. troops abroad lasting more than 60 days.

Alaska pipeline authorized (November 16); proposed 787-mile pipeline from northern Alaskan oil fields to port of Valdez has been bitterly opposed by environmentalists.

Gerald R. Ford sworn in as Vice President (December 6); he has been appointed by Nixon under Twenty-fifth Amendment and confirmed by Congress.

1974

Federal grand jury indicts seven key Nixon administration and CREEP officials for various felonies (March 1); grand jury wishes to indict President Nixon but is persuaded not to by Special Prosecutor Jaworski, who doubts constitutionality of indicting a President still in office.

Henry Aaron of Atlanta Braves hits 715th home run (April 8), breaking Babe Ruth's record of 714, which had stood for almost 40 years.

White House transcripts (April 30): Nixon releases heavily edited transcript of selected tape-recorded conversations, the coarseness of which offends many.

Supreme Court orders President Nixon to turn over 64 tapes requested by Special Prosecutor Jaworski (July 24); tapes, which provide incontrovertible evidence of Nixon's involvement in crimes for which his subordinates are now being tried, quickly erode his remaining support, making it plain that Senate will vote for his conviction if the impeachment process continues.

House Judiciary Committee votes three articles of impeachment (July 24–30); in televised proceedings committee finds Nixon guilty of three impeachable offenses: obstruction of justice, violation of his oath of office, and defiance of impeachment process.

President Nixon announces his resignation (August 8); resignation is to take effect at noon the following day and is formally tendered to Secretary of State Kissinger in a brief note: "Dear Mr. Secretary: I hereby resign the office of President of the United States. Sincerely, Richard M. Nixon."

Gerald R. Ford takes oath as thirty-eighth President (August 9).

President Ford issues unconditional pardon of Richard Nixon (September 8); in a separate agreement Ford gives Nixon title to the White House tapes but requires that they be preserved for three years.

Democrats score huge gains in congressional midterm elections (November 5); Democrats control 39 state governorships, including that of Connecticut, where Mrs. Ella Grasso becomes first woman to be elected governor in her own right.

Ella Grasso
ELLA GRASSO

Although U.S. has ceased combat role in Vietnam, military and economic aid has continued, amounting to nearly $5.4 billion in 1973-74.

Nelson A. Rockefeller is sworn in as Vice President (December 19); thus year ends with country in unprecedented position of having an unelected President and Vice President.

1975

"Blue-ribbon" commission, headed by Vice President Rockefeller, begins to investigate CIA activities (January 5); on June 10 commission issues report indicating that CIA has exceeded its charter by conducting intensive surveillance of U.S. citizens at home.

Remaining Americans (about 1,000) hastily evacuated from South Vietnam (April 29); in past month or so South Vietnamese regime under President Nguyen Van Thieu has undergone rapid and terminal military collapse; U.S. eventually provides asylum for approximately 120,000 South Vietnamese refugees; on April 30 South Vietnam surrenders unconditionally to Vietcong and North Vietnamese forces, thus ending a war that from the point of view of indigenous Communists has been going on since 1945. North and South Vietnam officially reunited as single nation, with Hanoi as capital, on July 2, 1976.

City of New York, nation's largest, rescued from virtual bankruptcy by New York State (June 10); on December 9 President Ford signs bill authorizing short-term federal loans to city to ease cash-flow problems, but city's financial difficulties, shared to a lesser degree by many other high-density American cities, are by no means solved.

U.S. *Apollo 18* spacecraft and Soviet *Soyuz 19* capsule achieve orbital rendezvous (July 17).

Helsinki Accords signed by U.S.S.R., U.S., and 33 other nations in Finland (August 1); agreements recognize existing borders of various Iron Curtain countries, pledge continued détente, renounce aid to terrorist groups, and commit signatories to respect human rights and freedoms at home and abroad.

UN General Assembly passes resolution condemning Zionism as a form of racism (November 10); vote, which is strong slap at Israel and United States, reflects a world order—and a U.S. place in that order—that has changed markedly in last 30 years; UN General Assembly now has almost three times as many members as in 1945, and many of them are poor, nondemocratic, nonwhite, and hostile to U.S.

Senate committee headed by Senator Frank Church releases report documenting CIA involvement in several plots to assassinate foreign leaders in Cuba, Zaire, Dominican Republic, South Vietnam, and Chile (November 21); Church committee later (December) clears CIA of direct responsibility for 1973 overthrow and murder of Chilean leader Salvador Allende but finds that CIA did indirectly encourage coup.

U.S. Senate votes to cut off support to U.S.-backed rightist faction in Angolan civil war (December 19); vote reflects public fears of another involvement of the Vietnam type and public embarrassment that U.S. has increasingly found itself supporting losing or least popular side in local civil or national-independence wars.

1976

U.S. Supreme Court upholds most parts of landmark Federal Election Campaign Act of 1974 (January 30); Court upholds portions of law that provide for public financing of presidential campaigns, limits on individual campaign contributions, and strict accounting procedures for candidates. Court invalidates part of law that had limited spending of personal or family money by candidates themselves and also rules that several of law's enforcement mechanisms need to be restructured.

Nation celebrates Bicentennial (July 4).

Democratic National Convention gathers in New York

Queen Elizabeth II visits Boston during the Bicentennial.
LOU JONES

City (July 12–15); convention nominates James Earl "Jimmy" Carter, Jr. (Georgia), and Senator Walter Mondale (Minnesota) on platform calling for fairer distribution of nation's wealth, tax reform, low unemployment, easier voter registration, national health-insurance plan, lower defense spending, and foreign policy reflecting more emphasis on human rights; Democrats oppose constitutional amendments outlawing abortion and busing schoolchildren for racial balance. Although Carter was virtually unknown nationally when he began campaign for nomination, he defeated several prominent candidates and by time of convention had put together F.D.R.-type coalition of northern and southern wings enjoying solid support of labor, minority, and urban-interest groups.

Viking 1 lands on Mars (July 20); robot landing craft, first to soft-land on another planet, sends back various

A photograph of Viking 1 *on the surface of Mars, July, 1976*
NASA

data on nature of "red planet," including some that suggest possibility of microscopic life there, but scientific consensus is that bulk of evidence seems to speak against it.

Republican National Convention (August 16–19): convention, held in Kansas City, nominates Gerald R. Ford and Senator Robert J. Dole (Kansas) on platform calling for reduced federal spending, tax cuts for industry, defense spending at current or higher levels, constitutional amendments against abortion and busing to achieve racial balance, and support for Ford-Kissinger foreign policy; platform opposes national health-insurance plan.

Campaign of 1976: Republicans, running incumbent, President Ford, are generally on defensive against Democratic challengers Carter and Mondale as a result of economic conditions (high prices, high unemployment, faltering stock market) and eight-year Republican tenure marred by Watergate, intelligence, and bribery scandals involving multinational corporations. A series of televised debates between Carter and Ford (September 23, October 7, and October 22) does not fully resolve doubts that many voters have about both candidates, although Carter probably emerges victor in two

out of three. Carter stresses fact that he has no political obligations to major organized interest groups (although he takes care to avoid offending them) and promises "compassionate" and "efficient" government; many voters remain undecided to the last moment, perceiving that Carter represents a perhaps needed change but uncertain about the nature or dimensions this change will have. Popular vote (November 2): Carter 40,287,283, Ford 38,557,855; electoral vote: Carter 297, Ford 241. Democrats retain control of Congress.

Jimmy Carter
THE WHITE HOUSE

Presidents of the United States

George Washington
1789–1797

John Adams
1797–1801

Thomas Jefferson
1801–1809

James Madison
1809–1817

James Monroe
1817–1825

John Quincy Adams
1825–1829

Andrew Jackson
1829–1837

Martin Van Buren
1837–1841

William Henry Harrison
1841
(*died in office*)

John Tyler
1841–1845

James K. Polk
1845–1849

Zachary Taylor
1849–1850
(*died in office*)

Millard Fillmore
1850–1853

Franklin Pierce
1853–1857

James Buchanan
1857–1861

Abraham Lincoln
1861–1865
(*assassinated*)

Andrew Johnson
1865–1869

Ulysses S. Grant
1869–1877

Rutherford B. Hayes
1877–1881

James A. Garfield
1881
(*assassinated*)

Chester A. Arthur
1881–1885

Grover Cleveland
1885–1889

Benjamin Harrison
1889–1893

Grover Cleveland
1893–1897

William McKinley
1897–1901
(*assassinated*)

Theodore Roosevelt
1901–1909

William Howard Taft
1909–1913

Woodrow Wilson
1913–1921

Warren G. Harding
1921–1923
(*died in office*)

Calvin Coolidge
1923–1929

Herbert C. Hoover
1929–1933

Franklin D. Roosevelt
1933–1945
(*died in office*)

Harry S. Truman
1945–1953

Dwight D. Eisenhower
1953–1961

John F. Kennedy
1961–1963
(*assassinated*)

Lyndon B. Johnson
1963–1969

Richard M. Nixon
1969–1974
(*resigned*)

Gerald R. Ford
1974–1977

James E. Carter
(1977–)

Wives of the Presidents of the United States

Martha Washington
(1731–1802)
Born Martha Dandridge; widow of Daniel Parke Custis, she married George Washington and presided as First Lady while the capital was under construction.

Abigail Adams
(1744–1818)
Born Abigail Smith; she was the first First Lady to live in the White House.

Martha Jefferson
(1748–1782)
Born Martha Wayles; widow of Bathurst Skelton, she married Thomas Jefferson but died before he became President; no portrait of her exists.

Dolley Madison
(1768–1849)
Born Dolley Payne; widow of John Todd, she married James Madison and is credited with saving Washington's portrait when the White House burned (1814).

Elizabeth Monroe
(1768–1830)
Born Elizabeth Kortright; she brought a new formality to White House entertaining.

Louisa Adams
(1775–1852)
Born Louisa Catherine Johnson; she was the only First Lady to be born abroad.

Rachel Jackson
(1767–1828)
Born Rachel Donelson; divorced from Lewis Robards, she married Andrew Jackson but died while he was President-elect.

Hannah Van Buren
(1783–1819)
Born Hannah Hoes; she died before Martin Van Buren became President.

Anna Harrison
(1775–1864)
Born Anna Tuthill Symmes; her husband's death occurred before she joined him at the White House.

Letitia Tyler
(1790–1842)
Born Letitia Christian; too ill to assume official duties, she died during her husband's Presidency.

Julia Tyler
(1820–1889)
Born Julia Gardiner; she married President Tyler and was First Lady during his last eight months in office.

Sarah Polk
(1803–1891)
Born Sarah Childress; she directed the first redecorating of the White House.

Margaret Taylor
(1788–1852)
Born Margaret Mackall Smith; no portrait of her exists.

Abigail Fillmore
(1798–1853)
Born Abigail Powers; she requested funds from Congress for a White House library.

Caroline Fillmore
(1813–1881)
Born Caroline Carmichael; widow of Ezekiel McIntosh, she married the former President in 1858.

Jane Pierce
(1806–1863)
Born Jane Means Appleton; grief-stricken by her son's death, she remained in seclusion as First Lady.

Mary Lincoln
(1818–1882)
Born Mary Ann Todd; she was much criticized for her extravagance as First Lady.

Eliza Johnson
(1810–1876)
Born Eliza McCardle; an invalid, she was not an active First Lady.

Julia Grant
(1826–1902)
Born Julia Boggs Dent; her years as First Lady were the happiest period of her life.

Lucy Hayes
(1831–1889)
Born Lucy Ware Webb; she was the first First Lady to have a college diploma.

Lucretia Garfield
(1832–1918)
Born Lucretia Rudolph; she was First Lady for only 200 days.

Ellen Arthur
(1837–1880)
Born Ellen Lewis Herndon; she died before her husband became President.

Frances Cleveland
(1864–1947)
Born Frances Folsom; she was the first bride of a President to be married in the White House. After her husband's death she married Thomas J. Preston, Jr.

Caroline Harrison
(1832–1892)
Born Caroline Lavinia Scott; she died during her husband's Presidency.

Mary Harrison
(1859–1948)
Born Mary Scott Lord; widow of Walter E. Dimmick, she married the former President in 1896.

Ida McKinley
(1847–1907)
Born Ida Saxton; an invalid, she still remained an active First Lady.

Alice Roosevelt
(1861–1884)
Born Alice Hathaway Lee; she died before Roosevelt became President.

Edith Roosevelt
(1861–1948)
Born Edith Kermit Carow; she supervised a remodeling of the White House while she was First Lady.

Helen Taft
(1861–1943)
Born Helen Herron; as First Lady she requested the planting of the famous cherry trees around the Tidal Basin.

Ellen Wilson
(1860–1914)
Born Ellen Louise Axson; she died during Wilson's first term.

Edith Wilson
(1872–1961)
Born Edith Bolling; widow of Norman Galt, she married Wilson and took an active part in government duties during his illness.

Florence Harding
(1860–1924)
Born Florence Mabel Kling; she worked diligently in Harding's presidential campaign and was an energetic First Lady.

Grace Coolidge
(1879–1957)
Born Grace Anna Goodhue; her energy and friendliness made her a popular First Lady.

Lou Hoover
(1874–1944)
Born Lou Henry; a graduate of Stanford, she was an intelligent and active First Lady.

Eleanor Roosevelt
(1884–1962)
Born Anna Eleanor Roosevelt; the first First Lady to hold her own press conferences, travel widely on lecture tours, and write a newspaper column, she championed humane causes and was respected throughout the world.

Elizabeth "Bess" Truman
(1885—)
Born Elizabeth Virginia Wallace; intelligent and witty, she was a valued adviser to her husband.

Mamie Eisenhower
(1896—)
Born Mamie Geneva Doud;
friendly and outgoing, she
enjoyed her role as First
Lady.

Jacqueline Kennedy
(1929—)
Born Jacqueline Lee Bou-
vier; she supervised a White
House redecoration and
planned the first guidebook
of the mansion.

Claudia "Lady Bird" Johnson
(1912—)
Born Claudia Alta Taylor;
an active First Lady, she
worked on a beautification-
of-America project.

Thelma "Pat" Nixon
(1912—)
Born Thelma Catherine
Ryan; she traveled more
than any other First Lady
and encouraged volunteer
work for the needy.

Elizabeth "Betty" Ford
(1918—)
Born Elizabeth Anne
Bloomer; divorced from
William Warren, she mar-
ried Gerald Ford. She actively supported the arts and
women's rights.

Rosalynn Carter
(1927—)
Born Rosalynn Smith; she
campaigned alone on her
husband's behalf in 36 states
during the presidential election and works actively for
the improvement of services
for the mentally and emo-
tionally handicapped.

Vice Presidents of the United States

Vice President	Birth and Death Dates	Term of Office	President
John Adams	(1735–1826)	1789–1797	George Washington
Thomas Jefferson	(1743–1826)	1797–1801	John Adams
Aaron Burr	(1756–1836)	1801–1805	Thomas Jefferson
George Clinton	(1739–1812)	1805–1809	Thomas Jefferson
(died in office)		1809–1812	James Madison
Elbridge Gerry	(1744–1814)	1813–1814	James Madison
(died in office)			
Daniel D. Tompkins	(1774–1825)	1817–1825	James Monroe
John C. Calhoun	(1782–1850)	1825–1829	John Quincy Adams
(resigned upon being elected senator)		1829–1832	Andrew Jackson
Martin Van Buren	(1782–1862)	1833–1837	Andrew Jackson
Richard M. Johnson	(1780–1850)	1837–1841	Martin Van Buren
John Tyler	(1790–1862)	1841 (Mar. to Apr.)	William Henry Harrison
George M. Dallas	(1792–1864)	1845–1849	James K. Polk
Millard Fillmore	(1800–1874)	1849–1850	Zachary Taylor
William R. D. King	(1786–1853)	1853	Franklin Pierce
John C. Breckinridge	(1821–1875)	1857–1861	James Buchanan
Hannibal Hamlin	(1809–1891)	1861–1865	Abraham Lincoln
Andrew Johnson	(1808–1875)	1865 (Mar. to Apr.)	Abraham Lincoln
Schuyler Colfax	(1823–1885)	1869–1873	Ulysses S. Grant
Henry Wilson	(1812–1875)	1873–1875	Ulysses S. Grant
(died in office)			
William A. Wheeler	(1819–1887)	1877–1881	Rutherford B. Hayes
Chester A. Arthur	(1830–1886)	1881 (Mar. to Sept.)	James A. Garfield
Thomas A. Hendricks	(1819–1885)	1885 (Mar. to Nov.)	Grover Cleveland
(died in office)			
Levi P. Morton	(1824–1920)	1889–1893	Benjamin Harrison
Adlai E. Stevenson	(1835–1914)	1893–1897	Grover Cleveland
Garret A. Hobart	(1844–1899)	1897–1899	William McKinley
(died in office)			
Theodore Roosevelt	(1858–1919)	1901 (Mar. to Sept.)	William McKinley
Charles W. Fairbanks	(1852–1918)	1905–1909	Theodore Roosevelt
James S. Sherman	(1855–1912)	1909–1912	William Howard Taft
(died in office)			
Thomas R. Marshall	(1854–1925)	1913–1921	Woodrow Wilson
Calvin Coolidge	(1872–1933)	1921–1923	Warren G. Harding
Charles G. Dawes	(1865–1951)	1925–1929	Calvin Coolidge
Charles Curtis	(1860–1936)	1929–1933	Herbert C. Hoover
John Nance Garner	(1868–1967)	1933–1941	Franklin D. Roosevelt
Henry A. Wallace	(1888–1965)	1941–1945	Franklin D. Roosevelt
Harry S. Truman	(1884–1972)	1945 (Jan. to Apr.)	Franklin D. Roosevelt
Alben W. Barkley	(1877–1956)	1949–1953	Harry S Truman
Richard M. Nixon	(born 1913)	1953–1961	Dwight D. Eisenhower
Lyndon B. Johnson	(1908–1973)	1961–1963	John F. Kennedy
Hubert H. Humphrey	(born 1911)	1965–1969	Lyndon B. Johnson
Spiro T. Agnew	(born 1918)	1969–1973	Richard M. Nixon
(resigned)			
Gerald R. Ford	(born 1913)	1973–1974 (Dec. to Aug.)	Richard M. Nixon
Nelson A. Rockefeller	(born 1908)	1974–1977	Gerald R. Ford
Walter F. Mondale	(born 1928)	1977–	James E. Carter

II
Thematic Chronologies

Significant Supreme Court Decisions

Included below are some of the major judgments rendered by the Supreme Court of the United States since its creation in 1789. In the broadest sense, the Supreme Court is a powerful political institution whose decisions, like those of the national legislature and national executive, not only govern the behavior of American individuals and groups but also are ultimately dependent upon the consent of the governed for acceptance and enforcement. Perhaps the most striking single fact about the Supreme Court is its wondrous capacity, as a nonelective governmental agency almost constantly making unpopular decisions, to persist in high dignity and almost never lose the respect—or even the reverence—of the American people.

Since the Court has always acted only when real litigation reached it, there is often an incongruous or even comic disparity between the actual disputes—involving, for example, a small-town mayor fining a bootlegger and collecting twelve dollars in court costs, a load of gravel being dumped next to somebody's pier, or an eccentric handing out leaflets on a street corner—and the momentous principles that the Supreme Court is charged to draw from these cases and shape into broad but clear guidelines affecting wide areas of national life. For this reason the facts involved in the decisions listed below are for the most part not given.

1793   *Chisholm* v. *Georgia*: Supreme Court decides that a state may be sued without its consent. Decision is one of three in Court's history that Congress has overridden by means of a constitutional amendment, in this case the Eleventh Amendment (1798).

1796   *Hylton* v. *U.S.*: for first time Court reviews an act of Congress (a tax on carriages) and finds it constitutional.

1803   *Marbury* v. *Madison*: Chief Justice Marshall rules that any act of Congress "repugnant" to the Constitution must be "void" and that Congress has no right to alter the Constitution by "an ordinary Act," that is, by simply passing a law rather than through the process of constitutional amendment. The Supreme Court does not declare another congressional act unconstitutional until 1857, in the Dred Scott decision, although lower courts occasionally do.

1810   *Fletcher* v. *Peck*: Court for first time invalidates a state law, on the grounds that it impairs the "obligation of contracts," which the Constitution expressly (Article I, Section 10) forbids the states to do.

1819   *McCulloch* v. *Maryland*: in another of his great nationalist opinions Marshall holds that the Constitution derives ultimately from the people, not from the states; that the powers of Congress, though limited and delegated, also imply certain other "incidental" powers—namely, the power to use legitimate, appropriate means to achieve ends that are themselves constitutional; and that the powers of the states do not include those whose function is to destroy or render nonfunctional agencies created by the national government. Decision upholds the right of Congress to create the unpopular Bank of the United States and denies the right of Maryland to tax bank into oblivion.

1824   *Gibbons* v. *Ogden*: in the first case in which Court rules squarely on power of Congress "to regulate Commerce . . . among the several States" (Article I, Section 8), Chief Justice Marshall denies the right of any state to grant a transportation monopoly interfering with the free flow of goods or passengers within or among the states. Called the first antitrust decision, it broadly construes the powers of Congress under interstate-commerce clause, a clause that subsequently, especially in the twentieth century, provides a major avenue for the expression of national power in economic and social issues, including civil rights.

1832   *Worcester* v. *Georgia*: Chief Justice Marshall, upholding supremacy of U.S. treaties as the law of the land, denies validity of Georgia law controlling missionaries in Cherokee lands and denies Georgia any control whatsoever of Cherokee territory. Decision is significant only in that it is ignored by executive (President Andrew Jackson) and by defendant (Georgia). Decision is of no practical interest to Congress, which has already passed a law providing for removal of Indians east of Mississippi River. This decision is a reminder that Court's power has severe practical limits when no popular or influential interest is involved that will compel enforcement.

1833   *Barron* v. *Baltimore*: in key civil-rights decision Chief Justice Marshall rules that Bill of Rights directly applies only to actions of the federal government, not to those of state governments, a ruling that the Court has not reversed to this day. It was not until the passage of the Fourteenth Amendment in 1868 that the Court had an "angle" from which to consider state laws in their relation to Bill of Rights guarantees and not until the twentieth century that the Court began to apply the "due process" and "equal protection of the laws" clauses of this amendment in defense of individual rather than corporate interests.

1837   *Charles River Bridge* v. *Warren Bridge*: Court, now under Chief Justice Roger Taney, modifies earlier position on "the obligation of contracts" and holds that public charters or contracts must be construed so as to give the benefit of any doubt to the public interest, in this case according Massachusetts the right to charter the building of a second bridge in competition with another bridge it had earlier contracted for. In this as in many other decisions the Taney Court tends to emphasize reservoir of state powers created in part by the Tenth Amendment, thus swinging somewhat away from strong emphasis on federal supremacy characteristic of Marshall Court.

1849   *Luther* v. *Borden*: decision is significant largely because it establishes a large, vague area called "political questions" in which Court will not venture to render judgment. In this case, involving rival governments in Rhode Island (in connection with Dorr's Rebellion), Court says Congress and President must decide which government is legitimate; for the most part, the Court subsequently holds for more than 100 years—until 1960's and *Baker* v. *Carr* decision—that various state issues involving referenda and the drawing of congressional and other electoral districts are "political questions."

1857   *Dred Scott* v. *Sandford*: Court declares in a number of separate opinions that probably no black—and certainly no slave—can be a citizen of the United States or of any particular state; also declares the Missouri Compromise of 1820 is unconstitutional in that Congress has no right to outlaw slavery from any territory (to do so is to violate the Fifth Amendment guarantee against deprivation of property). Actual judgment is simply that Dred Scott is not entitled to sue in federal court, but opinions of Chief Justice Taney and a majority of justices about black citizenship and unconstitutionality of Missouri Compromise cause tremendous controversy; this is the second time Congress has resorted to the amendment process to nullify a Court decision.

1861   *Ex parte* Merryman: Chief Justice Taney, as a circuit judge, rules that the executive (President Lincoln) does not have the right to suspend the writ of habeas corpus; Lincoln ignores Taney's judgment, and Taney does not press it further in this circuit-court case.

1863   Prize Cases: Court rules that President has wide latitude to respond to military emergency, in this case by ordering a naval blockade of Confederacy without specific congressional authority or a declaration of war.

1866   *Ex parte* Milligan: Court declares that President has no right to suspend habeas corpus and to set up military courts in areas where civil courts are functioning. A majority (5–4) declares that Congress does not have these rights either; this is the closest the Court comes to considering the constitutionality of the various Reconstruction laws, in which martial law and military courts play a large role.

1869   *Ex parte* McCardle: Court agrees to let Congress deprive it of its appellate jurisdiction over a case directly challenging congressional right to set up military courts in southern states, thus avoiding a head-on collision with the legislative branch.

1873   Slaughterhouse Cases: ruling for the first time on an issue pertaining to the Fourteenth Amendment, Court declares (5–4) that states are not bound to protect the various civil liberties guaranteed in the Bill of Rights. Slaughterhouse cases have nothing to do with rights of freedmen but rather involve monopoly granted by Louisiana to one slaughterhouse company. Court points out that Fourteenth Amendment was designed to protect freedmen, then makes distinction between national and state citizenship that in effect places most of the civil liberties associated with the Bill of Rights outside the reach of the Fourteenth Amendment.

1877   *Munn* v. *Illinois* (one of the Granger Cases): Court declares that states may regulate certain aspects of intrastate business (in this case setting maximum rates for grain storage) without violating due-process clause of Fourteenth Amendment or violating congressional control over interstate commerce.

1883   Civil Rights Cases: Court invalidates Civil Rights Act of 1875 on grounds that by outlawing discrimination against blacks in public accommodations, act exceeds provisions of Fourteenth Amendment, which prohibits discriminatory actions by states but not by individuals.

1884   *Ex parte* Yarbrough (one of Ku Klux Klan Cases): Court upholds right of Congress to pass laws punishing private citizens for interfering with right of citizens to vote in a federal election.

1886   *Santa Clara County* v. *Southern Pacific Railroad Co.*: Court accepts idea that a corporation is a legal "person" and that due-process clause of Fourteenth Amendment therefore protects such "persons" from actions by states that have the effect of depriving them of their property. In a series of decisions dating from this period and usually involving railroads, Court also broadens interpretation of the phrase "due process of law." Previously this phrase had meant only that various legal formalities were observed; after 1886, however, the phrase was given a "substantive" meaning in which the actual content or effect of a law was considered: if the effect of the law was confiscatory, unjust, or otherwise injurious, due process could be considered violated, however "legal" the law was.

1890   *Chicago, Milwaukee and St. Paul Railroad Co.* v. *Minnesota*: Court declares that state regulatory commissions have no right to fix rates and that courts must have final say on the reasonableness of rates if due-process clause of Fourteenth Amendment is not to be violated.

1895 *U.S.* v. *E. C. Knight Co.*: Court interprets Sherman Antitrust Act in such a way as to exclude virtually all federal control of interstate manufacturing monopolies (in this case makers of refined sugar). Court declares that Congress' power to regulate interstate commerce does not include power to regulate manufacturing, because commerce results from manufacturing.

Pollock v. *Farmers' Loan and Trust Co.* (one of the Income Tax Cases): Court declares income tax unconstitutional. Sixteenth Amendment later (1913) overrides this decision.

1896 *Plessy* v. *Ferguson*: Court holds that state laws requiring segregated public accommodations do not violate "equal protection of the laws" provision of Fourteenth Amendment as long as these accommodations are separate but equal. Decision is significant for dissent by Justice John Harlan (a Southerner): "The destinies of the two races in this country are indissolubly linked together, and the interests of both require that the common government of all shall not permit the seeds of race hate to be planted under the sanction of the law."

1898 *Holden* v. *Hardy*: in one of the first cases in which Court permits some state regulation of working conditions, it upholds a state law fixing maximum working hours for miners.

1903 *Champion* v. *Ames* (Lottery Case): Court upholds federal law banning distribution of lottery tickets through the mails. This key case involves the right of Congress, through its control of interstate commerce, to exercise a police power, that is, to outlaw dangerous, fraudulent, or otherwise objectionable commodities in an effort to protect the safety, health, morals, and general welfare of the public.

1905 *Lochner* v. *New York*: one of many cases in which Court invalidates a state law attempting to regulate industrial working conditions, it is primarily notable for Justice Oliver Wendell Holmes's exasperated dissent to the effect that the Court is deciding the case on the basis of socioeconomic theories that have slight relevance either to national needs or to the Constitution.

1908 *Muller* v. *Oregon*: Court upholds state law setting maximum working hours for women. Case is notable for first "Brandeis brief," named after argument prepared by counsel for state Louis D. Brandeis (later a Supreme Court justice himself). Since Court had

placed heavy burden of proof on those proposing various social-welfare laws, Brandeis presented this proof not in the form of legal argument but rather as data on the conditions that caused the state legislature to pass the disputed measure in the first place.

1911 *Coyle* v. *Smith*: for the first time since the founding of the Republic, Court deals directly with the issue of the Organic Acts by which Congress admits a state to the Union. In this case it holds that Congress may not impose upon Oklahoma conditions that deprive it of equal footing with existing states and specifically that Congress may not forbid a state to move its capital from one location (Guthrie) to another (Oklahoma City).

1915 *Guinn* v. *U.S.*: Court invalidates Oklahoma grandfather clause as a violation of the Fifteenth Amendment.

1918 *Arver* v. *U.S.* (one of Selective Draft Law Cases): Court upholds draft law as logical extension of congressional war powers.

Hammer v. *Dagenhart*: Court strikes down first congressional attempt to regulate intrastate working conditions (in this case the use of child labor) by means of the commerce clause. Court rules that Congress cannot prohibit interstate shipments of goods solely because they were manufactured by children.

1919 *Schenck* v. *U.S.*: Court upholds Espionage Act of 1917 as not abridging First Amendment guarantees of freedom of speech. Justice Holmes presents "clear and present danger" argument, in which he says Congress has the right to limit speech that clearly will bring about an "evil" which Congress is empowered to prevent—in this case resistance to the draft law.

1925 *Gitlow* v. *New York*: case is significant because it is the first of a now huge number of Fourteenth Amendment cases in which Court explicitly acknowledges that this amendment protects at least some of the individual citizen's federally guaranteed civil liberties against abridgment by the states. The key phrase in this decision is "we may and do assume that freedom of speech and of the press—which are protected by the first Amendment from abridgment by Congress—are among the fundamental personal rights and 'liberties' protected by the due process clause of the 14th Amendment from impairment by the states. . . ."

1927 *Nixon* v. *Herndon*: Court invalidates a Texas law barring black votes in Democratic primaries as a violation of the equal-protection clause of the Fourteenth Amendment.

1931 *Near* v. *Minnesota*: Court strikes down state law providing for censorship of newspapers or other periodicals that are "obscene, lewd, and lascivious" or "malicious, scandalous, and defamatory" as too broadly infringing upon the freedom of the press as guaranteed by the First Amendment through the due-process clause of the Fourteenth Amendment.

1932   *Powell* v. *Alabama* (one of Scottsboro Cases): Court rules that due-process clause of Fourteenth Amendment requires that defendants (in this case blacks charged with rape of white girls and sentenced to death) be given a fair trial and specifically that it requires that the Sixth Amendment guarantee of legal counsel for one's defense be protected against state abridgment.

1936–   *West Coast Hotel Co.* v. *Parrish*: one of several New
1937   Deal cases, culminating ultimately in *U.S.* v. *Darby*, in which Court reverses more than 50 years of opposition to most attempts by the national legislature to regulate parts of the economy in the public interest, that is, for the social and economic welfare of citizens. In these decisions Court generally grants Congress its powers to do so on the basis of the commerce clause and on the power to levy taxes in order to "provide for . . . the general Welfare of the United States" (Article I, Section 8), once again rooting a broad federal power in certain general constitutional propositions in a way somewhat reminiscent of the earlier Marshall era.

1937   *Palko* v. *Connecticut*: Court holds that Fifth Amendment guarantee against double jeopardy was not in this case included in Fourteenth Amendment. Case is significant, however, because it sets up a distinction between those liberties in Bill of Rights that are—or are not—essential to "the edifice of justice" and are—or are not—so fundamental to a "scheme of ordered liberty" that "neither liberty nor justice would exist if they were sacrificed." Court agrees in this decision that freedom of speech, thought, and press and the right to a fair trial have already met the test of being essential and hence have been included in the Fourteenth Amendment.

1938   *Missouri* ex rel. *Gaines* v. *Canada*: Court begins to re-examine the "equal" part of the "separate but equal" doctrine laid down in *Plessy* v. *Ferguson*. Court holds in this case that denying blacks entrance to University of Missouri law school but offering to pay their tuition in out-of-state law schools is neither "equal" nor constitutional.

1941   *U.S.* v. *Darby*: Court specifically and unanimously overrules the case of *Hammer* v. *Dagenhart* and upholds the Fair Labor Standards Act of 1938. Court here argues a broad construction of the commerce clause, holding that it gives Congress the right to prohibit interstate shipment of goods produced by

workers who earn less than a prescribed minimum wage or labor more than a prescribed maximum of hours. Decision recognizes that commerce is a vast communications and transportation network and recognizes that Congress alone has the constitutional authority to control this system. Decision specifically cites *Gibbons* v. *Odgen* and dismisses the argument that a construction of the commerce clauses gives the federal government police powers equivalent to those possessed by the several states over their own intrastate commerce.

1944   *Smith* v. *Allwright*: Court outlaws Democratic primary elections in Texas as a violation of the Fifteenth Amendment, ruling that party primaries in a state like Texas are tantamount to elections and that even though ruling members of the Democratic Party in Texas were acting in their capacity as private citizens rather than state officials, they were violating the Fifteenth Amendment by excluding black voters.

1947   *U.S.* v. *California*: Court rules that three-mile (oil-bearing) coastal shelf is national rather than state property. In 1954–60 Court upholds Congress' right to give these and tidelands back to the states if it so wishes, even to the extent of giving Florida and Texas a nine-mile jurisdiction so that their boundaries in effect stick out six miles beyond those of the rest of the states. In 1975 (*U.S.* v. *Maine*) Court rules that national government has title to Atlantic continental shelf beyond the three-mile limit.

1951   *Dennis* et al. v. *U.S.*: Court upholds 1946 Smith Act convictions of top eleven leaders of Communist Party on the grounds that act, which makes it a crime to teach and advocate the violent overthrow of the U.S. government, does not unconstitutionally abridge freedom of speech. Justices Black and Douglas dissent on the grounds that the "clear and present danger" test has been abandoned.

1952   *Youngstown Sheet and Tube Company* v. *Sawyer* ("Steel Seizure Case"): Court denies that President has the authority, in the absence of specific congressional consent, to seize private property for purpose of halting a labor dispute and thus forestalling a break in production. Court denies that President has inherent executive powers either as President or as Commander in Chief to take such an action.

1954   *Brown* v. *Board of Education of Topeka*: in this landmark case Court squarely faces issue of whether racial segregation in public schools, even if there is substantial equality in physical facilities, curricula, qualification of teachers, and other factors, is inherently unequal and denies black children equal protection of the laws under the Fourteenth Amendment. The

Court unanimously holds that it is and it does, in an opinion written by Chief Justice Warren: "Separate educational facilities are inherently unequal. . . . To separate [children in grade and high schools] from others of similar age and qualifications solely because of their race generates a feeling of inferiority as to their status in the community that may affect their hearts and minds in a way unlikely ever to be undone." Since Brown decision is technically applicable only to five school districts party to this case, the next twenty years have brought numerous cases based on the attempt to compel national compliance with Brown ruling.

1957 *Yates* v. *U.S.*: Court reverses several convictions of lesser Communist Party officials on grounds that federal government had too broadly interpreted 1946 Smith Act and was proceeding against Communists merely because of their ideas. Court in effect demands that more "clear and present danger" of actual incitement and action be demonstrated before First Amendment rights are suppressed.

Watkins v. *U.S.*: Court rules that congressional investigating committees (in this case the House Committee on Un-American Activities) do not have the right to expose publicly an individual's beliefs, behavior, or associations merely "for the sake of exposure" or in order extralegally to punish those being investigated for "dubious loyalty." Court holds that committee hearings must have some discernible connection with the lawmaking function and that the area of inquiry must be reasonably limited rather than general. Court retreats somewhat from this position in a 5–4 decision in *Barenblatt* v. *U.S.* (1959).

Roth v. *U.S.*: although Court has generally agreed that obscenity is not entitled to First Amendment protection, it has been difficult to define just what constitutes obscenity in particular instances. In Roth case Court proposes three tests: material (1) "appeals to a prurient interest in sex," (2) "affronts contemporary community standards," and (3) "is utterly without redeeming social value." Using these somewhat vague tests, Court has generally struck down bans on obscene books by recognized authors for which some legitimate case can be made for historical or literary value; in 1966, however, in what many critics regard as an aberration, the Supreme Court upholds (5–4) the conviction of a publisher on the grounds that the advertising in his publications was "permeated by the leer of the sensualist" (*Ginzburg* v. *U.S.*). In 1969 Court declares unconstitutional a state law making the mere possession (as opposed to publication or sale) of pornographic material in one's home a crime (*Stanley* v. *Georgia*); Court holds that such a law unconstitutionally violates right of privacy.

1962 *Engel* v. *Vitale*: Court rules that nondenominational prayer composed by school officials for use in public schools violates First Amendment prohibition against an established religion. Decision is one of a series involving religious issues under First Amendment dating back to 1943 case (*West Virginia State Board of Education* v. *Barnette*), in which Court held that state law requiring schoolchildren to salute the flag abridged religious freedom, and including a 1963 decision (*Abington School District* v. *Schempp*) that outlawed daily Bible readings in public schools. These decisions created a storm of protest in which Court was accused of trying to remove God from American life and which resulted in 5–4 ruling (*Board of Education* v. *Allen*) that use of public funds to supply parochial schools with textbooks does not violate separation of Church and State.

Baker v. *Carr*: in landmark decision Court rules that it does in fact have jurisdiction over cases involving alleged deprivation of equal protection of the laws under the Fourteenth Amendment when state legislatures are apportioned in such a way as to allow sparsely populated rural districts to dominate densely populated urban areas. Court thus retreats from its traditional position, first enunciated in 1849, that such matters were "political questions." In the next two years many states come up with reapportionment schemes, and in *Reynolds* v. *Sims* (1964) Court rules that the only fair and constitutional rules for such redistricting are (1) that both houses of state legislatures should be apportioned according to population and (2) that districts should be drawn in such a way that they contain about the same number of voters so that each vote will count equally in electing a representative ("one man, one vote" rule). In the Reynolds case some Alabama districts got one state senator for every 635,000 votes, and others got one senator for every 15,000 votes. As a result of various subsequent apportionment cases the courts have found themselves closely scrutinizing and evaluating complicated demographic schemes.

1965 *Griswold* v. *Connecticut*: Court strikes down as a violation of privacy state law that bans use of contraceptives and dissemination of information about birth control.

1966 *Miranda* v. *Arizona*: Court declares (5–4) that a criminal suspect must be apprised of certain procedural rights against self-incrimination; namely, he must be advised that he has the right to remain silent, that any statement he makes may be used as evidence against him, that he has a right to have an attorney present, and that although he may voluntarily waive his right to counsel, police questioning may not proceed if he indicates a wish to consult with counsel or to remain silent. Miranda case is culmination of long series of criminal-justice actions, beginning in 1961, in which Warren Court gradually extends Fourth, Fifth, and Sixth amendment guarantees, via the Fourteenth Amendment, to persons suspected or convicted of criminal offenses. Rulings include exclusion of evidence wrongfully seized and appointment by the courts of counsel in all cases involving crimes punishable by jail sentences; decisions are widely criticized as hamstringing law enforcement and allowing criminals to escape justice on legal technicalities. In 1976 Court retreats in a series of decisions from several of these rulings, particularly those relating to the exclusion of evidence, and allows police and court officers wider latitude in gathering and using evidence obtained in searches without warrants.

Sheppard v. *Maxwell*: Court declares that excessive pretrial publicity can violate a defendant's right to a fair and impartial trial. In a similar decision the year before (*Estes* v. *Texas*), Court had reversed the conviction of a swindler on the grounds that his televised trial made a mockery of due process.

1967   *In re* Gault: Court holds that juvenile courts must provide offenders many if not most of the fair-trial procedural safeguards (right to counsel, cross-examination, etc.) available to adult offenders.

1969   *Tinker* v. *Des Moines Community School District*: Court holds that children wearing black armbands in protest against Vietnam war are exercising right of free speech, which is protected by First Amendment. In similar case, however, Court holds that burning one's draft card is not so protected.

1970   *Oregon* v. *Mitchell*: in divided decision Court holds that Congress has right to lower voting age to eighteen in federal elections but not in state elections; issue is subsequently settled by ratification of Twenty-sixth Amendment in 1971.

1971   *New York Times Co.* v. *U.S.*: in "Pentagon Papers" case Court denies (6–3) government right to halt publication of stolen classified Pentagon report, largely on grounds that government has not demonstrated that publication would cause grave national harm.

1972   *U.S.* v. *U.S. District Court*: Court holds unanimously that government has no inherent right to conduct warrantless electronic surveillance of citizens, even on grounds of national security. Court holds in this case, as in another dating back to 1967 (*Katz* v. *U.S.*), that wiretapping and other forms of bugging conducted without first obtaining a warrant constitute "unreasonable search and seizure" under the Fourth Amendment.

Furman v. *Georgia*: in 5–4 decision Court outlaws capital punishment as constituting "cruel and unusual punishment," prohibited by Eighth Amendment, or as violating equal-protection clause of the Fourteenth Amendment, since in general only poor and ignorant people and members of minority groups actually have been executed. In 1976 Court upholds newly drafted capital-punishment laws of several states and strikes down others that mandate death penalty.

Branzburg v. *Hayes*: Court rules that reporters must divulge confidential sources of information to properly constituted grand juries or suffer the penalty of imprisonment for contempt of court.

1973   *Roe* v. *Wade*: Court declares that state antiabortion laws that interfere with a woman's right to seek an abortion, at least within first three months of pregnancy, are unconstitutional violations of privacy as guaranteed by the Fourteenth Amendment.

1974   *U.S.* v. *Richard Nixon*: Court declares unanimously that President has no constitutional right (based either on separation of powers or on inherent executive privilege) to withhold evidence in a criminal proceeding.

Wars in American History

Included in this list are all principal domestic and foreign wars in which Americans have participated from the early colonial period to 1976. Costs and casualties of the principal wars are generally based on Defense Department and Veterans' Administration estimates. Total military costs include veterans' benefits; since there are approximately thirty million veterans and sixty-four million veterans' dependents and survivors, costs given for the Spanish-American War (with approximately a thousand living veterans) and all later wars are projected figures. Death totals include battlefield deaths and "other deaths," meaning war-related deaths from disease or accident. (Until World War II disease usually took the lives of more combatants than actual warfare.)

Other wars included are some of the Indian wars that have for one reason or another impressed themselves upon the American imagination, at least to the extent of having been given a name. Indian wars involving principally Spanish or French explorers and colonists have not been included, nor have many of the extensive campaigns undertaken against the American Indian in various locales during the nineteenth century. It should be noted that many of the principal wars fought on American soil but involving foreign powers also included Indians as foes or allies and usually resulted in large land cessions or other substantial losses by the Indians. Casualties and costs for most of the Indian wars are not available.

This list also omits filibustering expeditions in the nineteenth century and twentieth-century interventions or occupations in Latin-American countries, of which at least seventeen occurred between 1900 and 1934.

An asterisk (*) indicates that no military operations of consequence occurred in what is now the continental United States.

1622–1624   Powhatan War. Principals: Virginia colonists against confederacy of some thirty tribal groups under leadership of Opechancanough, chief of Powhatan Indians. War begins with attack on Jamestown and other settlements (March 22, 1622), killing 357 settlers. Powhatans are defeated in two years, but war in effect goes on until 1644, when other tidewater Indians are greatly reduced in number.

1637   Pequot War. Principals: Connecticut and Massachusetts colonists and Mohegan and Narraganset allies against Pequot tribe. Begins with murder of Boston trader; Massachusetts declares war on Pequots (May 1, 1637); Pequot town on Mystic River, Connecticut, is destroyed, along with about 500 inhabitants; remainder of tribe is hunted down and killed or enslaved.

1675–1676   King Philip's War. Principals: New England colonists from Connecticut to Maine against New England Indians, including Wampanoags under Metacomet (King Philip), Narragansets, Nipmucks, Podunks, some Mohegans, and Abnakis. War begins in June with Wampanoag attack on Swansea, Massachusetts. War in Connecticut, Massachusetts, and Rhode Island ends by August 12, 1676, when King Philip is killed. War continues in Maine and New Hampshire until 1678, when a truce treaty is concluded (April 12). War costs colonists £150,000, 600 killed, and destruction of or damage to 64 towns (more than half of all settlements). Indian deaths probably total more than 3,000, with all New England tribes except Abnakis in Maine virtually destroyed.

1676   Bacon's Rebellion. Principals: Virginia frontiersmen led by Nathaniel Bacon against hitherto friendly Virginia Indians and established lower-tidewater planters under Governor Berkeley. Frontiersmen stirred up backcountry by slaughtering friendly Susquehannock Indians in 1675. Bacon's followers demand right to exterminate all Virginia Indians and are refused; in 1676 they make war on Indians and on Berkeley's forces, burning Jamestown (September 19). Rebellion collapses with Bacon's death (October 18).

1689–1697   King William's War. American phase of the War of the Grand Alliance (also called War of the League of Augsburg). Principals: England, American colonists, and Indian allies—chiefly Iroquois—against French, French colonists, and Indian allies—Abnakis in Maine and principally Hurons in Great Lakes region. Colonial war begins with Iroquois attack against French traders in Great Lakes region. War spreads from Hudson Bay in north to Schenectady, New York, and various Massachusetts settlements; includes temporary New England capture of Port Royal, Nova Scotia. War formally concluded by Treaty of Ryswick (September 30, 1697).

1702–1713   Queen Anne's War. American phase of the War of the Spanish Succession. Principals: England, American colonists, and Indian allies against France, Spain, French and Spanish colonists, and Indian allies. In 1702–03 Carolina settlers invade Florida and destroy St. Augustine and many Spanish missions but fail to reach French settlements in Louisiana. In New England, French and Indian allies destroy towns in Maine and along Massachusetts-New York border; New Englanders capture Port Royal (1710). War formally ends with Treaty of Utrecht (April 11, 1713).

1715–1716   Yamassee War. Principals: South Carolina colonists and Cherokee allies against Yamassees and Lower

Creeks. Yamassees are defeated, and many flee to Florida.

1739–1742
War of Jenkins' Ear. Principals: England, American colonists in Georgia, and Indian allies against Spain, Spanish colonists in Florida, and Indian allies. Colonists and allies under leadership of James Oglethorpe invade Spanish Florida in 1740 and smash Spanish counterattack in 1742.

1744–1748
King George's War. American phase of the War of the Austrian Succession. Principals: English, American colonists, and Indian allies—chiefly Iroquois—against France, French colonists, and Indian allies. French begin war with 1744 attack on British Annapolis Royal, Nova Scotia; colonists capture Fort Louisburg (1745). French and Indians raid Albany and Saratoga, New York, and Maine settlements. War ends formally with Treaty of Aix-la-Chapelle (October 18, 1748).

1754–1763
French and Indian War. Also known as the Seven Years War. Principals: England, American colonists, and Indian allies against France, French colonists, and Indian allies. Begins in Ohio Territory (July 3, 1754) with defeat of George Washington at Fort Necessity. Military operations cease in continental North America with French surrender of Quebec (September, 1759) and Montreal (September, 1760). War formally ends with Treaty of Paris, signed February 10, 1763.

1763–1764
Pontiac's War. Also known as Pontiac's Rebellion. Principals: England and American settlers against confederacy of Shawnee, Delaware, Chippewa, and other tribes of Great Lakes area under Ottawa war chieftain Pontiac. Begins with an Indian attack against Fort Detroit (May 7, 1763). Confederacy falls apart by summer, 1764. Pontiac signs final treaty with British at Oswego (July 24, 1766).

1774
Lord Dunmore's War. Principals: Virginia frontiersmen against Shawnees under Chief Cornstalk. Shawnees are defeated at Point Pleasant, West Virginia (October 9), and give up claims to Kentucky as a hunting ground.

1775–1783
Revolutionary War. Also known as the War for Independence. Principals: U.S.A., France, and Spain against Great Britain, American Loyalists (Tories), and Indian allies. Although often thought to have begun with the Declaration of Independence on July 4, 1776, military operations actually commence with the Battles of Lexington and Concord on April 18–19, 1775. Large-scale fighting ceases with British surrender at Yorktown (October 19, 1781). Definitive peace treaty is signed in Paris (September 3, 1783). Direct U.S. military costs: $101 million; total costs, including debt service and veterans' benefits: $255 million. Es-

timates of battle deaths range from about 4,400 to 6,800, with estimates of total deaths as high as 25,000; more than 8,000 were wounded.

1776–1781
Cherokee Wars. Principals: frontiersmen from Georgia, the Carolinas, and Virginia against Cherokee groups, Chickamaugas, and Creeks, occasionally joined by Tories and British. Cherokees are defeated in 1777, ceding large areas in Carolinas. Uprisings in 1779 are again put down, and land cessions of 1777 are reconfirmed by treaty in 1781.

1798–1800
*Naval War with France. Principals: U.S. Navy and merchantmen against French privateers and French navy. Undeclared war begins with French seizure of American vessels in West Indies and is concluded with pact on September 30, 1800.

1801–1805
*Tripolitan War. Also known as one of the Barbary Wars. Principals: U.S. Navy against forces of pasha of Tripoli.

1812–1815
War of 1812. Principals: U.S.A. and Indian allies against Great Britain, including Canada, and Indian allies, including confederacy organized by Shawnee chieftain Tecumseh. Congress declares war June 18, 1812; war officially ends with signing of Treaty of Ghent on December 24, 1814, although major battle occurs at New Orleans in January, 1815. Direct U.S. military costs: $93 million; total costs: $127 million. Estimated U.S. casualties: 2,260 dead in battle, 4,505 wounded.

1813–1814
Creek War. Principals: Tennessee militia under Andrew Jackson against "Red Stick" Creeks in what is now Alabama. Red Sticks are defeated at Battle of Horseshoe Bend (March 27, 1814); Creeks are then forced to cede large portions of Alabama and Georgia in treaty of Fort Jackson (August 9, 1814).

1815
*Algerine War. Also known as one of the Barbary Wars. Principals: U.S. Navy against dey of Algiers. Naval war against Algiers ends June 30. Other Barbary States, Tunis and Tripoli, sign treaties with U.S. on July 26 and August 5.

1816–1818
First Seminole War. Principals: U.S. soldiers and whites on Florida-Georgia border against Seminoles and escaped black slaves. Ends with invasion of Florida led by General Andrew Jackson.

1832
Black Hawk War. Principals: U.S. Army, Illinois settlers, and militia against about 1,000 Sauk and Fox Indians (of whom some 600 are women). War lasts from May to August, costing lives of at least 200 settlers and 850 of Black Hawk's group.

1835–1836
Texas Revolution. Principals: American and some Mexican colonists in Texas against the Mexican government. Clashes begin June 30, 1835. War ends with

Battle of San Jacinto (April 21, 1836) and treaty pledging Texas independence (May 14, 1836).

1835–1842 Florida War. Also known as Second Seminole War. Principals: U.S. Army and Florida and Georgia planters against Seminole Indians, last remaining tribe in Southeast. Seminoles, who are a mixture of ancient Florida tribes, Creek refugees, and escaped slaves, are mainly removed by 1842, although a few remain in Everglades. Savage war costs U.S. approximately 1,600 dead (Regular Army and volunteers).

1846–1848 Mexican War. Also known as Mexican-American War. Principals: U.S.A. and Mexico. Hostilities are begun April 25, 1846, in disputed area between Nueces and Rio Grande rivers; U.S. declares war May 13. War is formally ended by Treaty of Guadalupe-Hidalgo, signed February 2, 1848. Total U.S. military costs, including debt service and veterans' benefits: $109 million. Estimated U.S. casualties: total deaths 13,283, of which 1,733 are battle deaths; wounded, about 4,100.

1847–1864 Navaho Wars. Principals: U.S. Army against Navahos and Apache allies. War ends with destruction of Navaho settlements in Canyon de Chelly, Arizona, in 1864.

1848–1865 California Indian Wars. Principals: U.S. Army and Anglo-American miners and settlers in California against various California tribes. By 1873 the California Indian population was 17,000, reduced from the 1846 level of 250,000 by disease, warfare, and starvation.

1861–1865 Civil War. Also variously called the War Between the States, the War of the Rebellion, the War for Southern Independence, the Second American Revolution, and the War for Separation. Principals: U.S.A. against Confederate States of America. War actually begins with attack on Fort Sumter on April 12, 1861, but legally begins with President Lincoln's proclamation of insurrection on April 15, 1861. Military actions virtually end with surrender of Lee's army at Appomattox Courthouse on April 9, 1865, and with subsequent surrenders of remaining Confederate armies by May 26. Legal end of war held to be presidential proclamations of April 2 and August 20, 1866. Estimated direct U.S. military costs: $2 billion; total Union military costs, including debt service and veterans' benefits: $6.5 billion. Estimated total Confederate costs: $1–1.5 billion. Estimated U.S. casualties: total deaths 364,511, wounded 275,175. Estimated Confederate casualties: 260,000–270,000 total deaths, 100,000 wounded.

1861–1886 Apache Wars. Principals: U.S. Army and white settlers in New Mexico, western Texas, and Arizona against various Apache groups under leadership of Cochise, Victorio, Mangas Colorado, and Geronimo. Wars end in 1886 with final surrender of Geronimo and 24 warriors.

1864–1865 Cheyenne-Arapaho War. Principals: U.S. Army and Colorado militia against Cheyenne and Arapaho Indians in Colorado and Platte River Valley. War, which includes Sand Creek Massacre of 1864, ends with Indian cessions.

1865–1868 First Sioux War. Also known as the Red Cloud War. Principals: U.S. Army against Oglala Sioux under Red Cloud. War results in treaty signed November 6, 1868, guaranteeing Sioux permanent reservations in Black Hills, South Dakota, and Bighorn Mountains, Wyoming; also stipulates abandonment of attempt to build Bozeman Road through Wyoming to Montana. One of few Indian Wars that Indians won, even temporarily.

1868–1869 Washita War. Principals: U.S. Army and white settlers against Cheyenne, Arapaho, Kiowa, and Comanche bands in Kansas and Texas. War is virtually ended by slaughter along Washita River in Oklahoma on November 26, 1868.

1874–1875 Red River War. Principals: U.S. Army and buffalo-hide hunters against Kiowas and Comanches in Texas under Satenta and Quanah Parker. Ends in spring, 1875, when last warriors surrender.

1875–1877 Second Sioux War. Also known as the Sitting Bull War. Principals: U.S. Army and South Dakota miners against various Sioux groups under Crazy Horse and Sitting Bull. Includes annihilation of Custer's command (265 men) on June 25, 1876, along Little Bighorn River in Montana. Ends with surrender of Crazy Horse in April, 1877. Sitting Bull flees to Canada.

1877 Nez Perce War. Principals: U.S. Army (5,000 soldiers) against Oregon Nez Perces under Chief Joseph (250 warriors and 450 women, children, and old people). War begins in June and ends in October after 2,000-mile chase from Oregon to Montana.

1878 Bannock War. Principals: U.S. Army against Indians from Bannock and other reservations in Idaho. Is among the last of the flare-ups among Indians of Northwest.

1890 Ghost Dance War. Principals: U.S. Army against various groups of reservation Sioux. Ends in December with arrest and death of Sitting Bull and massacre at Wounded Knee Creek, South Dakota. Indian dead: more than 200 men, women, and children; army dead: 29, many of them killed by their own artillery fire.

1898 *Spanish-American War. Principals: U.S.A. against Spain. War begins with U.S. naval blockade of Cuban ports on April 22; Congress declares war on Spain on April 25. War is formally ended by Treaty of Paris, signed December 10, 1898. Direct U.S. military costs: $400 million; total costs, including veterans' pensions: about $2.5 billion. U.S. casualties: total deaths 5,462, of which 379 are battle deaths.

1899- *Philippine War. Principals: U.S.A. against Filipino
1902 rebels under leadership of Emilio Aguinaldo. U.S. employs 70,000 troops in suppressing rebellion. Scattered guerrilla resistance continues until 1906-07.

1900 *Boxer Rebellion. Principals: U.S.A., Great Britain, France, Germany, Japan, and Russia against Chinese revolutionists (Boxers). U.S. sends 5,000 troops as part of joint international expedition to raise siege of foreign legations in Peking (accomplished August 14). Affair is settled by Boxer Protocol (September 7, 1901).

1914- *World War I. Also known as Great War. Principals:
1918‘ Allies (England, France, Russia, Japan, and U.S.A. as an "associated power") against Central Powers (Germany, Austria-Hungary, Ottoman Empire). U.S. declares war against Germany on April 6, 1917, partly as a result of a series of German naval attacks against Allied shipping in which American civilians have been killed. Military hostilities cease with armistice signed November 11, 1918. U.S. fails to sign Versailles Treaty; Congress formally ends war by joint resolution (July 2, 1921). Direct U.S. military costs: $26 billion; estimated current costs to 1975, including veterans' benefits and interest on war debt: $49.2 billion. U.S. casualties: battle deaths 53,000; other deaths 116,195; wounded 204,000.

1918- *Siberian Expeditions. Principals: U.S.A., China, Ja-
1920 pan, and White Russian forces against Soviet Bolsheviks in northern Russia (Murmansk) and Siberia (Vladivostok). Last of approximately 8,500 troops withdrawn in April, 1920; 36 Americans killed.

1939- *World War II. Principals: Allies (or, as of 1942, the
1945 United Nations), whose 26 governments include those of U.S.A., Soviet Union, Great Britain (the "Big Three"), France, and China, against the Axis powers (principally Germany, Japan, and Italy until 1943). U.S. enters war against Japan following Pearl Harbor attack on December 7, 1941; Germany and Italy declare war on U.S.A. on December 11, 1941. War in Europe formally ends on May 7, 1945—V(ictory)-E(urope) Day; war in Pacific formally ends on August 14—V(ictory)-J(apan) Day. Direct U.S. military costs: $288 billion; estimated current costs through 1974: $530 billion. U.S. casualties: total deaths 405,399, wounded 670,846.

1950- *Korean War. Principals: Republic of Korea (South
1953 Korea) and United Nations forces, of which U.S. furnishes major part, against the People's Democratic Republic of Korea (North Korea), with the Soviet Union furnishing materiel and Red China providing substantial ground forces. U.S. enters undeclared war on June 27, 1950, by order of President Truman. War ends with armistice signed July 27, 1953. Estimated direct military costs: $54 billion; estimated current costs through 1974: $67.5 billion. U.S. casualties: total deaths 54,246, wounded 103,284.

1945- *Vietnam War. Also known as Indochina War. Princi-
1975 pals: France, U.S.A., and various South Vietnamese governments against the Democratic Republic of Vietnam (North Vietnam) and South Vietnamese guerrillas (Vietcong), who are aided materially by Soviet Union and Red China. War also involves Communist and anti-Communist elements in Cambodia and Laos. U.S. provided economic and military aid to French until 1954 and to South Vietnam from 1950 on. Major escalations: 1961 (first year in which there are U.S. casualties), 1964 (first U.S. bombing of North Vietnam), and 1965 (first substantial commitment of U.S. ground forces: 184,300). Last of American combat troops are removed August 13, 1972, but air war continues until January 15, 1973. Peace talks ending direct U.S. military involvement are signed January 27, 1973. Last Americans are evacuated by helicopter from South Vietnam on April 29, 1975; South Vietnam surrenders to Vietcong on April 30, 1975. U.S. casualties (1961–74): total deaths 56,758; total wounded 303,654. Direct U.S. military costs: $112 billion; estimated current costs through 1974: $118.5 billion.

Battles in U.S. Wars

Powhatan War

Date	Military Engagement	Location	Outcome
March 22, 1622	Surprise raid	Virginia Royal Colony, along James River	Indians led by Opechancanough massacre 357 men, women, and children in settlements.
1622–24	Indians are invited to draw up a treaty and are massacred in revenge; fall marches are organized to destroy Indian crops.		Result is peace for twenty years.
April, 1644	Surprise attacks	Virginia settlements, especially along York and Pamunkey rivers	About 500 settlers are killed in two days of fighting.

Pequot War

Date	Military Engagement	Location	Outcome
Summer of 1636	Gallup's naval engagement	Off Block Island, Rhode Island	Boat pirated by Indians is recaptured, and expedition is sent to Block Island to punish Indians.
May 25, 1637	Attack on Indians	Near Groton, Connecticut	180 Colonials, Mohegans, and Narragansets under Captain John Mason decimate Pequots' fortified stronghold.
July 13, 1637		Sasqua Swamp, near Southport, Connecticut	Remaining members of tribe are pursued and killed or captured and sold as slaves; Pequot culture ends, and peace comes to northern frontier for 40 years.

King Philip's War

Date	Military Engagement	Location	Outcome
December 19, 1675	Narraganset campaign	Great Swamp, near South Kingstown, Rhode Island	Force under Governor Josiah Winslow attacks main Narraganset fort and kills about 600 warriors.
February 9, 1676	Sack of Lancaster	Massachusetts	Town is destroyed, and a number of persons are taken captive.
May 18, 1676	Battle of Peskeompskut	Hadley, Connecticut	Wampanoags suffer severe losses.

Bacon's Rebellion

Date	Military Engagement	Location	Outcome
May, 1676		Roanoke River, Virginia	Force under Nathaniel Bacon decimates Occaneechi Indians, who had offered hospitality.
August, 1676		Upper York River, Virginia	Bacon leads another raid on Pamunkey Indians.
September 18, 1676		Jamestown, Virginia	Troops called by Governor William Berkeley to quash Bacon's Rebellion retreat after meeting resistance; Berkeley withdraws from Jamestown.

King William's War

Date	Military Engagement	Location	Outcome
February 9, 1690		Schenectady, New York	A force of 200 French and Indians attack the town, capture 80–90, and kill 60.
May 11, 1690		Port Royal, Nova Scotia	Massachusetts expedition under Sir William Phips captures city.
August 3– October 23, 1690		Quebec, Canada	Attack by New England expedition fails to take city.

Queen Anne's War

Date	Military Engagement	Location	Outcome
September, 1702		St. Augustine, Florida	Colonial force captures town but not fort.
August, 1703		Wells, Maine	Town is destroyed by force of French and Indians.
October 16, 1710		Port Royal, Nova Scotia	French town falls to colonial expedition after siege, the third of the war.

Yamassee War

Date	Military Engagement	Location	Outcome
April 15, 1715		Frontier settlements in South Carolina	About 90 traders and their families are slain by Indians.

Yamassee War

Date	Military Engagement	Location	Outcome
June, 1715		Near Charleston, South Carolina	Attack by Catawbas is repulsed.
Autumn of 1715			Expedition under Robert Daniel drives Yamassees into Florida.

War of Jenkins' Ear

Date	Military Engagement	Location	Outcome
June 14, 1740		Fort Moosa, Florida	Spaniards slip out of St. Augustine and recapture fort, which represents sharp setback to three-month siege of St. Augustine by much larger force of 2,000 under James Oglethorpe, governor of Georgia.
July 7, 1742	Battle of Bloody Marsh	Georgia	Large fleet and army under Florida's Governor Montiano are repulsed by smaller force under Oglethorpe, ending Spanish threat to British colony.

King George's War

Date	Military Engagement	Location	Outcome
Summer of 1744		Annapolis Royal (formerly Port Royal), Nova Scotia	French effort to capture town is a failure.
April 28–June 16, 1745		Fort Louisburg, Cape Breton Island	New England expedition under William Pepperell, in cooperation with British fleet, takes French city.
November 15, 1745		Saratoga, New York	Indians capture town and frighten settlers along Hudson River Valley.

French and Indian War

Date	Military Engagement	Location	Outcome
July 3, 1754		Fort Necessity, Pennsylvania	French defeat much smaller force led by George Washington.

French and Indian War

Date	Military Engagement	Location	Outcome
July 9, 1755	Battle of the Wilderness	Ohio	French and Indians defeat larger force led by General Edward Braddock.
September 8, 1755	Battle of Lake George	New York	French are defeated, thwarting their drive toward Lake Ontario.
July 8, 1758	Battle of Ticonderoga	New York	Marquis de Montcalm repulses British attack, thwarting plans to take fort and thus secure water route for attack on Canada.
July 26, 1758		Louisburg, Cape Breton Island	Town is taken by fleet under Jeffery Amherst and James Wolfe.
July 25, 1759		Fort Niagara, New York	British win and close in on St. Lawrence Valley.
September 12–18, 1759	Battle of Quebec	Canada	Both Wolfe and Montcalm die in this British victory, which paves way for later surrender of Montreal and English possession of Canada.

Pontiac's War

Date	Military Engagement	Location	Outcome
July 31, 1763	Battle of Bloody Ridge	Michigan	British are disastrously defeated in a sortie from Detroit against Pontiac.
August 2–6, 1764	Battle of Bushy Run	Pennsylvania	Indians are routed, and Fort Pitt siege is relieved.

Lord Dunmore's War

Date	Military Engagement	Location	Outcome
October 10, 1774	Battle of Point Pleasant	West Virginia	Whites win decisive victory when Indians withdraw after mistaking a flank attack for enemy reinforcements.

Revolutionary War

Date	Military Engagement	Location	Outcome
April 18–19, 1775	Battles of Lexington and Concord	Massachusetts	In Lexington, British attack American militia drawn up on common; in Concord they destroy some supplies, but 73 British soldiers die in process.

Revolutionary War

Date	Military Engagement	Location	Outcome
June 17, 1775	Battle of Bunker Hill	Massachusetts	General Thomas Gage seizes hill overlooking Boston Harbor from Americans who seek to fortify it.
August 27, 1776	Battle of Long Island	New York	British General William Howe routs General Israel Putnam on Brooklyn Heights.
October 11, 1776	Batle of Valcour Bay	New York	British decimate American flotilla in seven-hour battle on Lake Champlain.
October 13, 1776	Battle of Split Rock	New York	At Split Rock, British complete destruction of American flotilla on Lake Champlain.
October 28, 1776	Battle of White Plains	New York	Howe captures key hill positions.
January 3, 1777	Princeton	New Jersey	General George Washington inflicts heavy losses, recaptures much of New Jersey, and boosts Patriot morale.
October 4, 1777	Battle of Germantown	Pennsylvania	Washington attacks Howe, but offense loses coordination in heavy fog, and Continental army retreats to Valley Forge.
October 7, 1777	Battle of Bemis Heights	New York	General John Burgoyne surrenders with 5,700 men after suffering two defeats.
June 28, 1778	Battle of Monmouth	New Jersey	Washington pursues British, who are retreating to New York City to avoid being bottled up in Philadelphia by French fleet.
December 29, 1778	Fall of Savannah	Georgia	Lieutenant Colonel Archibald Campbell, under orders of General Sir Henry Clinton, lands near Savannah and crushes militia.
March 3, 1779	Briar Creek	Georgia	American effort to recapture Augusta fails.
August 29, 1779	Newtown (Elmira)	New York	Loyalists and Indians are defeated.
September 3–October 28, 1779	Savannah	Georgia	French fail to oust British from city.
May 12, 1780	Fall of Charleston	South Carolina	Clinton takes Charleston and captures 5,400-man garrison and four American ships in greatest British victory of war.

Revolutionary War

Date	Military Engagement	Location	Outcome
August 16, 1780	Battle of Camden	South Carolina	General Charles Cornwallis routs Americans under Horatio Gates.
October 7, 1780	Battle of Kings Mountain	South Carolina	Backwoodsmen rout Loyalist force of about 1,100.
January 17, 1781	Battle of Cowpens	South Carolina	General Daniel Morgan defeats larger British force under Colonel Banastre Tarleton.
March 15, 1781	Battle of Guilford Courthouse	North Carolina	Cornwallis fights larger force under Nathanael Greene; the battle is not decisive, but large British losses compel Cornwallis to leave the Carolinas.
September 18– October 19, 1781	Siege of Yorktown	Virginia	Cornwallis surrenders force of about 7,250 after failing to break through naval blockade.

Cherokee Wars

Date	Military Engagement	Location	Outcome
July 20, 1776		Eaton's Station, North Carolina	170 defenders of Eaton's Station beat off attack by 700 Indians under Chief Dragging Canoe.

Naval War with France

Date	Military Engagement	Location	Outcome
November 20, 1798	*Retaliation* v. *L'Insurgente* and *Volontaire*	Off Guadeloupe	*Retaliation* (U.S.) surrenders.
February 9, 1799	*Constellation* v. *L'Insurgente*	Near Nevis, in Caribbean	*L'Insurgente* is captured after two and a half hours of combat.
February 1, 1800	*Constellation* v. *La Vengeance*	Off Guadeloupe	Draw
October 12, 1800	*Boston* v. *Le Berceau*	Off Guadeloupe	Captain George Little captures *Le Berceau*.

Tripolitan War

Date	Military Engagement	Location	Outcome
July, 1801	*Enterprise* v. *Tripoli*	Mediterranean	*Tripoli* is heavily damaged by *Enterprise*.
February 16, 1804	*Philadelphia*	Off Tripoli	*Philadelphia,* which had run on a reef and been captured by Tripolitans (October, 1803), is recaptured and burned during a night attack by Lieutenant Stephen Decatur and force of 80 men.
April 27, 1805		Derna, Tripoli	Marines capture the city.

War of 1812

Date	Military Engagement	Location	Outcome
August 16, 1812		Detroit, Michigan	General William Hull surrenders 2,200 men without fighting opposing Canadian force.
August 19, 1812	*Constitution* v. *Guerrière*	Off Nova Scotia	Captain Isaac Hull blows up *Guerrière* (British) after damaging it heavily. The victory bolsters sagging American morale after the Detroit debacle.
October 25, 1812	*United States* v. *Macedonian*	Off the Madeira Islands	British frigate *Macedonian* is brought to New London as prize by Captain Stephen Decatur.
December 29, 1812	*Constitution* v. *Java*	Off coast of Brazil	*Java* (British) is destroyed in battle.
January 22, 1813	Battle of Frenchtown	Raisin River, at western end of Lake Erie	Kentucky force led by James Winchester is defeated in first battle of campaign to retake Detroit.
May 27–29, 1813	Battle of Sackets Harbor	New York	British landing force from Canada is repulsed.
June 1, 1813	*Chesapeake* v. *Shannon*	Off Boston	Americans led by James Lawrence (known for "Don't give up the ship") suffer heavy losses, and British capture the *Chesapeake*.
September 10, 1813	Battle of Lake Erie	Off Put-in-Bay	Captain Oliver Hazard Perry wins decisive victory over British squadron and forces evacuation of Detroit.
October 5, 1813	Battle of the Thames	Canada	General William Henry Harrison defeats British, and Indian chief Tecumseh dies, leading Indians to desert British cause.
October 25–26, 1813	Battle of Chateaugay	New York	Canadian forces compel General Wade Hampton to fall back.

War of 1812

Date	Military Engagement	Location	Outcome
November 11, 1813	Battle of Chrysler's Farm	Canada	Campaign to take Montreal ends as British defeat landing party of 1,700 Americans.
July 5, 1814	Battle of Chippewa	Canada	General Winfield Scott defeats British on open field.
July 25, 1814	Battle of Lundy's Lane	Canada	Battle is a draw and marks end of U.S. campaign to seize Canada.
August 24, 1814	Battle of Bladensburg	Maryland	Americans are routed, and British enter Washington, D.C.
September 11, 1814	Battle of Lake Champlain	Across bay from Plattsburg, New York	Captain Thomas Macdonough defeats British squadron, giving U.S. undisputed control of Lake Champlain.
September 12–13, 1814	Battle of Godly Wood	Maryland	British win but lose many men as they advance to Baltimore.
September 13–14, 1814	Bombardment of Fort McHenry	Maryland	British fail to take fort, and plans to take Baltimore are foiled; British return to Jamaica.
January 1–8, 1815	Battle of New Orleans	Louisiana	British lose many, and General Andrew Jackson emerges a military hero.

Creek War

Date	Military Engagement	Location	Outcome
August 30, 1813		Fort Mims, Alabama	Creek Indians kill 250 in fort and burn many others to death.
November 3, 1813		Talishatchee, Alabama	Indian village is destroyed, along with 200 defenders.
November 9, 1813		Talladego, Alabama	General Andrew Jackson destroys village, killing more than 500 Indian warriors.
March 27, 1814	Battle of Horseshoe Bend (Tohopeka)	Alabama	800 Indians die when Jackson attacks their fortified position.

Algerine War

Date	Military Engagement	Location	Outcome
June 17, 1815		Off Spain	*Mashuda* and *Estido,* Algerine warships, are seized by Captain Stephen Decatur's squadron.

First Seminole War

Date	Military Engagement	Location	Outcome
July 27, 1816		Fort Apalachicola, East Florida	U.S. expedition destroys fort.
May 24, 1818		Pensacola, Florida	Town is seized, and its Spanish governor is ejected by Andrew Jackson.

Black Hawk War

Date	Military Engagement	Location	Outcome
May 14, 1832		Dixon's Ferry, Illinois	Skirmish takes place after Black Hawk's offer to surrender is disregarded.
mid May–July, 1832	Indian raids occur in which 200 Indians and 200 settlers die.		
July 21, 1832		Wisconsin Heights, Wisconsin	Battle results are inconclusive, but Black Hawk manages to get his women and children across the Wisconsin River.
August 3, 1832		Bad Axe River, Wisconsin	Indians are slaughtered.

Texas Revolution

Date	Military Engagement	Location	Outcome
December 5–10, 1835		San Antonio, Texas	Mexicans are routed in attack on town, and 1,100 surrender.
February 23– March 6, 1836	Siege of the Alamo	San Antonio, Texas	3,000 Mexicans under Santa Anna massacre 187, including Davy Crockett, in garrison.
March 27, 1836		Goliad, Texas	Many of the 400 defenders of the town are massacred by Santa Anna's troops.
April 21, 1836	Battle of San Jacinto	Near Galveston Bay, Texas	Texans inflict disastrous defeat.

Florida War
(Second Seminole War)

Date	Military Engagement	Location	Outcome
December 28, 1835	Battle of Black Point	Florida	Indians led by Osceola ambush and capture a number of soldiers.

Florida War
(Second Seminole War)

Date	Military Engagement	Location	Outcome
December 31, 1835	Battle of Withlacoochee	Florida	Osceola's ambush of force that has come to destroy an Indian hideaway marks point when war becomes serious.
December 25, 1837	Battle of Okeechobee	Florida	Seminoles and U.S. troops under Colonel Zachary Taylor battle; issue remains unsettled.

Mexican War

Date	Military Engagement	Location	Outcome
May 8, 1846	Battle of Palo Alto	Contested Texas-Mexico area	General Zachary Taylor repulses larger Mexican force.
May 9, 1846	Battle of Resaca de la Palma	Contested Texas-Mexico area	Taylor, in pursuit of Mexicans, inflicts heavy losses and lifts siege of Fort Texas.
September 21–23, 1846	Battle of Monterrey	Mexico	Taylor seizes city after three-day siege.
February 22–23, 1847	Battle of Buena Vista	Mexico	Taylor, leading 4,700 men, defeats Santa Anna's 15,000 and terminates war in northern Mexico.
March 22–27, 1847	Battle of Veracruz	Mexico	General Winfield Scott besieges and occupies city.
April 18, 1847	Battle of Cerro Gordo	Mexico	Santa Anna is routed in battle with much hand-to-hand combat and loses large number of officers.
August 19–20, 1847	Battles of Contreras and Churubusco	Mexico	Heavy losses are inflicted on Santa Anna, who withdraws to Mexico City, five miles away.
September 8–14, 1847	Battle of Mexico City	Mexico	City is taken after Scott's troops storm fortified hill of Chapultepec.

Navaho Wars

Date	Military Engagement	Location	Outcome
February, 1860		Fort Defiance, Arizona	Manuelito and 500 warriors raid Army's herd of horses but capture few of them.
April 30, 1860		Fort Defiance, Arizona	An Indian attack is beaten off.

Navaho Wars

Date	Military Engagement	Location	Outcome
September 22, 1860		Fort Wingate, New Mexico	Several Navahos are killed in a melee over cheating in a horse race between Indians and soldiers.
January 12, 1864		Canyon de Chelly, Arizona	Soldiers under Kit Carson destroy Navaho crops and peach orchards, but there is no military engagement.

California Indian Wars

Date	Military Engagement	Location	Outcome
November 29, 1872	Battle of Lost River	California	Modocs under Captain Jack fight off 38 soldiers seeking to return them to an Oregon reservation.
January 17, 1873	Lava Beds	California	Force of 225 soldiers and 104 Oregon and California volunteers are beaten off.

Civil War

Date	Military Engagement	Location	Outcome
July 21, 1861	First Battle of Bull Run (Manassas)	Virginia	Union army led by Irvin McDowell faces Confederate army led by Pierre Beauregard and Joseph E. Johnston. After it fails to dislodge brigade led by Thomas J. Jackson (thus nickname "Stonewall"), Union army is routed.
August 10, 1861	Battle of Wilson's Creek	Missouri	Confederate victory is their first in Missouri.
February 12–16, 1862	Battle for Fort Donelson	Tennessee	In his first major Civil War action Ulysses S. Grant besieges and captures fort, with 11,500 defenders and all their equipment. This opens road to Vicksburg and control of the Mississippi River, while defense of New Orleans is weakened because Confederate forces are drawn north.
March 6–8, 1862	Battle of Pea Ridge	Arkansas	Confederate attack is repulsed in this border state.
March 9, 1862	*Merrimack* v. *Monitor*	Virginia	The battle is a draw but ends threat of *Merrimack* to Union shipping.
March 28, 1862	Battle of Glorietta Pass	New Mexico	Confederate threat to Far West is ended with defeat of a force led by General George Sibley.
April 6–7, 1862	Battle of Shiloh	Tennessee	23,000 die in bloodiest two days of the war; Shiloh is a strategic victory for Grant, who recoups after surprise attack.

Civil War

Date	Military Engagement	Location	Outcome
April 24–25, 1862	Battle of New Orleans	Louisiana	Commodore David G. Farragut captures city after earlier battles with Confederate vessels on Mississippi River. This action strengthens blockade.
May 25, 1862	Winchester	Virginia	Jackson forces retreat of Union forces across Potomac.
May 31–June 1, 1862	Battle of Fair Oaks (Seven Pines)	Virginia	Joseph Johnston loses his life as he leads this Confederate attack, which is repulsed.
June 25–July 2, 1862	Seven Days' Battles	Virginia	General Robert E. Lee, new chief of Army of Northern Virginia, fails to drive McClellan off peninsula, but Confederate victory costs McClellan his title as commander of all Union armies.
August 25–31, 1862	Second Battle of Bull Run (Manassas)	Virginia	Lee, Jackson, and James Longstreet drive Union army back to Washington.
September 17, 1862	Battle of Antietam	Near Sharpsburg, Maryland	McClellan forces Lee across Potomac during this bloody battle, which is militarily a draw.
October 8, 1862	Battle of Perryville	Kentucky	Battle is a Union victory.
December 13, 1862	Battle of Fredericksburg	Virginia	Ambrose Burnside, new chief of Army of Potomac, waits too long to attack, and attack fails.
December 29, 1862	Chickasaw Bluffs	Mississippi	General William Tecumseh Sherman is repulsed in attempt to seize Vicksburg.
December 31, 1862–January 2, 1863	Battle of Murfreesboro	Tennessee	Union forces compel General Braxton Bragg to withdraw from central Tennessee after this battle.
May 2–5, 1863	Battle of Chancellorsville	Virginia	General Joseph Hooker is defeated by Lee, but "Stonewall" Jackson dies after he is accidentally wounded by his own men.
May 22–July 4, 1863	Siege of Vicksburg	Mississippi	Town surrenders after Grant crosses Mississippi River and cuts off its supply base; this gives Union complete control of Mississippi and splits Confederacy.
July 1–3, 1863	Battle of Gettysburg	Pennsylvania	Lee is repulsed by George Meade in a decisive Union victory.
September 19–20, 1863	Battle of Chickamauga	Tennessee	General Braxton Bragg defeats Union army, pinning it down in Chattanooga.

Civil War

Date	Military Engagement	Location	Outcome
November 23–25, 1863	Battle of Chattanooga	Tennessee	Grant, now commander of all Union armies in West, forces Bragg to retreat into Georgia, leaving Union forces in full control of West.
May 5–6, 1864	Battle of the Wilderness	Virginia	Grant, in an indecisive, futile effort to flank Lee, tries to cut him off from lower South.
May 8–12, 1864	Battle of Spotsylvania	Virginia	J. E. B. Stuart is killed, a major loss to Confederacy.
June 1–3, 1864	Battle of Cold Harbor	Virginia	In another assault by Grant both sides lose heavily.
June 15–18, 1864	Siege of Petersburg	Virginia	Beauregard reinforces town and stands off attack by Grant, who besieges town thereafter.
June 19, 1864	*Alabama* v. *Kearsarge*	Off Cherbourg, France	Confederate raider *Alabama,* which had wrought havoc with Union ships, is sunk.
July 20–28, 1864	Battles around Atlanta	Georgia	Confederate John Hood fails in attempts to prevent encirclement of Atlanta by William T. Sherman.
August 23, 1864	Battle of Fort Morgan (Mobile)	Alabama	Union navy led by Farragut seizes Mobile and cuts Confederacy off from sea.
September 19, 1864	Winchester	Virginia	Philip H. Sheridan beats off attack by Confederate Jubal Early to drive him out of Shenandoah Valley.
December 15–16, 1864	Battle of Nashville	Tennessee	Union forces almost destroy Hood's army as an organization, though casualties are relatively light, and drive it out of Tennessee.
March 19, 1865	Battle of Bentonville	North Carolina	Sherman repulses attack, marking end of North Carolina campaign.
April 1, 1865	Battle of Five Forks	Virginia	In battle that comes after Lee's last assault, Sheridan routs forces under George Pickett.

Apache Wars

Date	Military Engagement	Location	Outcome
July 15, 1862		Apache Pass, Arizona	Indians are driven out by cannon fire, retreating after Apache chief, Mangas, is wounded.

Apache Wars

Date	Military Engagement	Location	Outcome
April 30, 1871	Camp Grant Massacre	Arizona	More than 100 Indians living near Camp Grant are slaughtered or die from wounds after surprise attack by Tucson posse.

Cheyenne-Arapaho War

Date	Military Engagement	Location	Outcome
November 29, 1864	Sand Creek Massacre	Colorado	Colonel John Chivington's troops massacre 450 Cheyenne Indians in dawn attack.
January 7, 1865		Julesburg, Colorado	Indians burn town and scalp defenders.

First Sioux War

Date	Military Engagement	Location	Outcome
December 21, 1866	Fetterman Massacre	Wyoming	Indians kill 81 soldiers and their leader, Captain W. J. Fetterman, who have been giving them chase, in worst army defeat in Indian wars thus far.
September 17, 1868	Battle of Beecher Island	Colorado	Indians' attack on General Sheridan's scouts is repulsed, and Chief Roman Nose is killed.

Washita War

Date	Military Engagement	Location	Outcome
November 27, 1868	Massacre at Washita River	Oklahoma	Custer's troops surprise Cheyennes and kill 103, of whom only 11 are warriors.

Red River War

Date	Military Engagement	Location	Outcome
June 27, 1874		Adobe Walls, Texas	Indians attack hunters who have been making a shambles of buffalo herds but are repulsed.
September 28, 1874		Palo Duro Canyon, Texas	Provisions of Comanches are destroyed in surprise attack.

Second Sioux War

Date	Military Engagement	Location	Outcome
June 17, 1876	Battle of Rosebud	Montana	Indians under Crazy Horse defeat General George Crook's attack on their village.
June 25, 1876	Battle of Little Bighorn	Montana	General George Custer's troops are wiped out by Sioux.

Nez Perce War

Date	Military Engagement	Location	Outcome
June 17, 1877		White Bird Canyon, Idaho	Troops under General O. O. Howard are defeated.
July 11, 1877		Clearwater River, Idaho	Draw
August 9, 1877		Big Hole River, Montana	Surprise attack led by Colonel John Gibbon is repulsed decisively.
September 13, 1877		Canyon Creek, Montana	Colonel Samuel D. Sturgis is beaten off.
September 30–October 5, 1877		Bear Paw Mountains, Montana	Indians are surrounded by Colonel Nelson A. Miles and troops and forced to surrender.

Spanish-American War

Date	Military Engagement	Location	Outcome
May 1, 1898	Battle of Manila	Philippines	Commodore George Dewey destroys ten-ship Spanish squadron and gains control of Philippine Archipelago.
July 1, 1898	Battles of El Caney and San Juan	Cuba	After the fall of El Caney, a fortified village with a garrison of 600, Colonel Theodore Roosevelt's Rough Riders charge up San Juan Hill.
July 3, 1898	Battle of Santiago Bay	Cuba	Spanish squadron is destroyed as it seeks to escape.

Philippine War

Date	Military Engagement	Location	Outcome
February 4–5, 1899	Second Battle of Manila	Philippines	Filipinos under Emilio Aguinaldo are crushed in their assault on General Elwell Otis' troops.

Boxer Rebellion

Date	Military Engagement	Location	Outcome
July 13, 1900		Tientsin, China	International relief expedition on the way to Peking captures city.
August 14, 1900		Peking, China	Expedition relieves besieged foreign legations.

World War I

Date	Military Engagement	Location	Outcome
June 4, 1918	Battle of Belleau Wood	France	After skirmish at Château-Thierry 2nd Division stops German drive that reaches almost within 50 miles of Paris.
July 18–August 6, 1918	Second Battle of the Marne	France	Nine U.S. divisions help turn back German attack across the Marne.
August 18–September 15, 1918	Oise-Aisne Offensive	France	U.S. troops take part in this drive, which approaches Belgian frontier.
August 19–November 11, 1918	Ypres-Lys Offensive	Belgium	In this drive, which is launched by Britain, 108,000 U.S. troops take part.
September 12–16, 1918	Saint-Mihiel Offensive	France	First Army, led by General John Pershing, takes this strong German salient, capturing 16,000 prisoners in the first distinctively American offensive.
October 4–16, 1918	Battle of the Argonne	France	In this battle, part of the larger Meuse-Argonne offensive, which ends with the signing of the armistice, the First Army captures all major German defense positions in the Argonne region, pivot of Germany's Hindenburg Line. This defeat forces General Erich von Ludendorff to request that talks be initiated for an armistice.
October 24–November 1, 1918	Battle of Vittorio-Veneto	Italy	1,200 U.S. troops (332nd Regiment) take part in this battle, which ends in rout of Austrian army.

World War II

Date	Military Engagement	Location	Outcome
December 7, 1941	Attack on Pearl Harbor	Hawaii	Japanese cripple U.S. Pacific fleet.
February 27–March 1, 1942	Battle of Java Sea	Pacific	Delaying action results in most severe losses since Pearl Harbor.

World War II

Date	Military Engagement	Location	Outcome
April–May 6, 1942	Corregidor	Philippines	Japanese capture island fortress and win control of Philippines.
May 7–8, 1942	Battle of the Coral Sea	Pacific	First major U.S. victory of war halts southward advance of Japanese on Australia.
June 3–6, 1942	Battle of Midway	Central Pacific	In this naval and air battle the Japanese, under Isoroku Yamamoto, seek to take island but are repulsed by Admiral Chester W. Nimitz's fleet, thus ending immediate threat of assault on Hawaii.
August 9, 1942	Battle of Savo Island	North of Guadalcanal	Japanese victory temporarily deprives U.S. forces on Guadalcanal of air and naval support.
November 12–15, 1942	Battle of Guadalcanal	Solomon Islands	Marines resist Japanese efforts to land reinforcements and dislodge U.S. forces, facilitating the conquest of Guadalcanal (February 9, 1943) and marking end of Japanese power in the Solomon Islands.
February 14–19, 1943	Battles of Faïd Pass and Kasserine Pass	Tunisia	Americans crumble under German attack by Rommel's Afrika Korps but then put up stiff resistance, thus slowing down effort to cut British communications lines.
March 2–4, 1943	Battle of Bismarck Sea	Pacific	Japanese convoy carrying reinforcements to New Guinea is destroyed by Allied aircraft.
May 7–13, 1943	Bizerte	Tunisia	Italian First Army surrenders to Allied forces.
May 11–30, 1943	Battle of Attu	Aleutian Islands	U.S. wipes out Japanese from this island, ending further landings in North America by Axis forces.
August 5–17, 1943	Messina	Sicily	Town is taken, marking end of Sicilian campaign.
September 9–18, 1943	Salerno	Italy	Anglo-American Fifth Army, led by General Mark Wayne Clark, lands at Salerno and repels German counterattacks.
October 1, 1943	Naples	Italy	City is taken by Fifth Army.
November 2, 1943	Battle of Empress Augusta Bay	Solomon Islands	Decisive Japanese defeat allows Allies to isolate enemy forces in Solomon Islands and to secure U.S. flank for advance on Philippines.
November 21–24, 1943	Makin and Tarawa	Gilbert Islands	Admiral Nimitz launches successful attack on these two key islands in Central Pacific.
January 22–May, 1944	Battle of Anzio	Italy	Surprise landing at Anzio, 30 miles from Rome, meets strong resistance from Germans until May 11, when Allies launch drive on Rome and main force of Fifth Army penetrates German defenses and links up with troops in Anzio.

World War II

Date	Military Engagement	Location	Outcome
February 1–22, 1944	Marshall Islands	Pacific	Kwajalein, Eniwetok, and other islands are taken after fierce fighting.
April 22, 1944	Hollandia and Aitape	New Guinea	MacArthur leapfrogs Japanese stronghold and outflanks the Japanese.
June 6, 1944	Omaha Beach	France	Troops under Omar Bradley's command establish beachhead despite strong resistance.
June 15–July, 1944	Saipan	Mariana Islands	Some of fiercest fighting in war takes place in effort to end Japanese resistance.
June 19–20, 1944	Battle of Philippine Sea	Pacific	Admiral Jisaburo Ozawa, bound for Saipan, withdraws his fleet after losing most of his planes.
June 27, 1944	Cherbourg	France	Allies storm city, taking 35,000 prisoners.
July 9, 1944	Caen	France	City is taken, and Rommel's panzer and land forces are beaten.
July 13–25, 1944	Saint-Lô	France	Allies break out of Normandy beachhead despite strong German defenses, allowing troops to move into open plains of central France and proceed toward Paris.
August 17–27, 1944	Falaise-Argentan	France	Parts of twelve to fourteen German divisions are surrounded by Bradley and Montgomery in worst German defeat since Stalingrad; General Patton helps close trap.
September 15, 1944	Peleliu	Palau Islands	Ring around Caroline Islands is completed, and bases closer to Philippines are provided.
September 17, 1944	Arnhem and Nijmegen	Netherlands	Attempt to outflank German defense (Siegfried Line) fails.
October 15–21, 1944	Aachen	Germany	First major German city is taken after seven days of house-to-house fighting.
October 23–25, 1944	Battle of Leyte Gulf	Philippines	Japanese fleet is dealt smashing defeat following land battles on Leyte, central island of the Philippines.
November 22–23, 1944	Metz-Strasbourg	France	Patton's Third Army captures Metz, and Alexander Patch's Seventh Army takes Strasbourg.
December 20–December 26, 1944	Bastogne	Belgium	In this important battle (part of Battle of the Bulge) Americans hold up against larger German force that surrounds them until Patton's armor breaks through encirclement.

World War II

Date	Military Engagement	Location	Outcome
mid-December, 1944–January, 1945	Battle of the Bulge	France, Belgium, Luxembourg	Germans fail in their last offensive in the Ardennes; objective was to gain vital seaport of Antwerp.
February 6–March 2, 1945	Corregidor	Philippines	Fortress is recaptured.
February 19–March 14, 1945	Iwo Jima	South of Japan	Very costly U.S. victory permits accelerated bombing of Japan.
April 1–June 21, 1945	Okinawa	Southwest of Japan	Japanese fight Tenth Army from fortifications and seek to destroy the American fleet off Okinawa through kamikaze attacks, which have caused heavy naval casualties in World War II.

Korean War

Date	Military Engagement	Location	Outcome
July 5, 1950	Osan	South Korea	American task force of 540 is overwhelmed by North Koreans in first battle.
July 16–20, 1950	Taejon	South Korea	Americans under General William Dean are routed, but they hold long enough to save vital port of Pusan, allowing landing of more divisions from Japan.
August 6–September 15, 1950	Battle of Pusan Beachhead	South Korea	UN forces repulse attack and launch counteroffensive.
September 26–28, 1950	Seoul	South Korea	Capital of South Korea is recaptured.
November 25, 1950	Chongchon River	North Korea	U.S. pulls back with light losses after Chinese divisions join war.
November 27, 1950	Yudam-ni	North Korea	U.S. forces fight way out of Chinese trap.
February 15, 1951	Chipyong	North Korea	Chinese army suffers first tactical defeat by Americans when a massive offensive is blunted by Eighth Army under General Matthew Ridgway.
May 16–21, 1951	Battle of the Soyang	South-North Korea	Second Division repulses North Koreans; Eighth Army moves north again.

Vietnam War

Date	Military Engagement	Location	Outcome
February 7, 1965	Pleiku	South Vietnam	In surprise attack U.S. suffers sharpest blow (8 dead and 60 wounded) since the intervention; attack leads to bombing of North Vietnam.
November 13–19, 1966	Ia Drang Valley	South Vietnam	In first fierce contact between U.S. and North Vietnamese troops 66th North Vietnamese inflicts 200 deaths and 2,000 wounded on U.S. 1st Air Cavalry.
July 2–7, 1967	Battle of Conthien	Demilitarized Zone	Marine base is subjected to surprise attack.
November 3–22, 1967	Battle of Dakto	South Vietnam	285 U.S. soldiers are killed and 985 are wounded in battle surrounding large U.S. military complex.
January 23– April 5, 1968	Siege of Khesanh	South Vietnam	A garrison of Marines is surrounded by a larger North Vietnamese force, and a potential Dien Bien Phu is averted by air attacks.
January 30– March 2, 1968	Tet Offensive	South Vietnam	Vietcong and North Vietnamese launch overwhelming attack on all major South Vietnamese cities and U.S. military bases, with major battles in Hue and Saigon; it is during this battle that Americans hear that at the Battle of Ben Tre in Mekong Delta 1,000 South Vietnamese were killed and 1,500 wounded in order to dislodge 2,500 Vietcong soldiers.
May 20, 1969	Battle for Hamburger Hill	South Vietnam	Nixon's handling of war comes under attack after this battle, in which U.S. and South Vietnamese troops capture Apbia Mountain in the Ashau Valley.

A Vietnam Chronology

1945 Vietminh, led by Ho Chi Minh, proclaim Vietnam independent republic following collapse of Japanese occupation of Indochina (September 2).

Ho writes first of several letters to President Harry Truman and United Nations, appealing for U.S. aid in struggle to prevent reconquest by former colonial power, France (October).

1950 Ho's Democratic Republic of Vietnam, which controls much of the north, is recognized by the Soviet Union and Red China (January).

U.S. recognizes regime of Emperor Bao Dai, based in Saigon and supported by French (February 7).

President Truman announces $10 million worth of economic and military aid to French in Vietnam and sends 35 military advisers (May–June).

1951 U.S. assistance to French in Indochina reaches $500 million mark.

1952 Bao Dai's Saigon regime collapses owing to lack of political support within Vietnam. French public opinion is increasingly opposed to the war, of which U.S. is now paying about 80 per cent of the costs (October).

1954 French suffer devastating military defeat at Dien Bien Phu (May 7). CIA group under Colonel Edward Lansdale begins covert operations against Communist forces in North Vietnam (June).

Geneva Agreements call for armistice in Indochina, partition of Vietnam into northern and southern halves separated by a demilitarized zone, and general elections in Vietnam in 1956. U.S. does not sign Geneva Agreements (July 20).

1955 U.S. military advisers are sent to train South Vietnamese army (February 23).

Ngo Dinh Diem, premier of South Vietnam, rejects reunification elections provided for in Geneva Agreements (the North would have won) and is supported in this decision by Eisenhower administration (July 16).

1960 U.S. increases military advisers in South Vietnam to 685 (May).

Vietcong (National Liberation Front of South Vietnam) is formed with South Vietnamese Communist guerrillas and North Vietnamese leadership (December).

1961 President Kennedy sends 400 members of the Special Forces (Green Berets) to train South Vietnamese in

guerrilla actions directed against North Vietnam (May 11).

U.S. advisers are permitted to support combat operations, leading to first U.S. casualties (fourteen) (November).

By year's end U.S. military and economic aid to various Vietnam governments since 1950 totals $3.7 billion.

1963 Unpopular Diem regime is overthrown by military coup, and Diem is killed (November 1); U.S. tacitly supported coup but opposed Diem's assassination.

U.S. military advisers in Vietnam now number 16,500; there have been 489 U.S. casualties this year (December 31).

1964 Congress passes Tonkin Gulf Resolution (August 7), authorizing President Johnson to take "all necessary measures" to protect U.S. forces from "any armed attack." Resolution is response to alleged attacks on U.S. destroyers in Gulf of Tonkin (August 2 and August 4), off North Vietnam, where destroyers had been associated with commando raids.

U.S. military advisers in South Vietnam now number 23,300, but they do not yet participate directly in combat (December 31).

1965 President Johnson orders continuous bombing of North Vietnam (February 13) after an attack on military advisers at Pleiku that cost eight American lives.

First U.S. Marines arrive in South Vietnam (March 8).

U.S. ground troops participate in first offensive "search and destroy" mission (June).

U.S. troops in South Vietnam number 184,300 (December 31).

1966 U.S. begins using B-52's for air strikes against Hanoi-Haiphong area in North Vietnam (June 29).

There are now 385,300 U.S. troops in South Vietnam (December 31).

1967 B-52 raids on North Vietnam now occur at the rate of 800 a month (February).

Public dissent in U.S. spreads from small demonstrations at universities to large-scale demonstrations involving 50,000–350,000 protesters in several cities. Congressional dissatisfaction with war effort increases, with doves calling for a winding down of U.S. commitment and hawks calling for all-out U.S. effort to smash North Vietnam (April–October).

Nguyen Van Thieu is elected president of South Vietnam (September 3).

There are now 485,600 U.S. troops in South Vietnam. This year's war costs: $20.1 billion (December 31).

1968   Tet offensive: major coordinated Vietcong and North Vietnamese attacks on all South Vietnamese cities and U.S. installations launched (January 30).

Antiwar candidate Eugene McCarthy makes strong showing in New Hampshire Democratic presidential primary, Senator Robert F. Kennedy announces his (antiwar) candidacy for Democratic presidential nomination, and President Lyndon Johnson announces he will not seek another term (March).

Preliminary peace talks between U.S. and North Vietnam begin in Paris (May 10).

Major police-demonstrator riots take place outside Democratic National Convention in Chicago (August 26–29).

U.S. commander in Vietnam has requested 206,000 additional troops, but he has been turned down; nevertheless U.S. troop levels reach near-peak of 536,100. This year's war costs: about $26.5 billion (December 31).

1969   Paris peace talks expanded to include Vietcong and Saigon regime (January 16).

Secret bombing of Cambodia begins (March).

President Nixon announces 25,000 U.S. troops will be withdrawn by end of August (June 8).

President Nixon announces Vietnamization program (November 3); program calls for gradual withdrawal of U.S. troops and turning over of combat operations to South Vietnamese army (ARVN).

Massive antiwar demonstrations continue, with 250,000 marchers gathering in Washington, D.C. (November 15).

Court-martial of Lieutenant William L. Calley begins for his role in massacre of 450 South Vietnamese civilians in village of My Lai (November 24). U.S. troops now number 475,200. This year's costs: about $30 billion (December 31).

1970   Invasion of Cambodia by U.S. and ARVN troops announced (April 30); intent is to destroy Vietcong sanctuaries, but real result is to strengthen Communist (Khmer Rouge) movement in Cambodia.

Students are killed at Kent State University, Ohio (May 4), and Jackson State College, Mississippi (May 14), during demonstrations against Cambodian invasion.

Congress repeals Tonkin Gulf Resolution (December 31). There are now 334,600 troops in South Vietnam. This year's war costs: $23.1 billion.

1971   ARVN, with U.S. air support, invades Laos (February 8); effort causes heavy South Vietnamese losses and ends earlier than projected; creates further domestic concern about what seems a widening of Vietnam war.

More than 12,000 people arrested during antiwar protests in Washington, D.C. (May 3–5).

"Pentagon Papers," classified Defense Department study of history of U.S. involvement in Vietnam, begin appearing in *New York Times* (June 13); study, leaked by Daniel Ellsberg, appears to suggest pattern of deliberate deception of U.S. public by Presidents Kennedy and Johnson.

There are now 156,800 U.S. troops in South Vietnam (December 31).

1972   Following large North Vietnamese push into South Vietnam, heavy U.S. air raids against North are resumed (April 15–16).

President Nixon announces mining of Haiphong, major North Vietnamese harbor, a naval blockade of North Vietnam, and heavier bombing of North (May 8).

Last U.S. combat troops leave South Vietnam (August 13).

President Nixon orders bombing halt in North Vietnam (October 23), and National Security Adviser Henry A. Kissinger announces that peace is at hand (October 26).

U.S. completes shipment to South Vietnam of $1 billion worth of military equipment (November 31).

Peace negotiations break down, and President Nixon orders heaviest bombing ever of North Vietnam (December 18); bombing is halted on December 30. There are now 24,200 U.S. troops stationed within South Vietnam (December 31).

1973   Peace talks resume in Paris (January 8).

Peace agreements signed; call for immediate cease-fire, withdrawal of remaining U.S. forces, release of American prisoners of war, end to foreign military operations in Laos and Cambodia, and some participation of the Vietcong in South Vietnamese politics (January 27).

Five hundred and ninety American POW's have been released by North Vietnam, and U.S. has withdrawn almost all of the U.S. troops remaining in South Vietnam (March 29).

1974   President Ford offers conditional amnesty to Vietnam draft evaders who will do up to two years of public service (September 16).

1975   ARVN forces begin rapid collapse (March 13); by April 22 Communist forces have advanced whole length of South Vietnam to within 40 miles of Saigon.

U.S.-supported Cambodian government surrenders to Communist Khmer Rouge (April 16–17).

U.S. helicopters evacuate 1,000 Americans and about 5,000 South Vietnamese (April 29); during next two weeks about 120,000 South Vietnamese flee or are evacuated by U.S.

South Vietnamese government surrenders to Vietcong (April 30).

U.S. merchant ship *Mayaguez* and crew of 39 are rescued from Cambodian capture, with at least 15 killed in operation (May).

Communist Pathet Lao assume complete control of Laos (August 23); military and economic aid to Laos in the years 1950–74: $2.5 billion.

1976   After several appeals the court-martial conviction of Lieutenant Calley is upheld (April 5); Army announces that it will parole Calley, who has served about three years.

South and North Vietnam officially reunited as one nation, with Hanoi as the capital, under the North Vietnamese flag (July 2).

Rumors and reports from Cambodia suggest that its leaders are instituting drastic measures involving the systematic extermination of ideological enemies and the relocation of vast segments of the population.

The American Intellectual Tradition

The list below gives a sampling of persons who have contributed to the development of an American intellectual tradition. Reflecting the fact that such a tradition embraces a broad spectrum of disciplines, the writings included here represent significant contributions to fields as diverse as medicine, law, botany, history, political science, biology, religion, literary criticism, psychology, and economics. The long-term importance of books of recent vintage, especially those published in the 1970's, is of course beyond prediction, but an attempt has been made to select a few that promise something of more than passing significance.

The nature of the writers' contributions to their respective disciplines is as varied as the fields themselves. To cite the single example of history: the historical texts on the list range from such multivolume analyses as Van Wyck Brooks's *Makers and Finders* to such primary sources as John Winthrop's *Journal* of 1630–49. As this latter title suggests, the American intellectual tradition is founded on the works of both professional and nonprofessional writers.

Although the books included feed an intellectual tradition that is distinctively American, this tradition cannot be understood as existing in splendid isolation. From the outset this American tradition has been nourished by much broader cultural currents, beginning with those that accompanied the first colonists across the Atlantic. The names of a number of these colonists, all native Englishmen, figure prominently in the first section of this list, and without them an American intellectual tradition would be inconceivable. Therefore being a native American has not been a criterion for inclusion. From start to finish the list contains writers born abroad—Haitian-born John James Audubon, German-born Franz Boas, and Canadian-born John Kenneth Galbraith among others. But in every case significant intellectual achievement has followed the writer's arrival in America and earned him his place on this list.

The authors are entered in chronological order according to their date of birth; when two or more were born in the same year, they are listed in alphabetical order.

1579?–1631	John Smith: *A True Relation of Such Occurrences and Accidents of Noate ... in Virginia ...* (1608), *A Description of New England* (1616), *The Generall Historie of Virginia, New England, and the Summer Isles* (1624)
1588–1649	John Winthrop: *Journal,* covering 1630–49, published in 1825–26 as *The History of New England from 1630 to 1649*
1590?–1657	William Bradford: *History of Plimmoth Plantation, 1620–1647,* published in full in 1856

1585–1652	John Cotton: *The Keyes of the Kingdom of Heaven* (1644), *The Way of the Churches of Christ in New England* (1645), *Milk for Babes, Drawn out of the Breasts of Both Testaments, Chiefly for the Spiritual Nourishment of Boston Babes ... but may be of like Use for any Children* (1646), *The Way of Congregational Churches Cleared* (1648)
1586–1647	Thomas Hooker: *A Survey of the Summe of Church Discipline* (1648)
1603?–1683	Roger Williams: *The Bloudy Tenent of Persecution* (1644), *Christenings Make Not Christians* (1645), *The Hireling Ministry None of Christs* (1652)
1604–1690	John Eliot: *A Primer or Catechism in the Massachusetts Indian Language* (1654), *The Christian Commonwealth* (1659), translation of the Bible into one of the Algonquian languages and first Bible printed in English colonies (1661–63)
1635?–1678?	Mary White Rowlandson: *The Soveraignty and Goodness of God: Together With the Faithfulness of His Promises Displayed; Being a Narrative of the Captivity and Restauration of Mrs. Mary Rowlandson* (1682), first nonfiction best seller not a theological work or textbook
1639–1723	Increase Mather: *A Brief History of the Warr With the Indians* (1676), *A Relation of the Troubles Which Have Hapned in New-England by Reason of the Indians There* (1677), *Cases of Conscience Concerning Evil Spirits* (1693)
1652–1730	Samuel Sewall: *Diary* (written 1673–1729, published in 1882), *The Selling of Joseph* (1700)
1663–1728	Cotton Mather: author of more than 470 books (in seven languages), including *Memorable Providences: Relating to Witchcrafts and Possessions* (1689), *Magnalia Christi Americana* (1702), and a great number of scientific communications to Royal Society of London, including an enthusiastic account of success of smallpox inoculation that he had long urged (1722)
1674–1744	William Byrd II: *History of the Dividing Line Between Virginia and North Carolina* (1728–29), *Diary* (written in shorthand, 1709–12 and 1739–41, partially published in 1941–42), *The Secret History of the Dividing Line* (published in 1929)
1688–1776	Cadwallader Colden: *The History of the Five Indian Nations* (1727), *Plantae Coldenghamiae,*

systematic classification of New York plants (1749)

1703–1758   Jonathan Edwards: "Sinners in the Hands of An Angry God" (1741), *A Careful and Strict Enquiry into the Modern Prevailing Notions . . . of Freedom of Will* (1754)

1706–1790   Benjamin Franklin: *Poor Richard's Almanack* (1732–57), *Experiments and Observations on Electricity* (1751–54), "Rules by which a Great Empire may be Reduced to a Small One" (1773), *Autobiography* (published partially in 1791, in full in 1867)

1710–1780   Jonathan Carver: *Travels Through the Interior Parts of North America in the Years 1766, 1767, 1768* (1778)

1711–1780   Thomas Hutchinson: *History of the Colony and Province of Massachusetts Bay* (3 vols., 1764, 1767, 1828)

1720–1772   John Woolman: *Some Considerations on the Keeping of Negroes* (1754, 1762), *Considerations on Pure Wisdom and Human Policy, On Labour, on Schools, on the Right Use of the Lord's Outward Gifts* (1758), *Journal* (written 1756–72, published in 1774)

1725–1783   James Otis: *The Rights of the British Colonies Asserted and Proved* (1764)

1732–1808   John Dickinson: *Letters from a Farmer in Pennsylvania to the Inhabitants of the British Colonies* (1767–68)

1735–1813   Michel Guillaume Jean de Crèvecoeur: *Letters from an American Farmer* (1782), *Sketches of Eighteenth-Century America* (published in 1925)

1737–1809   Thomas Paine: *Common Sense* (1776), *The Crisis* pamphlets (1776–83), *The Rights of Man* (1791–92), *The Age of Reason* (1794–96)

1743–1826   Thomas Jefferson: *A Summary View of the Rights of British America* (1774), Declaration of Independence (1776), *Ordinance for Religious Freedom* (1779), *Notes on the State of Virginia* (1785)

1754–1846   Benjamin Waterhouse: *Shewing the Evil Tendency of the Use of Tobacco* (1805), *Information Respecting the Origin, Progress, and Efficacy of the Kine Pock Inoculation* (1810)

1755–1804   Alexander Hamilton: *The Federalist* (1788); of these 85 essays Hamilton wrote more than 50, with James Madison contributing 29 and John Jay 5. Hamilton was also chief author of George Washington's Farewell Address (1796)

1758–1843   Noah Webster: *The American Spelling Book* (1783), *A Grammatical Institute of the English Language, II, III* (1784–85), *Brief History of Epidemic and Pestilential Diseases* (1799), *An American Dictionary of the English Language* (1828)

1763–1847   James Kent: *Commentaries on American Law* (1826–30)

1773–1838   Nathaniel Bowditch: *New American Practical Navigator* (1802)

1780–1842   William Ellery Channing: "The Moral Argument Against Calvinism" (1820), forceful summing up of Unitarianism

1783–1859   Washington Irving: *Salmagundi: Or the Whim-Whams and Opinions of Launcelot Langstaff, Esq. and Others* (1807–08), *History of New York from the Beginning of the World to the End of the Dutch Dynasty* (1809), *The Sketch Book of Geoffrey Crayon, Gent.* (1820), *History of the Life and Voyages of Christopher Columbus* (1828)

1785–1851   John James Audubon: *The Birds of America* (4 vols., 1827–38), *Ornithological Biography* (5 vols., 1831–39)

1785–1860   James Pollard Espy: *Philosophy of Storms* (1841)

1791–1871   George Ticknor: *History of Spanish Literature* (1849)

1792–1873   Sarah Moore Grimké: *An Epistle to the Clergy of the Southern States* (1836), *Letters on the Equality of the Sexes and the Condition of Woman* (1838)

1796–1872   George Catlin: *Letters and Notes on the Manners, Customs, and Condition of the North American Indians* (1841)

1796–1859   Horace Mann: *Twelve Annual Reports* (1837–48), issued when Mann was secretary of the Massachusetts State Board of Education

1796–1859   William Hickling Prescott: *History of the Reign of Ferdinand and Isabella, the Catholic* (1837), *History of the Conquest of Mexico* (1843), *History of the Conquest of Peru* (1847)

1798–1877   Charles Wilkes: *Narrative of the United States Exploring Expedition* (1844), *Meteorology* (1851), *Hydrography* (1861)

1800–1891   George Bancroft: *History of the United States* (10 vols., 1834–74)

1800–1873   William Holmes McGuffey: *Eclectic Readers* (1, 2, 1836; 3, 4, 1837; 5, 1844; 6, 1857)

1801–1882   George Perkins Marsh: *The Origin and History*

of the English Language (1862), *Man and Nature* (1864)

1803–1882 Ralph Waldo Emerson: *Nature* (1836), "The American Scholar" (1837), *Essays* (1841), *Essays* (1844), *Representative Men* (1850), *The Conduct of Life* (1860)

1803–1895 Theodore Dwight Weld: *The Bible Against Slavery* (1837), *American Slavery As It Is* (1839)

1805–1879 Angelina Emily Grimké: *An Appeal to the Christian Women of the South* (1836), *An Appeal to the Women of the Nominally Free States* (1837)

1805–1844 Joseph Smith: *The Book of Mormon* (1830)

1806–1873 Matthew Fontaine Maury: *Wind and Current Chart of the North Atlantic* (1847), *Physical Geography of the Sea* (1855)

1809–1894 Oliver Wendell Holmes: *The Contagiousness of Puerperal Fever* (1843), *The Autocrat of the Breakfast-Table* (1858)

1809–1865 Abraham Lincoln: Gettysburg Address (1863), Second Inaugural Address (1865)

1809–1849 Edgar Allan Poe: *The Philosophy of Composition* (1846), *The Poetic Principle* (1850)

1810–1850 Margaret Fuller: *Woman in the Nineteenth Century* (1845), *Papers on Literature and Art* (1846)

1810–1888 Asa Gray: *Elements of Botany* (1836), *Botanical Text-Book* (1842), *Manual of the Botany of the Northern United States* (1848)

1814–1877 John Lothrop Motley: *The Rise of the Dutch Republic* (1856)

1815–1882 Richard Henry Dana, Jr.: *Two Years Before the Mast* (1840)

1815–1902 Elizabeth Cady Stanton: Declaration of Sentiments (1848), resolution for first women's-rights convention at Seneca Falls, New York

1817–1895 Frederick Douglass: *Narrative of the Life of Frederick Douglass, an American Slave* (1845)

1817–1862 Henry David Thoreau: *A Week on the Concord and Merrimack Rivers* (1849), "On the Duty of Civil Disobedience" (1849), *Walden* (1854)

1821–1910 Mary Baker Eddy: *Science and Health* (1875), foundation text of Christian Science

1823–1893 Francis Parkman: *The California and Oregon Trail* (1849), *History of the Conspiracy of Pontiac* (1851), *Pioneers of France in the New World* (1865), and five other titles in monumental series *France and England in North America*, completed in 1892

1829–1909 Hinton Rowan Helper: *The Impending Crisis of the South: How to Meet It* (1857)

1834–1902 John Wesley Powell: *Explorations of the Colorado River of the West and Its Tributaries* (1875), *An Introduction to the Study of Indian Languages* (1877), *Report on the Lands of the Arid Region of the United States* (1878)

1836–1918 Washington Gladden: *Plain Thoughts on the Art of Living* (1868), *Applied Christianity* (1887)

1838–1918 Henry Brooks Adams: *History of the United States from 1801 to 1817* (9 vols., 1889–91), *Mont-Saint-Michel and Chartres* (1913), *The Education of Henry Adams* (1918)

1838–1914 John Muir: *The Mountains of California* (1894), *Our National Parks* (1901)

1839–1897 Henry George: *Progress and Poverty* (1879)

1839–1914 Charles Sanders Peirce: "How to Make Our Ideas Clear" (1878), *Chance, Love and Logic* (1923)

1840–1914 Alfred Thayer Mahan: *The Influence of Sea Power upon History, 1660–1783* (1890), *The Influence of Sea Power upon the French Revolution and Empire, 1793–1812* (1892)

1840–1910 William Graham Sumner: *What Social Classes Owe to Each Other* (1883), "The Forgotten Man" (1883), *Folkways* (1906), *The Science of Society* (1927–28)

1841–1913 Lester Frank Ward: *Dynamic Sociology* (1883)

1842–1914? Ambrose Bierce: *The Fiend's Delight* (1872), *Nuggets and Dust Panned Out in California* (1872), *The Devil's Dictionary* (1906)

1842–1910 William James: *The Principles of Psychology* (1890), *The Will to Believe and Other Essays in Popular Philosophy* (1897), *The Varieties of Religious Experience* (1902), *Pragmatism: A New Name for Some Old Ways of Thinking* (1907)

1848–1908 Joel Chandler Harris: *Uncle Remus: His Songs and His Sayings* (1880)

1848–1927 James Ford Rhodes: *History of the United States from the Compromise of 1850* (7 vols., 1893–1906), *History of the Civil War 1861–1865* (1917)

1849–1914 Jacob August Riis: *How the Other Half Lives* (1890), *The Children of the Poor* (1892), *Children of the Tenements* (1903)

1852–1916 Charles Taze Russell: *Food for Thinking Christians* (1881), one of foundation texts of Jehovah's Witnesses

1856–1915   Frederick Winslow Taylor: *The Adjustment of Wages to Efficiency* (1896), *Shop Management* (1903), *The Principles of Scientific Management* (1911)

1856–1915   Booker T. Washington: *Up From Slavery* (1901)

1857–1944   Ida Minerva Tarbell: *The History of the Standard Oil Company* (1904), *The Business of Being a Woman* (1912)

1857–1929   Thorstein Veblen: *The Theory of the Leisure Class* (1899), *The Theory of Business Enterprise* (1904)

1858–1942   Franz Boas: *The Mind of Primitive Man* (1911), *Anthropology and Modern Life* (1928), *Race, Language, and Culture* (1940)

1859–1952   John Dewey: *The School and Society* (1899), *Democracy and Education* (1916), *The Quest for Certainty* (1929)

1860–1935   Charlotte Perkins Gilman: *Women and Economics* (1898)

1861–1918   Walter Rauschenbusch: *Christianity and the Social Crisis* (1907), *Christianizing the Social Order* (1912)

1861–1932   Frederick Jackson Turner: "The Significance of the Frontier in American History" (1893), *The Frontier in American History* (1920), *The Significance of Sections in American History* (1932)

1863–1952   George Santayana: *The Sense of Beauty* (1896), *The Life of Reason* (1905–06), *The Realms of Being* (4 vols., 1927–40)

1865–1935   James Henry Breasted: *A History of Egypt* (1905), *Development of Religion and Thought in Ancient Egypt* (1912)

1866–1945   Thomas Hunt Morgan: *The Physical Basis of Heredity* (1919), *The Theory of the Gene* (1926)

1866–1936   Lincoln Steffens: *The Shame of the Cities* (1904), *The Struggle for Self-Government* (1906), *Upbuilders* (1909)

1867–1936   Finley Peter Dunne: *Mr. Dooley in Peace and in War* (1898), *Mr. Dooley's Philosophy* (1900)

1868–1963   W. E. B. Du Bois: *Souls of Black Folk* (1903), *Color and Democracy* (1945)

1869–1930   Herbert David Croly: *The Promise of American Life* (1909)

1869–1959   Frank Lloyd Wright: *An Organic Architecture* (1939), *An American Architecture* (1955)

1871–1929   Vernon Louis Parrington: *Main Currents in American Thought: An Interpretation of American Literature from the Beginnings to 1920* (1927–30)

1874–1948   Charles Austin Beard: *An Economic Interpretation of the Constitution of the United States* (1913), *The Rise of American Civilization* (with Mary Beard, 4 vols., 1927–39)

1874–1946   Gertrude Stein: *Composition as Explanation* (1926), *How to Write* (1931), *The Autobiography of Alice B. Toklas* (1933)

1874–1949   Edward Lee Thorndike: *Educational Psychology* (1913–14), *Human Nature and Social Order* (1940), *Man and His Works* (1943)

1878–1958   John Broadus Watson: *Psychology from the Standpoint of a Behaviorist* (1919), *Behaviorism* (1925), *Psychological Care of Infant and Child* (1928)

1880–1961   Arnold Gesell: *The First Five Years of Life* (1940), *The Child from Five to Ten* (with Frances Ilg, 1946)

1880–1956   Henry Louis Mencken: *Prejudices* (1919–27), *The American Language* (1919)

1883–1966   Margaret Higgins Sanger: *What Every Girl Should Know* (1916), *What Every Mother Should Know* (1917), *The Case for Birth Control* (1917), *Women, Morality, and Birth Control* (1922)

1885–1972   Ezra Pound: *ABC of Reading* (1934), *Impact, Essays on Ignorance and the Decline of American Civilization* (1960)

1885–1972   Harlow Shapley: *Galaxies* (1943), *Of Stars and Men* (1958)

1885—   Stith Thompson: *The Types of the Folktale* (1928), *Motif-Index of Folk Literature* (1932–36), *The Folktale* (1946)

1886–1963   Van Wyck Brooks: *The Ordeal of Mark Twain* (1920), *Makers and Finders* (5 vols., 1936–52, including *The Flowering of New England,* 1936)

1887–1948   Ruth Benedict: *Patterns of Culture* (1934), *The Chrysanthemum and the Sword: Patterns of Japanese Culture* (1946)

1887–1949   Leonard Bloomfield: *Language* (1933)

1887–1976   Samuel Eliot Morison: *Builders of the Bay Colony* (1930), *Three Centuries of Harvard* (1936), *Admiral of the Ocean Sea* (1942), *John Paul Jones* (1959), *The Oxford History of the American People* (1965), *The European Discovery of America* (2 vols., 1971–74)

1888–1965	T. S. Eliot: *The Sacred Wood* (1920), *The Use of Poetry and the Use of Criticism* (1933), *The Idea of a Christian Society* (1939), *Notes Towards the Definition of Culture* (1948), *On Poetry and Poets* (1957)
1888–1974	John Crowe Ransom: *The World's Body* (1938), *The New Criticism* (1941)
1889–1974	Walter Lippmann: *Public Opinion* (1922), *A Preface to Morals* (1929), *The Good Society* (1937)
1892–1971	Reinhold Niebuhr: *Moral Man and Immoral Society* (1932), *The Nature and Destiny of Man* (2 vols., 1941–43), *Man's Nature and His Communities* (1965)
1893–1970	Joseph Wood Krutch: *The Modern Temper* (1929), *The Twelve Seasons* (1949), *The Desert Year* (1952), *The Measure of Man* (1954), *The Gardener's World* (1959)
1894–1956	Alfred Kinsey: *Sexual Behavior in the Human Male* (1948), *Sexual Behavior in the Human Female* (1953)
1894–1961	James Thurber: *The Years with Ross* (1959)
1894–1964	Norbert Wiener: *Cybernetics; or, Control and Communication in the Animal and the Machine* (1948), *The Human Use of Human Beings* (1950)
1895—	Buckminster Fuller: *Nine Chains to the Moon* (1938), *Operating Manual for Spaceship Earth* (1969), *Earth, Inc.* (1973)
1895—	Lewis Mumford: *The Culture of Cities* (1938), *The Human Prospect* (1955), *The City in History* (1961)
1895—	Immanuel Velikovsky: *Worlds in Collision* (1950), *Ages in Chaos* (1952), *Earth in Upheaval* (1955), *Oedipus and Akhnaton* (1960)
1895–1972	Edmund Wilson: *Axel's Castle* (1931), *To the Finland Station* (1940), *The Wound and the Bow* (1941), *The Shock of Recognition* (1943), *The Scrolls from the Dead Sea* (1955), *Apologies to the Iroquois* (1959), *The Cold War and the Income Tax* (1963)
1897–1955	Bernard De Voto: *Mark Twain's America* (1932), *Across the Wide Missouri* (1947), *The Course of Empire* (1952)
1898—	Malcolm Cowley: *Exile's Return* (1934), *The Literary Situation* (1954), *Second Flowering* (1973)
1898—	Herbert Marcuse: *Eros and Civilization* (1955), *One-Dimensional Man* (1964)
1899—	Bruce Catton: *Mr. Lincoln's Army* (1951), *Glory Road: The Bloody Route from Fredericksburg to Gettysburg* (1952), *A Stillness At Appomattox* (1953), *This Hallowed Ground* (1956)
1900–1945	Ernie Pyle: *Here is Your War* (1943), *Brave Men* (1944), *Last Chapter* (1946)
1901—	Margaret Mead: *Coming of Age in Samoa* (1928), *Sex and Temperament in Three Primitive Societies* (1935), *Male and Female* (1949), *Culture and Commitment* (1970)
1902—	Henry Steele Commager: *Majority Rule and Minority Rights* (1943), *The American Mind* (1950), *Freedom, Loyalty, Dissent* (1954)
1902–1950	F. O. Matthiessen: *American Renaissance* (1941)
1903—	Benjamin Spock: *The Common Sense Book of Baby and Child Care* (1946), *Decent and Indecent* (1969)
1904–1967	Julius Robert Oppenheimer: *Science and the Common Understanding* (1954), *The Open Mind* (1955), *Some Reflections on Science and Culture* (1960)
1904—	B. F. Skinner: *The Behavior of Organisms* (1938), *Walden Two* (1948), *Beyond Freedom and Dignity* (1971)
1905–1963	Perry Miller: *The New England Mind* (1939)
1905–1976	Lionel Trilling: *The Liberal Imagination* (1950), *A Gathering of Fugitives* (1956), *Sincerity and Authenticity* (1972)
1906—	Dwight Macdonald: *Henry Wallace: The Man and the Myth* (1948), *The Root is Man* (1953), *Memoirs of a Revolutionist* (1957), *Against the American Grain* (1962), *Discriminations* (1974)
1907–1964	Rachel Carson: *The Sea Around Us* (1951), *Silent Spring* (1962)
1907–1977	Loren Eiseley: *The Immense Journey* (1957), *The Firmament of Time* (1960), *All the Strange Hours: The Excavation of a Life* (1975)
1908—	John Kenneth Galbraith: *The Great Crash: 1929* (1955), *The Affluent Society* (1958), *The New Industrial State* (1967), *Economics and the Public Purpose* (1973), *Money: Whence It Came, Where It Went* (1975)
1909–1955	James Agee: *Let Us Now Praise Famous Men* (1941), *Agee on Film* (2 vols., 1958–60)
1909—	David Riesman: *The Lonely Crowd: A Study of the Changing American Character* (with Nathan

Glazer and Reuel Denney, 1950), *Faces in the Crowd: Individual Studies in Character and Politics* (with Glazer, 1952), *Individualism Reconsidered* (1954)

1913— Lewis Thomas: *The Lives of a Cell: Notes of a Biology Watcher* (1974)

1914— Daniel J. Boorstin: *The Americans: The Colonial Experience* (1958), *The Americans: The National Experience* (1965), *The Americans: The Democratic Experience* (1973)

1914— John Hersey: *Into the Valley* (1943), *A Bell for Adano* (1944), *Hiroshima* (1946)

1915— Paul Samuelson: *Foundations of Economic Analysis* (1947), *Economics: An Introductory Analysis* (1948)

1916–1970 Richard Hofstadter: *The American Political Tradition and the Men Who Made It* (1948), *The Age of Reform* (1955), *Anti-Intellectualism in American Life* (1963)

1916— Jane Jacobs: *The Death and Life of Great American Cities* (1961), *The Economy of Cities* (1969)

1917— Barry Commoner: *The Closing Circle: Nature, Man, and Technology* (1971), *The Poverty of Power: Energy and the Economic Crisis* (1976)

1917— Arthur Schlesinger, Jr.: *The Age of Jackson* (1945), *The Age of Roosevelt* (vols. 1–3, 1957–60), *A Thousand Days* (1965), *The Imperial Presidency* (1973)

1919— Robert L. Heilbroner: *An Inquiry into the Human Prospect* (1974)

1923— Norman Mailer: *The Armies of the Night* (1969), *Of a Fire on the Moon* (1971), *Prisoner of Sex* (1971)

1924— James Baldwin: *Notes of a Native Son* (1955), *Nobody Knows My Name* (1961), *The Fire Next Time* (1963), *The Devil Finds Work* (1976)

1925–1965 Malcolm X: *The Autobiography of Malcolm X* (with Alex Haley, 1964)

1925— Gore Vidal: *Reflections Upon a Sinking Ship* (1969), *Homage to Daniel Shays: Collected Essays 1952–1972* (1972)

1928— Noam Chomsky: *Syntactic Structures* (1957), *Language and Mind* (1968), *American Power and the New Mandarins* (1969)

1928— James Dewey Watson: *The Double Helix* (1968)

1929–1968 Martin Luther King, Jr.: *Stride Toward Freedom* (1958), *Why We Can't Wait* (1964), *Where Do We Go From Here: Chaos or Community?* (1967)

1929— Edward O. Wilson: *The Insect Societies* (1971), *Sociobiology: The New Synthesis* (1975)

1934— Ralph Nader: *Unsafe at Any Speed* (1965)

1934— Carl Sagan: *The Cosmic Connection: An Extraterrestrial Perspective* (1973)

1938— William Irwin Thompson: *At the Edge of History: Speculations on the Transformation of Culture* (1971)

American Poets

Poets included in this survey are, with predictable colonial exceptions, native Americans who meet at least one of the following criteria: (1) they were at one time or continue to be popular among a fairly wide public, (2) at least some of their poems continue to appear in anthologies of serious American verse, and (3) their work has been collected and accorded professional critical attention. Titles given are usually volumes of verse rather than single poems, and some attempt has been made to bracket output by listing first important volumes and subsequent major collections. These major collections are of two types: those that have won prestigious literary awards, such as the Pulitzer Prize, and those that gather together poems published over an extended span of time.

The poets are entered in chronological order according to their date of birth; when two or more were born in the same year, they are listed in alphabetical order.

1612?-1672   Anne Bradstreet: *The Tenth Muse Lately Sprung up in America* (London, 1650), *Several Poems, compiled with great variety of Wit and Learning* (Boston, 1678)

1640   *The Bay Psalm Book (The Whole Booke of Psalms Faithfully Translated into English Metre),* translated by Thomas Welde, Richard Mather, and John Eliot

1644?-1729   Edward Taylor: works not published until 1937, collected as *The Poetical Works of Edward Taylor* (1939), *The Poems of Edward Taylor* (1960)

1752-1832   Philip Freneau: major output between 1772, "The Rising Glory of America," and 1788, "The Indian Burying Ground"

1753?-1784   Phillis Wheatley: *Poems of Various Subjects, Religious and Moral* (1773)

1794-1878   William Cullen Bryant: "Thanatopsis" (1817), "To a Waterfowl" (1818), *Poems* (1832), *The White-footed Doe and Other Poems* (1844)

1807-1882   Henry Wadsworth Longfellow: *Voices of the Night* (1839), *The Song of Hiawatha* (1855), *The Courtship of Miles Standish, and Other Poems* (1858), *Tales of a Wayside Inn* (1863)

1807-1892   John Greenleaf Whittier: *Legends of New England in Prose and Verse* (1831), *Voices of Freedom* (1846), *In War Time* (1864), *Snow-Bound* (1866)

1809-1894   Oliver Wendell Holmes, Sr.: "Old Ironsides" (1830), *Poems* (1836), "The Chambered Nautilus" (1858)

1809-1849   Edgar Allan Poe: *Tamerlane and Other Poems* (1827), *The Raven and Other Poems* (1845)

1819-1891   James Russell Lowell: *A Year's Life* (1841), *Under the Willows* (1869), *Three Memorial Poems* (1877), *Heartsease and Rue* (1888)

1819-1892   Walt Whitman: *Leaves of Grass* (1855; added to and revised until 1892)

1828-1867   Henry Timrod ("poet laureate of the Confederacy"): "Ethnogenesis" (1861)

1830-1886   Emily Dickinson: major output 1850-64; published in badly edited form 1890-96; definitive edition in Dickinson's own style and punctuation appeared in 1955

1842-1881   Sidney Lanier: "The Symphony" (1875), *Poems* (1884)

1849-1916   James Whitcomb Riley: *The Old Swimmin' Hole and 'Leven More Poems* (1883), *Home Folks* (1900)

1869-1950   Edgar Lee Masters: *Spoon River Anthology* (1915), *Illinois Poems* (1941)

1869-1935   Edwin Arlington Robinson: *The Torrent and the Night Before* (1896), *Collected Poems* (1921; complete with additional poems, 1937), *Tristram* (1927)

1872-1906   Paul Laurence Dunbar: *Oak and Ivory* (1893), *Lyrics of Lowly Life* (1896), *Complete Poems* (1913)

1874-1963   Robert Frost: *A Boy's Will* (1913), *Complete Poems* (1949), *Selected Poems* (1963)

1874-1925   Amy Lowell: *A Dome of Many-Coloured Glass* (1912), *Men, Women, and Ghosts* (1916), *What's O'Clock* (1925)

1878-1967   Carl Sandburg: *In Reckless Ecstasy* (1904), *Chicago Poems* (1916), *Cornhuskers* (1918), *Complete Poems* (1950)

1879-1931   Vachel Lindsay: *General William Booth Enters into Heaven* (1913), *Selected Poems* (1938)

1879-1955   Wallace Stevens: *Harmonium* (1923), *The Man with the Blue Guitar and Other Poems* (1937), *The Auroras of Autumn* (1950), *Collected Poems* (1954)

1883-1963   William Carlos Williams: *Poems* (1909), *Paterson* (1946-58), *Pictures from Brueghel, and Other Poems* (1962)

1885–1972	Ezra Pound: *Personae* (1909), *Hugh Selwyn Mauberley* (1920), *Cantos* (1925–60)
1886–1961	Hilda Doolittle ("H.D."): *Sea Garden* (1916), *Collected Poems* (1940)
1886–1918	Joyce Kilmer: *Summer of Love* (1911), *Trees and Other Poems* (1914)
1887–1962	Robinson Jeffers: *Tamar and Other Poems* (1924), *The Selected Poetry* (1939)
1887–1972	Marianne Moore: *Poems* (1921), *Collected Poems* (1951), *Complete Poems* (1967)
1888–1965	T. S. Eliot: "The Love Song of J. Alfred Prufrock" (1915), *The Waste Land* (1922), *The Four Quartets* (1935–42), *Collected Poems, 1909–62* (1963)
1888–1974	John Crowe Ransom: *Poems about God* (1919), *Selected Poems* (1945; revised and enlarged, 1963)
1892–	Archibald MacLeish: *Tower of Ivory* (1917), *Conquistador* (1932), *Collected Poems: 1917–1952* (1952)
1892–1950	Edna St. Vincent Millay: *Renascence and Other Poems* (1917), *The Harp-Weaver and Other Poems* (1923), *Collected Poems* (1956)
1894–1962	e. e. cummings: *Tulips and Chimneys* (1923), *Poems 1923–1954*, *95 Poems* (1958)
1898–1943	Stephen Vincent Benét: *Five Men and Pompey* (1915), *John Brown's Body* (1928), *Western Star* (1943)
1889–1973	Conrad Aiken: *The Jig of Forslin* (1915), *Selected Poems* (1929), *Collected Poems* (1953)
1899–1932	Hart Crane: *White Buildings* (1926), *The Bridge* (1930), *The Collected Poems* (1933)
1902–1961	Kenneth Fearing: *Angel Arms* (1929), *Collected Poems* (1940), *New and Selected Poems* (1956)
1902–1967	Langston Hughes: *The Weary Blues* (1926), *Ask Your Mama* (1961)
1903–1946	Countee Cullen: *Color* (1925), *The Medea and Some Other Poems* (1935)
1905–	Robert Penn Warren: *Thirty-Six Poems* (1935), *Promises: Poems 1954–1956* (1957), *Selected Poems, 1923–1975* (1976)
1908–1963	Theodore Roethke: *Open House* (1941), *The Waking* (1953), *Collected Poems* (1966)
1910–1970	Charles Olson: *The Maximus Poems* (1960, 1968)
1913–	Karl Shapiro: *Person, Place and Thing* (1942), *V-Letter and Other Poems* (1944), *Poems, 1940–1953* (1953), *Selected Poems* (1968), *Adult Bookstore* (1976)
1914–1972	John Berryman: *Poems* (1942), *Seventy-Seven Dream Songs* (1964), *His Toy, His Dream, His Rest* (1968), *Selected Poems* (1972)
1914–1965	Randall Jarrell: *Blood for a Stranger* (1942), *Selected Poems* (1955), *The Lost World* (1965)
1917–	Gwendolyn Brooks: *A Street in Bronzeville* (1945), *Annie Allen* (1949), *Selected Poems* (1963)
1917–1977	Robert Lowell: *Land of Unlikeness* (1944), *Lord Weary's Castle* (1946), *Life Studies* (1959), *Selected Poems* (1976)
1919–	Lawrence Ferlinghetti: *A Coney Island of the Mind* (1958), *An Eye on the World* (1967)
1920–	Howard Nemerov: *The Image and the Law* (1947), *New and Selected Poems* (1960), *The Winter Lightning: Selected Poems* (1968), *The Western Approaches: Poems 1973–1975*
1921–	Richard Wilbur: *The Beautiful Changes and Other Poems* (1947), *Advice to a Prophet and Other Poems* (1961), *Walking to Sleep* (1969)
1923–	James Dickey: *Into the Stone and Other Poems* (1960), *Buckdancer's Choice* (1965), *The Zodiac* (1976)
1926–	Robert Bly: *Silence in Snowy Fields* (1962), *The Morning Glory* (1969), *Sleepers Joining Hands* (1973)
1926–	Allen Ginsberg: *Howl and Other Poems* (1955)
1926–	James Merrill: *Water Street* (1962), *Nights and Days* (1968), *Divine Comedies* (1976)
1926–	W. D. Snodgrass: *Heart's Needle* (1959), *After Experience* (1968)
1927–	W. S. Merwin: *A Mask for Janus* (1952), *Lice* (1967), *The First Four Books of Poems* (1975)
1928–	Irving Feldman: *Works and Days, and Other Poems* (1961), *Leaping Clear, and Other Poems* (1976)
1928–1974	Anne Sexton: *To Bedlam and Part Way Back* (1960), *Love Poems* (1969)
1932–1963	Sylvia Plath: *The Colossus* (1960), *Ariel* (1965), *Uncollected Poems* (1965)

American Novelists

With certain exceptions, the novelists appearing in this list are those whose reputation and place in literary history have been secured by a substantial body of work that has been accorded the status of serious literature. The list does not include professional novelists whose work in genres like the detective story, science fiction, or the western usually gives great pleasure and sometimes powerfully impresses itself upon the imagination. Nor does it include writers whose reputation rests on only one novel, however popular or significant.

Again with certain exceptions, this list excludes the general category "men and women of letters," persons whose output has included fine or significant novels but whose place in the literary history of their time has been firmly secured by other means. An exception has been made for Washington Irving, whose tales first gained an international audience for American fiction and who was the first American man of letters to support himself wholly by his pen. Edgar Allan Poe and Sherwood Anderson have been included because their tales or short stories have not only earned them a place in the roster of important American fictionalists but also link together to form extended thematic surveys. William Hill Brown, Susanna Haswell Rowson, and Charles Brockden Brown have been included only because they were the first American novelists.

The authors are entered in chronological order according to their date of birth; when two or more were born in the same year, they are listed in alphabetical order. An asterisk (*) indicates that the writer has received the Nobel Prize for Literature.

1762?–1824   Susanna Haswell Rowson: *Charlotte, A Tale of Truth* (1791)

1765–1793   William Hill Brown: *The Power of Sympathy* (1789)

1771–1810   Charles Brockden Brown: *Wieland* (1799), *Arthur Mervyn* (1799–1800)

1783–1859   Washington Irving: *A History of New-York, by Diedrich Knickerbocker* (1809), *The Sketch Book of Geoffrey Crayon, Gent.* (1819–20; includes "Rip Van Winkle")

1789–1851   James Fenimore Cooper: *The Spy* (1821), the *Leatherstocking Tales* (1823; includes *The Pioneers*), *The Last of the Mohicans* (1826), *The Prairie* (1827), *The Pathfinder* (1840), *The Deerslayer* (1841)

1804–1864   Nathaniel Hawthorne: *Twice-Told Tales* (1837, 1842), *Mosses From an Old Manse* (1846), *The Scarlet Letter* (1850), *The House of the Seven Gables* (1851), *The Blithesdale Romance* (1852), *The Marble Faun* (1860)

1809–1849   Edgar Allan Poe: *The Narrative of Arthur Gordon Pym* (1838), *Tales of the Grotesque and Arabesque* (1840), *Tales* (1845)

1811–1896   Harriet Beecher Stowe: *Uncle Tom's Cabin* (1852), *Dred: A Tale of the Great Dismal Swamp* (1856), *Oldtown Folks* (1869)

1819–1891   Herman Melville: *Typee* (1846), *Omoo* (1847), *Moby Dick* (1851), *Pierre* (1852), *Billy Budd* (1891; not published until 1924)

1835–1910   Mark Twain: *The Celebrated Jumping Frog of Calaveras County, and Other Sketches* (1867), *Roughing It* (1872), *The Gilded Age* (with Charles Dudley Warner, 1873), *The Adventures of Tom Sawyer* (1876), *The Adventures of Huckleberry Finn* (1884), *A Connecticut Yankee in King Arthur's Court* (1889), *The Mysterious Stranger* (1898; published 1916), *The Man That Corrupted Hadleyburg* (1899)

1837–1920   William Dean Howells: *Their Wedding Journey* (1872), *A Modern Instance* (1882), *The Rise of Silas Lapham* (1885), *A Hazard of New Fortunes* (1890)

1843–1916   Henry James: *Roderick Hudson* (1875), *The American* (1877), *Daisy Miller* (1878), *The Portrait of a Lady* (1881), *The Princess Casamassima* (1886), *The Wings of the Dove* (1902), *The Ambassadors* (1903), *The Golden Bowl* (1904)

1849–1909   Sarah Orne Jewett: *Deephaven* (1877), *The Country of the Pointed Firs* (1896)

1862–1937   Edith Wharton: *The House of Mirth* (1905), *Ethan Frome* (1911), *The Age of Innocence* (1920), *Old New York* (1924)

1870–1902   Frank Norris: *McTeague* (1899), *The Octopus* (1901), *The Pit* (1903)

1871–1900   Stephen Crane: *Maggie: A Girl of the Streets* (1893), *The Red Badge of Courage* (1895)

1871–1945   Theodore Dreiser: *Sister Carrie* (1900; soon withdrawn because of censorship), *Jennie Gerhardt* (1911), *An American Tragedy* (1925), *The Stoic* (1947)

1873–1947   Willa Cather: *O Pioneers!* (1913), *My Antonia* (1918), *One of Ours* (1922), *A Lost Lady* (1923), *Death Comes for the Archbishop* (1927), *Shadows on the Rock* (1931)

1874–1945   Ellen Glasgow: *The Battle-Ground* (1902), *Virginia* (1913), *Barren Ground* (1925), *They*

Stooped to Folly (1929), *In This Our Life* (1941)

1876–1941   Sherwood Anderson: *Winesburg, Ohio* (1919), *The Triumph of the Egg* (1921)

1876–1916   Jack London: *The Call of the Wild* (1903), *The Sea-Wolf* (1904), *White Fang* (1906), *The Iron Heel* (1907), *The Valley of the Moon* (1913)

1878–1968   Upton Sinclair: *The Jungle* (1906), *Oil!* (1927), *Dragon's Teeth* (1942)

1885–1951   *Sinclair Lewis: *Main Street* (1920), *Babbitt* (1922), *Arrowsmith* (1925), *Elmer Gantry* (1927), *Dodsworth* (1929), *It Can't Happen Here* (1935)

1889–1973   Conrad Aiken: *Blue Voyage* (1927), *Great Circle* (1933), *King Coffin* (1935)

1890—   Katherine Anne Porter: *Pale Horse, Pale Rider* (1939), *Ship of Fools* (1962)

1892–1973   *Pearl Buck: *The House of Earth* (1935; trilogy consisting of *The Good Earth* [1931], *Sons* [1932], *A House Divided* [1935]), *Dragon Seed* (1942), *Letters from Peking* (1957), *The Three Daughters of Madame Liang* (1969)

1896–1970   John Dos Passos: *Three Soldiers* (1921), *Manhattan Transfer* (1925), *U.S.A.* (1937; trilogy consisting of *The 42nd Parallel* [1930], *1919* [1932], *The Big Money* [1936]), *District of Columbia* (1952)

1896–1940   F. Scott Fitzgerald: *This Side of Paradise* (1920), *The Beautiful and the Damned* (1921), *Tales of the Jazz Age* (1922), *The Great Gatsby* (1925), *Tender is the Night* (1934), *The Last Tycoon* (1941)

1897–1962   *William Faulkner: *Sartoris* (1929), *The Sound and the Fury* (1929), *As I Lay Dying* (1930), *Sanctuary* (1931), *Absalom, Absalom!* (1936), *The Hamlet* (1940), *Go Down, Moses, and Other Stories* (1942), *The Reivers* (1962)

1897–1975   Thornton Wilder: *The Bridge of San Luis Rey* (1927), *Heaven's My Destination* (1934), *The Ides of March* (1948), *The Eighth Day* (1967), *Theophilus North* (1974)

1899–1961   *Ernest Hemingway: *The Sun Also Rises* (1926), *A Farewell to Arms* (1929), *For Whom the Bell Tolls* (1940), *The Old Man and the Sea* (1952)

1900–1938   Thomas Wolfe: *Look Homeward, Angel* (1929),

Of Time and the River (1935), *You Can't Go Home Again* (1940)

1902–1968   *John Steinbeck: *Tortilla Flat* (1935), *In Dubious Battle* (1936), *Of Mice and Men* (1937), *Grapes of Wrath* (1939), *East of Eden* (1952)

1903—   Erskine Caldwell: *Tobacco Road* (1932), *God's Little Acre* (1933), *Trouble in July* (1940)

1903—   James Gould Cozzens: *Confusion* (1924), *The Last Adam* (1933), *Men and Brethren* (1936), *The Just and the Unjust* (1942), *Guard of Honor* (1948), *By Love Possessed* (1957)

1903–1940   Nathanael West: *The Dream Life of Balso Snell* (1931), *Miss Lonelyhearts* (1933), *A Cool Million* (1934), *The Day of the Locust* (1939)

1904—   James T. Farrell: *Studs Lonigan* trilogy (1932–35), *A World I Never Made* (1936), *No Star Is Lost* (1938), *Father and Son* (1940), *My Days of Anger* (1943), *The Face of Time* (1953)

1908–1960   Richard Wright: *Uncle Tom's Children* (1938), *Native Son* (1940), *The Outsider* (1953), *The Long Dream* (1958)

1909—   Eudora Welty: *The Robber Bridegroom* (1942), *Delta Wedding* (1946), *The Optimist's Daughter* (1972)

1915—   *Saul Bellow: *Dangling Man* (1944), *The Victim* (1947), *The Adventures of Augie March* (1953), *Henderson the Rain King* (1959), *Herzog* (1964), *Humbolt's Gift* (1975)

1917–1967   Carson McCullers: *The Heart is a Lonely Hunter* (1940), *Reflections in a Golden Eye* (1941), *The Member of the Wedding* (1946), *Clock Without Hands* (1961)

1924—   James Baldwin: *Go Tell It on the Mountain* (1953), *Another Country* (1962)

1930—   John Barth: *The Floating Opera* (1956), *The End of the Road* (1958), *The Sot-Weed Factor* (1960), *Giles Goat-Boy* (1966), *Chimera* (1972)

1932—   John Updike: *The Poorhouse Fair* (1959), *Rabbit, Run* (1960), *The Centaur* (1963), *Couples* (1968), *Bech: A Book* (1970), *Rabbit Redux* (1971), *Marry Me* (1976)

1937—   Thomas Pynchon: *V.* (1963), *The Crying of Lot 49* (1966), *Gravity's Rainbow* (1973)

Blacks in American History

The chronology below includes some of the events, contributions, and personalities associated with the history of Americans of African descent. It focuses on individual achievements, particularly in relation to the more than three centuries of black presence on North American soil before the Civil War; in the period following the Civil War—and especially since the 1930's—achievements have been limited to selected firsts.

1492   Pedro Alonzo Niño, possibly black, serves as a navigator during Columbus' first voyage.

1526   Spanish explorers in South Carolina bring with them black slaves, who almost immediately flee to the interior and intermarry with Indians.

1535   Esteban or Estevanico, one of the survivors of the ill-fated Narváez expedition to Florida (1528), joins Cabeza de Vaca in astonishing trek from Texas to Mexico City (1535–36) and is later killed by Zuñi Indians while guiding Fray Marcos de Niza to Háwikuh, a Zuñi New Mexico pueblo believed to be one of the fabled seven cities of gold, known as Cíbola (1539).

1539   Blacks accompany Hernando de Soto and his party in the explorations of the southeast (1539–43).

1619   First blacks arrive in Jamestown, Virginia; brought by Dutch pirate, twenty "negars" are sold to colonists as indentured servants, on same terms as white bonded servants. At this point blacks are not slaves but are simply another racial element in Jamestown colony; black slavery does not become institutionalized for another 40 to 50 years in English mainland colonies.

1624   William Tucker, first black child born in what was to become the United States, is born nonslave in Jamestown, Virginia.

1626   Black slaves appear in New Amsterdam; slaves are subsequently imported to Connecticut (1629), Maryland (1634), and Massachusetts (1638).

1641   Massachusetts becomes first state to recognize slavery legally.

1651   Anthony Johnson imports five slaves and receives 200-acre grant in what is now Northampton County, Virginia; other black landowners and owners of slaves or indentured servants also settle in this area.

1661   Virginia legally recognizes slavery.

1662   Virginia passes the following law: "Whereas some doubts have arisen whether children got by any Englishman upon a negro woman should be slave or free, *Be it therefore enacted* that all children borne in this country shall be held bond or free only according to the condition of the mother."

1663   Maryland law makes all newly imported blacks slaves.

1664   Maryland passes law banning marriage of black males and English women.

1668   Virginia passes law stating that if a slave dies as result of punishment inflicted for resistance or disobedience, the slave's death "shall not be considered a crime," on the theory that no one would maliciously destroy his own property.

1670   Free blacks in Virginia are forbidden to vote, in order, as a Virginia governor years later explained it, to "fix a perpetual brand upon Free-Negroes and Mulattos"; one reason for this was that free black voters "always did, and ever will, adhere to and favor the slaves," even to the point of aiding in slave revolts; second reason was "the Pride of a Manumitted Slave, who looks on himself immediately on Acquiring his freedom to be as good a Man as the best of his Neighbors. . . ." Virginia's black population is about 2,000, some 5 per cent of the total.

1672   Bounties are placed by Virginia on the heads of "Maroons," runaway slaves who have formed backcountry communities and sometimes raid the tidewater settlements.

1680   Virginia passes law forbidding slaves to gather "under pretence of feasts and burials" and forbids possession by a slave of any weapon, including clubs and staffs; act also makes it a crime punishable by "twenty lashes on his bare back well layd on" for any slave to be found off his master's plantation without a pass. Black population in Virginia is now about 3,000; white population is about 44,000.

1682   South Carolina legally recognizes slavery.

1688   Antislavery resolution, first in New World, is passed by Quakers in Germantown, Pennsylvania.

1691   Virginia bans all interracial marriages.

1700   Slave population is now 23,000 in southern colonies, 5,000 in northern colonies.

1705   Virginia House of Burgesses forbids all blacks, mulattos, and Indians to hold any public office or to belong to the militia; law also forbids blacks to be witnesses in legal cases. All blacks, unless Christians in their native land or born free in a Christian country, are to be slaves for life.

1712	Slave revolt in New York City: 9 whites are killed; 21 blacks are executed, and 6 others commit suicide.
1715	North Carolina legally recognizes slavery.
1723	Free blacks in Virginia are forbidden to carry weapons.
1739	Slave revolts in South Carolina result in deaths of 51 whites and many more slaves; most serious of these revolts occurs in town of Stono, in which at least 25 whites die (September 9).
1740	South Carolina prohibits slaves from owning or raising livestock of any sort.
1741	In race riot in New York, after series of fires is blamed on blacks, 31 slaves and 5 whites are executed.
1744	Virginia passes law enabling blacks to appear as witnesses in court cases that do not involve whites.
1746	Slave poet Lucy Terry writes commemorative poem "Bars Fight"; poem is not published, but Terry is often considered first black American poet.
1747	South Carolina permits black slaves to serve in militia so long as they never constitute more than a third of a given company; move comes about in recognition of "great faithfulness and courage" shown by some during King George's War.
1750	Trustees of Georgia colony rescind restrictions on large landholding, land speculation, and black slavery.
	Slave population is 236,400, with more than 206,000 living south of Pennsylvania; blacks represent about 20 per cent of total colonial population.
	Black population in Virginia is 101,452, up from 60,000 in 1740; now represents slightly more than 30 per cent of the total population.
1754	Benjamin Banneker, 22, a free black in Baltimore, Maryland, builds what is probably first clock in the English colonies; made of wood, clock works for more than twenty years.
1760	Jupiter Hammon, a slave on Long Island, New York, is author of "An Evening Thought. Salvation by Christ, with Penitential Cries," first poem by a black to be published in American colonies.
1767	Phillis Wheatley, fourteen, publishes her first poem; Wheatley, who belongs to wife of a wealthy Boston tailor, later attracts considerable notice when "A Poem by Phillis, A Negro Girl on the Death of Reverend George Whitefield" is printed in 1770; she becomes well known after publication of book of poems in 1773.
1770	Crispus Attucks, mulatto sailor and escaped slave (es-

caped from Framingham, Massachusetts), dies in Boston Massacre (March 5).

1772	Mansfield decision: English judge abolishes slavery in England and states that any slave taken there must be freed.
1773	Massachusetts slaves send first of eight petitions requesting their freedom to General Court (January 6).
	Massachusetts slave Caesar Hendricks, arguing that he is being denied his natural right to liberty, takes his master to court and is freed by the jury (November).
1775	At least ten black minutemen, including Peter Salem and Lemuel Haynes, participate in Battles of Lexington and Concord (April 19).
	Lemuel Haynes and two other black members of Ethan Allen's Green Mountain Boys, Primas Black and Epheram Blackman, take part in the capture of Fort Ticonderoga (May 10).
	Among the blacks who fight at Bunker Hill (June 17) Salem Poor is later specially commended for leadership and valor by fourteen officers, and Peter Salem is credited with killing British Major John Pitcairn.
1776	Declaration of Independence is published in Philadelphia (July 4); the promise of its famous second paragraph (all men are created equal and have God-given, inalienable rights, among them being rights to life, liberty, and the pursuit of happiness) does not escape anyone, including of course black men and women.
	Patriot spy Nathan Hale is hanged (September 22); executioner is fifteen-year-old Bill Richmond, a black Loyalist who later becomes heavyweight boxing champion of England.
	George Washington crosses the Delaware (December 25); manning a forward starboard oar of Washington's boat is Prince Whipple, bodyguard to one of Washington's staff officers.
1777	Virginia passes law permitting blacks to enlist in the militia only if they possess certificates from local magistrates attesting that they are freemen (May 6).
	Vermont, not yet admitted to statehood, abolishes slavery (July 2).
	General Philip Schuyler complains about large number of black reinforcements he is getting (August 4); under Horatio Gates this army soon wins the various engagements known as the Battle of Saratoga.
1778	Rhode Island allows slaves to enlist at same rate of pay as whites and promises them freedom if they serve for the duration (February 2); two black regiments are quickly formed, the 1st Regiment distinguishing itself

greatly against British and Hessian professionals at the Battle of Rhode Island (August 11).

The Revolutionary War

Despite valorous black participation in 1775 battles like Bunker Hill and Lexington and Concord, there was considerable early opposition to the use of slaves as combatants in the Revolutionary War. Some Patriots shrank from the idea of using slaves in the fight for independence. Slave owners were reluctant to lose their property on the battlefield and feared they would have to emancipate slaves who had served well. Many slave owners were reluctant to arm and train men they kept in bondage largely by force, and many others believed that blacks would not make good soldiers.

In October, 1775, the Continental Congress barred all blacks, free or slave, from service in the Continental army but left it up to the states to raise their militias as they chose. Virginia allowed free blacks to enlist in the militia but soon found that many slaves were joining up, using one subterfuge or another. In November, 1775, the Loyalist governor of Virginia promised freedom to all slaves who joined the Loyalist forces, and they flocked to his banner. Alarmed at this development, Washington urged a change in congressional policy, and in January, 1776, Congress permitted the re-enlistment of free blacks but never officially sanctioned the enlistment of slaves. However, after Valley Forge (1778–79), in which the desertion rate for blacks was lower than the rate for whites, General Washington accepted into the Continental army any able-bodied male, white or black, free or slave. In June, 1776, Spanish Louisiana contributed black troops, commanded by black officers, that swept the British out of the Mississippi Valley and Florida.

From the first, the Navy, beginning a tradition maintained until well after the Civil War, welcomed all blacks with seafaring experience. As a result there were blacks on John Paul Jones's ships, including the *Bonhomme Richard*. The states, which maintained privateering forces, frequently used blacks, sometimes as officers.

In all some ten thousand blacks from every one of the thirteen colonies served in the Revolutionary War and participated on the Patriot side in almost every major engagement, including the Battle of Yorktown. At least a thousand blacks served in the British forces, although rarely in combat roles, owing to the prejudice of British commanders. Many more blacks fought in various Loyalist commando and guerrilla groups.

1779 South Carolina's privy council recommends withdrawal from the Revolution after the Continental Congress urges South Carolina to enlist 3,000 slaves for the defense of Charleston (March 29).

1780 Paul Cuffe and six other free blacks demand relief from taxation in Massachusetts on grounds that they are denied privileges of citizenship (February 9); Cuffe, later a wealthy shipbuilder, is prominent in various African colonization movements.

Pennsylvania becomes first state to abolish slavery—though gradually—by providing that no child, regardless of parents' status, shall ever again be born a slave (March 1).

Charleston, South Carolina, falls (May 12); encircling British forces have made heavy use of black support personnel, and black runaways pour into city after its surrender.

Maryland, only southern state to do so, authorizes slave enlistments (October).

At the age of twenty-three James Robinson, a slave, was awarded a gold medal for valor at the Battle of Yorktown. His owner's heirs, defying a provision in the owner's will, sold Robinson down the river. At the age of sixty-seven—and still a slave—Robinson fought with Andrew Jackson in 1814–15 at the Battle of New Orleans. Robinson remained a slave until the Emancipation Proclamation and died in 1868, at the age of a hundred and fifteen, a free man at last.

1781 After surrendering at Yorktown (October 19) General Cornwallis is surprised to find James Armistead, whom he had earlier employed as a spy, in the headquarters of General Lafayette. Lafayette had planted Armistead on Cornwallis's staff as a double agent.

1782 British evacuate Savannah, Georgia (July 21); 5,000 escaped slaves choose to go with them.

British evacuate Charleston, South Carolina (December 16); 5,327 runaway slaves go with them, to be resettled in Nova Scotia, East Florida, or England.

1783 British begin evacuation of New York City (November 29); 2,772 blacks leave with them.

Washington bids farewell (December 4) to his officers at Fraunces Tavern in New York City, long a favored meeting place of the local Sons of Liberty and owned since 1762 by Samuel Fraunces, a black man.

Massachusetts court abolishes slavery, and blacks who meet property qualifications are given vote; New Hampshire institutes gradual emancipation measure.

James Derham, first black physician in U.S., establishes practice in New Orleans.

1784   Connecticut passes a gradual emancipation law.

Rhode Island passes a gradual abolition act.

1786   Lemuel Haynes, Revolutionary War veteran, becomes pastor of white congregation in Torrington, Connecticut.

1787   Richard Allen and Absalom Jones form Free African Society in Philadelphia (April 12); society is one of first black social organizations. Allen and Jones later (1794) found the African Methodist Episcopal Church, which not only provides blacks an opportunity to worship unmolested but also becomes leading black social and educational institution.

In Boston, Prince Hall, Revolutionary War veteran and civil-rights activist, holds first meeting of black Masonic Lodge No. 459 (May 6); fraternal orders like this one developed into mutual-aid societies and much later provided basis for black-owned, black-supported industries—especially banking and insurance.

Northwest Ordinance prohibits slavery in Northwest Territory (July 13).

Constitutional Convention approves U.S. Constitution (September 17); calls for the abolition by 1808 of the foreign slave trade (which twelve states have already abolished or heavily taxed) but contains several clauses protecting institution of human slavery, including one clause that counts five slaves as three voters for the purposes of congressional representation.

1790   There are 757,181 blacks in U.S., of whom about 9 per cent are free; blacks represent slightly more than 19 per cent of total U.S. population.

Jean Baptiste Pointe du Sable, French-speaking black fur-trapper, establishes trading post on what later becomes site of Chicago, Illinois.

1791   Massive slave uprising begins on the island of Hispaniola, part of which is now Haiti, with revolt of more than 100,000 slaves, the burning of 1,400 plantations, and the slaughter of whites (August 22); a succession of brilliant black leaders, including Toussaint L'Ouverture and Jean Jacques Dessalines, stand off assaults by English, Spanish, and French armies; Napoleon loses 60,000 crack troops in an unsuccessful attempt to retake Haiti (1802–03). The lesson of Haiti was not lost on southern plantation owners or southern slaves; both Gabriel Prosser and Denmark Vesey later consciously modeled their conspiracies after what they could learn about L'Ouverture's tactics.

Benjamin Banneker, mathematician and astronomer, first publishes his *Almanack and Ephemeris*, which enjoys wide American and European sales; he is also a member of the 1791 surveying team that lays out site of Washington, D.C., and is said to have reproduced from memory P. C. L'Enfant's plans for capital after L'Enfant withdrew from project; Banneker also writes a famous letter to Thomas Jefferson, taxing him with hypocrisy on slavery issue.

1793   Congress enacts its first fugitive slave law (February 12).

1797   Congress rejects first of many petitions from American blacks; petition, from escaped slaves, asks Congress to consider "our relief as a people."

1800   Black population in U.S. is now 1,002,037, slightly less than 19 per cent of the whole.

Gabriel Prosser's conspiracy, involving a planned attack on Richmond by at least 1,000 blacks, is foiled by informers and a huge storm that makes the roads and streams impassable (August 30); Prosser's plan called for the death of every white person in Richmond—except Frenchmen, Quakers, and Methodists.

1804   New Jersey passes a gradual emancipation law.

1807   Legislation outlawing slave trade as of 1808, in accordance with constitutional provisions, is signed by President Jefferson (March 2).

1813   Battle of Lake Erie (September 10): although blacks participated in all the major land and naval battles of the War of 1812, they were especially heavily represented in this crucial battle. Captain Oliver Hazard Perry had complained to his commanding officer, Isaac Chauncey, about the "motley" crews Chauncey was giving him; Chauncey rebuked him sharply, telling him that the black seamen he had sent Perry were experienced tars who were in fact among the finest he had at his disposal.

1816   Captain Paul Cuffe, Massachusetts shipping magnate, lands 38 U.S. black settlers at Freetown, Sierra Leone (February); Cuffe is one of several prominent American blacks who support efforts of the American Colonization Society (founded in December, 1816) to move U.S. blacks to colonies in Africa. Most black Americans are strongly opposed to colonization, but some, especially those of high accomplishment who have learned by bitter experience that success does not bring social acceptance by the white community, feel that African or other colonization is the best answer.

In First Seminole War, which ultimately gains U.S. the possession of Florida, Fort Blount, attacked in July,

1816, is manned almost exclusively by runaway slaves. War virtually ends in 1818 after Andrew Jackson defeats blacks and Indian allies (including Seminoles) at Battle of Suwannee (April 18), clearing way for seizure of Pensacola (May).

James P. Beckwourth, one of the first mountainmen, becomes a scout for the Ashley fur-trading expedition; Beckwourth, after whom Beckwourth Pass in the California Sierras is named, later becomes an honorary chief of Crow Indians.

1820   Black population in U.S. is now more than 1.7 million, about 18.5 per cent of total. American Colonization Society sends (January 31) 86 of these 1.7 million to Africa, where many of them die.

Missouri Compromise prohibits slavery north of 36°30' line (March 3).

1821   Liberia is founded when American Colonization Society is granted land by local chiefs; country is colonized in 1822; by 1834 it has 2,000 American black settlers.

1822   Denmark Vesey conspiracy is foiled in Charleston, South Carolina; plot, with cell-type organization, had been months in the planning and numbered as many as 9,000 slaves; attack on Charleston was planned for July 16—all whites were to be killed—but was given away by house slave. It took authorities about three weeks to crack through various cells and get to ringleader Vesey, a free carpenter, and his chief lieutenants. Vesey and his aides were hanged; second in command Peter Poyas, a ship's carpenter, instructed others: "Do not open your lips. Die silent as you shall see me do."

1827   *Freedom's Journal*, first black-owned newspaper, is published by Samuel Cornish and John B. Russwurm. Russwurm has the additional distinction of being one of the first two blacks to earn a college degree, having graduated from Bowdoin in 1826.

Abolition of slavery in New York, instituted in 1799, is finally completed (July 4); one of those set free is Isabella Baumfree, better known as Sojourner Truth.

1829   David Walker, freeborn secondhand-clothing merchant in Boston, publishes *Walker's Appeal*, a wrathful antislavery pamphlet in which he urges slaves to cut their masters' throats and "kill or be killed" (September 28); pamphlet causes great consternation in southern states.

1830   Black population in U.S. is now 2,328,642, slightly more than 18 per cent of the total population.

First national black conference is held in Philadelphia under leadership of Bishop Richard Allen (September 20).

1831   William Lloyd Garrison publishes first issue of *The Liberator*, radical abolitionist newspaper (January 1); newspaper, which has small circulation and is unprofitable, is supported financially by black Revolutionary War veteran James Forten, a wealthy Philadelphia sailmaker who employs 40 workers, black and white, in his firm.

Nat Turner's Rebellion in Southampton County, Virginia (August 22): beginning with six men, Turner slaughters his masters and their family and then goes from house to house gathering adherents and killing men, women, and children (as Turner later said, "It was my object to carry terror and devastation wherever we went"); his band ultimately numbers 60 or 70 and takes at least 55 white lives. A force of about 3,000, quickly raised against him from surrounding counties and adjoining states, kills many blacks thought to be involved. Uprising spreads fear throughout South—some whites even suffer heart attacks when Turner is rumored to be in the neighborhood. Turner and 19 other blacks are hanged after a trial. Revolt leads to tightened police codes, increased efforts to keep blacks illiterate, increased suspicion of free blacks, and a sharply intensified siege mentality, among both slaves and slave owners.

1833   American Anti-Slavery Society is organized in Philadelphia (December 4); among black founding members are Robert Purvis; James McCrummell, a dentist; James G. Barbadoes; Samuel E. Cornish, a minister and editor; Theodore S. Wright, a minister; and Peter S. Williams, an Episcopal priest.

Ira Aldridge, free black and one of leading tragedians of nineteenth century, makes debut in London at Theatre Royal in title role of Shakespeare's *Othello*.

1834   Slavery abolished in British Empire, including West Indies (August 1).

Henry Blair becomes first black to receive a patent, for a corn harvester he invented (October 14); there may have been other black inventors before him, but Patent Office did not record race of inventor.

1835   Antislavery pamphlets are removed from mails in Charleston, South Carolina, and burned in public (July 29).

Noyes Academy, integrated school in Canaan, New Hampshire, is attacked by mob and shut down (August 10).

1837   Battle of Okeechobee, in Florida (December 25): in one of many battles during long, costly Florida War (1835–42) a Seminole and black force clashes with U.S. troops; fighting is fierce, but the outcome remains unsettled.

James McCune Smith, who studied medicine in Scotland, establishes medical practice in New York City.

1838 *The Mirror of Liberty*, first black magazine, published in New York City by abolitionist David Ruggles (August).

Charles Lennox Remond, a freeborn Massachusetts black, becomes first black lecturer employed by an antislavery society, speaking for and becoming vice president of the New England Anti-Slavery Society.

1839 Liberty Party, first political party built around antislavery cause, organized in Warsaw, New York (November 13); two early and prominent black supporters are Samuel Ringgold Ward, an escaped slave who became a Presbyterian minister to a white congregation, and Henry Highland Garnet, born in slavery and carried to freedom, later also a Presbyterian minister; both are extremely effective speakers for abolitionist societies.

1841 Frederick Douglass, a slave who escaped from Maryland in 1837 at the age of 21, is hired to lecture by the Massachusetts Anti-Slavery Society (August).

Blacks on slave ship *Creole*, bound from Richmond, Virginia, to New Orleans, take over ship and sail to Nassau, Bahamas, where they are granted political asylum and freedom despite demands by Secretary of State Daniel Webster that they be returned. Although smuggling of slaves from Africa and South America continues until the Civil War—despite the abolition of foreign slave trade in 1808—the bulk of the slave trade is now domestic.

1845 In Worcester, Massachusetts, Macon B. Allen becomes first black to be admitted to the bar (May 3).

Norbert Rillieux of Louisiana invents vacuum pan evaporator that makes possible mass-production refining of sugar.

1847 Americo-Liberian settlers in Liberia declare country an independent republic (July 26).

Frederick Douglass publishes first issue of *North Star* in Rochester, New York (December 3).

1848 Massachusetts blacksmith Lewis Temple invents harpoon with a swiveling barb that becomes standard of whaling industry.

1849 Harriet Tubman escapes from Maryland slave owner at about age 29; she returns to South 19 times, leading more than 300 slaves to freedom by 1859, which results in a $40,000 price on her head. During Civil War she served in South Carolina as a nurse and spy for the Union. Tubman becomes perhaps most famous of black "conductors" on Underground Railroad.

Benjamin Roberts files first school-integration suit, in Boston, Massachusetts, on behalf of his daughter; Massachusetts Supreme Court decision in *Roberts* v. *Boston* allows state to establish separate but equal black schools.

> In his *North Star* editorials Frederick Douglass commented on a wide range of issues, including the impact of Irish immigrants on free black wage earners: "White men are becoming house-servants, cooks and stewards. . . . They are becoming porters, stevedores, wood-sawyers, hod-carriers, brick-makers, white-washers and barbers, so that the blacks can scarcely find the means of subsistence—a few years ago, a *white* barber would have been a curiosity—now their poles stand on every street. Formerly blacks were almost the exclusive coachmen in wealthy families: this is so no longer; white men are now employed, and for aught we see, they fill their servile station with an obsequiousness as profound as that of the blacks. The readiness and ease with which they adapt themselves to these conditions ought not to be lost sight of by the colored people. . . ."

1850 Black population in U.S. is now 3,638,808, slightly under 16 per cent of total population.

1851 Abolitionist and self-educated journalist William C. Nell publishes *Services of Colored Americans in the Wars of 1776 and 1812*, first historical treatment of black Americans. In 1861 Nell is appointed a post-office clerk, becoming first black to hold a federal civil-service job.

1852 Harriet Beecher Stowe's *Uncle Tom's Cabin* is published in book form (March 20); Stowe's model for the character Uncle Tom is Josiah Henson, a millowner and preacher who had led a group of slaves to freedom in 1830 and established a community of fugitive slaves in Dawn, Canada.

1853 *Clotel; or, the President's Daughter*, by William Wells Brown, first novel by a black American, is published in England.

1854 Lincoln University, first black college, is founded in Oxford, Pennsylvania, as the Ashmun Institute (January 1).

Anthony Burns, last fugitive slave to be returned from Massachusetts, is escorted out of Boston by 2,000 U.S. troops (June 2).

1855 John Mercer Langston, first black American to be elected to any public office, becomes town clerk of Brownhelm, Ohio.

Massachusetts abolishes separate black and white schools.

1856   Wilberforce University founded in Ohio by Methodist Episcopal Church (August 30).

1857   U.S. Supreme Court, in sweeping Dred Scott decision, pronounces that blacks cannot be citizens of the United States (March 6).

1859   Arkansas requires free blacks and mulattos to leave the state or become slaves (February).

John Brown raids federal arsenal at Harpers Ferry, Virginia (October 16–18); of the five blacks accompanying Brown two were killed in the shoot-out, and two were later (December 16) hanged.

1860   The black population of the U.S. is 4,401,830, about 14 per cent of the total; almost a half million blacks are nonslaves, and of these slightly more than half live in the southern states.

1861   Confederates attack Fort Sumter in Charleston, South Carolina (April 12); on hearing the news Frederick Douglass cries out: "God be praised!" Free blacks respond in large numbers to Lincoln's initial call for 75,000 volunteers but are turned down.

Congress outlaws slavery in Washington, D.C. (April 16).

Union General Benjamin Butler declares that slaves who flee from Confederate war work to Union camps in Virginia are "contraband of war" and thus will not be returned to their owners (May 25).

Continuing its egalitarian tradition, the U.S. Navy accepts black volunteers, and the Secretary of the Navy approves the enlistment of slaves (September 25).

In Missouri, General John C. Frémont issues military proclamation freeing slaves belonging to rebels (August 30); Lincoln, fearful of losing key border state, nullifies Frémont's order.

1862   Congress officially prohibits Union army from returning fugitive slaves (March 13).

Robert Smalls, black pilot, seizes Confederate gunboat *Planter*, sails it out of Charleston Harbor, and turns it over to U.S. Navy (May 13).

President Lincoln receives black delegation at White House, first time a U.S. President has conferred with blacks on public policy; Lincoln advises blacks to emigrate to Central America or Africa (August 14).

Lincoln issues preliminary Emancipation Proclamation (September 22).

First black regiment to be mustered into U.S. Army

(September 27) is 1st Louisiana Native Guards; regiment had originally offered its services to Confederacy but was never used.

First black regiment to engage in combat is 1st Kansas Colored Volunteers, which defeats a numerically superior force of Texans at Island Mound, Missouri (October 28).

1863   Lincoln signs Emancipation Proclamation (January 1); although proclamation actually freed no slaves, it greatly accelerated flight of slaves from rebel and border plantations.

Fifty-fourth Massachusetts Volunteers, first all-black regiment from the North, is organized (January 26); under white commander Colonel Robert Gould Shaw 54th covered itself with glory at Fort Wagner, South Carolina, in a doomed, valley-of-death charge that cost the lives of Shaw, two thirds of its officers, and one half of its men (July 18).

Confederacy passes law defining as criminals black Union soldiers and their white officers (May 1).

Milliken's Bend, Louisiana (June 7): 840 black troops rout 2,000 Texans in savage hand-to-hand combat.

Fall of Port Hudson, Louisiana (July 9): eight black regiments have participated in siege, begun in mid-May; two of these regiments were cut to pieces in series of gallant, suicidal charges on May 27.

New York draft riots (July 13–16): about 1,200 people are killed or wounded as working poor, mainly Irish, run amuck, lynching blacks from lampposts and setting fire to a black orphanage; mobs also kill Chinese and Germans.

Lincoln threatens (July 30) that U.S. will kill or sentence to life at hard labor one Confederate prisoner of war for every black soldier murdered or enslaved after surrender.

1864   Confederate force under command of General Nathan Bedford Forrest captures Fort Pillow in Tennessee and puts its 300 black defenders to death, in some cases by nailing the men to logs and burning them (April 12).

Congress passes bill providing for equal pay, equipment, and medical attention for black soldiers (June 15).

Black infantrymen and cavalry join Grant in sieges of Petersburg and of Richmond (June 15–18, 1864, and April 2–4, 1865); take part in many sharp engagements, including brilliant assault on New Market Heights and repulse of Confederate counterattack at Fort Harrison (September 29–30), both of which took place within eyeshot of besieged Confederate capital;

thirteen blacks earned Medals of Honor in these two engagements.

John Lawson, gunner on Admiral Farragut's flagship U.S.S. *Hartford*, earns Medal of Honor during Battle of Mobile Bay (August 5).

Two brigades of black troops, under overall command of General George H. Thomas, play significant role in Battle of Nashville (December 15–16).

1865 Black division participates in major amphibious assault on Fort Fisher, North Carolina (January 13–15), closing last major Confederate loophole in Union blockade.

Congress passes Thirteenth Amendment, abolishing human slavery in the U.S. (January 31).

John S. Rock becomes first black lawyer admitted to practice before the U.S. Supreme Court (February 1).

Congress establishes Freedmen's Bureau (March 3).

After repeated pleas by Robert E. Lee, Jefferson Davis signs law authorizing use of slaves as combat troops (March 13).

Troops of the all-black XXV Corps are among the first to enter Petersburg (April 2) and Richmond (April 3) and are in the vanguard of the forces moving in on Lee's army at Appomattox Courthouse when Lee orders the white flag (April 9).

Lincoln asks General Benjamin Butler to calculate possibilities of using naval vessels and merchant marine to "export" southern blacks; Butler reports that it is a logistic impossibility (April).

In various southern cities blacks hold series of mass meetings demanding the vote and equal rights (May 11–November 25).

Mississippi enacts series of statutes enforcing segregation on public transportation, binding out black minors as apprentices, fining unemployed blacks for vagrancy and then auctioning them to anyone who will pay the fines, restricting black rights to own land, punishing interracial marriage with life imprisonment, requiring blacks to have licenses to move about, depriving blacks of right to own or carry weapons, and punishing a variety of infractions including "insulting gestures" (November); various other southern states pass similar black codes.

Thirteenth Amendment is ratified (December 18).

1866 Fisk School opens in Nashville, Tennessee (January 9).

Radical Republican Thaddeus Stevens proposes measure redistributing land to freedmen in 40-acre

plots (February 5); defeat of this measure by an overwhelming vote kills the only truly radical economic solution to the problem posed by millions of propertyless, illiterate freedmen having agricultural skills but no land.

Civil Rights Act passed over President Johnson's veto (April 9).

Race riots in Memphis, Tennessee (May 1–3), and New Orleans, Louisiana (July 30), take a combined toll of 81 dead and more than 175 wounded. Black homes, schools, and churches are burned.

Edward Walker and Charles L. Mitchell are elected to Massachusetts House of Representatives, first blacks elected to any lawmaking assembly; in most northern states, however, blacks are still denied not only the right to hold public office but also the right to vote in local and state elections; in 1865 and 1866 Connecticut, Ohio, Michigan, Minnesota, and Kansas all reject proposals calling for black suffrage.

The Civil War

In all, 178,975 blacks served in the Union army; they were organized into 166 all-black regiments, of which 145 were infantry, 7 cavalry, 13 artillery, and 1 engineering. Blacks participated in a total of 449 engagements; 68,178 lost their lives in the war. No more than 100 blacks had the rank of captain or above; two of the highest-ranking officers were Major Alexander T. Augusta, a surgeon, and Major Martin R. Delaney, who was trained at Harvard Medical School and also served in the Medical Corps. Some 200,000 black civilians worked for the United States Army as cooks, teamsters, laborers, and servants. Until 1864, when Congress equalized pay, equipment, and medical services, black soldiers were paid seven dollars a month, six dollars less than the rate for white soldiers.

One out of every four U.S. seamen during the Civil War was black. Blacks participated in most of the naval engagements, including the famous *Monitor* battle, Farragut's "damn the torpedoes" assault at Mobile Bay, and the sinking of the C.S.S. *Alabama* by the U.S.S. *Kearsarge*; they also manned the blockade ships that slowly strangled the Confederacy. Five black seamen earned the Congressional Medal of Honor.

1867 Bill granting male blacks the vote in Washington, D.C., is passed over Johnson's veto (January 8).

Morehouse College opens in Augusta, Georgia (February).

First of Reconstruction Acts passed by Congress (March 2); freedmen are given right to vote for delegates to constitutional conventions.

Knights of the White Camellia, white supremacist organization, is founded in Louisiana.

Howard University opens in Washington, D.C. (May 1).

1868   South Carolina constitutional convention meets in Charleston (January 14); a voter registration of 80,000 blacks and 46,000 whites has elected 76 black delegates and 48 white delegates. The state constitution drawn up by this convention was generally a conservative and orthodox one, but it extended civil and political rights to blacks, changed gerrymandered districts that had disenfranchised rural whites, broadened rights of women, and reformed the penal codes, expanded public education, provided for an integrated school system, and increased facilities for the mentally and physically handicapped. South Carolina was the only state in which black delegates outnumbered whites; in Louisiana there was an even split. In all, the constitutional conventions produced sane, democratic, moderate, workable state constitutions and produced them quickly and in an orderly fashion.

Newly elected South Carolina Reconstruction government meets in Columbia (July 6); black representatives are in an 84–73 majority but do not control upper house. In this government blacks were elected lieutenant governor, secretary of state, and treasurer; one black sat on the state supreme court.

Blacks in Congress

South Carolina sent eight blacks—all Republicans—to the U.S. House of Representatives from 1870 to 1876. Mississippi provided two black U.S. senators: Hiram Revels, who filled out Jefferson Davis' term (1870–71), and Blanche K. Bruce, the only American black to serve a full term in the U.S. Senate during the nineteenth century (1875–81). Other southern states provided U.S. representatives as follows: Mississippi one, Louisiana one, Florida one, North Carolina four, Alabama three, Georgia one, and Virginia one. Louisiana's acting governor, P. B. S. Pinchback, was elected a U.S. senator, but the Senate ultimately refused to seat him. Of the twenty-two blacks sent to Congress by Reconstruction governments most had more formal education than Lincoln had; ten had attended college, and one, Robert Brown Elliot, was an Etonian.

Jonathan C. Gibbs, Dartmouth graduate, becomes

Florida secretary of state.

The Fourteenth Amendment, which taken in connection with the Bill of Rights has proven perhaps the single most vital amendment to the national charter, is ratified (July 28).

1870   Black population in the U.S. is now 4,901,000, representing somewhat less than 13 per cent of the total; for the first time in about 300 years not one of these human beings is a slave.

Jonathan Jasper White becomes an associate justice of the South Carolina supreme court (February 2).

Hiram R. Revels is seated as U.S. senator from Mississippi, becoming the first American black to be a member of Congress (February 25).

Fifteenth Amendment becomes part of the law of the land (March 30).

Joseph H. Rainey is first black to be seated in U.S. House of Representatives (December 12).

1871   Fisk Jubilee Singers begin first international tour (October 6); group, which raised money to save Fisk University from bankruptcy, introduced black spirituals and other black religious music to white public in North and in Europe.

1872   Charlotte Ray becomes first black woman lawyer and first woman to graduate from a university law school, receiving her degree from Howard University Law School (February 27).

Elijah P. McCoy patents first of 57 inventions, most relating to automatic lubrication of heavy machinery (July 2).

1873   P. B. S. Pinchback, acting governor of Louisiana, is elected to U.S. Senate (January 15); after three years of senatorial debate he is not seated (1876).

Richard T. Greener, first black Harvard graduate, becomes professor of metaphysics at the University of South Carolina (November).

Dr. Susan McKinney becomes first black woman formally certified as a physician, although Dr. Rebecca Cole, who practiced in New York City (1872–81), is considered first black woman physician.

1874   Patrick Francis Healy becomes president of Georgetown University (July 31).

1875   Civil Rights Act becomes law (March 1); the passage of this law had at least one interesting moment associated with it: on January 6, 1874, Robert Brown Elliot, graduate of Eton and black congressman from South Carolina, took the floor of U.S. House of Representatives and argued eloquently for the bill's passage against Alexander H. Stephens, former vice president of the Confederate States of America.

Blanche Kelso Bruce begins his term as U.S. senator from Mississippi (March 5).

James Augustine Healy becomes first black Roman Catholic bishop in U.S., in Portland, Maine (June 2).

"Mississippi plan," systematic campaign of ballot fraud, economic and social ostracism, torture, and murder, begins against black and white Republicans in Mississippi with a race riot that leaves ten to twenty blacks dead (September 1).

1876   Isaiah Dorman, black scout and interpreter, dies with Custer at Little Bighorn (June 25); it is said that Sitting Bull, a friend of Dorman's, intervened to prevent mutilation of his body by Indian women; all others were scalped and otherwise mutilated.

Edward A. Bouchet receives Ph.D. in physics from Yale University; Bouchet is first black to receive doctorate from an American university.

1877   As a result of Compromise of 1877 federal troops are withdrawn from South Carolina (April 10) and Louisiana (April 24), and Reconstruction governments in these states fall.

President Hayes appoints Frederick Douglass U.S. marshal for Washington, D.C. (March 18).

Henry O. Flipper becomes first black graduate of West Point (June 15).

1879   "Exodus of 1879," series of migrations out of now increasingly repressive South into American West (1879–81): one large group is led by Benjamin "Pap" Singleton, but most of so-called Exodusters— 20,000–40,000—pack up and move out spontaneously, many settling as homesteaders, or sodbusters, in Kansas and Nebraska, in some cases setting up all-black communities, as in Nicodemus, Kansas.

1880   Black population is 6,580,793; total U.S. population is about 50.2 million.

1881   Booker T. Washington opens Tuskegee Institute in Alabama (July 4).

1882   George Washington Williams, black lawyer and Civil War veteran, publishes *History of the Negro Race in America*; scholarly two-volume work is first comprehensive history of American blacks.

1883   In one of two court decisions that open way for modern Jim Crow legislation in southern states, most of it coming after 1885, U.S. Supreme Court declares Civil Rights Act of 1875 unconstitutional (October 15). Segregation on public transportation sets in in the late 1880's and is followed in late 1890's by a rash of

state and municipal statutes setting up segregated toilets, drinking fountains, eating places, public telephones, textbooks, and even separate Bibles for black and white witnesses in the courtroom.

Jan Matzeliger patents shoe-making machine that revolutionizes mass production in shoe industry.

1884   Lewis H. Latimer, inventor and electrical engineer who had previously assisted Alexander Graham Bell in preparing telephone patent applications, joins Edison Company, becoming only black member of "Edison pioneers."

1887   Granville T. Woods patents device allowing stations to telegraph moving trains (November); a prolific inventor—egg incubator, improved air brakes for trains, developments related to third rail—Woods successfully sued Thomas Edison twice for patent infringements.

1889   Charles D. Young becomes third black to graduate from West Point and last black to enter Point until the 1930's.

1890   Black population in U.S. is 7,488,676, slightly less than 12 per cent of the total. Approximately nine out of ten blacks live in South, most of them in rural areas.

Second "Mississippi plan" inaugurated (August 12– November 1); plan is systematic attempt to exclude blacks from southern political life through various voter-registration subterfuges that enable poor and illiterate whites to vote but not blacks, however qualified. Other southern states follow (1895–1910).

1892   Ida B. Wells (later Wells-Barnett), editor of *Free Speech*, black newspaper in Memphis, Tennessee, demonstrates that lynching is sometimes merely a way for white businessmen to eliminate black competitors.

1893   Black group, Creole Show, opens at Chicago World's Fair; introduces ragtime music to vast new audience.

In Provident Hospital, Chicago, Dr. Daniel Hale Williams performs (July 10) one of world's first successful operations on the human heart. Williams had founded Provident Hospital because Chicago hospitals did not at that time permit black doctors to use their facilities.

1895   North Carolina, last southern state to have a legislature with black and white populist members, adjourns out of respect for death the preceding day of Frederick Douglass, aged 78 (February 21).

Booker T. Washington delivers "Atlanta Compromise" speech at Cotton Exposition in Atlanta, Georgia (September 18); in speech Washington urges black people in South to "cast down your bucket where you are" (learn industrial and agricultural skills) and remain, in things "purely social," as separate as fingers on a hand. Washington says that "the agitation of questions of social equality is the extremest folly" and that privileges cannot come by "artificial forcing"; he in effect urges southern and northern blacks not only to cease pressures for social equality (for example, to stop fighting Jim Crow laws) but also to abandon struggle for elementary political rights already guaranteed by Fourteenth Amendment. One reporter noted that although whites listening to speech produced a "delirium of applause . . . most of the Negroes in the audience were crying, perhaps without knowing just why." Speech makes Washington preeminent spokesman for blacks for next twenty years and brings him enormous economic and political power.

1896   *Plessy* v. *Ferguson* (May 18): decision by Supreme Court sets seal of approval on various Jim Crow laws and encourages mass of further legislation segregating hospitals, sports, funeral homes, cemeteries, morgues, and so on (one city, Birmingham, Alabama, even passed law forbidding interracial checker games).

George Washington Carver, born a slave during Civil War, joins chemistry department of Tuskegee Institute; Carver grapples successfully with chronic problem of soil exhaustion in South and is largely responsible for making peanuts and soybeans multimillion-dollar cash crops.

Paul Laurence Dunbar publishes *Lyrics of Lowly Life*; work enjoys wide readership and gains Dunbar appointment to position with Library of Congress.

1897   Andrew J. Beard is awarded $50,000 for invention of automatic coupler for railroad cars; cars had previously had to be coupled with a pin as they came together, and workers were often crushed or killed.

1898   Units of black 9th and 10th Cavalry units participate in charge on San Juan Hill (July 1) during Spanish-American War.

1899   Composer Scott Joplin publishes ragtime composition "Maple Leaf Rag."

1900   Black population is 8,833,994, about 11.5 per cent of total. Although vast majority of blacks at this time are rural sharecroppers, there is also a small elite of businessmen, scientists, and educators. At least one black is a millionaire. There are at least two black-owned insurance companies and four black banks; funeral homes are a major source of wealth for middle-class black entrepreneurs. There are more than 21,000 teachers, about 16,000 preachers, about 1,750 doctors, 212 dentists, 310 journalists, 728 lawyers, about

2,000 entertainers, actors, and minstrels, 236 artists, sculptors, and art teachers, and 247 photographers.

National Negro Business League founded in Boston (August 23–24) by Booker T. Washington and others.

1901   George H. White of North Carolina is last black to sit in U.S. House of Representatives until 1929; shortly before his term expired (March 4), White addressed the House, saying in part: "This, Mr. Chairman, is perhaps the Negro's temporary farewell to the American Congress; but let me say, Phoenix-like he will rise up some day and come again. These parting words are in behalf of an outraged, heartbroken, bruised and bleeding, but God-fearing people . . . full of potential force."

1903   Dr. William Edward Burghardt Du Bois, graduate of Harvard and University of Berlin, publishes collection of essays, *The Souls of Black Folk*. In one essay Du Bois sharply challenges Booker T. Washington for leadership of black American intellectuals: "But so far as Mr. Washington apologizes for injustices, North or South, does not rightly value the privilege and duty of voting, belittles the emasculating effects of caste distinctions, and opposes the higher training and ambitions of our brighter minds,—so far as he, the South or the Nation, does this,—we must unceasingly and firmly oppose them."

Harlem is opened to black residents by black real-estate broker; formerly New York City's 23,000 blacks had been concentrated mainly in mid-Manhattan.

1905   Niagara movement is organized near Niagara Falls (July 11–13); meeting is held on Canadian side of river because U.S. hotels in area deny delegates rooms; movement, of which W. E. B. Du Bois is one of leaders, stresses aggressive search for political, civil, and social equality.

1906   Brownsville riot in Texas: some black soldiers are involved in riot with local white townspeople, one of whom is killed; President Theodore Roosevelt orders dishonorable discharge of three companies of 25th Regiment; dishonorable discharges are reversed by Army in 1972.

1908   Jack Johnson becomes world heavyweight boxing champion in Sydney, Australia (December 26).

1909   Matthew Henson, black assistant to Robert E. Peary, reaches North Pole (April 6).

National Association for the Advancement of Colored People (NAACP) organized in New York City (May 30); W. E. B. Du Bois, sole black officer of new organization, becomes director of research and publicity and editor of NAACP monthly journal *The Crisis*, which he molds into extremely influential publication.

1910   Black population of U.S. is now 9,827,763, somewhat less than 11 per cent of the total.

1911   William H. Lewis is appointed Assistant Attorney General of the U.S. (March 26).

National Urban League organized in New York City (April).

1912   W. C. Handy's "Memphis Blues" is first blues composition to be published (September 27).

1913   Black Americans in many states celebrate fiftieth anniversary of signing of Emancipation Proclamation. Black gains since Civil War were impressive and included a large gain in literacy rate (now 70 per cent of black population was literate, as opposed to 5 per cent in 1863) and a net black wealth estimated at $700 million. On the other hand, discrimination was still rampant, and 51 blacks were lynched in this year.

1914   William Monroe Trotter, heading a delegation bearing protest petitions signed by more than 20,000 blacks, is told by President Woodrow Wilson that "segregation is not humiliating but a benefit, and ought to be so regarded by you gentlemen" (November). Wilson's appointees—with his knowledge and approval—had instituted Jim Crow regulations in federal government, especially Treasury and Post Office departments, which had been relatively free of segregation; Wilson subordinates had also begun to downgrade or dismiss black employees, especially in South.

1915   "Great Migration" begins; mass movement of rural southern blacks to northern cities results from complex pressures, including (1) increased manpower needs of northern industry, especially in war-related fields; (2) black disgust at southern Jim Crow obsession; (3) severe boll-weevil infestations of southern cotton crop, which wiped out many independent small farmers and sharecroppers; (4) enthusiastic urging of influential northern black newspapers, especially Robert S. Abbott's Chicago *Defender*; (5) relative absence of grosser forms of Jim Crow in northern cities; (6) aggressive recruitment in South by representatives of northern manufacturers, who promised and mainly delivered higher wage rates and better working conditions; and (7) drains on labor force caused by U.S. mobilization and entry into World War I. Some estimates place total black immigration to northern industrial cities as high as 1 million persons during years 1915–20; by 1918 Philadelphia, Chicago, New York, and Washington, D.C., had largest black communities in the country.

NAACP wins first significant legal victory when U.S.

Supreme Court rules in *Guinn* v. *U.S.* that grandfather clause is unconstitutional (June 21).

Harvard-educated black historian Carter G. Woodson founds Association for the Study of Negro Life and History (September 9).

NAACP organizes protest demonstrations against D. W. Griffith's *Birth of a Nation*, which was a great film but also embodied classic Reconstruction myths and black stereotypes.

NAACP presents first annual Spingarn Medal to Ernest E. Just, biologist who made important contributions to cytology.

1917   Race riot in East St. Louis, Illinois (July 1–3): an estimated 100 blacks die during three-day attack on black ghetto; riot started when blacks fired on police car that they believed had earlier shot up black neighborhood.

Woodrow Wilson asks Congress for a declaration of war against Germany (April 2); highest-ranking black officer in Army, Colonel Charles Young, is promptly retired on patently false grounds of high blood pressure, setting general administration tone for duration. Black units are trained for combat but assigned mainly labor and orderly tasks; black units sent to France (more than 200,000 troops) are often assigned to French command and are, among other things, forbidden upon pain of arrest to speak to French women. Army makes no effort to protect black soldiers in training camps at home from abuse and other indignities heaped on them by local whites; as a result several serious riots occur. Nevertheless, black combat units earn great distinction at Château-Thierry, Belleau Wood, Saint-Mihiel, Vosges, the Argonne Forest, and Metz. First Americans to receive French Croix de Guerre are black infantrymen, Private Henry Johnson and Private Needham Roberts.

Three black regiments—the 369th, 371st, and 372nd—are awarded Croix de Guerre.

NAACP organizes silent parade in which 10,000 blacks in New York City march in protest against lynchings (38 in 1917) and riots (July 28).

Race riot in Houston, Texas (August 23), involves black soldiers of 24th Infantry Regiment and leaves two blacks and seventeen whites dead. Quick army court-martial sentences forty-one soldiers to life imprisonment and hangs thirteen.

Joseph "King" Oliver moves his Creole Band from New Orleans to Chicago, bringing new music north; other outstanding jazz artists, including Louis Armstrong, join Oliver in Chicago.

1918   Military order, "Secret Information Concerning the Black American Troops," is circulated to French commanders (August 7); order, emanating from American headquarters, instructs French officers not to eat meals with black officers, shake hands with them, or otherwise affiliate with them because that will "deeply wound" white American officers; it further states that black troops are not to be commended "too highly," especially when whites are present, and that French officers must especially beware of any "public expression" of intimacy between French women and black soldiers because that "greatly incenses" white Americans. On Thanksgiving Day, near recaptured Metz, 3,000 black American soldiers refuse to sing the words to "My Country, 'Tis of Thee."

1919   The "Red summer" (July–October): horrible race riots, 25 in all, erupt in American cities, north and south; one of the worst, in which six people are killed and at least 150 wounded, occurs in Washington, D.C.(July 19–23); another happens in Chicago (July 27), with more than 500 wounded and 15 whites and 23 blacks killed. Riots are result of many factors, including attempts of large numbers of Great Migration blacks in crowded northern ghettos to move into previously all-white neighborhoods, severe economic competition as jobs in defense industries vanish and millions of soldiers return to labor market, and a resurgence of Ku Klux Klan activity.

1920   Black population in U.S., at 10,463,131, falls below 10 per cent of total population for first time in history of U.S. Census.

        Marcus Garvey, Jamaica-born founder and leader of Universal Negro Improvement Association (UNIA), addresses 25,000 blacks in New York's Madison Square Garden (August 2); appealing powerfully to despair and bitterness of many American blacks, Garvey builds first extensive black nationalist, black separatist movement, telling his audiences that they cannot hope for justice and decency from white America and must focus their dreams on a united African kingdom; Garvey raised at least $1 million to further his plans for a back-to-Africa movement and founded various enterprises, including a steamship line, the Black Star. Garvey also exploited class differences within the black community, excoriating the middle class, especially the intelligentsia, who not infrequently practiced caste discrimination based not only on wealth and education but also on relative lightness of skin.

1921   Missouri Congressman L. C. Dyer, a white, introduces antilynching bill that passes House but is killed by Senate filibuster.

1922   "Harlem renaissance": a great outpouring of black creative talent, with the community of Harlem as its nexus, the renaissance begins, in a sense, with the publication of Claude McKay's *Harlem Shadows* (1922); in part a literary movement dominated by educated, middle-class novelists, poets, and intellectuals, the renaissance was also characterized by great music making and vastly increased black participation in the Broadway theater and other entertainments.

The Harlem Renaissance

Among the writers and poets associated with the Harlem renaissance are Jean Toomer, Langston Hughes, Countee Cullen, James Weldon Johnson, Arna Bontemps, Walter White, and Jessie Fauset. Among the musical artists who earned wide public acclaim during the decade-long renaissance, which also saw royalty and smart New York café society regularly visiting Harlem, were "Ma" Rainey, Bessie Smith, Louis Armstrong, "Fats" Waller, Fletcher Henderson, Jimmie Lunceford, and "Duke" Ellington. Ellington began appearing before all-white audiences in Harlem's Cotton Club in 1927. During this era the actor Charles Gilpin was a great critical success in Eugene O'Neill's *Emperor Jones,* as was Paul Robeson in Jerome Kern's *Show Boat* (1927); and Marc Connelly's *Green Pastures* (1929–30) was an enormously popular showcase for black talent. After this era American society became more accessible to black men and women of talent, and many black writers, artists, and entertainers have since become household names.

1923   Garret A. Morgan, inventor of the Morgan inhalator, an early type of gas mask that was later adapted for military use in World War I, invents automatic traffic signal.

1925   Asa Philip Randolph founds International Brotherhood of Sleeping Car Porters, the strongest black labor union of its time.

        Dr. Ossian Sweet is arrested in Detroit for murder (September 8); white mob that had gathered in front of his home in white neighborhood was driven off by gunfire, leaving one dead. Dr. Sweet, defended by Clarence Darrow, is eventually acquitted.

1927   In another significant NAACP victory U.S. Supreme Court in *Nixon* v. *Herndon* voids Texas law excluding blacks from Democratic primaries (March 7).

1929   Oscar De Priest of Chicago, a Republican, becomes first black to sit in U.S. House of Representatives since 1901 (April 15).

1930   U.S. black population is 11,891,143, out of total of almost 123 million.

After long and well-organized campaign by NAACP, U.S. Senate blocks confirmation of racist appointee to U.S. Supreme Court (April 21), providing one of first concrete examples of growing political clout of American blacks.

1931   Temple of Islam is founded in Detroit; Black Muslim movement is later (1934) taken over by Elijah Muhammad, who builds strong black-separatist organization.

First trial of "Scottsboro boys" begins in Scottsboro, Alabama (April 6); although defendants are quickly convicted of rape—on dubious testimony—case is given wide publicity by American Communists, and a series of appeals and U.S. Supreme Court decisions brings rural southern justice into national limelight; widespread northern liberal outrage marks significant shift in public attitudes.

Arrowsmith, directed by John Ford, is first film to present competent, sympathetic, dignified black character, a physician; role is played by Clarence Brooks.

1932   Bill Pickett, black ranch hand and rodeo star, dies (April 21); Pickett invented technique of bulldogging steers (jumping from galloping horse, grabbing steer by horns, and twisting it down).

Blacks vote in considerable numbers for Democratic presidential candidate Franklin Delano Roosevelt, marking the beginning of new political alliance and abandonment of party of Lincoln (November 8).

1934   NAACP plans coordinated, aggressive, nationwide legal campaign to combat discrimination and Jim Crow, concentrating particularly on segregation in graduate education (October 26); in this effort they are considerably aided by a young white man, Charles Garland, who brusquely gave away a million-dollar inheritance he had come into, setting up a fund to aid "unpopular causes," of which black organizations like the NAACP were principal beneficiaries.

1935   National Council of Negro Women founded (December 5); Mary McLeod Bethune becomes first president.

Dr. Percy Julian synthesizes drug physostigmine, used in treatment of glaucoma.

Frederick McKinley Jones, inventor, adapts mechanical refrigeration units for use on trucks and trains, eliminating need for packed ice.

1936   Jesse Owens wins four gold medals at Munich Olympic games (August 9).

Blacks vote overwhelmingly for Democratic candidates, Franklin D. Roosevelt in particular (November 3); landslide shift in black voting pattern reflects fact that many blacks benefited from New Deal programs and that these programs, when federally administered, were relatively free of discrimination.

Mary McLeod Bethune is appointed director of Division of Negro Affairs of the National Youth Administration.

1937   William H. Hastie becomes first black jurist appointed to federal bench (March 26).

Joe Louis becomes world heavyweight boxing champion (June 22).

Antilynching bill is killed once again in Senate; by this time F.D.R. is increasingly dependent upon conservative southern Democrats for his war-preparedness policies and is unwilling to alienate them.

1938   NAACP legal campaign begins to succeed when U.S. Supreme Court, in *Missouri* ex rel. *Gaines* v. *Canada*, rules that states must provide equal graduate educational facilities for blacks or else admit them to existing facilities (December); Missouri had barred blacks from state law school but offered to pay tuition to out-of-state schools.

In Pennsylvania, Crystal Bird Fauset becomes first black woman to be elected to a state legislature (November 8).

1939   Marian Anderson gives concert on steps of Lincoln Memorial in Washington, D.C. (Easter Sunday); Daughters of the American Revolution had refused to allow Miss Anderson to use their Constitution Hall, whereupon Eleanor Roosevelt resigned her membership in the D.A.R. and arranged to make Lincoln Memorial available; 75,000 Americans gathered to hear the concert.

Jane Matilda Bolin is appointed New York City judge, becoming first black woman jurist in U.S. (July 22).

Hattie McDaniel becomes first black to win an Academy Award, receiving an Oscar for best supporting actress in film *Gone With the Wind*.

1940   Black population of U.S. is now 12,865,518, out of total population of 132,122,000; black percentage of total has risen slightly since all-time low of 1930 but is still not quite 10 per cent.

Richard Wright publishes *Native Son* (February).

Dr. Charles R. Drew, an American black, becomes director of British blood-bank program as result of his pioneering research efforts in this field (October 1). Drew later sets up American blood-plasma program, which is responsible for saving the lives of thousands of combat casualties; American Red Cross, which later administers program, segregates black and white blood.

Brigadier General Benjamin O. Davis, Sr., becomes first black general in U.S. armed forces (October 16).

Virginia chooses as its official state song "Carry Me Back to Ole Virginny," written by James A. Bland, a New York black composer.

1941   Under threat of lawsuit the War Department establishes first Army Air Corps squadron for black fliers (January 16).

Dr. Robert Weaver named head of section of Office of Production Management designed to further integration of blacks into defense effort (April 18).

President Roosevelt meets with A. Philip Randolph at White House in showdown over black role in defense effort (June 18); blacks want assurances that they will get an equal chance at defense-industry jobs, officer training, and combat roles requiring instruction in the use of sophisticated weaponry; F.D.R. assures Randolph that something will be done but says the government is not going to be pressured; Randolph replies that something will have to be done or he will march 100,000 blacks on Washington, D.C., on July 1.

President issues Executive Order 8802, which bans discrimination in war industries and military training programs (June 25); Randolph then calls off threatened march.

First school for black pilots established at Tuskegee Institute (July 19).

Black and white soldiers shoot at each other in a bus in North Carolina (August 6); one black and one white killed; first of many such incidents throughout the war involving racial conflicts between soldiers or between soldiers and civilians.

Dorie Miller of U.S.S. *Arizona*, on which he served as messman, shoots down four Japanese fighters during Pearl Harbor attack (December 7); he had no antiaircraft training but took gun over from wounded crewman. After Pearl Harbor, Secretary of War Henry Stimson and Secretary of the Navy Frank Knox both make public statements questioning whether blacks have ability or courage to make combat contributions.

1942   Bernard W. Robinson commissioned an ensign in U.S. Naval Reserve, thus becoming first black naval officer (June 18).

Congress of Racial Equality (CORE), an interracial group dedicated to nonviolent direct action, holds first sit-in, in Chicago restaurant (June).

Federal government threatens to sue black newspapers said to be guilty of sedition in their harsh criticism of racial policies in armed forces.

World War II

On the home front thousands of blacks entered skilled trades in the war industries; the percentage of blacks employed in such trades rose from 4.4 in 1940 to 7.3 in 1944. By 1945, 394,500 blacks were members of CIO-affiliated unions. As a result of President Roosevelt's Executive Order 8802 and of war-related labor shortages many blacks found employment in defense industries but often got the most onerous or dangerous jobs—on dockyards, loading ammunition ships, or in munitions factories.

Also as a result of 8802, blacks received nonsegregated officer training, except in the air arm; they received training in machine gunnery, communications, antiaircraft, and other aspects of warfare. Black units continued to be segregated, however, although usually under black officers; training, housing, and recreational facilities were often inferior.

Most black units were placed in labor or service battalions, although this service often tended to involve sophisticated tasks, given the nature of modern warfare. Most black units that did see combat, however, performed with high valor and effectiveness in such battles as the Normandy invasion, the Battle of the Bulge, Bougainville, Saipan, Okinawa, and Guadalcanal. Especially noteworthy were the combat records of the 99th Pursuit Squadron under Colonel Benjamin O. Davis, which by 1945 had flown sixteen hundred combat missions, including raids on Berlin, and the 761st Tank Battalion, which was among the finest of Patton's elite corps. About twenty-four thousand blacks served in integrated crews in the Merchant Marine, sometimes under black officers. The Navy did not accept blacks for combat roles until 1944, however, and most blacks saw service in the Navy as messmen.

In all more than a million blacks were drafted during World War II, and of these about seven hundred thousand saw actual service in the Army. In addition, about seventeen thousand served in the Marines and about a hundred thousand in the Navy.

Captain Hugh Mulzac becomes first black to command a Liberty Ship (September 29); his vessel, S.S.

Booker T. Washington, was one of eighteen Liberty Ships to be named after prominent American blacks.

John H. Johnson publishes *Negro Digest* in Chicago; three years later he follows with *Ebony*.

1943 William H. Hastie, aide to Secretary of War, resigns in protest against army segregation policies (January 5).

George Gershwin's *Porgy and Bess* opens on Broadway (February 28); Anne Brown and Todd Duncan star.

Detroit race riot (June 21): 34 blacks and whites are killed, and riot must be suppressed by federal troops; riot stemmed in part from second Great Migration by rural blacks to urban industrial areas (estimated 2.5 million blacks moved from rural areas to cities in North, South, and West in years 1939–50).

Paul Robeson stars—to rave reviews—in title role of New York production of *Othello* (October 19); production sets record run (296 performances) for Shakespeare on Broadway.

1944 Adam Clayton Powell, Jr., of Harlem becomes first black U.S. congressman from a northeastern city (August 1).

Battle of the Bulge (December 16–26): military emergency causes Army temporarily to abandon its segregation policies and use interracial units.

1946 Senate confirms appointment of William H. Hastie as governor of the Virgin Islands (May 1).

Supreme Court bans segregation on interstate buses (June 3).

President Truman issues Executive Order 9802 and creates President's Committee on Civil Rights (December 5) as a result of Congress' failure to pass an antilynching bill, put an end to the poll tax, and set up a permanent Fair Employment Practices Commission; among black committee members is Mrs. Sadie T. M. Alexander, Philadelphia lawyer.

1947 CORE sends first freedom riders through South on interstate buses (April 9).

Jack Roosevelt "Jackie" Robinson joins Brooklyn Dodgers, becoming first black ballplayer in previously all-white major leagues (April 11); earns "Rookie of the Year" honor.

President's Committee on Civil Rights issues report "To Secure These Rights" (October 29); report includes many recommendations long urged by NAACP.

Southern Regional Council estimates that as a result of legal and extralegal discouragements only 12 per cent of all southern blacks are registered to vote; in Louisiana, Alabama, and Mississippi voter registration

is about 3 per cent of black population.

Tuskegee Institute estimates that 3,426 blacks have been lynched since 1882.

1948 Lieutenant Nancy C. Leftenant becomes first black in Army Nurse Corps (February 12).

A. Philip Randolph, in testimony before Senate, threatens that unless draft laws and army training programs are desegregated, he will urge black youths to resist draft (March 31).

U.S. Supreme Court rules that racially restrictive housing covenants cannot be enforced by federal or state courts (May 3); decision does not actually declare covenants themselves illegal.

President Truman issues Executive Order 9981 (July 30), which bans segregation in U.S. armed forces, thus allowing ordinary black and white soldiers to train together. Truman also issues order making U.S. government equal-opportunity employer, with result that large numbers of blacks enter civil service.

Ralph J. Bunche becomes acting UN mediator in Palestine (September 18).

U.S. Supreme Court voids California statute prohibiting interracial marriage (October 1).

1949 William L. Dawson, congressman from Chicago, becomes first black to head a standing congressional committee, the House Expenditures Committee (January 18).

Wesley A. Brown becomes first black graduate of U.S. Naval Academy (June 3).

First black-owned radio station (WERD) begins broadcasting in Atlanta, Georgia (October 3).

Entertainer Bill "Bojangles" Robinson dies in New York City (November 25).

Motown Records is founded in Detroit by several black automobile workers, including Berry Gordy, Jr.

Dr. William A. Hinton, who developed standard test for detection of syphilis, becomes first black professor at Harvard Medical School.

1950 Black population in U.S. is 15,042,286, about 10 per cent of total.

Charles Hamilton Houston dies in Washington, D.C. (April 22); Houston, who was chief legal counsel of the NAACP, was architect of its campaign against segregation in education.

Gwendolyn Brooks is awarded Pulitzer Prize in poetry for volume *Annie Allen* (May 1); Brooks is first black to receive a Pulitzer.

U.S. Supreme Court rules, in *Sweatt* v. *Painter*, that new segregated Texas law school was inferior "in those qualities .. which make for greatness in a law school" and because it was segregated did not provide plaintiff Sweatt access to the Texas law establishment—the vast majority of white individuals and institutions with which a member of the Texas bar would have to interact professionally (June 5); as a result of this decision Herman Marion Sweatt became the first black to enter a southern white university since the Reconstruction period.

Black infantry regiment—the 24th—captures Yech'on in first UN victory of Korean War (July 21).

Althea Gibson becomes first black woman tennis player to compete in national championships of United States Lawn Tennis Association in Forest Hills, New York (August).

Edith Sampson, Chicago lawyer, is appointed an alternate U.S. delegate to the United Nations (August 24).

Ralph Bunche is awarded Nobel Peace Prize for his role in negotiations between Arabs and Jews in Palestine (September 22).

Singer-actor Paul Robeson, who has long been associated with leftist causes, is denied a passport because he refuses to sign an affidavit about whether he was ever a member of the Communist Party.

1951   Private William Thompson is posthumously awarded Congressional Medal of Honor for heroism in Korean War (June 12); Thompson, who sacrificed himself in order to cover the retreat of his comrades, thus became first black recipient of Medal of Honor since Spanish-American War.

Harry T. Moore, NAACP official, is killed in bombing of his home in Mims, Florida (December 25); his wife is seriously injured in explosion.

1952   Sergeant Cornelius H. Charlton of New York City, Korean War combatant, is posthumously awarded Congressional Medal of Honor (February 12).

At the age of 48 Satchel Paige is named to American League all-star baseball squad.

Tuskegee Institute, which has been monitoring lynchings in U.S. since 1882, reports that 1952 is first year since then in which no one has been lynched (December 30).

1953   Supreme Court rules that Washington, D.C., restaurants cannot refuse to serve blacks (June 8).

1954   J. Ernest Wilkins nominated Assistant Secretary of Labor (March 4).

In *Brown* v. *Board of Education of Topeka* U.S. Supreme

Court rules (May 17) that segregation in public-school education violates the Constitution.

First White Citizens Council organized in Indianola, Mississippi (July 11); councils, which spread quickly, were composed of prominent community leaders; goal was to resist integration by "every lawful means."

Benjamin O. Davis, Jr., becomes first black general in U.S. Air Force (October 27).

1955   Marian Anderson, at the age of 52, makes her debut at New York City's Metropolitan Opera (January 7); she is first black singer ever to appear on the stage of the Metropolitan.

Fourteen-year-old Emmett Till is kidnapped and lynched in Money, Mississippi (August 28); Till had, it was claimed, whistled at a white woman.

U.S. Supreme Court bans segregation in recreational facilities supported by public tax dollars (November 7).

Mrs. Rosa Parks refuses to yield her seat to a white passenger in a Montgomery, Alabama, bus (December 1); after her arrest and fine Dr. Martin Luther King, Jr., minister of Dexter Avenue Baptist Church, organizes year-long boycott of bus system by most of black community of Montgomery (December 5). Buses were integrated on December 21, 1956.

1956   Manifesto denouncing Supreme Court desegregation rulings is issued by 101 southern U.S. senators and representatives (March 12).

Dynamite blast destroys home of Rev. F. L. Shuttlesworth in Birmingham, Alabama (December 25); involvement of black churches and religious leaders in black movement to gain civil rights in South was a decisive factor in the struggle.

1957   Southern Christian Leadership Conference is organized in New Orleans (February 14); Martin Luther King, Jr., becomes president.

Alvin Ailey, dancer and choreographer, forms Alvin Ailey Dance Theater; largely black in membership, company is soon acknowledged to be one of the finest in America.

U.S. soldiers from 101st Airborne Division escort nine black children to school at Little Rock Central High in Little Rock, Arkansas (September 25); this is first time since Reconstruction that federal government has placed its military power in service of the civil rights of black Americans.

1959   Lorraine Hansberry's *Raisin in the Sun* opens on Broadway (March 11); first play by black woman to reach a Broadway stage, it won New York Drama

Critics' Circle Award.

Charles Sifford is first black to win major professional golf tournament, the Long Beach Open in California.

1960   Black population of U.S. is 18,871,831, representing a proportional increase to about 10.5 per cent of whole.

Sit-in movement begins when four black college students sit in whites-only Woolworth lunch counter in Greensboro, North Carolina (February 2); movement spreads quickly to fifteen other southern cities; by March 22 more than 1,000 blacks have been arrested for sit-ins; by October three national chains have announced the elimination of Jim Crow from their southern branches.

Student Nonviolent Coordinating Committee (SNCC) is organized at Shaw University (April 15–17); although SNCC participates in many civil-rights tests, it has as an initial primary goal the assertion of political rights, especially voter registration.

1961   Soprano Leontyne Price makes triumphant Metropolitan Opera debut as Leonora in *Il Trovatore* (January 27).

Thirteen freedom riders begin southern interstate bus trip to test or force compliance with various court decisions banning segregation on buses and in bus stations, rest rooms, and other facilities connected with interstate travel (May 4); bus is bombed and burned ten days later near Anniston, Alabama; freedom-ride movement spreads, and federal government eventually dispatches federal marshals to protect riders.

Board of Education of New Rochelle, New York, is ordered to integrate its schools (May 31); case is among first in which de facto racial segregation in northern and western schools is attacked; such segregation is not mandated by state law but reflects segregated residential patterns, sometimes with a boost from gerrymandered school-district lines.

1962   Lieutenant Commander Samuel L. Gravely becomes captain of destroyer U.S.S. *Falgout* (January 31); Gravely thus becomes first black in twentieth century to command U.S. warship.

Federal marshals escort James H. Meredith to University of Mississippi (September 30–October 1); riot occurs in which 2 people are killed and more than 100 wounded; 5,000 federal and national guard troops are required to suppress riot. Defiance of court-ordered admission of Meredith had been announced on TV by Mississippi governor, Ross R. Barnett, who subsequently twice physically prevented Meredith from

entering "Ole Miss" (September 20 and 25) and ordered a blockade by state patrolmen (September 26). Both Barnett and Lieutenant Governor Paul B. Johnson were found in contempt of court.

1963   The hundredth anniversary of the Emancipation Proclamation is celebrated (January 1).

Anti-Jim Crow campaign, led by Martin Luther King, Jr., begins in Birmingham, Alabama (April 3); Birmingham was deliberately chosen as focus for confrontation, in part because of growing black impatience with pace of change and pressure from younger, more militant groups and in part because Alabama's Governor Wallace and Birmingham's Police Commissioner Eugene "Bull" Connor were national symbols of violent opposition to integration. King is arrested (April 12); confrontations and arrests continue. Large numbers of schoolchildren are employed in massive demonstration and about 700 are arrested (May 2). Police turn fire hoses and attack dogs on marchers as appalled nation watches on TV (May 3). Violent confrontations continue until May 7, when a tentative accord is reached with city leaders. On May 11 campaign headquarters and home of Dr. King's brother are bombed, which produces a two-day riot. Violence in Birmingham stimulates black demonstrations all over the country, many joined now by sympathetic whites sickened by what they have seen at Birmingham.

Medgar W. Evers, Mississippi field secretary for NAACP, is gunned down in front of his home in Jackson (June 12).

Demonstrations occur in virtually every major city in U.S. (June–August); reflect rage at Evers' murder and other southern violence and also a growing determination among nonsouthern blacks to seek economic justice in form of equal pay and equal access to job opportunities.

In march on Washington (August 28), organized by A. Philip Randolph, about 200,000 people, most of them blacks, gather before Lincoln Memorial.

Black church in Birmingham is bombed, and four little girls are killed during Sunday school (September 15).

1964   Malcolm X resigns from Black Muslims (March 14); he later (June) founds Organization for Afro-American Unity; rejecting Black Muslim notion that whites are devils and not eliminating possibility of political action with whites, Malcolm appeals most strongly for "black power," namely, for black control over local public and private community institutions that affect day-to-day lives of black Americans.

Murder of civil-rights workers Andrew Goodman,

Michael H. Schwerner, and James E. Chaney near Philadelphia, Mississippi (June 21): Goodman and Schwerner, whites from New York, and Chaney, a Mississippi black, were illegally arrested and then released after a group had been formed to follow and shoot them; their bodies are later (August 5) found under an earthen dam.

Riots begin in New York City: riots, which began in Harlem (July 18), spread to Bedford-Stuyvesant ghetto in Brooklyn and mark beginning of "long, hot summer" of 1964.

Dr. Martin Luther King, Jr., is awarded Nobel Peace Prize (October 14).

1965 Malcolm X, who had publicly expressed fears of an attack on his life by Muslims after his break with Elijah Muhammad, is assassinated in New York City (February 21); two of three assailants are Black Muslims; all three are sentenced to life imprisonment.

Selma, Alabama, march (March 21–25): marchers, led by Martin Luther King, Jr., and ultimately numbering 25,000, walk 54 miles, from Selma to Montgomery, Alabama's capital, to dramatize demand for elimination of restrictions on black voter registration; many whites, especially clergymen, join march. First attempt at Selma march had been brutally turned back (March 7), drawing protest and public rebuke of Alabama authorities by President Lyndon Johnson (March 9); a number of demonstrators, including white clergymen, are injured in association with Selma marches, and two demonstrators, both white, are killed.

Martin Luther King, Jr., threatens economic boycott of Alabama (March 28).

Deacons for Defense and Justice, black group in Louisiana that has renounced King's nonviolent approach and dedicates itself to protecting blacks against white terrorism, gains wide publicity (June); issue of what is proper and appropriate response to white violence, including police violence, tends increasingly to split black leadership and organizations.

Mass demonstration in Chicago (June 10–16) leads to arrest of more than 500 persons, including well-known blacks Dick Gregory, entertainer, and James Farmer, CORE director.

Thurgood Marshall is nominated to post of Solicitor General of the U.S. (July 13).

Second massive demonstration is led in Chicago by Martin Luther King, Jr. (July 24–26).

Riot in Watts area of Los Angeles (August 11–16), which kills 35, leaves 1,032 injured, results in the arrest of more than 3,400 adults, and causes millions of dollars in property damage, starts when white police officers arrest young black drunken driver and rumors of police brutality spread. Although Watts area does not resemble typical dense northern inner-city ghetto, it is in fact a severely blighted area economically; much of looting and burning is directed at typically hated ghetto institutions—pawnshops, liquor stores, and credit-extending furniture and clothing stores.

In New Orleans, Harold R. Perry is first black to become Roman Catholic bishop in America in twentieth century (October 2).

House Un-American Activities Committee votes full investigation of Ku Klux Klan, whose members have been involved in deaths of several civil-rights workers in Alabama.

1966 Robert Weaver becomes Secretary of Housing and Urban Development and first black cabinet member (January 13).

Constance Baker Motley is first black woman to become a federal judge (January 25).

Andrew Brimmer becomes first black member of Federal Reserve Board (February).

Emmett Ashford of American League is first black to umpire in a major-league baseball game (April 12).

Private First Class Milton L. Olive III is posthumously awarded Congressional Medal of Honor and is first black so to be honored for action in Vietnam (April 21); Olive threw himself on a grenade in order to shield his companions from the explosion.

Stokely Carmichael becomes new head of SNCC (May 16).

James Meredith is shot and wounded during solo march "against fear" from Memphis, Tennessee, to Jackson, Mississippi (June 6); march is then taken up and concluded by variety of civil-rights organizations.

Black Panthers founded by Bobby Seale and Huey P. Newton (October); movement stresses revolutionary rhetoric, but much of Panthers' activity concerns efforts to improve early childhood education, provide free milk and breakfasts to schoolchildren, and so on.

Edward W. Brooke of Massachusetts becomes first black elected to U.S. Senate since Reconstruction (November 8).

Bill Russell, center for Boston Celtics, becomes first black to coach big-league professional basketball team when he becomes Celtics' player-coach.

1967 Adam Clayton Powell, Jr., is barred from House of Representatives by 307–116 vote (March 1); Powell, who has served in Congress since 1945 and has become head of House Committee on Education and Labor, is accused of padding congressional payroll with friends and relatives, absenting himself too often from roll-call votes, and being a playboy; he has also been successfully sued for libel by one of his constituents.

In rally and demonstrations in New York City (April 15–24) Martin Luther King, Jr., attacks U.S. policy in Vietnam, thus clearly linking civil-rights movement with antiwar movement, to discomfiture of many who feel issues should be kept separate.

H. Rap Brown becomes head of SNCC and announces continuation of militant program, including now strong antiwar emphasis (May 12–16).

Devastating riot rages in Newark, New Jersey (July 12–17); riots and disorders also occur in many other cities, including Boston, Massachusetts, Buffalo, New York, Tampa, Florida, and Cincinnati, Ohio.

Thurgood Marshall is appointed a justice of the U.S. Supreme Court; Marshall is first black to become member of Court.

SNCC publishes anti-Zionist article accusing Israelis of atrocities and discrimination against Israeli Arabs and dark-skinned Jews (August); controversy alienates many middle-class liberal Jewish supporters of civil-rights movement.

All-white Mississippi jury convicts seven out of 21 men accused of murdering civil-rights workers Chaney, Schwerner, and Goodman in 1964 (October 20); two of those convicted are a chief deputy sheriff and a high-ranking Ku Klux Klan member.

Carl Stokes is elected mayor of Cleveland, Ohio (November 7); Stokes is first black mayor of major U.S. city.

Richard Hatcher is elected mayor of Gary, Indiana.

1968 Black playwright Imamu Amiri Baraka (formerly Leroi Jones) is sentenced to two to three years in prison for illegal possession of firearms during the 1967 Newark, New Jersey, riot (January 4); other militant leaders, including Stokely Carmichael and H. Rap Brown, have also been indicted or convicted for offenses relating to civil disturbances, leading some blacks and whites to believe that a government conspiracy to eliminate militant black leadership is afoot.

Lucius Amerson is elected sheriff of Macon County, Alabama (January 16), becoming first black sheriff in South since Reconstruction.

National Advisory Commission on Civil Disorders

(Kerner commission) issues report blaming wave of urban riots, especially in North, on white racism; holds racism responsible for discrimination, poverty, and frustration in black ghettos, which are, commission reports, created, maintained, and condoned by white society (February 29).

Dr. Martin Luther King, Jr., is assassinated in Memphis, Tennessee, where he had been leading protest in support of strike by Memphis sanitation workers, most of whom are black (April 4). Riots erupt in more than 100 American cities, including Washington, D.C., as a result of black anger at King's murder. Riots are suppressed by a total of 70,000 federal troops and guardsmen.

Poor People's Campaign in Washington, D.C. (May 11–June 10): large numbers of blacks gather in Resurrection City, temporary shantytown near White House, to call for an end to poverty in U.S.; several schisms occur within leadership of campaign, leading to resignation of Bayard Rustin.

Private First Class James Anderson, Jr., is posthumously awarded Congressional Medal of Honor, becoming first black Marine ever to receive it (August 21).

Teachers' strike begins in New York City (September 9); strike by mainly white teachers crystallizes issue of community control in Ocean Hill-Brownsville school district, where pupils are largely black and Puerto Rican. Issue is subtle and complex, involving on one hand academic freedom and on the other black dissatisfaction with quality of education in primarily black schools and determination ultimately to control school establishment in local communities.

More than half of all professional basketball players are black; about one third of all professional football players and baseball players are black.

1969 Charles Evers, brother of slain civil-rights worker Medgar Evers, is one of several blacks elected to public posts in the South, becoming mayor of Fayette, Mississippi (May 13).

Howard Lee is elected mayor of predominantly white city of Chapel Hill, North Carolina.

Black and white civil-rights lawyers protest Nixon administration policy of slowing down federally instituted integration suits in South (August 26–27).

Dr. Clifton R. Wharton becomes president of Michigan State University (October 17); Dr. Wharton is first black to head major university in which majority of students are white.

Black soldiers in Vietnam account for 13.5 per cent of

battle deaths, although only 9.7 per cent of troops in Vietnam are black, leading to charges that blacks are being assigned in disproportionate numbers to combat units and to especially hazardous missions.

1970   Black population of U.S. is now approximately 22.6 million, about 11 per cent of total.

NAACP kicks off campaign to prevent Senate confirmation of G. Harrold Carswell as justice of U.S. Supreme Court (January 21); Carswell nomination is ultimately blocked by broad coalition of interests—black, labor, and legal.

Presidential adviser Daniel P. Moynihan suggests in memo to Nixon that race issue in U.S. could benefit from period of "benign neglect"; memo is leaked to press (February 28) and sets off uproar among civil-rights advocates, but it does reflect substantial white consensus that great strides forward have been made and that these gains should be consolidated.

Detroit school board approves plan calling for busing of 3,000 students—black and white—to achieve racial balance in city schools (April 7); more than 60 per cent of schoolchildren in Detroit system are black, and achieving integrated schools requires that some white students be bused to previously all-black schools from schools in white enclaves; white parents fiercely resist such busing, fearing that their children will be sent to inferior schools and thus be handicapped.

Busing controversy in Pontiac, Michigan (October): white parents attack buses and chain themselves to fences in protest against court-ordered busing to achieve racial balance in Pontiac school system.

1971   Rev. Leon Howard Sullivan elected to board of directors of General Motors, Inc. (January 4).

Blacks now occupying elective offices in U.S. number 1,860, about a fourfold gain over 1967; black percentage of officeholders remains well below black percentage of total U.S. population, however.

James Meredith announces that he is leaving New York to live in Mississippi because South now has better race relations than North (June 27).

Voter registration among southern blacks is now almost 59 per cent, up from 29 per cent in 1961.

1972   *Apollo 16* moon mission places ultraviolet camera-spectrograph designed by Dr. George Carruthers on lunar surface (April 16–27).

Frank Wills, black security guard at Watergate complex in Washington, D.C., foils attempt by burglars to bug Democratic National Committee headquarters and has them arrested (June 17).

Andrew Young of Atlanta, Georgia, and Barbara Jordan of Houston, Texas, become first southern blacks to be elected to U.S. House of Representatives since Reconstruction (November 7); there are now fifteen black members of Congress.

1973   Blacks holding elective office in United States number 2,621; five states having greatest number of black officeholders are Michigan, New York, Mississippi, Alabama, and Arkansas.

Thomas Bradley is elected mayor of Los Angeles, California (May 29).

Rutgers University honors alumnus Paul Robeson on his seventy-fifth birthday (April).

Governor George Wallace of Alabama receives warm welcome and applause following speech in Tuskegee to National Conference of Black Mayors.

Maynard Jackson is first black to be elected mayor of major southern city, Atlanta, Georgia (October 16).

1974   Henry Aaron of Atlanta Braves surpasses home-run record of Babe Ruth, hitting his 715th career home run in Atlanta (April 8); Aaron finishes his career with 755 home runs. (As of 1976 three of the five top home-run leaders in baseball history are blacks—Hank Aaron, Willie Mays, and Frank Robinson.)

Frank Robinson becomes first black manager of major-league baseball team, the Cleveland Indians (October).

Busing riots erupt in Boston, Massachusetts (December); riots result from court-ordered busing of black students into tightly knit lower-class Boston neighborhoods.

Top eight black-owned businesses in terms of 1973 annual sales are Motown Industries, Johnson Publishing Co., Inc., Fedco Food Corp., Johnson Products Co., Inc., The Stax Organization, F. W. Eversley & Co., Inc., Jenkins Electric Co., Inc., and H. G. Parks, Inc., with combined annual sales of more than $196 million.

1975   Black unemployment rate during 1975 recession is 15 per cent, in contrast to 9 per cent for whites.

William T. Coleman is appointed Secretary of Transportation (March) and becomes second black to hold cabinet post.

Wallace Muhammad, new leader of Nation of Islam, announces that Muslim movement is open to members of all races (July 1).

General Daniel James becomes commander in chief of North American Air Defense Command (NORAD) and nation's first black four-star general (August 29).

WGPR-TV in Detroit becomes first black-owned, black-run TV station in U.S. (September 29).

Federal judge Arthur Garrity places Boston school system under court control after hearing testimony by black students that they had been beaten by students and ignored by teachers in previously all-white school (December 9).

1976   U.S. Supreme Court rules that blacks must be awarded retroactive seniority and benefits if they can prove that their initial job applications were rejected as a result of racial discrimination (March 24).

U.S. Supreme Court rules that private, nonreligious schools may not bar students solely on basis of race (June 25); Court also rules that 1866 Civil Rights Act protects whites as well as blacks from racial discrimination.

At the Democratic National Convention, held in New York City, at which Jimmy Carter, former governor of Georgia, is nominated, Barbara Jordan delivers one of two keynote speeches, first black ever to do so, and the Reverend Martin Luther King, Sr., delivers the benediction (July 12–15).

Secretary of Agriculture Earl Butz is forced to resign after the fact that he has told derogatory joke about blacks is made public (October 4).

Jimmy Carter becomes first President to be elected from Deep South since before the Civil War (November 2); wins with overwhelming black support in both North and South.

Women in American History

This chronology represents a sampling of the roles played by American women, particularly in relation to the attempt to achieve social, political, and economic equity. It should not be considered a survey or even an indication of the total contribution of women to the founding, growth, quality, or arts of the American nation.

1587 Virginia Dare is first English child born in what is now the United States, on Roanoke Island (August 18).

1608 First women recorded to have arrived in Jamestown, Virginia, are Mistress Forrest and her maid, Anne Burras.

1609 Twenty women and children arrive in Jamestown (August); within the next year at least another 100 women are on board ships heading to Jamestown plantation.

1614 Pocahontas, a hostage in Jamestown and beloved daughter of Powhatan, marries John Rolfe. John Smith later claims that Pocahontas, soon to become Lady Rebecca, had intervened during Smith's capture by the Indians and caused his life to be spared.

1619 House of Burgesses petitions London Company to grant equal lots of land to wives "because that in newe plantation it is not knowen whether man or woman be the most necessary"; the petition was granted.

1620 London Company has by now sent total of 140 unmarried women to Jamestown; planters who marry women pay 150 pounds of tobacco for each, to defray transportation costs; women are, according to company instructions, to be married only to "honest and sufficient men."

1637 In two separate trials (1637–38), one civil and one ecclesiastical, Anne Hutchinson is found guilty of heresy and banished from Massachusetts Bay Colony. A forceful and well-informed speaker, Hutchinson had succeeded in interesting a number of leading persons, including the colony's governor, in her ideas. She also urged that women be allowed to become preachers (Puritan doctrine was ambiguous on this point); she attracted a wide following among colonial women, speaking to gatherings as large as 60 women, a fact that deeply alarmed Puritan leaders.

1638 Margaret Brent arrives in Maryland, where she establishes manorial estates in her own name; in 1647 she becomes executor of estate of Governor Leonard Calvert; in 1648 she demands and is refused the right to vote in the colonial assembly.

1648 First woman convicted of witchcraft is executed in Massachusetts Bay Colony.

1656 First Quakers, Mary Fisher and Ann Austin, arrive in American colonies from England; Massachusetts authorities clap them in jail and then banish them.

1657 First American jury consisting entirely of women is empaneled in Maryland to try case of woman accused of murdering her child; jury finds accused not guilty.

1692 *Ornaments for the Daughters of Zion* by Cotton Mather is published in Cambridge, Massachusetts; originally written for the education of Mather's daughters, pamphlet cites many and varied roles, especially in the learned arts, played by women in antiquity; it also urges women not to overlook among other studies "arithmetic, accounting and such business matters."

Salem witch trials, based on accusations of a group of young girls, begin; most of those accused and most of those executed are women.

1696 Dinah Nuthead, who had inherited a printing press from her husband, successfully petitions Maryland assembly to allow her to act as public printer in capital, Annapolis; Nuthead herself was apparently unable to read or write but hired journeymen printers to set type while she managed the business affairs of the press.

1697 Hannah Dustin, a Haverhill, Massachusetts, housewife, is captured by Indians; while in custody she slips her bonds and tomahawks her captors—two braves, three women, and seven children, of whom she spares one wounded woman and one small child, scalping the rest in order to collect the bounty Massachusetts has set on Indian scalps.

1707 Henrietta Johnson of South Carolina becomes first woman painter in American colonies.

1715 Patent issued to "Thos. Masters, for an Invention found out by Sibylla his wife" for a method of cleaning and curing maize.

1718 Mary Butterworth of Massachusetts, using an ingenious cloth-copying process, becomes successful counterfeiter of paper money.

1733 Some New York City women place a notice in a New York newspaper, publicly calling attention to the fact that as taxpaying "she merchants" they "in some measure contribute to the support of the government [and] ought to be entitled to some of the sweets of it."

1737 While still a teen-ager Eliza Lucas Pinckney takes over management of her father's South Carolina plantation, expanding the holdings; by about 1745 she has almost single-handedly developed indigo as a cash crop in the southern mainland colonies.

1738   Elizabeth Timothy of South Carolina becomes first American woman to publish a newspaper, *South Carolina Gazette,* taking over after death of her husband.

1745   Christine Zeller of Lebanon, Pennsylvania, drives off band of attacking Indians, killing three with an ax.

1760   Barbara Heck founds Methodism in America, organizing first Methodist meetings and causing the first Methodist church in America to be built.

1774   In New York State, Ann Lee founds Shaker sect in America.

1776   New Jersey briefly extends franchise to women who meet property qualifications; franchise is later withdrawn.

       Abigail Smith Adams writes (March 31) to her husband, John, urging him to "remember the ladies" in any new code of laws he and the other patriots might draw up for the fledgling United States. "Do not," she says, "put such unlimited power into the hands of the husbands. Remember, all men would be tyrants if they could. If particular care and attention is not paid to the ladies, we are determined to foment a rebellion, and will not hold ourselves bound by any laws in which we have no voice or representation." Although Abigail Adams took a joshing tone in her letters to John on this subject, she was serious.

       Margaret Corbin earns right to be first woman to receive a Revolutionary War veteran's pension after being shot and lamed in combat against Hessian mercenaries.

1778   Mary Ludwig Hays—"Molly Pitcher"—becomes famous at Battle of Monmouth, first as water carrier and then by taking over cannon from fallen husband and continuing to fire on enemy.

1784   Hannah Adams, first American woman to attempt a career as a professional writer, publishes *An Alphabetical Compendium of the Sects.*

1794   Susanna Haswell Rowson writes *Charlotte, a Tale of Truth,* first best-selling American novel.

       Elizabeth Hog Bennett is operated on by her husband; operation is first successful Caesarean section.

1795   Sarah Waldrake and Rachael Summers become first women to work for new federal government; they are employed in Philadelphia mint.

The Colonial Period

Throughout the American colonies women were relatively scarce. In the southern colonies—particularly in Virginia—the initial settlements were almost exclusively a male enterprise. In the New England colonies, however, the first settlers were for the most part family units, and Puritan leaders usually insisted that married male immigrants bring their families with them.

Until about the middle of the eighteenth century American women were freer to engage in a broad range of occupations than at almost any time since then. Women were blacksmiths, gunsmiths, hunters, butchers, lawyers, innkeepers, silversmiths, ferrymen, and so on; a considerable number of women were midwives, and not a few practiced other forms of medicine, including "chirurgery" (surgery). In the Puritan New England colonies few distinctions based on sex alone were applied in the matter of education; it was not considered inappropriate that daughters learn Greek, Hebrew, or Latin. Before 1776 at least eleven women ran printing presses, and ten were newspaper publishers.

In Puritan New England especially, sexual relations seem to have been reasonably free of the various inhibitions associated with the nineteenth century and with Victorianism in particular; relationships were often entered into on the basis of mutual sexual attraction, wives were sometimes granted divorces for inadequate sexual performance by their husbands, and a good many Puritan women seem to have enjoyed nonspecialized roles within the family as mothers, sexual partners, business associates, and intellectual companions. In the southern colonies neither men nor women had yet settled into the pre-Civil War roles of southern gentleman and southern belle, and the primary social expectations there seem to have involved competence at a wide range of tasks.

In many colonial courts married and unmarried women could sue and be sued. Courts generally did not permit a husband to dispose of a wife's property without her consent. Women could and did enter into legal contracts. Some courts allowed wives to testify against their husbands, not automatically assuming that their interests were or should be identical.

By the mid-nineteenth century, however, the egalitarianism in some ways typical of earlier colonial America had begun to wane, especially within the middle class, though it persisted—of economic and social necessity—on the frontier.

1801   Boston Female Society for Propagating the Diffusion of Christian Knowledge is founded, first of several groups that will send missionaries to American Indians and abroad.

1804   In North Dakota, Sacajawea, a Shoshone woman, joins Lewis and Clark expedition as guide; with her two-month-old papoose on her back, she leads party from Fort Mandan, North Dakota, across the continental divide.

1807   New Jersey withdraws franchise from women.

1808   Elizabeth Ann Bayley Seton founds Sisters of Charity of St. Joseph; community moves to Emmitsburg, Maryland, in 1809.

1809   Dr. Ephraim McDowell operates on Jane Todd Crawford, performing first removal of ovarian tumor in medical history (December 13) in Danville, Kentucky; Crawford does not have the benefit of anesthetic but is up and about some five days later.

Mary Kies becomes first U.S. woman awarded a patent, for a method of weaving.

1818   Hannah Mather Crocker of Boston publishes *Observations on the Real Rights of Women,* in part modeled after *Vindication of the Rights of Women,* Mary Wollstonecraft's famous 1792 treatise.

1821   Emma Willard founds Troy Female Seminary, first institute of higher learning (a kind of advanced high school), in Troy, New York; it is later (1895) known as the Emma Willard School.

1825   In Troy, New York, Hannah Lord Montagu invents detachable shirt collar for men; she cut off several collars from her husband's shirts after getting tired of washing whole shirt when only collar was dirty.

First women's labor union, The United Tailoresses Society of New York, is founded. By 1831 it has more than 600 members.

1827   Sarah Josepha Hale becomes editor of *Ladies' Magazine* and first woman magazine editor.

1828   Needleworkers in Dover, New Hampshire, organize first labor strike by women in America; they strike against a wage cut and ten-hour day.

1833   Oberlin College, first co-educational college, opens as Oberlin Collegiate Institute, in Oberlin, Ohio.

1834   Hymn "Nearer, My God, to Thee" is composed by Sarah Flower Adams.

1836   Methodist missionary Dr. Marcus Whitman and his wife begin journey from St. Louis to Oregon (March 31) with another married couple; two wives are the first white women to make the overland wagon trek across plains and Rockies.

1837   *Ladies' Magazine* is absorbed by *Godey's Lady's Book*; under editorship of Sarah Josepha Hale *Godey's* becomes most influential women's publication in America.

Mount Holyoke College opens its doors as the South Hadley Female Seminary, in Massachusetts; founded by Mary Lyon, Mount Holyoke is first women's college in U.S. and is swamped with applicants.

1838   Angelina Grimké, bearing antislavery petitions signed by 20,000 Massachusetts women, addresses Massachusetts legislature; she explicitly connects abolitionist and feminist causes by asserting women's rights to involve themselves in antislavery issue because it is political and because women "are citizens of this republic and as such our honor, happiness and well-being are bound up in its politics, government, and laws."

Sarah Moore Grimké publishes in book form *Letters on the Equality of the Sexes and the Condition of Women.*

1840   Elizabeth Cady Stanton and Lucretia Mott are among the female delegates who travel to London to attend the World Anti-Slavery Convention, only to be refused admittance on account of their sex.

1843   Dorothea Dix publishes *Memorial to the Legislature of Massachusetts,* a description of conditions in insane asylums; Dix is influential in reform of these and other institutions.

1845   Margaret Fuller publishes *Woman in the Nineteenth Century,* hitting all the main feminist issues of the time; book is an expanded version of an essay she published in 1843 in the *The Dial,* transcendentalist publication of which she was the editor for several years.

1846   Under Sarah Bagley the Lowell Female Labor Reform Association, a labor organization formed in 1844 to combat deteriorating wages and conditions in New England mills, purchases *Voice of Industry,* a labor-oriented paper; *Voice* urges women to abjure "false delicacy" and fight—especially in and through primarily male unions—for higher wages and shorter hours.

1847   Astronomer Maria Mitchell discovers a comet.

1848   First Women's Rights Convention is held in Seneca Falls, New York (July 18–19); an unexpectedly large crowd of about 300, including about 40 men, gathers at the Wesleyan Chapel; because it is considered outrageous for a woman to preside over such a gathering, chairman is John Mott, husband of Lucretia Mott. Meeting gets a lot of publicity, most of it negative; one local newspaper calls it "the most shocking and unnatural incident ever recorded in the history of womanity."

Boston Female Medical School, first of its kind in U.S., is founded.

New York passes Married Women's Property Act, one of first laws affording women some legal protection over property possessed in their own right.

1849   Lydia Sayer Hasbrouck, who later becomes editor of feminist publication *The Sibyl,* fights against current women's fashions by publicly appearing in style later publicized by Amelia Bloomer.

Elizabeth Blackwell becomes first woman in America to earn modern medical degree, at Geneva Medical School of western New York. She later (1857) establishes a private clinic in New York City that becomes New York Infirmary and College for Women.

1850   Women's Medical College of Pennsylvania is founded as Female Medical College of Pennsylvania.

1851   First National Woman's Rights Convention meets in Worcester, Massachusetts (October 23–24); this is first gathering of women specifically concerned with achieving vote for women.

1852   Susan B. Anthony organizes first New York women's temperance society.

Harriet Beecher Stowe's *Uncle Tom's Cabin* is published in book form (March 20).

1853   Antoinette "Nette" Brown Blackwell is ordained a minister in Congregational Church of South Butler, New York, thus becoming first woman minister of recognized church in U.S.

Mount Vernon Ladies' Association is organized for purpose of buying Mount Vernon, George Washington's estate, for national shrine; association ultimately raises $200,000 and makes purchase in 1859.

Rebecca Pennell conducts classes as professor of physical geography and other subjects at Antioch College, which has this year also opened its doors to female students; Pennell has same professional prerogatives as male colleagues, first woman professor to achieve this equality.

1855   Reformers and women's-rights advocates Henry Blackwell and Lucy Stone marry and publish document in which they jointly protest current laws giving the husband (1) "custody of the wife's person," (2) exclusive custody of children born of the marriage, (3) exclusive ownership or use of the wife's property (unless that property has been placed in trust), and (4) a larger share of a deceased wife's property than a widow would get of her husband's property if he died intestate; document also criticizes legal system that in many states prevents a married woman from making a will, inheriting property, and suing in court; document urges all married couples to submit marital disputes to mutually chosen arbitrators and to avoid all "legal tribunals."

1856   Mrs. Joshua Patten, nineteen, takes command of clipper ship *Neptune's Car,* bringing it into San Francisco Bay from Cape Horn when the captain, her husband, became ill; the first mate had been clapped in the brig, and the second mate could not navigate, so Mrs. Patten did it all.

University of Iowa becomes first public university to admit women as students.

1860   At tenth annual National Woman's Rights Convention some successes are noted, especially those relating to property laws (in five states—Indiana, Maine, Missouri, Ohio, and New York—married women now have right to keep money they earn); Elizabeth Cady Stanton drops bombshell, however, by proposing that divorce laws be liberalized (for the most part a woman lost home and children in a divorce, regardless of cause, and was usually unable to initiate divorce proceedings); issue sets up fierce split among feminists, many of whom consider divorce—or even discussion of it—immoral.

Female shoe workers participate in strike and demonstration in Lynn, Massachusetts; strike ultimately involves nearly 20,000 workers. In northeastern factories 65 per cent of work force are either women or children under twelve.

Sculptor Harriet G. Hosmer's statue *Puck* becomes enormously popular; she employs twenty stonecutters to make reproductions.

1863   Recruiting posters for Civil War army nurses require that applicants be at least 30 and be "very plain-looking women."

1865   Mary Surratt is tried and executed for her never substantially proven role in the conspiracy to assassinate President Abraham Lincoln.

Vassar College, in Poughkeepsie, New York, first of full-program women's colleges, opens its doors to students.

Belle Boyd, Confederate spy now living in England, writes autobiographical account, *Belle Boyd, in Camp and Prison.*

Maria Mitchell becomes first woman professor of astronomy, at Vassar.

1866   First American Young Women's Christian Association is formed in Boston.

Victoria Woodhull and sister Tennie C. Claflin open

first Wall Street brokerage house owned and managed by women; business is highly successful for a time, in part because Cornelius Vanderbilt is known to have financial interest in the firm.

Lucy Hobbs is first woman to earn degree in dentistry, from Ohio College of Dental Surgery.

1867   Mary Louise Booth becomes editor of newly formed *Harper's Bazaar* magazine; she remains its editor for 22 years.

Pennsylvania College of Dental Surgery graduates its first woman dentist.

1868   First issue of *The Revolution* appears (January 1); edited by Elizabeth Cady Stanton and managed and published by Susan B. Anthony, paper consistently takes up controversial feminist causes, linking them in public mind with suffrage, and thus is one source of the split between more radical New York feminists (Stanton, Anthony, Lucretia Mott) and more moderate Boston group (headed by Lucy Stone and enjoying support of prominent male reformers, including Horace Greeley).

1869   Women's movement formally splits, with New York group forming National Woman's Suffrage Association and Boston group forming American Woman Suffrage Association, which is open to men and has Henry Ward Beecher as its first president. National group concerns itself with all issues affecting women, including a new federal constitutional amendment for suffrage; American eschews most controversial feminist issues and concentrates on getting suffrage at state and local levels.

Catharine Beecher publishes *The American Woman's Home: or Principles of domestic science; being a guide to the formation and maintenance of economical, healthful, beautiful and Christian homes*; book is very influential in providing sensible "how-to" information about nutrition, child rearing, health, cooking, ventilation and furnishing of homes, etc. Catharine Beecher, like many women of talent and accomplishment, was uninterested in and somewhat critical of the suffrage movement.

Daughters of St. Crispin, first national women's labor union, is organized by shoe workers in Lynn, Massachusetts; Carrie Wilson becomes first president.

1870   Sophia Smith provides in her will for the establishment of a college for women: "It is my opinion that by the higher and more thoroughly Christian education of women, what are called their 'wrongs' will be redressed, their wages will be adjusted, their weight of influence in reforming the evils of society will be greatly increased; as teachers, as writers, as mothers, as members of society, their power for good will be incalculably enlarged."

Radicals and Moderates

The Fifteenth Amendment, which granted suffrage to black males, was sent to the states for ratification in February, 1869. Moderate feminists reluctantly agreed that Reconstruction was and should be "the Negro's hour" and worked for the ratification of this amendment. However, the fact that males were willing to grant political equality to illiterate former slaves but not to the educated middle-class women who formed the backbone of the women's-rights movement profoundly wounded such women and radicalized not a few of them, including Elizabeth Cady Stanton, who came to believe that men could never be trusted in relation to issues impinging on the rights and aspirations of women.

The more radical feminists like Stanton and Anthony were less than enthusiastic about the Fifteenth Amendment and were now suspicious of male participation in the women's-rights movement. Furthermore, they increasingly felt that a woman's right to vote was only one of several important issues that deserved attention and began to consider profound and controversial questions having to do with social definitions of the home and family, appropriate occupational roles, a woman's sexual rights with respect to her husband or males in general, and other of the feminist issues that later surfaced again as part of the women's-liberation movement of the 1960's and 1970's.

Such differences between the moderate and radical wings of the organized women's-rights movement, as well as certain personal estrangements among some leading moderates and radicals, contributed to the formal split that occurred in 1869 and was not healed until 1890.

Ellen Swallow, Vassar graduate with degree in chemistry, is admitted to Massachusetts Institute of Technology; although she gains an M.S. there, Swallow quits M.I.T., claiming that instructors have blocked her progress toward Ph.D. because they do not want first M.I.T. doctorate in chemistry to go to a woman.

Claflin sisters publish *Woodhull and Claflin's Weekly,* radical feminist journal espousing free love, women's rights, legalized prostitution, spiritualism, and a variety of other causes, in New York City.

1871   Catharine Beecher publishes *Woman Suffrage and Woman's Profession,* in which she argues that it is more important for women to acquire professional-level skills in the home-management arts than to gain the vote.

Victoria Claflin Woodhull testifies before House Judiciary Committee that in her opinion the Fourteenth Amendment confers upon women the right to vote; it is the first time Congress formally considers issue of woman suffrage.

1872   Louisa Lee Schuyler forms New York State Charities Aid Association.

Victoria Claflin Woodhull nominated by Equal Rights Party as candidate for Presidency of U.S.; party nominates Frederick Douglass for Vice President.

1873   Susan B. Anthony is tried and convicted of violating laws of the state of New York by registering and voting in 1872 election; she is sentenced to $100 fine and court costs, which she refuses to pay: "All the stock in trade I possess is a debt of $10,000 incurred by publishing my paper—*The Revolution*—the sole object of which was to educate all women to do precisely as I have done, rebel against your man-made, unjust, unconstitutional forms of law, which tax, fine, imprison and hang women, while denying them the right of representation in the government; and I will work on with might and main to pay every dollar of that honest debt, but not a penny shall go to this unjust claim."

1874   Mary Outerbridge plays first lawn-tennis match in America, on Staten Island in New York City; Outerbridge introduced game to U.S. from Bermuda.

1875   Lydia Pinkham produces famous "female remedy" patent medicine.

Smith College opens its doors in Northampton, Massachusetts.

1876   Professional acrobat Maria Spelterini walks across tightrope stretched across Niagara Falls.

1877   Helen Magill gets Ph.D. in Greek from Boston University, becoming first woman to be awarded doctorate by an American university.

1879   Frances Willard becomes president of Women's Christian Temperance Union (WCTU); a strong feminist, Willard persuades conservative WCTU to back suffrage movement and is responsible for making WCTU a powerful engine of reform.

Belva Bennett Lockwood is first woman lawyer to argue a case before U.S. Supreme Court.

Mary Baker Eddy, author of *Science and Health with Key to the Scriptures,* founds First Church of Christ, Scientist, in Boston.

The 1880's and 1890's

In the 1880's and 1890's relatively large numbers of middle-class women were entering colleges and universities. By 1886 there were 266 women's colleges, 207 co-educational institutions, and 56 specialized technical and professional schools that accepted women. Some highly educated women found appropriate professional places. For example, perhaps as many as five hundred women had become dentists by 1890, and one of them, Elizabeth Morey, invented the dental cap. But the opportunity for educated women to employ college-acquired skills remained fairly limited.

As a result some of the brightest and most ambitious college graduates entered the foreign-missionary movement. This movement, which had its beginnings in the early 1800's, had ceased to be a male-dominated affair by the mid-nineteenth century and had expanded into a worldwide organization providing educational and health services. In many countries of Africa and Asia, American women were teachers, doctors, and administrators in thousands of mission-supported institutions providing, among other things, what was probably the best free elementary or secondary education available anywhere in the world. Many of the twentieth-century leaders in the so-called Third World received their primary educations in mission schools.

At home some educated women went into the settlement-house movement. The settlement houses, of which Jane Addams' Hull House in Chicago and Lillian Wald's Henry Street Settlement in New York City are perhaps the best-known examples, offered a broad range of social services to the poor, services later institutionalized by various state and federal agencies and performed by professional social workers, many of whom continue to be women. The settlement houses played an important role in easing the transition of many immigrant poor people into the fabric of American life and also provided the means by which numbers of talented young women could lead useful, rewarding lives rich in companionship.

A third major outlet for female talent was the club movement, including organizations like the Women's Christian Temperance Union, whose reform and social-service activities extended far beyond the temperance issue. The club movement, consisting by 1900 of many local and state groups loosely organized into a national organization, had a total membership greatly outnumbering that of the suffrage or feminist organizations. Though largely conservative with respect to feminist issues, this membership threw itself into most of the progressive reforms—from conservation to the Pure Food and Drug Act—and was one of the principal supporters of charitable and legislative efforts to improve the living and working conditions of lower-class women and children.

Illinois passes labor law barring women from employment in coal mines.

By this year about 35,000 American women are enrolled in various colleges and other institutions of higher learning and constitute one third of collegiate student body in U.S.

1880   The saying "The hand that rocks the cradle rules the world" comes into wide use, in some ways replacing the quote from *Hamlet* ("Frailty, thy name is woman") against which Margaret Fuller and others inveighed in the pre-Civil War era.

1881   Clara Barton organizes and becomes president of American Red Cross, U.S. branch of the International Red Cross; she is primarily responsible for policy shift enabling Red Cross to become active in domestic emergencies unrelated to war.

Helen Hunt Jackson publishes *A Century of Dishonor,* a savage indictment of policies toward American Indians and revelation of the desperate conditions on reservations.

Louise Blanchard Bethune becomes first woman architect in U.S., opening an office in Buffalo, New York.

1883   American Anti-Vivisection Society is founded by Caroline Earle White in Philadelphia.

1884   In San Francisco, Equal Rights Party nominates Belva Bennett Lockwood for President; vice-presidential nominee is Amarietta Stow.

1885   Playground for children is created by Boston women's group, which has a large pile of sand dumped in the yard of the Children's Mission on Parmenter Street; before this time no provision for organized outdoor play areas for children had been made in U.S.

Annie Oakley joins Buffalo Bill's Wild West show and becomes one of its stars.

1886   The poet Emily Dickinson dies in Amherst, Massachusetts (May 15).

Women get right to vote in Kansas municipal elections.

1887　Susanna Salter is first woman to be elected mayor of a U.S. town, Argonia, Kansas; her name was placed on the ballot by the Women's Christian Temperance Union without her knowledge, and she got two thirds of all votes cast.

1889　Jane Addams and her friend Ellen Starr open Hull House, at 335 Halsted Street, in a Chicago slum area; the Hull House settlement, ultimately comprising fourteen buildings, provided many immigrant children with their first exposure to books, magazines, and art, as well as to nourishing food and fresh-air play; Hull House ran day-care centers for working mothers and organized self-help classes of various sorts for all age groups, including the old, who had many remunerative folk-art skills.

Journalist Elizabeth Cochrane Seaman ("Nellie Bly") beats fictional Jules Verne around-the-world record of 80 days by making trip in 72 days, 6 hours, and 11 minutes.

1890　General Federation of Women's Clubs is organized. By 1892 its membership included 190 clubs, with 20,000 members; by 1900 it had about 150,000 members and had become one of most influential women's organizations.

National Woman's Suffrage Association and American Woman Suffrage Association merge as National American Woman Suffrage Association (NAWSA), with Elizabeth Cady Stanton (75) as president, Susan B. Anthony (70) as vice president, and Lucy Stone (72) as chairman of executive committee.

Wyoming is admitted to statehood, with a constitution granting woman suffrage (as a territory Wyoming had allowed women to vote since 1869).

1891　Josephine Shaw Lowell is principal founder of Consumer's League and becomes its first president; movement is primarily concerned with bettering pay rates and working conditions of women; it agitates for various reforms and publishes annual "white lists," lists with names of stores having acceptable labor policies, urging public to patronize only such approved stores.

1892　Elizabeth Cady Stanton addresses House Judiciary Committee; instead of rehashing suffrage arguments, of which she is heartily tired, she gives a great and lovely speech, "The Solitude of Self," in which she sums up her reasons for a long lifetime's work in the cause of women's rights.

Elizabeth Cady Stanton retires from the NAWSA.

1895　First volume of *The Woman's Bible*, with translations made under editorship of Elizabeth Cady Stanton,

appears and creates a scandal; it analyzes biblical passages usually cited as support for keeping women subordinate and analyzes them not as the word of God but as writings and compilations of men, patriarchs at that.

From "The Solitude of Self" by Elizabeth Cady Stanton:

"No matter how much women prefer to lean, to be protected and supported, nor how much men desire to have them do so, they must take the voyage of life alone. . . . The talk of sheltering woman from the fierce storms of life is the sheerest mockery, for they beat on her from every point of the compass, just as they do on man. . . .

"Whatever the theories may be of woman's dependence on man, in the supreme moments of her life he can not bear her burdens. . . . We may have many friends, love, kindness, sympathy and charity to smooth our pathway in everyday life, but in the tragedies and triumphs of human experience each mortal stands alone.

"But when all artificial trammels are removed, and women recognized as individuals . . . thoroughly educated for all positions in life they may be called to fill; with all the resources in themselves that liberal thought and broad culture can give . . . and stimulated to self-support by a knowledge of the business world and the pleasure that pecuniary independence must ever give; when women are trained in this way they will, in a measure, be fitted for those years of solitude that come to all, whether prepared or otherwise."

1896　Evylyn Thomas, a bicyclist in New York City, earns unfortunate distinction of being first person in America to be run over by an automobile; she suffers fractured leg as a result of collision with a Duryea Motor Wagon.

1898　Charlotte Perkins Gilman publishes *Women and Economics,* a classic analysis that still deserves to be read.

1899　Generva Mudge becomes first woman automobile racer, participating in a New York City race; her Locomobile spins out into several spectators.

1900　General Federation of Women's Clubs denies a delegate's seat to Mrs. Josephine St. Pierre Ruffin, a Massachusetts black woman active in Massachusetts club affairs, thus resolving a major tactical and philosophical crisis in GFWC; organization decides to exclude black women in order to keep and gain support among southern clubwomen.

Divorce rate in U.S. is 4 per 1,000 marriages; two thirds of these are granted to wives; rate is more than twice as high as the highest in Europe.

1901 General Federation of Women's Clubs is granted national charter by U.S. Congress.

Anna Taylor becomes first woman to go over Niagara Falls in a barrel; she is one of few, male or female, to survive such an attempt.

Everleigh sisters open Everleigh Club in Chicago; one of most famous and lavish brothels in the world, club featured, among other high-priced attractions, solid gold spittoons.

1903 National Women's Trade Union League is organized in Boston by, among others, Mary Kenney O'Sullivan, a unionist with strong ties to the settlement-house movement.

Maggie Lena Walker founds the Saint Luke Penny Savings Bank in Richmond, Virginia; a black, Walker becomes first woman bank president in U.S.

1906 Elsie Parsons publishes *The Family,* a scholarly anthropological and sociological study that gains popular notoriety because it contains a suggestion that trial marriages might be encouraged.

1908 Rose Knox becomes president of Knox Company, a gelatin-manufacturing firm, after the death of her husband; she later institutes five-day work week and other reforms and more than trebles assets of the business between 1908 and 1915.

1910 Emily James Putnam, a classics scholar and first dean of Barnard College, publishes *The Lady,* a historical study of upper-class women from Grecian times to the ante-bellum South.

1912 Harvard astronomer Henrietta Leavitt publishes analysis of "period-luminosity" phenomenon having to do with relative energy and brightness of stars and later playing important role in calculations of the dimensions of the Milky Way galaxy and ultimately of the universe.

Juliette Gordon Low founds Girl Scouts in America, at first known as the Girl Guides.

Annie Peck becomes first person to climb 21,250-foot Mount Coropuna in Peru; Peck, who is 61 years old, plants "Votes for Women" banner at summit.

1913 Anna Garlin Spencer publishes *Woman's Share in Social Culture,* a wide-ranging study of role of women in human culture.

Alice Paul, Crystal Eastman, and Lucy Burns form the militant Congressional Union for Woman Suffrage

and march 5,000 women through Washington, D.C., on day before inauguration of Woodrow Wilson; marchers are subjected to mob violence.

1914 Margaret Sanger publishes *Woman Rebel,* which is seized as obscene because it includes the new term "birth control" and relates several circumstances in which birth control should be practiced.

For first time General Federation of Women's Clubs passes resolution in support of woman suffrage; this vote is an indication that suffrage has become respectable and safely divorced from its long association with other feminist issues, especially those having to do with marriage, family, divorce, and sex.

1915 Woman's Peace Party is organized (January 19); platform urges speedy end to World War I through a conference of neutral nations and an eventual end to all war by various means, including the creation of an international police force. Jane Addams is elected party chairman.

1916 Henrietta "Hetty" Green, reputedly the richest woman in America, dies; she substantially increased a fortune inherited from her family, through long career as financier and speculator.

1917 Mary Lathrop becomes first woman member of the American Bar Association.

Jeannette Rankin, Republican from Montana, becomes first woman to sit in U.S. Congress. She casts a nay vote against America's entry into World War I, for which she is defeated next term; she also casts the only nay vote in the House of Representatives against World War II, for which she is again defeated.

For second time Carrie Chapman Catt becomes president of National American Woman Suffrage Association; she engineers successful national campaign to finally get vote; campaign is a masterful, expensive job involving efforts of perhaps 2 million women and expenditure of many millions of dollars.

Alice Paul, whose Congressional Union for Woman Suffrage has now become equally militant National Women's Party, some of whose members are Quakers and opposed to World War I, begins with other militants to picket White House, demanding suffrage, attacking "Kaiser Wilson," and later expressing antiwar sentiments; pickets are beaten, brutalized, and jailed, beginning in June. In order not to jeopardize suffrage campaign Carrie Chapman Catt and National American Woman Suffrage Association condone brutal treatment of militants but continue to put pressure on President Wilson.

1918 Margaret Sage, philanthropist, dies; she gave away

about $80 million to various causes.

President Wilson urges Senate to pass a woman-suffrage law as "vital to the winning of the war" (September 30).

1920   Nineteenth Amendment, giving women right to vote, is ratified (August 26).

1922   Rebecca Latimer Felton of Georgia, 88, is first woman to occupy a seat in U.S. Senate (November 21); she is appointed to fill vacancy caused by death of incumbent and serves one day, then resigning her seat to newly elected candidate for vacancy.

Florence Allen is first woman judge in America to sentence a man to death.

1923   Through the efforts of Alice Paul first equal-rights amendment is introduced in Congress; it does not pass.

1924   Nellie Ross Taylor is elected governor of Wyoming (November 4) following death of her husband; on taking office in January, 1925, she became first woman governor.

Studies made of the 1922 and 1924 elections show that women are not voting as a bloc and that married women are not voting in greater numbers than their husbands or voting in opposition to them; as a result most political leaders write women off as a political force to be reckoned with.

1928   Amelia Earhart is first woman to fly across the Atlantic; in 1932 she is first woman to fly nonstop across U.S. and in 1935 becomes first woman to fly solo across the Pacific—an eighteen-hour flight from Honolulu to Oakland, California. In 1937 she disappears in Pacific during attempt to fly around the world.

1929   Mrs. Dorothy Eustis becomes president of Seeing Eye organization, which she founded to train dogs to lead the blind.

Josephine Roche becomes president of the Rocky Mountain Fuel Company, a large western coal company; immediately after gaining control of the company she encouraged the miners to unionize; she raised wages and at the same time decreased operating costs and introduced enlightened marketing procedures.

1930   Helen Church becomes first airline stewardess.

1933   Dorothy Day is instrumental in founding the Catholic Worker movement, out of which came the *Catholic Worker,* a radical, anticapitalist, anti-Communist monthly newspaper, and a variety of facilities dispensing food, clothing, and shelter to the poor.

Mary R. Beard publishes *America Through Women's Eyes,* an important collection of diaries and other documents relating women's historical experience in America.

Ruth Bryan Owen becomes first female diplomatic minister when Franklin D. Roosevelt appoints her envoy extraordinary and minister plenipotentiary to Denmark and Iceland.

President Roosevelt appoints Frances Perkins Secretary of Labor; she is first woman cabinet officer.

1936   Mary McLeod Bethune, president and founder of Bethune-Cookman College, is appointed director of Division of Negro Affairs in the National Youth Administration.

1938   Julia Cherry Spruill publishes *Women's Life and Work in the Southern Colonies,* a valuable work of scholarship on seventeenth- and eighteenth-century colonial America.

1939   Eleanor Patterson forms Washington *Times-Herald,* which by 1943 is city's largest. Patterson had a reputation for executive ruthlessness that led *Time* to call her "the most hated woman in America."

1947   Florence Blanchfield is commissioned a colonel in U.S. Army, first woman to receive regular army commission.

1948   Eleanor Roosevelt, as chairman of the UN Commission on Human Rights, plays major role in drafting and getting the United Nations to adopt the Universal Declaration of Human Rights.

1950   Senator Margaret Chase Smith, Republican from Maine, is one of few in Senate to speak out against Senator Joseph McCarthy: "I don't want to see the Republican Party ride to political victory on the Four Horsemen of Calumny—Fear, Ignorance, Bigotry, and Smear."

1953   Frances Willis, career diplomat, is first foreign-service professional to achieve rank of ambassador (to Switzerland).

Dr. Alfred Kinsey's *Sexual Behavior in the Human Female* is published; data reveal that nearly 50 per cent of American women studied (statistical analysis based on 5,940 cases) had engaged in premarital intercourse, 26 per cent had had extramarital relationships, 62 per cent practiced masturbation, and 20 per cent had had some homosexual experience; study provokes heavy criticism.

Oveta Culp Hobby is appointed Secretary of Health, Education, and Welfare.

1955   There are now sixteen female members of U.S. House

of Representatives and two female U.S. senators.

1960 Women now make up 24.2 per cent of all college presidents, professors, and instructors, down from the 1930 peak of 31.9 per cent; women make up 2.3 per cent of all dentists, down 3.3 per cent from 1920; women make up 6.9 per cent of all physicians, up from 5.0 per cent in 1920 and 4.4 per cent in the 1930's and 4.7 per cent in the 1940's; 6.9 per cent of industrial managers are women, which represents a slow but steady gain since the 1.7 per cent of 1910; 36.6 per cent of editors and reporters are women, also a steady increase from the 12.2 per cent of 1910. There are 23,272,000 women in the labor force, representing 32.3 per cent of the total force and about 38 per cent of all women of working age; of these working women 30.5 per cent are married.

1961 President Kennedy establishes Commission on the Status of Women to find out why educated women are being underutilized in economy; commission eventually discovers widespread discrimination in professions and begins to reveal whole pattern of unequal job opportunity.

Jane Jacobs publishes *The Death and Life of Great American Cities*; pioneering book speaks out powerfully against destructive forms of urban renewal and against forms of urban planning that tend to destroy vital neighborhoods.

1962 Rachel Carson publishes *The Silent Spring,* a book that in effect launches modern environmental concern.

1963 Betty Friedan publishes *The Feminine Mystique,* a book that is usually considered to have initiated the modern women's-rights movement.

Congress passes Equal Pay Act (June 10), which requires equal pay for equal work in industries engaged in interstate commerce.

1964 Civil Rights Act of 1964 (July 2): Title VII of this act prohibits discrimination in employment on the basis of sex and sets up Equal Opportunity Commission to monitor compliance and investigate complaints.

Alice Rossi publishes "Equality Between the Sexes: An Immodest Proposal," one of the pioneering essays on the subject.

1966 The National Organization for Women (NOW) is formed in Washington, D.C.; Betty Friedan is elected first president. The particular concern of NOW is the achievement of equal representation for women in all jobs and equality in pay rates.

1968 Dr. Elizabeth Boyer and others form Women's Equity Action League (WEAL) after policy disagreement with NOW about making abortion-law repeal part of official program.

1969 Cornell University offers first women's-studies course.

Diana Crump becomes first female jockey to race at major U.S. track.

1970 Elizabeth P. Hoisington (Women's Army Corps) and Anna Mae Hays (Army Nurse Corps) become first women generals in U.S. Army (June 11).

In Women's Strike for Equality (August 26) mass demonstrations are held in several cities to dramatize demand for equality of job opportunity, free 24-hour day-care service, and free abortions on demand.

Median income for women is $5,440 as opposed to $9,184 for men.

Shulamith Firestone publishes *The Dialectic of Sex,* one of the important documents of the women's-liberation movement.

1971 National Women's Political Caucus (NWPC) is formed in Washington, D.C.

1972 *New York Times* predicts that American women will bear an average of 2.08 children during 1970's, a rate somewhat below the replacement level; should this rate continue for 70 years, the U.S. will achieve zero population growth.

Joann Pierce and Susan Lynn Roley become first female FBI agents.

Senate approves Equal Rights Amendment (House had approved ERA in 1971) and passes amendment to states for ratification; initial reaction by state legislatures is favorable.

Equal Employment Opportunity Act specifically gives Equal Opportunity Commission power to force compliance through court action in sex-discrimination cases.

U.S. Supreme Court rules that a state may require a woman to use her husband's surname on certain documents (case involved an Alabama married woman who wished to take out a driver's license in her own name).

1973 American Telephone and Telegraph (ATT) is ordered to pay damages of $15 million in back pay to female employees as result of discriminatory salary practices.

"Ms." receives approval as an acceptable title from the Government Printing Office.

U.S. Supreme Court declares current antiabortion laws unconstitutional.

Women now make up 44.7 per cent of total U.S. work

force; 15 per cent are in professional or technical class; salary differences between men and women in the same jobs range up to 20 per cent.

1974   Ella Grasso of Connecticut is first woman to be elected governor of a state in her own right (November 5).

Of the 19,440,000 families classified as poor by the U.S. Census Bureau, 10,877,000 are headed by males, and 8,563,000 are headed by females. Of families headed by women, 24.9 per cent of those headed by white women are poor, and 52.8 per cent of those headed by black women are poor.

1975   Women outnumber men 109,377,000 to 103,760,000 as of mid-July; this disparity is partly a result of longer female life span (an average of 74.6 years, almost 8 years greater than average male life expectancy).

Average annual salaries of female faculty members in public and private universities are $14,710 and $12,968, respectively; average male salaries are $17,558 and $16,676, respectively. The disparity between male and female salaries has increased slightly in the past three years.

Elizabeth Ann Bayley Seton is elevated to sainthood by the Roman Catholic Church (September 14); she is first U.S.-born person to be canonized.

The percentage gap between female and male median incomes has increased by approximately 2 per cent since 1970, so that the average female worker earns only 57 per cent of what the average male earns.

Mary P. Ryan publishes *Womanhood in America: From Colonial Times to the Present,* a powerful, complex survey of the social-historical role of American women.

1976   Barbara Walters becomes the first woman to co-anchor a prime-time national news program, reportedly at a salary of $1 million a year.

As result of suits by Equal Employment Opportunity Commission nation's largest stock brokerage agrees to pay $1.9 million in damages to minority and female employees it had underpaid or underpromoted; company also agrees to institute $1.3 million five-year affirmative-action program.

According to the Center for the American Woman and Politics at Rutgers, less than 5 per cent of all elective offices in the U.S. are held by women.

The Equal Rights Amendment ("equality of rights under the law shall not be denied or abridged by the United States or by any state on account of sex"), proposed in 1971, is running into increasingly stiff opposition, although 34 states out of a needed 38 have approved it.

The United States in Space

With the exception of several pioneering Soviet efforts and later joint U.S.-U.S.S.R. ventures, only major U.S. space achievements are included here. Unless otherwise noted the initial date in parentheses is the launch date.

1957   *Sputnik 1* (October 4): Soviet satellite, first human artifact to achieve orbit around the earth, weighs 184 pounds.

       Sputnik 2 (November 3): 1,120-pound Soviet satellite carries dog, Laika.

1958   *Explorer 1* (January 31): first U.S. satellite, weighing 18 pounds, detects Van Allen belts.

       Vanguard 1 (March 17): 3¼-pound satellite confirms slight irregularities in the earth's shape.

       National Aeronautics and Space Administration (NASA) formed (July 29).

       Pioneer 1 (October 11): aimed at moon, rocket gets 70,700 miles from earth, a record at this time.

       Score (December 18): Atlas missile weighing more than 8,700 pounds is placed in orbit.

1959   NASA picks seven astronauts for Mercury program from ranks of military test pilots (April 9).

       Explorer 6 (August 7): 142-pound satellite is first to be a complete NASA operation from start to finish; all previous U.S. space ventures were essentially army or navy operations.

1960   *Tiros 1* (April 1): first U.S. weather satellite takes almost 23,000 photographs of earth's cloud cover.

       Discoverer 13 (August 10): first orbiting payload to be recovered from outer space is fished out of Pacific on August 11.

1961   *Vostok 1* (April 12): Soviet Major Yuri Gagarin becomes first human being to orbit the earth.

       Mercury 2 (May 5): Commander Alan B. Shepard, Jr., is first American in space; suborbital flight lasts about 15 minutes and takes Shepard about 116 miles above earth.

1962   *Mercury 6* (February 20): Colonel John H. Glenn, Jr., becomes first American to orbit the earth.

       Telstar 1 (July 10): solar-powered communications satellite, developed and owned by International Telephone and Telegraph Company and Bell Laboratories, is world's first, at least for civilian use; relays TV signals from U.S. to France and Britain.

Mariner 2 (August 27): after in-flight connection, unmanned probe passes within 21,645 miles of Venus after 180-million-mile journey and transmits (December 14) first fly-by information about planet, including amazingly high (800°F) surface temperature.

1963   *Telstar 2* (May 7): second communications satellite can relay color TV signals between U.S. and Europe.

       Mercury 9 (May 15): Major L. Gordon Cooper becomes first American to remain in space for more than 24 hours (22-orbit flight lasts about 34 hours).

       Vostok 6 (June 16): Soviet Valentina V. Tereshkova, first woman in space, makes 48 orbits, remaining in space almost three days (approximately 71 hours).

       Syncom 2 (July 26): second of series of communications satellites designed to achieve synchronous earth orbit (at a distance of about 22,000 miles from earth, satellite makes one revolution per day, so it in effect stays over same point on earth's surface), *Syncom 2* achieves synchronous orbit August 15 and transmits radio signals between U.S. and Nigeria; *Syncom 2* is first to function; *Syncom 3* is launched August 19, 1964.

1964   *Echo 2* (January 25): communications satellite is first joint U.S.-Soviet space venture.

       Ranger 7 (July 28): crashes on moon (July 31); transmits 4,316 photographs of moon before impacting; previous Rangers have malfunctioned or have otherwise not provided as much data as expected, but subsequent 1965 missions (*Ranger 8* and *Ranger 9*) send back more than 13,000 photos, some extremely detailed, before crashing.

       Nimbus 1 (August 28): first of series of weather satellites designed to achieve circular orbit around earth and relay information on cloud cover.

1965   *Gemini 3* (March 23): Virgil I. Grissom and John W. Young are first to maneuver a manned spacecraft out of its original orbital path; *Gemini 3* is first U.S. two-man flight.

       Early Bird (April 6): first commercial communications satellite, owned by private consortium, relays telephone, teletype, and television signals.

       Gemini 4 (June 3): four-day flight by James A. McDivitt and Edward H. White II is marked by first U.S. space walk, White spending twenty minutes outside space capsule.

       Mariner 4 approaches Mars (July 15); begins transmitting photos; gets to within 6,000 miles of "red planet."

Gemini 7 (December 4): Frank Borman and James A. Lovell, Jr., remain in space for fourteen days in longest flight yet; *Gemini 7* is met by *Gemini* 6A eleven days after launch.

Gemini 6A (December 15): Walter M. Schirra, Jr., and Thomas P. Stafford achieve first space rendezvous; *Gemini* 6A comes within one foot of *Gemini 7* and flies along with it, demonstrating feasibility of docking.

1966 *Gemini 8* (March 16): Neil A. Armstrong and David R. Scott achieve first docking of two space vehicles; malfunction causes docked craft to tumble, but mission is aborted safely.

Surveyor 1 (May 30): makes soft landing on moon June 2; transmits about 11,000 close-up photos of moon; six more Surveyors are launched (1966–68).

Lunar Orbiter 1 (August 10): sent into orbit around moon August 14 with purpose of investigating landing sites; sends back TV pictures and also takes first pictures of earth as it appears from moon.

Lunar Orbiter 2 (November 6): goes into moon orbit November 17; discovers mascons, high-density concentrations of matter beneath lunar surface.

1967 *Apollo 1*: astronauts Virgil I. Grissom, Edward H. White II, and Roger B. Chaffee are killed (January 27) when sudden fire flashes through Apollo capsule during ground tests at Cape Kennedy, Florida. These are the only astronauts to die in U.S. space program.

Outer Space Treaty signed by U.S. (January 27); treaty, embodying principles of 1963 UN declaration, stipulates that no nation may claim sovereignty over a celestial body (moon or other planets), prohibits military use of outer space, provides for return of astronauts or equipment forced to land on foreign territory, and makes launching country liable for any damage caused by its rockets, satellites, or other space vehicles. U.S.S.R. and 58 other countries are signatories.

Mariner 5 (June 14): flies by Venus (October 19) and confirms high temperature and carbon-dioxide atmosphere.

1968 *Apollo 8* (December 21): Frank Borman, James A. Lovell, Jr., and William A. Anders make first flight to the moon; command module orbits moon ten times (December 24–25) and broadcasts TV views of moon and earth; Apollo module returns safely December 27. Flight is first in which human beings can see earth as it appears from a vantage point more than 200,000 miles in space; astronauts at one point jokingly ask: "Is it inhabited?"

1969 *Apollo 11* (July 16): astronauts Neil A. Armstrong and Edwin E. Aldrin, Jr., make first landing on the moon in lunar module *Eagle* on July 20. Armstrong becomes first human being to set foot on moon and is soon joined by Aldrin; live TV broadcasts are sent back to earth, where an estimated audience of 600 million people around the world watch astronauts set up experimental equipment and collect samples from lunar surface. *Eagle* remains on moon for about 21½ hours and then blasts off, rejoining Apollo command module, which has been orbiting moon with Michael Collins in command. Astronauts return to earth July 24, splashing down in Pacific; they are quarantined to guard against possible lunar microorganisms, but there are none.

Apollo 12 (November 14): astronauts Charles Conrad, Jr., and Alan L. Bean make second moon landing (November 19–20), in lunar module *Intrepid*; spend almost 32 hours on moon and make two excursions on surface, collecting about 75 pounds of moon rocks; Apollo command module, piloted by Richard F. Gordon, Jr., splashes down November 24.

1970 *Apollo 13* (April 11): third moon mission, with astronauts James A. Lovell, Jr., Fred W. Haise, Jr., and John L. Swigert, Jr., runs into trouble when Apollo command module malfunctions; astronauts circle moon and head back to earth, using power and oxygen from lunar module, and splash down safely April 17.

1971 *Apollo 14* (January 31): third moon landing, with Alan B. Shepard, Jr., and Edgar D. Mitchell in lunar module *Antares* and Stuart A. Roosa in command module; Shepard and Mitchell remain on moon 33½ hours, collecting 96 pounds of samples in excursions lasting total of nine hours (February 5–6); command module splashes down February 9.

Mariner 9 (May 30): achieves orbit around Mars (November 13); transmits photographs and other data showing that Mars is evolving geologically (it is not old and "dead" like the moon) and has features suggesting water erosion. Ceases operation October 27, 1972.

Apollo 15 (July 26): fourth moon landing, with David R. Scott and James B. Irwin, Jr., in lunar module *Falcon* and Alfred M. Worden in command module; Scott and Irwin remain on lunar surface more than two days, exploring surface in four-wheeled Lunar Rover and gathering data and 170 pounds of samples. Return August 7.

1972 *Pioneer 10* (March 2): 570-pound probe, designed to leave solar system, is first to pass asteroid belt beyond Mars; achieves fly-by of Jupiter (December 3, 1973, closest approach 81,000 miles, after 620-million-mile journey from earth) and transmits data; by 1987 should enter interstellar space.

Apollo 16 (April 16): fifth moon landing; John W. Young and Charles M. Duke, Jr., are in lunar module, with Thomas K. Mattingly II in command module. Young and Duke spend about 20 hours exploring lunar surface and bring back 213 pounds of samples. Return to earth April 27.

Apollo 17 (December 7): sixth moon landing and last of Apollo lunar missions; in lunar module *Challenger* are Eugene A. Cernan and Harrison H. Schmitt, first civilian and first professional scientist (geologist) to visit moon; Ronald E. Evans pilots command module; Schmitt and Cernan gather data and samples (250 pounds); remain on moon more than three days, returning December 19. Total cost of Apollo project, largest scientific and technological program in history: about $25 billion.

1973   *Skylab 1* (May 14): unmanned 85-ton Skylab space station is boosted into orbit but is damaged. First crew—Charles Conrad, Jr., Joseph P. Kerwin, and Paul J. Weitz—is sent up May 25 (mission becomes *Skylab 2* on arrival of crew) and makes repairs. Crew remains in Skylab 28 days, a record at this time, conducting many experiments, one of which is to observe the effects on human beings of 28 days of weightlessness. First Skylab crew returns to earth June 22.

Skylab 3 (July 28): second crew—Alan L. Bean, Jack R. Lousma, and Owen K. Garriott, a civilian solar physicist—is sent up to Skylab; crew spends record 59½ days in Skylab, gathering enormous amounts of data on earth, sun, and human beings. Crew returns September 25.

Mariner 10 (November 3): achieves fly-by of Venus (February 5, 1974) and Mercury (March 29); reveals that Mercury has atmosphere.

Skylab 4 (November 16): third and final Skylab crew—Gerald P. Carr, William R. Pogue, and Edward G. Gibson, a civilian physicist—is sent up to Skylab; mission lasts a record 84 days, and crew returns to earth February 8, 1974.

1975   *Apollo 18-Soyuz 19* (July 15): joint U.S.-Soviet venture involves rendezvous and docking of two spacecraft in earth orbit (July 17); Soviet and American crew members (Vance D. Brand, Thomas P. Stafford, Donald K. Slayton, Alekseiy A. Leonov, Valeriy N. Kubasov) exchange visits and share meals. American crew returns to earth July 24.

1976   *Viking 1* soft-lands on Mars (July 20); Viking lander, after an eleven-month journey, begins transmitting first color photos on following day; tests conducted by robot lander (July 26–August 26) provide contradictory data on possibility of microscopic life.

Viking 2 soft-lands on Mars (September 3); robot lander conducts atmospheric and other tests showing that Martian ice cap at North Pole was frozen water and that trace elements in atmosphere suggest planet earlier had richer atmosphere.

A Watergate Chronology

1972 Five men are caught with cameras and bugging equipment inside the Democratic National Committee headquarters in the Watergate apartment-hotel complex in Washington, D.C. (June 17); one of the burglars, James W. McCord, Jr., is soon identified as an ex-CIA employee now in charge of security at the Committee to Re-elect the President (CREEP), Nixon's 1972 campaign organization (CREEP has virtually no connection with the ordinary machinery of the Republican Party, of which President Nixon is both candidate and titular head).

Evidence disclosed (June 19) linking Watergate burglars with E. Howard Hunt, Jr., who had an office in the White House and had connections with Charles W. Colson, special counsel to the President.

John Mitchell, former Nixon Attorney General, resigns as head of CREEP, citing family obligations (July 1).

It is disclosed (July 22) that G. Gordon Liddy, a lawyer for CREEP, was fired in June for refusing to answer FBI questions about the Watergate break-in.

President Nixon denies that anyone in the administration was involved in the Watergate affair (August 29).

Seven Watergate defendants—Hunt, Liddy, and the five burglars—are indicted by a federal grand jury (September 15); since investigative reporters are already in possession of evidence and testimony that clearly suggest involvement of John Mitchell and Maurice Stans, finance chairman of CREEP, suspicions are aroused that the FBI's investigation has been limited and that perjury has been committed during the grand-jury hearings.

Carl Bernstein and Bob Woodward, reporters for the Washington *Post*, begin a series of stories reporting that John Mitchell while Attorney General had controlled a secret (and illegal) fund to finance intelligence-gathering operations and "dirty tricks" against Democrats (September 29); key White House aide Dwight Chapin, a subordinate of Nixon's chief of staff, H. R. Haldeman, is subsequently identified as White House contact man for the dirty-tricks campaign.

1973 Watergate trial (January 8–30): McCord and Liddy plead not guilty but are found guilty by jury; E. Howard Hunt and four burglars plead guilty, arousing suspicion that they have been bought off by promises of financial aid and executive clemency. Judge John J. Sirica is openly dissatisfied with prosecution approach, asks his own questions, and states at end of trial that he is not sure that "all the pertinent facts" have come out.

Senate establishes (February 7) Select Committee on Presidential Campaign Activities; seven-man committee soon becomes known as the Ervin committee, after its chairman, Senator Sam J. Ervin, Jr., of North Carolina.

L. Patrick Gray, testifying before Senate Judiciary Committee considering his nomination as director of the FBI, says that he turned over results of FBI Watergate investigation to John Dean, counsel to President Nixon (February 28); on March 6 Gray releases FBI materials directly confirming a link between Nixon's personal lawyer, Herbert Kalmbach, and Dwight Chapin and the dirty-tricks campaign, thus backing up the Bernstein-Woodward reports and indirectly suggesting a conspiracy on the part of the White House to obstruct justice.

Judge John Sirica releases letter of March 19 from James McCord stating that others had been involved in Watergate bugging, that pressures had been applied for guilty pleas, and that perjury had been committed during trial (March 23); McCord later names John Dean and Jeb Stuart Magruder as among those having advance knowledge of burglary.

It is reported that James McCord, testifying behind closed doors before the Ervin committee, said that hush money for Watergate burglars came directly from CREEP fund; McCord repeated this testimony before federal grand jury (April 9).

President Nixon announces that he has undertaken "intensive new inquiries" of the whole Watergate matter as of March 21 and will allow key aides to testify in various forms (April 17).

It is reported that Magruder has testified that both Mitchell and Dean were in on the planning of the Watergate burglary and that both had caused hush money to be funneled to the burglars (April 19); subsequent stories relate that John Dean will testify that Haldeman was fully privy to and had approved the various Watergate illegalities.

President Nixon announces the resignations of John Ehrlichman, H. R. Haldeman, and Attorney General Richard Kleindienst; John Dean is fired; Nixon says there was an "effort to conceal the facts" from the public and from himself but that "in any organization, the man at the top must bear the responsibility" (April 30).

Charges against Daniel Ellsberg and Anthony J. Russo, on trial for leaking the "Pentagon Papers," are thrown out of court by Judge W. Matthew Byrne, Jr., who reveals that Ellsberg's telephone had been illegally wiretapped and that the government prosecutors had failed to inform Ellsberg's defense attorneys about the wiretap information (May 11); reports in press had already indicated that the office of Ellsberg's psychiatrist had been burglarized by Hunt and Liddy on the authority of John Ehrlichman and that Ehrlichman had tried to influence Judge Byrne by offering him the post of FBI director.

Acting Director of FBI William D. Ruckelshaus reveals that seventeen wiretaps on telephones of government officials and reporters had been ordered in 1969–71 (May 14); logs of these wiretaps have been found in John Ehrlichman's office, and subsequent reports in press suggest that Henry A. Kissinger had played a role in the wiretapping.

Public televised hearings are begun by Ervin committee (May 17–August 7); pattern is to start with small fry and gradually work up to the key figures; by the end of June one of the crucial questions before the committee—and the public—is, as Senator Howard Baker, ranking Republican member of Ervin committee, puts it, "What did the President know, and when did he know it?" Nixon's position is that he knew nothing about Watergate or its cover-up until March 21, 1973, at which time he ordered a new investigation that turned up "new" information; with certain exceptions big fry—Mitchell, Maurice Stans, John Ehrlichman, and H. R. Haldeman—stonewall, denying culpable involvement, whereas lesser figures generally confess to legal and moral errors. Chairman Sam Ervin, despite wry references to himself as a mere "country lawyer," does much to emphasize broad moral, political, and constitutional implications of the testimony given.

Professor Archibald Cox is appointed special prosecutor, with the purpose of seeking and getting criminal convictions, where appropriate, in whole Watergate affair (May 18); new Attorney General, Elliot L. Richardson, has promised Senate during confirmation hearings that he will give Cox a free hand in investigating Nixon administration.

John Dean testifies before Ervin committee (June 25–29) that President had been part of cover-up almost from beginning, as had John Ehrlichman and H. R. Haldeman; reveals White House "enemies" list, names of those critical of Nixon administration who were to be targets of government harassment or investigation by Internal Revenue Service, other government agencies, or special White House group called

Plumbers, an extralegal group originally formed to stop leaks to the press. Question after Dean's testimony is whether Dean or President is telling the truth and whether Dean's testimony can be substantiated or refuted by subsequent witnesses.

In testimony before Ervin committee presidential aide Alexander Butterfield, in charge of internal security, reveals that Nixon had installed a tape system capable of monitoring conversations and phone calls in the President's offices in White House and Executive Office Building; existence of tape system was unknown to all except Nixon, Haldeman, Butterfield, a few aides, and a few Secret Service men who maintained it (July 16); from this point on main focus of various Watergate investigations is to get relevant tapes and find out what is on them.

Judge John Sirica orders President Nixon to turn over to him various tapes requested in subpoenas by Special Prosecutor Cox and by the Ervin committee (August 29); Nixon has claimed executive privilege and has asserted that national security will be endangered if the tapes are released. Sirica says he will listen to tapes in question to see if in fact they contain material prejudicial to national security. Sirica's decision is upheld on October 12 by the U.S. Circuit Court of Appeals for the District of Columbia.

Vice President Spiro T. Agnew resigns (October 10); Agnew pleads no contest to charge of income-tax evasion and receives a $10,000 fine and a suspended three-year sentence. Although not a part of the various Watergate scandals, Agnew's resignation and conviction add to public sense of something deeply wrong with whole Nixon administration and in that sense contribute to general Watergate malaise.

"Saturday Night Massacre" (October 20): Special Prosecutor Cox has turned down Nixon's proposal to hand over summaries of the tapes, and Nixon orders Attorney General Richardson and Deputy Attorney General William Ruckelshaus to fire Cox; both men refuse and resign; Solicitor General Robert H. Bork becomes acting Attorney General and fires Cox. Result is a storm of public protest and outrage.

House of Representatives decides to instruct House Judiciary Committee, under Chairman Peter Rodino (New Jersey), to investigate possible impeachment of President Nixon (October 22–30).

Leon Jaworski, a Houston lawyer, is appointed new special prosecutor (November 1); new Attorney General, Senator William B. Saxbe, asserts that Jaworski's investigations will be unimpeded.

Watergate sentences (November 9): original break-in defendants get final sentences from Judge Sirica: Hunt gets two and a half to eight years with $10,000 fine; McCord gets one to five years; four other burglars get sentences of one to four years; G. Gordon Liddy, who has refused to cooperate in any way with Watergate investigation, has been sentenced to a maximum of twenty years in prison.

Tape gap revealed (November 21); one of nine tapes Sirica has ordered turned over contains eighteen-and-a-half-minute gap, thought by many to have been caused by deliberate erasure.

Egil Krogh, Jr., presidential aide and Ehrlichman subordinate, pleads guilty to involvement in Plumbers' burglary of the office of Ellsberg's psychiatrist (November 30) and is later sentenced to six months in jail.

In response to reports suggesting something questionable about his personal finances, President Nixon turns over his tax returns and other financial records to the joint congressional committee on internal revenue taxation (December 8).

1974   House of Representatives votes overwhelmingly to instruct Rodino's Judiciary Committee to begin full impeachment inquiry (February 6).

Herbert Kalmbach, Nixon's personal lawyer and fund raiser, pleads guilty to two violations of the federal law concerning campaign funds: (1) to raising $3.9 million for a secret congressional campaign committee in 1970 and (2) to accepting $100,000 in campaign contributions with promise of ambassadorship (February 25); is later sentenced to six to eight months in jail and $10,000 fine.

Federal grand jury indicts seven former officials of Nixon's administration or of CREEP: H. R. Haldeman, John D. Ehrlichman, ex-Attorney General John N. Mitchell, Charles W. Colson, Robert C. Mardian, Kenneth W. Parkinson, and Gordon C. Strachan (March 1); grand-jury report, which cites President Nixon as an unindicted coconspirator and contains substantial evidence of criminal behavior on Nixon's part, is later (March 26) turned over to House Judiciary Committee by Judge Sirica; Special Prosecutor Jaworski recommends that grand jury not actually indict Nixon, which it had wished to do, because he doubts that such an indictment is constitutional.

Congressional committee investigating Nixon's finances reports that Nixon improperly deducted $576,000 from his 1969–72 income and that he owes the government $476,431 in back taxes and interest (April 3); Nixon announces he will pay all moneys owed; although committee did not deal with issue of fraud, Nixon's tax preparer, Edward L. Morgan, later (November 8) pleads guilty to having illegally pre-

dated Nixon's gift of his vice-presidential papers, which formed the basis for the deduction.

John Mitchell and Maurice Stans are acquitted in New York trial of charges that they conspired to block a Securities and Exchange Commission investigation of Robert Vesco, shady financier, in return for $200,000 campaign contribution (April 28); Vesco case was one of Watergate-related scandals.

President Nixon releases White House transcripts, 1,308 heavily edited pages of 46 tape-recorded conversations, four more than were subpoenaed (April 30); coarseness and vulgarity of many of the conversations (the notation "expletive deleted" often occurs) shock many Americans, including many Nixon supporters; transcripts contain many indications of presidential involvement (later comparisons with actual tapes show that much had been distorted or suppressed) and furthermore suggest little presidential concern for legal principles or the public interest. Nixon has refused since April 4 to turn over actual tapes to House Judiciary Committee and releases transcripts instead, but how—or indeed whether—he expects transcripts to help his cause remains a mystery.

House Judiciary Committee begins formal, closed-door impeachment hearings (May 9).

Former Attorney General Richard Kleindienst pleads guilty to minor misdemeanor charge in Watergate-related International Telephone and Telegraph (ITT) scandal (May 16); 1971 antitrust action against ITT was dropped after ITT offered to pledge $400,000 toward costs of 1972 Republican National Convention; several members of Congress question Jaworski decision to prosecute a misdemeanor, since there is clear evidence of perjury, a felony; nevertheless Kleindienst becomes first former U.S. Attorney General to be convicted of a crime.

Judge Sirica orders Nixon to turn over 64 tapes to Special Prosecutor Jaworski (May 20); Nixon appeals order, and U.S. Supreme Court agrees to consider appeal directly.

Jeb Stuart Magruder, key CREEP official, receives jail term of ten months to four years for his role in Watergate burglary and cover-up (May 21).

Charles W. Colson, key presidential adviser, pleads guilty to obstructing justice in Ellsberg case (June 3); other charges against him are dropped, and he gets one to three years in jail and $5,000 fine.

John Ehrlichman is convicted by California jury of conspiracy in Ellsberg case (July 12); Ehrlichman is sentenced to twenty months to five years in jail.

U.S. Supreme Court rules unanimously in *United*

States v. *Richard Nixon* that Nixon must turn over 64 tapes requested by Jaworski (July 24); Court holds that executive privilege does not extend to criminal proceedings, that even a President cannot withhold evidence, and that the Supreme Court, not the President, must be the final judge of what is constitutional.

Televised House Judiciary Committee hearings (July 24–30): during debates remarkable for their substance, dignity, and anguish the committee votes three articles of impeachment: first, that Nixon had criminally conspired to obstruct justice in Watergate break-in and other unlawful activities (July 27, by a vote of 27–11); second, that Nixon had violated his sworn oath to preserve the Constitution and take care that the laws are faithfully executed (July 29, by a vote of 28–10); third, that Nixon had unconstitutionally defied the committee's subpoenas (July 30, by a vote of 21–17). Other articles, relating to secret Cambodian bombing and personal finances, are voted down by committee.

John Dean, former counsel to President, is sentenced to one to four years in jail for conspiracy to obstruct justice (August 2).

"Smoking gun" (August 5): at the insistence of his lawyer, James St. Clair, President Nixon releases transcripts of three conversations between himself and Haldeman that took place on June 23, 1972, five days after the Watergate break-in, in which Nixon ordered that the CIA try to block FBI investigations of the Watergate leads on the grounds that national security was involved. The transcripts provide proof (the so-called smoking gun) of a conspiracy to obstruct justice. Nixon, who had expected to be impeached by the full House but thought that in the absence of clear-cut proof the Senate would not muster the two-thirds vote necessary to convict, now sees his political support vanish. Republicans on the Judiciary Committee change their votes to ayes on the impeachment articles, and it becomes clear that the Senate will vote heavily for conviction. Lawyer St. Clair, a man of impeccable reputation, had been hired to represent Nixon but had not listened to the tapes until after the Supreme Court decision of July 24.

Nixon announces resignation (August 8); Vice President Gerald R. Ford sworn in as President (August 9) about a half hour after Nixon's resignation is delivered to Secretary of State Kissinger.

House of Representatives votes 412–3 to accept report of Judiciary Committee (August 20); since Nixon has resigned, the impeachment issue is moot. Technically, however, Nixon was not impeached by the House of Representatives.

President Ford grants Nixon an unconditional pardon for all crimes he may have committed while President (September 8); many Americans, though deeply troubled at the prospect of trying a former President of the United States as a felon, are equally troubled by the pardon. Ford White House also announces that Nixon papers and tapes will be held for three years and then returned to him.

1975   Haldeman, Ehrlichman, Mitchell, and former Assistant Attorney General Robert Mardian are convicted of Watergate-related crimes (January 1); Judge Sirica later sentences Haldeman, Ehrlichman, and Mitchell to two and a half to eight years in jail for perjury, obstruction of justice, and conspiracy; Mardian gets ten months to three years for obstruction of justice. Mitchell thus becomes second former U.S. Attorney General to be convicted of a crime.

Former Secretary of Commerce and CREEP Finance Chairman Maurice Stans, having pleaded guilty to misdemeanor violations of federal campaign laws (May 14), is fined $5,000; with the Stans sentencing the Watergate toll stands as follows: three former cabinet members, including two former Attorneys General of the United States, convicted of crime; seven key members of the White House staff, most of them lawyers, convicted of crime; seven top members of the Committee to Re-elect the President and several lesser members convicted of crime; one Vice President of the United States resigned and convicted of crime; one President of the United States resigned and pardoned for crimes he committed or may have committed while holding the highest office in the land.

Sports in America

700 Adult North American Indians play a variety of rule-governed games, including lacrosse, ball games (sometimes played in large enclosed courts), foot racing, archery, and chenco, which is played with throwing sticks and rolling stones.

1611 Lawn bowls are played in Jamestown, Virginia.

1650 Colonial Americans engage in a wide variety of European games, including bowls, pitching the barre, billiards, trictrac, rounders, several forms of games resembling golf and field hockey, cockfighting, bearbaiting, horse racing, fox hunting, sleighing, sledding, quoits, and horseshoes.

1665 Horse racing is formally organized as a sport with rules and prizes.

1673 Fencing school is established in Boston, Massachusetts.

1706 Closed hunting season is declared on deer, turkey, heath hen, partridge, and quail in New York City area and on Long Island (1706–08).

1732 First bowling green is laid out in New York City.

First fishing club is formed in Philadelphia.

1734 First jockey club is organized in South Carolina.

1759 Football (a form of kickball) is played at Yale.

1766 First fox-hunting club is established in Philadelphia.

1788 Messenger, famous English trotter, is brought to America for breeding purposes.

1793 Justin Morgan, foundation sire of Morgan horses, is born in Vermont.

1798 Systematic breeding of racehorses begins in Virginia.

1810 In England ex-slave Tom Molineaux, unofficial heavyweight boxing champion (bare knuckles), loses disputed match to English champion after 40 rounds (December 10).

1811 Rowing races enjoy vogue in New York-New Jersey area.

1818 First recorded public trotting race for a stake is run.

1820 Football (kickball) becomes popular as a form of hazing at American colleges (freshmen kick ball; sophomores kick freshmen).

1823 Twenty-thousand-dollar-purse horse race is run on Long Island between American Eclipse, of the North, and Sir Henry, of the South; northern horse wins, before 100,000 spectators (May).

1825 First gymnasium opens in Northampton, Massachusetts, and introduces new German gymnastics.

1826 Physical education is introduced to Harvard curriculum.

1827 First swimming school opens in Boston.

1828 First archery club is organized in Philadelphia.

American missionaries and traders in Hawaii observe surfing.

1829 *American Turf Register and Sporting Magazine*, first periodical devoted to sports (horse racing, hunting, fishing), is published in Baltimore, Maryland.

1832 William T. Porter becomes first sports editor on an American newspaper (*The Traveller*).

1833 Fly-fishing becomes important part of angling.

1834 First written rules for rounders, an old ball game somewhat like stickball with cricket influences, appear in Robin Carver's *Book of Sports*.

1835 Ten-mile footrace ($1,000 prize) is watched by 30,000 spectators at Union Course on Long Island.

1839 First baseball field in the shape of a diamond is laid out at Cooperstown, New York.

1843 Rowing in shells is introduced at Harvard and Yale.

1844 New York Yacht Club, first in U.S., is founded (July 29).

1845 Alexander Joy Cartwright writes first formal rules for baseball, including required dimensions of the diamond.

1846 First recorded baseball game is played at Elysian Fields, Hoboken, New Jersey (June 19).

1851 Yacht *America* wins race at Isle of Wight, gaining trophy now known as the America's Cup (August 22).

1852 First intercollegiate rowing race takes place between Harvard and Yale (August 3).

1856 John A. "Snowshoe" Thomson begins delivering mail on skis to miners in California; shortly thereafter first formal cross-country skiing contests are held in Carson Valley, California.

1857 American Chess Association is organized in New York City; Paul C. Morphy wins first national championship (October 6).

1858 First formal baseball organization, National Association of Base Ball Players, is formed by 25 amateur clubs.

Admission is charged to a baseball game for the first time (July 20).

1859   First national billiards championship is held in Detroit (April 12).

First intercollegiate baseball game is played between Amherst and Williams (July 1).

International cricket match takes place in Hoboken, New Jersey, between England and U.S. (October 3–6).

1863   Roller skating is introduced to U.S. by James Plimpton, inventor of the four-wheel skate.

Courts for rackets are built in New York City; English professional is hired.

1864   First croquet club is founded in Brooklyn, New York.

Al Reach becomes first professional baseball player.

Saratoga racetrack is opened; first thoroughbred stakes race is organized.

1865   Scaling by Edward Whymper of Matterhorn in Switzerland vastly increases interest in sport of mountain climbing.

1866   First transoceanic yachting race takes place from New Jersey to England.

First unofficial baseball championship is held, on Long Island, between Brooklyn Atlantics and Philadelphia Athletics.

New York Athletic Club is founded (June 17).

1867   First running of the annual Belmont Stakes is held at Jerome Park, New York.

Edward P. Weston wins $10,000 by walking from Portland, Maine, to Chicago in 26 days.

1868   First baseball uniforms (with knickers) are worn by Cincinnati Red Stockings.

American Skating Congress meets in Pittsburgh to formulate regulations for ice skating.

Bicycling (velocipeding) enjoys first great vogue.

First indoor amateur track-and-field meet is held by New York Athletic Club (November 11).

1869   Cincinnati Red Stockings pay players on a regular basis, becoming first professional team.

First international bare-knuckles boxing match is held in U.S. (June 15).

First intercollegiate football game (a soccerlike form

of kickball) is held between Rutgers and Princeton (November 6).

1870   Roller skating (especially figure skating) enjoys great vogue.

Pimlico racetrack is built in Baltimore.

1871   National Rifle Association is formed.

Iceboating on Hudson River enjoys vogue.

1872   First U.S. ski club is formed in Berlin, New Hampshire.

Grand Teton (13,766 feet) is scaled in Teton Range, Wyoming.

1873   President White of Cornell refuses to allow Cornell team to play Michigan: "I will not permit 30 men to travel 400 miles to agitate a bag of wind."

Bookmakers appear at U.S. racetracks, replacing informal wagering among owners and spectators.

First running of the annual Preakness Stakes is held at Pimlico.

First set of rules for football is drafted in New York City by Yale, Princeton, Rutgers, and Columbia for a game resembling soccer (October 19).

1874   Rugby is introduced in a game between Harvard and McGill University; rules developed by Rugby Football Union, under which this game was played, heavily influence development of modern football.

Lawn tennis is introduced to U.S. from Bermuda by Mary Ewing Outerbridge.

U.S. team defeats Ireland in Grand International Rifle Match at Creedmore, Long Island, before more than 5,000 spectators. Riflemen and oarsmen are most popular athletic heroes of the time.

1875   Baseball glove (unpadded) is used for the first time, in Boston.

First running of the Kentucky Derby is held (May 17) at Churchill Downs, Kentucky.

1876   Polo is introduced to U.S. from England.

National League of professional baseball teams is formed; first official NL game is played on April 12.

Horace Lee becomes first American to sprint 100 yards in ten seconds flat.

Intercollegiate Association of Amateur Athletes of America, first such organization, is founded in Saratoga, New York (July 20).

Rules for game resembling modern football (egg-shaped ball, running with ball, tackling) are drawn up and adopted in Springfield, Massachusetts, by Princeton, Yale, Harvard, Rutgers, and Columbia (November 23).

1878   U.S. manufacture of bicycles (with extremely large front wheels) begins.

1879   National Archery Association is formed.

1880   An American, Paddy Ryan, wins world heavyweight (bare-knuckles) championship in 87th round, in West Virginia (June 21); boxing, though widely reported in newspapers, continues to be illegal throughout U.S.

Walter Camp of Yale introduces rules creating ball snap and quarterback in football.

1881   United States Lawn Tennis Association is formed; first national championship is held August 31 at Newport, Rhode Island.

American Angler, first fishing journal, is published in Philadelphia (October 15).

1882   Handball is introduced to U.S. from Ireland by Phil Casey, who builds first court and opens school.

John L. Sullivan, world bare-knuckles champion, tours U.S., boxing in gloves under Marquis of Queensberry rules.

Baseball umpire is expelled from National League for dishonesty, the first and last ever to be so expelled (June 24).

The American Association, second baseball league, is founded.

U.S. Intercollegiate Lacrosse Association is formed.

First major-league double-header is played (September 25).

Walter Camp institutes system of yards and downs in football.

1883   First recorded bicycle race is held in Springfield, Massachusetts.

First recorded interranch rodeo takes place near Pecos, Texas.

1884   Moses Fleetwood Walker of Toledo, Ohio, becomes first black to play on a major-league (American Association) baseball team.

Baseball regulation is adopted that allows pitchers an overhand or sidearm delivery.

1886   First Tournament of Roses is held in Pasadena, California (January 1).

1887   Foxburg Golf Club is founded in Pennsylvania.

American Trotting Association is organized in Detroit (March 2).

Ellen F. Hansell becomes first U.S. women's lawn-tennis champion.

1888   Amateur Athletic Union is founded (January 21).

First recorded American golf match on a permanent course is played at St. Andrews Golf Club in Yonkers, New York.

Softball is invented in Chicago as an indoor game.

1889   Large-scale U.S. manufacture of "safety" (modern) bicycles is begun.

First All-American football team is selected by Casper Whitney and Walter Camp.

Last bare-knuckles championship fight is won in Mississippi by John L. Sullivan after 75 rounds (July 8).

1890   Badminton is introduced to U.S. from England.

Water polo, in version using soft ball and allowing underwater tackling, is introduced to U.S.

First Army-Navy football game is played at West Point, New York (November 29).

1891   Basketball is invented by Dr. James A. Naismith at YMCA Training College in Springfield, Massachusetts.

Modern low-wheel sulky is introduced in harness racing.

1892   James Corbett becomes first heavyweight boxing champion under Marquis of Queensberry rules (gloves, timed three-minute rounds, no wrestling); defeats John L. Sullivan in New Orleans after 21 rounds (September 7).

1893   Ice hockey is introduced from Canada at Yale and Johns Hopkins.

First national fly-casting tournament is held at Chicago World's Fair.

1894   United States Golf Association is formed (December 22).

1895   First United States Golf Association amateur and open golf championships are held at Newport, Rhode Island.

Volleyball is invented by William G. Morgan in Holyoke, Massachusetts.

First professional football game is played in Latrobe, Pennsylvania (August 31).

American Bowling Congress is organized; standardizes rules and equipment for modern ten-pin game (September 9).

1896 U.S. athletes participate in first modern Olympic games, held in Athens, Greece, winning nine out of twelve events (April 6).

Amateur Hockey League, first in U.S., is organized in New York City.

1897 Prize fight is photographed for the first time by motion-picture camera (March 17).

More than 1 million bicycles are in use in U.S.

Mt. St. Elias (18,008 feet) in Alaska is climbed.

1900 Davis Cup in tennis is established.

American League of baseball is formed in Chicago (January 29).

First well-organized automobile race is won in Springfield, New York, with an average speed of 25 mph (April 15).

1902 First postseason football game is played at Tournament of Roses.

1903 National Commission, ruling body of organized baseball, is established.

First annual World Series of baseball is held (October 1–13, between Boston and Pittsburgh).

Harvard Stadium is dedicated (November 14).

World's first professional hockey team is formed in Houghton, Michigan.

1904 National Ski Association is formed.

Vogue for jujitsu is started by President Theodore Roosevelt.

Olympic games are held in St. Louis, Missouri (May 14), first time they have been held in U.S.

First Vanderbilt Cup automobile race is held (October 8).

1905 President Theodore Roosevelt threatens to abolish college football on account of violent play (18 deaths, 159 serious injuries).

1906 Intercollegiate Athletic Association (later renamed National Collegiate Athletic Association) is founded.

Rule changes in football are made (forward pass legalized, flying wedge formations banned) in order to cut down injuries; overall advantage shifts to defense.

1908 Around-the-world auto race (New York to Paris via Alaska and Siberia) is won by American driving team (February 12–July 1).

Irving Brokaw popularizes sport of figure skating.

In Sydney, Australia, Jack Johnson becomes first black

world heavyweight boxing champion (December 26).

1911 World championship wrestling match is held in Chicago (September 4).

First running of the Indianapolis 500 auto race is held; winning average is 74.59 mph.

1912 American Indian James Thorpe is proclaimed world's greatest athlete after winning decathlon and pentathlon events at Olympic games; honors are later rescinded because of semiprofessional involvement in college baseball.

Mt. Blackburn (16,390 feet) in Alaska is climbed.

1913 Mt. McKinley (20,320 feet) in Alaska is climbed by Hudson Stuck, an English-born American.

1914 First national figure-skating tournament is held in New Haven, Connecticut.

Yale Bowl is opened.

1916 First of annual postseason football games is held (January 1) at Rose Bowl, in Pasadena, California.

Professional Golfers' Association of America is formed (January 17); first PGA tournament is held on April 10 at Bronxville, New York.

1917 National Hockey League is founded; Stanley Cup is awarded to winner of NHL play-offs.

1919 Dog racing (greyhounds) becomes increasingly popular after invention of mechanical "bunny," which replaces live rabbits.

1920 Boxing is fully legalized in New York State, with other states soon following suit.

Eight players of Chicago White Sox are indicted for throwing 1919 World Series (September 18).

Judge Kenesaw Mountain Landis is appointed commissioner of baseball (November 8).

American Professional Football Association is formed; is renamed National Football League in 1922.

1921 First $1 million gate is attained at heavyweight boxing match in Jersey City, New Jersey, between Jack Dempsey and Georges Carpentier (July 2).

Commissioner Landis bans eight indicted White Sox players even though they have been acquitted of charges against them (August 3).

1922 Baseball game is broadcast on radio for the first time (October 4).

1926 Gertrude Ederle is first woman to swim the English Channel.

1927 First Golden Gloves boxing matches are sponsored by

New York *Daily News.*

Babe Ruth hits 60 home runs in one season, the sixtieth on September 30.

United States Professional Lawn Tennis Association is formed.

1928 U.S. Volleyball Association is formed.

1929 Rodeo becomes nationally organized sport.

1930 Bobby Jones completes "grand slam" of golf, winning British Open, British Amateur, U.S. Open, and then U.S. Amateur.

1932 First Winter Olympics to be held in U.S. open at Lake Placid, New York (February).

Soaring Society of America is founded (regulates sailplanes, or gliders).

1933 First totalizator is used at an American racetrack (Arlington Park, Chicago).

First annual All-Star baseball game is held at Comiskey Park, Chicago (July 6).

First National Football League championship game takes place in Chicago (December 17).

U.S. Table Tennis Association is founded.

1934 Amateur Softball Association of America is formed.

First Masters Tournament in golf is held in Augusta, Georgia.

College basketball games are held in Madison Square Garden, New York City.

1935 Skin diving with snorkel, face mask, and swim fins gains popularity.

Babe Ruth ends career with a lifetime total of 714 home runs.

First Heisman Trophy is awarded to outstanding college football player.

First night baseball game is played in Cincinnati, Ohio.

Top money winner in professional golf is Johnny Revolta, with $9,543.

1936 Basketball is included for first time as an Olympic sport.

Jesse Owens wins four gold medals at Munich Olympic games (August 9).

Associated Press conducts first poll of sportswriters to rank best ten teams in college football.

1937 In Chicago, Joe Louis becomes second black heavyweight boxing champion (June 22).

Basketball rule change eliminates center jump after each score, greatly increasing pace of the game.

1939 First NCAA basketball championship is held.

American Water Ski Association holds first annual championship.

Baseball's Hall of Fame is established at Cooperstown, New York.

1941 Joe DiMaggio hits safely in 56 consecutive games (July 16).

1945 Second professional football league, All-American Football Conference, is formed; first season of actual playing begins in 1946.

1947 Jackie Robinson becomes first black baseball player in modern major leagues, joining Brooklyn Dodgers.

1949 National Basketball League and Basketball Association of America merge into the National Basketball Association.

1950 American Football Conference merges with National Football League.

1951 Citation becomes first racehorse to win more than $1 million in purses (July 14).

Bobby Thomson of New York Giants hits ninth-inning pennant-winning home run against the Brooklyn Dodgers.

Scandal hits college basketball as some players are found guilty of accepting bribes from gamblers to fix games or point spreads.

1953 AAU recognizes judo as a sport; intercollegiate competitions are organized.

1956 Scuba diving becomes increasingly popular sport.

1957 In Stockton, California, Don Bowden becomes first American to run the mile in under four minutes (July 19).

Althea Gibson becomes first black to win U.S. lawn tennis women's singles championship.

1958 Sugar Ray Robinson regains middleweight boxing crown for record fifth time (March 25).

1959 A new professional league, American Football League, is organized.

1960 Dolph Shayes becomes first professional basketball player to score more than 15,000 career points (January 12).

Floyd Patterson is first heavyweight boxing champion ever to regain his crown (June 20).

Skydiving, or sport parachuting, gains adherents.

Surfing enjoys tremendous vogue, especially in California.

1961 Roger Maris of New York Yankees hits 61 home runs in one season, breaking Babe Ruth's record.

1962 Wilt Chamberlain becomes first basketball player to score 100 points in one game (March 2).

1963 Arnold Palmer becomes first professional golfer to win more than $100,000 in one year.

1965 Arthur Ashe becomes first black tennis player selected for American Davis Cup team.

1967 Heavyweight boxing champion Muhammad Ali is stripped of his title after refusing to be drafted into U.S. Army.

First annual Super Bowl in professional football is held; NBC and CBS pay total of $2 million for TV rights (January 15).

American Basketball Association is formed (February 2).

1968 International Lawn Tennis Federation opens its tournaments, including Wimbledon and the U.S. National, to professionals.

Jogging enjoys great vogue.

U.S. track stars are suspended from Olympic competition after giving black-power salute during victory ceremony in Mexico City (October 18).

Hang gliding becomes popular, especially in California.

1969 In Hialeah, Florida, Diana Crump is first woman jockey to race at major U.S. track (February 7).

Barbara Jo Rubin becomes first woman jockey to win a thoroughbred horse race (February 22).

American and National baseball leagues expand, each splitting into eastern and western divisions, with play-offs to determine pennant winner.

1970 Curt Flood, outfielder, files antitrust suit against organized baseball, challenging the reserve clause.

American Football League merges into the National Football League, forming two conferences of thirteen teams each; football becomes top professional sport in terms of media attention.

Martial arts, especially karate and kung fu, enjoy vogue.

All-woman group of mountain climbers ascends Mt. McKinley.

1971 "Ping-Pong diplomacy" begins as a U.S. table-tennis team visits Communist China for seven days of competition (April).

First legal system of offtrack betting opens for business in New York City (April).

Pat Matzdorf breaks world high-jump record, leaping 7'6¼" in Berkeley, California (July).

1972 Basketball's Los Angeles Lakers are defeated after a 33-game winning streak, the longest in the modern history of professional sports (January).

Major-league baseball players strike and delay opening of the season for ten days.

Bobby Fischer becomes first American world chess champion (September).

Swimmer Mark Spitz wins seven Olympic gold medals, breaking all-time record (September).

New Jersey Interscholastic Athletic Association approves program allowing girls to try out for school varsity sports.

1973 Average qualifying speed for the Indianapolis 500 soars to 192.3 mph (May).

Sue Schneider becomes a trainer for the Michigan State football team.

Secretariat is first horse since 1948 to win the Triple Crown after triumphing at the Belmont Stakes (June).

Golfer Jack Nicklaus establishes a record by winning his fourteenth major title.

Bobby Riggs is sobered when defeated by Billie Jean King in a $100,000 winner-take-all tennis match (September).

1974 Henry "Hank" Aaron of Atlanta Braves slams his 715th home run, breaking Babe Ruth's long-standing record (April).

Frank Robinson is major-league baseball's first black manager.

World heavyweight boxing championship is fought in Zaire, Africa, at 4:00 A.M. so it can appear on prime-time American television.

Because of a shortage of horsehide, baseballs are covered with cowhide; 453 fewer home runs are scored than in 1973.

Little League Baseball, Inc., accepts girls after a court ruling in New Jersey (June).

1975 UCLA wins its tenth NCAA basketball championship in twelve seasons.

Soccer's popularity grows, especially on the West Coast.

Cincinnati Reds capture their first World Series in 35 years (October).

Graduate student Will Rodgers wins the seventy-ninth Boston Marathon, becoming the fastest American marathon runner on record.

1976 President of the American Power Boat Association, Bob Nordskog, sets offshore speed record of 90.55 mph.

Major-league baseball attendance record is set with 31,320,592 spectators, 1,200,000 more than the previous high in 1973; American League adds two teams scheduled to begin play in 1977.

U.S. comes in second in the Montreal Olympics, winning 94 medals, far behind the Soviet Union's 125.

Tennis star Chris Evert is voted athlete of the year by *Sports Illustrated* magazine (December).

American Nobel Prize Winners

Two or more persons whose names are linked by a brace are members of an American team that won a prize for its work. An asterisk (*) preceding a name indicates that the winner shared the prize with another winner who was not an American. Where names linked by a brace are also preceded by asterisks, a Nobel Prize-winning team has shared the prize with a non-American person or team.

Economic Science

1970	Paul A. Samuelson (1915—)
1971	Simon Kuznets (1901—)
1972	*Kenneth J. Arrow (1921—)
1973	Wassily W. Leontief (1906—)
1975	*Tjalling C. Koopmans (1910—)
1976	Milton Friedman (1912—)

Literature

1930	Sinclair Lewis (1885–1951)
1936	Eugene O'Neill (1888–1953)
1938	Pearl S. Buck (1892–1973)
1949	William Faulkner (1897–1962)
1954	Ernest Hemingway (1899–1961)
1962	John Steinbeck (1902–1968)
1976	Saul Bellow (1915—)

Chemistry

1914	Theodore W. Richards (1868–1928)
1932	Irving Langmuir (1881–1957)
1934	Harold C. Urey (1893—)
1936	Peter J. W. Debye (1884–1966)
1946	{ John H. Northrop (1891—) / Wendell M. Stanley (1904–1971)
1949	James B. Sumner (1887–1955) / William F. Giauque (1895—)
1951	{ Glenn T. Seaborg (1912—) / Edwin M. McMillan (1907—)
1954	Linus C. Pauling (1901—)
1955	Vincent du Vigneaud (1901—)
1960	Willard F. Libby (1908—)
1961	Melvin Calvin (1911—)
1965	Robert B. Woodward (1917—)
1966	Robert S. Mulliken (1896—)
1968	Lars Onsager (1903–1976)
1972	{ Christian B. Afinsen (1916—) / Stanford Moore (1913—) / William H. Stein (1911—)
1974	Paul J. Flory (1910—)
1976	William N. Lipscomb, Jr. (1919—)

Physiology and Medicine

1912	Alexis Carrel (1873–1944)
1930	Karl Landsteiner (1868–1943)
1933	Thomas H. Morgan (1866–1945)
1934	{ George R. Minot (1885–1950) / William P. Murphy (1892—) / George H. Whipple (1878–1976)
1943	*Edward A. Doisy (1893—)
1944	{ Joseph Erlanger (1874–1965) / Herbert S. Gasser (1888–1963)
1946	Hermann J. Muller (1890–1967)
1947	{ *Carl F. Cori (1896—) / *Gerty Theresa Radnitz Cori (1896–1957)
1950	{ *Philip S. Hench (1896–1965) / *Edward C. Kendall (1886–1972)
1952	Selman A. Waksman (1888–1973)
1953	*Fritz A. Lipmann (1899—)
1954	{ John F. Enders (1897—) / Thomas H. Weller (1915—) / Frederick C. Robbins (1916—)
1956	{ *Dickinson W. Richards, Jr. (1895–1973) / *André F. Cournand (1895—)
1958	{ George W. Beadle (1903—) / Edward L. Tatum (1909–1975)
	Joshua Lederberg (1925—)
1959	{ Severo Ochoa (1905—) / Arthur Kornberg (1918—)
1961	Georg von Bekesy (1899–1972)
1962	*James D. Watson (1928—)
1964	*Konrad E. Bloch (1912—)
1966	{ Charles B. Huggins (1901—) / Francis P. Rous (1879–1970)
1967	{ *Haldan K. Hartline (1903—) / *George Wald (1906—)
1968	{ Robert W. Holley (1922—) / Har Gobind Khorana (1922—) / Marshall W. Nirenberg (1927—)
1969	{ Max Delbrück (1906—) / Alfred D. Hershey (1908—) / Salvador E. Luria (1912—)
1970	*Julius Axelrod (1912—)
1971	Earl W. Sutherland, Jr. (1915–1974)
1972	*Gerald M. Edelman (1929—)
1974	{ *Albert Claude (1899—) / *George E. Palade (1912—)
1975	{ David Baltimore (1938—) / Renato Dulbecco (1914—) / Howard M. Temin (1934—)
1976	{ Baruch Blumberg (1925—) / Daniel C. Gajdusek (1923—)

Physics

1907	Albert A. Michelson (1852–1931)

1923	Robert A. Millikan (1868–1953)
1927	*Arthur H. Compton (1892–1962)
1936	*Carl D. Anderson (1905—)
1937	*Clinton J. Davisson (1881–1958)
1939	Ernest O. Lawrence (1901–1958)
1943	Otto Stern (1888–1969)
1944	Isidor I. Rabi (1898—)
1946	Percy W. Bridgman (1882–1961)
1952	Felix Bloch (1905—) Edward M. Purcell (1912—)
1955	Willis E. Lamb (1913—) Polykarp Kusch (1911—)
1956	William Shockley (1910—) Walter H. Brattain (1902—) John Bardeen (1908—)
1957	Tsung Dao Lee (1926—) Chen Ning Yang (1922—)
1959	Emilio Segrè (1905—) Owen Chamberlain (1920—)
1960	Donald A. Glaser (1926—)
1961	*Robert Hofstadter (1915—)
1963	*Eugene P. Wigner (1902—) *Maria Goeppert-Mayer (1906–1972)
1964	*Charles H. Townes (1915—)
1965	*Julian S. Schwinger (1918—) *Richard P. Feynman (1918—)
1967	Hans A. Bethe (1906—)
1968	Luis W. Alvarez (1911—)

1969	Murray Gell-Mann (1929—)
1972	John R. Schrieffer (1931—) Leon N. Cooper (1930—) John Bardeen (1908—)
1973	*Leo Esaki (1925—) *Ivar Giaever (1929—)
1975	*James Rainwater (1917—)
1976	Samuel Chao Chung Ting (1936—) Burton Richter (1931—)

Peace

1906	Theodore Roosevelt (1858–1919)
1912	Elihu Root (1845–1937)
1919	Woodrow Wilson (1856–1924)
1925	*Charles G. Dawes (1865–1951)
1929	Frank B. Kellogg (1856–1937)
1931	Jane Addams (1860–1935) Nicholas Murray Butler (1862–1947)
1945	Cordell Hull (1871–1955)
1946	John R. Mott (1865–1955) Emily G. Balch (1867–1961)
1947	*The American Friends' Service Committee
1950	Ralph J. Bunche (1904–1971)
1953	George C. Marshall (1880–1959)
1962	Linus C. Pauling (1901—)
1964	Martin Luther King, Jr. (1929–1968)
1970	Norman E. Borlaug (1914—)
1973	*Henry A. Kissinger (1923—)

Admission to the Union

1787	Delaware*	1792	Kentucky	1837	Michigan	1876	Colorado
	New Jersey*	1796	Tennessee	1845	Florida	1889	Montana
	Pennsylvania*	1803	Ohio		Texas		North Dakota
1788	Connecticut*	1812	Louisiana	1846	Iowa		South Dakota
	Georgia*	1816	Indiana	1848	Wisconsin		Washington
	Maryland*	1817	Mississippi	1850	California	1890	Idaho
	Massachusetts*	1818	Illinois	1858	Minnesota		Wyoming
	New Hampshire*	1819	Alabama	1859	Oregon	1896	Utah
	New York*	1820	Maine	1861	Kansas	1907	Oklahoma
	South Carolina*	1821	Missouri	1863	West Virginia	1912	Arizona
	Virginia*	1836	Arkansas	1864	Nevada		New Mexico
1789	North Carolina*			1867	Nebraska	1959	Alaska
1790	Rhode Island*						Hawaii
1791	Vermont						

*One of the thirteen original states

Gross National Product (1869–1975)

The gross national product (GNP) is the total market value of all goods and services produced by a national economy during a specified period. The per capita GNP is arrived at by dividing the GNP by the number of people in a nation and is usually considered a somewhat more accurate measure of a nation's relative wealth. GNP is a measure developed in the late 1940's, so figures before that time involve a certain amount of guesswork. The figures in the columns below (sources, *Historical Statistics of the United States: Colonial Times to 1970* and *Statistical Abstract of the United States: 1976*) labeled "GNP" and "Per Capita GNP" represent yearly averages for each decade. Although the figures are given in dollars unadjusted for inflation in relation to today's dollar, some indication has been given of the inflation rate since 1940. The figures in the last column represent the value of a dollar in a given year as it compares to the value of a dollar in 1967; for example, a dollar in 1940 was worth $2.38 in relation to what a dollar would buy in 1967.

	GNP (in billions of dollars)	Per Capita GNP (in dollars)		GNP (in billions of dollars)	Per Capita GNP (in dollars)	
1869–78	7.4	170	1939	90.5	691	
1879–88	11.2	205	1940	99.7	754	$2.38
1890	13.1	208	1945	211.9	1,515	
1900	18.7	246	1950	286.2	1,887	$1.39
1910	35.3	382	1955	399.3	2,416	
1920	91.5	860	1960	506.0	2,801	$1.13
1929	103.1	847	1965	688.1	3,541	
1930	90.4	734	1970	982.4	4,795	$.86
1931	75.8	611	1972	1,171.1	5,608	
1932	58.0	465	1973	1,306.6	6,209	
1933	55.6	442	1974	1,413.2	6,640	
1934	65.1	514	1975	1,516.3	7,016	$.62

National Debt (1791–1975)

	National Debt (in thousands of dollars)	Per Capita Debt (in dollars)		National Debt (in thousands of dollars)	Per Capita Debt (in dollars)
1791	75,463		1900	1,263,417	16.60
1800	82,976		1915	1,191,264	11.25
1810	53,173		1918	12,455,225	119.13
1816	127,335		1920	24,299,321	228.23
1820	91,016		1930	16,185,310	131.51
1830	48,565		1933	22,538,673	179.48
1840	3,573		1936	33,778,543	263.79
1850	63,453		1940	42,967,531	325.23
1860	64,844	2.06	1942	72,422,445	537.13
1861	90,582		1944	201,003,387	1,452.44
1862	524,178		1946	269,422,099	1,905.42
1863	1,119,774		1950	257,357,352	1,696.67
1864	1,815,831		1955	274,374,223	1,660.11
1865	2,677,929	75.01	1960	286,330,761	1,584.70
1870	2,436,453	61.06	1965	317,273,899	1,630.46
1880	2,090,909	41.60	1970	370,918,707	1,811.12
1890	1,222,397	17.80	1975	533,200,000	2,496.00

Exports and Imports (1697–1975)

The figures below give the total estimated value of goods and services exported and imported by the United States from 1697 to 1975. For the colonial years, 1697–1790, the figures give trade with England only and represent value in pounds sterling (the bulk of American trade prior to the Revolution was with the mother country; a pound was worth something like forty of today's dollars). Many factors influence the import-export balance sheet—tourism, military goods and services whose value may be subject to a variety of accounting methods, and so on. As a result the net inflow or outflow of payments may not tally with the total value of goods and services exchanged. Nevertheless the figures below, taken from *Historical Statistics of the United States: Colonial Times to 1970* and *Statistical Abstract of the United States: 1976*, will serve to give a rough indication of the volume and direction of United States international trade.

	Exports	Imports		Exports	Imports
1697	279,852*	140,129*	1864	304	418
1700	395,021	344,341	1865	279	343
1710	249,814	293,659	1870	507	608
1720	468,188	319,702	1880	963	848
1730	572,585	536,860	1890	960	1,109
1740	718,416	813,382	1900	1,686	1,179
1750	814,768	1,313,083	1910	2,160	2,114
1760	761,099	2,611,764	1915	3,948	2,200
1770	1,015,538	1,925,571	1916	6,029	2,927
1775	1,920,950	196,162	1917	7,072	3,597
1776	103,964	55,415	1918	7,272	4,814
1777	12,619	57,295	1919	10,776	5,908
1778	17,694	33,986	1920	10,264	6,741
1779	20,579	349,797	1930	5,448	4,416
1780	18,560	825,431	1943	19,134	8,096
1785	775,892	2,078,744	1944	21,483	8,986
1790	1,043,389	3,258,238	1945	16,273	10,232
1800	107**	108**	1950	13,893	12,001
1810	117	110	1960	27,490	23,383
1820	84	84	1970	62,483	59,545
1830	86	79	1971	65,614	65,870
1840	160	134	1972	72,664	78,618
1850	166	210	1973	102,154	98,249
1860	438	438	1974	144,773	141,187
1861	303	406	1975	148,410	132,141

*In pounds sterling
**In millions of dollars

Income Distribution in the U. S.
(1929–1975)

There are a number of ways of describing how income is distributed in the United States. Income is defined as money coming in from wages, dividends, interest, and the like, and must be distinguished from wealth, or the total value of one's property. That is, two families or unrelated individuals may have identical incomes of ten thousand dollars a year, but family A may derive this income solely from wages and may have a wealth equivalent to the value of its home, car, and other property, while family B has a wealth of a million dollars—in municipal bonds, for example—of which its ten-thousand-dollar income represents dividends of 1 per cent. One family is rich and the other is not,

although their incomes are identical. The chart below shows what portion of all income in the United States is earned by the top 5 per cent of all families and unrelated individuals, the top 20 per cent of these families or individuals, and the bottom 20 per cent. As can be seen from these figures (sources, *Historical Statistics of the United States* and *Statistical Abstract of the United States: 1976*), the top 5 per cent was more affected by World War II than by the Depression; it can also be seen that since 1950 the relative shares of the top and bottom fifths have remained fairly constant. For 1975 the income ranges for families in these groups have been given.

	Percentage of national income received by top 5% of U.S. families and unrelated individuals	Percentage of national income received by top 20% of U.S. population	Percentage of national income received by bottom 20% of U.S. population
1929*	26.4	54.4	under 4.0
1933	25.3		
1936	24.4	51.7	4.1
1941	22.7	48.8	4.1
1945	17.4		
1950	18.2	45.0	4.5
1960	17.0	44.0	4.8
1965	16.6	43.6	5.2
1970	16.9	44.1	5.4
1975**	15.5	41.1	5.4
	($34,144 and above)	($20,690 and above)	(0–$6,914)

*Estimate
**Not strictly comparable with earlier years due to revised procedures

Energy Consumption and Environmental Pollution (1940–1975)*

Included in this chart are some figures indicating the environmental impact of an energy-intensive society. It should be noted that the measurement of pollution, particularly in relation to air and water pollution, did not begin until the early 1950's.

	Energy consumption (in trillions of Btu's)	Polluting discharges into coastal and inland waters (in thousands of gallons)	Synthetic organic pesticides (in millions of pounds purchased)	Commercial fertilizers (in thousands of tons purchased)
1940	23,908			9,360
1945	31,541			
1950	33,992			17,904
1955	39,703			21,935
1960	44,569		570	23,499
1965	53,343		764	30,315
1970	67,143	15,253	881	38,292
1971	68,698	8,840	946	
1972	71,946	18,806	1,002	39,896
1973	74,755	24,315	1,199	41,822
1974	72,933	16,916		44,964
1975	71,078			40,596

	Air pollutants (in millions of tons)				
	Sulfur oxides	Carbon monoxide	Particulates	Hydrocarbons	Nitrogen oxides
1940	23.0	73.0	45.0	17.0	7.0
1945					
1950	25.0	83.0	33.0	22.0	9.0
1955					
1960	23.0	99.0	30.0	26.0	11.0
1965					
1970	34.3	107.3	27.5	32.1	20.4
1971	33.5	104.9	25.2	31.4	20.8
1972	32.6	104.9	23.2	31.3	22.2
1973	33.2	100.9	21.0	31.3	23.0
1974	31.4	94.6	19.5	30.4	22.5
1975					

*Source: Environmental Protection Agency, U.S. Department of Agriculture

Horsepower of U. S. Prime Movers
(1850–1975)

Horsepower is a nonmetric measure of power equivalent to the power needed to move 550 pounds one foot in one second, or to 746 watts. This chart includes most of the machines that produce most of the power or do most of the work in the United States. Not specifically included are electric motors, which so to speak feed secondhand on power produced in electric power plants and are in effect subsumed in that category.

A great deal can be read in these figures about the socioeconomic development of the United States, including, of course, the enormous role played by the internal-combustion engine. Of particular interest is the huge (more than 500 per cent) increase in power output and consumption between 1950 and 1975, mainly in the automotive,

farming, and power-plant categories. In the same twenty-five years the population of the United States increased about 40 per cent.

The chart also indicates some of the principal sources of energy and the periods in which they were in widest use or began to be used widely. In general, the 1870's or thereabouts saw the beginnings of a massive shift from renewable to nonrenewable sources of energy. By 1976 a slight trend back to renewable energy sources—especially various forms of solar energy—had begun to manifest itself, but not really enough to measure.

The sources for these figures are *Historical Statistics of the United States: Colonial Times to 1970* and *Statistical Abstract of the United States: 1976*.

Total Horsepower (1850–1975) (in 1000's)

Year	Total	Cars & Trucks	Railroads	Airplanes	Merchant Ships (Powered)	Sailing Ships	Windmills	Work Animals
1850	8,495		586		325	400	14	5,960
1860	13,763		2,156		515	597	20	8,630
1870	16,931		4,462		632	314	30	8,660
1880	26,314		8,592		741	314	40	11,580
1890	44,086		16,980		1,124	280	80	15,970
1900	63,952	100	24,501		1,663	251	120	18,730
1910	138,810	24,686	51,308		3,098	220	180	21,460
1920	453,450	280,900	80,182		6,508	169	200	22,430
1930	1,663,944	1,426,568	109,743	3,382	9,115	100	200	17,660
1940	2,773,316	2,511,312	92,361	7,455	9,408	26	130	12,510
1950	4,754,038	4,403,617	110,969	22,000	23,423	11	59	7,040
1960	11,007,889	10,366,880	46,856	36,534	23,890	2	44	2,790
1970	20,408,000	19,325,000	54,000	183,000	22,000			1,500
1975	25,100,000	23,752,000	62,000	185,000	22,000		15	1,400

Principal Energy Sources

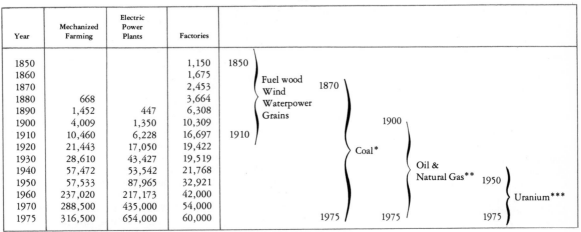

Year	Mechanized Farming	Electric Power Plants	Factories
1850			1,150
1860			1,675
1870			2,453
1880	668		3,664
1890	1,452	447	6,308
1900	4,009	1,350	10,309
1910	10,460	6,228	16,697
1920	21,443	17,050	19,422
1930	28,610	43,427	19,519
1940	57,472	53,542	21,768
1950	57,533	87,965	32,921
1960	237,020	217,173	42,000
1970	288,500	435,000	54,000
1975	316,500	654,000	60,000

1850 — 1910: Fuel wood, Wind, Waterpower, Grains (1870)

1870 — 1975: Coal*

1900 — 1975: Oil & Natural Gas**

1950 — 1975: Uranium***

*In 1975 coal provided about 26% of all energy consumed.
**In 1975 oil and natural gas provided about 66% of all energy consumed.
***In 1975 nuclear fission provided less than 3% of all energy consumed.

Index

A

Bland-Allison Act, 118
"Bleeding Kansas," 82
Bloomfield, Leonard, 248
Bloody Marsh, Battle of, 224
Bloody Ridge, Battle of, 225
Blue-Backed Speller (Webster), 44
Bly, Nellie, *see* Seaman, Elizabeth Cochrane
Bly, Robert, 252
Board of Education v. *Allen*, 216
Boas, Franz, 150, 248
Bolin, Jane Matilda, 268
Bonhomme Richard, 42
Bontemps, Arna, 267
"Bonus army," 162
Bonus Bill: *1817*: 66; *1924*: 155
Books, *see* Literature; Publishing
Boone, Daniel, 32, 33
Boonesborough, Ky., 33
Boorstin, Daniel J., 250
Booth, John Wilkes, 102, **102**
Booth, Mary Louise, 281
Bootlegging, 157
Border Ruffians, 82
Bork, Robert H., 293
Borman, Frank, 290
Boston, 53, 67, 81, 152, 275; colonial period, 14, 20;
   in Revolution, 32, 33, 35; population, 53, 67
Boston, 227
Boston Female Medical School, 280
Boston Female Society for Propagating . . . Christian
   Knowledge, 279
Boston Massacre, 32, **32**
Boston Tea Party, 32, **33**
Bouchet, Edward, 264
Boundaries, U.S.; *1783*, 44; Maine-New Brunswick,
   74; Mexico, 76, 80; Oregon, 75
Bowden, Don, 300
Bowditch, Nathaniel, 246
Bowling, 298
Boxer Rebellion, 133, 134, **134**, 237
Boxing, 296–99
Boyd, Belle, 281
Boyer, Elizabeth, 287
Boy Scouts of America, 139
Braddock, Gen. Edward, 26, **26**
Bradford, William, 19, 245
Bradley, Thomas, 275
Bradstreet, Anne, 21, 23, 251
Bragg, Gen. Braxton, 99, 233
Brand, Vance D., 291
Brandeis, Louis D., 145, Brandeis brief, 214
Branzburg v. *Hayes*, 217
Breasted, James Henry, 248
Breckinridge, John C., 85, 210
Bremer, Arthur, 197

Brent, Margaret, 21, 277
Bretton Woods Conference, 175
Brezhnev, Leonid I., 198
Briand-Kellogg Pact, 157
Bricker, John W., 175
Brimmer, Andrew, 273
Brock, Gen. Isaac, 63
Brokaw, Irving, 299
Brooke, Edward, 193, 273
Brook Farm, 73
Brooklyn Bridge, 120
Brooks, Clarence, 268
Brooks, Gwendolyn, 252, 270
Brooks, Preston S., 82
Brooks, Van Wyck, 245, 248
Brown, Anne, 270
Brown, B. Gratz, 114
Brown, Charles Brockden, 253
Brown, H. Rap, 274
Brown, John, 82; Harper's Ferry raid, 84–85, 261
Brown, Wesley A., 270
Brown, William Hill, 253
Brown, William Wells, 260
Brownsville, Tex., race riot in, 137, 265
Brown University, 25
Brown v. *Board of Education*, 185, 215
Bruce, Blanche K., 263, 264
Bryan, William Jennings, 126, 133, 142, 143; Scopes
   trial, 156, **156**
Bryant, William Cullen, 251
Buchanan, James C., 82; presidency, 83–85, 92, 93,
   203
Buck, Pearl, 254
Budget and Accounting Act, 154
Buena Vista, Battle of, 231
Buffaloes, exterminated, 114
Buffalo, N.Y., 64, **132**
"Buffalo Soldiers," 105
Bulganin, Nikolai, 185
Bulge, Battle of the, 175, 239–40
"Bull Moose" Party *see* Progressive Party
Bull Run, Battle of, first, 94, **94**, 232–33; second, 96,
   233
Bunche, Ralph J., 270, 271
Bunker Hill, Battle of, 34, 35, **35**, 226, 256
Bunker Hill Mine, 121
Bureau of Budget, 154
Bureau of Corporations, 135
Burgoyne, Gen. John, 39, 41, **41**, 226
Burns, Anthony, 81, 260
Burns, Lucie, 285
Burnside, Gen. Ambrose, 97, **97**, 233
Burr, Aaron, 48, 56; duel with Hamilton, 62; treason
   trial, 62; vice-president, 58

Conestoga wagon, 26
Confederate States of America, 87–89; foreign policy, 89, 94, 99; money, 88; population, 87; raiders, 100
Confederation of the U.S., 42, 44, 45
Confiscation Act, 96
Congress, first under Constitution, 45; gag rule, 72
Congress of Industrial Organizations, 165, 186
Congress of Racial Equality (CORE), 189, 269, 270
Congressional Union for Woman Suffrage, 285
Conkling, Roscoe, 118
Connecticut, 22–23, 258; Fundamental Orders of, 21; settlement, 20, 21
Connecticut Compromise, 45
Connecticut Land Co., 56
Connelly, Marc, 267
Connor, Eugene ("Bull"), 272
Conrad, Charles, Jr., 290, 291
Conscription Act, 98
Conservation, 106, 114, 138, 195
Constellation, 57, 227
Constitution, U.S.: Amendments, *see* Amendments, Bill of Rights, 50, 52; ratification, 45, 52
Constitution, 49, 57, **57**, 63, 64, **64**, 228
Constitutional Convention, 39–40, 44–45
Consumer's League, 284
Continental Congress, 33, 34, 39, 41; and Articles of Confederation, 42; and Declaration of Independence, 17, 35; war debt, 52
Contract Labor Act, 120
Convention of *1800*, 58
Conway Cabal, 41
Coogan, Jackie, **151**
Coolidge, Calvin, 152, 153, 210; presidency, 154–156, **204**
Coolidge, Grace, **208**
Cooper, Gordon L., 289
Cooper, James Fenimore, 253
Cooper, Peter, 69, 117
Copperheads, 100, 108
Copyright law, 52
Coral Sea, Battle of, 173, 238
Corbett, James, 298
Corbin, Margaret, 278
CORE, 189, 269, 270
Corn, 18, 19
Cornell, Ezra, 82
Cornell University, 82, 297
Cornish, Samuel, 259
Cornwallis, Gen. Charles, Lord, 38, 42, 43, **43**, 227, 257
Coronado, Francisco Vásquez, 8
Corregidor, 173, 238
Corte-Real, Gaspar, 7
Cortes, Hernando, 7

Cotton, 50, **50**, 53
Cotton, John, 245
Cotton gin, 50, 54
Coughlin, Charles E., 164
Council for New England, 19
Council of Economic Advisers, 180
Council of National Defense, 145
Cowley, Malcolm, 249
Cowpens, Battle of, 227
Cox, Archibald, 198, 293
Cox, James M., 153
Coxey, Jacob (Coxey's Army), 125–126, **125**
Coyle v. *Smith*, 214
Cozzens, James Gould, 254
Crane, Hart, 252
Crane, Stephen, 253
Crapsey, Algernon S., 137
Crawford, Jane Todd, 279
Crawford, William, 67
Crédit Mobilier, 114
Creek Indians, 52, 64, **64**; war with, 219, 229
Creel, George, 146
Creole affair, 73
Creole Show, 264
Crèvecoeur, Michel Guillaume Jean de, 246
Cricket, 297
"Crime of '73" 114
Crisis, The, 139, 266
Crittenden, John, 92
Crocker, Hannah Mather, 279
Crockett, Davy, 71, **71**
Croly, Herbert David, 248, 139, 140
Croquet, 297
Crump, Diana, 287, 301
Cuba, 80, 126, 134; Bay of Pigs invasion, 189; Castro government, 187–89; exploration, 7; missile crisis, 190; in Spanish-American War, 127–28, **127**, **128**
Cuffe, Paul, 257, 258
Cullen, Countee, 252, 267
Cumberland Gap, 32
Cumberland Landing, Va., 98
Cumberland Road (National Road), 63
Cummings, e.e., 252
Curtis, Charles, 157, 162, 210
Curtis, Cyrus H.K., 120
Custer, Gen. George A., **116**, 235, 236
Czolgosz, Leon F., 134

D

Dakota: territory, 93, 110
Dallas, George, 74
"damn the torpedoes," 101, 262
Dana, Richard Henry, 247
Danbury Hatters' Case, 138
Daniel, Robert, 224

Dare, Virginia, 277
Darrow, Clarence, 156
Dartmouth, 33
Dartmouth University, 25
Daughters of the American Revolution, 268
Davis, Gen. Benjamin O., Sr., 269
Davis, Gen. Benjamin O., Jr., 271
Davis, Henry G., 136
Davis, Jefferson, **92**, 98, 101, 102, 111
Dawes, Charles G., 210
Dawes, William, 34
Dawes Plan, 157
Dawes Severalty Act, 121
Dawson, William L., 270
Day, Dorothy, 286
Daylight Saving Time, 147
Dayton, William L., 82
D-Day, 174
DDT, 197
Deacons for Defense and Justice, 273
Dean, John, 292–95
Dean, Gen. William, 240
Deane, Silas, 42
Debs, Eugene, 126, 136, 147, 148
Decatur, Capt. Stephen, 65, 228, 229
"Declaration of Constitutional Principles," 186
Declaration of Independence, 17, **28**, 35, 256
Declaration of Rights: Continental Congress, 33; of
    Women, 76
Declaration of Sentiments, 280
Declaratory Act, 31
Deere, John, 72
Defense Production Act, 182
Delaney, Major Martin R., 262
Delaware: in Civil War, 88, 92
Delaware Indians, 23, 43
De La Warr, Thomas, Lord, 18
De Lôme, Dupuy, letter, 127
Democratic Party, 60, 72, 75; and free silver, 126; and
    slavery, 75–76, 80, 83; *see* also Elections, presi-
    dential
Democratic Party (Jacksonian), 68
Dempsey, Jack, 299
Denmark, 145
Dennis et al v. *U.S.*, 215
Department stores, 83
Dependent Pension Act, 123
De Priest, Oscar, 267
Derham, James, 258
Description of New England, A, 18
Desert Land Act, 117
DeSoto, Hernando, 8, 8, 255
Dessalines, Jean Jacques, 258
Detroit, Mich., 24, 174, 194, 196, 219; in War of 1812,
    63, 228

De Voto, Bernard, 249
DEW (Distant Early Warning), 185
Dewey, Commodore George, 127, 236
Dewey, John, 248
Dewey, Melvil, 117
Dewey, Thomas E., 175, 181
Dial, The, 72, 279
Diaz, Adolfo, 140
Dickey, James, 252
Dickinson, Emily, 252, 283
Dickinson, John, 246
Dien Bien Phu, 184
Dies, Martin, 167
Dillinger, John, 164
Di Maggio, Joe, 300
Dingley Tariff, 127
Diplomatic Appropriations Act, 125
Direct primary, 135
Disarmament: London Naval Conference, 160; Wash-
    ington Conference, naval limits, 154; SALT, 197
Discoverer satellite, 289
Disney, Walt, 150
Displaced Persons Act, 181
District of Columbia, 45, 118, 109; slavery in, 77, 79,
    261; voting in, 189
Dix, Dorothea, 74, 94, 279
Dixiecrat (States' Rights) Party, 181
Dixon-Yates contract, 185
Dog racing, 299
Dole, Robert J., 201
Dole, Sanford B., 125, 126
Dominican Republic, 113, 136, 146
Dominion of New England, 23, 24
Domino theory, 184
Donelson, Andrew, 82, 83
Doolittle, Hilda, 252
Doolittle, Gen. James, 157, 173
Dorman, Isaiah, 264
Dorr, Thomas W., (Dorr's Rebellion), 73, 213
Dos Passos, John, 254
Douglas, Stephen A., 78, **80**, 85; Lincoln debate,
    83–84, 84
Douglas, William O., 215
Douglass, Frederick, 75, 247, 260, 264, 282
Dow, Neal, 119
Draft; 214; in Civil War, 98, 99, 261; termination, 198
    in World War I, 146, **146**; in World War II, 171
Drake, Edwin L., 84, **84**
Drake, Sir Francis, 9
Dred Scott v. *Sandford*, 83, 212, 213, 261
Dreiser, Theodore, 253
Dressler, Marie, 144
Drew, Charles R., 269, 270
Du Bois, W.E.B., 135, 139 248, 265–66; and Niagara
    Movement, 137

Fort Niagara, 225
Fort Orange, 19
Fort Ross, 63
Fort Scott, Kans., **82**
Fort Stanwix, 41
Fort Sumter, S.C., 85, 87, 92–93, **93**, 261
Fort Ticonderoga, 27, 34, 256
Fort Wagner, 98, **98**
Fort William and Mary, 33
Fort Wingate, N.M., 232
Foster, William Z., 152, 162
Four Freedoms, 171–72
Foxburg Golf Club, 298
Fox hunting, 296
France: alliance with U.S., 42; in American Revolution, 35, 38, 41–43; in colonial wars, 24–27, 218, 219, 223–25; and Louisiana Purchase, 61; undeclared naval war, 57, 219, 227, 228; U.S. relations with, 49, 56; in World War II, 175, 237; *see also* World War I
Franciscans, 11
Franklin, Benjamin, 17, 25, 42, **42**, 52, 246; confederacy plan, 26; electricity experiment, 26; and peace negotiations, 43
Fraunces, Samuel, 257
Fraunces Tavern, N.Y., 44
Fredericksburg, Battle of, 97, 233
Free African Society, 258
Freedmen's Bureau, 101, 108, 109, 262
Freedom riders, 189–90, **189**, 270, 272
Freedom's Journal, 259
Freeport doctrine, 84
Free-Soil Party, 76, 80, 81
Frelinghuysen, T., 74, 75
Frémont, John C., 76, 82, 83, 261
French and Indian War, 26, 27, 219, 224–25
Frenchtown, Battle of, 228
Freneau, Philip, 53, 251
Friedan, Betty, 287
Fries Rebellion, 57
Frobisher, Sir Martin, 9
Frontenac, Louis de Buade, Comte de, 24
Frost, Robert, 251
Fugitive Slave Act, 77, 79, 84,
Fugitive Slave Law, *1793*, 258
Fulbright, J. William, 180
"Full Dinner Pail," 133
Fuller, Buckminster, 249
Fuller, Margaret, 72, 247, 279
Fulton, Robert, 62
Furman v. *Georgia*, 217
Fur trade, 18–19; conflict with French, 22, 25; in Oregon, 54

G

Gadsden Purchase, 80
Gagarin, Yuri, 289
Gage, Gen. Thomas, 226
Gag rule, 72
Galbraith, John Kenneth, 249
Garfield, James A., assassinated, 119, **119**; presidency, 119, **203**
Garfield, Lucretia, **207**
Garner, John Nance, 162, 165, 210
Garnet, Henry Highland, 260
Garriott, Owen K., 291
Garrison, William Lloyd, 69, 71, 78, 258
Garrity, Arthur, 276
Garvey, Marcus, 267
Gary, Elbert H., 134
Gaspee, 32
Gates, Gen. Horatio, 41, 227
Gault, *in re*, 217
Gazette of the United States, 53
Geary Chinese Exclusion Act, 124
Gemini space flights, 289, 290
General Accounting Office, 154
General Federation of Women's Clubs, 284; and suffrage movement, 285
General Motors, 181
General Staff Corps, 135
Genêt, Edmond Charles (Citizen), 49, 54
Geneva, summit meeting at, *1955*: 185
Geneva Agreements on Vietnam, 185
George, David Lloyd, **152**
George, Henry, 118, 247
George III, king of England, 30, 33, 34
Georgia, 25, 52; in Civil War, 92, 234; Indians, 69, 70, 72, 212; Yazoo land fraud, 55
Germantown, Battle of, 226
Germany, 122, 148, 167; immigration from, 73, 79, 85, 112, 171; World War I, 143–48, **148**; World War II, 172, 176, **176**
Germany, West (Federal Republic), 181, 182
Geronimo, 113, 121
Gerry, Elbridge, 56, **56**, 64, 210
Gershwin, George, 270
Gesell, Arnold, 248
Gettysburg, Battle of, 98, **99**, 233
Ghent, Treaty of, 65, 219
Ghost Dance War, 124, 221
Gibbons v. *Ogden*, 212, 215
Gibbs, Jonathan C., 263
GI Bill of Rights, 183
Gibson, Althea, 271, 300
Gibson, Edward G., 291
Gilbert, Sir Humphrey, 9
Gilman, Charlotte Perkins, 248, 284
Gilpin, Charles, 267

Ginsberg, Allen, 252
Ginsburg v. *U.S.*, 216
Girl Scouts, 285
Gitlow v. *New York*, 214
Gladden, Washington, 247
Glasgow, Ellen, 253–54
Glass-Steagall Act, 161, 163
Glenn, John H., 190, **190**, 289
Glidden, Joseph F., 115
Glorietta Pass, Battle of, 97, 232
Glover, Mrs. Jose, 21
Goddard, Robert H., 144, 150
Godey's Lady's Magazine, 279
Goethals, George, 138
Gold: from Hispaniola, 7; discoveries, 76, 84, 127; as political issue, 111, 126
Gold Reserve Act, 163
Gold Standard Act, 133
Golf, 298, 301
Goliad, Tex., 71, 230
Gompers, Samuel, 133
Goodman, Andrew, 272, 274
Goodyear, Charles, 74
Gordy, Berry, Jr., 270
Gorgas, William, 138
Gosnold, Bartholomew, 10
"Gospel of Wealth, The," 123
Gould, Jay, 112
Grand Alliance, 24
Grand Banks, 6, 7
Grand Canyon, 8
"Grandfather clause," 128, 144, 145, 214
Granger Cases, 213
Granger laws, 117
Grangers (Patrons of Husbandry), 110, **110**
Grant, Julia, **207**
Grant, Ulysses S., in Civil War, 95, 99–102, **99**, 232–34; presidency, 111–17, **203**
Grasso, Ella, 199, **199**, 188
Gravely, Lt. Com. Samuel, 272
Gray, Asa, 247
Gray, L. Patrick, 292
Gray, Capt. Robert, 54
Great Awakening, 25
Great Britain; *Alabama* claims, 114; in Civil War, 94, 97; immigration from, 73, 79, 85; Jay's Treaty, 49; naval limits, 154; in Northwest, 43, 48, 53, 55; peace treaty, 43–44; in Revolution, *see* American Revolution; rivalry with French, 24–26; Venezuela dispute, 126; War of 1812, 63–65
Great Depression, 158–67, **158,161**
"Great Migration," 19
"Great Society," 192
Great Train Robbery, The, 136

Greeley, Horace, 73, 281
Green, Henrietta (Hetty), 285
Greenback Labor Party, 115, 117–20
Greenbacks, **88**, 98, 111, 115, 118
Green Berets, 242
Greene, General Nathanael, 41–42
Greener, Richard T., 263
Greenland, 5–7
"Green Mountain Boys" 31, 34
Greensboro, N.C., 188
Greenville, Treaty of, 55
Greer, 172
Gregory, Dick, 195, 273
Grey, Edward, 145
Griffith, D.W., 144, 266
Grimké, Angelina Emily, 72, 247, 279
Grimké, Sarah, 72, 246, 279
Grissom, Virgil I., 289–90
Griswold v. *Connecticut*, 216
Grosseilliers, Médard Chouart, Sieur de, 22
Guadalcanal, Battle of, 173, 238
Guadalupe-Hidalgo, Treaty of, 76, 80
Guam, 128, 175
Guatemala, 185
Guerrière, 63, **64**, 228
Guilford Courthouse, Battle of, 227
Guinn v. *U.S.*, 214, 266
Guiteau, Charles J., 119
Guns: Colt, 71; Gatling, 97; manufacture of, 50; as sport, 297; Winchester, 97
Guthrie, Okla., **122**, 123
Gymnasium, 296

H

Hague Conference: *1899*: 133; *1907*, 138
Hague Tribunal, 141, 156, 164
Haiti, 49, 61, 144, 258
Haldeman, H.R., 198, 292–95
Hale, John P., 80
Hale, Nathan, 41, 256
Hale, Sarah Josepha, 279
Halfway Covenant, 21
Hall, Prince, 258
Hamilton, Alexander: duel with Burr, 62; *Federalist* essays, 45; Jefferson's feud with, 48; secretary of the treasury, 47–48, **48**, 52–55
Hamlin, Hannibal, 85, 93, 210
Hammarskjöld, Dag, **188**
Hammer v. *Dagenhart*, 214, 215
Hammon, Jupiter, 256
Hampton Roads, Va., 101
Hancock, John, 32, 34
Hancock, William S., 119
Handball, 298
Handy, W.C., 266

Java, 63, 228
Java Sea, Battle of, 237
Jaworski, Leon, 199, 293-95
Jay, John, 43, 52; and *Federalist* essays, 45; negotiates treaty, 48-49, 55
Jay Treaty, 49, 55
Jeffers, Robinson, 252
Jefferson, Martha, **206**
Jefferson, Thomas, 17, 47-49, 50, 53, 55, 81; Hamilton's feud with, 48; presidency, 58, 61-63, **202**; secretary of state, 52, 54; and Statute of Religious Freedom, 44
Jesuits, 11, 12
Jewett, Sarah Orne, 253
Jews, 21, 141
"Jim Crow," 264, 265
Jockey, 296
Jodl, Gen. Alfred, **176**
Johnson, Andrew, 100-101, 210; impeachment, 110-11, **111**; presidency, 102, 107-11, **203**
Johnson, Anthony, 255
Johnson, Claudia ("Lady Bird"), **209**
Johnson, Eliza, **207**
Johnson, Henrietta, 277
Johnson, Herschel B., 85
Johnson, Hiram W., 142, 152
Johnson, Jack, 139, 265, 299
Johnson, James Weldon, 267
Johnson, Lyndon B., 189, 210; presidency, 191-95, **191**, **204**; and Vietnam War, 192-94
Johnson, Richard M., 72
Johnston, John H., 270
Johnston, Gen. Joseph E., 94, 102, 232
Johnston, John H., 270
Joint Committee of Reconstruction, 107, 108, 110
Joint Committee on the Conduct of the War, 94, 95
Joliet, Louis, **12**, 23
Jolson, Al, 157
Jones, Absalom, 258
Jones, Bobby, 300
Jones, Capt. John Paul, 42
Jones, Frederick McKinley, 268
Jones, Leroi, 274
Joplin, Scott, 265
Jordan, Barbara, 275, 276
Joseph, Chief, 117, **117**, 220
Juárez, Benito, 98
Judiciary Act: *1781*, 52, 61; *1800*, 58
Jujitsu, 299
Julian, Dr. Percy, 268
Jupiter, space observation, 290
Just, Ernest E., 266

K

Kalmbach, Herbert, 292, 294
Kanagawa, Treaty of, 81
Kansas, 283; slavery struggle in, 82-83; territory, 80; statehood, 92
Kansas-Nebraska Act, 80, 81
Karlsefni, Thorfinn, 5
Katz v. *U.S.*, 217
Kearsarge, 234
Kefauver, Estes, 186
Kennebec River, 10
Kennedy, Jacqueline, **209**
Kennedy, John F., **204**; assassinated, **191**; foreign policy, 189-90; presidency, 189-91
Kennedy, Robert, 190, 195
Kent, James, 246
Kent State University, 196, **196**
Kentucky, 32, 33; in Civil War, 88, 92; statehood, 54
Kentucky Derby, 297
Kentucky Resolutions, 50, 57
Kentucky rifle, 25
Kern, John W., 139
Kerner Commission, 274
Kerwin, Joseph P., 291
Key, Francis Scott, 64
Khmer Rouge, 244
Khrushchev, Nikita, **188**, 190; in kitchen debate, 188
Kid, The, **151**
Kidnappings, laws on, 164
Kies, Mary, 279
Kilmer, Joyce, 147-48, 252
King, Billie Jean, 301
King, Martin Luther, Jr.; 186, 192, **194**, 271-73; assassinated, 194; Nobel Peace Prize, 273
King, Rev. Martin Luther, Sr., 276
King, Rufus, 62, 63, 66
King, William R., 80
King George's War, 25, 219, 224
King Philip's War, 22, **22**, 23, 218, 222
King William's War, 24, 218, 223
Kings Mountain, Battle of, 42, 227
Kinsey, Alfred, 181, 249, 286
Kissinger, Henry A., 197, 198, 293
Kitty Hawk, N.C., 136
Kleindienst, Richard, 198, 292, 294
Knights of Labor, 105, 112
Knights of the White Camellia, 263
Know-Nothing Party (American Party), 81, 82
Knox, Frank, 165
Knox, Gen. Henry, 35, 52
Knox, Rose, 285
Korea, North, 182, 240; *Pueblo* affair, 194
Korea, treaty with, 120

Monroe Doctrine, 67, 126; Roosevelt's Corollary, **129**, 136, 157
Montagu, Hannah Lord, 279
Montana, 107; statehood, 122
Montcalm, Louis Joseph, Marquis de, 27, 224
Monterey, Cal., 10, 32
Monterrey, Mex., 231
Montgomery, Gen. Richard, 35
Montreal, 21, 25, 27, 219; in Revolution, 35
Moon: landing on, 195, 290, 291; missions to, 187, 195, 289
Moore, Harry T., 271
Moore, Marianne, 252
Moore's Creek Bridge, Battle of, 35
Morehouse College, 262
Morgan, Gen. Daniel, 227
Morgan, Garret A., 267
Morgan, J.P., 126, 134, 137, 144
Morgan, Thomas Hunt, 248
Morgan horses, 296
Morison, Samuel Eliot, 248
Mormons, 68, 69, 75, 126
Morphy, Paul C., 296
Morrill Tariff, 93, 96
Morris, Gouverneur, 45
Morris, Robert, 53
Morristown, N.J., 41
Morse, Samuel F.B., 74, 74
Morton, Levi P., 122, 210
Morton, Thomas, 20
Moscow Conference, 175
Mother's Day, 143
Motion pictures, 136, 144, 157, 266
Motley, Constance Baker, 273
Motley, John Lothrop, 247
Motown Records, 270
Mott, Lucretia, 76, 279
Mountain climbing, 297, 299, 301
Mount Holyoke College, 72, 279
Mount Vernon Ladies Association, 280
Mount Wilson Observatory, Cal., 136
Moynihan, Daniel P., 275
Muckrakers, 136
Mudge, Generva, 284
Mugwumps, 120
Muhammad, Wallace, 275
Muhammad Ali, 301
Muir, John, 247
Muller, Hermann J., 150
Muller v. *Oregon*, 139, 214
Mulzac, Capt. Hugh, 269-70
Mumford, Lewis, 249
Mundt, Karl, 184
Munich Agreement, 167
Munn v. *Illinois*, 117, 213

Murchison, Charles F. (Murchison letter), 122
Murfreesboro, Battle of, 233
Muscle Shoals, Tenn., 160
Muskie, Edmund, 195
My Lai massacre, 195

N

NAACP, *see* National Association for the Advancement of Colored People
Nader, Ralph, 193, 250
Nagasaki, atomic attack on, 176
Naismith, James A., 298
Nantucket, 16
Napoleon, 49, 55, 58, 63; and Louisiana Purchase, 61
Narraganset Indians, 21, 30, 222
Narrative of . . . Frederick Douglass . . ., 75
Narváez, Pánfilo de, 8, 255
Nashville, Battle of, 101, 234, 261
Natchez Indians, 25
National Advisory Commission on Civil Disorders, 274
National Aeronautics and Space Agency, 187, 289-91
National American Woman Suffrage Association, 284-85
National Association for the Advancement of Colored People (NAACP), 137, 139, 145, 265-68, 270
National Association of Baseball Players, 296-97
National Collegiate Athletic Association, 299
National Commission (baseball), 299
National Conservation Commission, 138
National Council of Negro Women, 268
National Debt, 47, 52
National Defense Act, 145
National Defense Education Act, 187
National Environmental Policy Act, 196
National Football League, 299, 300
National Foundation of the Arts and Humanities, 193
National Guard, 145; and racial conflicts, 186-87, 192
National Hockey League, 299
National Industrial Recovery Act, 163-64
National Gazette, 53
National Labor Relations Act, 64
National Labor Relations Board, 164
National Labor Union, 108
National League (baseball), 297
National Liberation Front of South Vietnam, 242
National Monetary Commission, 138
National Negro Business League, 265
National Organization for Women, 287
National Progressive Republican League, 140
National Prohibition Party, 112
National Republican Party, 68, 70

Northwest Passage, 8, 9
Nova Scotia, 11; in intercolonial wars, 24, 25, 223, 224
NOW, 287
Noyes Academy, 259
Nuclear Nonproliferation Treaty, 195
Nullification, Ordinance of, 70
Nullification doctrine, 68
Nuthead, Dinah, 277
Nye, Gerald P. (Nye Committee), 163
nylon, 164

O

Oakley, Annie, 283
Oberlin College, 70, 279
Observer, 72
Occupational Safety and Health Act (OSHA), 196
Ocean Hill-Brownsville School District, N.Y., 274
O'Conor, Charles, 114
Office of Price Administration, 172, 175
Oglethorpe, James, 13, 25, 219, 224
Ohio, 85, 112; statehood, 61; territory, 55
Ohio Valley, 25; French in, 26, 27
Oil industry, 84, 84, 109, 134, 195; embargo, Middle East, 198
Okeechobee, Battle of, 231
Okinawa, 176, 240
Oklahoma, 214, settlement, 122–23, 122; statehood, 138
"Old Deluder Satan Act," 21
Oldfield, Barney, 140
"Old Ironsides," *see Constitution*
Oliver, Joseph ("King"), 266
Olive, Milton K., III, 273
"Olive Branch" Petition, 34
Olney, Richard, 126
Olson, Charles, 252
Olympic Games, 299, 301, 302
Omaha Beach, France, 239
"Omaha Program," 124
Omnibus Bill: *1850*, 79; *1889*, 122
Omnibus Housing Act, 192
Oñate, Juan de, 10
Opechancanough, 218, 222
Open Door Policy, 133, 147
"Open Skies" plan, 185
"Operation Torch," 173
Oppenheimer, Julius Robert, 185, 249
Ordinance of 1785 (western lands), 44
Oregon, 74, 74, 75; initiative and referendum introduced, 135; territory, 54; statehood, 84
Oregon v. *Mitchell*, 217
Organic Acts, 120, 146; court decision, 214
Orlando, Vittorio, **152**
Osceola, 71, 230

OSHA, 196
Oskar II, 144
Ostend Manifesto, 81–83, **81**
O'Sullivan, Mary Kenney, 285
Oswald, Lee Harvey, 191
Otis, Gen. Elwell, 236
Otis, James, 31, 246
"Our country . . . right or wrong," 65
Outerbridge, Mary Ewing, 282, 297
Outer Space Treaty, 290, 297
Owen, Ruth Bryan, 286
Owens, Jesse, 268, 300

P

Pacific Ocean, 7
Pacific Railroad Act, 96
Paige, Satchel, 271
Paine, Tom, 29, 246; *Crisis* pamphlet, 41; *Common Sense*, 35
Palko v. *Connecticut*, 215
Palmer, A. Mitchell, 152, **152**
Palmer, Arnold, 301
Palo Alto, Battle of, 231
Palomares incident (Spain), 193
Panama, 135–36; treaty with, 167
Panama Canal, 135, 138; construction of, **135**, 136; opening, 143
Panama Canal Act, 142
Pan American Union, 123
Pan American World Airways, 167
Panay, 166
Panics: *1819*, 66; *1837*, 71, 72, **72**; *1857*, 83; *1873*, 114, 115; *1893*, 125; *1907*, 138; *1929*, 157
Parcel post, 142
Paris: Peace Conference, *1919*, 152, **152**; Summit Conference, *1960*, 188; Vietnam peace talks, 198; in World War II, 175, **175**
Paris, Treaty of: *1763*, 27, 219; *1783*, 43–44, **43**, 219; *1898*, 128, 133
Parker, Alton B., 136
Parker, Bonnie, 164
Parker, Quanah, 220
Parkinson, Kenneth W., 294
Parkman, Francis, 247
Parks, Rosa, 186, 271
Parrington, Vernon Louis, 248
Parsons, Elsie, 285
Patents: U.S., first in, 53; *see also* specific inventions
Pathet Lao, 244
Patroons, 20
Patten, Joshua, 281
Patterson, Eleanor, 286
Patterson, Floyd, 300
Patton, Gen. George S., Jr., 239, 269

Postal savings system, 140
Postal system: air mail, 147; parcel post, 142
Postmaster general, 53
Post Office Dept., 53, 55, 124, 150, 187–88
Pottawatomie massacre, 82
Pound, Ezra, 248, 252
Powell, Adam Clayton, Jr., 270, 273, 274
Powell, John Wesley, 247
Powell v. *Alabama*, 215
Power boating, 302
Powers, Francis Gary, 188
Powhatan Indians, 18, 19, 218, 222, 277
Preakness Stakes, 297
Preemption Law, 73
Prescott, Samuel, 34
Prescott, William Hickling, 246
Presidential Succession Act, 121
Presidents, chronology of, **202–205**; message to
   Congress, 143, **191**; two term limit, 182; wives,
   chronology of, **206–209**
Press, freedom of, 25; court decisions, 214–17
Price, Leontyne, 272
Price controls: in Korean War, 183; in Nixon admin-
   istration, 197; in World War II, 172
Prigg v. *Pennsylvania*, 74
Princeton, N.J., Battle of, 41, 226
Princeton University, 25
Prize Cases, 213
Proclamation of Amnesty and Reconstruction, 99
Proclamation of 1763, 31
Professional Golfers' Association, 299
Progress and Poverty, 118
Progressive movement, 130–32
Progressive Party, 142, 155, 181
Prohibition, 147, 152, 157; and crime, 160; repeal of,
   163
Prohibition Party, 117, 119, 120, 122, 125
Promontory Point, Utah, **106**, 111
Prosser, Gabriel, 258
Prostitution, 51, 140, 285
Providence, R.I., 20
Public Credit Act, 111
Publicity Act, 140
Public Works Administration, 158, 159
Publius essays, 45
Pueblo incident, 194
Pueblo Indians, 12
Puerto Rico, 133, 146; ceded, 128; commonwealth,
   183; exploration and conquest, 7
Pulitzer, Joseph, 120, **120**, 126
Pullman, George, 90
Pullman strike, 126
Pure Food and Drug Act, 137
Puritans, 15, 19–21, 23, 24; and women, 277

Purvis, Robert, 259
Pusan Beachhead, Battle of, 240
Putnam, Emily James, 285
Putnam, Gen. Israel, 226
Pyle, Ernie, 249
Pynchon, Thomas, 254

Q

Quakers, 22, 26, 255, 277
Quarantine speech, 166
Quartering Act, 31
Quebec (city), 18, 24
Quebec (province), in colonial wars, 24, 25, 27
   219, 223, 225; in Revolution, 35
Quebec Act, 33
Queen Anne's War, 24, 218, 223
Quivira, 8
Quota Acts, 154, 155

R

Racial discrimination: in armed services, 181, 267,
   269, 270; *see also* Blacks in American history,
   255–76
Radical Republicans, *see* Republican Party
Radio, 137, 153; and Federal Communications Com-
   mission, 163, 164
Radio Act, 156
Radio broadcasting, 141, 156
Radisson, Pierre-Esprit, 22
Railroad Administration, 147
Railroads, 68, 80, 90; regulation of, 137, 145; subsi-
   dies, 196, 197; transcontinental, 92, 96, **106**, 111
Railway Labor Board, 153
Railway Rate Regulation Act, 137
Rainey, Joseph H., **103**, 263
Raleigh, Sir Walter, 9
Rankin, Jeannette, 172, 285
Randolph, Asa Philip, 172, 267, 269, 270, 272
Randolph, Edmund, 52
Ranger spacecraft, 192, 289
Ransom, John Crowe, 249, 252
Rauschenbusch, Walter, 248
Ray, James Earl, 195
Rainey, "Ma," 267
Reach, Al, 297
Re-apportionment, 216
Reciprocal Trade Agreements Act, 164
Reclamation Act, 135
Reconstruction, 107–113
Reconstruction Acts, 109
Reconstruction Finance Corp., 161
Reconstruction proclamation, 107
Red Cloud, 107, 108
Red Cross, 119, 283
Red River War, 220, 235

"Red scare" (1919–20), 152–53, 267
Reed, Walter, 138
Referendum, 135
Refugee Relief Act, 183
Regulators, 32
Reid, Whitelaw, 125
Religion: 20, 23, 44; court ruling, 216; Great
  Awakening, 25; Scopes trial, 156; see also Jews and
  Roman Catholic Church
Remond, Charles Lennox, 260
Report on Manufactures, 54
Report on Public Credit, 52
Republican Party, 118, 119; founded, 81; radical
  Republicans, 95, 97, 99, 107, 109; stalwarts, 118;
  see also Elections, presidential
Republican party (Jeffersonian), 48, 50, 67; founded,
  53
Resaca de la Palma, Battle of, 231
Reservations, 71, 72, 110, 121
Reserve Officers Training Corps, 145
Resettlement Administration, 164
Retaliation, 227
Reuben James, 172
Revels, Hiram, **103**, 263
Revenue Acts, 156, 164, 167
Revenue Sharing Act, 197
Revere, Paul, 12, 32, 34
Revolta, Johnny, 300
Revolution, American, *see* American Revolution
Revolution, The, 281, 282
Reynolds v. *Sims*, 216
Rhode Island, 73, 213, 256
Rhodes, James Ford, 247
Ribaut, Jean, 8
Richardson, Elliot L., 198, 293
Richmond, Bill, 256
Richmond, Va., 86, 88, 100–102
Ridgway, Gen. Matthew, 240
Riesman, David, 249–50
Rifle (as sport), 297
*Rights of the British Colonies Asserted and Proved,
  The*, 31
Riis, Jacob August, 124, 247
Riley, James Whitcomb, 251
Rillieux, Norbert, 260
Riots, 76, 174, 194, 261, 262, 274, 265, 266
Ripon, Wis., 81
Roanoke Island, 9–10, 277
Roberts v. *Boston*, 260
Roberval, Jean François de la Rocque, Sieur de, 8
Robeson, Paul, 267, 270, 271
Robinson, Bernard W., 268, 275
Robinson, Bill ("Bojangles"), 270
Robinson, Edwin Arlington, 251
Robinson, Frank, 301

Robinson, Jack Roosevelt ("Jackie"), **180**, 181, 270,
  300
Robinson, James, 257
Robinson, Joseph T., 157
Robinson, Sugar Ray, 300
Robinson-Patman Act, 165
Rock, John S., 262
Rockefeller, John D., 112, 124, 143, 180
Rockefeller, Nelson A., 199, 210
Rockefeller Foundation, 143
Rodeo, 298, 300
Rodino, Peter, 293, 294
Roethke, Theodore, 252
Roe v. *Wade*, 217
Roley, Susan Lynn, 287
Rolfe, John, 18, 277
Roman Catholic Church, 20, 81, 157, 189
Roman Nose, Chief, 235
Rommel, Gen. Erwin, 175, 239
Roosa, Stuart A., 290
Roosevelt, Alice, 208
Roosevelt, Edith, 208
Roosevelt, Eleanor, **208**, 286
Roosevelt, Franklin D., 153, 158, 159; court contro-
  versy, 166; presidency, 162–76, **162**, **171**, **174**,
  175, **204**
Roosevelt, Theodore, 129, 140, 210, 299; presidency,
  134–38, **203**; and Progressive Party, 141–42; in
  Spanish-American War, **128**, 236
Roosevelt Corollary to Monroe Doctrine, **129**, 136,
  157
Root, Elihu, 142
Rose Bowl (football), 299
Rosebud, Battle of, 236
Rosenberg, Julius and Ethel, 182
Rossi, Alice, 287
Rostow, Walt W., 190
Roth v. *U.S.*, 216
Rough Riders, 128, **128**, 236
Rounders (sport), 296
Rowing, 296
Rowlandson, Mary White, 245
Rowson, Susanna Haswell, 253, 278
Rubber (vulcanized), 74
Rubin, Barbara Jo, 301
Ruby, Jack, 191
Ruckelshaus, William D., 198, 293
Ruffin, Josephine St. Pierre, 284
Rugby, 297
Ruggles, David, 260
"Rum, Romanism, and Rebellion," 120
Rural Electrification Administration, 164
Rush-Bagot Agreement, 66
Russell, Bill, 273
Russell, Charles Taze, 247

Russia (Empire): Alaska purchased from 102; exploration and trade in North America, 25, 63; immigration from, 153; in World War I, 148; U.S. relations with, 141; *see also* Soviet Union
Russo, Anthony, 293
Russwurm, John B., 259
Rutgers University, 25
Ruth, George Herman ("Babe"), 150, 199, 300
Ryan, Mary B., 288
Ryan, Paddy, 298
Ryswick, Treaty of, 218

S

Sable, Jean Baptiste Pointe du, 258
Sacajawea, 61, 279
Sacco, Nicola, 153, **153**
Sacco-Vanzetti case, 153, 154, 157
Sackets Harbor, Battle of, 228
Sagan, Carl, 250
Sage, Margaret, 286
St. Augustine, Fla., 9, 218, 223, 224
St. Clair, Gen. Arthur, 53, 57
St. Clair, James, 295
St. Crispin, Daughters of, 281
St. John, John P., 120
St. Lawrence River, 27; exploration, 8, 10
St. Lawrence Seaway, 184, 188
St. Louis, Mo., 81, 115
Saint Luke Penny Savings Bank, 285
Saint-Mihiel salient, 148, **148**, 237
St. Valentine's Day Massacre, 157
Saipan, 239
"Salary Grab Act," 114
Salem, Mass., 20, 277
Salem, Peter, 256
Salk vaccine, 184, 185
SALT, 197
Salter, Susanna, 284
Salvation Army, 119
Samoa, 118, 122
Samuelson, Paul, 250
San Antonio, Tex., 13, 25
Sandburg, Carl, 251
Sand Creek Massacre, 91, 235
San Diego Bay, Cal., 10
San Francisco, 35; earthquake, 137, **137**
San Francisco Bay, 32
San Francisco Conference, **170**, 176
Sanger, Margaret Higgins, 144, **144**, 248, 285
San Ildefonso, Treaty of, 58
San Jacinto, Battle of, 71, 230
San Juan, Battle of, 128, 236
San Lorenzo, Treaty of, 55
San Salvador, 7
Santa Anna, Antonio Lopez de, 71, 72, 230

Santa Barbara spill, 195
Santa Catalina Islands, 10
Santa Clara County v. *Southern Pacific Railroad Co.*, 121, 213
Santa Fe, N.M., 18
Santa Maria, 7
Santayana, George, 248
Santiago Bay, Battle of, 128, 236
Saratoga, N.Y., 224; racetrack, 297
Saratoga campaign, 39, 41, **41**
Sarnoff, David, 141
Satellites, 289–91; artificial, 289–90; communications, 289; weather, 289
"Saturday Night Massacre," 198, 293
Savannah, Ga., 25; in Civil War, 101; in Revolution, 226, 257
Savo Island, Battle of, 238
Saxbe, William B., 293
Schenck v. *U.S.*, 149, 214
Schine, G. David, 184
Schirra, Walter M., 290
Schlesinger, Arthur, 250
Schmitt, Harrison, 291
Schneider, Sue, 301
Schuyler, Louisa Lee, 282
Schwerner, Michael H., 273–74
Scopes, John T., trial of, 156
Scott, David R., 290
Scott, Dred, 83, **83**; *see Dred Scott* v. *Sandford*
Scott, Gen. Winfield, 73, 80, 229
Scottsboro Cases, 215
scuba diving, 300
Seale, Bobby, 273
Sealing, 141
Seaman, Elizabeth Cochrane, 123, 284
Sears, Roebuck Co., 126
SEATO, 185
Secession, 85, 92
Secretariat, 301
Securities and Exchange Commission, 164
Sedition Act: *1798*: 57, **57**; *1918*, 147
Selective Draft Law Cases, 214
Selective Service Act, *1917*, 146; expires, 198
Selective Training and Service Act, *1940*, 171
Selma, Ala., 192, 273
Seminole War: (1st) 66, 219–20, 230; (2nd) 71, 220, 230–31
Senate, 39, 45; popular election of, 140, 143
Seneca Falls, N.Y., 76, 279–80
Sennett, Mack, 144
Seoul, S. Korea, 240
Serapis, 42
Serra, Father Junipero, 32
Seton, Elizabeth Ann Bayley (Saint), 279, 287
Settlement houses, 283

Truth-in-Lending Act, 195
Tubman, Harriet, 80, 259
Tucker, William, 255
Tunis, 65
Turner, Frederick Jackson, 248
Turner, Nat, 69, 259
Tuskegee Institute, 119, 264, 269, 271
TVA, 160, 163
Twain, Mark, 90, 253
Tweed, William Marcy, 113, **113**
Tydings-McDuffie Act, 163
Tydings, Millard, 182
Tyler, John, presidency, 73–75, **202**
Tyler, Julia, **206**
Tyler, Letitia, **206**

U

U-2 incident, 188
Uncle Tom's Cabin, 80, **80**, 260, 280
Underground Railroad, 79, 260
"Understanding clause," 123, 124
Underwood-Simmons Tariff, 143
Unemployment: in Coxey's Army, 125–26; in Great
    Depression, 158–60, 162, 164, 166
Union Pacific R.R., 91, 96, 111
Unions, 71, 74, 108, 138; national, 121; origins of,
    105, 112; racketeering in, 188; Taft-Hartley Act
    and, 180; in World War I, 147; in World War II,
    173; women and, 279, 281
Union Stockyards, 107
United Automobile Workers, 166, 181
United Colonies of New England, 21
United Fruit Co., 138
United Mine Workers, 135
United Nations, 180, 200; Declaration, 172; and
    Korean War, 183
United Nations Relief and Rehabilitation Administra-
    tion, 174
United Negro Improvement Association, 267
United States, 57, 63
United States Golf Association, 298
United Tailoresses Society of New York, 279
University of Chicago, 124
University of Georgia, 44
University of Iowa, 281
University of Pennsylvania, 25
Unknown Soldier, Tomb of, 154
Updike, John, 254
U.S. Lawn Tennis Association, 200, 298
U.S. Steel Corp., 134, 190
U.S. Telegraph Co., 108
U.S. v. California, 215
U.S. v. E.C. Knight Co., 214
U.S. v. Maine, 215

U.S. Volleyball Association, 300
U.S. v. Richard Nixon, 217, 295
U.S. v. U.S. District Court, 217
Utah, 79; settlement, 75; statehood, 126
Utrecht, Treaty of, 24, 218

V

Valcour Bay, Battle of, 226
Valley Forge, Pa., 41–42, 226
Van Buren, Hannah, **206**
Van Buren, Martin, 69, 70, 210; presidency, 72, 73,
    202
Vanderbilt, Cornelius, 82
Vanderbilt Cup, 299
Vanguard satellite, 289
Vanzetti, Bartolomeo, 153, **153**
Vassar College, 92, 281
Veblen, Thorstein, 248
Velikovsky, Immanuel, 249
Venezuela, 126
Vengeance, La, 227
Venus, spacecraft observations, 290–91
Veracruz, Mex., 7; Battle of, 231
Verdun, 147
Vermont, 31, 41, 256; statehood, 53
Verrazano, Giovanni da, 7, 8
Versailles Treaty, 152–53
Vesco, Robert, 294
Vesey, Denmark, 67, 258
Vespucci, Amerigo, 7, **8**
Veterans: bonus, World War I, 155, 165; GI Bill of
    Rights, 183; number of, 218; pensions, 123
Veterans' Administration, 160
Veterans' Bureau, 154
Vice presidents: chronology of, 210
Vicksburg, Miss., 99, **99**, 232, 233
Vidal, Gore, 250
Vietnam: Eisenhower policy, 184, 242; France in,
    182, 184; Geneva Agreements, 185
Vietnam War: battles, 241; costs, 196, 199, 221;
    escalation, 190–93, 242–43; losses, 194, 196, 221;
    protest, 193, 196, 243; Tet offensive, 194, 241;
    withdrawal, 197, 241
Vikings, 5, 6
Viking satellites, 200, **200**, 291
Villa, Francisco ("Pancho"), 145
Villard, Oswald Garrison, 139
Vincent, John H., 115
Vinland, 6
Vinson Naval Act, 167
Virginia: in Civil War, 92, 93, 232–34; colony, 14, 18;
    House of Burgesses, 18, 19; Indians, 4, 218; in
    Revolution, 42, 226; slavery debate, 69; slaves,
    255–56
Virginia (formerly *Merrimack*), 95

XYZ

XYZ Affair, 49, 56

Yachting, 296-97
Yale College, 24, **24**; and sports, 296-98
Yalta Conference, 175
Yalu Valley, 182
Yamamoto, Adm. Isoroku, 238
Yamassee Indians, 25; war with, 218-19, 223-24
Yarbrough *ex parte*, 213
Yates v. *U.S.*, 216
"Yellow Press," 120, **120**, 126
Yellowstone National Park, 114
York, James Stuart, duke of, 22, 23; *see* also James II, king of England
Yorktown, Va.; surrender of Cornwallis, 38, 42, 43, 227
Young, Andrew, 275
Young, Brigham, 75
Young, Charles D., 264, 265
Young, John W., 289
Young Plan, 157
Youngstown Sheet and Tube Company v. *Sawyer*, 215
Young Women's Christian Association, 281
Yucatán, 7
Yukon gold rush, 127

Zeller, Christine, 278
Zenger, Peter, 25
Ziegfeld's Follies, 138
"Zimmerman note," 146
Zuñi Indians, 255

In this index the use of boldface type for a page number indicates that an illustration appears on that page.

The names of individuals included in such lists as the roster of American Nobel Prize winners have not been indexed, nor have the names of the works of authors, poets, and novelists appearing in the various chronologies in the second section of this book; it was felt that to index this material would only have resulted in unnecessary duplication and would not have contributed to the usefulness of the book.

For the location of tabular and statistical material, the reader should consult the table of contents.